Proceedings of the Tolkien 2019 Conference

Edited by
Will Sherwood

Foreword by
Shaun Gunner

Academia Lunare
Luna Press Publishing

First published in 2025 by Luna Press Publishing, Edinburgh

ISBN-13: 978-1-915556-41-7

www.lunapresspublishing.com

Contents

Foreword

In 2014 The Tolkien Society had an idea: whereas previous conferences had celebrated anniversaries of Tolkien's life and works, we should now hold a dedicated conference to celebrate an anniversary of the Society's life: our 50th birthday. Taking the best from the Tolkien Centenary Conference in 1992, The Ring Goes Ever On in 2005, and The Return of the Ring in 2012, we built the event with two objectives in mind: honouring the Society and its history; and honouring Tolkien and his works.

The Society's history goes back to November 1969 when an advert appeared in *The New Statesman* inviting people to join a brand-new society devoted to promoting Tolkien's works. Since its foundation in 1969, the Society has consistently sought to promote – and encourage research into – the life and works of J.R.R. Tolkien. From our humble beginnings we have grown to become a worldwide community that fosters Tolkien scholarship whilst giving our members the opportunity to become part of our global fellowship. We do all of this in honour of a man who is one of the world's best-selling and most-loved authors whose contributions have helped to shape modern literature, our understanding of the history of the English language, and even 21st century cinema.

The aims of our Society were recognised by Tolkien himself, who consented to be our honorary president (a title he retains in perpetuo) whilst his daughter Priscilla became our honorary Vice-president (a title she also retains since her sad passing in 2022). In our 55-year history the Society has published over 400 journals, bulletins, books and proceedings in order to advance our aims, including our bimonthly bulletin *Amon Hen*, our annual journal *Mallorn*, and our regular shorter academic books in the Peter Roe series. Through our events, publications, and community, we are proud that our support has gone into nurturing some of the best-known Tolkien scholars.

Recognising our 50-year heritage, Tolkien 2019 took place on 7th-11th August 2019 at the Macdonald Burlington Hotel, Birmingham, UK, with 550 attendees from over 30 countries. Over the course of the 5 days, we had hundreds of hours of talks, panels, signings, coffee klatches, games, and quizzes, all running alongside an exhibition of the Society's history and a public exhibition of Tolkien art. We also spent our evenings banqueting, enjoying an orchestra, being wowed by a performance of *Leaf by Niggle*, and transporting attendees to Middle-earth. We wanted to create a truly wholesome conference that honours Tolkien, the Society, and its members.

It is undoubtedly the case that the event will stay alive in people's memories for decades to come. But that was not just because of the evening entertainments. We had the pleasure of welcoming some of the most notable Tolkien scholars, including Dimitra Fimi, John Garth, Wayne G. Hammond, Christina Scull, Tom Shippey, and Brian Sibley, as well as artists including Jenny Dolfen, Anke Eissmann, Jay Johnstone, Alan Lee, and Ted Nasmith. The scale of the event was unparalleled in the Society's history, and may never be matched again.

At any given point in time, there could have been up to eight activities for attendees to choose from, so any publication will struggle to recreate the excitement and scale of the event, never mind the feeling of warmth about being around so many like-minded people. However, what we can recreate is the scholarship on offer at the event by asking speakers to contribute to these Proceedings – making their thought and effort available for future generations, and those unable to attend the event. This is particularly important to us as the Society exists, under law of England and Wales, "to educate the public in, and promote research into, the life and works of J.R.R. Tolkien". This volume delivers those objectives.

Many of the authors you will recognise, but many you will not. Not only does this reflect the size of the event, and the breadth and depth of Tolkien scholarship, it also shows how things have changed. More and more is Tolkien an accepted topic of academic study, and more and more scholars are doing so. As much as Tolkien 2019 reflected on the previous 50 years of the Society's history, it also showcased new scholars who will come to shape our academic thinking over the next 50 years.

The 61 authors of these papers owe a great deal of thanks to Will Sherwood for editing these Proceedings, and going through the hard toil to make them possible. Aside from being a Trustee of the Society and our Education Secretary, Will is studying for a PhD on the intersections of British Romanticism and J.R.R. Tolkien's Middle-earth corpus at the University of Glasgow. That Will has been able to edit these whilst working in a secondary school and completing a PhD is surely a testament to his personal skill and commitment. Aside from Will, I owe a great deal of thanks to Francesca Barbini for managing the production and design of this volume and to Daniel Helen for his support. As Chair of the Society, I am grateful that we have so many willing and able volunteers, and it is proof of the strength of the organisation that we continue to have such volunteers.

I am sure you would agree that this volume represents an impressive collection of thought and scholarship on Tolkien and his works. I hope you find these Proceedings as enjoyable, educational, thought-provoking, challenging, and inspiring as the event itself. I am proud to be able to present them to you.

Shaun Gunner
Chair of the Tolkien Society
November 2024

Introduction

Will Sherwood

These conference proceedings have been a long time in the making. I took over as editor in January 2021 during an intense period of the COVID-19 pandemic and have continued to work on the many wonderful papers since.

This volume consists of sixty-one papers that celebrate the breadth, knowledge, and passion of the Tolkien community who attended Tolkien 2019. We have chosen to reflect the diverse authorship represented in the volume; the writing style, tone, and spelling are all personal to each author and so there is no consistent UK or US system applied across these proceedings. It also includes a mixture of papers that were originally twenty and forty minutes in length. The versions that appear in this volume may also accordingly vary in length as many authors have added additional material during the editorial process. The views and opinions expressed in these papers are those of the authors and do not necessarily reflect the position of The Tolkien Society.

The *Proceedings of the Tolkien 2019 Conference* are structured in nine sections: Biography; Tolkien's Theoretical and Creative Practices; Mythical, Folkloric, and Literary Traditions; Cities and Environments; Religion, Spirituality, and Faith; Politics and Law; Identity; Art and Music; and Reception, Fandom, and Legacy. In each section the papers have been organised in alphabetical order.

On behalf of the Society, I would like to thank all the presenters of Tolkien 2019, without whom the event would not have been possible. Furthermore, thank you to all the authors of these proceedings for their patience and perseverance to ensure that the volume the very best that it can be. I am thankful to the continued patience of the Society's committee regarding the editing and publishing of this proceedings. Special thanks go to Hannah McDonald and Luke Shelton who both helped to edit the final drafts. The publication itself is made possible by the generosity of the Peter Roe Memorial Fund, for which I am grateful.

On a personal note, I wish to dedicate this volume to Francesca Barbini at Luna Press Publishing. Fra, your tireless dedication to the Society's publications has long deserved acknowledgement and I could not ask for a greater publisher. Thank you for all your support, advice, and friendship over the years.

Abbreviations

A&I	*The Lay of Aotrou and Itroun*
Arthur	*The Fall of Arthur*
AW	*Ancrene Wisse*
B&L	*Beren and Lúthien*
Beowulf	*Beowulf: A Translation and Commentary, together with Sellic Spell*
Bombadil	*The Adventures of Tom Bombadil and other verses from the Red Book*
CoH	*The Children of Húrin*
Exodus	*The Old English Exodus*
Father Christmas	*Letters from Father Christmas*
FoG	*The Fall of Gondolin*
FoN	*The Fall of Númenor and Other Tales from the Second Age of Middle-earth*
FR	*The Fellowship of the Ring*
FS	*Tolkien on Fairy-stories*
GGK	*Sir Gawain and the Green Knight, Pearl, and Sir Orfeo*
Hobbit	*The Hobbit*
Jewels	*The War of the Jewels*
Kullervo	*The Story of Kullervo*
Lays	*The Lays of Beleriand*
Letters	*The Letters of J.R.R. Tolkien*
Lost Road	*The Lost Road and Other Writings*
Lost Tales I	*The Book of Lost Tales, Part One*
Lost Tales II	*The Book of Lost Tales, Part Two*
Maldon	*The Battle of Maldon: Together with the Homecoming of Beorhtnoth*
Monsters	*The Monsters and the Critics and Other Essays*
Morgoth	*Morgoth's Ring*
Nature	*The Nature of Middle-earth*
OFS	*Tolkien On Fairy-stories*
P&S	*Poems and Stories*
Peoples	*The Peoples of Middle-earth*
Perilous Realm	*Tales from the Perilous Realm*
RK	*The Return of the King*
Silmarillion	*The Silmarillion*
Sauron	*Sauron Defeated*
Secret Vice	*A Secret Vice: Tolkien on Invented Languages*
Shadow	*The Return of the Shadow*
Shaping	*The Shaping of Middle-earth*
S&G	*The Legend of Sigurd and Gudrún*
SWM	*Smith of Wootton Major*
TL	*Tree and Leaf*
TT	*The Two Towers*
Treason	*The Treason of Isengard*
UT	*Unfinished Tales of Númenor and Middle-earth*
War	*The War of the Ring*

BIOGRAPHY

Tolkien's Birmingham

Bob Blackham

The talk was accompanied by around sixty pictures and maps, mostly from the 1890s-1920s, and was based on my book, *The Roots of Tolkien's Middle-earth*, but more facts and information have come to light since it was published and some of this has been included in this paper.

1 – The Story Begins

In March 1891 a young woman, Mabel Suffield, left the Moseley Village near Birmingham. She was leaving the family home at Malvern House in Trafalgar Road, number 90, to travel to southern Africa to marry Arthur Tolkien who she had been engaged to for just over three years. There was a small modern housing development in Trafalgar Road called Sarehole Mill Gardens which appeared to celebrate Tolkien's mother's connection with the road – it may have been better to call it Suffield Gardens!

Arthur Tolkien had moved to southern Africa a year before, leaving his position at Lloyds Bank in Birmingham to seek a better life in southern Africa which at the time was having a mining boom. He had obtained a position in the Bank of Africa and during his first year had a number of temporary positions in branches across a wide area of southern Africa but had finally been appointed manager in the Bloemfontein branch. The bank was on Maitland Street in the heart of Bloemfontein and there was living accommodation over the bank.

Mabel's family travelled with her to Southampton, to wave her off, where she boarded the Roslin Castle steamer for the twenty-one days voyage to the Cape of Africa, the ship would have called at a number of ports on the voyage to drop off and pick up mail.

The couple married on the 16th April 1891 in Cape Town Cathedral and honeymooned at Sea Point (Afrikaans; *Seepunt*) located between Signal Hill and the Atlantic Ocean a short distance west of Cape Town's city centre. They travelled by train to Bloemfontein, a distance of almost 700 miles, to start their married life together over the bank and this was to be their only home together. Bloemfontein with its modern public buildings was still a bit of a frontier town with veldt on the edge of town still roamed by wild animals.

Mabel soon became pregnant and gave birth to her first son on the 3rd of January 1892 and he was christened John Ronald Reuel Tolkien on the 31st of January 1892 in Bloemfontein Cathedral. He was to use Ronald as his first name for most of his life. Mabel became pregnant again and gave birth to their second son on the 17th February 1894 and he was christened Hilary Arthur Reuel Tolkien.

Mabel and the boys set sail on the S. S. Guelph in early April in 1895 for the voyage to England. Arthur had hired a nurse to help Mabel look after the boys on the voyage and after around twenty-one days they docked at Southampton. Arthur was to remain in Bloemfontein for the time being as he was unwilling to leave others in the bank to deal with the current crop of business. He would also have been on half salary while away from the bank (something he felt he could not afford at the time) but he did plan on joining Mabel and the boys in England later. Ronald Tolkien's last and only memory of his father was watching him paint his name 'A.R. Tolkien' on the family trunk.

2 – King's Heath

Mabel, Ronald and Hilary were met at Southampton by Mabel's younger sister Jane who was to play a major role in the brothers' later life. They all travelled by train from Southampton to most likely Birmingham New Street Station, a place that was very familiar to Jane as she had used the station on her journey to and from school and had even passed letters from her sister Mabel to Arthur Tolkien. From here they would have taken the steam tram along the Moseley Road, through Moseley Village, then up the hill on Alcester Road to the lower end of King's Heath High Street and alighted the steam tram by King's Heath Railway Station. Then a short walk up Valentine Road and turned left into Ashfield Road to Mabel's parent's new home at number 9 Ashfield Road. Back in the late Victorian period most people rented their home and this was the case with Mabel's parents who had moved from their home in Trafalgar Road, Moseley while she had been in Bloemfontein. Her father was John Suffield, who at the time was sixty-three and had a Jeyes Fluid franchise in Birmingham.

Mabel and the boys were now living in King's Heath. At the time it was on the edge of the countryside but it was growing, and all around the area new houses were being built, and a short walk from the busy High Street would find them in the Worcestershire countryside.

Bad news reached Ashfield Road in the November of that year, Arthur had suffered an attack of rheumatic fever and he was over the worst of the illness but was not well enough to make the long journey to England to join his family. By January Mabel was making plans to return to Bloemfontein to look after Arthur who was still unwell. In mid-February Ronald got his nurse to write a letter to his father to tell him they were returning home and how he may not recognize him and his brother Hilary as they have grown much in their time in England. Sadly, the letter was never sent as a telegram arrived at Ashfield Road to tell Mabel that Arthur had suffered a haemorrhage, he died the next day the 15th of February 1896 and was buried in Bloemfontein.

3 – Sarehole

Mabel needed to set up home on her own to escape her extended Suffield family in Ashfield Road but not too far away from her family. So in the summer of 1896 she rented 5 Gracewell Cottages, we would call it a semi-detached house, on Wake Green Road in the hamlet of Sarehole. This hamlet was outside Birmingham in the county of Worcestershire at the time the Tolkien family lived there and was around two miles from Mabel's parent's home in King's Heath.

They most likely walked there, going up Ashfield Road turning left into School Road, walking up the hill to walk down Greenhill Road or Cotton Lane. Tolkien's Suffield grandfather moved to Cotton Lane after Ashfield Road where he lived till 1930, dying at the age of 97. He was also a skilled draftsman and sent Tolkien hand drawn Christmas 'cards' for many years. He would write the Lord's Prayer in copperplate inside a circle drawn around a sixpence on these cards; his drawing skills and even his style of drawing appear to have been inherited by Ronald. Both these names were to appear in *The Lord of the Rings* as Greenhill Country, and Farmer and Rosy Cotton, one a place at the start of the books and the other a family of Hobbits.

Probably the first place that drew Ronald's attention was Sarehole Mill and mill pond as this was clearly visible, back then, from the front of 5 Gracewell Cottages. There has been a mill on the site from at least the 16th century but most of the three storey brick mill buildings and chimney dates from between 1760 to the 1850s. Originally the name Sarehole was spelt as two words Sare Hole with the 'hole' part of the word coming from '*holm*' which means flood meadow in Old English.

The mill had two large water wheels, a steam engine, boiler, and chimney to power the mill's machinery at times when water levels were too low to power the mill. Ronald and later his brother Hilary would have peered through the dusty windows of the mill and marvelled at the mill machinery turning around and around as the corn was ground into flour. Or on other days the mill would be grinding up bones for fertilizer for local farms – back then you could sell the bones from your kitchen waste to the rag and bone man. The mill also ground peas and beans for animal feed. This produced much dust and the miller would come out of the mill to chase off the Tolkien boys, for their own safety, covered in dust and surrounded in clouds of dust. They nicknamed his son George Andrew junior 'The White Ogre'.

The mill, with its smoking chimney, makes several appearances in *The Lord of the Rings*. When Sam is looking into Galadriel's mirror he sees the mill of Hobbiton with a smoking chimney discharging pollution into the environment:

> But now Sam noticed that the Old Mill had vanished, and a large red–brick building was put up where it had stood. Lots of folk were busily at work. There was a tall red chimney nearby. Black smoke seemed to cloud the surface of the Mirror. (*FR*, 'The Mirror of Galadriel', 362-3)

This is a vision of the Mill as it becomes in *The Return of the King* when the Hobbits return to The Shire:

> 'Take Sandyman's mill now. Pimple knocked it down almost as soon as he came to Bag End. Then he brought in a lot o' dirty-looking Men to build a bigger one and fill it full o' wheels and outlandish contraptions.' (*RK*, 'The Scouring of the Shire', 1013)

So the mill we see today at Sarehole with its three-story brick building and chimney is Ted Sandyman's mill in *The Lord of the Rings*.

In a rare interview in 1966, reproduced in *The Guardian* in 1991, Tolkien described how important the little Worcestershire hamlet of Sarehole on the rural edge of Birmingham had been in the development of his fictional vision:

> It was a kind of lost paradise [...] There was an old mill that really did grind corn with two millers, a great big pond with swans on it, a sandpit, a wonderful dell with flowers, a few

> old-fashioned village houses and, further away, a stream with another mill [...] I could draw you a map of every inch of it. I loved it with an (intense) love. (qtd. in Ezard 1991)

Further on in the article he re-emphasizes the importance of his childhood memories of the area:

> I was brought up in considerable poverty, but I was happy running about in that country. I took the idea of the hobbits from the village people and children (1991)

Further up the River Cole (the name '*Cole*' is pre-Saxon and means hazel) you reach Little Sarehole, a farming hamlet, and here was (and still is) the spillway for the headrace taking water from the River Cole to Sarehole Mill. The flow of water to the mill was controlled here by planks across the spillway that could be raised or lowered by the miller. These planks were stolen in 1917, most likely for firewood, and this may have been one of the things that led to the mill stopping milling.

4 – Bill the Pony

In February 2010 I received an email from Ian Collier asking if I could help Rob Brooke who was writing a book about a Warwickshire cricketer called Frank Foster. Foster had lived in a house called Mel Valley on Wake Green Road in Birmingham from 1894 to the 1920s and Rob had seen the name Mel Valley on one of the maps in my book *The Roots of Tolkien's Middle-earth.*

I got out 'The Godfrey Edition' map of Hall Green 1903 which luckily contained Kelly's entry for Wake Green Road for around the same time. Kelly's was a yearly book that listed house names or numbers and who was living there that year. I located the house called Mel Valley from Kelly's and the site of the house on the map, but the house was not shown on the map as it was not built at the time the map was surveyed.

Now, what lit a light bulb was a line in an email from Rob Brooke: "Incidentally William Foster (that's the cricketer's father) bred Hackney Ponies at Mel Valley, and when he died in 1914 he was a breeder and judge of international repute". This is because in 1910 he sold five Hackney Ponies in New York for $20,000, a huge sum of money at the time. The ponies, which all had the first name Mel Valley's, were called Master, Masterpiece, Masterkey, Masterman and Tissington Belief. Mel Valley's Master won his class in the horse show in New York being thirteen hands in height which is fifty-two inches from the ground to where the back joins the neck, so he was a sturdy chap.

Now where these ponies were being kept is only a short walk from 5 Gracewell Cottages where Mabel, Ronald, and Hilary Tolkien were living from 1896 till 1900 and I bet you that Mabel would have taken the two brothers to see the ponies many times while living there. Could it be that one night while writing *The Lord of the Rings* in his study in Northmoor Road Oxford Tolkien's mind went back to his childhood days at Sarehole and Bill and all the other ponies in *The Lord of the Rings* were born into the books?

5 – Moseley and King's Heath

In 1900 Ronald passed his examination for King Edward's School on New Street in Birmingham city centre. Travelling from Sarehole to school was a problem for the boys so Mabel decided to move to Moseley Village to access the steam-powered tram system. They packed their belongings up and most likely loaded them onto a horse-drawn cart or even a handcart, and travelled up Wake Green Road to Moseley Village.

The house they rented was on the hill leading out of the village towards King's Heath and was on the route of the steam trams ploughing back and forth in and out of the city centre. The houses on the tram route were blighted because of the noise and smoke the trams produced and the rents were lower. But this was not a bad thing for Mabel who by this time had been a widow for nearly four years and money must have been tight with two young sons to bring up. She had converted to Roman Catholicism just before leaving Sarehole and the church at St Anne's Alcester Street was a short tram ride away. Ronald did not like the house in Moseley, he thought it to be 'dreadful' and Moseley, with the noise, smoky chimneys, horse-drawn traffic, and lots of people, was such a change from the rural surroundings of Sarehole. Where-ever he had moved to in the Victorian Birmingham suburbs, in the type of housing Mabel could afford, he would have had the same reaction.

After a very short time in the house in Moseley they moved to King's Heath to Westfield Road on the Grange Estate. This house backed on to the railway line and looked across fields to two grand mansions, Highbury and Uffculme. Coal was king in those days and coal trucks from the South Wales coalfields were coming and going from King's Heath Station a short way from their house. The strange sounding names on the trucks led to Ronald discovering the Welsh language. The Tolkiens were attending the small Catholic church of St Dunstan's on the corner of Station Road and Westfield Road. The church was a small iron building with a pine-board interior opened in 1896. It was destroyed by bombing in the Second World War and the new church is on Institute Road, King's Heath.

6 – Edgbaston

In 1902 Mabel, Ronald, and Hilary moved to Oliver Road in Edgbaston because Mabel did not like the house in King's Heath or St Dunstan's Church. In Edgbaston they were able to attend the Birmingham Oratory and maybe get support from the priests that ran it. Also, the brothers could attend the Grammar School of St Philip, a Catholic school, where the fees were less than King Edward's.

Mabel may also have been having money problems because by 1902 the Boer War in southern Africa had already been raging for three years and much if not all of her independent income was coming from share dividends in gold mines that Arthur Tolkien had purchased during his time in southern Africa. While living on Oliver Road, Mabel, Ronald, and Hilary became friendly with Father Francis Xavier Morgan who was the local parish priest.

The house in Oliver Road was of poor quality, almost a slum, and this poor housing and a possible poor diet was to have a toll on the whole family's health. Early in 1904

Ronald and Hilary came down with measles followed by whooping-cough and in Hilary's case this became pneumonia. Nursing the boys had put a great strain on Mabel and in April 1904 she was ill with diabetes and spent some time in hospital. The house was abandoned and Hilary went to stay with his grandparents, probably in King's Heath. Ronald stayed with his Aunt Jane and Edwin Neave in Hove on the south coast. Back in the early part of the twentieth century many illnesses that today can be controlled or even cured could be fatal and one of the best prescriptions for recovery after an illness was fresh air. Sometime after Mabel came out of hospital, the family moved just out of Birmingham and stayed in Woodside Cottage in the large grounds of Oratory House in Rednal. Oratory House stood on the wooded slopes of Rednal Hill, part of the Lickey Hills and was used as a retreat by members of the Oratory community.

Here they had a couple of rooms in the cottage where a local postman and his wife lived, who provided them with their daily meals. But after a wonderful summer in the woods and fields of the Lickey Hills and the glorious colours of the trees in the autumn, Mabel's diabetes overcame her and she died on the 14th November. Mabel in her will had made Fr. Francis the two Tolkien brothers' guardian, a role he was to undertake with great dedication. Mabel is buried in the Catholic churchyard at Bromsgrove, her grave is marked with a stone cross of similar design to that used to mark the graves of the Oratory priests at their Rednal cemetery. After a short time living in Barnt Green and Middleton Hall Road, Cotteridge, Ronald and Hilary returned to Edgbaston to live with their aunt Beatrice Suffield in Stirling Road, a short distance from the Oratory. Ronald had returned to King Edward's in autumn 1903, having won a Foundation Scholarship earlier in the year.

Living on the other side of the road was the widow of the locally famous surgeon Dr. Joseph Sampson Gamgee. He founded the Birmingham Hospital Saturday Fund in 1873 which helped members with hospital bills as it still does today. He also invented Gamgee tissue, cotton dressing used for dressing wounds, which is still used today. Dr. Sampson died in 1886, but his name becomes that of a major character in *The Lord of the Rings*, as Frodo's companion on the quest is Samwise Gamgee who is also a Ring bearer for a short time in the book. There is a plaque located on the Repertory Theatre building in Centenary Square in the city centre, the site of his home.

At the end of Stirling Road stood a tall chimney, one of many that formed a forest of chimneys on the Birmingham skyline. This was not your common circular brick chimney but a beautiful Italianate style red brick chimney with ornamental cream brickwork built in 1862. Standing next to the chimney was the boiler house, engine room and workshops of the Edgbaston Water Works that was pumping water day and night to supply water to Birmingham and Aston from bore holes. This would have been a busy site at the time when the Tolkien brothers lived in Edgbaston in the early 1900s with much horse-drawn traffic coming and going from the site. The carts would have been carrying coal, most likely from the canal a short distance away, to feed the ever-hungry boilers that supplied steam for the beam engines that pumped the water.

From outside, the great chimney would have sometimes belched black smoke and the sound of the engines pumping would have been felt and heard. In the engine house men would have been oiling the great engines as the connecting rods moved up and down and beams rocked like giant see-saws. The spinning weights of the engine governors would flash in the light as they controlled the speed of the engines. In the boiler house there would be rows of boilers supplying steam to the engines.

A short distance further down the aptly named Waterworks Road, just before the junction of Monument Road, stood a second tower but this was a true tower in every sense. This beautiful jewel of architecture was built in brick in 1758 for Humphrey Perrott next to his hunting lodge. The tower known as Perrott's Folly has a spiral staircase of one hundred and thirty-nine steps with small rooms on each floor and the roof of the tower is a stone-embattled parapet with the height of the tower being ninety-six feet. In the later part of the nineteenth century the tower became one of the world's first weather stations under the guidance of the pioneering meteorologist A. Follett Osler. The two towers are locally believed to be Minas Morgul and Minas Tirith but Tolkien himself was very ambiguous about which pair of towers the second volume of *The Lord of the Rings*, *The Two Towers*, is named after.

While living in Stirling Road, Ronald would most likely have walked past a Victorian public house on the corner of Monument Road and Hagley Road as he went to and from school in the centre of Birmingham. The public house is called the Ivy Bush and this would reappear many years later as the Ivy Bush Tavern in Hobbiton.

7 – King Edward's VI School

School must have been a 'rock' in Tolkien's life after his mother's death. He had many friends there and the school held many after-hours activities for the boys. Tolkien was in Mr Measures' House, and eventually became house-captain. Tolkien played Rugby football for his house but there was a price to pay for this. He was slight of build but by force of mind he drove himself on, taking some knocks and injuries on the way, one of which almost caused him to lose his tongue. Tolkien also played Rugby football for the school first team and eventually became the Football Secretary. He was a member of the School Debating Society and later its secretary and also a member of the School Literary Society, where he presented a paper on Norse Sagas. He also performed in school plays. For a while he was a member of The King Edward's School Officer Training Corps and took part in a number of camps and exercises with the corps.

In 1911 Tolkien was a senior boy and had been appointed as a Librarian in the school library along with some of his school friends, Christopher Wiseman, Robert Quilter Gilson, who was the headmaster's son, and a number of other senior boys. These young men had time on their hands as most of the school in the summer term was taking examinations. Tolkien had secured his place at Exeter College, Oxford back in December 1910. They entertained themselves with jokes and fun but Birmingham, along with the rest of the country, was suffering a heat-wave and maybe this drove them into making tea on a spirit-stove fuelled by alcohol or methylated spirits. This is a dangerous practice in a library full of books. Members of the group, by this time known as the 'Tea Club', were taking it in turn to bring in nibbles and were also meeting out of school hours in Barrow's Store just round the corner from the school in Corporation Street. (Mr Barrow's full name was Richard Cadbury Barrow and was a member of the Cadbury family who did not move to Bournville). This became known first as the 'Barrovian Society', then as the 'Tea Club and Barrovian Society' and later just as the 'TCBS'.

Tolkien went to Exeter College, Oxford, in the October of 1911 and the 'TCBS' friends carried on meeting in various forms and at various locations, into the Great War. Geoffrey Bache Smith, a King Edward's 'boy' some two years younger than Tolkien, joined the group after the death of member Vincent Trought. Smith was at Corpus Christi College, Oxford, and because of their school connections became friends with Tolkien while Tolkien was at Exeter College.

Gilson and Smith both died in The Battle of the Somme in 1916. Smith had a work of poetry, *A Spring Harvest*, published posthumously in 1918 and Tolkien wrote the preface.

In 1908 Ronald and Hilary moved from Stirling Road to Duchess Road, to Mrs Faulkner's house and living there at the time was Edith Bratt, also an orphan, and romance started to blossom between Ronald and Edith. In the autumn of 1909 Edith and Ronald set off for a bicycle ride to the Lickey Hills; they set off separately but came together after a short distance. They spent the afternoon in the wooded hills before going to the village of Rednal for a cup of tea, which they got at a house where Ronald had stayed at while working for his scholarship for Oxford. They were to become undone by this visit as the lady who gave them tea told Mrs Church, the caretaker at Oratory House, who told the cook at the Oratory in Edgbaston, who told Fr. Francis.

This relationship was frowned upon by Fr. Francis, the boys' guardian, and he had Hilary and Ronald moved out of Duchess Road into a house in Highfield Road just across from the Oratory. This was the last house in Birmingham Tolkien would stay in. While living at this house, Fr. Francis Morgan banned Ronald from carrying on with this relationship and Edith moved away from Birmingham to live in Cheltenham. But before Edith left Birmingham, she and Ronald had a chance meeting at The Prince of Wales Theatre on Broad Street, one lunchtime. Ronald had been to see Peter Pan in April 1910 at The Prince of Wales Theatre and had been greatly impressed by the performance, in which Pauline Chase had played Peter Pan: seeing her 'fly' on stage was a wonder of the age.

Fr. Francis Morgan's ban may well have caused Ronald to fail his scholarship exam for Oxford later in the year. This in a way may have saved his life because if he had gone to Oxford in 1910 and followed the same path at university as he did one year later, he would have graduated in the summer of 1914. He may well have volunteered to join the army that summer at the start of the Great War, and could well have been killed during the longer time he would have served in the army. However, at the age of twenty-one, while still at Oxford University, he made contact with Edith who was about to get married to someone else and restarted the spark of romance with her. Ronald finished at Oxford in the summer of 1915, at which time the Great War was raging away, and joined the Lancashire Fusiliers. They married in the spring of 1916.

The couple returned to Birmingham in June 1916 and stayed at the Plough and Harrow hotel just over the road from the Oratory and stopped for one night only. Ronald was most likely on embarkation leave as he was shortly to go to the Western Front and they may have returned to the places of their childhood sweetheart days. They stayed in room 116 in the Plough and Harrow where there is now a Blue Plaque recording their short stay. Tolkien returned to Birmingham in 1933 to show his children his childhood haunts, only to find that much has been built over and a suburb called Hall Green has spread across the farms and fields of his childhood.

Today time and trees have mellowed it and it has become one of Birmingham's leafy suburbs; many of the places have survived to this day.

In April 1944 Ronald returned to Birmingham for a school reunion and went to visit the old school site in New Street and was not very impressed with the building that had replaced King Edward House:

> I then strolled about my 'home town' for a bit. Except for one patch of ghastly wreckage (opp. My old school's site) it does not look much damaged: not by the enemy. The chief damage has been the growth of great flat featureless modern buildings. The worst of all is the ghastly multiple–site erection on the old site. I couldn't stand much of that or the ghosts that rose from the pavements; so I caught a tram (*Letters*, Letter 58, 70)

Once again Birmingham had stirred his imagination in the writing of *The Lord of the Rings*. The vision of the ghosts rising from the pavement broke his writing block and he rapidly wrote the chapters 'The Passage of the Marshes' and 'The Black Gate is Closed' in The Two Towers. Both these chapters draw heavily on his experiences in the Battle of the Somme with water filled shell holes and blasted chalk landscapes.

Acknowledgement

This paper is dedicated to the memory of Dr. Chris Upton 1959-2015 who wrote *The Tolkien Discovery Trail, Birmingham* (1992), that inspired me and many people in the Birmingham area to research and celebrate Tolkien's life and times in and around this great city.

Bibliography

Ezard, J., 'Tolkien's Shire', *Weekend Guardian*, 28/29 December 1991, p. N.A.

Tolkien, J.R.R., *The Letters of J.R.R. Tolkien*, ed. H. Carpenter with the assistance of C. Tolkien (London: HarperCollins, 2006).
— *The Lord of the Rings*, (London: HarperCollins, 2010).

Tolkien's First Job:
Experiences in France Linked to his 1913 Trip

José Manuel Ferrández-Bru

Tolkien is one of the authors whose life has been analysed in detail. But there are still moments that have not been reviewed in depth. One of them is his trip to France during the summer of 1913. This trip, together with his travel to Switzerland in 1911, are two of the main experiences of his formative period. At the beginning of 1913 Tolkien had resumed his love affair with Edith, which had been interrupted for three years. Tolkien couldn't have contact with Edith until his coming of age, so exactly on his 21st birthday (January 3, 1913) he wrote a letter to Edith asking her to marry him, and a few days later, they were engaged to be married.

Presumably, Tolkien wanted to generate his own economic resources but the description by the man in whose house Edith lived then (something like her guardian) was devastating:

> I have nothing to say against Tolkien, he is a cultured gentleman, but his prospects are poor in the extreme and when he will be in a position to marry I can not imagine. Had he adopted a profession it would have been different. (Tolkien and Tolkien 1992, 34)

Tolkien did not have a profession and he hadn't even finished his studies. The truth is that he had never worked or earned his own money, but lived thanks to his scholarship and the help of Fr. Francis Morgan. Surely the restart of the relationship was the key factor that led Tolkien to perform his best in Oxford and even to look for options to earn some money. However, even though he was an educated young man and a student at a university as prestigious as Oxford, there were few practical jobs for him. In this circumstance, he got a job as escort and tutor on a pleasure trip to Paris for three brothers and two of their aunts, from a wealthy Mexican family. He would travel with the two older brothers to Paris where they would meet a younger brother and the aunts. In Paris Tolkien would have the mission of guiding and accompanying the children on their excursions.

The boys came from a Catholic boarding school in Lancashire and the youngest brother had arrived in Paris with the aunts and would join the same school as his brothers after the summer. Their names were Ventura (1896-1954), Jose Pablo (born in 1900), and Eustaquio (1902-1936) Martínez del Río Bermejillo. It is curious that Tolkien was barely four years older than Ventura.[1] The boys attended Stonyhurst in Lancashire,

1. At this point, and for a better understanding, it is necessary to go in depth about the use of surnames in the Hispanic world. The tradition is that each person always has two surnames, the first comes from the father and the second from the mother. In addition, it can happen that some (or both) of the surnames are composed. In this case, Martínez del Río was the surname of the boys from his father's side and Bermejillo from his mother's side (women retain their surnames after marriage). It also admits the option of joining the surnames with the conjunction "y" (that

the same school where years later Michael Tolkien would develop part of his teaching career. It was a Jesuit boarding school very popular among the Spanish-speaking young people who came to study in England (and one of the most outstanding Catholic schools alongside Beaumont and the Birmingham Oratory School).

The aunts were Ángela and Julia Martínez del Río Pedemonte, sisters of the boys' father. Both were widows: Ángela, the oldest, was 64 years old and Julia was 46. Julia, who had just been widowed a few months earlier, was still in mourning. She was the twin of the childrens' father. As Tolkien would directly experience, both had a snobbish and capricious character probably derived from their high social status. Regarding the parents of the boys, both had died, the mother in 1905 and the father in 1906. So, they were orphans and their family had taken care of them. Surely, like their relatives, the boys would have a considerable fortune, which they would enjoy when they came of age. Meanwhile they were educated in England following a family tradition.

The family on the father's side (the Martínez del Río family) was one of the most prominent in Mexico. The patriarch, the grandfather of the boys, was a famous doctor and landowner. His sons were also landowners and his successor at the head of the family was his first-born son, Pablo. Ventura, the father of the children, was the youngest of the brothers. The mother's side (the Bermejillo Martínez-Negrete) was also a family of Mexican high society. They were of Spanish origin (the mother of the boys belonged to the first generation born in Mexico) and their fortune was due mainly to the industrial initiatives they had carried out.

Both families were 'Criollos' (Creole), which in Mexico meant that they were families whose members, probably to maintain their elitism, only married into other families of European origin or directly to Spaniards. That is why the Martínez del Río and the Bermejillo families had a high degree of 'Spanishness', especially in some branches. In fact, many members of both families settled in Spain.

It is unknown how Tolkien heard about, applied, and got this job. We may never discover how Tolkien came into contact with the boys' family. However, we can speculate! One option is that Tolkien knew Pablo Martínez del Río Vinent, the boys' cousin, as he was a student at Oxford at the same time as him. Both were Catholics and frequented the same places, for example the Oxford University Newman Society. It is plausible that they knew each other and maybe Pablo told him about the need for an escort for his cousins and aunts. Pablo Martínez del Río Vinent became, years later, an important Mexican scholar (historian and anthropologist).

On the other hand, it is also possible that the contact came through Francis M. Killion, a 'Scholastic Guardian' from Chiswick as it appears in the British census of the time. Killion, of Irish origin and Catholic, acted as the delegate of the families of many young foreigners who studied in the United Kingdom, especially of Hispanic origin. Due to the distance with their families, Killion was in charge of managing matters related to their education and he solved problems and practical issues.

---

is "and"), so that Martínez del Río Y *Bermejillo* could be used. Furthermore, sometimes only the first surname is indicated in order to shorten. It's important to clarify this because we will talk later about other members of his family who share some of the surnames but not both, as they were cousins, aunts or other relatives.

Killion was of a similar age to that of Fr. Francis Morgan (Killion was born in 1862 and Fr. Francis in 1857) and they had common interests as Fr. Francis was very involved in matters related to Catholic education and with young people of Spanish origin (many of them from his own family). It is possible, therefore, that both knew each other and maybe Tolkien was aware of the job through his own guardian. Additionally, there is a more convoluted third possibility. The best friend of Father Francis's mother was Catalina des Fontaines y Barron. Catalina's family, in the Barron branch, was engaged in banking and one of her uncles settled in Mexico in the mid-nineteenth century and there he devoted himself to this activity. His name was Eustace Barron and later his nephew William followed him. In Mexico his name was transformed, and Eustace became Eustaquio.

He did business and established a great friendship with the Martínez-Negrete family (maternal grandmother in the family of the boys). In fact, one of their uncles was godson of Eustace, and Eustaquio, the youngest of the boys, received his name from him. It is possible therefore, that the connection was produced due to these relationships and from a possible contact from the Bermejillo family with Francis Morgan.

In any case, it is evident that Tolkien had the right qualities to perform the job. First of all, he was Roman Catholic like the boys, which seemed to be a fundamental requirement. He was also well qualified because he was an Oxford student who also had some knowledge of French (thanks to his mother's teachings) and Spanish (through Fr. Francis), although he later realised that he was not proficient in any of these languages. Tolkien had good credentials and references as well, no matter how he had known the existence of the job. Additionally, he was very motivated, since this job would represent his first income and it was a fundamental step in order to achieve his goal of forming a family with Edith.

The trip began on July 29th at Charing Cross station. Tolkien met Mr Killion, Ventura and José Pablo and left with the boys for Paris. He described them as "quite jolly & good & most submissive and quiet, especially little Jose who never speaks" (qtd. in Hammond and Scull 2017, 50). After crossing the English Channel, the three arrived by train to Paris the next day. There, Tolkien met the little brother, Eustaquio, and the aunts who had just arrived from Mexico. Eustaquio was described as: "the nicest child I have ever met" (50).

As tourists, they remained in Paris for ten days, staying at two hotels near the *Arc de Triomphe*. However, the aunts planned a trip to Brittany and, although Tolkien imagined the possibility of visiting the Celtic area of the country, the idea was rather to go to a fashionable place on the coast, Dinard, near Saint Malo. Tolkien probably did not know that the Martínez del Río family had spent long stays in Biarritz and now the aunts just wanted to enjoy the new fashionable tourist destination.

On August 10th, all of them left for Dinard, except Julia, the youngest aunt (we must remember that she was in mourning). During their stay, Tolkien complained bitterly by letter to Edith:

> To see nothing but trippers and dirty papers and bathing machines instead of enjoying the atmosphere and culture of the real Brittany. (51)

On Wednesday, August 13th, a fatality occurred: Aunt Ángela died after being hit by a car. Tolkien had to face a complicated situation, especially considering the wish expressed by the dying Ángela that her remains be moved to Mexico. Events and decisions followed one another. On Thursday Julia arrived from Paris and on Friday Tolkien and Ventura (the eldest of the brothers) returned to Paris to begin the bureaucratic formalities for moving Ángela's body to her country.

For several days Tolkien and Ventura made mortuary arrangements to transfer the coffin to Mexico. During this period, they went to Mass and Communion at the English church in Paris, and to Mass at the Spanish church. On the nights of the 16th and the 17th, they dined at the home of Madame Cervantes (María Manuela Cervantes Cortazar) – a rich Mexican landowner dedicated to the production of *pulque* (an extremely popular alcoholic beverage produced with the sap of the agave). The great Mexican *haciendas* were frequently attacked at the time due to political instability and, for this reason, Mrs. Cervantes decided to move her residence to Paris, although her property continued to produce great benefits.

After several days, the coffin arrived in Paris at the *Gare de Montparnasse* and was sent to Mexico with Julia, whilst the boys and Tolkien remained behind. During the previous days, Tolkien had been in contact with Mr Killion and different options had been studied. For example, it was suggested that the children return to Mexico accompanied by Tolkien and subsequently come back for the new term in January. However, the unstable situation in Mexico, in the midst of a social revolution, led them to travel to England to spend the rest of their vacations (to the relief of Tolkien). The place chosen was Bournemouth in Dorset, a town where Tolkien would spend part of his last years, more than half a century later. There, they spent two weeks staying at Mrs Fisher's house, a small and typical lodging. There is an image of them in the town because on September 3rd they took a bus tour and were photographed in 'The Square', a public square marking the centre of the city.[2]

On September 15th the boys returned to school and Tolkien to Oxford. It was the end of an experience that deeply marked Tolkien (probably due to the unfortunate circumstances of the trip), who even said, "Never again except I am in the direst poverty will I take any such job." (52)

Life went on and the boys grew up. After having contacted their relatives, it is possible to know what happened to them, although the main thing is that the three returned to Mexico after finishing their studies. Thanks to Jaime Martínez del Rio Romero-Vargas, son of Ventura, we know that he devoted himself to business and married twice. He died in January 1954 at fifty-seven years of age:

> Ventura (my father), after studying in England, returned to Mexico, and later married to Dolores Icaza and they had three children Ventura, Xavier and Rosa. On the death of my father's wife, he married my mother Eugenia Romero-Vargas Iturbide and they had four children, Eugenia, Julio, Jaime and Virginia.[3]

2. This picture is available in The Tolkien Family Album, but it is wrongly located in Paris.
3. Personal correspondence with Jaime Martínez del Rio Romero-Vargas.

José Pablo, the middle child, got married but had no children. His relatives remember him as very reserved, 'very English', which matches Tolkien's description when he pointed out that Jose Pablo never spoke. For his part, Eustaquio ("the nicest child I have ever met") died prematurely at thirty three of a heart attack. He left a son and a daughter (Eustaquio and Lourdes).

However, there is another branch of the family that is of interest. This is the main branch, that of Pablo Martínez del Río Vinent (the cousin of the boys who studied in Oxford at the same time as Tolkien, cited before). There is a 'family legend' about the possibility that Pablo and Tolkien exchanged correspondence. However, they can't prove it, since all the historical family documents had been donated to an entity that wishes to preserve the history of Mexico (Centro de Estudios de Historia de México).

As of today, these letters have not been found. It is possible that they are still to be catalogued, or they may have been lost or they may simply not exist. On the website of this organisation hundreds of documents can be consulted, but almost all of them are related to family businesses and there are hardly any personal documents.[4] Through the Archive we learn that in the Martínez del Río family there was a world celebrity. Jaime, the brother of Pablo Martínez del Río Vinent (another cousin of the boys) married a young Mexican woman. Years later she would become a movie star under the stage name of Dolores del Río.

Bibliography

Hammond, W.G., and C. Scull, *The J.R.R. Tolkien Companion and Guide: Volume 1: Chronology*, (London: Harper Collins, 2017).

Tolkien, J., and P. Tolkien, *The Tolkien Family Album*, (London: HarperCollins, 1992).

4. Through the Archive we learn that in the Martínez del Río family there was a world celebrity. Jaime, the brother of Pablo Martínez del Río Vinent (so another cousin of the boys) married a young Mexican woman. Years later she would become a movie star under the stage name of Dolores del Río.

Tolkien in East Yorkshire, 1917-18: A Hemlock Glade, Two Towers, The Houses of Healing and a Beacon[1]

Michael Flowers

"Lordynges, ther is in Yorkshire, as I gesse, A mersshy contree called Holdernesse" (Chaucer 1987, 129)

Dr. Stuart Lee has recently reconstructed as much of the 'lost' television interviews Tolkien gave in March 1968 for the BBC film *Tolkien in Oxford*, as is possible more than half a century after the event. Towards the end of the reconstruction the interviewer asks "about places in Tolkien's fictions that are linked to Oxford" (2018, 162). Rather surprisingly, Tolkien did not mention somewhere like the Radcliffe Camera or Addison's Walk, or one of the colleges. The first location he mentioned was far from Oxford. Outside of Oxford it may have been expected that he would initially think of Sarehole Mill, or Cannock Chase, or the village of Great Haywood in Staffordshire. However, Tolkien replied that there was "nothing which is highly derivative", but then he added "mostly places fairly remote from here. Like a little place on the extreme Yorkshire east coast called Roos, r-double o-s" (162). This placing of Roos first among all other locations highlights the importance of Roos in particular, and East Yorkshire in general, to Tolkien as an inspiration for his legendarium.

Although Tolkien's eighteen months in East Yorkshire have been examined previously, it is the contention of this paper that there are reasons why earlier accounts provide only a partial picture. Humphrey Carpenter is very sketchy on Tolkien's residence in the area, and at the time his biography was written Tolkien's war record was not yet available for inspection, so his account has since been proved to include some chronological errors. For instance, Carpenter dated Edith Tolkien's inspirational dance among the 'hemlocks' to the painful period after her first child's birth, but anyone with a basic knowledge of natural history and Edith's medical condition would rule out the possibility of it taking place during the winter of 1917-1918 (Carpenter 1977, 95-8). John Garth in his *Tolkien and the Great War* corrected Carpenter's guesswork, and undertook considerable original research when he was examining Tolkien's period in Holderness, but has admitted that he only spent one day on the ground visiting East Yorkshire's Tolkien locations. Of course, his work was also more broadly focused on the whole of Tolkien's Great War experience than a specific look at Tolkien's time in Holderness. In contrast, Phil Mathison knows Holderness intimately, but he has confided that he has not read any fiction written by Tolkien. This approach means that aspects of Tolkien's fiction which appear to have been directly inspired by East Yorkshire locations have been neglected.

The following account comes from the viewpoint of a reader with a deeper knowledge of Tolkien's fiction than Mathison, coupled with an attempt to follow Tolkien's actual footsteps in more detail than was possible for either Garth or Carpenter.

1. This essay was originally published in "Something has gone crack": *New Perspectives on J.R.R. Tolkien in the Great War*, Walking-Tree Publishing, 2019.

Holderness is still a forgotten, hidden, and neglected part of the country in 2020, as it was when Tolkien was stationed there just over a century ago, but he would have been aware of its existence before he arrived. Tolkien had studied Chaucer at both school and university, so he would have known the above lines, which are the first two from 'The Summoner's Tale' in Chaucer's epic work, *The Canterbury Tales*. This is almost certainly the earliest reference to Holderness in English Literature. Since Chaucer's time extensive drainage of Holderness has been undertaken, so when Tolkien arrived it was no longer quite the "mersshy contree" of Chaucer's time. Many readers of biographies of Tolkien probably have a fairly accurate image of Oxford in their minds, and Birmingham is also quite a well-known English city. However, East Yorkshire is virtually unknown in comparison. Holderness would have been a relatively sparsely inhabited area between the only large city of Kingston-upon-Hull and the sea. The roads were unmetalled at that time, which meant that travelling away from the rail network was slow and uncomfortable. Tolkien would have been able to travel by rail from Hull to Hornsea, and from Hull to Withernsea, but there was no rail link between these two coastal towns which were to be significant locations for Tolkien while he remained in East Yorkshire. Holderness was (and still is) a relatively flat country with big skies, very little substantial woodland, and was predominantly an area where cereal crops were produced.

Once Tolkien was stationed in East Yorkshire, he was living for the first time in his life in an area in which an extremely high proportion of the surviving place-names are Scandinavian or Anglian in origin. This would have appealed to the philologist in Tolkien. Locations with which Tolkien became acquainted in East Yorkshire include Thirtle Bridge, the army camp in which he was based. Thirtle derives from the Old Norse of *Thorkell*, which is a shortened form of *Thorketil*. The first element comes from the Norse God *Thor*, and the second, *ketill*, is from cauldron ("Last Name: Thirtle"). Danthorpe, which is a few miles north-west of Roos, means village of the Danes (Kent 2002, 57), and Hilston, which is even closer to Roos, means Hildof's farm (50). Hildof is believed to be a Scandinavian and Anglian hybrid. Finally, Frodingham south-east of Roos is derived from "the settlement of Froda's people" (Allison 1984, 85). Tom Shippey explained in *The Road to Middle-earth* that "Frodo" is an English form of [the] original Froda. Shippey points out the parallels between Froda, a character mentioned in passing in Beowulf, and Tolkien's protagonist (2005, 232-7). However, the proximity of Frodingham to Roos, and Tolkien's known interest in Yorkshire place-names in particular, indicates that he may well have also been thinking about this name associated with an historical Froda, and a place he knew during the Great War, when he was writing *The Lord of the Rings* nearly thirty years later. Tolkien would urge us "not to desire to see the bones of the ox" from which the soup has been boiled, but it is a possible ingredient, so is included here (*OFS*, 39). The name Roos itself is unusual in that it has Celtic origins, but this will be examined later.

Of course, Tolkien originated in the West Midlands where smaller divisions of counties were referred to as hundreds, which date from the late Saxon period. However, Holderness was a division of the East Riding of Yorkshire that was known as a *wapentake* until quite late into the nineteenth century. This is a term used in several other northern counties. It was this word Tolkien appropriated for his "weapontake," which he transformed from its original meaning to refer to the mustering of armed warriors in Rohan. It should be pointed out that the Old Norse equivalent of the word also had three distinct other meanings which Tolkien would have encountered (Hammond and Scull 2014, 528). However, what cannot be disputed is that Tolkien modelled the four farthings of the Shire on the divisions in Yorkshire of the three 'thridings,' or what have become known as 'the Ridings' (32).

1 – Hornsea

In 1916 Tolkien participated in the "animal horror" of the Battle of the Somme as a signaller for the 13th Lancashire Fusiliers (*Letters*, Letter 61, 72), but contracted trench fever, and was invalided home on 9 November 1916 (Scull and Hammond 2017a, 102). He was hospitalised at Edgbaston (Birmingham) from which he travelled on occasion to Great Haywood (Staffordshire) to see Edith, but at the end of February 1917 he was transferred to Harrogate, and after a medical examination was ordered to join the 3rd Reserve Battalion of the Lancashire Fusiliers at Thirtle Bridge, near Withernsea (Garth 2003, 234). Tolkien was sent to East Yorkshire for "hardening," and with the ultimate intention that he would be passed fit to participate on the frontline again. Tolkien actually arrived in Hornsea by train from Hull on 19 April 1917 (Mathison 2015b, 34). Hornsea is a coastal resort sixteen miles from the city of Hull. Tolkien seems to have spent some time initially at the fifty-two-acre Hornsea Musketry Camp, which was based at the small hamlet of Rolston nearly one mile to the south of Hornsea (54). Tolkien would have received consolidation of firearms training here. Edith, with her cousin Jennie Grove, took lodgings close to the station in Hornsea by 5 May 1917, presumably to be close to him.

Hornsea is perhaps the most picturesque location at which Tolkien stayed in East Yorkshire. This is largely provided by the natural wonder which is the tree-lined Hornsea Mere–the largest natural freshwater lake in Yorkshire. Hornsea Mere belonged to the Roman Catholic Strickland-Constable family, whose seat of Wassand Hall lies on the western fringes of the Mere. Margaret Strickland-Constable, the wife of the incumbent at that time, would later be in charge of the Brooklands hospital in which Tolkien would subsequently be a patient. Her diaries offer glimpses of life at an Officers' Hospital, but are also an invaluable record of various Zeppelin raids on the east coast during the war, and inexperienced English pilots ditching their planes in the mere (Chichester-Constable). Incidentally, the suffix 'sea' in East Yorkshire locations, such as Hornsea, Skipsea, Withernsea, and Kilnsea, does not refer to their proximity to the sea, but to their freshwater lakes or inland seas which were left behind after the last Ice Age. Over recent centuries most of these have either been swallowed up by the eroding coastline, or have silted up, and only the largest at Hornsea was present in 1917 and is still present today.

When Tolkien was transferred permanently from the Musketry Camp thirteen miles south-east to Thirtle Bridge, Edith moved out of her lodgings in Hornsea. Phil Mathison has discovered that her final letter from there was dated 1 June 1917 (34). The next surviving envelope was sent from her Withernsea lodgings on 12 July 1917. For the intervening nearly six weeks her residence is unknown, and as there is no extant correspondence, the suggestion is that for this brief period the Tolkiens did not need to correspond. 'The Horns of Ulmo,' rewritten about this time from the earlier 'Sea Chant of an Elder Day,' includes a note that its "[p]resent shape [was] due to rewriting and adding [an] intro[duction] [...] in a lonely house near Roos, Holderness ["] Spring 1917" (*Shaping*, 215). As Tolkien's residence in other locations in spring 1917 may be inferred by the survival of envelopes addressed to him by Edith, it seems highly likely that during the period 1 June to around 12 July 1917 the Tolkiens were either living together or were in close proximity somewhere in the Roos area.

2 – Roos

> The leaves were long, the grass was green,
> The hemlock-umbels tall and fair,
> And in the glade a light was seen
> Of stars in shadow shimmering.
> (*FR*, 'A Knife in the Dark', 191)

Tolkien mentions Roos three times in his published *Letters*. On the first occasion in 1955 he informed his American publishers: "The kernel of the mythology, the matter of *Lúthien Tinúviel* and *Beren*, arose from a small woodland glade filled with 'hemlocks' (or other white umbellifers) *near* Roos on the Holderness peninsula– to which I occasionally went when free from regimental duties while in the Humber Garrison in 1918" (*Letters*, Letter 165, 221; emphasis mine). His 1964 letter to Christopher Bretherton gives a largely similar account as does his 1972 epistle to his youngest son, Christopher, after Edith's death (*Letters*, Letter 257, 345). However, there is one subtle difference, because in the final "Roos" letter Tolkien informs his son that the woodland glade was "*at* Roos" (*Letters*, Letter 340, 420; emphasis mine). Tolkien may have been slightly more precise with words in correspondence with Christopher. There are a few possible candidates in the Roos area, but John Garth identified the wooded area of Dents Garth near All Saints' Church in Roos as the correct location (2003, 238). Dents Garth is on the extreme south-east edge of the village, from which it would have been possible to see Thirtle Bridge, where Tolkien was stationed several times while in the area.

According to a popular wild flower guide, "many other umbellifers are loosely referred to as hemlock", and Tolkien's letter quoted above indicates this was precisely the case with him (Blamey, Fitter, and Fitter 2003, 180). Rather surprisingly, the linguistically precise Tolkien was vague about this particular subject. However, Christopher Tolkien explained his father "regarded the restriction of a vernacular name to this or that species within a large group of plants not easily distinguishable to the eye as the pedantry of popularising botanists–who ought to content themselves with the Linnean names" (qtd. in Garth 2003, 238). He evidently called all similar umbellifers 'hemlocks,' and what was good enough for him was also good enough for his story of tragic lovers.

John Garth identified Tolkien's 'hemlocks' as Queen Anne's Lace or cow parsley (2016, 238), and Dinah Hazell in her *Plants of Middle-earth* concurs (2006, 54). The most recent reference work on this subject also believes cow parsley is the "more likely" species Tolkien encountered (Judd and Judd 2017, 185). It may be possible to estimate the date of Edith's dance by comparing the flowering period of cow parsley at Roos in the springs of 2014-2018 and extrapolating that back to 1917. In 2014 the white umbels began to open in sheltered spots around 1 May, and by 10 May it was a fine spectacle–it remained in this condition for most of the rest of the month. However, in Dents Garth, the supposed site of Edith's dance in Roos, the flowering was definitely beginning to look tired and faded in most places of the woodland by 27 May. Heavy rain both on and subsequent to that date ensured it did not survive into June. It is unlikely that Tolkien would have commented favourably on the beauty of the whiteness of the 'hemlocks' if it had already begun to fade, so at a first glance a date in June seems rather unlikely. However, in 2018 after a very cold February and March the umbels didn't really begin to flower until 10 May, and they were largely intact at the end of May. Similarly, in late May 2015 the flowers were still in excellent condition at the end of May. The earliest-surviving 'Tale of Tinúviel' mentions that Beren and Tinúvel met "on a time of June", and as it is in prose there was no reason for Tolkien to alter the month for it to scan or rhyme in verse (*Lost Tales II*, 10; *B&L*, 41). It would therefore seem almost certain that the real-life inspiration also took place in June 1917. The clues from the natural world such as the chestnut blossom and the main flowering dates of cow parsley both suggest an earlier date in the month, so the most probable time for the dance would be quite early in June before the cow parsley faded completely, and the chestnut blossom had begun to die back–the first ten days of June are the most likely.

Anyone with a Classical education in the early-twentieth century would have been aware that Socrates was sentenced to death, and was poisoned by a fatal drink of hemlock. Socrates, despite the urging of his friends, accepted the court's decision and nobly drank the fatal dose whilst still discoursing to his disciples. Hemlock is therefore associated from ancient times with a story of noble self-sacrifice, and it seems highly appropriate that Tolkien utilised the name hemlock at the very commencement of his great story of love and self-sacrifice. It appears Tolkien selected the name 'hemlock,' either from a lack of precise botanical knowledge of the exact species he saw, or because he felt that that word fitted best within his story.

Cow parsley must be the species Tolkien intended as the "great misty growth of white umbels [...] were like a cloud about the boles of the trees" (*Lost Tales II*, 10; *B&L*, 41). However, unless further documentary evidence becomes available the absolute certainty of the identification of the woodland will have to remain conjectural, nevertheless there are several striking local landmarks, which would seem to support the identification. Dents Garth and Roos churchyard contain beech, horse chestnut, and all the other tree and plant species mentioned in the various versions of the encounter between Beren and Lúthien. The only exception is a mature elm tree–Beren leans on a young elm in the earliest surviving version of the text – but mature examples of this species were probably lost in the devastating effects of the Dutch Elm disease of the 1970s and 1980s (*Lost Tales II*, 11; *B&L*, 42). A sapling, probably growing from a sucker of one of the original trees, was found just south of the church car park in 2015. The continued presence of an active rookery in Dents Garth indicates the previous presence of elms in the woodland, as traditionally this is the tree species in which these corvids prefer to nest. This evidence is bolstered by the nearest property to the church, which in Tolkien's time, as now, was simply called "The Elms" with "Elm Farm" the adjacent property to the north.

About five metres away from the cow parsley in the churchyard is a railed off area, which contains a damp subterranean staircase surmounted by an escutcheon depicting the palm of a hand above three circular features containing wavy lines, which represent water. This is the heraldic device of the Sykes family (the hand denotes a baronet), who commissioned the exterior stairs down to the crypt probably during the restoration of the church in 1842. Of course, in Tolkien's mythology Beren had to make the much more perilous journey down to Melko's underground fortress of Angamandi (later Angband), and his heraldic device, drawn by Tolkien much later, features a disembodied hand, because his hand clasping a Silmaril was lost to the ravening wolf Karkaras (later Carcharoth).

A further plausible link to Tolkien's fiction is a three-trunked tree, which is the nearest tree to the church, to the south-east between the church and the entrance in the southern exterior churchyard wall. In the earliest-surviving version of Tolkien's story, Tinúviel [Lúthien] is imprisoned by her father Tinwelint (later Thingol) in Hírilorn, a mighty Beech tree: "so deeply cloven was her bole that it seemed as if three shafts sprang from the ground together and they were of like size, round and straight, and their grey rind was smooth as silk, unbroken by branch or twig for a very great height above men's heads" (*Lost Tales II,* 18; *B&L,* 53). John Garth remarked that the "three-trunked tree does seem such a specific and seemingly random detail to have [been] included in the story", so the finding of such a tree actually in Roos near the genesis of the tale is suggestive (2015). This tree is over one-hundred-and-fifty feet in height in Roos churchyard, and would certainly have been there in Tolkien's time. It has some similarities to his description, including the cloven bole, the three shafts of equal size, the grey bark, and branches above the height of men, although now there are also some more recent younger lower twigs. The fairly smooth bark is now partly obscured by ivy stems, but crucially this tree is a lime, or more poetically a linden-tree, not a beech. The tree adjacent to this lime tree is a beech. Of course in the poem about Beren and Lúthien in *The Fellowship of the Ring*, the original version of which dates back to around 1919, Tinúviel's feet are described as a "light as leaf on lindentree" (Hammond and Scull 2014, 172). The leaves of both the beech and the lime are at their freshest green when the cow parsley is in bloom.

On the southern side of the church car park is a meagre, unimpressive waterway heading south out of the village. This is very difficult to see in the summer as it is concealed by the heavy undergrowth, and as it is often a mere trickle it is very easy to ignore. It only becomes slightly more visible in the winter. In Tolkien's forest of Neldoreth in which the tree Hírilorn grows is a river called Esgalduin. By no stretch of the imagination could the tiny Roos Beck be classified as a river, but the hidden aspect of the beck may have more significance. In Tolkien's tale there was no tiny hidden stream, but the far more majestic river Esgalduin, which flowed through Neldoreth. The 'esgal' element in Esgalduin means 'screen' or 'hiding,' and Esgalduin actually translates as "River under veil", so as unlikely as it sounds Roos Beck may have been part of the 'cauldron of soup' in the back of Tolkien's mind when he created the far more magical River Esgalduin (*Silmarillion*, 329, 358).

In All Saints' church is an item of high-quality but now foxed framed calligraphy on one of the walls. It post-dates Tolkien's time in the area, but it is of interesting local historical value, and it contains etymological information which would have interested him. It reveals that the original spelling of the village name was *Ros*, and that the name is unusual in the area as being of Celtic origin and means either marsh or moorland. Tolkien had a known interest in Yorkshire place-names, so he may have researched this information himself. After the Norman Conquest the name of the village was utilised by major landowners, so in c.1158 a Robert de Ros took the title of Baron of Helmsley (Kent 2002, 88). The editors of *Parma Eldalamberon* 11 examined the meaning of *ros*, and their suggested derivations include the Welsh *rhôs*, which meant 'moor, heath or plain'; or the Breton word *ros*, which meant 'hillock,' and the Irish word *ros*, which meant 'promontory' (Gilson et al 1995, 6n7). This latter definition may have some significance because in notes about the conclusion of 'The Book of Lost Tales' in the Faring Forth, Tol Eressëa was to be "uprooted and dragged near to the Great Lands, nigh to the promontory of Rôs," which was to be followed by the "Battle of Rôs" in which the Elves were to be defeated (*Lost Tales II*, 283). Christopher Tolkien proposed that Rôs may be Brittany (283), but the editors of *Parma Eldalamberon* postulated that "the promontory of Rôs may have been suggested to Tolkien by Roos" (Gilson et al 1995, 6n7). It could be argued that Roos, which is slightly higher than some of the immediately surrounding area, lies at the head of the promontory of Holderness, which dribbles away to the elongated sand spit of Spurn Point.

Tolkien clearly had a romantic experience in Roos, which remained with him all his life until the event was even obliquely memorialised on his own gravestone. In the more immediate aftermath of Edith's dance he worked on his Goldogrin vocabularies and grammar and even invented a meaning for 'rôs,' with an exceedingly romantic flavour: "embrace" (66). However, this may have been an extremely temporary definition. It is known that in due course 'rôs' evolved in the etymologies to be equivalent to "foam, spindrift, [and] spray" (*Silmarillion*, 441). This later definition of 'rôs' could actually be an oblique reference to the hemlocks because 'foam' is an effective synonym for Tolkien's own 'cloud-like' or 'mist.'

Tolkien's linguistic invention may also have attempted to memorialise Dents Garth in another respect. Lúthien's father's realm was named Doriath and in the etymologies, Doriath is also known as Garthurian, meaning fenced realm (*Lost Road*, 358). However, it should also be emphasized that 'garth' is not a particularly rare Northern word, and Tolkien would have encountered it before. In *The Lord of the Rings* 'garth' is used on a couple of occasions by Treebeard. Towards the end of the narrative Treebeard renames the area around Isengard as "The Treegarth of Orthanc" (*RK*, 'Many Partings', 979), and earlier when singing of the entwives, their part of the song mentions spring returning to "garth and field" (*TT*, 'Treebeard', 477). In Tolkien's writing 'garth' clearly has positive connotations, as of course Dents Garth did in Tolkien's remembrance of his past life with Edith. In the early period of Tolkien's writings he often utilised real-life locations with changes of name to fit his secondary world. For instance, it is now generally accepted that Kortirion is Warwick and Great Haywood became Tavrobel in 'The Book of Lost Tales', and that "Great Haywood is recognizable [...] At the place where the rivers Trent and Sow meet, the grey stone of Essex Bridge, with its fourteen arches, leaps the 'joining waters' to Shugborough Hall, the 'House of the Hundred Chimneys' on the far side" (McIlwaine 2018, 212). These examples illustrate it is possible that he also may have utilised some of the Roos landmarks to provide firm foundations in the physical world with which to anchor the emerging mythological narrative of Beren and Lúthien. The 'hemlocks,' the three-trunked tree, the heraldic hand, the elm trees and a single beech next to a 'linden-tree', the concealed appearance of Roos Beck, all within fifty metres of Dents Garth, may seem insignificant or coincidental in isolation; but taken in conjunction with each other and combined with his positive use of the word garth, Dents Garth does seem to be the most likely venue for the location for Edith's dance, and therefore the inspiration for the meeting of Beren and Lúthien in the legendarium.

Mathison believes that Tolkien's clue on the manuscript of 'The Horns of Ylmir' that it was rewritten "in a lonely house near Roos" refers to Tolkien's billet at Thirtle Bridge Camp, but the linguistically-precise Tolkien would never have described a location at which over one thousand five hundred men were stationed as "a lonely house near Roos" (*Shaping,* 215). On balance he was probably based away from the camp and in a house not adjacent to other dwellings, but not too far from Roos. One possibility is a building on the outskirts of Halsham, a village less than two miles from Roos, which had a few isolated buildings at that time, as it does now. It is a much smaller village, and more strung-out than the comparably more tightly-knit Roos.

3 – Halsham

Even if Tolkien wasn't actually living in Halsham, it is likely he would have been drawn to the village in his free time, as it is a fairly short walk of about two miles from Roos across the fields. The strength of Tolkien's Roman Catholic faith must never be underestimated. According to the *Victoria County History*, there "is little evidence of Roman Catholicism" in Roos, but Halsham is quite a different matter (Kent 2002, 93). In medieval times Halsham was the seat of the Constable family, and after the Reformation the family remained loyal to their Roman Catholic faith, and they kept links to the parish even when they moved to their impressive new Elizabethan Hall on the Burton Constable estate. Halsham had recusants in 1595-1596, and between eight to sixteen in the 1660s and 1670s. As late as the eighteenth century eight Roman Catholics were still living in the village (Allison 1984, 39). There is still visible evidence of the faith in Halsham. The most striking reminder is the mausoleum of the Constable family. This was constructed between 1792 and 1802, and it had been restored as recently as c.1900 (32). It has marked similarities to Sauron's temple in Númenor, as it is described in the *Notion Club Papers*. When Lowdham sees the Radcliffe Camera in Oxford he is reminded of Sauron's temple, which apart from the blackened colouration perhaps better fits the description of Halsham Mausoleum rather than the Radcliffe Camera. However, in Tolkien's fiction the dimensions have become truly monumental: "it was in the form of a circle at the base, and the walls were fifty feet in thickness, and the width of their base was five hundred feet across the centre, and they rose from the ground five hundred feet, and they were crowned with a mighty dome; and it was wrought all of silver, but the silver was turned black" (*Sauron*, 367). Tolkien had utilised the Radcliffe Camera library when he studied for his degree in Oxford, and at that time it was black from industrial soot, so if he saw the Halsham Mausoleum he would have been immediately reminded of the Oxford building. When he returned to Oxford after the war he was almost in the same position as Lowdham, as he was confronted with the sooty Radcliffe Camera, and would no doubt remember the Halsham equivalent, although that was of course almost pristine in comparison. In an earlier Old English version of a text a further relevant aspect to Halsham appears: "it was built in the midst of the town [...] on the high hill which before was undefiled but now became a heathen fane" (384). As mentioned earlier Halsham is a small settlement not a town, but the mausoleum was built on the highest point of land in Halsham. When it was being constructed evidence was discovered of a possible prehistoric burial site. Would Tolkien have disapproved of ancient remains being disturbed to construct a Roman Catholic monument to the dead, to such an extent that he would consider it a heathen fane? A clue as to Tolkien's possible stance may be gathered from a letter in which he discussed the Númenóreans of Gondor's "great interest in ancestry and in tombs," which he declared was "proud, peculiar, and archaic" (*Letters*, Letter 211, 281). The implication is that he disapproved of lavish funerary monuments, and he went on to have a simple grave himself.

The original order for Tolkien's posting to Holderness was made on 27 November 1916 from the headquarters of the Lancashire Fusiliers, which at that time was actually in Halsham (Mathison 2015b, 12). However, by the time Tolkien had arrived only a few months later the HQ had been moved to Tunstall, which was more convenient for Thirtle Bridge Camp. Nevertheless, it is entirely possible that the military maintained some presence in the village. The most likely building in Halsham for the HQ is the oldest residence, now known as Halsham House, but previously it was a former almshouse and school. Halsham House, is immediately south-west of the mausoleum, and has a strange small alcove built into the side of an exterior wall, possibly present at the time of original construction, which contains a small statue. On closer examination this proves to be a figure of the Virgin Mary. The Catholic credentials of Halsham are plain to see after a little investigation, but whether this or a similar statue was present when Tolkien was in the area is probably a question which may never be answered. At an exhibition at Burton Constable in 2014 an information panel stated that during the Great War the Constable family encouraged Roman Catholic soldiers to join them at mass (Reynolds 2015). At the present time it is not known where Tolkien worshipped while in Holderness.

4 – Thirtle Bridge

After the idyllic period near Roos, it is believed Tolkien had his first lengthy stint at Thirtle Bridge Camp, which is approximately 1¼ miles south-east of Roos. Rather confusingly, Tolkien was based at Thirtle Bridge at various times during his eighteen months in Holderness. On some detailed old maps Thirtle Bridge is marked, but there were no buildings in that area before the Great War, it was simply a bridge over the Tunstall drain on the road to Withernsea. The nearest place of habitation before the war was an isolated farmhouse at Renish. However, for the duration of hostilities a temporary camp was installed on the higher ground above Thirtle Bridge catering for 1,500 men. (Garth 2003, 234). A rough idea of what was present at Thirtle Bridge during Tolkien's time may be gleaned from a local paper which advertised the auctioning off of "the whole of the existing hutments" of both Thirtle Bridge and the smaller Dimlington site, which consisted of: "about 40 sectional wooden huts of various sizes, 50 armstrong sectional canvas huts, bath houses, cook houses, several brick buildings, cooking ranges, boilers, a No. 5.0 Bno independent boiler and connections, and 1.25 inch iron piping" (*Yorkshire Post* 1919, 3). Today very little survives of the camp. However, the southernmost section of the present Mona House is believed to incorporate the Officer's mess and the footprint of the former cookhouse survives as a corrugated barn. The bridge over the drain has a dedicated keystone bearing the date 1833, so the bridge looks very much as it would have in Tolkien's time, although some red bricks higher than the dated stone are probably 1950s in date.

Thirtle Bridge was an army camp, and Tolkien was there at a time of war, but when not actually engaged in repelling Zeppelin attacks or involved in physical activity time hung heavy on the hands of the "inmates." The only known surviving letters written at Thirtle Bridge from an independent source describe duties at the camp as "tedious, and boredom was rife" (Mathison 2015b, 64). This implies that Tolkien would certainly have had time to mull over his emerging mythology, and even to have managed to write. This is confirmed by his Gnomish Lexicon which is dated Withernsea 1917. At no known period did Tolkien live in Withernsea, so the use of it here translates to the nearby camp of Thirtle Bridge. Tolkien's handwritten note accompanying a contemporary photograph shows that Withernsea was synonymous with Thirtle Bridge for Tolkien. The Tolkien Estate have confirmed that a photograph of Tolkien in an army hut published on page 38 of *The Tolkien Family Album* is accompanied by Tolkien's handwriting which says: "Self in Hux's and my cubicle, Withernsea [Thirtle Bridge] 1917" (Blackburn 2015b). "Hux" must refer to Tolkien's long-time comrade and friend Leslie Risdon Huxtable, with whom he had also shared quarters on Cannock Chase. Huxtable was another signalling officer, and was believed to have been trained to be Tolkien's deputy at one time, ready to take over if anything happened to Tolkien. Ironically, he was injured in an explosion, and he returned to England before Tolkien. Garth mentions him as being based at Tunstall Hall after receiving an injury in France, and he was present at the Minden Dinner with Tolkien on 1 August 1917 (Garth 2003, 23).

5 – Withernsea

When Tolkien was based at Thirtle Bridge, Edith moved into lodgings in Withernsea three miles to the south-east. It is known she was installed there by 12 July 1917 (Mathison 2015b, 54). Phil Mathison discovered that Edith's lodgings in Withernsea were at 76 Queen Street on the corner of Queen Street and Hull Road, which is now the Lifeboat Café. The back of this property may still be seen from the top of Withernsea Lighthouse. John Garth has shown that Withernsea had a temporary significance in Tolkien's developing mythology. In a Gnomish lexicon he was compiling he wrote under the title and the name of Eriol, the mariner, the words "Tol Withernon (and many places besides), 1917" (Garth 2003, 236). Eriol is significant because in some respects he can be seen as a self-portrait, and in early versions of the legendarium his arrival in Eressëa provides the framing-story of *'The Book of Lost Tales'*. Unfortunately for East Yorkshire, Tol Withernon (almost certainly inspired by Withernsea) was never mentioned again in any writings, which have been published so far.

Edith's lodgings at 76 Queen Street are about two hundred yards away from Withernsea's only monolithic structure, the lighthouse completed in 1894. The lighthouse is one hundred and twenty-seven feet high and is at least three times the height of any of the surrounding buildings. The lighthouse is a striking structure in what is an otherwise unremarkable town made even more so by being painted brilliant white. The lighthouse is unusual in being built well inland from the sea ("About the Lighthouse"), and Edith's lodgings were slightly nearer to the lighthouse than the sea. Today the white tower is surrounded by domestic dwellings, but in 1917 the adjacent area was much less cluttered, as contemporaneous postcards show. Since completion it has always dominated the surrounding town and countryside.

When the light was working the beam could be seen for a radius of seventeen miles, but even unlit as it is today, the lighthouse as a structure may still be observed from the southern edge of Roos. The road leaving Roos undulates slightly, so in the hollows the lighthouse is lost to sight, but it comes back into view again as soon as height is regained. The lighthouse would have been visible to Tolkien from the Thirtle Bridge camp as long as the sightlines were not blocked by the temporary camp buildings.

Shortly after the outbreak of war the *Hull Daily Mail* reported that Withernsea lighthouse had been in darkness for a fortnight, so when Tolkien was in Holderness three years later the light would still have been doused for most of the time (19 Sep 1914, 3). However, the beam was permitted to glow again during the Second World War if a special convoy needed escorting through the hazardous shallows off the Yorkshire coast. The evidence is lacking for the Great War, but the Withernsea Museum assumes that the situation would have been almost identical during the earlier conflict (Simpson 2015).

Although Tolkien explicitly states in his interview with Denys Gueroult that he did not think in symbols (BBC 1964), when he caught sight of the brilliant white lighthouse from anywhere in Holderness after 12 July 1917, surely he would be reminded of Edith, especially while she was lodged virtually at the lighthouse's foot? Indeed, it seems highly probable that even after Edith left for Cheltenham that this striking white structure would still remind Tolkien of his wife's former sojourn in the town.

There is only one direct route Tolkien could have used from Thirtle Bridge to Withernsea when he wished to visit his wife or when he needed to catch a train to Hull for monthly medical examinations, and that is the twisting, undulating road now known as the B1242. For over a mile after leaving the camp there would hardly have been a single man-made structure visible between Thirtle Bridge and Withernsea in what was, and still is, a completely rural landscape. However, 1¼ miles south-east of Thirtle Bridge on the edge of a small settlement called Waxholme is a hill, on the summit of which is a ruined mill, variously called Withernsea Mill, Waxholme Mill, Owthorne Mill, and more often simply the Black Mill. The mill last ground corn in 1892, and its sails were removed in 1904. In 1917 the black-painted windmill was still at its full height of approximately sixty feet, and was being used as a watch-tower by the army (Chapman and Chapman 1996, 30). It can safely be assumed that on the summit guns were mounted as a defence against low-flying Zeppelins or potential invaders on foot from the beach at Waxholme. Only a few years ago the family who own the mill discovered a box of Great War ammunition in its foundations (Mathison 2015a). As the road from Thirtle Bridge approaches the mill it dips into a deep depression, so the final ascent to the mill becomes quite steep, and the black mill on the summit would have loomed larger than if it had been approached on the level. A century later the badly ruined mill is just a presence on a hazardous bend, but in 1917 and 1918 as a contemporary newspaper report makes clear, the whole coastal road running from Easington through Withernsea, up to Hornsea and finishing in Skipsea was under military control (*Hull Daily Mail* 29 Apr 1916, 2), so there would have been a series of road blocks at significant junctions, and one of the most prominent was at this point (*Hull Daily Mail* 6 Dec 1917, 4). Tolkien stated in his 1972 letter to his youngest son that he was "for a brief time in command of an outpost of the Humber Garrison in 1917"; the finding of the ammunition adds weight to the theory that the Black Mill was an outpost of the Humber Garrison, but further evidence would have to come to light before it could be proved conclusively that this was the outpost Tolkien mentioned (*Letters*, Letter 165, 420).

From the Black Mill it is possible to see both the white spike of Withernsea lighthouse over a mile distant in a south-easterly direction, but also a quite different white structure about 1½ miles away to the south-west. The latter was new when Tolkien was in the area–the gleaming white water-tower at Rimswell was completed in 1916. Although it is clear that Tolkien would have seen and journeyed past many of these white and black towers during his war service, there is absolutely no similarity between the white tower at Rimswell and any of the white towers in his fiction.

6 – Brooklands Officers' Hospital

While Edith was still lodging beneath the shadow of the white tower of Withernsea Lighthouse, by 13 August 1917 her husband had a recurrence of trench fever and was sent to the first of the two hospitals or 'Houses of Healing' he would become acquainted with in East Yorkshire: Brooklands Officers' Hospital on Cottingham Road in Hull. This ten-week stay was the first of two long stints lasting in total for nearly eighteen weeks at this convalescent home, and his time spent there was extremely productive. In the first instance he was able to spend long periods working on the building-blocks of his emerging language, known at the time as Goldogrin. There have been many writers who have attempted to follow Tolkien in writing fantasy narratives, but none of them have matched his care in creating grammars and languages. His fiction was "*fundamentally linguistic* in inspiration", the language, as he often attested–words or names came first–and stories followed afterwards (*Letters*, Letter 165, 219; emphasis original). In addition to the time spent on the foundation of his lexicons, vocabularies, and grammars Tolkien also wrote down for the first time the earliest versions of two stories which he continued to write, rework, and re-imagine for almost the whole of his writing life: 'The Tale of Tinúviel' and 'The Tale of Turambar.' The central importance of Lúthien Tinúviel is exemplified by his placing of the fictional name Lúthien under his wife's name on their gravestone more than half a century later. In addition to what were to become major works in his legendarium, he is known to have composed at least two new poems at Brooklands: 'The Companions of the Rose' and 'The Grey Bridge of Tavrobel' (Scull and Hammond 2017b, 1455). In August 1917 he explained to Christopher Wiseman that the former was the only poem he had written so far that year (Garth 2003, 231, 240). This seems to have spurred him on as 'Sea-Song of an Elder Day' was rewritten between 31 August and 2 September and retitled 'The Horns of Ylmir', and a little later he also revised 'The Mermaid's Flute' (Scull and Hammond 2017a, 109).

Brooklands was operated by Margaret Strickland-Constable (née Pakenham), who was actually the commandant, not the matron as stated by some earlier researchers. She was proficient in German, French, Swedish, Danish, and Norwegian, and she is thought to have worked for the censor department during the war. Her knowledge of these languages would have provided a little common ground between her and Tolkien on her brief visits to the hospital. However, in his second long stay at Brooklands Tolkien was said to have learnt a little Russian and improved his Spanish and Italian–not languages in which Strickland-Constable excelled. Margaret Strickland-Constable was soon to be a war widow, as her husband killed himself in a London hotel on his return from the front in December 1917.

Brooklands was only officially opened as a hospital for officers as late as 31 July 1917 by Major General Sir Stanley von Donop (*Hull Daily Mail* 1 Aug 1917, 2). Recent research has revealed that almost all of the personnel associated with Brooklands mentioned in a newspaper article written to mark its opening were Roman Catholics. It is not known if Tolkien's faith helped him to gain a place here, as this was the only hospital for officers in the immediate area. On completion accommodation was provided for only seventeen patients, and on the opening day three were installed (*Hull Daily Mail* 1 Aug 1917, 2), to be joined by Tolkien only a fortnight later (Garth 2003, 236). Brooklands enjoyed a good reputation amongst local officers, as an overheard comment by Margaret's brother, which Strickland-Constable proudly included in her diary, implies: "What you want to do is arrange to have a good crash, so as to get sent to Brooklands" (Chichester-Constable). Likewise, Tolkien found the surroundings congenial, and surviving ordnance survey maps from 1910 show that the substantial grounds contained several mature trees. The map also shows that the conservatory was there as early as 1910, which must have been another boon for the invalids. Only the western half of the detached building including the conservatory was utilised as the hospital; the remainder was a private dwelling known as the Cedars, named after the large tree in its garden. Cottingham Road itself was at that time a fairly quiet leafy-lined thoroughfare, and opposite it on the other side of the road was the recently-founded municipal college, later the Hull University campus, but in 1917 that area consisted mainly of large open fields.

As mentioned earlier Strickland-Constable's diaries for the time survive, and although she does not refer to Tolkien by name we do know that he was in Brooklands for the second long period when the Zeppelin raid of 6 August 1918 took place in Hull. She mentions two majors with neurasthenia who hid under their beds when the bombardment took place, but the remainder, including Tolkien, were said to be "quite calm" (Chichester-Constable). This second summer Tolkien was incarcerated in Brooklands was probably the longest period free from distractions he would enjoy for the remainder of his life. There is no evidence that Edith, their first child, John, nor Jennie Grove moved up north again to be near Tolkien once she left for Cheltenham around the third week of August 1917. Once he returned to Oxford, and later academic duties, his spare time for working on his language-creation would have been severely curtailed by both work commitments and the demands of his ever-increasing family. The almost two months at Brooklands in the summer of 1918 gave him a real opportunity for constructing the strong foundations of language creation and for time spent on writing some of the central narratives of what would become *'The Book of Lost Tales'*.

Although Tolkien shared some of his time at Brooklands with an officer friend, and was able to produce some good work on his emerging mythology, it seems the diet there could have been a lot more nutritious. On 11 October 1918, a month to the day after Tolkien left Brooklands for the final time, Colonel Easton wrote to the local newspaper asking for presents of game (presumably birds like pheasant, and possibly meat like venison) to be donated to the institution, which he pointed out was the only officers' hospital in Hull and the surrounding district (*Hull Daily Mail* 12 Oct 1918, 2). A medical report notes Tolkien lost two stone in weight after his attack of gastritis and during his second stay at Brooklands, so some of this weight loss may have been due to insufficiently nutritious food. Tolkien's emaciated frame around this time can be easily gauged by examining the photograph published on page 41 of *The Tolkien Family Album*. This likeness depicts a very thin uniformed Tolkien on a seashore with Edith. When Phil Mathison wrote his book, he assumed that this was taken at Hornsea (2015b, 35). However, the Tolkien Estate revealed that on the back of the photograph Tolkien had added the following words: "Withernsea/July (?)/1917./ taken by L.R. Huxtable" (Blackburn 2015a).

7 – Easington

On the 16 October 1917 Tolkien was discharged from Brooklands for the first time and he initially returned to Thirtle Bridge. However, by 16 November he had already been transferred to the 9th Battalion, Royal Defence Corps, and they were based ten miles further south down the coast at Easington. There are only a few clues as to where Tolkien lived or what he worked on at this time. One of the manuscripts of what became 'The Song of Eriol' includes a later note, which says "Easington, 1917-18" (Mathison 2015b, 91). In addition, a note on a manuscript of 'Elf Alone' (formerly entitled 'The Lonely Harebell') explains it was written at a "farmhouse near Easington" (91). One of the largest landowners in the area was a Robert Walker who owned a substantial property, called 'The Tower' in Easington, which has changed very little since 1918 (88). Walker, who left diaries which have been examined, is known to have rented out some of his properties to army personnel, but it is not known for certain if one of these was Tolkien. On a modern Ordnance Survey map there are only a handful of farms and farmhouses in the Easington area, bounded as it is on one side by the sea, and on the other by the proximity of the Humber estuary, so theoretically it should be possible to determine exactly where Tolkien lived during the winter of 1917 to 1918.

As a man steeped in history, Tolkien was almost certainly aware that at the time of the *Domesday Book* most of the land around Easington, indeed the whole of Holderness, which was not owned by the church, belonged to the Earl of Holderness, a certain Drogo (English 1991, 7). It is rather surprising that he would choose Frodo's father's name from a hated Norman overlord if Tolkien "felt that his true culture had been crushed and forgotten" by the Norman Conquest (Garth 2003, 52). Whether Tolkien recalled this name when he was writing *The Lord of the Rings* and selecting a name for Frodo's father is debatable. However, East Yorkshire contains both North and South Frodingham, and was controlled by Earl Drogo, so there does appear to be at the least a tenuous link between these two members of the Baggins family in the landscape of the East Riding.

8 – Kilnsea

When trench fever or other illnesses returned over the winter of 1917-18 he was sent another two miles further south to Kilnsea for treatment at the hospital at the Godwin Battery (Mathison 2015b, 90). This "House of Healing" was very different from the other in the quiet leafy suburbs of Hull. At that time it was approximately 250 yards from the sea, and, it being winter, some of Tolkien's visits must have coincided with pounding waves. Tolkien as far as his memory went back could remember a "terrible recurrent dream" of a "Great Wave, towering up, and coming in ineluctably over the trees and green fields" (*Letters*, Letter 163, 213). Although Tolkien's nightmare predated his internment in Kilnsea hospital, it was probably intensified by his proximity to what had until relatively recently been called the German Ocean. The Godwin Battery hospital, as is evident from contemporary aerial photographs, was built very close to North Marsh Lane, and at the southern end of the lane about 550 feet away from the hospital is the Blue Bell public house, which had a very clear proof embedded in its side of the destructive power of the sea. The plaque states that the inn was built in 1847, and at that time was 534 yards from the sea. When Tolkien was there in early 1918 he would have been able to calculate, should he have wanted to, that the inn was already much closer to the sea.

As Tolkien made clear in his interview with Denys Gueroult he was always "historically minded", and he would no doubt have heard of examples of the destruction of historical artefacts (BBC 1964). The tower of Old Kilnsea church was finally swallowed up by the sea in 1831 (Crowther 2006, 176, plate 3), and in 1818 an old ornate medieval cross was removed inland to safety (plate 1). This cross is thought to have either commemorated the landing of the future Henry IV at Raverspurn in 1399, or the return of King Edward IV from exile in 1471. Photographs survive of Easington being almost submerged by severe flooding in 1906, and it is likely this most recent inundation would have been brought to Tolkien's attention. The recurrent great wave dream continued to haunt Tolkien until he managed to exorcise it from his system by writing the 'Downfall of Númenor' in the 1930s (*Letters*, Letter 163, 213). John Garth has shown that the storm poem 'Sea Chant of an Elder Day' became more violent in the rewriting in Holderness, and Tolkien's proximity to destructive seas may have had an effect on his subsequent maritime writing.

In Wayne G. Hammond and Christina Scull's *The Lord of the Rings: A Reader's Companion* when Tolkien mentions the Beacons of Gondor, which were lit to summon aid from Rohan, the authors quite rightly note that "almost every English man, woman, and child would immediately think of the beacons lit in 1588 to warn of the approach of the Spanish Armada" (2014, 509). The authors go on to mention earlier beacons in antiquity, but they fail to refer to Tolkien's personal association with a beacon during the Great War. The Kilnsea Beacon was originally erected in Napoleonic times and was constructed of wood, but when Tolkien was in Holderness it had been moved westwards from its earlier location on a hill, because otherwise it would have been lost to the sea many years earlier. By 1917 the wooden beacon had been replaced by a very distinctive metal structure. The Kilnsea Beacon during the Great War was situated north of the Godwin Battery, but nearer the battery than Easington. It was finally dismantled in the

Second World War, as it was thought to be a too readily identified landmark for enemy planes (Crowther 2006, 136).

When Tolkien was with the Humber Garrison, he travelled to Dunstable to sit a signalling course exam in the second half of July 1917. It is possible that Tolkien's duties as a signalling officer may have been connected with one of the most striking surviving remnants of the Great War in the area. In 1916 an Acoustic Sound Mirror was erected at Kilnsea to listen out for approaching aircraft, which at that time effectively meant Zeppelins, as German planes were unable to travel across the North Sea to Yorkshire (Crowther 2006, 89). The sound was focussed by the concave dish to the 'collector's head' mounted on the metal pipe still visible in 2019, on which was attached a rudimentary microphone. Wires from this led down into a trench in which an operator with headphones would listen for approaching aircraft, and would provide an early warning–actually of only four minutes. We will probably never know if Tolkien was one of these 'listeners', but even if not, when he was in the Kilnsea area he could not have failed to see this monumental concrete structure. As a trained signalling officer, he must have been aware of how this structure operated and was utilised.

Kilnsea is the southernmost inhabited village in that part of East Yorkshire, and marks the end of Tolkien's known physical association with Holderness. Admittedly, Tolkien only spent eighteen months in East Yorkshire, but these were crucial in the development of his emerging mythology. The dance of Edith in the "hemlock glade" signifies both an idyllic period in his married life, and simultaneously an inspirational turning point in his mythological world-building. Additionally, it also symbolises a return to a much-needed calmer period of recovery after the ravages of surviving the Somme. Arguably, just as crucial were the nearly twenty weeks of recuperation over two summers spent in Brooklands Officer's Hospital. This gave him the invaluable concentrated time to build up and construct his complex vocabularies and grammars of Goldogrin languages; compose new poems or rework older examples, and write the earliest versions of 'The Tale of Tinúviel' and 'The Tale of Turumbar.' These two Great Tales of his legendarium were to stay with him for the remainder of his life, but their dissemination to a wider and very appreciative public was more than half a century in the future. Indeed, the fullest narratives of both of these stories were only published posthumously. On 11 September 1918 Tolkien was transferred to the Savoy Convalescent Hospital in Blackpool, and by early November he had recovered enough to accept work on the *New English Dictionary* in Oxford (Scull and Hammond 2017a, 113-4). The armistice was signed on 11 November 1918, by which time Tolkien had resumed his married family life and commenced his long academic career in Oxford.

Bibliography

"About the Lighthouse", *Withernsea Lighthouse Museum*, 2016, <https://www.withernsealighthouse.co.uk/about-the-lighthouse/> [accessed 7 January 2018].

Allison, K.J., ed., *A History of the County of York, East Riding, Vol. V. Holderness: Southern Part*, (Oxford: Oxford University Press, 1984).

BBC *Author Archive Collection*, Professor J.R.R. Tolkien interviewed by Denys Gueroult, 26 November 1964, <https://www.bbc.co.uk/programmes/p021jx7j> [accessed 3 January 2024]

Blackburn, C., "Re: Tolkien in East Yorkshire", Email to Phil Mathison, 17 November 2015a.
– "Re: J.R.R. Tolkien in Staffordshire", Email to Scott Whitehouse, 9 April 2015b.

Blamey, M., R. Fitter, and A. Fitter, *Wild Flowers of Britain & Ireland*, (London: A & C Black, 2003).

Carpenter, H., *J.R.R. Tolkien: A Biography*, (London: George Allen & Unwin, 1977).

Chapman, M. and B. Chapman, eds., *The Archive Photographs Series: Withernsea*, (Stroud: Chalford, 1996).

Chaucer, G., *The Riverside Chaucer*, ed. by F.N. Robinson, 3rd edn, (Oxford: Oxford University Press, 1987).

Crowther, J., *The People Along the Sand: The Spurn Peninsula and Kilnsea: A History*, 1800-2000, (Andover: Phillimore, 2006).

English, B., *The Lords of Holderness, 1086-1260: A Study in Feudal Society*, (Hull: Hull University Press, 1991).

Easton, G., "Brooklands Officers' Hospital", *Hull Daily Mail*, 12 Oct 1918, p.2.

Garth, J., *Tolkien and the Great War: The Threshold of Middle-earth*, (London: HarperCollins, 2003)
— 'Esgalduin aside, I'm delighted that my brief investigations 15 years or so – and at slightly the wrong time of year – are inspiring and seemingly being borne out by your further research, Michael. I'm intrigued by the linden tree idea too, because the three-trunked tree does seem such a specific and seemingly random detail to have included in the story. But I do wonder how large and noticeable the lime tree in Dents Garth might have been in 1917. Even if it's more than 100 years old, could it have been mature by that time? Is there any way of finding out? – short of chopping it down, of course!' Comment on Tolkien Society Facebook Group Page, 29 May 2015. <https://m.facebook.com/groups/6522796067?view=permalink&id=10153240175736068&_ rdr> [accessed 7 January 2019].
— "Re: Roos Extra", Email to author, 16 September 2016.

Gilson, C., C.F. Hostetter, P. Wynne, and A. Smith, eds. *Parma Eldalamberon*, 11 (1995).

Hammond, W. G. and C. Scull, *The Lord of the Rings: A Reader's Companion*, (London: HarperCollins, 2014).

Hazel, D., *The Plants of Middle-earth: Botany and Sub-creation*, (Kent: Kent State University Press, 2006).

Judd, W. and . Judd, *Flora of Middle-earth: Plants of J.R.R. Tolkien's Legendarium*, (Oxford: Oxford University Press, 2017).

Kent, G.H.R., ed. *A History of the County of York, East Riding, Vol. VII. Holderness: Middle and North Divisions*, (Oxford: Oxford University Press, 2002).

"Last Name: Thirtle." *Surname DB: The Internet Surname Database*. 2017. <www.surnamedb.com/Surname/Thirtle> [accessed 7 January 2019].

Lee, S.D., "'Tolkien in Oxford' (BBC, 1968): A Reconstruction", *Tolkien Studies*, 15 (2018), 115-176.

Mabey, R., *Flora Britannica*, (London: Sinclair Stevenson, 1996).

Mathison, P., "Re: Tolkien Seminar–Phil M", E-mail to the author, 5 Jul. 2015a.
– . *Tolkien in East Yorkshire, 1917-1918: An Illustrated Tour*, (Newport: Dead Good, 2015b).

McIlwaine, C., *Tolkien: Maker of Middle-earth*, (Oxford: Bodleian Library, 2018).

Noad, C., "Re: Halsham Mausoleum", Email to author, 2 May 2015.

Our own correspondent, 'Withernsea Council. Lead pipes and the Water Supply', *Hull Daily Mail*, 6 December 1917, p.4.

"Paul Pry", 'Our Holderness Letter', *Hull Daily Mail*, 19 September 1914, p.3.

"Paul Pry", 'Our Holderness Letter', *Hull Daily Mail*, 29 April 1916, p.2.

Reynolds, P., "Re: Burton Constable", Email to author, 5 Aug 2015.

Scull, C. and W. G. Hammond, *The J.R.R. Tolkien Companion and Guide: Chronology*. 2nd edn. (London: HarperCollins, 2017a).
– . *The J.R.R. Tolkien Companion and Guide: Reader's Guide*. 2nd edn. (London: HarperCollins, 2017b).

Shippey, T., *The Road to Middle-earth*, 3rd edn. (London: HarperCollins, 2005).

Simpson, T., "Re: Withernsea Lighthouse", Email to the author, 24 February 2015.

Tolkien, J. and P. Tolkien, *The Tolkien Family Album*, (London: HarperCollins, 1992).

Tolkien, J.R.R., *The Silmarillion*, ed. by Christopher Tolkien (London: George Allen & Unwin, 1977).
— *The Book of Lost Tales, Part Two*, ed. by Christopher Tolkien (London: George Allen & Unwin, 1984).
— *The Lays of Beleriand*, ed. by Christopher Tolkien (London: George Allen & Unwin, 1985).
— *The Shaping of Middle-earth*, ed. by Christopher Tolkien (London: HarperCollins, 1986).
— *The Lost Road*, ed. by Christopher Tolkien (London: Unwin Hyman, 1987).
— *Sauron Defeated*, ed. by Christopher Tolkien (London: HarperCollins, 1992).
— *The Letters of J.R.R. Tolkien*, ed. by H. Carpenter with the assistance of C. Tolkien, (London: HarperCollins, 1999).
— *The Lord of the Rings*, 50th Anniversary edition, (London: HarperCollins, 2004).
— *Tolkien On Fairy-stories*, eds. Douglas Anderson & Verlyn Flieger (London: HarperCollins, 2008).
— *Beren and Lúthien*, ed. by Christopher Tolkien (London: HarperCollins, 2017).
The Treasure House, Beverley, *Diaries of Margaret Chichester-Constable*, DDST/NA1640.
Unsigned, 'By Direction of the Disposal Board', *Yorkshire Post*, 2 August 1919, p.3.
Unsigned, 'Hospital for Officers', *Hull Daily Mail*, 1 August 1917. p.2.

Chronological Order of HDM articles

"Paul Pry", 'Our Holderness Letter', *Hull Daily Mail*, 19 September 1914, p.3.

"Paul Pry", 'Our Holderness Letter', *Hull Daily Mail*, 29 April 1916, p.2.

Unsigned, 'Hospital for Officers', *Hull Daily Mail*, 1 August 1917. p.2.

Our own correspondent, 'Withernsea Council. Lead pipes and the Water Supply', *Hull Daily Mail*, 6 December 1917, p.4.

Easton, G., "Brooklands Officers' Hospital", *Hull Daily Mail*, 12 Oct 1918, p.2.

Appendix: Tolkien in East Yorkshire Chronology

(compiled from Scull and Hammond, *Chronology*, Garth, Mathison and my own research)

1917	
19 April	Tolkien posted to Hornsea Musketry Camp. He joins 3rd Reserve Battalion.
1 May	Tolkien attends a medical board examination. Tolkien spends some time at Hornsea Musketry camp.
5 May	Edith lodging at 1 Bank Terrace, Hornsea on this date. Tolkien posted to Thirtle Bridge, but is actually based at Hornsea Musketry Camp.
12 May	Tolkien declared fit for home service.
c.1-10 June	Edith Tolkien dances in a glade of Cow Parsley at or near Roos.
1 June	Tolkien found fit for general service during a medical board examination. Edith still at 1 Bank Terrace, Hornsea.
2 June	Edith leaves 1 Bank Terrace, Hornsea.
2 Jun-11 July	Tolkien may have been able to lodge with Edith for 6 weeks near Roos when put in charge of an outpost.
12 July	Edith lodging at 76 Queen Street, Withernsea by this date.
13 July	Tolkien at 'Waverley,' Cliff Road, Hornsea, on route for Dunstable.
14-21 July	Tolkien sits a signalling exam at Dunstable.
31 July	Brooklands Officers' Hospital opens with 3 patients.
1 August	Tolkien attends annual Minden Day dinner at Thirtle Bridge or Tunstall Hall?
13 August	Tolkien admitted to Brooklands Officers' Hospital by this date.
21-4 August	Edith leaves Withernsea for Cheltenham sometime about this date.
22 August	Zeppelin raid on Hedon, but there are no casualties.
Late August	Tolkien admits to C. Wiseman he has only written 1 poem so far in 1917: "The Companions of the Rose."
25 September	Zeppelin raid on Hull.
16 October	Tolkien leaves Brooklands Officers' Hospital for Thirtle Bridge.
16 November	Tolkien attends a medical board examination. His address is 9th Royal Defence Corps, Withernsea. He still requires some indoor hospital treatment. John Francis Reuel Tolkien born in Cheltenham.
19 November	Tolkien's address is 9th Royal Defence Corps, Kilnsea.
24 November	Tolkien promoted to Lieutenant.
1918	
19 January	Tolkien attends a medical board examination and is still based with 9th Royal Defence corps at Easington.
19 February	Tolkien attends a medical board examination.
10 March	Zeppelin raid on Hull; a woman died of shock 2 days later.
19 March	Tolkien attends a medical board examination. 9th Royal Defence corps is disbanded and Tolkien is to be based at Thirtle Bridge.
10 April	Medical board decides Tolkien fit for general service.
10-28 June	Tolkien at Penkridge Camp and Brocton Camp, Cannock Chase.
29 June	Tolkien succumbs to gastritis at Brocton Camp.

12 July	Tolkien back at Brooklands Officers' Hospital by this date. He develops his Qenya and Goldogrin lexicons and brushes up his Italian and Spanish.
26 July	Tolkien ordered to embark for Boulogne, even though still in hospital.
4 September	Tolkien attends a medical board examination and is considered 100% disabled after losing 2 stones in weight.
11 September	Tolkien is released from Brooklands Officers' Hospital and transferred to Blackpool Savoy Convalescent Hospital.
19 November	Tolkien is in Oxford on this date.

"I will do my duty to God and the King" – J.R.R. Tolkien and R.S.S. Baden-Powell

Troels Forchhammer

In May 1909 the parishioners of the Birmingham Oratory could, in the Parish Magazine, read a brief notice stating that

> Three patrols of Scouts under the Brothers Tolkien, have been started, and they marched smartly in the wake of the Boys Brigade on Easter Monday. When they have done a little more drill, we shall ask some of our friends to help towards providing them with shirts, haversacks, etc. (Oratory 2019)

Discussing Tolkien's *Book of the Foxrook*, Dimitra Fimi in *Tolkien, Race and Cultural History* speculated whether Tolkien had been involved with the Boy Scout Movement. I, too, have previously noted similarities between Scouting and Tolkien (Forchhammer 2012), but since discovering the above notice on the Birmingham Oratory website in 2013 (Forchhammer 2013), I have been trying to wring out the meaning of this brief note.[1]

Nancy Bunting also explored aspects of Tolkien's involvement with the Scout Movement in her 2015 paper, 'Tolkien and the Boy Scouts' (2015). Here she mentions the note from the Oratory website, briefly notes the *Book of the Foxrook*[2] as well as Tolkien's evolving relationship with Edith Bratt[3] and the character of Bard from *The Hobbit*.

This paper, however, focuses on various topical, ethical and other parallels between Tolkien and the founder of the Scout Movement, R.S.S. Baden-Powell, 1st Baron Gilwell. This paper will argue that Tolkien must have read Baden-Powell's book, *Scouting for Boys*, and will explore parallels between Baden-Powell's book and Tolkien's personal ethos and his writings.

1 – History of B-P and Scouting

Before moving on, however, I will provide a brief sketch of the early history of the Scout Movement and of its founder, General Lieutenant R.S.S. Baden-Powell, first Baron Baden-Powell, to whom I shall henceforth refer, in proper Scouting manner, simply as "B-P".

1. I would like to thank Professor Dimitra Fimi for her support and encouragement with respect to this investigation.
2. I will discuss the links between *Scouting for Boys* and the *Book of the Foxrook* in detail, relying heavily on the analysis by Smith and Wynne (Smith & Wynne) for details about Tolkien's notebook.
3. Bunting's argument builds on the assumption that Tolkien's participation in the Boy Scout programme would make him hungrier due to increased physical activity – something I find rather unlikely as the programme would not usually result in a significant increase of physical activity outside of some infrequent longer hikes during weekend camps.

Robert Stephenson Smyth Baden-Powell was born 4 days after Arthur Reuel Tolkien in 1857 (Boehmer 2004; The Famous People 2017; Scull & Hammond 2017). In the summer of 1870, half a year after the birth of Mabel Suffield (later Mabel Tolkien), he received a scholarship to the public school, Charterhouse. In 1876 B-P joined the 13th Hussars in India as a lieutenant, and over the following years he was stationed in India, Africa, and Malta as he rose through the ranks.

B-P was absent from southern Africa from 1890 until 1896, during which period Arthur Tolkien became the manager of the Bloemfontein branch in the Orange Free State, of the Bank of Africa. Arthur and Mabel Tolkien were married in the Cape Town Cathedral on 16 April 1891, and Ronald Tolkien and his brother, Hilary, were born on 3 January 1892 and 17 February 1894 respectively in Bloemfontein, Mabel and the boys returned to England, and Arthur Tolkien died in Bloemfontein (Boehmer 2004; The Famous People 2017; Scull & Hammond 2017).

After yet another stint in India as commander of the 5th Dragoon Guards, B-P, now a Colonel, was once more posted to southern Africa. At the beginning of the Boer war, B-P was sent to Mafeking (now Mahikeng) in the Cape Colony – a railway junction close to the borders of both the South African Republic and British Bechuanaland.

On the 13th October 1899 the Boer army besieged Mafeking – a siege that would last 217 days, during which the besieged garrison of Mafeking would hold out due primarily to the strategies of B-P. By coincident a couple of journalists for London papers had been in the town when the attack started, and though they were stuck in Mafeking, they nonetheless managed to get reports of the siege out by using native runners, allowing their audiences back in Britain to follow the siege in reports that certainly did not belittle the import of the commanding officer, Colonel Baden-Powell (Johnston 2015; Baden-Powell 1933).

Regarding the siege of Mafeking, Christina Scull and Wayne Hammond note that "because Ronald had been born in the Orange Free State, he and his mother would have a special interest in events occurring there" (Scull & Hammond 2017, 7).

The siege, and the associated media coverage, made B-P a national hero and earned him the rank of Major General. However, B-P's media-created popularity also earned him some antipathy in the military top, and after a few other positions, he found himself side-ways promoted to the position of Inspector General of the Cavalry with rank of General Lieutenant (Johnston 2015; Baden-Powell 1933).

At that time, however, he had started taking an interest in the British youth. He studied various organisations for boys and began to develop some ideas of his own to supplement ideas taken from a variety of sources. In 1907, B-P was ready to test out his ideas on a group of boys. He selected twenty boys, twelve of whom were public school boys and eight were grammar school boys from Boys Brigade companies in Poole and Bournemouth, and he brought them together for an experimental camp on Brownsea Island lying in Poole Harbour (The Famous People 2017; Baden-Powell 1933; Reynolds 1943).

The camp was a huge success, and, in the words of B-P's biographer, E.E. Reynolds:

> B.-P. decided to make the general scheme more widely known. While he was looking about for means to do this he met Mr. Arthur Pearson, the head of the publishing firm of that

> name. He was at once interested, and arranged for B.-P. to go about the country lecturing to audiences of interested people, and at the same time to write a handbook for the boys. Mr. Pearson himself undertook to publish the book, and to start a paper, The Scout, in which B.-P. promised to write a weekly yarn – this he continued to do for many years, and some of his best articles on Scouting are to be found in old volumes of The Scout.
>
> [...]
>
> *Scouting for Boys* was published in six fortnightly parts, the first appearing in January, 1908, at a cost of four-pence. The first issue of The Scout was published on 14th April, 1908. Then the fun began! B.-P. still thought of Scouting as an extra activity that could be done by existing clubs and other boy organizations, but the boys themselves soon made it necessary to begin a separate movement. (1943, 64)

Through its many editions *Scouting for Boys* is today estimated to have sold nearly as many copies as *The Lord of the Rings*.

In 1909, on Saturday, 4 September, a rally of Boy Scouts – and unofficial Girl Scouts – was held at Crystal Palace in London. An estimated 11,000 Scouts attended, including several hundred Girl Scouts.

2 – The Birmingham Oratory Troop

Ending the summary of the early history of Scouting, I return to the notice in the Birmingham Oratory Parish Magazine in May 1909 (The Oratory of Saint Philip Neri 2017).

One thing that I note, which has nothing to do with Scouting, is the underlying assumption that the parishioners would know enough about "the Brothers Tolkien" to identify them. At this point Ronald was 17 years old, while Hilary was 15. They had been orphaned five years before on the 14th of November 1904, and they were, of course, now under the guardianship of Fr. Francis Morgan, a priest of the Birmingham Oratory (Scull & Hammond 2017; Garth 2003), who is likely to have viewed the Scout Movement positively.

The notice lets us know that three patrols had been formed, and it hints that the Tolkien brothers were in some way in charge of this new troop of Scouts. Given the organisation of the Scout Movement at this early stage, the phrasing of the notice, and the age of each of the Tolkien boys, the most likely roles for the "Brothers Tolkien" would have been as Assisting Scoutmaster and Patrol Leader respectively, though other options are also possible.

It would be interesting to know if any of the Birmingham Oratory patrols went to the Scout Rally in Crystal Palace in September, but I have not been able to discover any evidence in that regard.

3 – The Scout's Oath

When being initiated into the Scouts, Tolkien must have taken the Scout's Oath as it was then:

On my honour I promise that

1. I will do my duty to God and the King
2. I will do my best to help others, whatever it costs me.
3. I know the scout law, and will obey it (Baden-Powell 1908, 36)

Looking at the Scout's Oath, the first promise would seem to resonate well with Tolkien's personal ethos. Promising to "do my duty to God and the King" would undoubtedly feel right to the orphaned boy who was being raised by a Catholic Priest, and who would later go on to say that "Touching your cap to the Squire may be damn bad for the Squire but it's damn good for you" (Carpenter 2002, 174).

Looking deeper into the patriotic element of the Scouting ethos at the time, B-P was very much a son of the British Empire. He had become an officer in the cavalry and fought in the colonies under Queen Victoria, and he was a personal friend of Rudyard Kipling, the author of *White Man's Burden*. During the first years of Scouting, he promoted a kind of imperial patriotism within the Scout Movement (Johnston 2015), though there is a clear preference for the English, which is seen in his making St. George the patron saint of Scouting, but also in his preference, in *Scouting for Boys*, for using history and myth more closely tied with England (Baden-Powell 1908). Also, in his manuscripts, many instances of "England" were replaced by "Britain".

On Tolkien's views, Scull and Hammond note for 16 November 1914, (a few months after the start of the Great War), that Tolkien, when writing a letter to Christopher Wiseman, expressed patriotism and a fierce belief in nationalism but denied that he was a militarist: "'I no longer defend the Boer War! I am a more & more convinced Home Ruler'" (qtd. in 2017, 63).

This, of course, also implies that Tolkien had previously been able to defend the Boer War, and given the long-standing friendship between Tolkien and Wiseman, it seems to me likely that Tolkien is here describing a more recent development on the nature of his patriotic views. I would, therefore, assume that he had, more than five years earlier, been fully able to "defend the Boer War" when he took the Scouts' Oath.

When writing to his son, Christopher, in 1944, Tolkien would go on to insist that his views during the Second World War were not indicating a lack of patriotism, "For I love England (not Great Britain and certainly not the British Commonwealth (grr!))" (*Letters*, Letter 53, 65), and later he would explain to Christopher that "barring the Tolkien (which must long ago have become a pretty thin strand) you are a Mercian or Hwiccian (of Wychwood) on both sides" (*Letters*, Letter 95, 108). When he stayed with Priscilla at New Lodge, Stonyhurst, in August 1947, they would sign their nationality as 'English' in the guest book, not 'British' (Scull & Hammond 2017, 341).

Despite Tolkien's 1914 sentiments in the letter to Wiseman, it seems likely that this Midlands-centric type of patriotism was founded already in his early years. Indeed, some of his reminiscences in the published letters could indicate that this particular love for the English West Midlands was founded already in his childhood.

B-P and Scouting, on the other hand, would, in the inter-war period, go on to extend the views on patriotism to a kind of internationalism – a belief that if only we could let young people meet at camps to work and have fun together, then they would be able to prevent future war. In 1926, B-P would address the Guide and Scout Commissioners

Conference saying, “Patriotism for one’s country is not only narrow but harmful, if it does not see beyond its own horizon and recognise and appreciate good in other nations” (Sica 1984, 157).

While Tolkien’s personal patriotism seems to have narrowed into a very localised love for the English West Midlands, and Scouting seems to have widened their concept into an idea of global citizenship, Tolkien’s later openness and respect for e.g. German and Jewish culture seems to me to practise the modern idea in Scouting of being better able to tolerate and respect that which is different when doing so from a position of knowing and loving your own roots (Vallory 2012, 108).

The second promise of the Scout’s Oath: to help others at whatever the cost to himself, along with its practical implementation in the ‘good deed’ has been coupled with the parable of the Good Samaritan – a parallel that I am sure would not have escaped Tolkien, even at the age of 17.

The third promise deals with the Scout Law, which, in the 1908 version, stipulated that:

1. A Scout’s Honour is to be Trusted.
2. A Scout is Loyal.
3. A Scout’s Duty is to be Useful and to Help Others.
4. A Scout is a Friend to All, and Brother to Every Other Scout, no matter to what Social Class the Other Belongs.
5. A Scout is Courteous.
6. A Scout is a Friend to Animals.
7. A Scout Obeys Orders.
8. A Scout Smiles and Whistles.
9. A Scout is Thrifty. (Baden-Powell 1908, 44-6)

I am sure that readers of Tolkien’s works will recognise virtues such as honouring one’s word, loyalty, helpfulness, a friendly approach to all (other than Orcs, Trolls, and suchlike, of course), courteousness, friendship with nature, obedience, cheerfulness, and thriftiness without needing me to provide detailed examples of them all, but a few examples might be in place.

The Oathbreakers, who broke their oath of loyalty and obedience to Isildur in the Second Age, is a fine example of what happens when you break your word, and for more about loyalty, obedience and oath-taking, Deborah Higgens explores Tolkien’s use of the Anglo-Saxon comitatus oath (Higgens 2014).

Aragorn embodies the virtues of Men, and incidentally also of Scouting: he is friendly to all that he meets, whether lowly Hobbits, barkeeps, or the lord of the Hall, and he is even on friendly terms with the good animals of the land. He is born to rule, but his history as captain under the king in Rohan and the Steward in Gondor shows that he is also capable of obeying orders.

4 – Scouting

We know nothing about the other Scouts of the Birmingham Oratory Troop in 1909, and it seems doubtful to me that Tolkien struck up any lasting friendships in Scouting;

he was already too deeply engaged with the T.C.B.S. (Tea Club and Barrovian Society) (Garth 2003). I do, however, think that the idea of the Scout Patrol with its close-knit fellowship would have appealed to him, and helping other boys form fellowships of this kind must have pleased him (Tan, et al. 2017).

Nature plays an essential role in Scouting, being the primary locus for the essential activities of the programme (Tan, et al. 2017). B-P would write that "The study of nature brings into a harmonious whole the question of the infinite, the historic, and the microscopic as part of the Great Creator's work" (Baden-Powell 1919, 40). About the forests, B-P would say that "Man seems all out of place and a trespasser here. It is mainly a plant kingdom where insects are admitted." (Baden-Powell 1922, 181)

These ideas seem to resonate well with Tolkien's personal ethos. Where the Scout Law speaks of being "a friend to animals", Tolkien's love seems to have been given primarily to the wild flora, and in particular to the trees (to which a part is also dedicated in *Scouting for Boys*), but B-P's words about the forest could just as well have been written by Tolkien, and I am sure that Tolkien would have agreed with B-P's idea that "For those who have eyes to see and ears to hear, the forest is at once a laboratory, a club and a temple" (181).

It would be tempting for me to claim that Scouting was a formative influence in the shaping of Tolkien's love of nature but looking at his letters and elsewhere this love seems, just as his love for the West Midlands, to have been founded earlier – particularly when he lived with his mother and brother around Sarehole and Moseley. Nonetheless, I think the ideas about nature that are built into Scouting would have resonated with Tolkien's thinking already at seventeen, and possibly have made his involvement with the early Scout Movement just a bit more attractive.

We do not know how long Tolkien stayed in the Birmingham Oratory troop, but he would, at the latest, have stopped when he went up to Oxford in October 1911. His involvement with the Scout Movement, however, did not stop there. When Tolkien, in 1923, contributed the poem *The City of the Gods* to the Leeds literary charity periodical, *The Microcosm*, the proceedings from that year were to benefit the Boy Scout Movement in the North Riding (*The Yorkshire Post* 1923). In that same issue of *The Microcosm*, Tolkien would appear in print alongside Lord Baden-Powell, who contributed a foreword on "the building of sound citizenhood" (4). The original title of Tolkien's poem was 'Kôr', it was first composed in April 1915, and it belongs to some of the very earliest work on what would grow into his great legendarium (Scull & Hammond 2017, 71).

Another interesting parallel between Tolkien and B-P lies in their interaction with English fairy lore. Fimi has discussed how Tolkien's early ventures into Faëry draw on the Victorian and Edwardian era fairy lore of fluttering sprites and pixies with antennae (Fimi 2008, 28ff), and it is interesting to see how B-P put that same fairy lore into use for his pedagogical purposes when he organised the "Brownies" as a branch of Girl Guiding in 1914 (Baden-Powell 1918, 11–48). Here we find the adult leader in the role of the "Brown Owl", and the pack organised in sixes with names such as Sprite, Elf, Gnome, Fairy, Pixie, and Imp. The other parts of Great Britain were not forgotten either; there, sixes could be called Leprechaun, Ghillie Dhu or Tylwyth Teg. The Brownie pack should have their own Toadstool around which they would gather, and at times dance in a circle around the toadstool (15ff).

I do not propose any connection between the two authors, and their interactions with this Edwardian fairy world are in many ways very different, but it does show them both engaging with the same theme and suggests another level of resonance between the two.

5 – *Scouting for Boys*

Whether as a senior patrol leader or as Scoutmaster, it is extremely likely, given the way things worked in the Scout Movement at the time, that Tolkien would have read *Scouting for Boys* when he joined the Scout Movement. In essence, reading that book was what defined Scouting at that time. Let us therefore take a brief look at the first edition of this book as it would have appeared in May 1909.

Having tried out his ideas during the camp at Brownsea Island in the summer of 1907, B-P wanted to share them more widely. After the camp, and with the help and encouragement of the London publisher Arthur C. Pearson, B-P began to set down his ideas in a form fit for publication. *Scouting for Boys* was first published in six parts between January and April 1908 at the price of 4 pennies for each instalment. In May 1908 it was published as a single cloth-bound volume of 288 pages for 2 shillings. The second, revised edition – the first revision of many – would appear in June 1909 (Boehmer 2004, xi; Reynolds 1943, 64).

In the 2004 annotated edition by Oxford University Press, Elleke Boehmer says that "the Scouting handbook as it first appeared is in every part a fragmentary, porous, noncohesive mishmash of other texts" (2004, xiii). This, however, did not matter for the success of the book: written by the hero of the siege of Mafeking, the book responded powerfully to the British national uncertainties, and in discussion of the book's reception, Boehmer explains that

> Baden-Powell's handbook is the direct product of a turn-of-the-century social imagination moulded by the Victorian thinker John Ruskin's pre-modern nostalgia and the Arts and Crafts Movement's respect for manual skills and vernacular forms. Aversions to urbanized society found expression in the back-to-nature movements, outdoors clubs, and enthusiasm for the open air that proliferated both in Britain and on the Continent in this period. (xxiiif)

Of the six parts in which the book was originally sold, the first five are primarily addressed at the Scouts, while the last part is exclusively addressed at the instructor (Baden-Powell 1908).

The style of the first five parts of B-P's book is conversational and very accessible.

Most of the time he addresses the Boy Scouts directly, urging them to go out and practise the skills of the Scout, with occasional boxes addressed "to the instructor".

Throughout the book, B-P offsets his imperialist nationalism with a focus on woodcraft and the outdoors in an almost anti-industrialist resistance to some of the perceived weaknesses ailing Great Britain. B-P also promulgates a public-school ethos of "playing the game", encouraging Scouts to not just be spectators, but to take part in the game, sacrificing themselves for the team, but also to "play" in a wider sense as play-acting, drama, and to engage their imagination in make-belief exercises of stopping smugglers, or rescuing an abducted child, as demonstrated in the early silent film, Scouts to the Rescue from 1908 (Boehmer 2004, xxi). Along with the rules for a large number of games, *Scouting for Boys* thus contains scripts for several small plays to be played out by the Scouts and promoting or exemplifying the Scouting virtues.

The first five parts are further subdivided into nine chapters and twenty-eight "camp fire yarns". The chapters bear the titles "Scoutcraft", "Tracking", "Woodcraft", "Camp life", "Campaigning", "Endurance for Scouts", "Chivalry of the Knights", "Saving Life", and "Patriotism".

Already in these titles, we find a series of skills and virtues that are displayed by Aragorn in *The Lord of the Rings* – in many ways Aragorn appears as the perfect embodiment of not just the Scouting ethos, but also of the Scouting skill-set. Again, however, it would go too far to claim that Aragorn is directly shaped by the ideal Boy Scout as portrayed by B-P in *Scouting for Boys*, but I find it somewhat difficult to accept that the book played no role at all in helping the young Tolkien at least express, and possibly shape, his own thinking about a number of these skills and virtues.

In *Scouting for Boys*, B-P encourages the Scouts to study closely the wildlife of their region; not just to get to recognise them from each other, but to know their behaviour, to stalk them to their lair or nest etc. (Baden-Powell 1908).

The book also contains practical advice for moving in the wild, "pathfinding" – leaving little marks to show where you went and which way, how to judge heights and distances, and how to find the corners of the compass. There is practical first aid, and advice on how to stay healthy and strong in body as well as in mind and spirit. Once more, the Dúnedain Rangers of Eriador come to mind as exemples of the Scouting skill-set.

6 – The Private Scout Code

In the chapter on "Campaigning" in part III, we find camp fire yarn no. 16 on "Information by Signal", which deals with 'Hidden Dispatches', 'Signalling' and 'Wistle and FlagSignals' (Baden-Powell 1908, 173).

Opening with the claim that "Scouts have to be very clever at passing news secretly from one place to another" (173), this particular yarn is a celebration of secret codes, secret signs and secret languages. *Scouting for Boys* contains a set of signs that B-P invites the Scouts to "Practise with chalk on floor or walls, or with a stick on the sand or mud." (43) , and in this yarn, the Scouts are presented with ideas to convey messages in secret codes such as Morse code or Semaphore.

> If you want to write a dispatch that will puzzle most people to read, use the Morse or Semaphore letters in place of the ordinary alphabet. It will be quite readable to any of your friends who understand signalling.
> Also if you want to use a secret language in your patrol you should all set to work to learn "Esperanto." It is not difficult, and is taught in a little book costing one penny. This language is being used in all countries so that you would be able to get on with it abroad now. (177)

This brings me back to Tolkien. In 1909 (most likely around 10th June) – the year of the start of the Birmingham Oratory Scout Troop – Tolkien created a writing system in a notebook entitled the *Book of the Foxrook*. The writing system was headlined privata kodo skaŭta, Esperanto for 'private scout code', and it is the earliest known example of a writing system devised by Tolkien (Smith & Wynne 2000; Fimi 2008). The word "skaŭta" which Tolkien uses for English "scout" is his own invention and is at least once misspelt with a "c" instead of a "k" ("scaŭta"), showing the derivation from English "scout". Smith & Wynne note that "Apparently Tolkien was unable to find a suitable Esperanto word for "scout" in the reference works available to him at the time (the usual word for "scout" is now skolto, but this may not have existed in 1909), and he was obliged to coin his own." (Smith & Wynne 2000, 31).

In the tradition of Animalic, which Tolkien had learned from his Incledon cousins, the *Book of the Foxrook* identifies "scout" with "fox", and Smith & Wynne express the opinion that it is likely that "Foxrook" simply meant "Scout-code" (32).

The writing system consisted of 'monographs' representing entire words, and a "rune-like alphabet" representing the letters of the English alphabet, only to be used for spelling out names for which no monograph was available. Tolkien makes it clear that the signs were meant, like the Scouts' signs proposed by B-P (Baden-Powell 1908, 43), "for inscribing on trees or making with sticks and straws" (Smith & Wynne 2000, 30).

Most of *The Book of the Foxrook*, including the messages written in the code, is in English, but one page is almost entirely written in Esperanto. We know that Tolkien had discovered Esperanto during the Autumn term of 1907, so there can be no question of Tolkien taking up the language itself because of B-P's prodding, but the use of it in association with the construction of a private writing system for use with primitive writing tools (such as sticks on the ground or chalk on walls) in a "private Scout code" is undoubtedly a direct response to reading *Scouting for Boys* with its call to use Esperanto for private messages and its use of secret codes for concepts or phrases, both as simple ideographs and as e.g. whistle and flag signals (Scull & Hammond 2017, 15).

In conclusion, the Birmingham Oratory has informed us that Tolkien was involved with Scouting in 1909. There he would have found a movement, the ethos of which would have resonated well with him on many levels.

Because he had a senior role, whether as patrol leader, as assisting Scoutmaster, or as Scoutmaster, it is very nearly certain that he did indeed read *Scouting for Boys*. In that book, he would have found descriptions of many of the skills used for surviving in the wild that we also see displayed in his literature, particularly by the Dúnedain Rangers.

He also found encouragement to study and practise Esperanto as a secret Scout code, and he found secret ideograms to be used to communicate between scouts, designed to be produced by sticks on the ground or by chalk on a wall.

I propose that this was the direct inspiration that caused Tolkien to create the Book of the Foxrook – his "Private Scout-code".

7 – A Reflection

Scouting affects every Scout differently; for some it becomes a short encounter, quickly forgotten, while for others, such as myself, it becomes a lifelong journey of learning and service. However, regardless of the length of the involvement, the main objective of Scouting is to promote its values system in the hearts of those it touches.

For Tolkien, the involvement with Scouting was short, but it did not lead to an estrangement or resentment on his part as demonstrated by his contribution to *The Microcosm* in 1923, and it would seem that Tolkien's personal ethos, such as it emerges in his writings, remained reasonably well aligned with that of Scouting, though it seems likely that this alignment predates Tolkien's involvement with the Scout Movement (*The Yorkshire Post* 1923).

While I remain convinced that Tolkien must have read Scouting for Boys, any impact on his life beyond the creation of *The Book of the Foxrook* must remain conjecture. It is, in my view, unlikely that the Boy Scout programme and *Scouting for Boys* had any direct impact on his later writings, such as e.g. modelling a character after the ideal Boy Scout, or having any of the many stories B-P tell or retell in *Scouting for Boys* as a direct source for a narrative element.

It could be interesting to discover what other interactions, if any, there were between Tolkien (or the Tolkien family) and the Guide and Scout Movement. Carpenter does not mention the Boy Scouts at all, Scull and Hammond do not mention any other interactions, and Garth only mentions "scouting" in relation with the military discipline (for which Baden-Powell's text, *Aids to Scouting for NCOs and Men*, would long have been one of the standard textbooks).

I would also be interested in investigating if Tolkien, in his *privata kodo skaŭta*, used any of the signs – or 'monographs' – that B-P shows in *Scouting for Boys*.

Bibliography

Baden-Powell, R.S.S., *Scouting for Boys*, ed. Boehmer, E. (London: Oxford University Press, 2004).
— *Girl Guiding*, (London: C. Arthur Pearson, 1918).
— *Aids to Scoutmastership*, (London: C. Arthur Pearson, 1919).
— *A Handbook for Brownies*, (London: C. Arthur Pearson, 1920).
— *Rovering to Success*, Rev edn. (London: Herbert Jenkins Limited, 1930).
— *Lessons from the 'Varsity of Life'*, (London: C. Arthur Pearson, 1933).

Boehmer, E., 'Introduction', in *Scouting for Boys: The Original 1908 Edition* by R.S.S. Baden-Powell. (Oxford: Oxford University Press, 2004), pp. xi–xxxix.

Bunting, N., "Tolkien and the Boy Scouts", in *Lembas Extra 2015, Unexplored Aspects of Tolkien and Arda*, 2015, pp. 75–87.

Carpenter, H., *Tolkien: A Biography*, (London: HarperCollins Publishers, 2002).

Fimi, D., *Tolkien, Race and Cultural History: From Fairies to Hobbits*, (Basingstoke: Palgrave Macmillan, 2008).

Forchhammer, T., 'Scouting and Tolkien', *Parma-kenta*, 10 March 2012, <http://www.parmakenta.com/2012/03/scouting-and-tolkien.html> [Accessed 29 12 2019].
— 'Brilliant! I have just discovered that JRR Tolkien was a boy scout in Brum. The Parish Magazine of the Birmingham Oratory reported in May 1909 that "Three patrols of Scouts

under the Brothers Tolkien, have been started, and they marched smartly in the wake of the Boys Brigade on Easter Monday. If my smile gets any wider, I fear I shall split ', Facebook post, 7 April 2013, <https://www.facebook.com/troels.forchhammer/posts/176067042547659> [Accessed 29 12 2019].

Garth, J., *Tolkien and the Great War*, (London: HarperCollins Publishers, 2003).

Higgens, D. A., *Anglo-Saxon Community in J.R.R. Tolkien's The Lord of the Rings*, (Toronto: Oloris Publishing, 2014).

Johnston, S., 'Courting Public Favour: The Boy Scout Movement and the Accident of Internationalism, 1907–29', Historical Research, 88.241 (2015), 508–529. < https://doi.org/10.1111/1468-2281.12079>

Reynolds, E., B-P: *The Story of His Life*, (Oxford: Oxford University Press, 1943).

Scull, C. & Hammond, W. G., *The J.R.R. Tolkien Companion and Guide*, (London: HarperCollins Publishers, 2017).

Sica, M., *Footsteps of the Founder*. 2nd edn. (Milano: Editrice Àncora Milano, 1984).
Smith, A. R. & Wynne, P., 'Tolkien and Esperanto'. VII: An Anglo-American Literary Review, 17 (2000), 27–46.

Tan, M., Díaz, R.L., Soares, A., Kattan, S., Forchhammer, T., Nakano, M., Gonçalves, J.A., Abdulmonem, H., and Peck, S., *The Scout Method Review*. (2017). World Scout Conference document.

'Kuala Lumpur: The World Organisation of the Scout Movement', <https://www.scout.org/node/335131/> [Accessed 29 12 2019]

The Famous People, 'Robert Baden-Powell, 1st Baron Baden-Powell', *The Famous People*, 2017, <https://www.thefamouspeople.com/profiles/robert-baden-powell- 1st-baron-baden-powell-6686.php> [Accessed 29 12 2019].

The Oratory of Saint Philip Neri, 'Tolkien and the Oratory', *The Oratory, Birmingham*, 2017, <https://www.birminghamoratory.org.uk/tolkien-and-the- oratory> [Accessed 29 12 2019].

The Yorkshire Post, 'The Microcosm', *The Yorkshire Post and Leeds Intelligencer*, 14 March 1923, p. 4.

Tolkien, J.R.R., *The Letters of J.R.R. Tolkien*, ed. by Humphrey Carpenter with the assistance of Christopher Tolkien (London: HarperCollins, 1995).

Vallory, E., World Scouting – Educating for Global Citizenship. (New York: Palgrave Macmillan, 2012).

THE MICROCOSM.
The charitable efforts of "The Microcosm" are only equalled by its literary excellence. In 1921.

North-country charities benefited to the extent £100; in 1922, increased sales enabled not less than £250 to be disbursed. The 1923 spring number retains all the merits of its predecessors. The black and white illustrations are good and varied, the lithograph of "Bootham Bar, York," reproduced by the courtesy of Sir Edward Brotherton, being particularly striking. As this issue is to be sold in the interests of the Boy Scout movement in the North Riding, the foreword Sir Robert Baden-Powell on the building of sound citizenhood comes aptly. The late Alice Meynell's sonnet, "The Young Neophyte," has a delicate charm that alone would lend distinction to any literary journal. In "Jak and Anne," Wilfred Rowland displays good deal of subtle humour, and a nice sense of ballad rhythm and simplicity. The editor contributes a dainty little essay "About Fans," and a one-act fantasy in verse. Many not less notable North-country litterateurs, such Mr. Keighley Snowden, Mr. T. Wray Milnes, Mr. J.R.R. Tolkien, and Mr. J. Machereth, add their efforts the growing list of contents, which in prose and verse make this literary publication so remarkable among its kind.

The Yorkshire Post and Leeds Intelligencer for (14 March 1923), p. 4 (*The Yorkshire Post*).

The Two Towers of Birmingham and other follies

John Garth

1 – The 'two towers' of Birmingham

It seems widely regarded as a marvel that there are two towers in the title of volume two of *The Lord of the Rings* and two towers in the small area of Edgbaston, Birmingham, where Tolkien lived in his youth. One of the two real towers is the 96ft, six-storey Perrott's Folly, built by a local gentleman in 1758 to look over his hunting park. Properly called 'the Monument', it had been used since 1884 as a pioneering weather-forecasting station. The other, an object of architectural beauty and industrial smoke, is not really a tower but a chimney for Edgbaston Water Works pump-house. Both were noteworthy features of Edgbaston, where he lived at various addresses for most of the period from 1902 to 1911. Indeed, both could be seen from the far end of Stirling Road, Tolkien's home for nearly four years, from 1904 to 1908, between the ages of 12 and 16.

All this is certainly marvellous for Birmingham tourism officials. The so-called 'two towers' of Birmingham appear unfailingly in news features about his youth there, in online reference works like Wikipedia, and in tourist maps of the city. To lend extra credence to the claims made for these towers, there are very attractive models of them at Sarehole Mill, a place with indisputable Tolkien connections.

But do such claims help anyone who seriously wants to understand Middle-earth or Tolkien's life and inspirations?

Tolkien's books are so rich in striking details, and they touch us so closely, that many readers have the experience of seeing something in real life and thinking, *Wow, that reminds me of Rivendell, or Lothlórien, or Minas Tirith* – or whatnot. It is all too easy to leap to the conclusion that Tolkien must have seen the same thing and been inspired by it. So many hypotheses have been made about his inspirations, you could drown in them.

In this paper I will also try to answer a couple of important questions about the search for sources of inspiration. First: for an author as cagey as Tolkien, can such searches ever be more than blind guesswork? Second: can knowing a source of inspiration really enrich our appreciation of his writing, whether by revealing his conscious intentions or by illuminating his contexts?

Without giving too many spoilers, I'll tell you the answers right now, as I see them. Yes, yes, and yes.

But I believe that the source hunter or literary investigator should not be afraid of these questions, should not look upon them as obstacles to be dodged or weapons in the hands of the enemy. Anyone interested in inspiration should see these questions as tools always to be kept close at hand to help separate the wheat from the chaff. They can help us see where there are reasonable grounds for recognising an external influence, and they can help us see which influences enhance our appreciation of Tolkien's writing.

Let us set aside for a moment the thorny question of which two Middle-earth towers Tolkien actually meant to indicate in the volume title *The Two Towers*. First, we must deal with a different question of origins. Where did the Birmingham claim come from?

It seems to have emerged in 1991. And it turns out that The Tolkien Society inadvertently propagated the idea that Perrott's Folly and the pumphouse inspired Tolkien's 'two towers'. That's because the connection was first made among Tolkien Society officers that August, when they were reconnoitring the city to prepare bus tours for the following year's Tolkien Centenary Conference. The idea was meant as *a joke*.

However, the Two Towers claim was then taken up and promoted by Peter Leather, an expert on Birmingham buildings who conducted Tolkien tours in 1992. According to the *Guardian* newspaper, "He is an archaeologist with a passionate interest in buildings, ancient and modern, who prefers to leave discussions on the finer points of Tolkien's prose to colleagues in literature and creative writing. Very sensible in the circumstances, as it transpires that he has read neither *The Hobbit* nor *The Lord of the Rings* trilogy" (Arnot 2003). Leather researched Tolkien's Birmingham background in Humphrey Carpenter's authorised biography of Tolkien. "It led me to the archives to harden up the Tolkien reference points in Birmingham for a column I write for a local newspaper," he said, "As a result, I was asked to be the guide on the Tolkien Society's centenary tour" (Arnot 2003).[1]

The Two Towers claim seems to have floated around, fairly inoffensively, for a decade. Then, in 2003, Leather went on to be involved in a three-day 'Tolkien in Birmingham' course. Peter Jackson's *The Two Towers* movie had recently come out. This is when the claim began to gather real momentum. In fact it went viral. And ever since, no article about Tolkien and Birmingham will omit to mention that the folly and the waterworks *are said* or *thought* to have inspired his fictional 'two towers'.

Are said. Are thought. These are words much favoured by journalists who do not have the time, energy, interest or expertise to try and verify the claims that they are passing on to their readers. They are also favoured by anyone with a stake in the game, such as promoters of local tourism, publicans and so forth. And they are favoured by Wikipedia writers. So a circle has been born, in which news media, interested parties, and the world's default online reference work buttress each others' unsubstantiated claims. Indeed, the question of Tolkien and the 'two towers' is just one tiny facet of that vastly bigger and more serious problem. But that's not going to stop me from subjecting it to interrogation here.

Because the 'two towers' connection is flawed however you look at it.

Tolkien never truly considered any *The Lord of the Rings* towers as a pair. The title *The Two Towers* emerged only *after* the text was finished. Rayner Unwin, of the publishers George Allen & Unwin, had insisted that as a point of commercial practicality the huge story must be broken up into three instalments. Struggling to think of any title that might adequately cover the adventures in Rohan as well as the borders of Mordor, someone – Tolkien or Unwin – suggested *The Two Towers*. Exactly which two towers were meant could "be left ambiguous", said Tolkien; "it might refer to Isengard and Barad-dûr, or to

1. I am grateful to Alan Reynolds for drawing my attention to this article.

Minas Tirith and B[arad-dûr]; or Isengard and Cirith Ungol" (*Letters*, Letter 140, 170). Whoever suggested the title, that comment sounds like a mixture of desperation and chagrin, as if to say: if you pose a ridiculous problem, you'll get a ridiculous solution. There are actually no fewer than five candidate towers – Tolkien somehow omitted Minas Morgul in his list.

When it came to designing the dust jacket, he was forced to begin making a choice. His own draft sketches first depicted the 'two towers' as Minas Tirith and Barad-dûr, and later as Minas Morgul and Orthanc (Hammond and Scull 1995, 180–1; Catherine McIlwaine 2018, 369–71). It was the latter two that ended up being named in the note at the end of volume one of *The Lord of the Rings*: "*The second part is called* THE TWO TOWERS, *since the events recounted in it are dominated by* ORTHANC, *the citadel of Saruman, and the fortress of* MINAS MORGUL *that guards the secret entrance to Mordor.*" Yet the process by which this emphatic identification was reached shows that any search for a pairing of real towers that inspired Orthanc and Minas Morgul is a futile exercise.

To compound the problem, there is no sign that Tolkien (or anyone else) thought of the two Birmingham landmarks as a pair, let alone referred to them as 'the two towers'. You can certainly argue that there are similarities between one or other of the Birmingham towers and one of the towers in *The Lord of the Rings*. But a pair inspiring a pair becomes more complex to argue and defend. The most salient similarity between Tolkien's *The Two Towers* title and the 'two towers' of Birmingham is this: each pairing was established arbitrarily *after* Tolkien had finished writing the story.

The urge to find the inspiration for the towers is understandable, and it can sometimes reveal the workings of a creative process, or turn up other unexpected benefits too. That is what I hope to show now. We will briefly look at what is already known about the links in the chain of creative developments that led to one of those five *The Lord of the Rings* towers, Orthanc. Then I will reveal what I believe to be the vital missing links at the beginning of that chain.

2 – The shape of Orthanc

First of all, let us recognise that any attempt to identify the inspirations for Orthanc has to take into account that Tolkien's tower completely changed shape several times. To return to Perrott's Folly, as it is documented on Wikipedia: "The windows down the side of Perrott's Folly are similar to Tolkien's sketches of Orthanc."[2] And you can judge for yourselves by looking at reproductions in any of several books.

Tolkien's first idea for Orthanc was a tower of stacked cylinders. His second was a tall, slender cone, which he considered poising upon a stone arch. His third, final and far more unique idea was a tower of black, glass-like rock that seems "a thing not made by the craft of Men, but riven from the bones of the earth in the ancient torment of the hills" (*TT*, 'The Road to Isengard', 555).

The windows on Perrott's Folly are arranged more vertically than horizontally.

2. https://en.wikipedia.org/wiki/Talk%3APerrott%27s_Folly.

It is interesting to hazard a guess at inspirations for these versions of Orthanc. Christina Scull has tentatively likened the first one, the stacked drum, to the Great Mosque at Samarra in Iraq (1993, 47). You might also wonder whether the Tower of Babel as depicted by Bruegel the Elder goes into the mix. Can it be that there is a glimmer of the Eiffel Tower in the arch-footed version? As for the final version, the idea that it comes from the 'ancient torment of the hills' prompts me to turn to Sian Pehrsson, geologist and Tolkienist. She points out the similarity with the lava spine that rose 1,000ft above the reeking ruins left by the 1902 eruption of Mount Pelée on the Caribbean island of Martinique.

Can it be that Tolkien blindly clutched at one idea then another, then another, like some whirling dervish of indecision, until he had simply run out of steam? The care he took over the drawing and accompanying description at each stage, and the final success of Orthanc as a memorable feature of the published *The Lord of the Rings*, suggest to me that it didn't happen like that. Perhaps it was a case of deciding between competing inspirations, each with its rationale. Or perhaps it was a gradual metamorphosis, an inner vision coming into clearer focus step by step as the silhouette became more conical and the bedrock element – present even at the start as the base for the masonry structure – steadily took over. Either way, it was a process in which thought and feeling both played their part.

3 – Towers of the Númenórean exiles

Next, let's go a step further into the past, before Tolkien began designing Orthanc, and sum up what Christopher Tolkien, in his meticulous in-depth studies of his father's draft writings, has revealed about the emergence of Saruman's tower as a narrative idea.

Orthanc is so named as soon as it first appears, along with the whole story of Gandalf's captivity there by Saruman, in the fourth version of 'The Council of Elrond' written in 1940 or 1941. As in the final published version, Frodo realises that one of his dreams during the journey to Rivendell must have been a vision of Gandalf held captive on the tower's pinnacle. If he had understood it, he would have known why Gandalf had not turned up at Bag End to accompany the hobbits.

However, as we know from *The Treason of Isengard*, volume seven of *The History of Middle-earth*, it had taken major convolutions before Tolkien conceived of Saruman, the renegade wizard, as the reason for Gandalf's delay. In one earlier conception, Black Riders besiege Gandalf in one of the Elf-towers in the Tower Hills west of the Shire. This scene, too, is glimpsed by Frodo in a matching dream-vision. Curiously, even though Tolkien scrapped the idea of the siege of the Elf-tower, this prototype dream partly survives as a kind of literary fossil in the published *The Lord of the Rings*, where Frodo at Crickhollow in the Shire dreams that "He was on a dark heath, and there was a strange salt smell in the air. Looking up he saw before him a tall white tower, standing alone on a high ridge" (*FR*, 'A Conspiracy Unmasked', 108).

Christopher Tolkien maps these developments masterfully. In *The Lost Road and Other Writings*, volume five of *The History of Middle-earth*, he identifies an even earlier link in the chain. This comes in the second version of *The Fall of Númenor*, where the world has been made round, Númenor has been destroyed, and its survivors are exiled in Middle-earth but still yearn for their lost land and 'the True West' beyond it. The story says, "Therefore they built very high towers in those days", hoping to catch a glimpse along the Straight Way, the mystical plane of air that still exists, like a memory of the old world before it was made round (*Lost Road*, 28). As Christopher observes, this reference to the Númenóreans building towers "must be the first reference to the White Towers on Emyn Beraid, the Tower Hills" (30). As first conceived, then, they were not Elf-towers, but Númenórean towers. Their purpose was the same – to look west across the Sea.

However, Christopher Tolkien has not noted the peculiar origin of the idea of the 'high towers' from which the yearning Númenóreans look west across the Great Sea. Perhaps it occurred to him but he felt it beyond the remit of his study of the legendarium texts; because this further link in the chain takes us outside the mythology. Not only that, it takes us *outside* fiction or myth or what Tolkien called feigned history, and into a literary territory which is often seen as foreign to him – allegory.

4 – The Allegory of the Tower

The Allegory of the Tower is familiar to generations of students of *Beowulf*, and familiar also to readers of Tolkien's essays. It appears in his landmark essay '*Beowulf*: The Monsters and the Critics'. Tolkien delivered this as a lecture to the British Academy on 25 November 1936. And, crucially, this was just days before he wrote the blurb for *The Hobbit* from which, as I have pointed out elsewhere, the idea of Númenor first sprang.[3] But I have not previously pointed out how one spark of inspiration leapt the gap between Tolkien's strictly academic work and Middle-earth.

Tolkien's lecture is an attack on the critics and scholars who studied the Old English poem *Beowulf* but had missed the point of the poem. He felt that in their search for clues to history, language, archaeology, and so forth, they had overlooked the fact that it is a work of art. After a brief foray into another allegory, he writes:

> I would express the whole industry in yet another allegory. A man inherited a field in which was an accumulation of old stone, part of an older hall. Of the old stone some had already been used in building the house in which he actually lived, not far from the old house of his fathers. Of the rest he took some and built a tower. But his friends coming perceived at once (without troubling to climb the steps) that these stones had formerly belonged to a more ancient building. So they pushed the tower over, with no little labour, in order to look for hidden carvings and inscriptions, or to discover whence the man's distant forefathers had obtained their building material. Some suspecting a deposit of coal under the soil began to dig for it, and forgot even the stones. They all said: 'This tower is most interesting.' But they also said (after pushing it over): 'What a muddle it is in!' And even the man's own descendants, who might have been expected to consider what he had been about, were heard to murmur: 'He is such an odd fellow! Imagine his using these old stones just to build a nonsensical tower! Why did not he restore the old house? He had

3. See 'When J.R.R. Tolkien bet C.S. Lewis: The wager that gave birth to *The Lord of the Rings*', *Sunday Telegraph*, 11 December 2016 Available at: www.telegraph.co.uk/books/what-to-read/jrr-tolkien-bet-cs-lewis-wager-gave-birth-lord-rings/). See 'When Tolkien reinvented Atlantis and Lewis went to Mars', blog post, 31 March 2017, Available at: https://johngarth.wordpress.com/2017/03/31/when-tolkien-reinvented-atlantis-and-lewis-went-to-mars/

> no sense of proportion.' But from the top of that tower the man had been able to look out upon the sea. (*Monsters*, 7-8)

This neat little scenario conveys its underlying, allegorical sense by way of a kind of substitution code. The old stone is the ancient legendary lore predating *Beowulf*. The tower is the same material transformed into *Beowulf*; the builder is the poet himself. The scornful outsiders are the latter-day critics of who ignore the art in search of unliterary insights. This act of substitution is what makes it an allegory.

5 – The Allegory of the Rock Garden

The Allegory of the Tower seems perfectly characteristic of Tolkien, who constructed so many fictional towers and who conveys the awe and lure of the sea so hauntingly. But the 1936 British Academy lecture was itself the distillation of lectures on *Beowulf* that Tolkien had been delivering to undergraduates at Oxford from as early as 1933. So we can go back another step to those lectures, preserved in manuscript in the Bodleian Library, Oxford, and published as *Beowulf and the Critics* in an edition by Michael D.C. Drout. And here we find a further surprise. The allegory is in place in the undergraduate versions of the lectures, and it has the same basic message, but there is no tower.

Here is the first version of the allegory:

> A man found a mass of old stone in an unused patch, and made of it a rock-garden; but his friends coming perceived that the stones had once been part of a more ancient building; and they turned them upsidedown to look for hidden inscriptions; some suspected a deposit of coal under the soil and proceeded to dig for it. They all said 'this garden is most interesting,' but they said also 'what a jumble and confusion it is in!'
> – and even the gardener's best friend, who might have been expected to understand what he had been about, was heard to say: 'He's such a tiresome fellow – fancy using these beautiful stones just to set off common-place flowers that are found in every garden: he has no sense of proportion, poor man!' (*Beowulf* 2011, 68)

Rock gardens do not belong in Anglo-Saxon times but, as Drout points out, they were a very fashionable middle-class English pursuit in the twenties and thirties.

Although utterly different in mood from the famous tower, the rock garden image is Tolkienian too, in its own way. Finding some pretty stones to offset his flowers is just the kind of thing the fashionable middle-class but slightly eccentric Bilbo Baggins might have done, probably to the irritation of his less imaginative neighbours. "You will notice already," we are told during Bilbo's first conversation, "that Mr. Baggins was not quite so prosy as he liked to believe, also that he was very fond of flowers" (*Hobbit*, 'An Unexpected Party', 7). Tolkien had either finished *The Hobbit* or written most of it by January 1933, when C.S. Lewis read it. This first version of the *Beowulf* undergraduate lecture text is thought to have been prepared for lectures on 'Beowulf: General Criticism' which Tolkien delivered in October that year.[4] The connecting tissue between Bilbo and

4. The lecture's A-text seems likely to have been written for Tolkien's Oxford lectures on '*Beowulf*: General Criticism', delivered in Michaelmas Term 1933. See Scull and Hammond 2017, 133.

the creator of the rock garden is simply the flower-loving Tolkien himself, inwardly extraordinary but outwardly ordinary, apart from a taste for colourful waistcoats.

A source for the tower allegory has been found in an influential comment by Matthew Arnold on the Welsh *Mabinogion*. Lecturing seventy years before Tolkien 'On the Study of Celtic Literature', the Victorian poet and critic had said "the mediæval story-teller is pillaging an antiquity of which he does not fully possess the secret; he is like a peasant building his hut on the site of Halicarnassus or Ephesus; he builds, but what he builds is full of materials of which he knows not the history, or knows by a glimmering tradition merely – stones [...] of an older architecture, greater, cunninger, more majestical" (1962, 322).[5] In *Beowulf and the Critics*, Drout points out that the Arnold passage appears in W.P. Ker's 1904 book *The Dark Ages*, which Tolkien used extensively for his own lecture (*Beowulf* 2011, 6-7, 182-3).[6]

So Matthew Arnold is clearly the first cause of Tolkien's allegory: if he had not known Arnold's, Tolkien would not have written his. Tolkien transfers the allegory to *Beowulf*, turns Arnold's critique on its head by focusing his ire on the critics rather than the medieval author, and transforms the imagery of re-used rubble. Tolkien's counterblast against Arnold is that even a writer who knows only fragments of the more ancient stock of myth and history can create something wonderful out of those fragments. That was what Tolkien believed the Beowulf poet had achieved – and of course it was what Tolkien had always hoped to achieve himself with the legendarium that began as 'The Book of Lost Tales'.

Arnold's Ephesian hut is not Tolkien's tower, and Tolkien does not get the tower image itself from Arnold, only the idea of a builder re-using the rubble of some once-great edifice.

Let's return to Tolkien's allegory of the rock garden. It survived into a second, considerably expanded version of the lectures for undergraduates, probably prepared in 1934 or 1936. But Tolkien returned to this second manuscript and pencilled a close series of changes, transforming the rock garden with flowers into a tower with a sea-view.[7] It is the most reworked passage of the manuscript. And this modified text was what he distilled to create the November 1936 British Academy lecture.

---

5. In his choice of a peasant at Halicarnassus or Ephesus – ancient Greek sites in what is now Turkey – Arnold is not bewailing simply the loss of Greek wisdom, but the fact that Greek heritage was in the hands of the Ottomans.

6. Ker quotes the Arnold passage just a short paragraph after the discussion of the Doom of the Gods in Norse myth, including this key passage quoted by Tolkien in 'Beowulf: The Monsters and the Critics': "The Northern Gods have an exultant extravagance in their warfare which makes them more like Titans than Olympians; only they are on the right side, though it is not the side that wins. The winning side is Chaos and Unreason' – mythologically, the monsters – 'but the gods, who are defeated, think that defeat no refutation." (Ker 1904, 57–9).

7. The emendations, on fol. 95 of the MS, are recorded by *Beowulf and the Critics*, 385. The MS is in ink, with most changes also in ink (and therefore in most cases probably made at the time of writing). Other pencil changes are minor – a phrase or sentence inserted. But the change from rock garden to tower involves many alterations to the passage in question. It is complemented by a further pencil change, on fol. 139 (*Beowulf and the Critics*, 403), from 'he gave them flowers and they wanted only stones', replacing 'flowers' with 'a tower'. There is no clear indication of when these changes were made. But another pencil annotation, on fol. 125, refers to an article published in the *Proceedings of the British Academy* 21, with the dateline 1935.

With the Allegory of the Tower, the allegorical implications are the same, but now the Beowulf poet is a tower builder and *Beowulf*'s literary quality is represented by a view of the sea. The rock garden and tower are the same material in different arrangements, but the shaping decision is quite different. Tower-building has a medievalesque resonance that rock gardens lack, and the sea is a recurrent motif in *Beowulf*. The tower is both an impressive edifice in itself and a vantage point for a new and wider perspective, if you bother to climb the stairs. A rock garden may be seen by passers-by too, but you would not see anything new by climbing on top of it. The tower embodies grandeur and stature, the sea view encapsulates vision and wonder – qualities the critics lack, scrabbling about with their noses to the ground. The revised allegory divides the Beowulf poet from his critics much more sharply than the original.

The tower builder is also far more extraordinary than the gardener. Rock gardens are conventional ways of cultivating beauty or showing off. A rock garden made with ancient stone may be Bilbo-like, but otherwise rock gardens evoke his Baggins side – staid, middle-class, commonplace. The building of a grand edifice that flouts the norms and flamboyantly overtops any middle-class pretensions – this is an action more Took-like than Baggins-like. But no hobbit would construct a tower.

6 – Why not a tower?

If the tower is such an apt image for what Tolkien wanted to convey, why didn't he come up with it immediately? Why did he make do with the rock garden through his undergraduate lectures, then suddenly decide it should be a tower instead? After all, hadn't the maker of Middle-earth always been prone to construct imaginary towers at the drop of a hat?

In fact, no, he had not. Compared to the era of *The Lord of the Rings* and afterwards, towers are relatively sparse in his writings up to the mid-1930s. The Gothic literary obsession with castles and towers was not such a productive force in the early legendarium.

Most of the towers that Tolkien had invented up to this point were not individualised. Among the many towers of Gondolin, only the tower of Turgon is specially marked out (the king dies defending it). Nargothrond is guarded by "tower-crowned" hills and Thangorodrim has "great towers" built on its mountain-flanks (*Lays*, 214, 282). But the only tower with character and a key role is the one on the island of Tol Sirion, in which Beren is captured by Thû, Lord of Wolves – the later Sauron.

A bigger role in the early mythology is played by subterranean strongholds – Nargothrond, Doriath, Angband and the Elf-kingdom in Mirkwood – strongholds for which Tolken drew variously on mythological underworlds and fairy-mounds, and probably on his honeymoon visit to Cheddar Caves.

Still, several of Tolkien's earlier towers actually have views over the sea – from the Tower of Pearl in the Twilit Isles of 'The Book of Lost Tales', to the Tower of Ingwë in Elvenhome, to the tower of Benwick where, in *The Fall of Arthur* (mid-1930s), the exiled Lancelot yearns for England. On the face of it, all this makes it even odder that Tolkien initially picked a rock garden for his *Beowulf* allegory rather than a tower.

But actually all of those earlier towers are quite different from the tower in the *Beowulf* allegory. Tolkien grew up in the heyday of the lighthouse, and all those earlier towers stand, like lighthouses, on the seashore, where inevitably the sea will be visible or its presence will be palpable even before you climb the winding stairs to the top.

By contrast, the whole point of Tolkien's allegorical tower is to provide a seaview that simply cannot be had from ground level. In allegorical terms, it elevates the spirit and extends the reach of the imagination.

This point is directly tied in with another one factor that is lacking in the towers of the earlier legendarium or *The Fall of Arthur*. It is a factor, indeed, that feels far too mundane, too un-epic, too bourgeois – one might almost say too suburban – for any of those settings. The factor is this: unpopularity with the neighbours.

The neighbours cannot see the sea or feel its influence. Their spirits are landlocked. They cannot understand the benefit of the Beowulfian tower.

It is this unpopularity factor, nicely ramped up in the tower version of the allegory, that makes it work so well as an attack on the critics of *Beowulf* who, as Tolkien earnestly believed, missed the beauty of the Old English poem.

7 – Faringdon Folly and Tolkien's tower

Again we come back to the twin questions of why Tolkien didn't come up with the tower image immediately and why he scrapped the original rock garden idea in 1934 or 1936. It's evident that something *clicked* and Tolkien realised what an improvement a tower would be. But was that realisation prompted by mere instinct, groping slowly towards a better literary symbol? Or was there some outside trigger?

In fact, as I suddenly realised while researching an entirely different paper on Tolkien, the theme of unpopularity with the neighbours points directly to such a trigger – one that was local to Tolkien, contemporary with his Oxford and British Academy *Beowulf* lectures, and great fun.

In the vocabulary of British architecture, a tower without purpose is called a folly. *Folly* in the older sense just means 'foolishness' or, as the *Oxford English Dictionary* adds, "a foolish action, error, idea, practice, etc.; a ridiculous thing, an absurdity" (*OED*). The *OED* defines folly in its specialised later sense as "a popular name for any costly structure considered to have shown folly in the builder" (*OED*). The oldest recorded use of this sense, from 1654, is very pertinent to Tolkien's theme: "[He] buryeth it [his wealth] [...] in Buildings needlesse, vain, or ill contrived [...] being called by his kind Gossip-neighbours his Folly" (qtd. in Whitlock 1654, 502).

It might be said that a folly's very purpose is its purposelessness. Follies were built all over Britain in the eighteenth and nineteenth centuries. Perrott's Folly in Edgbaston may (perhaps) have been the first folly to make an impression on Tolkien, but in its purpose and its purposelessness, it was typical of a huge number of buildings nationwide. Tolkien probably knew several others, which I will mention soon. But if these had any impact on Tolkien it is likely to have been years before his work on the *Beowulf* lectures. None answers the conundrum of why he exchanged his allegorical rock garden for a tower some time between 1934 and 1936.

By the 1930s the era of folly-building was almost over. Britain's follies were widely – though certainly not universally – cherished as part of the national heritage, and celebrated in a series of paintings commissioned by the petroleum company Shell for its motoring advertisements and guides.

The example which should command our attention is the 100-foot tower constructed in 1935 by Lord Berners on an historic hill fort site at his estate in Faringdon, Berkshire, 18 miles from Oxford.[8] Faringdon Folly was so unpopular with some of its neighbours that the controversy was reported in newspapers nationally – "a rare fuss through much of 1935", in the words of *The Times* many years later (Dickinson 2010, 92).[9] No doubt it featured in local news for a considerable period, as planning controversies do (and on this I speak as a former London local newspaper reporter who attended many a council planning meeting). John Betjeman, later Poet Laureate, uses the tower to open a 1938 essay on 'Gentlemen's Follies'. It appears in Nancy Mitford's 1945 novel *The Pursuit of Love*, as Lord Merlin's folly (Harris 2010, 221).[10] Faringdon Folly is still famous now, partly because it marked the end of the era of folly building but partly because the story behind it is so entertaining.

Lord Berners bought Faringdon House in 1920, the year after he was elevated to the peerage. He also acquired a nearby hill. The story goes that when he commented how nice it would be to have a tower on the hilltop, locals were not happy, and their reaction determined Berners to build one.

Berners was a noted composer, an accomplished artist, a diplomat and a poet and novelist. He had worked with ballet impresario Sergei Diaghilev and novelist Gertrude Stein, and was admired by composer Igor Stravinsky. His circle – to which Tolkien did not belong – included Nancy Mitford, Diana Mosley, Rosamund Lehmann, John Betjeman and Osbert Sitwell. Visitors to Faringdon House included H.G. Wells and Salvador Dalí (who once climbed the Folly). Berners was gay, publically flamboyant, and sardonically witty, but made little attempt to curry favour with neighbours. By the 1930s he was as well known for his eccentricities as for his accomplishments.

Berners engaged his architect friend, Lord Gerald Wellesley, to draw up plans. In 1934 the council considered them and voted to refuse planning permission (*Times*, 19 July 1934, 4).[11] The council said it "failed to see the object or benefit of the Tower if erected" (Dickinson 2010, 73). Berners responded that "the great point of the Tower is that it will be entirely useless" (73). But he reduced the height so that the tower would barely peep above the trees. Perhaps more crucially, he invited a government minister to lunch (73). Planning permission was granted late in 1934. The opening party, complete with grand fireworks display, was held on 5 November 1935, Guy Fawkes' Night. Guests were invited to bring effigies of their enemies to burn, but no more than six each.

8. For what follows, sources include: Dickinson, P., *Lord Berners – Composer, Writer, Painter* (Boydell Press, 2010); Wise, M., 'Lord Berners' Folly' (2004) Available at: www.faringdon.org/uploads/1/4/7/6/14765418/building_the_folly.pdf); Hayhurst-France, C. 'Lord Berners' Folly' (Publisher unknown, 1989).

9. See also 'Follies can be fun', *Times*, 9 October 1959, 14. William Hickey's society column in the *Daily Express*, 19 April 1934, reported on the folly plan before the controversy even erupted.

10. Here Harris cites *Oxford Mail*, 5 November 1936; *Daily Express* article cited by Sofka Zinovieff, *The Mad Boy, Lord Berners, My Grandmother and Me* (London: Jonathan Cape, 2014) 134; November 1937 *Tatler* article reproduced at http://www.faringdonfolly.org.uk/folly-history.html

11. A 1934 *Oxford Mail* article was titled 'High Words over Lord Berners's Tower' (Zinovieff 2014, 132).

And thanks to the very public row, the tower did acquire a purpose. During the planning dispute, the former High Sheriff of Berkshire had complained that the tower would ruin the view from his house. The architect, Lord Wellesley, had pointed out that even to see the tower from the former High Sheriff's house, nearly four miles away, you would have to be scanning the landscape through a telescope. The former High Sheriff – who was also a former naval Vice-Admiral – had replied that this was precisely his daily habit.[12]

So Wellesley cunningly appealed to the idea that everyone should be able to enjoy fine views like the former High Sheriff's, and that the tower was the way to provide them. The top of the tower had "a chamber fitted with a telescope".[13] The *Tatler* magazine claimed that "on a clear day six counties can be seen from the top" (Hayhurst-France 1935, 299). Faringdon Folly was finally embraced by Faringdon's people, who were able to enjoy its views for a small fee that went to charity.[14]

Tolkien might well have disliked much of what the Berners set represented, in its extravagance, its shallowness and vanity, its modernist cultural values.[15] But he took an interest in current affairs, he knew Oxford gossip, and there is no way that he can have missed the tower controversy. Bureaucracy and town planners were two of Tolkien's pet hates, so he may well have favoured Berners.

I imagine that the folly controversy also brought to mind other follies. I have even read one claim that you could see the sea from the top of Faringdon Folly, though I don't know whether this circulated in Tolkien's day, and it's certainly not true. But Beckford's Tower at the southern edge of the Cotswolds, near Bath, commands views of the Bristol Channel 16 miles away, and may have been known to Tolkien from his courtship with Edith in 1913, when she lived in Cheltenham, or from their 1916 honeymoon at Clevedon on the Bristol Channel. Tolkien surely knew Broadway Tower, which stands at the second-highest point of the Cotswolds above the Vale of Evesham

12. *Who's Who* puts Vice-Admiral F. Clifton Brown's address in the village of Buckland, though I don't think this has anything to do with Tolkien's choice of the Shire place-name (see *The Worlds of J.R.R. Tolkien* 2019, 126–8). An unidentified 1980s article that has been given to me, possibly from the *Oxford Times*, says the vice-admiral was also vice-chairman of the rural district council. Another complainant was Vivian Lobb, who lived at Kelmscott Manor with May Morris, the daughter of William and Jane Morris, and who wrongly believed that a siren was to be sounded from the tower every two hours (Dickinson 2010, 82). Incidentally or otherwise, in 1929 the Tolkiens had obtained their first Icelandic au pair via May Morris (see Benedikz 2008, 11).

13. 'Hundreds thrilled as Folly Tower opens in 1935', Newspaper unknown, July 2007. This was a reprinting of the 1935 *Faringdon Advertiser* article.

14. Hayhurst-France records that during the Second World War the folly was used for Royal Artillery wireless training. Berners died in 1950 and the tower fell into disuse until 1983, when his lover and heir, Robert Heber-Percy, renovated it and gave it to the Faringdon Folly Tower Trust for public enjoyment.

15. C.S. Lewis, at least, loathed John Betjeman, a former undergraduate pupil and a friend of Berners. The only other similar connection between Berners and Tolkien came later: in the 1940s Lord David Cecil was not only a friend of the Faringdon peer but also a member of the Inklings. It is useless to conjecture what Tolkien would have thought about Berners' sexuality: it was not publicised, and we know neither Tolkien's views on homosexuality nor whether he would have allowed any prejudice or religious scruple to colour his personal views of an individual.

where his brother Hilary had his farm. It had been frequented in the 1870s by William Morris of the Arts and Crafts Movement and Edward Burne-Jones of the Pre-Raphaelite Brotherhood – both of whom impressed and influenced Tolkien.[16]

At any rate, the Faringdon Folly controversy of 1935 is enough to explain why Tolkien changed the object of controversy in his *Beowulf* allegory from a rock garden into a tower with a view prior to his 1936 British Academy lecture. The local planning row was all about the two attitudes embodied in Tolkien's existing rock garden allegory – the eccentric with an imagination and the critics without one – but the tower was simply a much more fruitful image.

Many in Tolkien's audience in Oxford and at the British Academy in London will also have heard about the folly row. There is a very good chance that Faringdon Folly would have come to mind for anyone hearing Tolkien deliver his tower allegory in 1935 or 1936. He could depend on many in his audience recognising that it chimed with a real, recent and thoroughly entertaining case. Indeed, if he was not aware of the controversy, he might have wondered why people in his audience were chuckling at his allegory. But it seems certain that Tolkien did know about it, and very likely he played it for laughs. It's a good strategy for the opening of a paper.

8 – Further effects of Faringdon Folly

I first came across the existence of Faringdon Folly when I saw a picture that Lord Berners painted – a long view of his tower – for a 1936 poster used as part of the Shell advertising campaign (Harris 2010, 221). I was immediately struck by its similarities with *The Hill: Hobbiton across the Water*, which Tolkien is thought to have first drawn in mid-January 1937 and which he turned into a painting later that year (Scull and Hammond 2017, 203-4).[17] The Berners and the Tolkien image share a sky with scattered cumulus clouds; a landscape of trees, hedgerows and bosomy green fields; and a road that bisects the view from the foreground and runs through clustering village buildings towards the central hill. It is not essential to look for an inspiration in Berners' Faringdon Folly painting. Both pictures are typical of English landscape illustration. But there seems a very good chance Tolkien saw it. The Shell posters appeared on the sides of the trucks that delivered Shell supplies to petrol stations, and Berners' view of Faringdon Folly was new and current when Tolkien was drawing Hobbiton. We know, of course, that Tolkien used others' artwork to guide his own for *Beorn's Hall*, *Bilbo Woke Up with the Early Sun in His Eyes*, and other *Hobbit* illustrations.

Perhaps, to hypothesise further, Tolkien still had Faringdon Folly at the back of his mind in December 1937 when he began *The Lord of the Rings*. After all, it begins with a local eccentric winning over his sceptical neighbours, however briefly, with a grand display of fireworks. It may not have escaped Tolkien's notice, either, that Lord Berners lived with a younger male companion upon whom he doted.

---

16. It inspired Morris to found the Society for the Protection of Ancient Buildings. http://www.visit-broadway.co.uk/blog/history-of-broadway-tower.php.

17. Scull and Hammond suggest it was drawn after pictures previously submitted to George Allen & Unwin had been accepted (7 January). Tolkien told C. A. Furth on 13 August that he had made a painting of the scene.

9 – The meme of the tower

But let's return to the tower image in Tolkien's writings. And let's now stop running the clock backwards and look at the stages of inspiration again, in the right order – the order in which Tolkien developed his ideas from the allegorical *Beowulf* tower to the tower of Orthanc. Some very interesting features become apparent.

Pleased with the tower scenario in the *Beowulf* lecture delivered in November 1936, Tolkien very quickly grafted it onto his legendarium with 'The Fall of Númenor'. Towers are built near the western shores of Middle-earth by certain enlightened Númenórean survivors hoping to catch a vision of the True West along the Straight Way. Already, we can detect an echo of the allegory. But the resonance goes further. Like the purblind neighbours who can't see the point of the *Beowulf* tower, the majority of the other Númenórean survivors, lacking vision or imagination, are said to have "scorned the builders of towers" (*Lost Road*, 28).

And the scenario – the tower, the visionary builder or occupant, and the sceptical outsiders – proceeded to reappear in new guises in different Middle-earth situations. For Tolkien, it became what we might call a meme.

In 1938 drafts for *The Lord of the Rings*, Tolkien reimagined the Númenórean towers as elf-towers and planted them on the Tower Hills west of the Shire. But the symbolic package from Tolkien's Beowulf lecture is largely still intact – with the hobbits themselves as the unimaginative outsiders:

> The tallest was furthest away, standing alone on a hill. The hobbits of the Westfarthing said that you could see the Sea from the top of that tower: but no hobbit had ever been known to climb it [...] They did not go in much for towers. (*Shadow*, 312-3)

Then, when Tolkien temporarily decided that the Black Riders had besieged Gandalf in the tallest elf-tower, the Riders look up at the topmost chamber with "mocking laughter" (*Treason*, 34). So a resonance persists, even though it is Gandalf they mock, not the tower.

In 1940, when Tolkien came up with the definitive reason for Gandalf's delay, the wizard is still held captive on top of a tower – Orthanc – amid a "crying of fell voices" from below, though these are the voices of orcs and wolves, not Black Riders (*FR*, 'In the House of Tom Bombadil', 127-8). The faintest hints of the *Beowulf* allegory can still be discerned in Frodo's dream-vision of all this – the good man, the tower, and the sound of hostile voices.

Obviously, on the road to Isengard many elements of the symbolic pattern have been discarded or mutated almost out of recognition. But this method of substituting parts of a working structure is something already seen in the way Tolkien methodically altered his *Beowulf* allegory of the rock garden into the Allegory of the Tower.

At the same time, Tolkien preserved the Elf-towers in the Tower Hills, and their symbolism remains much as it was for the *Beowulf* tower. It seems especially significant that Sam Gamgee's descendants move to Westmarch beneath those towers. The old scepticism and suspicion about towers and the sea might linger among the majority of Hobbits, but at least now some of the neighbours are enlightened.

10 – Allegory and feigned history

Tolkien had deliberately vaulted the barrier between two kinds of writing that he tended to separate: allegory and what he called feigned history. This is to understate the magnitude of the leap; because the idea that Tolkien hated allegory has become one of his most famous literary pronouncements. In his Foreword to the second edition of *The Lord of the Rings*, he wrote:

> I cordially dislike allegory in all its manifestations, and always have done so since I grew old and wary enough to detect its presence. I much prefer history, true or feigned, with its varied applicability to the thought and experience of readers. I think that many confuse 'applicability' with 'allegory'; but the one resides in the freedom of the reader, and the other in the purposed domination of the author. (*FR*, 'Foreward to the Second Edition', xxiv)

This is often boiled down simply to 'Tolkien hated allegory', and is used to try and shut down all discussion of how his writing may have been influenced by his life and times. 'Tolkien never wrote allegory', it is said – a problematic point, if you know about the Allegory of the Tower or *Leaf by Niggle*. Evidently, though Tolkien claimed to dislike allegory in all its forms, actually he thought it had its uses, but he liked it lean, stripped down, pared to the essentials. If the extraordinarily complicated *The Lord of the Rings* were an allegory, it would be an absurdly complex one, going far beyond the significations that Tolkien mocks in his Foreword, such as whether the Ring 'equals' the atomic bomb and Sauron 'equals' Hitler or Stalin. But his complaint about allegory has a particular fitness for *The Lord of the Rings*. Allegory, he says, "resides [...] in the purposed domination of the author". In other words, allegory is alien to the spirit of a story about tyranny, in which the war for freedom is conducted by volunteers who are always at liberty to turn back.

But the great thing about the tower with the view over the sea is that it helps us understand the difference between allegory and what Tolkien called feigned history. That's because he uses the same scenario in both these forms of literary expression. In the *Beowulf* lecture's allegory the meaning of the scenario is heavily signalled, transparent. In the Middle-earth version it is not so. Yet some of the same meaning remains, if we want to find it. It is offered to us rather than thrust upon us. Even if we are not looking for it, we may appreciate it subliminally, as one of the effects of the story we are enjoying. Absence of allegory does not mean absence of symbolism, which is one of the rhetorical devices essential to literary art, to imagination and to language itself.

[Note. Some of the sources cited in notes are cuttings kindly provided to me but which are annotated either imperfectly or not at all, so that the provenance is not always clear.]

Bibliography

Anon. 'Faringdon Folly', *Times*, 19 July 1934, 4.

Anon. 'History of Broadway Tower', *Broadway Tower*, 2 January 2016, <http://www.visit-broadway.co.uk/blog/history-of-broadway-tower.php> [accessed 13 June 2021].

Anon. 'Hundreds thrilled as Folly Tower opens in 1935: An Extract from Faringdon Advertiser 2007 Newspaper account of the Firework display', *Faringdon Folly*, <https://www.faringdonfolly.org.uk/ uploads/1/4/0/4/14041893/folly_tower_opens_1935_folly_news_nov_07.jpg>.

Anon. 'The Higher, the Newer', *Tatler*, 13 November 1935, 299 <http://www.faringdonfolly.org.uk/ folly-history.html> [accessed 13 June 2021].

Arnot, C., 'Lord of the ring road', *Guardian*, 5 August 2003 <theguardian.com/education/2003/aug/ 05/schools.schooltrips> [accessed 13 June 2021].

Aslet, C., 'Pavilioned in extravagant splendour', *Times Saturday review*, 1 October 1983, 1.

Benedikz, B.S., 'Some Family Connections with J.R.R. Tolkien', *Amon Hen*, 209 (2008), 11.

Dickinson, P., *Lord Berners – Composer, Writer, Painter,* (Suffolk: Boydell Press, 2010).

Garth, J., 'When J.R.R. Tolkien bet C.S. Lewis: The wager that gave birth to *The Lord of the Rings*', *Sunday Telegraph*, 11 December 2016, <www.telegraph.co.uk/books/what-to-read/jrr-tolkien-bet-cs- lewis-wager-gave-birth-lord-rings/> [accessed 13 June 2021].
— 'When Tolkien reinvented Atlantis and Lewis went to Mars', *John Garth*, 31 March 2017 <https://johngarth.wordpress.com/2017/03/31/when-tolkien-reinvented-atlantis-and-lewis-went-to-mars/> [accessed 13 June 2021].
— *The Worlds of J.R.R. Tolkien: The Places that Inspired Middle-earth,* (London: Frances Lincoln; Princeton: Princeton University Press, 2019).

Hammond, W. G. and C. Scull, *J.R.R. Tolkien: Artist and Illustrator,* (London: HarperCollins, 1995).
— *The Art of The Lord of the Rings,* (London: HarperCollins, 2015).

Harris, A. *Romantic Moderns: English Writers, Artists and the Imagination from Virginia Woolf to John Piper,* (London; Thames & Hudson, 2010, paperback edition 2015).

Hayhurst-France, C., *Lord Berners' Folly*, (Publisher unknown, 1989).

Ker, W.P., *The Dark Ages,* (New York: Scribner, 1904).

McIlwaine, C., *Tolkien: Maker of Middle-earth,* (Oxford: Bodleian Publishing, 2018).

s.v. folly (n.1). *Oxford English Dictionary* 2nd ed. (1989) <https://www.oed.com/oedv2/00087457>

Scull, C., 'The Influence of Archaeology and History on Tolkien's World', in *Scholarship and Fantasy: Proceedings of the Tolkien Phenomenon*, ed. K. J. Battarbee (Turku: University of Turku Press, 1993).

Scull, C. and W. G. Hammond, *J.R.R. Tolkien Companion and Guide: Reader's Guide and Chronology*, 2nd edn, (London: HarperCollins, 2017).

Taylor, A.J.P., *An Old Man's Diary,* (London: Hamish Hamilton, 1984).

Tolkien, J.R.R., *Beowulf and the Critics*, ed. Michael D. C. Drout, 2nd edn, (Tempe: Arizona Center for Medieval and Renaissance Studies, 2011).
— *The Treason of Isengard*, ed. by Christopher Tolkien (London: Unwin Hyman; Boston: Houghton Mifflin, 1989).
— *The War of the Ring*, ed. by Christopher Tolkien (London: Unwin Hyman, 1990; Boston: Houghton Mifflin, 1990).

Various authors, 'Talk: Perrott's Folly', *Wikipedia* <https://en.wikipedia.org/wiki/Talk%3APerrott%27s _Folly> [accessed 13 June 2021].

Whitlock, R., *Zootomia, or, Observations on the Present Manners of the English,* (London: Thomas Roycroft, 1654).

Wise, M., 'Lord Berners' Folly', *Faringdon Online*, 2004, <www.faringdon.org/uploads/1/4/7/6/14765418/ building_the_folly.pdf> [accessed 13 June 2021].

Zinovieff, S., *The Mad Boy, Lord Berners, My Grandmother and Me,* (London: Jonathan Cape, 2014).

Tolkien and His Publishers

Wayne G. Hammond

My title is 'Tolkien and His Publishers', but it could as well have been 'Tolkien's Publishers and Their Author', for publishing is a collaborative effort, at any rate in its traditional form. Rayner Unwin once advised my wife and me that publishers need authors as much as authors need publishers; he was referring to the bargain by which authors provide content, and publishers put it before the public. One may argue how much this still applies in an age when so much is self-published, but it is generally true even now, and at any rate it was true for Tolkien. In this paper I would like to say a few words about Tolkien's relationships with some of his publishers, a subject about which his biographers have not said nearly as much as might be said, and about his desire to publish, which has been a point of discussion among critics.

Charles Dickens is said to have been overwhelmed at the sight of his first work in print (a brief sketch), so that his eyes were "dimmed with joy and pride". One has to wonder what Tolkien felt when his poem *The Battle of the Eastern Field* appeared in the magazine of King Edward's School, Birmingham, in March 1911 – this was his first published imaginative work, following some reports of the school debating society – or when *Goblin Feet* was chosen for *Oxford Poetry 1915*, his first work to appear in a book, published by B.H. Blackwell. Presumably on both occasions it was a feeling of accomplishment.

Tolkien's friends G.B. Smith and H.T. Wade-Gery, who also had poems in *Oxford Poetry*, felt that they and Tolkien were the best of its contributors; Tolkien may have agreed. At least, he seems to have been proud of his achievement, at that time if not years later, when he wished that *Goblin Feet*, that "unhappy little thing […] could be buried forever" (*Lost Tales I*, 32). By the first appearance of *Goblin Feet* in December 1915 he had written a number of poems and was eager to see them published. He sent them to friends for comment, and to his former King Edward's School master R.W. Reynolds. In January 1916 he shared his work also with Dora Owen, who had read *Goblin Feet* and wanted to include it in an anthology she was preparing for Longmans.

In August 1915 Reynolds had advised Tolkien to proceed with the collection of poems he was then planning, but warned that he shouldn't be disappointed if it fell flat. Under normal circumstances, as a matter of wise marketing, Tolkien would first have published single poems in weekly or monthly magazines (of which there were many) to establish his reputation before considering a volume of collected verse. Apart from *The Battle of the Eastern Field* he had published only one other poem, or rather part of one (its editor had lost half of it), 'From the Many-Willow'd Margin of the Immemorial Thames' in the *Stapeldon Magazine* of Exeter College, Oxford. The World War, however, in 1915 was then nearly into its second year, Tolkien was on active service, and his desire to be a published poet was driven by an understandable urgency. He had not yet entered the trenches, but would do so before long, and the life-expectancy of a junior officer at the front was not great.

Another Exeter College student, H.R. Freston, had already published in 1915 his first collection of verse, about which Tolkien delivered a paper to an Oxford society. (A second collection, in 1916, would be posthumous.) Tolkien was also energized by his friendship with schoolmates G.B. Smith, Rob Gilson, and Christopher Wiseman, and considered poetry his "weapon" (as Wiseman put it) in their agreed mission to raise up art and beauty (qtd. in Scull and Hammond 2017, 1285).

Tolkien's friends encouraged him to submit his poems to either of the London publishers Hodder & Stoughton or Sidgwick & Jackson. Dora Owen also suggested Sidgwick & Jackson, or Elkin Matthews or John Lane – there would have been several possibilities. I suspect that Tolkien chose Sidgwick & Jackson because they were the publisher of Rupert Brooke, a poet well loved by G.B. Smith as by many others and an early literary martyr of the war, who had died on active service (though not in battle) in April 1915. On the third of February 1916 Smith, already posted to France, urged Tolkien to publish by whatever means: "Make haste, before you come out to this orgy of death and cruelty" (85). Tolkien sent his collection, called *The Trumpets of Faerie*, to Sidgwick & Jackson within the week. At the end of March it was rejected.

He did not send it to another publisher at once. According to Douglas A. Anderson in the *J.R.R. Tolkien Encyclopedia*, Tolkien tried twice more to publish a selection of his early poems, twice more without success, but not until the 1920s (2007, 549). In 1916 he had much else on his mind. He had married Edith Bratt in late March; in early June, after a period of army training, he left England for France; Rob Gilson was killed in July, on the first day of the Somme offensive; Tolkien, contracting trench fever, was evacuated to hospital in England in early November; and G.B. Smith was hit by shrapnel at the end of November and died a few days later. Ironically, Smith received a (posthumous) printed collection of his poetry when Tolkien did not: *A Spring Harvest*, published in 1918, was edited by Tolkien and Wiseman as a memorial to their friend. It was probably subsidized by R.W. Reynolds. *A Spring Harvest* was itself considered, and evidently rejected, by Sidgwick & Jackson, who were one of the two major publishers of soldier-poets. Instead, it was issued by their unscrupulous rival Erskine Macdonald, who published books when their costs were paid by the author himself (if he survived), or by his family or friends, and then largely without royalties.

Illness having saved him from the trenches, Tolkien in convalescence found more time to write, notably beginning the prose 'The Book of Lost Tales'. Thus he went further down a road he had begun to follow in his poetry, ultimately developing a private mythology with attendant languages and stories. But we must not forget that he had prepared at university to lead the life of a scholar, and with the end of the war he joined the staff of the *Oxford English Dictionary* (*OED*) and established himself as a private tutor. In 1920 he moved to Leeds as part of the faculty of the new English school there, and in 1925 returned to Oxford, where he would have two long professorial careers.

Then as now, academics were expected to contribute to the literature of their fields. That Tolkien published relatively little in his was a source of dismay to his colleagues and of guilt to himself, even though those works of scholarship he did produce, such as his landmark lecture on *Beowulf*, were widely influential. His failure to produce in greater quantity was not, as some believe, solely or even mainly because he was too occupied with his imaginative writings. Rather, like colleagues such as George Gordon and Elaine Griffiths, he was a conscientious teacher and administrator, who paid as much or more attention to his students' work as to his own. Also significantly, as a writer he took remarkable pains in all that he did. Humphrey Carpenter says in his *Biography* that

> Tolkien had a passion for perfection in written work of any kind, whether it be philology or stories. This grew from his emotional commitment to his work, which did not permit him to treat it in any manner other than the deeply serious. Nothing was allowed to reach the printer until it had been revised, reconsidered, and polished. (1977, 138)

One case in point is Tolkien's *Middle English Vocabulary*, the glossary for *Fourteenth Century Verse & Prose*, edited by Kenneth Sisam, who had tutored Tolkien at Oxford. Sisam's collection had begun as a joint effort with A.S. Napier of the Oxford English School, intended "for the use of language students [...] with an apparatus strictly linguistic", but was abandoned when Napier died in 1916 and Sisam took a wartime government post (Sisam 1921, xxxliii). (On the same page in his book, Sisam thanks "Mr. J.R.R. Tolkien who has undertaken the preparation of the Glossary, the most exacting part of the apparatus", evidently hoping, when he wrote these words, that the glossary would still be included with the first printing (xxxliii). When after the war students returned to university in great numbers, Oxford University Press revived *Fourteenth Century Verse & Prose* as part of an effort to dominate the academic market in texts for the study of Middle English.

By June 1919 it was apparent that Sisam, then assistant to the chief executive of Oxford University Press, would not himself have time to compile the glossary for his book, as he had intended to do. The task was given instead to Tolkien, whose philological talents Sisam had recognized and who had proved himself on the *OED*; and it was apparently because he recognized the importance of this commission, (which would become his first academic publication) that Tolkien set aside, for the most part, work on 'The Book of Lost Tales'.

That he began to work on the *Vocabulary* that autumn and winter is evident from annotations he made to related words in office copies of the *Oxford English Dictionary*, Tolkien still being on the *OED* staff through May 1920. But it is also clear that work did not progress as quickly as Sisam and Oxford University Press had hoped, or in the manner they expected. Tolkien was meant to compile a straightforward glossary to Sisam's text, and to do so quickly. Instead, as he wrote a year later, the "mole-hill glossary" grew "into a mountain by accumulated domestic distractions" (qtd. in Scull and Hammond 2017, 785). These included his continuing work on the *OED*, as well as obtaining his academic post at Leeds, moving house, and teaching a heavy load, and the birth of his son Michael. He was able to hand over some material for the glossary only in February 1921. By then, Sisam's book was already in production, and when it appeared that October it was without Tolkien's part. Not until the following year did he complete the *Vocabulary*, which was issued separately and only later still as an appendix to Sisam's text.

Peter Gilliver, Jeremy Marshall, and Edmund Weiner in their book *The Ring of Words* describe Tolkien's completion of *A Middle English Vocabulary* even by 1922, with so many other responsibilities, as "an astonishing achievement" (2006, 35). They explain that he would have had to consider each of some 43,000 words in Sisam's text for possible inclusion in the glossary, from which he produced 4,740 entries and nearly 6,800 definitions, as well as references and cross-references. Nor was Tolkien content with simply glossing major words; rather, as he wrote in his introduction to the *Vocabulary*, he held that a good working knowledge of Middle English depends

> less on the possession of an abstruse vocabulary than on familiarity with the ordinary machinery of expression — with the precise forms and meanings that common words may assume; with the uses of such innocent-looking little words as the prepositions of and *for*. [...] So in making a glossary for use with a book itself designed to be a preparation for the reading of complete texts, I have given exceptionally full treatment to what may rightly be called the backbone of the language. (1922, 3)

Providing such 'full treatment' was typical of Tolkien, as Carpenter has suggested. *A Middle English Vocabulary* was far more than he had been commissioned to produce. It was created over a much longer period of time than was expected or convenient. It was more complex and time-consuming than even Tolkien himself foresaw. Writing in *The Year's Work in English Studies* for 1920–1921, Margaret L. Lee praised *A Middle English Vocabulary* for doing things Kenneth Sisam certainly had not meant it to do, such as devoting "much space and care to the various meanings of the preposition to, and the various forms of the pronoun *he*, or the verb *habben*, rather than to suggested etymologies of the rare and obscure words contained in his texts" (1920-1, 43). This, said Lee, gave the work "a value independent of the extracts to which it is appended" (43).

As an executive of Oxford University Press, Sisam was naturally concerned with budgets, deadlines, and potential sales. No doubt, economic factors influenced his ideas about scholarly books, but in his correspondence he expressed strong personal views about their design and publication. In particular, he preferred that they have a limited number of notes, and he was none too keen about glossaries, which because of their complex structure were expensive to set in type. After Sisam's death the scholar Eugene Vinaver wrote to the *Times* to defend Sisam's practice of thinning or dispensing with apparatus, what he called the "undergrowth of scholarship", removing "the outward appearance of learning" to restore "to the concept of scholarship its true meaning" (1971, 14).

Others looked upon Sisam less kindly. As Peter Sutcliffe wrote in his history of Oxford University Press:

> To some of his contemporaries [...] Sisam seemed a hard man. His many acts of generosity were seen as exceptions to a general rule of sternness bordering on parsimony. [...] He was certainly unyielding, often stubborn, and on the rare occasions when he was persuaded to change his mind there was a rumbling and creaking of machinery unaccustomed to shifts of gear. (Sutcliffe 1978, 270)

Raymond Edwards remarks in his biography of Tolkien that Sisam was known for "a briskly ruthless approach to philology", and was "temperamentally unsympathetic to Tolkien's more expansive and comprehensive approach" in *A Middle English Vocabulary* (2014, 116). Edwards also suggests, though I am inclined to consider this more a matter of opinion than of fact, that Sisam's introductions to the individual texts in *Fourteenth Century Verse & Prose* "have an undercurrent of robust Protestant, or at least anti-Roman, sentiment [...] which Tolkien [as a devout Catholic] can hardly have relished" (116).

Despite their differences, Tolkien and Sisam remained on good terms. They were scholars in the same field and gentlemen of their time. It was Sisam who alerted Tolkien to the opening at Leeds; and when Tolkien was named Rawlinson and Bosworth Professor of Anglo-Saxon at Oxford, a chair for which both were finalists, Sisam seems not to have held it against his rival. In any case, to return to Rayner Unwin's advice: as author and publisher, they needed each other. Tolkien, well respected for his learning and abilities, was consulted by Oxford University Press, and in mid-1921, even as he was still at work on the *Vocabulary*, he was recruited to help prepare an edition of the Middle English poem *Sir Gawain and the Green Knight* (*GGK*), which the Press wanted badly to compete with the standard edition by Gollancz.

For this he was partnered with E.V. Gordon, one of the best recent linguistic graduates in English. Gordon had been at Oxford, in part under Tolkien's tutelage, and became his colleague at Leeds. The two optimistically planned to produce *Sir Gawain* in a matter of months. Oxford University Press approved, provided that the book not exceed 160 pages, which Sisam had established as the standard for works in the Oxford series. But Tolkien and Gordon concluded that if they were forced to keep to this limit, they would have to curtail their apparatus, and the result would be merely a junior university textbook rather than a superior contribution to scholarship.

Sisam was not pleased to be asked for another 40 pages, nor to hear that both Tolkien and Gordon had heavy teaching schedules, which prevented them from finishing *Sir Gawain* as quickly as they had hoped. Sisam disagreed with their estimate of length for their text proper, and he objected to a large glossary. The length of the book, he warned, had to be controlled in order to keep its price within the reach of university students. But he was willing to accept 200 pages if the manuscript of the book was so accurate that proof correction at the Press would be negligible (that is, relatively cost-free). Tolkien and Gordon argued that the language of *Sir Gawain* – a Midlands dialect of Middle English, not that of Chaucer and the *Canterbury Tales* – was so different that it needed an unusual amount of glossing. They must have made their case, or Sisam was overruled from above, for their edition ran to 235 pages, including a 76-page glossary which Tolkien, who wrote it, had promised to keep to 50.

As I have said, Tolkien has been criticized for not publishing more within his academic disciplines. It was not that he lacked ambition – he certainly wished to publish. Rather, he tried to do more than was feasible. He had many ideas, some of which came to nothing, such as his suggestion – while still struggling to complete *Sir Gawain* – that he write an *Introduction to German Philology*; Sisam expressed interest, provided that the book not be too long or too unreadable. In the event, Tolkien did not endear himself to his academic publishers, gaining a reputation as a scholar who, though brilliant, was not to be trusted to meet deadlines or keep to established forms.

From around 1923, for example, also while he was still engaged with *Sir Gawain*, until the 1960s, Tolkien was responsible for editing a selection of texts by Chaucer together with his colleague George S. Gordon. Neither was able to bring the work to a conclusion, and it became a derelict at Oxford University Press and the subject of complaints by Sisam in internal memos, which blamed Tolkien for slow progress and for excessive correction of the base text (by Skeat).

Also, in 1935 Tolkien formally agreed to produce for the Early English Text Society an edition of *Ancrene Wisse* (*AW*), the important Corpus Christi College, Cambridge manuscript of the *Ancrene Riwle*, a medieval set of rules for anchoresses (female religious recluses); but this work was not published until 1962, and only after many heated letters passed between Tolkien and his editors arguing how the manuscript should be presented. Tolkien had worked on a line by line transcription at great length before being engaged to publish his work for the Society: to then have to alter it, as well as thousands of references already keyed to folio and line, to suit the Society's house form for editions – which was not line by line – seemed onerous, merely (as it seemed to Tolkien) for the sake of consistency by the publisher. Tolkien also argued that a line by line transcription would better suit the scholar interested in the finer points of the original manuscript.

In 1937 the Society's governing committee, probably weary of debate, gave way to Tolkien. But when, after many delays, the work resurfaced in 1958, a new editor, R.W. Burchfield, unaware of the decision made some twenty years earlier, expressed his own view that the transcription should be changed, and the debate began anew. Burchfield's diplomacy was severely tested, as was Tolkien's composure in the face of late changes to his work made without his knowledge or consent. Burchfield, like Sisam, was a fellow scholar of Middle English, and as a student at Oxford had been one of Tolkien's loyal followers, entranced by his lectures, especially those on the late 12th-century *Ormulum*, which became the subject of Burchfield's postgraduate work under Tolkien's supervision. It may be ironic that Burchfield, though otherwise accomplished, even distinguished in his field, never completed his D.Phil. – surely a reflection of how industrious he was with other matters.

Tolkien's failures in regard to the 'Chaucer' and *AW* – the former abandoned after much work, the text of the latter completed (and presented as Tolkien preferred) though he never wrote a formal introduction – cannot be explained wholly by perfectionism, or crowded teaching schedules, or 'domestic distractions' such as the illnesses that often struck down Tolkien or his family, though they had these in abundance. For his critics are not wrong to say that the 'Matter of Middle-earth' often occupied his thoughts, and at length, Tolkien's imaginative fiction also found a publisher, though he wasn't seeking one.

Probably in 1935 – and you will remember that this is the same year that Tolkien agreed to produce an edition of *AW*, and when he was still theoretically responsible for the 'Chaucer' – Elaine Griffiths, one of his B.Litt. students, suggested to the London publisher George Allen & Unwin that Tolkien prepare a new edition of John R. Clark Hall's Modern English translation of *Beowulf*, last revised in 1911. Wisely judging that he did not have time to spare for it, Tolkien suggested that the work be done by Griffiths herself, under his direction. In the event, she failed to complete the revision, and although Tolkien offered to put the work in order, feeling an obligation to Allen & Unwin as he had vouched for his student, he too was unable to proceed. In the end, the project was turned over to his Oxford colleague C.L. Wrenn. Tolkien at last (in 1940) wrote a preface on translating *Beowulf* which is brief but valuable.

But in the process, something even more important occurred. Susan Dagnall, a representative of Allen & Unwin, visited Oxford probably early in 1936, probably to speak with Elaine Griffiths or with Tolkien himself about the Clark Hall volume, and in some manner (accounts vary) saw the typescript of *The Hobbit* that Tolkien circulated to friends. Dagnall herself read it, and convinced Tolkien that it should be published. How much convincing this took, no one has said; I suspect that not much was needed. Unfortunately, Tolkien's earliest correspondence with Allen & Unwin has been lost. Certainly he did not write *The Hobbit* for publication; it had been a story for his sons, and for himself, and latterly for his friends. If he ever thought to publish it before Susan Dagnall came to call, it is not recorded. But it is clear, from the care he took in preparing its circulating typescript, with maps and illustrations, that he looked upon it as if it could be already a published book.

By 1936 Tolkien was no stranger to publishing academic work. Production of *The Hobbit*, though, was a very different experience. For one thing, the process moved far more swiftly than it had at Oxford University Press for *A Middle English Vocabulary* or *Sir Gawain*. For another, there was no one at Allen & Unwin who was remotely like Kenneth Sisam, ruling with a firm hand and giving ground only grudgingly. For *The Hobbit* Tolkien worked closely with Susan Dagnall as a general editorial assistant, with Charles Furth, head of production, and with Stanley Unwin, chairman of Allen & Unwin, who took a personal interest in all of his firm's business.

These were three members of a house which Stanley Unwin's son Rayner later described as "editorially-led, medium-sized, and self-financing. It published according to merit rather than market, and maintained trust with its authors and with its bookselling customers" (1999, viii). By no means averse to publishing books that sold very well, Allen & Unwin nevertheless stood by their motto by which they published 'books that matter'. George Allen had been the publisher of John Ruskin; Stanley Unwin, after forming Allen & Unwin, had Sigmund Freud and Bertrand Russell, even Lenin and Trotsky. He did not himself necessarily subscribe to his authors' views, but he felt that they deserved to be read.

As for *The Hobbit*, it was of no consequence that Allen & Unwin had no dedicated children's books department. Tolkien's work was judged to be one of quality, worthy of the publisher's attention. Rayner Unwin, who joined his family's firm in 1951 and himself rose to be its chairman, maintained this healthy attitude towards books for the rest of his days, even as the world of publishing changed drastically with mergers and mega-corporations. I am too young to have known Allen & Unwin first-hand in the period when they were still George Allen & Unwin, but I was honoured to be able to do research in the files of their successor, Unwin Hyman, even as their offices were being cleared after their sale to HarperCollins, and I like to think that something of the air of the firm's history, when it worked directly with Tolkien, still lingered. At least, that was my impression while working in the firm's rooms in Soho, with Rayner Unwin's permission, reading Tolkien's correspondence with Dagnall, Furth, et al. You too will have a sense of what Allen & Unwin was like if you have read the printed volume of Tolkien's letters, nearly a third of which are addressed to the publisher.

I will spare you the full length of the story of Tolkien's dealings with Allen & Unwin for *The Hobbit*, which you can read in The *J.R.R. Tolkien Companion and Guide*, but will trust that the shade of Rayner Unwin won't mind if I quote a few words about the subject from his memoir, *George Allen & Unwin: A Remembrancer*. "By the end of 1936", he wrote,

> the typescript of *The Hobbit* had gone to the printers and a long, patient and courteous dialogue began to build up between author and publisher in order to ensure that this children's book by an unknown author was prepared for press in exactly the way that Tolkien wanted. The dialogue was almost entirely conducted by letter. In 1937 alone Tolkien wrote 26 letters to George Allen & Unwin and received 31 letters in return. On Tolkien's part these were all in handwriting, often up to five pages long, detailed, fluent, often pungent, but infinitely polite and exasperatingly precise. The time and patience that his publishers devoted to what should have been a straightforward typesetting job is astonishing. I doubt whether any author today, however famous, would get such scrupulous attention. It is too glib to assume that this all happened in a more leisurely age. Charles Furth was probably seeing forty or fifty other books through the press, often of far greater complexity and on a wide spectrum of subjects, during the same period in which he was dealing with *The Hobbit*. The telephone was seldom used: it was considered something of an intrusion and anyway far too extravagant to use at all frequently for long-distance calls. Charles Furth once visited Tolkien in Oxford, and twice in the autumn of publication Tolkien came to London by train where he met my father for the first time and was 'overwhelmed' by his kindness; but most of the business was conducted by correspondence. (1999, 75)

Although Allen & Unwin staff were diplomatic about it, Tolkien caused a great deal of trouble for them and for their printer. He altered so much of *The Hobbit* in proof that its first typesetting had to be completely revised, and even Tolkien's corrected proofs did not make for perfect copy. He drew his initial maps in multiple colours, and his dust-jacket design likewise had more colours than Allen & Unwin's production budget could bear; but he worked with Charles Furth and revised his art. He had not at first submitted illustrations, in addition to maps, but then sent a few, which were accepted though the publisher had not allowed for them in costs; and when those too were accepted, Tolkien sent still more. Susan Dagnall cheerfully allowed that this was not economical for Allen & Unwin, but the art was too delightful not to include – indeed, it makes for a superior book. Tolkien was disappointed, however, that the 'moon-runes' on *Thror's Map* had to be printed on its face rather than on its back, to be seen only when held up to a light, more or less as in the story. Allen & Unwin finally had to hold firm with costs at least to the extent that *Thror's Map* was printed as an endpaper rather than a separate sheet.

In his memoir Rayner Unwin marvels "that George Allen & Unwin really thought they were economising by using the author as an amateur designer-cum-illustrator. But in those happy days cost-benefit analysis had scarcely been invented" (78). In fact, there were very successful precedents for this further author–publisher collaboration, such as Hugh Lofting who illustrated his own 'Doctor Dolittle' books, and Arthur Ransome whose pictures came to be standard in his own 'Swallows and Amazons' series. Their art was sometimes amateurish, but it suited their stories down to the ground. And Tolkien genuinely had a talent for art and design, especially pattern-designing and lettering, so to have him illustrate and decorate his own story was not only aesthetically correct, it also pleased the author to have a measure of control over the appearance of his work.

In the *J.R.R. Tolkien Encyclopedia* Douglas A. Anderson states that "the most striking fact of Tolkien's publishing history is how little he sought publication for his creative writings" (2007, 549). But Tolkien was not a professional writer; he was a professional scholar and teacher, and until *The Hobbit* was published he had no reason to think that his imaginative amateur fiction and poetry would generate interest outside his small circle of family and friends. The urgency he felt to publish in 1915–1916, to put his poems at least before the public, had diminished with the years as he settled into life as a husband and father and into the routine of an academic, and as his creative interests were focused for the most part on his private legendarium.

But in 1937, with a successful children's title in the shops, Stanley Unwin asked for another book about hobbits. At first Tolkien had nothing more to say on the subject, but had other writings in his files. "I should rather like an opinion", he wrote to Unwin,

> other than that of Mr C.S. Lewis and my children, whether it has any value in itself, or as a marketable commodity, apart from hobbits. […] At the moment I am suffering like Mr Baggins from a touch of 'staggerment', and I hope I am not taking myself too seriously. But I must confess that your letter [asking for a sequel to *The Hobbit*] has aroused in me a faint hope. I mean, I begin to wonder whether duty and desire may not (perhaps) in future go more closely together. I have spent nearly all the vacation-times of seventeen years examining, and doing things of that sort, driven by immediate financial necessity (mainly medical and educational). Writing stories in prose or verse has been stolen, often guiltily, from time already mortgaged, and has been broken and ineffective. I may perhaps now do what I much desire to do [that is, to publish his works of the imagination, while performing his academic tasks at Oxford], and not fail of financial duty. Perhaps! (*Letters*, Letter 17, 24)

This was easier said than done. Tolkien offered Allen & Unwin a buffet of writings, parts of '*The Silmarillion*', for example, which the publisher's reader found incomprehensible, and *Mr. Bliss*, which was then too expensive to print. Little of the material was for children, and Stanley Unwin expected Tolkien to make his name as a children's writer, *The Hobbit* having been written and marketed as a children's book.

But Tolkien was soon inspired to begin his 'new *Hobbit*', *The Lord of the Rings*. As he had been for other works, he was too optimistic about how quickly he could write it, and he underestimated its final length; nor was he any less busy in his Oxford duties, especially during the fraught years of the 1939–1945 war. With completion of *The Lord of the Rings* delayed, Allen & Unwin published, in 1949, Tolkien's *Farmer Giles of Ham* (*FGH*), a shorter work he had in hand, unrelated to hobbits. The book trade found it bewildering, and Tolkien remarked to Stanley Unwin his belief that the publisher had not done enough to promote it.

This complaint was part of a distrust by Tolkien of Allen & Unwin which had begun to mount twelve years before, when the publisher turned down '*The Silmarillion*' – rightly so, with the work still far from complete, let alone 'commercial', but that was not how Tolkien saw it. On their part, Allen & Unwin found Tolkien, as Rayner Unwin has said, "an author of undoubted talent but of distracted and disorganised achievement"

(1999, 90). The two books they had published for him, *The Hobbit* and *FGH*, "though successful, had absorbed more time in overheads than, say, the entire output of Bertrand Russell" (90). Moreover, by October 1949, when he finished a draft of *The Lord of the Rings*, he had come to feel strongly that that work should be published with '*The Silmarillion*' as "one long Saga of the Jewels and the Rings" (*Letters*, Letter 126, 139). At this time he also made the acquaintance of Milton Waldman, a senior editor at the London publisher Collins, who read *The Lord of the Rings* and parts of '*The Silmarillion*' and expressed an interest in publishing both. This was enough to convince Tolkien to change publishers, if he had not had that thought already.

A draft of a letter by Tolkien to Milton Waldman suggests that he was of two minds about the morality of his decision. He would be glad to leave Allen & Unwin, he wrote,

> as I have found them in various ways unsatisfactory. But I have friendly personal relations with Stanley (whom all the same I do not much like) and with his second son Rayner (whom I do like very much). [...] Sir Stanley has long been aware that *The Lord of the Rings* has outgrown its function [as a children's book], and is not pleased since he sees no money in it for anyone (so he said); but he is anxious to see the final result all the same. If this constitutes a moral obligation then I have one: at least to explain the situation. (*Letters*, Letter 123, 135)

This he did. And the Unwins, father and son, in reply and with due diligence explored how their firm might publish so massive and therefore costly a work. They were concerned especially with *The Lord of the Rings*, less so with '*The Silmarillion*'. But Tolkien gave them an ultimatum – publish both works, or none – which Stanley Unwin had no choice but to decline. As Rayner Unwin put it: "Father felt hurt, but there was little he could do about it. He pointed out that he was being forced to make a decision about books that he had not even seen, and whose extent he had had no opportunity to check [...] [but] he was always ready to renew the search for 'ways and means'" to publish (1999, 95).

Tolkien seems not to have considered that the same calculations of cost and marketability for his book would be made also by Collins, or that at Collins, only Milton Waldman was enthusiastic about the project, and he was abroad most of the time. In the event, Collins demanded cuts, which Tolkien did not want to make. Humbled, he returned to Allen & Unwin through his long friendship with Rayner Unwin, who at age ten had written a positive review of *The Hobbit* which clinched his father's decision to publish it. But *The Lord of the Rings*, lengthy as it was by itself, would have to be published alone.

Rayner now took the lead, convincing his father to approve publication of *The Lord of the Rings*, though Allen & Unwin stood to lose money on it. It was an unusual book, but (as in the publisher's slogan) one that mattered. It was divided into three volumes, to be published at intervals so that readers' interest could be gauged with each part and the costs of printing spread. On his part, Tolkien was persuaded to accept a profit-sharing agreement whereby he would receive no advance or royalty until prime costs of production were made back, but then returns on sales would be split equally between author and publisher. This proved to be a very good decision indeed for Tolkien, and latterly for his estate.

Production did not move as quickly as it had done for *The Hobbit*. There were delays of revision, and of the completion of the Appendices in *The Return of the King*, so that the third volume of *The Lord of the Rings* appeared more than a year after the first. As in 1937, there were questions of design, for again Tolkien took an interest in the appearance of his book, down to the choice of typefaces, and he contributed to its decoration, while his son Christopher drew its maps. He made no illustrations as he had done for *The Hobbit*, which was just as well, for the publisher's budget allowed for only minimal art (two inscriptions and a drawing of the 'Doors of Durin'), and under no circumstances for colour reproductions of Tolkien's laborious 'facsimiles' of pages from the Dwarves' ruined Book of Mazarbul.

In *George Allen & Unwin: A Remembrancer* Rayner Unwin provides a good summary of the years following the publication of *The Lord of the Rings*, when Tolkien's life became more complicated by fame, issues of American copyright, the Ace Books 'piracy' of *The Lord of the Rings*, negotiations over film contracts, and difficulties with the Puffin Books *Hobbit*, in which the printers took it upon themselves to 'correct' Tolkien's spelling 'dwarves' to 'dwarfs'. Through all of this, Allen & Unwin staff, not only Rayner Unwin and his assistant Joy Hill, supported and protected Tolkien to the best of their ability and published further, small books by him, such as *Smith of Wootton Major*, while waiting in vain for him to complete '*The Silmarillion*'.

It has been suggested that Tolkien did not want to finish his legendarium because he did not want to give up the process of its creation, with which he had lived for so long. We need not think this, although it may have been true as well, when it was patently difficult for Tolkien to integrate satisfactorily the mythological and historical aspects of '*The Silmarillion*', which towards the end of his life had come into conflict, and how laborious – and yet how essential – it was to make the older tales of Middle-earth consistent with the settled (published) text of *The Lord of the Rings*. In any case, it cannot be doubted that Tolkien wanted '*The Silmarillion*' to be published. This is clear at least from his offer of parts of it to Allen & Unwin in 1937 and to Allen & Unwin and Collins in 1950, from his return to the mythology after the success of *The Lord of the Rings* ensured that *The Silmarillion* would have a guaranteed audience, and from his appointment of his son Christopher to manage his literary estate and bring, if he would, the scattered and various parts of the legendarium into a coherent whole.

This latter act of foresight gave rise, as Rayner Unwin said, to

> a new relationship […] between the executors [of Tolkien's estate] […] and the publisher: a relationship that has proved just as close and co-operative as it was with the original author, and which has resulted […] in the unique situation in which not only have more books by Tolkien been published after his death than during his life-time, but the sale of all his books has continued to increase year by year" (1999, 135)

It is a curious feeling to think that I myself, and others at this conference, through our work with Tolkien's writings have become at least tangentially part of this same relationship between author and publisher, which meant so much to Tolkien and has been of such great meaning and benefit to us all.

Bibliography

Anderson, D.A., 'Publishing History', in *J.R.R. Tolkien Encyclopedia: Scholarship and Critical Assessment*, ed. M.D.C. Drout (New York: Routledge, 2007), 549–50.

Carpenter, H., *J.R.R. Tolkien: A Biography* (London: George Allen & Unwin, 1977).

Edwards, R., *Tolkien* (London: Robert Hale, 2014).

Gilliver, P., J. Marshall, and E. Weiner, *The Ring of Words: Tolkien and the Oxford English Dictionary* (Oxford: Oxford University Press, 2006).

Lee, M.L., 'Middle English', *The Year's Work in English Studies*, 2, (1920–1), 41–53.

Scull, C. and W.G. Hammond, *The J.R.R. Tolkien Companion and Guide* (Chronology and Reader's Guide), rev. and expanded edn, 3 vols, (London: HarperCollins, 2017).

Sisam, K., ed., *Fourteenth Century Verse & Prose* (Oxford: Clarendon Press, 1921).

Sutcliffe, P., *The Oxford University Press: An Informal History* (Oxford: Clarendon Press, 1978).

Tolkien, J.R.R., *A Middle English Vocabulary* (Oxford: Clarendon Press, 1922).
— *The Letters of J.R.R. Tolkien*, ed. by H. Carpenter with the assistance of C. Tolkien (London: George Allen & Unwin, 1981).
— *The Book of Lost Tales, Part One*, ed. by Christopher Tolkien (London: George Allen & Unwin, 1983).

Unwin, R., *George Allen & Unwin: A Remembrancer* (Ludlow: Merlin Unwin Books, 1999).

Vinaver, E., 'Mr Kenneth Sisam: Encouraging True Scholarship', *The Times* (London), 2 September 1971, p. 14.

Hobbit Holes in Hove?
On the trail of the young Tolkien in Sussex

Mick Henry

For Christmas 2018, my wife bought me *The J.R.R. Tolkien Miscellany* (2012) by Robert S. Blackham and it was not until 2019, when I was thumbing through it, that I came upon this sentence. “Ronald was sent to stay with the family of his Aunt Jane’s future husband, Edwin Neave, in Hove” (87). As I live in Brighton, the thought that Tolkien had a connection to Sussex excited me.

After researching Tolkien’s time in Sussex, I regrettably found sparse material that is wanting and occasionally contradictory. This is not completely surprising as Tolkien’s visit took place in 1904 when he was twelve years old. There is a general consensus that he stayed with Edwin Neave, whom the young Tolkien had befriended when Edwin’s parents had lodged with John & Emily Suffield, Tolkien’s Grandparents on his mother’s side.

In 1901 the Suffield’s lived at 9 Ashfield Road, Kings Heath, Worcestershire, which was just a few minutes away from where the Tolkien’s were living, at 85 Westfield Road. The 1901 census documents Edwin as a twenty-nine year old insurance inspector and his soon to be wife, Emily Jane Suffield, as a twenty-eight year old school teacher. It is reported that Tolkien’s aunt, Emily Jane, was quite taken by the sandy haired insurance clerk who played Polly-Wolly-Doodle on his banjo on the stairs. Then in the spring of 1904 Tolkien’s mother became seriously ill with diabetes and could no longer look after her two sons. The Oliver Road house where they lived was closed, the furniture was stored, and the boys were sent away: Hilary to his Suffield grandparents and Ronald to Hove to stay with Edwin.

Edwin had moved down to Sussex the year before and had been promoted to Secretary of the Guardian Life and Fire Assurance Company which is documented in one of the early Brighton Street Directories of 1904. The Towners’ Directory entry for that year lists Edwin Neave, Secretary at 82 East Street Brighton, which was the home of the Guardian Life & Fire Assurance Company Ltd. There is, however, some confusion over Edwin’s marital status in 1904. There is a presumption by some that as Tolkien came to stay with Edwin in 1904 that he had already married Emily Jane and that she was with him in Hove.

This is not borne out by the facts. Emily and Edwin were married on the 3rd August 1905 at St Mary’s St Deny’s and St George, Manchester. Their marriage certificate records that they were both thirty-three years old and that Edwin was living at The Mitre Hotel and Emily at Ivy Cottages, Mosley, Birmingham. Evidence by Tolkien also exists to prove this. The title of one of his 1904 drawings is “What is a home without a mother or a wife” not only reflecting Tolkien’s situation but also that of his soon to be uncle Edwin (McIlwaine 2018, 133-4).

Another of Tolkien’s sketches “For men must work as seen daily at 9.00am” shows Tolkien and Edwin walking towards the offices of Guardian Assurance Company in East

Street, Brighton (133-4). But this raises questions such as where did they come from? Where were they living at the time? If you look closely at the picture you can make out an embossed address on the top right and it clearly says 20 St Catherines Terrace, Hove, so we finally know where Tolkien and Edwin were living. 20 St Catherine's Terrace was split into at least five dwellings in the 1900s and the house now has seven separate flats. Whether it is possible to find out exactly which one they stayed in cannot be determined.

It took me just over an hour to walk from St Catherine Terrace to East Street where Edwin worked. One may speculate that Tolkien must have gone with Edwin on weekdays. The last of Tolkien drawings from his stay in Hove is "Working over time S.P.Q.R" and it shows Edwin in his office in the Guardian Assurance building in East Street, Brighton. This must have been what Tolkien encountered every day when he accompanied Edwin to work. The building was known as Clarendon Mansions and still stands today, you can still make out the place where the words 'GUARDIAN ASSURANCE' once were.

There can be no doubt that Edwin had a transformative effect on the young Tolkien and the death of his mother on 14th November 1904 must have impacted the young Tolkien greatly. Just five years later he was to lose Edwin, who sadly passed away from pneumonia and heart failure on 8th May 1909, he was aged just thirty-seven years.

Bibliography

Blackham, R.S. *The J.R.R.Tolkien Miscellany* (Cheltenham: The History Press, 2012).

Hammond, W.G. and C. Scull, *The J. R. R. Tolkien Companion and Guide: Volume 1: Chronology* (London: HarperCollins. 2017).

McIlwaine, C. *Tolkien: Maker of Middle-earth* (Oxford: The Bodleian Library, 2018).

Tolkien, J.R.R. *Working over time S.P.Q.R.* © Tolkien Estate. (Postcard held at the Bodleian Library Oxford)

The Wright Stuff

Ian Spittlehouse

1 – A Yorkshire Tease

A portrait of Joseph Wright, M.A., Ph.D., Hon.D.Litt. hangs in the Lecture Hall of the Taylor Institute, Oxford. The Institute has been the location for the study of Modern languages for over a century. Professor Wright was an established member of the Faculty in the early twentieth century and a respected authority in Oxford and beyond. Wright features in Humphrey Carpenter's 1977 biography of Tolkien where his presence is marked both before and during Tolkien's time in Oxford. Carpenter writes,

> One of his school-friends had bought a book at a missionary sale, but found that he had no use for it and sold it to Tolkien. It was Joseph Wright's Primer of the Gothic Language. Tolkien opened it and immediately experienced 'a sensation at least as full of delight as first looking into Chapman's *Homer*. (1995, 45)

The presence and personality of Wright show through in the interest and encouragement he had for the undergraduates he tutored. Carpenter notes Tolkien's impression of,

> the vastness of Joe Wright's dining-room table, when I sat alone at one end learning the elements of Greek philology from glinting glasses in the further gloom. [...] the huge Yorkshire teas given by the Wrights on Sunday afternoons. (1995, 64)

More than this, Wright's influence would feature in Tolkien's life, and his family's life, for many years.

> but even then Ronald had to take her to the Wrights' front door himself and ring the bell before hurrying away round the corner. [...] huge house built to Joe's design in the Banbury Road. (157)

The Wright's house on the Banbury Road in north Oxford is one of the many properties lost from the leafy suburbs within the mile and a half radius of Carfax tower.[1] These suburbs, in many respects, no longer represent the Oxford of the early twentieth century. The changes of ownership of private and college properties and the redevelopment of the plots have changed the urban character of Park Town and Summertown on the Banbury Road.

One of the more egregious examples is the current development on the plot at 119 Banbury Road. The very same plot was purchased by the Wrights in 1904 from St Hilda's College and Wright commissioned the construction of a large detached house befitting his status as an Oxford don. The property was designed by the architect Edward Ould

1. Professors were obliged to live within the 'University Radius'.

and named Thackley after Wright's hometown. Built in the Georgian style the house in its own grounds was built to Wright's requirements with,

> a study big enough to hold all his [Wright's] books and leave plenty of space for him to live and work in it. […] "None of your casement and leaded-panes for me! I'm a book man and want plenty of light." (Wright 1932, 582)

He also oversaw the materials used in its construction from the Dorsetshire (probably Portland) stone for the walls to the teak frames of the windows. The building was finished with a magnificent stone roof with stone quarried at Idle Moor in West Yorkshire.

Those with an interest in what this grand design looked like can consult the pages of *The Life of Joseph Wright* the two-volume biography published by Elizabeth Wright in 193 and the Special Collections of the Bodleian Library, Oxford hold 'The Wright Papers'. These were left to the Library by Elizabeth and include an album of photographs of Thackley, 119 Banbury Road taken in 1905.[2]

2 – 'Donkey-boy to Oxford don'

Who was Joseph Wright and where did he come from? Why did he choose an academic career? What motivated him? An invaluable resource for these enquiries is the aforementioned two-volume biography, *The Life of Joseph Wright* published after his death in 1930.

Wright was born on 31 October 1855 at Parkhill Farm in Airedale near Idle, midway between Bradford and Leeds in West Yorkshire and in later years he would revel in saying, in good faith, "I have been an idle man all my life, and shall remain an idle man till I die" (Wright 1932, 1).

The tenancy of Parkhill Farm was held by his grandfather, James Wright and was worked by his sons. Joseph was the second son of Dufton and Sarah Wright and their work on the farm was supplemented with piece-work for the cloth manufacturers in the area. It was the proficiency of the locals with small hand-looms that led to them being referred to as 'little masters'.[3]

Though the cottage where Joseph, his parents and siblings lived has long since been demolished, Parkhill House itself still stands on the corner of Ellar Carr Lane and Parkhill Road. As one of James Wright's many grandchildren Joseph would go up to the main house to visit. Such audiences were remembered by Wright with his grandfather, "an old man with a broken leg, who sat in his kitchen smoking a long clay pipe" and that lighting his grandfather's pipe meant that "he had been a smoker ever since he was three years old" (16).

James kept his sons short of money and for Dufton's growing family the financial situation was such that in 1860, having secured a job at an ironstone quarry in Eston near Middlesborough, the family moved away from James Wright's patronage. This venture

2. Oxford, Bodleian Library Special Collections, Post Medieval Western Manuscripts, The Wright Papers, Item 40442.

3. Tolkien readers will recall Barliman Butterbur using a similar epithet when greeting to the hobbits at the Prancing Pony, Bree.

proved too much of a strain for Sarah (who was expecting her fourth child) and in early 1861 Sarah and the children returned to Idle. The only support was the Workhouse and this is where Joseph's youngest brother Dufton Jnr was born. With a newborn and her three sons Jim, Joseph and Tom (aged six, five and two years respectively) Sarah left the Workhouse and found accommodation in a 'Spite and Malice house'.[4] This was a one bedroom cottage just off the main road by the side of the mill-dam in Woodend.

It was around this time that both Jim and Joseph started work to earn a few pence toward the maintenance of the home. Jim was old enough to be employed in the mill, but was never suited to work and especially 'indoors employment'. He ran away to sea and was never heard of again.

Joseph earned eighteen pence per week driving a donkey-cart, carrying quarrymen's tools from the stone quarry at Woodend to the local smithy until aged seven when he started working at Sir Titus Salt's mill in Saltaire. He was underage but still found employ as a doffer[5] starting as a half-timer and then moving on to full-time. During his time, like many children employed in the textile industry, he had access to the schooling provided by the mill-owners. The education there was basic and relied on rote-learning. By the time he moved to full-time he could only recite various scriptural passages.

In 1863 Dufton Wright returned to West Yorkshire but his health was not good and he died soon after. This meant that providing for the household fell to Joseph and his mother. Of his siblings Dufton (Jnr) was most like his elder brother and worked in the quarries and the mill and later became caretaker of the Windhill Free Library.

Dufton (Jnr) also visited his brother in Oxford and in *The Life of Joseph Wright* there is an account of an incident from one of these visits,

> Dufton Wright, was distressed to see Oxford Colleges built of stone which had been cut the wrong way of the grain, so that the face of it exposed to the weather peeled and crumbled. With the hand of a pained connoisseur he was feeling the surface of an ancient wall when a policeman came up, supposing him to be some rude country bumpkin about to deface an academic shrine by inscribing thereon his trumpery initials. Dufton Wright quickly explained, and the incident terminated with mutual affability. (5)

On reading this account, presented as an example of character and practical experience in a location famed for its academic excellence, it is not difficult for the reader to draw a parallel with a similar scene in *The Lord of the Rings*

> Together the Elf and the Dwarf entered Minas Tirith, [...] Gimli stalked beside [...] stroking his beard and staring about him. 'There is some good stone-work here,' he said as he looked at the walls; 'but also some that is less good, and the streets could be better contrived. When Aragorn comes into his own, I shall offer him the service of stonewrights of the Mountain, and we will make this a town to be proud of. (*RK*, 'The Last Debate', 1141)

4. 'Spite and Malice house', these were built quickly and quickly rented out usually to prevent the widening of a roadway.
5. 'doffer', doffers removed the full bobbins from the spindle of the spinning frame and replaced them with empty ones. There were 144 spindles per frame, 72 on each side.

But this event was a long way away from the life that Joseph, Dufton (Jnr), Tom and their mother were making for themselves in Windhill, West Yorkshire in 1869. Joseph had moved from Salt's mill in Saltaire to Baildon Bridge Mill and then to a new mill in Bingley. He had also moved vocation, becoming an apprentice wool-sorter. Wool sorting (grading fleeces) was a lucrative job and highly specialised. With the increase in responsibility and wage the family were now renting a terrace house in Wellington Street, Windhill. This was a significant improvement to their domestic life over the cottage at Woodend. Number 6 Wellington Street had a parlour, two bedrooms, a kitchen and a cellar. Joseph bought furniture, a rocking-chair for his mother, a parlour suite, a chest of drawers and a "seeming-glass", a big one, with a marble slab at the bottom" (Wright 1932, 35).

Joseph was attending night-schools run by some of the teachers from the mill schools. He had also been taking courses at the Mechanical Institute in Bradford. This was driven by his own ambition and willingness to 'do some work' along with the recognition by his tutors of his aptitude for the subjects he engaged in. By 1873 he was studying languages (French and German) both written and spoken, along with Arithmetic, Euclid and Algebraic mathematics as it was taught at the time. For more general studies he took to purchasing *Cassell's Popular Educator*, a fortnightly publication that could cover anything from calligraphy to history or for that matter geography, agricultural science, literature or politics in any given issue. He was also running (and charging for) his own night-classes for his fellow apprentices.

In 1875 Joseph passed his first certificated qualification. This was in the Pitman system of phonography and phonetic shorthand. He had taken the course with the idea that he might become a newspaper reporter. This formal qualification along with Wright's aptitude for languages is certainly an interesting combination. The discipline required to transcribe spoken language for later study, married to a curiosity about the mechanics of language may have laid the foundations for Wright's future academic achievements.

In 1876 there was a shortage of work in the mills. Wright had saved around forty pounds and in the early spring of that year decided to invest in a term at a German University.[6] He settled on Heidelberg and after consulting one of the many German émigrés living in Bradford set out from Harwich to Rotterdam, travelling on to Antwerp and Cologne and completing the journey on foot, for the sake of economy. Part of this journey was corroborated in a later correspondence of dated 7 June 1931 that reports,

> In February 1876 when I was 26 years old, I travelled via Harwich and Rotterdam to Hamburg. On board the steamer soon after leaving Harwich when I stood on deck enjoying the sea-air and above all the freedom of a holiday after 4 years uninterrupted drudgery in a London office, a young man entered into conversation with me. He told me he was a wool-sorter in Bradford, that he had a holiday and meant to spend a week in Cologne in order to try and learn German, that he already could speak French and that he acquired his knowledge by hard study and by burning the midnight oil. He told me his hopes and of his prospects of earning £150 as a correspondent in a merchant's office if he could succeed. (58)

6. £2,700 (2017).

A term at a German University was roughly fourteen weeks and Wright could only afford to spend about eleven weeks in Heidelberg. He attended lectures in mathematics and while there extended his knowledge of the German language. On returning to Windhill he resolved to use his gift for imparting knowledge and decided at the age of twenty-one to, "give up working in a mill and make a career for himself in scholarship" (60).

Wright's first step was to seek out posts at schools in Bradford. The headmaster of a school on Horton Road recommended he apply at a school on Manningham Lane. It was here at Springfield School that Wright was engaged as school-master on a wage of forty pounds a year.[7] The post included board and lodging at the school from Monday morning to Friday evening. He returned to Wellington Street, Windhill at the weekends, where he continued the tutorial sessions he had established while working in the mills.

The transition from wool-sorter to school master meant a reduction in income but it also provided further motivation to attain further academic qualifications. He kept on with German and he also began to learn Greek. He also resolved to prepare for the London Matriculation Examination and attended evening classes at the Yorkshire College of Science, now Leeds University. By 1877 Wright had formal qualifications in Mathematics, Chemistry and by 1878 he had matriculated as a student at the University of London with the subjects ranging from French, German and Latin to Natural Philosophy, Arithmetic and Chemistry.

In 1879 Wright left Springfield School (at the encouragement of the head master) to better himself but also because there was little prospect of a higher salary in his current post. Wright's next post was as a resident assistant master at Grove Park School, Wrexham where many of the pupils were Welsh speakers and, unsurprisingly, he took this opportunity to learn some Welsh.

After taking a sabbatical in France in 1881 he returned to England and secured a post in a private school in Margate with a salary of one hundred pounds a year including full board and lodging.[8] In 1882 he passed the intermediate exam for the London B.A. but Wright decided to leave his teaching post. He turned his ambitions to other ventures and again resolved to study to improve his prospects of an academic career.

Wright, aged 27 returned to Germany to further his studies and this was the beginning of a sojourn that would last six years. He matriculated in Heidelberg with the view to studying mathematics. It was after an introduction to Professor Hermann Osthoff (who had lectured in Comparative Philology since 1877) and the invitation to attend his lectures that Wright decided to change the course of his studies. He was fascinated by the subject of philology and observed that, "Everybody who would be a philologist must have done mathematics, or be capable of doing mathematics" (74).

At the time the undergraduate students studying the subject of philology under Professor Osthoff were known as Junggrammatiker. Osthoff's approach to comparative philology addressed some of the existing philological rules on sound shifts in the development of language. The most important of these principles was that "the laws of sound change admit of no exception" (74). Many of Osthoff's students were German scholars and for Wright this tutelage would prove invaluable on his return to England.

7. £2,700 (2017).
8. £6,000 (2017).

While studying he supplemented his income by teaching mathematics at Neuenheim College, a boarding school for English boys. Wright was also earning commission proofreading grammars and translating the German philological texts he was studying into English.

In 1885 Wright graduated from Heidelberg with the Degree of Ph.D, Class II 'Insignia cum Laude' with the following subjects,

- Principle: The Comparative Philology of the Indo-Germanic languages;
- First Secondary: The Comparative and Historical Grammar of the Germanic languages in detail;
- Second Secondary: Anglo-Saxon language and literature.

Wright continued his studies at the University of Leipzig with further studies of language notably Lithuanian and phonetics along with German literature. He supplemented his income tutoring, but he was also retained by a publisher in Heidelberg to revise and correct educational books for English, French, German and Italian markets. He was paid a yearly sum of DM 1000 in half-yearly instalments, whether the firm sent books or not. Between 1886 and 1912 Wright supervised the issue of twenty-nine books for the firm.

In addition to his academic studies and tutoring Wright was writing his own primers for students of the Germanic languages. He was also compiling a study of the grammar and dialect of Windhill. This study would of course include many of the dialect words familiar to him from childhood and his own use of such vocabulary is an indication of the grounded nature of his approach to academic discourse.

In a letter discussing the review and reception of a publication of 1888 Wright commented that, "The book *went down* with the people so well [...] because it was puffed up by the Lobesversicherungsgesellschaft auf Gegenseitigkeit. (This is a jaw-cracker, nicht wahr!)" (112).

The German language is renowned for its compound words, but it is Wright's use of the dialect term 'jaw-cracker' that stands out. It is a Yorkshire dialect word and *The English Dialect Dictionary* (1905) defines it as 'a long word, difficult to pronounce'. In *The Lord of the Rings* the same expression is used by Samwise Gamgee in assessing the names (in Dwarvish) of the peaks of the Misty Mountains, "I thought at first that this here Redhorn, or whatever its name is, might be it, till Gimli spoke his piece. A fair jaw-cracker dwarf-language must be!" (*FR*, 'The Ring Goes South', 372).

By the summer of 1887 Wright had had offers of academic posts in both England and America but in September of the same year he returned to England and his connection with Oxford began. In 1888 he travelled up from London to teach and in Easter 1888 he was appointed Deputy-Teacher of German at the Taylorian Institute and by the Summer of 1888 he was living in Oxford.

In 1888 the Clarendon Press published his primers for Middle High German and Old High German and he was engaged to teach Old English Grammar and continued teaching these subjects till he was elected to the post of Deputy-Professor of Comparative Philology in February of 1891.

In March of 1894 Wright was made an Honorary M.A. by decree of Convocation and in November he matriculated as a Non-Collegiate member of Oxford University. Of the primers he had published, most notable at this time is his Gothic Primer, published in 1892.

It was *The Grammar and Dialect of Windhill, in the West Riding of Yorkshire* in 1893 though that marks his journey, from donkey-boy to Oxford don. It was the first publication of its kind in England, a scientific study of a living dialect;

> Professor Holthausen noted in the later testimonial he wrote in 1901, that it had received most cordial recognition from competent judges in Germany. Joseph Wright had heard and spoken this particular dialect from his childhood, and had then set himself to study it from the standpoint of the newest and most scientific philology. He maintained that living speech was in many ways of more value to a philologist that the written word of dead languages, and this was his first contribution in support of the theory. (Wright 1932, 138)

Wright dedicated the book to his mother and the motto (in German) on the title page is indicative of the ethos that motivated Wright.

> Nur das beispiel furht zum licht,
> vieles redden thut es nicht.

In English,

> Only example leads to the light,
> much talking does not do it.

3 – The English Dialect Dictionary

Most of the achievements in Wright's long academic career were born of necessity or they were the product of his own ambition to improve his lot. Of these successfully completed works the one that stands out is *The English Dialect Dictionary*. The dictionary was published as a six volume set in 1905 and the project itself was long in the planning and demanded dedication, clear objectives and pragmatism by those who worked on it. The final publication had to satisfy its patrons as much as it did its Editor.

The idea of a Dialect Dictionary was proposed at a meeting of the Philological Society in 1858 by Professor Walter William Skeat (1835 – 1912) specifically that "instead of the *Supplement* to the standard English Dictionaries [...] a *New Dictionary of the English Language* should be prepared under the authority of the Philological Society" (349).

In his later role as Editor of the Dictionary, Wright acknowledged in its dedication that Skeat was, "The unwearied Worker in the varied field of English Scholarship to whose patient industry and contagious enthusiasm in connexion with the laborious task of accumulating dialect material, the possibility of compiling an adequate English Dialect Dictionary is mainly due" (Wright 1905).

Skeat's proposal in 1858 led to the creation of the Early English Text Society and the establishment of the English Dialect Society for which Skeat wrote the prospectus. The society's first meeting was in Cambridge in 1873 and a year later had over two hundred and sixty members. The study of dialects was seen as essential to larger works including the *New English Dictionary*, later known as the *Oxford English Dictionary*. For the Early English Text Society and the newly formed Dialect Society some knowledge of modern English dialects was essential in compiling this new dictionary and for the Dialect Dictionary itself there were a number of prerequisites,

> The whole work is very extensive, dealing [...] with the dialect of every district in which varieties of English speech are found, whether in Great Britain, or Wales, or Ireland. Perhaps some nine or ten years may see the chief part of the work accomplished, after which will come the labour of compiling a complete and exhaustive provincial glossary, probably of considerable size. (Wright 1932, 350)

Skeat put an estimate on the financing required for such a dictionary of at least £410,000 in today's money. The Dialect Society created a designated fund and began canvassing the leading authorities in the study of language.

In 1887 Professor Skeat contacted Wright with news of two upcoming opportunities. One was the position of Professor of English at the University of Toronto. The other was the offer of the Editorship of the Dialect Dictionary,

> We hope to have some day a big Dialect Dictionary. [...] we want a good man for final editor. He should be a phonetician, a philologist, & shd. Have some dialect knowledge. I cannot tell whether you consider it within your power or not. Do you think you could do it: & if so, will you undertake it? (353)

Wright's response was not immediate and his resolve to take on the Editorship appeared in a letter dated 1889 to Professor Holthausen, "I shall edit the projected Dialect Dictionary" (353). In the same letter Wright also sounded a note of defiance especially towards those who were, "callous or scornful about 'English dialects', and who looked down on the serious philologist as 'at least eccentric if not quite a lunatic" (354).

When Wright took over the post of Editor in 1890 the Dialect Society had already collected a substantial amount of material for the dictionary. This consisted of slips about the size of a half-sheet of ordinary notepaper for each word. These slips were the reference for the entry that would appear in the dictionary and along with the word was its pronunciation, meaning, the county where the word was used along with an illustrative sentence. There were over a million such slips and the weight of the collected material topped the scales at over a thousand kilograms, the slips for the letter S alone weighed over one hundred kilograms. Though this represented a remarkable achievement Wright estimated that before the work of compiling the entries could begin, they would need twice that amount. There was enough material for Wright to produce a specimen page for the dictionary, and to encourage submissions he sent out circulars and addressed public meetings.

The production of the dictionary would require staff and eventually a printer and publisher and these both required a reliable source of finance. Wright approached the Clarendon Press but they were already compiling and publishing the *New English Dictionary* so they were unable to help, but also unwilling to support the publication of another dictionary. There was the risk that the Press would be held responsible for it if the proposed method of financing failed.

Wright proposed that the Dialect Dictionary should be funded by subscription and that having at least one thousand subscribers (receiving at least two parts of the dictionary per year) at the outset would make the publication viable. In 1895 the prospectus for subscribers was published and by April that year two hundred and eighty were signed-up. By the middle of the same year the numbers were up to six hundred and Professor Skeat was predicting, "You [Wright] will certainly get to your 1000 subscribers, and more: probably 1200. So do not trouble" and by December, "Dr. Wright is now about to make his final effort to start the work by getting 1000 subscribers" (374).

Henry Frowde was engaged as the publisher and the Clarendon Press provided rooms for a workshop where the Dialect Dictionary's staff would compile and edit the sections.

Wright made a point of writing to many institutions and patrons in the United Kingdom, on the continent and further overseas. He wrote directly to Queen Victoria, "The subscription form came back duly filled up!!! Vivat Regina!" (375).

The list of subscribers included well known authors, although one did decline

1 *Marloes Road. Kensington W. March* 5 [1895]

Dear Sir,

I fear I have no desire to be one of the subscribers to a Dialect Dictionary. I have really no room for the books I *do* need, and I always lose all books that come out in parts. Moreover English dialects are of a wonderful hideousness, and one sees only too much of them in novels. For these reasons I am not anxious to connect in any way with a work on Dialects.

Believe me,

Faithfully yours,

A. Lang (378)[9]

Of course if my mere *name* is of any use, the makers of the Dictionary are welcome to it, but I am obliged to give up taking books that come out in parts, and Dialect (in which I do not include the Scottish language) is a subject which rather repels that attracts me (378).

With subscriptions arriving and material for the dictionary available to sort, Wright started interviewing for the staff that would assist in the compilation of the dictionary. The position of senior assistant in the workshop was offered to Miss J. B. Partridge who had a B.A. degree at London University in Mental and Moral Science and was recommended by Professor C. H. Herford, Professor of English Philology at Aberystwyth. The workshop opened with one senior lady assistant and two unskilled juniors and in July the preliminary sorting began.

By September of 1896 the staff on the dictionary consisted of Miss Partridge, Miss Harris and Miss Hart (all Senior Assistants and graduate scholars), Miss Horsley and Miss Eagleston (Junior Assistants), Mr Mayhew (Senior Assistant, mornings only) and the Editor.

Wright had this to say regarding the work on Dictionary at this time in a letter, "I won't give up the proprietorship now on any terms. I purchased it at a very high price, for it took a big slice out of my life; I can never be the same man I was two years ago" (366).

9. Andrew Lang: poet, novelist and literary critic, also a collector of folk and fairy tales.

Even though the staff engaged to compile the dictionary did not have any previous experience in this field as Miss Partridge noted, "The staff were left to make their own mistakes in editing the material. Those mistakes were sometimes big ones – but, whether big or little, they never escaped the Editor's notice. 'This mustn't happen again' was heard very often in those days" (381).

The terms of the subscription meant that starting in July of 1896 those signed up expected to receive parts of the dictionary and the final part was issued in February 1905 with the dialect grammar published in September of the same year completing the project. The cost of the subscription today puts the cost of buying the dictionary at around £986. There was a limited edition bound set (numbered and signed) and this was also funded by subscription and cost around £1,450. The parts of the dictionary could be bought without subscription and the total cost here was around £1,750. Original bound sets of *The English Dialect Dictionary* have appeared on the second-hand market for between £600 and £2,500.

The response to the finished Dictionary by those who had invested in the project either by acquaintance or from academia was effusive as were the press reviews on its completion, "a work of national importance, a storehouse of folk-lore, a mine of learning for philologists and other scholars" (397).

To quote from the preface, "a work that can never become antiquated, the largest and most comprehensive dialect dictionary ever published in any country" (Wright 1905, v).

The preface also contains statistics of entries for letters 'A', 'B' and 'C', where for simple and compound words alone the sections ran to 1,508, 7,789 and 8,222 entries respectively. It will come as no surprise that many of the entries are familiar to English speakers, whether they are recognised for their regional use or not.

In both *The Hobbit* and *The Lord of the Rings* Tolkien's readers are challenged with what many commentators term 'archaic' uses of language. Many of these would be more accurately described as the use of dialect vocabulary. This is not an unreasonable assertion as Tolkien was familiar with Wright's work before and during his time as an undergraduate at Oxford University. Wright was one of Tolkien's tutors and he was in Oxford at the start of Tolkien's academic career, from his appointment at Leeds in 1920 through to his Professorship at Oxford. The connection with the Wright's would continue into the late 1950s.

What follows are a few examples of Tolkien's use of dialect and other interesting and applicable entries from *The English Dialect Dictionary*. Starting with *The Hobbit* there is Bilbo's confrontation with the spiders of Mirkwood and his mocking of the dwarves' assailants with the following song

Old fat spider spinning in a tree!
Old fat spider can't see me!
Attercop! Attercop!
Won't you stop,
Stop your spinning and look for me!
Old Tomnoddy, all big body,
Old Tomnoddy can't spy me!
Attercop! Attercop!

> Down you drop!
> You'll never catch me up your tree! (*Hobbit*, 'Flies and Spiders', 145)

What *Attercop* and *Tomnoddy* (and the variant *Tommy-noddy*) have in common in dialect terms is that they can be both used as insults and the entry for Attercop; a spider, continues with the figurative use, 'a small, insignificant person'. Tom-noddy; a tadpole, as used in 'a tom noddy, all head and no body' and the variation, 'Tommy-noddy; big heed an' little body' are identified as insults to persons of abnormal appearance.

Another entry under A is *Auction* with its use as a substantive noun, 'A dirty or untidy place, room'. An auction appears at the end of *The Hobbit* when Bilbo returns to find, "a great commotion" with, "people of all sorts […] going in and out not even wiping their feet on the mat, as Bilbo noticed with annoyance. If he was surprised, they were more surprised. He had arrived back in the middle of an auction!" (*Hobbit*, 'The Last Stage', 270).

The narrative has an actual auction (as in the selling of goods by lots) but interestingly the dialect dictionary definition goes on to have *Auction* as, 'a disorderly crowd' as well, which more accurately describes the scene.

There are entries that point to the influence that dialect words may have had on Tolkien's invented languages. For example the word *Aigle*, another substantive noun from the Midlands (Shropshire, also Devon) a dialect word for 'An icicle'. Tolkien uses a similar construction for 'Aiglos' or 'Aeglos' the name of Gil-galad's spear that translates as 'snow-point' or 'icicle'.

There are many notable examples of dialect terms in Tolkien's text and *Baggins* is the next on the list. In this case it is the use of dialect that is important with *baggins* as one of the uses of the word 'Bagging' for 'Food […] provisions'. Then there is the compound word *Jaw-cracker* (as mentioned earlier) 'a long word, difficult to pronounce'. Finally, under this brief exploration of the uses of dialect terms there is the adverb *strangely*, meaning 'very much, greatly, exceedingly'. The use of *strangely* appears when King Théoden of Rohan comments on the difference between the name *Holbytlan* and *Hobbit*, "'Hobbits?' said Théoden. 'Your tongue is strangely changed; but the name sounds not unfitting so. Hobbits!" (*TT*, 'The Road to Isengard', 557).

Many of the occurrences of dialect words in Tolkien's texts are made by or are about Hobbits and the last three presented here continue in this vein. There is *Worrit*, 'To worry' as used by Farmer Maggot, "Mrs. Maggot will be worriting with the night getting thick." (*FR*, 'A Short Cut to Mushrooms', 97). In South Oxfordshire dialect *Potato* is *tater* and *Taters* are on Sam Gamgee's wish list when cooking up a stew, "'What a hobbit needs with coney,' he said to himself, 'is some herbs and roots, especially taters – not to mention bread.' […] 'Sméagol won't grub for roots and carrotses and – taters. What's taters, precious, eh, what's taters?' 'Po-ta-toes,' said Sam." (*TT*, 'Of Herbs and Stewed Rabbits', 654). On the other hand a *Daffodil* is known in dialect in various counties including West Yorkshire, Leicestershire and Warwickshire as *Daffadowndilly*, and here it is in Sam Gamgee's description of Galadriel to Faramir, "sometimes like a white daffadowndilly, small and slender like" (*TT*, 'The Window on the West', 680).

This paper concludes with *The English Dialect Dictionary* entry for *Hobbit*. It is recorded as a unit of measurement in Wales and specifically North Wales. Those consulting this dictionary to see if the word *Hobbit* had been submitted to the compilers might also note that this section of the 'H' entries (and specifically those starting 'Hob-') also includes the folkloric creatures Hob, Hobbedy's Lantern (Will-o'-the Wisp), Hobgoblin and Hob-thrush. On the same page as the entry for *Hobbit* the compilers have recorded that one of the documented sources for these creatures is, 'Denham Tracts (ed. 1895)' and yet it would appear that there was not enough corroborating material to link the use of *hobbit* to the folklore. To quote Miss Partridge of the Dictionary staff from *The Life of Joseph Wright*

> The amount of work put into the E.D.D. cannot be judged by an outsider. The big words, which spread over perhaps two or three pages, and loom large, were the easiest of all to edit, because there was so much evidence for them.
> It was the smaller words which gave the most trouble and anxiety, both to Editor and staff. (Wright 1932, 387).

Or as Tolkien writes in the opening passage of *The Hobbit*,

> I suppose hobbits need some description nowadays, since they have become rare and shy of the Big People, as they call us. They are (or were) a little people [...] There is little or no magic about them, except the ordinary everyday sort which helps them to disappear quietly and quickly when large stupid folk like you and me come blundering along (*Hobbit*, 'An Unexpected Party', 4)

Bibliography

Carpenter, H., *Tolkien: A Biography*, (London: HarperCollins, 1995).

Tolkien, J.R.R., *The Hobbit*, (London: HarperCollins, 1995).
— *The Lord of the Rings*, (London: HarperCollins, 1997).

Wright, E., *The Life of Joseph Wright*, (London, Oxford University Press, 1932).

Wright, J., *The English Dialect Dictionary*, (London, Henry Frowde, 1905).

A comparison of *The Lord of the Rings* with some of the themes identified in Paul Fussell's *The Great War* and *Modern Memory*

Kate Wilkins

In 1975 Paul Fussell published *A Great War and Modern Memory* (*GWMM*). The book is about the troops' experiences during World War One and is mostly concerned with their experience of trench life. As Fussell says although the war was also fought in the air, at sea and even on horseback he "chose to stay with the foot troops in the trenches: that is the setting that comes to mind instantly when the war is mentioned" (1975, 337).

In his preface, Fussell (who had seen active service as an American airman in World War Two) explains that *GWMM* concerns "some of the literary means by which it (the war) has been, remembered, conventionalised and mythologised [...] It is about the literary dimensions of the trench experience itself" (337). Fussell reviews writers who have "most effectively memorialised the Great War as a historical experience with conspicuous imaginative and historical meaning" (337). These include authors such as `classic memorists' Edmund Blunden, Robert Graves, Siegfried Sassoon and Wilfred Owen. In addition to the more famous war authors, Fussell also looked at "amateur memoirs lodged in the collections of the imperial war museum" (337). I should say that Fussell does not mention Tolkien but does briefly reference C.S. Lewis.

As Tolkien fans will already know from John Garth's *Tolkien and the Great War*, Tolkien's own "statements on the influence or otherwise of the First World War on Lord of the Rings are few and wary" (2003, 311). However we do know from his letters that he said:

> Personally I do not think that either war had any influence upon either the plot or the manner of its unfolding. Perhaps in landscape. The Dead Marshes and the approaches to Mordor owe something to Northern France after the Battle of the Somme. (*Letters*, Letter 226, 303)

This of course hasn't stopped others talking about the impact of the Great War on *The Lord of the Rings*. To take but one well known example from none other than C.S. Lewis:

> The War has the very quality of the war my generation knew. It is all here: the endless unintelligible movement, the sinister quiet of the front [...] the lively vivid friendships; the background of something like despair and the merry vivid foreground. (qtd. in Loconte 2015, 53)

In my talk and paper I describe how despite Tolkien's denial, several of the key themes that Fussell argues are common to WW1 writers are also applicable to *The Lord of the Rings*. An obvious theme identified by Fussell is that concerning the Troglodyte World. He reminds his readers of the following quote from Siegfried Sassoon who said "The war was actually a matter of holes and ditches" (1975, 43).

One specific application (other than the more obvious fact that many of the inhabitants of middle earth live underground) is the comparison of Hobbit holes with trenches. Fussell describes how the "exhibition trenches on display at Kensington Gardens for the edification of the homefront" were "clean, dry and well furnished" (43). In reality though the British trenches were "wet, cold, smelly, and thoroughly squalid" (43). Reading this you can't help but think of the description of Bilbo's hobbit hole and its comparison with a nasty alternative:

> In the hole there lived a hobbit. Not a nasty dirty, wet hole, filled with the ends of worms and an oozy smell, nor yet a dry, bare sandy hole, but a hobbit hole and that means comfort. (*Hobbit*, 'An Unexpected Party', 1)

Remaining on the subject of holes, Fussell adds how German trenches discovered by the British at the Somme were:

> Deep, clean, elaborate, and sometimes even comfortable.They had door bells, water tanks with taps, cupboards and mirrors, finished wooden staircases, electric lights, real kitchens and overstuffed furniture. (1975, 43)

This bares a remarkable similarity to Bilbo's residence:

> A very comfortable tunnel without smoke, with panelled walls, and floors tiled and carpeted, provided with polished chairs [...] bedrooms, bathrooms, cellars, pantries [...] Wardrobes, kitchens, dining rooms. (*Hobbit*, 'An Unexpected Party', 1)

Further exploring the Troglodyte World and the troops' lives in the trenches, Fussell describes how "the exploitation of moments of waxing or waning half lights is one of the distinct hallmarks of Great War rhetoric" (1975, 43). He reminds us of the quote by Hugh Quigley who said "we have a unique opportunity of viewing sunset and sunrise in the trenches owing to the decree that men stand to at day break and nightfall" (43).

The waxing and waning of light, in particular dawn and also sunset can be found in a number of places in *The Lord of the Rings* including in the following (of many) examples:

> The great horn of the Helm rang out [...] `Helm, Helm! the riders shouted. `Helm is arisen and comes back to war [...] And with that shout the King came. Light sprang in the sky. Night departed. (*TT*, 'Helm's Deep', 540)

> And in that very moment [...] a cock crowed. Still and clear he crowed. Welcoming only the morning that in the sky far above the shadows of death was coming with the dawn. [...] Rohan had come at last. (*RK*, 'The Siege of Gondor', 829)

> Then suddenly Merry felt it at last, beyond doubt: a change. Wind was in his face! Light was glimmering. Far, far away in the South the clouds could be dimly seen as remote, grey shapes, rolling up drifting: morning lay beyond them. (*RK*, 'The Ride of the Rohirrim', 838)

Shortly after this we hear the cry `Arise, Arise, Riders of Théoden' (838). This is similar to Edward Thomas's poem 'The Trumpet' where, as Fussell reminds us, dawn is also a signal to action:

> Up with the light
> To the old wars
> Arise, Arise

According to Fussell, along with the dawn and sunset, "Morning and evening stand to's were the occasions when the sky especially offered itself for observation and interpretation" (1975, 43). We see the sky often in *The Lord of the Rings*, such as at Helms' Deep Aragorn is looking out to see the dawn and sees "the eastern sky grow pale" (*TT*, 'Helm's Deep', 539). Eomer, during the battle of the Pelennor fields speaks of both the morning; the evening and the sky:

> Out of doubt, out of dark to the day's rising
> I came singing in the sun, sword unsheathing
> To hope's end I rode and to the heart's breaking
> Now for wrath: now for ruin and a red nightfall
> (*RK*, 'The Battle of the Pelennor Fields', 847)

Another of Fussell's identified themes concerns Arcadian Resources. Within this there is a brief reference to the WW1 writers referencing the Golden Summer of 1914. A classic example of this (although not mentioned by Fussell) is Vera Brittain in *Testament of Youth*:

> Looking back on those radiant days of July 1914 it seems to me that an ominous stillness, an atmosphere of brooding expectations, must surely have hung about the sunlit flower gardens and the shining green fields (2014, 72)

As Brittain further describes how:

> I have written so much of Uppingham Speech Day because it was the one perfect summer I ever experienced as well as my last care-free entertainment before the flood. (72)

In a similar vein we find Frodo, prior to leaving on his quest, wanting to "savour as much as he could of his last summer in the Shire" (*FR*, 'Three is Company', 65). We note a few pages later that "The Shire had seldom seen so fair a summer of so rich an Autumn" (67).

Fussell says "Recourse to the pastoral is an English mode of both fully gauging the calamities of the Great War and imaginatively protecting oneself against them" and "the Standard Great War memoir provides bucolic interludes or pastoral oases between bouts of violence and terror" (1975, 235).

War poets such as Owen, Blunden, Sassoon, Brooke and Graves, all referenced the pastoral and contrasted the war with the English countryside. To give a couple of examples Graves, in *Goodbye to All That* looking at the German trenches via a periscope, describes how between himself and the Germans "lay a flat meadow with cornflowers, marguerites and poppies growing in the long grass" (1960, 89). Brittain, at the point immediately after she receives the news of her brother Edward's death, describes how she sees a bowl of blue delphiniums "their intense colour vivid, ethereal, seemed too radiant for earthly flower" (2014, 401).

Further emphasising the point Fussell adds that if the opposite of war is peace, the opposite of experiencing moments of war is pastoral. Amongst other things, he cites a poem by Max Plowman 'Going Into the Line'. Plowman imagines a pastoral oasis while coming under shell fire:

> And slowly in his overheated mind
> Peace like a river through the desert flows,
> And sweetness wells and overflows in streams
> That reach the farthest friend in memory (qtd. in 1975, 241)

Pippin, believing he is about to die, thinks: "I wish I could see cool sunlight and green grass again" (*RK*, 'The Black Gate Opens', 892) and Frodo at his lowest ebb says he has "No memory of tree or grass or flower" (*RK*, 'Mount Doom', 938). Sam whose first thoughts, following his rescue from Mount Doom and "the slow rivers of fire [...] and a rain of hot ash" are of "wide beechen boughs, through whose young leaves sunlight glimmered green and gold" (*RK*, 'The Field of Cormallen', 951).

Tolkien's friends G.B. Smith and Rob Gilson were no exception to the contrast of war with the pastoral. The following is an extract from Smith's *A Spring Harvest*

> Now spring has come upon the hills in France,
> And all the trees are delicately fair,
> As heeding not the great guns' voice by chance,
> Brought down the valley on a wandering air. (1918)

Tolkien's places of respite in *The Lord of the Rings* include Lothlórien, the Shire and Rivendell which are all rural idylls and set within nature. At one point or another our Hobbit heroes (and others) end up here following bouts of fighting, running or generally having a bad time at the hands of the enemy. A classic example is Ithilien, which as we know is a country right next to Mordor, which has a two-page description of its flora and fauna.

While we are still considering Arcadian Resources, it is also worth looking at both the importance of gardens as well as the appearance of the gardener-solider. Fussell reminds us of Stephen Graham's concept: 'Soldiers camouflaged as gardeners taken'. The following was taken from a Private in the Guards (qtd. in Fussell 1975, 234).

> Of course he (Armstrong) found kindred spirits, and the other gardeners of the battalion shone out through their camouflage of khaki. Gardeners camouflaged as soldiers, I hear the hard voice of the R.S.M. a-saying. But before long every man had become a gardener, and was co-operating to work the miracle amid the ruins. (234)

It is worth noting that Blunden's batman was a gardener. Sam Gamgee, also a gardener and a reflection of the batmen Tolkien knew and considered superior to himself.

As Fussell says "even in Trenches, the English idea of domesticity was inseparable from the image of a well-kept gardening allotment" (1975, 234). A quick search of Google produces several images of gardening soldiers.

Finally while still in Arcadia we will have a quick look at shepherds. Fussell points us towards Gladden in *Ypres 1917: A personal account* which describes the following scene:

> Then among the broken trees not far ahead we saw a tall figure, moving like a shepherd with the aid of a simple staff, a shepherd looking for his lost sheep! We recognized the brigadier general, alone and quite unconcerned. (1975, 240)

This is, arguably, not so far removed from Gandalf the White who

> looked and beheld a bent figure moving slowly. It was not far away. It looked like an old beggar man, walking wearily, leaning on a rough staff (*TT*, 'The White Rider', 492)

Moving entirely away from the pastoral, Fussell, in a chapter concerning Myth, Ritual and Romance, describes the frequent occurrence and importance of the number three. He explains how there were three separate lines of trenches – namely front, support and reserve and how:

> The routine in each line was similar: the unit was divided into three groups, one of which kept alert while the other two stood down. Three men to every bay, one on sentry the other two resting or sleeping. (1975, 125)

He also explains how it was natural to divide everything by three. For example: "Infantry, artillery, cavalry as well as sleep, food, women" (125).

I have had hours of fun looking at threes in *The Lord of the Rings* and came up with the following: the three volumes; various points where there are three key characters; Sam, Frodo, Gollum; Pippin, Merry, Treebeard; Aragorn, Gimli, Legolas and maybe even Gandalf, Pippin and Shadowfax not to mention the chapter 'Three is Company'. No doubt there are plenty of other places too.

To conclude, *GWMM* was an award-winning work but which was later criticized for a number of reasons and by various academics and historians. However, in my opinion these criticisms were more than adequately addressed by Fussell himself in later editions. Although due to the time available I have cherry picked some of his themes to compare with *The Lord of the Rings*, I do believe that they can be applied and can shed further light on Tolkien's masterpiece.

Bibliography

Brittain, V., *Testament of Youth*, (London: Virago Press, 2014).

Fussell, P., *The Great War and Modern Memory*, (Oxford: Oxford University Press, 1975).

Garth, J., *Tolkien and the Great War*, (London: Harper Collins, 2003).

Graves, R., *Goodbye to All That*, (London: Cassell, 1960).

Loconte, J., *A Hobbit, A Wardrobe and a Great War*, (London: Harper Collins 2015).

Smith, G.B., *A Spring Harvest*, 1918, < https://andrewdunning.ca/spring-harvest/>

Tolkien, J.R.R., *The Hobbit* (London: George, Allen & Unwin, 1995).
— *The Letters of J.R.R. Tolkien*, ed. H. Carpenter with the assistance of C. Tolkien (London: HarperCollins, 2006).
— *The Lord of the Rings*, (London: HarperCollins, 2010).

TOLKIEN'S THEORETICAL AND CREATIVE PRACTICES

Depth by Paratext: How Forewords and Footnotes Helped J.R.R. Tolkien Develop a Secondary World in *The Lord of the Rings*

Lorenzo Gammarelli

The first idea of this essay was seeded in me by Allan Turner's lecture 'Putting the Paratext in Context' (2008), which I heard in 2005 at the *Return of the Ring* conference in Birmingham.

1 – What is paratext?

The concept of *paratext* was first defined by French literary theorist Gérard Genette in 1981 as those devices and conventions, like: "a title, a subtitle, intertitles; prefaces, postfaces, notices, forewords, etc.; marginal, infrapaginal, terminal notes; epigraphs; illustrations; blurbs, book covers, dust jackets, and many other kinds of secondary signals, whether allographic or autographic" both within and outside a book, that "provide the text with a (variable) setting and sometimes a commentary, official or not" (Genette 1997a, 3). In 1987 he further developed the concept, as "a certain number of verbal or other productions" that accompany the text: "they surround it and extend it, precisely in order to present it, in the usual sense of this verb but also in the strongest sense: to make present, to ensure the text's presence in the world, its 'reception' and consumption in the form (nowadays, at least) of a book" (3). In short: paratext is "what enables a text to become a book and to be offered as such to its readers and, more generally, to the public" (Genette 1997b, 1).

Paratext can be split up between *peritext* (paratext that is "around the text, in the space of the same volume, like the title or the preface, and sometimes inserted into the interstices of the text, like the titles of chapters or certain notes") and *epitext* ("all the messages which are situated, at least originally, outside the book"); in this paper, I shall almost only consider peritext (Genette 1997a, 3).

Genette shows a fascination for texts that are lost, or never existed, of which we only have a title: "a text without a paratext does not exist and never has existed. Paradoxically, paratexts without texts do exist, if only by accident: there are certainly works – lost or aborted – about which we know nothing except their titles" (1997a, 3-4); this resonates with Tolkien's fascination for "asterisk-realities" (Shippey 2005, 22-6). It is also worth noting that according to Genette: "in the course of time and by losing its initial pragmatic function, the paratext, unless it disappears, is 'textualized' and incorporated into the work", and this may well have happened to the paratext of *The Lord of the Rings* (1997a, 177).

2 – Use of paratext by Tolkien

Remarkable uses of paratext in Tolkien's work, that show a deep knowledge and understanding of the concept, are to be found in *Farmer Giles of Ham* and in *The Adventures of Tom Bombadil*.

The Farmer Giles foreword, where Tolkien pretends to be the editor and translator of an ancient text, is satirical: according to Janet Brennan Croft it "mocks the sort of critics Tolkien scorned in 'Beowulf: The Monsters and the Critics' for considering the poem only for the light it could shed on history" (2018, 190), admitting a value of the tale only as source of information on the origin of some place-names, even when conceding that "some may find the character and adventures of its hero attractive in themselves" (*Perilous Realm*, 101). Just compare this with the Foreword to the second edition of *Lord of the Rings* where Tolkien wrote: "The prime motive [for writing *The Lord of the Rings*] was the desire of a tale-teller to try his hand at a really long story that would hold the attention of readers, amuse them, delight them, and at times maybe excite them or deeply move them" (*FR*, 'Foreword', xvi). At least as important as the foreword, are Pauline Baynes' illustrations, which helped lengthen the short tale enough to be published by itself as a book, and which Tolkien (or his friends) famously described as "a collateral theme" (*Letters*, Letter 120, 133).

The foreword to *Tom Bombadil*, even if Tolkien himself described it as a "ridiculous editorial fiction" (*Letters*, Letter 237, 315), has a different meaning: according to Croft it explains "the textual history of the collection, considering Hobbitish linguistic and poetic preferences, and taking the poems seriously as historical evidence for the widening of the horizons of the Shire and Frodo's mental state after the events of the end of the Third Age", giving a unity and a sense to the whole collection of poems (2018, 189). Randel Helms claims that it may act "as self-parodying 'protection' against charges of bad poetry – because the verses are presented as the work of hobbits, not Tolkien's own – *and as a means of establishing* [...] *Secondary Belief*" (qtd. in Scull and Hammond 2014, 118; emphasis mine).

Additionally 'The Silmarillion', the great work of Tolkien's life, is a collection of texts (see Nagy 2014) in various degrees of completeness: there are many reasons why it was never published during Tolkien's life, but I think that one of them is because it lacked a convincing paratextual frame, and Tolkien never succeeded in writing one that he could find satisfactory.

3 – Paratext in *The Lord of the Rings*

Of course *The Lord of the Rings*, being the longest work, has the most complex and intricate paratext, to such an extent that it sometimes becomes part of the text itself. Tolkien was very concerned with the problem of *tradition*: how the texts that we read in *The Lord of the Rings* arrive to us from their remote fictional authors (Elves, Hobbits, Gondorian scribes and so on). To solve the problem, he built a complex framework of books, codices and manuscripts with many authors, writers, copyists; each of those has its paratext, and all these paratexts form a complex *paratextual architecture*, of which we only get a fleeting glimpse every now and then. Following Genette's book step by step, I will shortly describe the noteworthy uses of paratext, with special attention to those instances where it acts like a threshold between real and fictive texts.

3.1 – Publisher's peritext

"We are dealing here with […] the book's material construction (selection of format, of paper, of typeface, and so forth)" (Genette 1997b, 16).

The format of *The Lord of the Rings* has been the subject of discussion: Tolkien wanted it to be published as a single book, the publisher (Unwin) chose to split it in three volumes, giving them different titles, and starting the misunderstanding of calling it a trilogy (*Letters*, Letter 136, 166). Even after the problem of the format was settled, Tolkien continued to ponder over other aspects of the publisher's peritext. He proposed illustrations for the covers of the three volumes, trying to keep a unity of design, and at the same time caring to make them different enough to keep them distinguished, for example by changing the colour of the sub-title in *The Two Towers*.

3.2 – Name of the Author

It may seem like there is not much to talk about the name of the author, as we all know it: it is J.R.R. Tolkien. Or is it? The concept of Author is tightly interlaced with that of Narrator, which in *The Lord of the Rings* is not to be taken for granted: there are different narrators in different parts of the tale.[1]

There are episodes of which no character may possibly be the narrator, as none were present or awake to know what happened and to tell it (for example the famous fox-passing-through-the-wood episode in chapter III of *The Fellowship of the Ring*); these could be seen as embellishments by the fictional author (unlikely), or as later insertions by a fictional editor, namely Tolkien himself, when he translated and edited the Red Book of Westmarch.

3.3 – Titles

For titles, Tolkien had the same concern as for covers, or even more. Initially, he was against the idea of giving each of the three volumes a different subtitle: "I am not wedded to any of the suggested sub-titles; and wish they could be avoided." In particular, he was bothered by the title of volume two, *The Two Towers*, "For it is really impossible to devise ones that correspond to the content", and never really found a definite answer to the question of which were the two towers mentioned in the title (*Letters*, Letter 139, 170). He even worried about the possible spoiling effect of the title of volume three, *The Return of the King*, and considered *The War of the Ring* instead.

He gave titles to the six books in which *The Lord of the Rings* is divided, but they were never used (and strictly speaking, according to Genette these would be intertitles, not titles). The problem of the overall title of the book is also reckoned with in the text, when Frodo gives to Sam his and Bilbo's diary:[2]

---

1. But this falls outside the scope of this essay. See Vanderbecke and Turner (2012), Saxton (2013) and Pezzini (2018).
2. This being both a text and its own paratext, I suspect it could start a strange loop in the sense developed by Hofstadter (1979), but this may be the subject of a future study.

The title page had many titles on it, crossed out one after another, so:

My diary. My Unexpected Journey. There and Back Again.
And What Happened After.

Adventures of Five Hobbits. The Tale of the Great Ring, compiled by Bilbo Baggins
from his own observations and the accounts of his friends.
What we did in the War of the Ring.

Here Bilbo's hand ended and Frodo had written:

THE DOWNFALL
OF THE
LORD OF THE RINGS
AND THE
RETURN OF THE KING

(as seen by the Little People; being the memoirs of Bilbo and Frodo of the Shire, supplemented by the accounts of their friends and the learning of the Wise.)

Together with extracts from Books of Lore translated by Bilbo in Rivendell.
(*RK*, 'The Grey Havens', 1004)

3.4 – Dedication

In the foreword to the First Edition, *The Lord of the Rings* is dedicated "to all admirers of Bilbo, but especially to my sons and daughter, and to my friends the Inklings" (*FR*, 'Foreward', 7). It is a pity that the dedication disappeared from the foreword to the Second Edition because, even if a bit naive, it acted as *a means of establishing Secondary Belief.*

3.5 – Foreword and prologue

Apart from some minor changes, there are two forewords: one to the first edition, and one to the second and subsequent editions. The foreword to the first edition is kind of fictive, as it takes for true that the book is a translation from the Red Book of Westmarch;[3] the foreword to the second edition instead gives up the pretence of the translation.[4]

3. According to Genette's taxonomy, it is a "disavowing authorial preface", because it claims that the text that follows is not written by the author who really wrote it.
4. And for this reason according to Genette it is an "assumptive authorial preface". The old Italian edition of *Il Signore degli Anelli* before 2019 was, as far as I know, the only one to have an introduction which spoiled the ending of the story: it outright told that Frodo arranges to let the Ring fall into the fires of Mount Doom, and that when the Hobbits go back to the Shire, they find it full of Saruman's thugs (Zolla 1970, 19).

After the foreword, there is also a prologue, which Tolkien considered essential for the information it gives to the reader about the story so far, answering questions like what is a hobbit, what is pipe-weed, how the Shire is ordered, how the ring was found.[5] Except maybe for the finding of the ring, none of these pieces of information are really essential to understand the story that follows, and all of them could have easily been inserted in the tale, without even lengthening it too much: they are there only to provide background, to help with the world-building. They are, once again, only *a means of establishing Secondary Belief.*

3.6 – Notes

Editorial foot- or end-notes are loathed by most authors of narrative, because they remind the reader that she is actually reading a book, and not living in the story that is being told. In terms of Tolkien's 'On Fairy-stories', they pull her out of the Secondary World and back to the Primary one. There are exceptions, especially in the fantasy genre: Terry Pratchett's *Discworld* series, Jonathan Stroud's *Bartimaeus Sequence* and Susanna Clarke's *Jonathan Strange & Mr Norrell* come to mind first, but in all three cases the notes have a very ironic purpose.

Tolkien's footnotes do not have any kind of irony, and they look just like the notes that an editor could add to a text about a faraway or ancient civilization, to provide some context and give some explanations to the reader. There are seven footnotes in the text of *The Lord of the Rings*:[6] six are linguistic, giving the explanation of names or grammatical quirks of the hobbit language, and one is about the hobbit calendar. None is essential for the telling or the understanding of the tale, but they are useful to avoid later info-dumping, and as *a means of establishing Secondary Belief.*

3.7 – Public and private epitext

Ever since its publication, *The Lord of the Rings* attracted the attention and the comments of literary critics, who either loved it or loathed it. And even before *The Fellowship of the Rings* was actually published, Tolkien started writing letters to proof-readers and reviewers, explaining and sometimes justifying his work. Letters, articles, interviews: all the material Tolkien wrote about *The Lord of the Rings* is epitext, and with the passing of years it has become essential to fully understand and enjoy the book (just think of the *Letters* edited by Humphrey Carpenter, and of all that they reveal about Tolkien's intentions and the book's meanings).

There is also that which Genette calls pre-text: the various preliminary and alternate versions of the manuscripts that Christopher Tolkien collected in *The History of the Lord of the Rings* section of *The History of Middle-earth. The History of Middle-earth* itself might also be considered as the world's longest paratext.

5. Analysing the identity of the authorial voice of the prologue would take too much time, and would fall beyond the scope of this essay.

6. There are also four notes in the Prologue, which add to its scholarly aesthetic.

3.8 – Other aspects

Maps, family trees, chronologies are aspects of paratextuality that Genette explicitly omits to consider in his book, but are very important in *The Lord of the Rings*. Likewise, Genette left out other practices whose paratextual relevance seemed to him undeniable, but "investigating each one individually might demand as much work as was required here in treating this subject as a whole", so he only mentions them in the Conclusion of his book (1997b, 405).

The first one is *translation*; *The Lord of the Rings* is not really a translation, but it claims to be one, and the whole translation process, with the shift from Westron and related languages to English and all related languages like Old English, Norse, etc., is essential for the linguistic aesthetic effect that Tolkien wanted to achieve (see Honegger 2004). The second is *illustration*. It can be noted that, contrary to *The Hobbit*, *The Lord of the Rings* does not have any authorial illustrations, except for three: the inscription on the Ring, the Doors of Moria and the tomb of Balin. The inscription on the Ring can barely be considered an illustration, as it is a text (even if in an Elvish script). The Doors of Moria and the tomb of Balin, on the other hand, are extremely schematic, and are similar to epigraphic squeezes: they are the kind of illustration that can be found in an academic essay on archaeology, not in a narrative text.

There are many sketches that Tolkien jotted down while he was writing, as a remind or a help to envision some places, or as partial maps: these, as well as the three pages of the *Book of Mazarbul* that after some consideration were not included in the published book, belong rather to the pre-text (Hammond and Scull 2015).

Other kinds of paratext that Genette doesn't even consider, as they would not normally belong in a narrative book, but that play a considerable role in building the world of *The Lord of the Rings* and as *a means of establishing Secondary Belief*, are the notes on writing and spelling, and the notes on the languages and peoples of the Third Age.

4 – Conclusions and further studies

Further studies should comprise a thorough analysis of the use of paratext and pseudo-paratext[7] in *The Hobbit*,[8] in *The Lord of the Rings* and in Tolkien's other works (mainly *Farmer Giles of Ham* and *The Adventures of Tom Bombadil*); and a study about how the lack of a "good" paratextual frame may have been one of the causes why Tolkien never managed to publish 'The Silmarillion'. Tolkien didn't know the term paratext, as the name and the idea itself were only developed by Genette many years after his death, but he was absolutely aware of the concept and of its importance, and indeed he used many paratextual tricks to build the "sense of depth" in his works, or at least to help sustain it.

Among other purposes, paratext in *The Lord of the Rings* acts as a safety net. If ever a reader should waver in her secondary belief, the paratextual architecture devised by

---

7. With *pseudo-paratext* I mean the paratext to a pseudo-book, i.e. to a fictional text, which only exists in the fancy of an author. In this sense, the prefaces and notes to The Red Book of Westmarch are pseudo-paratext.

8. For time constraints I could not consider it, but I should at least mention its authorial illustrations, its gnomic chapter titles, and its foreword, evolving from absent in the first edition to complete in the third.

Tolkien would keep her from falling back to the Primary World, and leave her in limbo, whence she can rise up to Secondary World again.

In the conclusion to *Paratexts*, Genette wrote: "the paratext provides an airlock that helps the reader pass without too much respiratory difficulty from one world to the other, a sometimes delicate operation, especially when the second world is a fictional one" (1997b, 408). I doubt that Genette ever read *The Lord of the Rings* or "On Fairy-stories", but I find it hard not to consider this like a reference to Tolkien's Secondary World.

Bibliography

Brennan Croft, J., 'Doors into Elf-mounds: J.R.R. Tolkien's Introductions, Prefaces, and Forewords', *Tolkien Studies*, 15 (2018), 177-195.

Genette, G., *Palimpsests: Literature in the Second Degree*, trans. by C. Newman and C. Doubinsky, (Lincoln and London: University of Nebraska Press, 1997a).
— *Paratexts. Thresholds of interpretation*, trans. by J.E. Lewin, (Cambridge: Cambridge University Press, 1997b).

Hammond, W.G. and C. Scull, *The Art of The Lord of the Rings*, (London: HarperCollins, 2015).

Hofstadter, D., *Gödel, Escher, Bach: An Eternal Golden Braid*, (New York: Basic Books, 1979).

Honegger, T., 'The Westron Turned into Modern English: The Translator and Tolkien's Web of Languages', in *Translating Tolkien: Text and Film*, ed. Thomas Honegger, Cormarë Series 6,(Zurich: Walking Tree, 2004), 1-20.

Nagy, G., '*The Silmarillion*: Tolkien's Theory of Myth, Text, and Culture', in *A Companion to J.R.R. Tolkien*, ed. by S.D. Lee (Oxford: Wiley-Blackwell, 2014), 107-118.

Pezzini, G., 'The Authors of Middle Earth: Tolkien and the Mystery of Literary Creation', *Journal of Inklings Studies*, 8.1 (2018), 31-64.

Saxton, B., 'J.R.R. Tolkien, Sub-Creation, and Theories of Authorship', *Mythlore*, 31.3 (Spring/Summer 2013), 47-59.

Scull, C. and W.G. Hammond, 'Commentary', in J.R.R. Tolkien, *The Adventures of Tom Bombadil*, ed. by C. Scull and W. G. Hammond, (London: HarperCollins, 2014), 115-270.

Shippey, T., *The Road to Middle-Earth: How J.R.R. Tolkien Created a New Mythology*, 3rd edn, (London: HarperCollins, 2005).

Tolkien, J.R.R., *The Fellowship of the Ring*, (London: George Allen and Unwin, 1954).
— *The Two Towers*, (London: George Allen and Unwin, 1954).
— *The Return of the King*, (London: George Allen and Unwin, 1955).
Turner, A., 'Putting the Paratext in Context', in *The Ring Goes Ever On: Proceedings of the Tolkien 2005 Conference*, ed. by S. Wells, (Coventry: The Tolkien Society, 2008), 283-288.

Vanderbeke, D. and A. Turner, 'The One or the Many? Authorship, Voice and Corpus', in *Sub-creating Middle-earth*, ed. by J. Klinger, Cormarë Series 27, (Zurich: Walking Tree, 2012), 1-20.

Zolla, E., 'Introduzione', in J.R.R. Tolkien, *Il Signore degli Anelli*, (Milano: Rusconi, 1970), 5-19.

Memory, Lore, Knowledge

Thomas Honegger

Hidden away in Appendix A of *The Lord of the Rings* we find a short text of some seven pages which is identified as "Here Follows a Part of the Tale of Aragorn and Arwen" (*RK*, 'Appendix A', 1057). It contains, arguably, some of the most romantic and heart-wrenching scenes between Aragorn and Arwen, which is probably one of the reasons why Tolkien exiled it into Appendix A – the other reason being that Arwen came in as a rather late addition to the plot.[1] When Aragorn feels the end of his long life approaching, he addresses Arwen and tells her: "'The uttermost choice is before you: to repent and go to the Havens and bear away into the West the memory of our days together that shall there be evergreen but never more than memory; or else to abide the Doom of Men'" (1062-3). Arwen, however, is aware that the former is no longer an option and that she must, indeed, "abide the Doom of Men [...] the loss and the silence" (1063). She is, understandably, not happy with this prospect, yet does not comment on the (no longer) available alternative of living alone in the West with an evergreen memory of their days together. We cannot know for certain whether Arwen would have found such an option attractive – or whether the thought of having "never more than memory" would have made her opt for the Doom of Men anyway.

1 – Memory

Indeed, *The Lord of the Rings* could be and has been seen as an 'essay' on memory, commemorating, and letting go – an elegiac epic on the *ubi sunt* theme,[2] yet with a healthy dose of vigorous hobbit-sense and *joie de vivre* to make it bearable. And though the implied hobbit-centric point of view does not allow open reference to the consolation of the Gospel, Aragorn's answer to Arwen, in the tradition of the *anima naturaliter christiana*, contains more than a vague hint at the promise of a transcendental existence:[3] "'Behold! we are not bound for ever to the circles of the world, and beyond

---

1. Peter Jackson, in his movie-trilogy, transferred some of its content to the main storyline and thus used authentic material in his attempt to render his protagonists more appealing to a twenty-first century audience and to increase the visibility of women in Tolkien's epic. Thanks to Christopher Tolkien's endeavours, we can study the development of the writing of *The Lord of the Rings* in detail in volumes 6-8 of *The History of Middle-earth*, also referred to as *The History of The Lord of the Rings* (cf. Tolkien *Shadow*, *Treason*, and *War*).
2. See, among others, Honegger 2006. Tolkien himself characterized "the real theme" of his *opus magnum* as "Death and Immortality: the mystery of the love of the world in the hearts of a race 'doomed' to leave and seemingly lose it; the anguish in the hearts of a race 'doomed' not to leave it, until its whole evil-aroused story is complete" (*Letters*, Letter 186, 246). The question of the variegated generic nature of *The Lord of the Rings* has been discussed in depth by Simonson 2008.
3. The question of the possible salvation of Men and other metaphysical problems are discussed in 'Athrabeth Finrod Ah Andreth' (*Morgoth*, 303-66).

them is more than memory. Farewell!'" (1063). I have been wondering for quite some time what Aragorn's 'more than memory' implies. We know that the existence of the Elves in their serial immortality is linked to Arda itself and their souls cannot leave the circles of the world,[4] while Men are prone to die, and their souls leave Arda – whither is not known. The Elves, as a consequence, cannot escape time although they may manipulate and try to slow it down.[5] This means that a thing or event past no longer has the same reality and may be accessed merely with the help of one's memory, which, in the case of the Elves, may lead to impressively realistic acts of sub-creation. However, those products of Faërian Drama[6] lack the ultimate degree of reality that only the Flame Imperishable can convey. As a consequence, even the Elves cannot go back in Time and the best they can achieve is a re-creation in the form of a living memory – but memory it remains. Men, by contrast, seem to depart to a place beyond the circles of the world and thus, possibly, leave the realm of Time. Once outside its realm it is possible for ideas, thoughts, and memories to attain a new reality that is indeed more than memory – not unlike Niggle's Tree in Niggle's Parish.[7]

How, then, do Men, Elves and other *longaevi*[8] organize their memory? Unfortunately, we have no Middle-earth *artes memoriae* so I have to rely on the few instances where some of the protagonists demonstrate feats of memory. I would like to start with Elrond Half-elven since his memory seems to function much like our own, in spite of his serial longevity. We hear about oral transmission of lore in the Hall of Fire (*FR*, 'Many Meetings', 233-8), but also about Elrond's "books of lore" (*FR*, 'The Council of Elrond', 242).[9] Whether these books add up to a library is not explicitly stated, but the mention of books and maps seems to imply so.[10] The scanty evidence suggests that the Elves have a memory-culture relying primarily on their own personal recollections, on written texts, and, parallel to and in addition to these two forms, also on songs/poems. For the former, Elrond is a prime example since he remarks at the Council of Elrond:

> 'But my memory reaches back even to the Elder Days. [...] I have seen three ages in the West of the world, and many defeats, and many fruitless victories. I was the herald of Gil-galad and marched with his host. [...] I beheld the last combat on the slopes of Orodruin, where Gil-galad died, and Elendil fell, and Narsil broke beneath him; but Sauron himself

4. See the discussion on *fëa* ('spirit, soul') and *hröa* ('body, bodily form') in *Morgoth* (217-25).

5. The classical and, to my mind, best study on this topic is (still) Verlyn Flieger's *A Question of Time. J.R.R. Tolkien's Road to Faërie* (1997).

6. On Faërian Drama and sub-creation, see *OFS* (59-66).

7. See *TL* (88-9). There is, of course, a strong whiff of Platonic ideas to the entire episode, which would need another paper to discuss.

8. Loosely based on C.S. Lewis's chapter 'The Longaevi' in his *The Discarded Image* (1964, 122-38), I use the term *longaevi* in order to refer not only to Elves but also to the lesser spirits who populate Arda.

9. "Then through all the years that followed he traced the Ring; but since that history is elsewhere recounted, even as Elrond himself set it down in his books of lore, it is not here recalled" (*FR*, 'The Council of Elrond', 242).

10. Cf. "Aragorn and Gandalf walked together or sat speaking of their road and the perils they would meet; and they pondered the storied and figured maps and books of lore that were in the house of Elrond" (*FR*, 'The Rings Goes South', 277).

> was overthrown, and Isildur cut the Ring from his hand with the hilt-shard of his father's sword, and took it for his own.' (243)

Here we have someone who was not only contemporaneous with the (by now) semi-legendary and semi-historical figures such as Gil-galad, Elendil, Sauron, and Isildur, but who actually participated in several of the key events shaping the history of Middle-earth and who thus met the persons mentioned. Elrond's references to Gil-galad, Elendil, Isildur and the Ring are not the only ones in *The Lord of the Rings* but constitute a sort of nexus for earlier and later mentions of these elements. Indeed, Tolkien skilfully constructs the tale of the Ring by means of varying sources, presented by several protagonists, and by accessing different forms of memory. The first mention of the events connected with Gil-galad, Isildur, Sauron and the Ring occurs in the chapter 'The Shadow of the Past' where Gandalf, another *longaevus*, briefly sketches the Ring's history to Frodo (*FR*, 'A Long-expected Party', 52). The wizard's account may be best characterized as a re-oralized history since he himself has not been an eyewitness to the events but must have gathered the information from a variety of sources, oral and written, which he then synthesizes into a coherent narrative.[11]

Another type of memory is at work in the second mention of Gil-galad – this time in the form of the lines which Sam recites in response to Merry's question "'Who was Gil-galad?'":

> *Gil-galad was an Elven-king*
> *Of him the harpers sadly sing:*
> *the last whose realm was fair and free*
> *between the Mountains and the Sea.*
> (*FR*, 'A Knife in the Dark', 185)

Sam's rhymes are, as we are told by Strider, "part of the lay that is called 'The Fall of Gil-galad', which is in an ancient tongue. Bilbo must have translated it" (186). These rhymes illustrate several points that are important for our discussion. To start, a historical event, i.e. the defeat of Sauron by the Last Alliance, is shown as having inspired a, probably Elvish, poet to commemorate the main Elvish protagonist Gil-galad and his deeds in a song.[12] This then has been translated into the Common Tongue by Bilbo, who later taught it to Sam. History has thus joined forces with poetry, and the text-based literary account has passed over into a largely oral culture, so that the historical events are now remembered in rhymed couplets.[13] Handing down historical (and other) information in a poetic form was, of course, a practice prevalent not only

11. However, all the narratives we get, be this from Gandalf himself in the early chapter 'The Shadow of the Past' or from multiple narrators in 'The Council of Elrond', preserve a fair amount of insecurity and incompleteness and thus resist the temptation of imposing the unified view of a master narrative.

12. A lay is a short narrative poem. Famous are, for example, the French lays of Marie de France (c. 12th century) and their translation-adaptations into Middle English.

13. Like Tacitus's Germanic tribes: "Celebrant carminibus antiquis, quod unum apud illos memoriae et annalium genus est" (Tacitus, *Germania,* 4-6).

in antiquity, but also in the Middle Ages, and examples can be found even in the modern era.[14] This tradition, although ultimately based on the prose accounts found in the books of history, relies heavily on a (re-)oralization of events and information. Thus, the key feature of this lay is the poetic form, a characteristic shared with other mnemonic texts in *The Lord of the Rings*, such as Treebeard's alliterative 'Lore of the Living Creatures' (*TT*, 'Treebeard', 464). Just as in the real-world, the passing on or retention of information within living memory[15] is marked by its special form which helps to structure, organize, store and, finally, to recall the information wanted. Treebeard, for example, is not only able to quote from memory the list of creatures he learned when he was young, which "was a long, long time ago" (464), but he is also able to complement and expand the list by incorporating newcomers such as the hobbits by adding, as suggested by Pippin, the line: "*Half-grown hobbits, the hole-dwellers*" (465). The formal framework of the alliteration and the new line's placement in the appropriate hierarchical position – "next to Man" (465) – helps to organize the information and makes it easier to recall it at a later time. A good memory resembles a well-kept archive or storeroom[16] – or, in Treebeard's case, a pleasantly shaped tree with a straight trunk and branches sprouting at regular intervals.

The importance of keeping one's memory both well-organized and in use is illustrated by the third account connected to the Ring in the form of Isildur's scroll addressed to his nephew Meneldil. The text contains vital information on how to identify the One Ring by means of its inscription, which shows only when the Ring is heated up. The scroll – or a copy – has been kept in the archives of Minas Tirith, but we are not told whether these archives resemble more a lumber-room where a "thing wanted [is] always buried" or whether they are well-organized and kept in good order (*FR*, 'Strider', 167). Whichever the case, it seems that at least some of the archives have become what I would call dormant memory, i.e. information stored can still be retrieved, yet its existence is largely forgotten – as can be inferred by Gandalf's statement that Isildur's text had been "unread [...] by any save Saruman and myself" (*FR*, 'The Council of Elrond', 252). It takes someone like Gandalf to kiss awake this Sleeping Beauty and to bring it back into living memory.

This raises the question of how to maintain and cultivate the different forms of memory. On the one hand, we have the outsourced forms of memory such as archives or libraries. They need people who not only preserve the material from decay but who also read the texts and feed it into contemporary discourse, so that the public remains aware of the existence of the knowledge stored there. On the other hand, there is the

14. Such as Tennyson's famous poem 'The Charge of the Light Brigade' (published 9 December 1854), commemorating the charge of the Light Brigade at the Battle of Balaclava (25 October 1854).

15. This in contrast, on the one hand, to those instances of living-memory persons such as Elrond, who have been actual eye-witnesses to events, and on the other to those passing down information via dead memory in the form of books or scrolls.

16. Treatises and handbooks teaching the art of memory as part of the art of rhetoric have used the method of *loci* ever since the Classical *Rhetorica ad Herennium* (90 BC). Gandalf's comment on Butterbur is, of course, to be understood against the background of this method: "A worthy man, but his memory is like a lumber-room: thing wanted always buried" (*FR*, 'Strider', 167).

information kept in a person's individual memory, which also requires maintenance, and Tolkien provides us with at least one glimpse of how this is done. When Gandalf and Pippin ride on Shadowfax towards Minas Tirith, Pippin

> heard Gandalf singing softly to himself, murmuring brief snatches of rhyme in many tongues, as the miles ran under them. At last the wizard passed into a song of which the hobbit caught the words: a few lines came clear to his ears through the rushing of the wind:
>
> *Tall ships and tall kings*
> *Three times three,*
> *What brought they from the foundered land*
> *Over the flowing sea?*
> *Seven stars and seven stones*
> *And one white tree.*
>
> 'What are you saying, Gandalf?' asked Pippin.
> 'I was just running over some of the Rhymes of Lore in my mind,' answered the wizard. (*TT*, 'The Voice of Saruman', 597)

Gandalf, during his ride, revises some of the 'Rhymes of Lore' by retrieving them from his memory and by murmuring or even singing them. Especially the former is an instance of "subvocalization, a murmur, [which] was a persistent and apparently necessary feature of memory work" and may be considered an equivalent to reading a text again (Carruthers 2008, 7). Furthermore, the lines are characterized by formal elements such as rhyme and (partial) alliteration and, like Sam's rhymes about Gil-galad, they are enigmatic in their allusiveness. Gandalf, in response to Pippin's questions, explains some of the references, yet others remain opaque.[17] Again, like in Sam's case, the information preserved is sufficient to piece together the backbone of the story, but many elements are merely alluded to.

It is characteristic of mnemonic devices – and of our actual memory – that they do not store the information in its full form but retain only selected key-elements. The full account is only reconstructed once the process of retrieval has been triggered by the partial information preserved in the mnemonic devices.[18] Furthermore, poetic memory tends to preserve partial and largely unintelligible information even when access to the full story is no longer available, and mnemonic texts often survive solely thanks to their poetic form.[19] Formal elements like end-rhyme or alliteration help to preserve the content even when it no longer makes sense. The German idiomatic expression *Mit Kind und Kegel*, for example, is still in frequent use in sentences such as *Wir gingen nach Italien mit Kind und Kegel* ('We went to Italy with all junior members of the family.'). Now *Kind* as 'child' poses no problem, but the appropriate meaning of the

17. See Hammond and Scull for a discussion of the meaning of at least some of the elements mentioned (2005, 436).
18. This is true for the individual memory as well as for the cultural memory.
19. The Man in the Moon nursery rhymes and poems, for example, preserve ancient mythological lore no longer understood. See Honegger 2005 for an in-depth discussion of this tradition.

second term *Kegel* is no longer remembered by any speaker of German. It originally meant 'illegitimate child' and would thus stand in contrast to the *Kinder* as the progeny born within wedlock. Thus *Kind und Kegel* means indeed 'with all junior members of the family', yet the full expression remains in use only because the k-alliteration, linking *Kind* to *Kegel*, guarantees the survival of the nonsense element *Kegel*.

Similar phenomena occur in Middle-earth where rhymes of lore survive without being understood any more. The theme is mentioned explicitly for the first time when Celeborn admonishes Boromir: "But do not despise the lore that has come down from distant years; for oft it may chance that old wives keep in memory word of things that once were needful for the wise to know" (*FR*, 'Farewell to Lórien', 374). And indeed, Celeborn's prophetic words find their fulfilment many leagues from Lórien and some five hundred pages later when

> an old wife, Ioreth, the eldest of the women who served in that house, looking on the fair face of Faramir, wept, for all the people loved him. And she said: 'Alas! if he should die. Would that there were kings in Gondor, as there were once upon a time, they say! For it is said in old lore: *The hands of the king are the hands of a healer*. And so the rightful king could ever be known.' (*RK*, 'The Houses of Healing', 860)[20]

The full implications of this alliterative line (***h****ands* – ***h****ands* – ***h****ealer*) of "old lore" are no longer clear to those who remember it. Yet it triggers Gandalf's memory and makes him draw the correct conclusions and act accordingly. The theme is repeated once more a few pages later, when the herb-master in the Houses of Healing discourses wordily on the different names of *athelas* and its uses, and remarks to Aragorn that there is no known medical application for it, "[u]nless, of course, you give heed to rhymes of old days which women such as our good Ioreth still repeat without understanding" (865). Ironically, he then repeats some of these rhymes yet denigrates them as nothing "but a doggrel, I fear, garbled in the memory of old wives", without realizing that they contain the remedy for saving those who suffer from the effects of the black breath (865).

These ancient and often no longer fully understood rhymes of lore are, to borrow from another fantasy epic, like fossilized dragon's eggs – beautiful to behold but not actually expected to ever hatch. Yet, as we have seen, they sometimes do – which brings us to the matter of lore.

2 - 'knowledge' vs. 'lore'

It may be largely coincidental that lore, in the example discussed before, is closely connected to healing, i.e. the restoration of the patient's mental and physical health. This is certainly very appropriate since lore itself focuses on the continuation or restoration of a former state of being – as a contrastive analysis with the term 'knowledge' shows.[21]

20. As Shippey points out, Tolkien's "old wife" is most likely an allusion to Jacob Grimm's *ammen und spinnerinnen* ('nannies and spinstresses') mentioned in the 'Preface' to his *Deutsche Mythologie* (1875-1878) (2007, 303).
21. I am indebted to Dirk Vanderbeke's illuminating analysis of Tolkien's stance towards modern science in his paper 'Language, Lore and Learning in *The Lord of the Rings*' (2005).

An electronic search of the full PDF of the 2004 one-volume edition of *The Lord of the Rings* yields 67 occurrences of 'lore', including some compounds such as 'herblore', 'ring-lore', or 'lore-master'. 'Knowledge', by contrast, occurs only 38 times. In some instances, the two terms are used largely as synonyms and Tolkien must have chosen them for stylistic reasons. Firstly, in order to avoid repetition of the same word, and secondly because some idiomatic combinations require one word and not the other. Thus, when Gandalf talks about hobbits, he uses 'lore' first and then 'knowledge' in the ensuing phrase: "Among the Wise I am the only one that goes in for hobbit-lore: an obscure branch of knowledge, but full of surprises" (*FR*, 'The Shadow of the Past', 48). Of course, neither 'hobbit-knowledge' nor 'branch of lore' would be idiomatic and thus the differentiation is very much pre-determined by the rules of English usage. In this, as well as in some other instances, reasons of style and language usage account for the occurrences of lore and knowledge. By far the greatest part of the examples, however, follows a differentiation in semantics. Lore in the sense of 'handed down information', is used either with a neutral meaning or, predominantly, with a positive connotation. Thus, Boromir praises his father Denethor as "wise in the lore of Gondor" and Elrond as "greatest of lore-masters" (*FR*, 'The Council of Elrond', 246). There are instances where protagonists use lore negatively, as we have seen, yet even then the positive meaning wins out in the end – as is the case in the example of Ioreth and her "old lore".

Knowledge, on the other side, occurs as a term denoting 'information gained by means of observation, reasoning, or scientific inquiry' and is used primarily in a neutral manner, such as when Merry refers to his gathering information about the Ring and about Frodo in order to prevent him from leaving the Shire on his own (*FR*, 'A Conspiracy Unmasked', 104-5). Yet Tolkien subtly influences our perception of the term and the underlying concept by associating it with situations, events and protagonists that are somewhat flawed. Thus, when Saruman proclaims the pursuit of "Knowledge, Rule, Order" as the "high and ultimate purpose" condoning the deplorable "evils done by the way", we all know that we should be on our guard (*FR*, 'The Council of Elrond', 259). Indeed, Gandalf has already linked Saruman's striving for knowledge with the less savoury development of his character when he tells Frodo: "His [i.e. Saruman's] knowledge is deep, but his pride has grown with it, and he takes ill any meddling" (*FR*, 'The Shadow of the Past', 48). Similarly, Gandalf comments about Denethor, whose frequent use of the Palantir to gather information proved fatal: "The knowledge which he obtained was, doubtless, often of service to him; yet the vision of the great might of Mordor that was shown to him fed the despair of his heart until it overthrew his mind" (*RK*, The Pyre of Denethor', 856). These examples illustrate how knowledge, although not made explicitly responsible for the Deadly Sins of Pride and Despair, respectively, is too closely linked to them for comfort. In Appendix A, as if to confirm this connection, the chronicler-narrator gives the following assessment, linking knowledge, pride, and despair:

> In this way Denethor gained his great knowledge of things that passed in his realm, and far beyond his borders, at which men marvelled; but he bought the knowledge dearly, being aged before his time by his contest with the will of Sauron. Thus pride increased in Denethor together with despair. (*RK*, 'Appendix A', 1056)

The theme of dangerous knowledge runs through *The Lord of the Rings* like a *leitmotiv*, and it could be argued that it lies at the very origin of the Ring-problem since, as Elrond recounts, it is "the Elven-smiths of Eregion['s] [...] eagerness for knowledge, by which Sauron ensnared them" (*FR*, 'The Council of Elrond', 242). Yet the real elephant in the room, for whom knowledge is merely a stand-in, is never addressed directly, though the dialogue between Gandalf and Saruman provides a very clear pointer to those who can read the message. Gandalf's account made at the Council of Elrond is worth quoting in full:

> 'For I am Saruman the Wise, Saruman Ring-maker, Saruman of Many Colours!'
> I looked then and saw that his robes, which had seemed white, were not so, but were woven of all colours, and if he moved they shimmered and changed hue so that the eye was bewildered.
> 'I liked white better,' I said.
> 'White!' he sneered. 'It serves as a beginning. White cloth may be dyed. The white page can be overwritten; and the white light can be broken.'
> 'In which case it is no longer white,' said I. 'And he that breaks a thing to find out what it is has left the path of wisdom.' (259)

Vanderbeke, in his essay 'Language, Lore and Learning in *The Lord of the Rings*', points out that

> Gandalf's last line echoes Wordsworth's famous romantic critique of modern science from the poem 'The Tables Turned',[22] [...] But more important is the example chosen by Tolkien, for the passage refers to one of Newton's major discoveries – white light can be split up into the rainbow colours – and thus it links Saruman's turn to evil to the beginning of modern science. (Vanderbeke 2005, 145-6)

Thus, without explicitly linking the two, the passage makes clear that knowledge is often used as shorthand for modern science and the modern scientific approach with its master-narrative of progress, systemic growth, and development. For the scientifically minded Saruman,[23] the passing of time means indeed an accumulation of knowledge, which is why he offers Théoden "all the aid that my knowledge, founded in long years, can bring" (*TT*, 'The Voice of Saruman', 579). This master-narrative of scientific growth and progress stands in opposition to the one underlying the concept of lore, which is, in our world, characterized mostly by stagnation or threatened by a "[fall] from its fullness

22. The relevant stanza reads as follows: "Sweet is the lore which Nature brings; / Our meddling intellect / Mis-shapes the beauteous forms of things: – / We murder to dissect." (Wordsworth 1994, 481). See also Weinreich's (2008) discussion of Tolkien's poem 'Mythopoeia' and its critique of modernity and modern science.

23. Cf. Treebeard's telling characterization of Saruman as having "a mind of metal and wheels; and he does not care for growing things, except as far as they serve him for the moment" (*TT*, 'Treebeard', 473).

of old" (*RK*, 'The Houses of Healing', 860).[24] Any growth of lore is organic and focuses rather on the filling of gaps in the tradition, as we have seen in Treebeard's 'Lore of the Living Creatures', than in attempting a radical departure from the handed-down frameworks. The underlying master-narrative is linked to and shares key elements with the concept of *mundus senescit* (see Wiemann 2011) and the *topos* of the decline from a Golden to a Silver etc. Age which is, at least partially, related to the biblical narrative of the fall (see Honegger 2011). The basic assumption of all these concepts is that our present-day world is a long way from its original state of perfection and grace – often due to a fall for which the early humans must take the blame.

Tolkien's Middle-earth itself is no different and though the early history of Men is in the dark, the world of *The Lord of the Rings* is clearly a fallen world.[25] Such a view establishes a culture that does not follow the master-narrative of scientific progress, and therefore changes the way in which we should evaluate things past. For someone adhering to a *mundus senescit* framework, any radical departure from the original state of perfection cannot be but a deplorable decline from the fullness of being and knowledge, and the further we move away from the paradisiacal point of origin, the greater the loss.[26] As a consequence, the best we can do is to preserve as well as possible the original information (that is: lore), which awards memory a central role since it enables us to reach back to a "fullness of old".[27] Indeed, within such a framework the idea of *regression* acquires a positive connotation, and *progression*, by contrast, is seen negatively. Furthermore, being of a conservative persuasion within such a context means something entirely different than within a progressive framework. Saruman's complaint that he had been "hindered rather than helped by our weak or idle friends" makes sense primarily when interpreted with the master-narrative of progress vs. regress (*FR*, 'The Council of Elrond', 259). His words disclose Saruman as a believer in the perfectibility of things and beings by means no longer dependent on metaphysical support but which can be achieved by qualities innate in Man (or Wizard etc.) himself.[28] It also becomes clear that he sees himself as

24. The statement is taken from the narratorial comment about the Gondorian medical traditions which, in full, reads as follows: "For though all lore was in these latter days fallen from its fullness of old, the leechcraft of Gondor was still wise, and skilled in the healing of wound and hurt, and all such sickness as east of the Sea mortal men were subject to" (*RK*, 'The Houses of Healing', 860).

25. Tolkien's most theological piece is the posthumously published 'Athrabeth Finrod Ah Andreth' (*Morgoth* 303-66). The metaphysical framework of Arda is best presented and commented on by Tolkien himself in his long letter to Milton Waldman (late 1951, in *Letters*, Letter 131, 143-61), in which he writes: "There cannot be any 'story' without a fall – all stories are ultimately about the fall" (*Letters*, Letter 131, 147).

26. Verlyn Flieger's study of the motif of 'Splintered Light' in her eponymous book (2002) explores the importance and ramifications of this concept for Tolkien's entire work.

27. Such a diminishing can be seen even in individual words of a language. Thus, when discussing his choice of 'Elves' for translating 'Quendi', Tolkien comments: "This old word was indeed the only one available and was once fitted to apply to such memories of this people as Men preserved, or to the makings of Men's minds not wholly dissimilar. But it has been diminished, and to many it may now suggest fancies either pretty or silly, as unlike to the Quendi of old as are butterflies to the swift falcon" (*RK*, 'Appendix F', 1137).

28. In Jackson's adaptation of Tolkien's work, Saruman's creates the Uruk-hai by means of

the leader of the progressive party,[29] which makes him a natural ally of Sauron, since "in those days all the enemies of the Enemy revered what was ancient, in language no less than in other matters" (*RK*, 'Appendix F', 1134). Accordingly, the aim of Sauron's major opponents in Middle-earth in the Third Age, Gandalf and Aragorn, is not to establish a new and progressive order or utopia, but to restore the Gondorian realm. This comprises not only the preservation of the Númenórean heritage, but also the active management of the transmission from the Third to the Fourth Age, the Age of Men, in form of a *translatio imperii*[30] or, more accurately, a *continuatio imperii*. As a consequence, Aragorn appears not as a founding-father figure like Aeneas or Romulus, but rather as a *renovator imperii* such as Charlemagne.

The truly wise also know that they may be able to preserve some of the primordial perfection, but that they cannot and must not make the mistake of trying to stop the progression of time completely. Tolkien, in his letter to Milton Waldman, criticized the Elves for becoming "obsessed with 'fading', the mode in which the changes of time (the law of the world under the sun) was perceived by them. They became sad, and their art (shall we say) antiquarian, and their efforts all really a kind of embalming" (*Letters*, Letter 131, 151). Indeed, it is this desire for stopping or at least slowing the passing of time that Sauron uses to entice both Elves and Men. He does so by means of the Rings of Power, whose "chief power [...] was the prevention or slowing of *decay* (i.e. 'change' viewed as a regrettable thing), the preservation of what is desired or loved, or its semblance" (152). Similarly, he goads Tar-Calion/Ar-Pharazôn and the greater part of the Númenóreans into open revolt against the Valar by instrumentalizing their desire to "wrest from the gods 'everlasting life within the circles of the world'" (156). These events teach us to avoid the wrong kind of conservatism, which is actually a sort of covetousness since, as Tolkien remarked in his letter to Milton Waldman, the Númenóreans' long life not only leads to greater wisdom and skill, but also "breeds a possessive attitude to these things, and desire awakens for more *time* for their enjoyment" (154).[31] Men, but also Elves, have thus two options: either to accept "the loss and the silence" and the fading respectively – and to hope for a better life at the end of time or beyond the spheres of the world (*RK*, 'Appendix A', 1063). Or they decide to reject such a passive attitude and try to change things with the help of whatever power and the means at their disposal.

---

genetic engineering and, in his own words, thus perfects what Melkor had started: "Do you know how the Orcs first came to being? They were Elves once, taken by the dark powers, tortured and mutilated. A ruined and terrible form of life. And now, perfected. My fighting Uruk-hai." (Saruman in the movie adaptation of *The Fellowship of the Ring*, chapter 27 'The Fighting Uruk-hai').

29. See Curry 1997 and 2014 for a discussion of Modernity and all it implies in Tolkien's work.

30. See Gandalf's advice to Aragorn on Mount Mindolluin: "it is your task to order its [i.e. the Fourth Age's] beginning and to preserve what may be preserved" (*RK*, 'The Ride of the Rohirrim', 971). On the concept of the *translatio imperii* in Tolkien's work, see Honegger 2011, 90-6.

31. Aragorn resists this temptation and does not show covetousness for eternal life (cf. *RK*, 'Appendix A', 1062-3). The theme of covetousness (for life) is also central to Tolkien's interpretation of the Middle English poem *Sir Gawain and the Green Knight* (see especially *Monsters,* 97-100).

This is the point of view of the scientifically minded Saruman, who, in his hubris, believes himself to be able to construct a utopian order of his own making – never mind the collateral damage. Knowledge (that is: science) of the Sarumanian persuasion holds the promise of transforming the Vale of Tears into an unspecified utopia and offers to solve every problem by means of technological-scientific progress on a never-ending upward climbing trajectory. The underlying master-narrative of lore, by contrast, suggests a spiralling development that leads first downwards (the Fall), continues with a long period of imperfection and suffering, but completes in the end on a higher level with the restoration of the original perfection. Gandalf, in opposition to Saruman, acknowledges and embraces the imperfectability of things temporal and points out the importance of recognising and accepting one's limits:

> Yet it is not our part to master all the tides of the world, but to do what is in us for the succour of those years wherein we are set, uprooting the evil in the fields that we know, so that those who live after may have clean earth to till. What weather they shall have is not ours to rule. (*RK*, 'The Black Gate Opens', 879)

This is just one of many references towards a greater plan, whose nature has not yet been revealed to us.[32] What is needed is trust in a divine power and the hope in a restoration of the original perfection or, to use the language and imagery of the Bible, in the establishment of 'Paradise regained' [33]and the coming of the Kingdom of God. The Christian promise of salvation has its counterpart in "the Second Music of the Ainur", which seems to presage the re-establishment of Arda Unmarred (*Silmarillion*, 42). Memory is thus key in helping not only to prevent the loss and the silence by preserving and handing down in the form of lore the recollection of the First Music and later states of (near) perfection,[34] but also since this holds out a vague and dimly perceived promise of a return to a prelapsarian state of being in the form of the Second Music. As a consequence, lore can help Men and Elves in Middle-earth to endure the decline, fading, or loss while fighting the long defeat,[35] and the memory of the First Music can provide at least some consolation.

There is, however, at least one protagonist who is not satisfied with memory only: Gimli the Dwarf. Upon departing from Lothlórien, he laments "the danger of light and

32. A very illuminating and approachable discussion of the workings of providence and predestination in *The Lord of the Rings* is given in Dickerson 2003.

33. See Isaiah 65: 17-25.

34. This, in the world of *The Lord of the Rings*, is done almost exclusively by means of lore, and I know of only one prominent instance of remembrance by means of a ritual, namely when Faramir and the Rangers of Ithilien face west before sitting down to their meal. Afterwards Faramir explains to Frodo and Sam: "'So we always do [...] We look towards Númenor that was, and beyond to Elvenhome that is, and to that which is beyond Elvenhome and will ever be" (*TT*, 'The Window on the Past', 676). Tolkien intentionally avoided mentioning or describing elements of institutionalised religions and their rituals in *The Lord of the Rings* (see *Letters*, Letter 142, 172), which meant that he also cut out most cultural-religious practices such as the religious holidays that focus on commemoration.

35. Galadriel characterizes history as a long defeat: "and together through ages of the world we have fought the long defeat" (*FR*, 'The Mirror of Galadriel', 357).

joy" and is deeply distraught about having to leave behind Lothlórien and the Lady Galadriel (*FR*, 'Farewell to Lórien', 378). His friend Legolas tries to console him with the following words:

> 'But you have not forsaken your companions, and the least reward that you shall have is that the memory of Lothlórien shall remain ever clear and unstained in your heart, and shall neither fade nor grow stale.'
> 'Maybe,' said Gimli; 'and I thank you for your words. True words doubtless; yet all such comfort is cold. Memory is not what the heart desires. That is only a mirror, be it clear as Kheled-zâram. Or so says the heart of Gimli the Dwarf. Elves may see things otherwise. Indeed I have heard that for them memory is more like to the waking world than to a dream. Not so for Dwarves.' (378-9)

And Arwen might have added: 'And not so for the Peredhil, or Half-Elven of Middle-earth!'

Bibliography

Carruthers, M.J., *The Book of Memory. A Study of Memory in Medieval Culture*, 2nd edn (Cambridge: Cambridge University Press, 2008).

Curry, P., *Defending Middle-earth. Tolkien, Myth and Modernity*, (Edinburgh: Floris Books, 1997).
— 'Modernity in Middle-earth', in *Deep Roots in a Time of Frost. Essays on Tolkien*, Cormarë Series, xxxiii (Zurich: Walking Tree Publishers, 2014), 43-47.

Dickerson, M., *Following Gandalf. Epic Battles and Moral Victory in The Lord of the Rings*, (Grand Rapids: Brazos Press, 2003).

Flieger, V., *A Question of Time. J.R.R. Tolkien's Road to Faërie*, (Kent: Kent State University Press, 1997).
— *Splintered Light. Logos and Language in Tolkien's World*, 2nd rev edn (Kent: Kent State University Press, 2002).

Hammond, W.G. and C. Scull, *The Lord of the Rings. A Reader's Companion*, (London: HarperCollins, 2005).

Honegger, T., 'The Man in the Moon: Structural Depth in Tolkien', in *Root & Branch: Approaches towards Understanding Tolkien*, ed. by T. Honegger, 2nd edn, Cormarë Series, ii (Zurich: Walking Tree Publishers, 2005), 9-70.
— 'The Passing of the Elves and the Arrival of Modernity: Tolkien's "Mythical Method"', in *Tolkien and Modernity* 2, ed. by T. Honegger and F. Weinreich, Cormarë Series, x (Zurich: Walking Tree Publishers, 2006), 211-233.
— 'Time and Tide – Medieval Patterns of Interpreting the Passing of Time in Tolkien's Work', *Hither Shore*, 8 (2011), 86-99.
Lee, S.D., "Tolkien in Oxford' (BBC, 1968): A Reconstruction', *Tolkien Studies*, 15 (2018), 115-176.
Lewis, C.S., *The Discarded Image*, (Cambridge: Cambridge University Press, 1964).

Shippey, T., "A Fund of Wise Sayings': Proverbiality in Tolkien', in *Roots and Branches: Selected Papers on Tolkien by Tom Shippey*, Cormarë Series, xi (Zurich: Walking Tree Publishers, 2007), 303-319.

Simonson, M., *The Lord of the Rings and the Western Narrative Tradition*, Cormarë Series, xvi (Zurich: Walking Tree Publishers, 2008).

Tacitus, *Germania*, ed. and trans. by M. Fuhrmann (Stuttgart: Philipp Reclam Jun., 2000).

Tolkien, J.R.R., *The Lord of the Rings*, 50th anniv. edn (Boston: Houghton Mifflin, 2004).
— *The Silmarillion*, ed. by C. Tolkien (Boston: Houghton Mifflin, 1977).
— *The Letters of J.R.R. Tolkien*, ed. by H. Carpenter, with the assistance of C. Tolkien, Reprinted edition (Boston: Houghton Mifflin, 2000).
— *The Return of the Shadow*, ed. by C. Tolkien, P.b. edn. (London: Grafton, 1994).
— *The Treason of Isengard*, ed. by C. Tolkien, P.b. edn. (London: Grafton, 1993).
— *The War of the Ring*, ed. by C. Tolkien, P.b. edn. (London: Grafton, 1992).
— 'Leaf by Niggle' in *Tree and Leaf*, (London: Grafton, 1992), 75-95.
— *Morgoth's Ring*, ed. by C. Tolkien, P.b. edn. (London: HarperCollins, 1994).
— 'Sir Gawain and the Green Knight', in *The Monster and the Critics and Other Essays*, ed. by C. Tolkien (London: HarperCollins, 1997), 72-108.
— *Tolkien On Fairy-stories*, ed. by V. Flieger and D. A. Anderson, Expanded edn. with commentary and notes (London: HarperCollins, 2008).

Vanderbeke, D., 'Language, Lore and Learning in *The Lord of the Rings*', in *Reconsidering Tolkien*, ed. by T. Honegger, Cormarë Series, viii (Zurich: Walking Tree Publishers, 2005), 129-151.

Weinreich, F., 'Metaphysics of Myth: The Platonic Ontology of 'Mythopoeia'', in *Tolkien's Shorter Works. Essays of the Jena Conference 2007*, ed. by M. Hiley and F. Weinreich, Cormarë Series, xvii (Zurich: Walking Tree Publishers, 2008), 325-347.

Wiemann, D., 'Mundus senescit: Tolkien and the Allure of Medieval Nostalgia', *Hither Shore*, 8 (2011), 24-38.

Wordsworth, W., *The Works of William Wordsworth*, (Ware: Wordsworth Editions, 1994).

On the Nature and Corporeality of Elves, according to Tolkien

Massimiliano Izzo

1 – Motivation

Papers about the role and significance of Elves and Fairies in Tolkien's work abound. However, in this paper, I hope to highlight a new facet of Tolkien's thought on this subject, one closer to our Primary World rather than his Secondary World of Eä. Before I introduce my argument, I must begin with a premise or assumption. Throughout this paper I will use the terms 'fairy' and 'elf' interchangeably, as I assume that Tolkien considered them to be equivalent, as words or terms that refer to the same class of beings. This equivalence was explicit in his early poetry and in 'The Book of Lost Tales' and related writings, documents and lexicons. However, even though the term 'fairy' was subsequently dropped in his legendarium since the early 'Sketch of the Mythology' written in 1926, the equivalence between the two terms still held true for him, in particular when discussing folklore and fairy-stories in the Primary World. We can find evidence of this assumption in the essay 'On Fairy-stories' published in 1945 and later revised for publication in *Tree and Leaf* in 1963: "Stories that are actually concerned primarily with 'fairies', that is with creatures that might also in modern English be called 'elves', are relatively rare, and as a rule not very interesting" (*OFS*, 32). The equivalence between fairies and elves still held true for Tolkien towards the end of his life. In the 1960s, in an essay that he wrote as a commentary for his short story *Smith of Wootton Major*, he stated: "This short tale is not an 'allegory' [...] It is a 'Fairy Story', of the kind in which beings that may be called 'fairies' or 'elves' play a part and are associated in action with human people" (*Smith*, 111). A more thorough discussion on this topic can be found elsewhere (De Rosario Martinez 2010, 79-82).

Taking the previous assumption, at least for the scope of this paper, what can we say about the nature and corporeality of Tolkien's Secondary World Elves, the creatures known under the name of Eldar, or, more correctly, Quendi? The matter might seem moot and well established. The Eldar are a class of incarnated rational beings similar ('biologically' speaking) to Men. The difference is that they are immortal, or more correctly they enjoy a 'serial longevity' co-extensive with the life of the world of Arda (*Letters*, Letter 208, 267). Their soul (what in the later versions of the legendarium went under the Quenya name of *fëa*) is bound to the World until the end of time (at least until the end of the physical Earth). Their bodies can be killed by hurt or extreme suffering, but, under specific conditions, may undergo reincarnation. The detail of this reincarnation changed over the various versions of the legendarium, but the overall conception was very established in Tolkien's mythology since 'The Book of Lost Tales'.

Looking at how consistent and stable Tolkien's view on his Secondary World Elves was, it is even more remarkable that the Professor expressed a very different idea when he speculated on the 'real' nature of fairies or elves as, and if, they exist in our Primary World. He made this speculation while he was reworking and expanding 'On Fairy-stories' for publication in the early 1940s in some drafts expunged from the so-called 'Manuscript B' of the essay. In these drafts, Tolkien put into words what it seems to be his most private beliefs and speculations on the nature of Faërie and its inhabitants:

> If Fairies exist they are bound by the Moral Law as is all the Created Universe; but their duties and functions are not ours. They are not spirits of the dead, nor a branch of the human race, nor devils in fair shape whose chief object is our deception and ruin. These are either human ideas out of which the Elf-idea has been separated, or if Elves really exist mere human hypotheses (or confusions). They are a quite separate creation living in another mode. [...] For lack of a better word they may be called spirits, daemons: inherent powers of the created world, deriving more directly and 'earlier' (in terrestrial history) from the creating will of God, but nonetheless created, subject to Moral Law, capable of good and evil, and possibly (in this fallen world) actually sometimes evil. They are in fact non-incarnate minds (or souls) of a stature and even nature more near to that of Man (in some cases possibly less, in many maybe greater) than any other rational creatures, known or guessed by us. They can take form at will, or they could do so: they have or had a choice. (*OFS*, 254–5)

The passage is remarkable as it presents ideas and concepts that do not appear elsewhere in Tolkien's writings. Most noticeably, the Elves/Fairies are here posited to be spiritual, non-incarnate beings, able to assume form at will and subject to moral judgement. They are completely different from the creatures of flesh and blood that we are familiar with from *The Hobbit*, *The Lord of the Rings* and *The Silmarillion*.

In a subsequent passage from the same manuscript page, Tolkien offered the example of a tree-fairy, equated to the Greek semi-divine dryad, as a minor spirit devoted to bringing to accomplishment part of the 'divine Tree-idea', but acting on a small scale, such as a single individual tree. The role of Fairies seems then to be 'sub-creational', the act of making effective a (divine) idea as through an act of love, an act which binds the fairy to the created world until the end of time. The remarkable quality of this entire passage has been already noted by scholars such as Verlyn Flieger and Dimitra Fimi (Fimi 2010, 49; Flieger 2017, 29, 145–6). Among other things, it is worth to note the references to Greek mythology (the terms *daemon* and *dryad*) rather than the Germanic tradition, and the reference to the 'Platonic' – as well as 'Augustinian' – theory of the (divine) ideas. But what are the sources of this theory of Primary World Fairies? Why did Tolkien choose to underline the term *daemon* in the manuscript and why did he associate it to the beings known as fairies or elves? Was he the first one to conceive this link or was there a tradition that associated the two terms? To answer these questions, we must first see where the term *daemon* comes from and to what end it was used from Antiquity to Modern times.

2 – On daemons

Daemon originates from the Ancient Greek word δαίμων and was used in its earliest written records, such as in Homer's *Odyssey*, as a synonym of θεός (theos), god. It was Plato, in the IV century BC, who systematised and rationalised the role of daemons and their relation to gods and men in his dialogues. In the Symposium he defined daemons as intermediate beings (or 'spirits') between the mortal beings living on Earth and the divine beings living in Heaven.[1] More details on daemons are offered in the pseudo-Platonic dialogue *Epinomis*, which was considered an authentic work of Plato throughout Antiquity and had a great influence on many disciples of the great philosopher. In the *Epinomis*, the class of intermediate beings between mortal Men and immortal Gods are further refined into three categories: (1) the daemons proper, living in the aetherial regions below the heavenly stars, (2) a class of 'air born beings', and (3) a water kind of semi-divine beings, which were subsequently interpreted by the Middle Platonist philosopher Plutarch as nymphs. These three classes of intermediate beings shared the characteristic of possessing invisible bodies, but the third one could make themselves visible and lure humans with the beauty of their visible appearance (Timotin 2012, 86–93).

Many Greek and Latin philosophers and authors of the Ancient Times further elaborated with great details Plato's ideas on daemons. Here, I will briefly mention two Latin authors who were the most influential on this subject in the Medieval West: Apuleius and Calcidius. Apuleius (II century A.D.), in his treatise 'De Deo Socratis', reiterated the intermediate nature of daemons, stated that they inhabited the aerial regions, and affirmed that they were rational creatures who possessed the eternal nature of the gods, and the emotional mind of Men (gods being imperturbable). Calcidius (IV-V century A.D.) was the author of a Latin translation and commentary of Plato's cosmological dialogue *Timaeus* that became one of the main sources, and the only available primary source, of Platonic philosophy in Western Europe during the Middle Ages. Calcidius devoted a large section of his *Timaeus* commentary to describing the nature of daemons and he defined them as "invisible divine powers" (Calcidius 2016, 318-47). He was the first one who clearly stated that they were ontologically different from the souls of the dead and that, rather than being utterly incorporeal, they possessed invisible 'subtle' bodies. Reworking the hierarchy first exposed in the *Epinomis*, he distinguished three classes of daemons: (1) the aetherial, the most pure (whom he equated to Judaeo and Christian daemons), (2) the aerial and (3) those living the 'moist substance' (*humecta essentia*) region situated above the Earth surface. For Calcidius, as it was for Apuleius, daemons could be either good or bad; he even explicitly associated the good daemons to the holy angels of the Hebrew tradition (338-41). A very different stance was taken by St. Augustine, a contemporary of Calcidus, who considered all daemons evil, equating them to proper 'demons' as they are now considered according to the Christian canon. Augustine indicted as well various semi-divine creatures from Classical folklore and literature – such as Sylvans, Fauns, and Incubi – claiming that they were nothing else but malignant demons capable of assuming visible bodies to lure and tempt both male and female individuals.

St. Augustine notwithstanding, the idea of good daemons still lingered during the Middle Ages, though the concept of demons (in the modern sense) as evil spirits became more and more prevalent as the years passed. Medieval Cosmological Models – such

1. As a side note, Plato speculated in the *Cratylus* whether the term *δαίμων* could be related to the term *δαήμων* (knowing or wise), an interesting coincidence with the meaning of the Quenya word *Ñoldo*, referring to the second clan of the Elves.

as the one described in Bernardus Sylvestris's *Cosmographia* (XII Century) – , under the influence of Plato, Apuleius and Calcidius, placed daemonic spirits in the air regions below the Moon, as intermediate beings between Men and Angels, as the latter now tended to replace the role of the pagan deities. These medieval models tried to assimilate with little success other classical semi-divine beings, such as silvans and fauns. These creatures proved difficult to systematise, though Bernardus Sylvestris tried to solve the issue claiming that they lived on the remote regions of the Earth and their body was 'of elemental purity', thus anticipating the elemental theories of Cornelius Agrippa and Paracelsus (XVI century). The influence of these models of the world and its supernatural 'daemonic' inhabitants was pervasive in Late Medieval and in Early Modern Literature.[2] However, their relevance as far Tolkien is concerned is probably not uniquely due to the Literary Canon, but to the fact that C.S. Lewis taught and discussed extensively the medieval Model of the Universe, its sources and its influence while lecturing in Oxford in the 1930s. His lectures were the basis for his book *The Discarded Image*, which contains different sections devoted to the role of daemons in the Model. It is worth to note that Lewis chose to spell these creatures as 'daemons' rather than 'demons', to better distinguish them from their Christian devilish counterpart.

3 – On Elves and Fairies

What I have offered you so far is a short comprehensive account of the concept of daemons, highlighting some associations to semi-deities of classical folklore such as nymphs and fauns. But what can we say about daemons in relation to the elves of the Germanic tradition? There is good evidence that, originally, elves, both in Old English (O.E.) as *ælfe* and in Old Norse (O.N.) as *álfar*, were conceived as human-like 'otherworldly' or 'super-natural' beings, aligned with gods and men against monsters (e.g. giants, ogres). At that stage, elves were not conceived as particularly invisible or incorporeal, thus matching the Eldar (or Quendi) of Tolkien's Secondary World (Hall 2007, 68). However, this conception changed when the Germanic pagan tradition came into contact with Christianity and the Classical heritage. The causes for this change are multiple, but we can point with a certain degree of confidence to two of them, at least in the Anglo-Saxon world. First, the Elves, across all Germanic folklore traditions, had the power to send spirit-like creatures called *mære* (O.E) or *maran* (O.N.) to torment the sleep of human victims (124-6). The modern German world for nightmare, *Alptraum* still bears witness to this connection. Now, some Anglo-Saxon scribe glossed *mære* to Latin using the word *incubi*, a class of creatures that, as I have mentioned in the previous section, St. Augustine associated with evil demons. Second, some other Old English glossator used the word *ælfenne* and compounds of *ælfenne* to translate minor deities of Classical folklore such as nymphs, dryads and oreads (78–88). We can thus see two, albeit tenuous, links between elves and creatures with daemonic connotations. It must be noted that, besides the daemonic/demonic association, the elves were

2. In English Literature only has to look at Chaucer (*The House of Fame*, II, 929; see also R.F. Green 2016, 39), Shakespeare's Ariel in *The Tempest* (see Shakespeare and Kermode 1975, 142-45), Spenser (see Russel, 2020), Milton (*Paradise Regained*, I, 46).

sometimes associated with angels as well, especially in Scandinavia. In the *Snorra Edda* (XIII century) we encounter the *ljos-alfar*, the Light Elves, who inhabit Andlangr, the second heavenly realm. Their description by Snorri Sturluson brought Jacob Grimm to claim that "the Elves of light, of a pure colour, seem nearly transparent, quite ethereal, with white garments, shining like silver, as in the Irish legend" (Grimm 1838, 65). However, the *ljos-alfar* were not a genuine product of mythology or folklore: they were most likely a creation of Snorri modelled on the Christian Angels as described in the medieval treatise *Elucidarium*, as first shown by Anne Holtsmark and reported by Shippey and Hall (Shippey 2005, 181; Hall 2007, 25). Even so, we can conclude that, across the Germanic world, elves were being equated at different stages both to angels and classical daemons.

By the Late Middle Ages, the English word *elf* was increasingly being replaced by the Anglo-Norman loan-word *faerie*. By the XIV century, elves had acquired inherently daemonic (good/neutral) or demonic (evil) traits: in the *South English Legendary*, the eluene are lesser devils staking visible form to lure humans into temptation (Hall 2007, 141–2); in *Sir Orfeo*, the Fairy King and his retinue are invisible to mortal men and remain so to Orfeo until he hasn't spent ten years in exile in the woods; in the XV century (1438 AD), John Stafford, the Bishop of Bath, refers in his Register to "spirits of the airs, whom the common folk calls 'feyry'' a clear echo of Apuleius's and Calcidius's theories on aerial daemons (Stafford 1915, 226). Two centuries later, in 1691, in the first systematised account of British fairy lore, Robert Kirk's *The Secret Commonwealth of Elves, Faun and Fairies*, the creatures referred in the title are "said to be of middle nature between Man and Angel, as were Daemons thought to be of old; of intelligent fluid Spirits, and light changeable bodies (lyke those called Astral)" (1893, 5). Here we finally have the link between elves/fairies and daemons explicitly stated. It is relevant to note that Kirk's book was among the ones consulted by Tolkien when working on 'On Fairy-stories' and was cited by Lewis in *The Discarded Image* (Lewis 1964, 134-5). In the XIX Century, Jakob Grimm wrote in the chapter "Wights and elves" of his seminal *Teutonic Mythology* that these creatures "are what we should call *spiritus* nowadays. But the word spirit (geist, ghost) like the Greek *δαίμων*, is too comprehensive […] The Lat. *genius* would more nearly hit the mark." (Grimm 1883, 439). Grimm's quote, with its mention of "spirit" and "δαίμων", echoes in Tolkien's passage from the 'Manuscript B' drafts, though the Professor seems to draw quite a different conclusion, finding daemon a suitable term to describe the elves.

4 – On C.S. Lewis's eldila

Both angels and daemons were a source of inspiration for C.S. Lewis when he conceived the *eldila* (see Sick 2008). They first appeared in *Out of the Silent Planet*, the opening book of Lewis's *Space Trilogy*, originally published in 1938. In the trilogy, the eldila are non-incarnate semi-divine rational beings inhabiting the Fields of Arbol, our Solar System. In Out of the Silent Planet Lewis wrote that "the body of an *eldil* is a movement swift as light; you may say its body is made of light, but not of that which is light for the *eldil*" (Lewis 2005, 118). This is a modern description compatible with the Classical and Medieval description of the daemon's subtle bodies. It seems very likely that Tolkien and Lewis discussed the nature of elves, eldila and daemons during some of their meetings in the late 1930s or early 1940s. Tom Shippey proposes a similar kind of discussion when he refers to C.S. Lewis's mention of 'albs' (Elves) and 'devas' ('the shining ones' in Sanskrit, the celestial beings of the Hindu tradition) in relation to the possible appearance of eldila on Earth (Shippey 2004, 1-2). Such a discussion might have triggered some of Tolkien's speculations on the 'real' 'daemonic' nature of Fairies as outlined in the drafts of 'Manuscript B' of 'On Fairy-story'. The timeline of these events does not contradict this hypothesis: Tolkien read *Out of the Silent Planet* sometime in 1937-38 (Scull and Hammond 2006, 203), he wrote 'Manuscript B' in the early 1940s, possibly in the first half of 1943 (258).

5 – On Tolkien's En-keladim

But, even if this is the case, and Plato, the Late antiquity and Middle Age Platonists, Robert Kirk, and C.S. Lewis were either direct or indirect sources of inspiration, did Tolkien explore this idea further? Did he ever try to depict non-incarnate 'daemonic' Elves at least once in his stories? He did so, and the context where these creatures appear seem to support the speculation of some influence from C.S. Lewis and *The Space Trilogy*. A short time after his revisions of 'On Fairy-stories', while taking a break from writing *The Lord of the Rings*, the Professor attempted – for a second time, after the abandoned 'The Lost Road' – to write a science-fictional thriller. This novel, called 'The Notion Club Papers', follows the weekly meeting of a group of Oxford scholars that, through lucid dreams and other recollection techniques, recover images and records of places and events far aways in space and time. The second part of the 'Papers', culminates with an account of the Downfall of Númenor, described as the 'real' Atlantis. But our interest lies in the first part, 'The Ramblings of Ramer' (interestingly subtitled 'Out of the Talkative Planet'). Here, Nicholas Ramer, a professor of Finno-Ugric [sic], narrates his lucid dreams about travels to distant – and possibly imaginary – stars and planets. At a certain point, he describes a great waterfall on a planet called Ellor Eshúrizel, and he affirms that creatures called *En-keladim* live there. A few pages later he describes them: "My En-keladim I see in humane forms of surpassing and marvellously varied beauty. But I guess that their true types, if such there be, are invisible, unless they embody themselves by their own will, entering into their own works because of their love for them. That is, they are elvish. But very different from Men's garbled tales of them; for they are not lofty indeed, yet they are not fallen" (*Sauron*, 206). Here we have found our non-incarnate elves, very well matching Tolkien's description in the 'On Fairy-stories' drafts expunged from 'Manuscript B'.

These En-keladim are "not bound to a given body", but make their own or walk unembodied (206-7). According to Ramer, their languages shift and evolve continuously, another striking difference with the Eldar, whose languages are quite conservative, even across the Ages. The role of the En-keladim is the governance of matter on a small scale, focusing on the aesthetic aspects of sub-creation; their relation to their works is one of love. The most noteworthy characteristics of the daemonic faeries from 'Manuscript B' are all present in the brief description of the En-keladim. Both types of creatures are not embodied, but can take shape at will; both have (small) sub-creative powers on matter to enhance its beauty, and their relationship with their creations is one of love, not possession or domination. Tolkien makes various explicit references to *Out of the Silent Planet* in this section of 'The Notion Club Papers', which strengthens the idea that Lewis might have been providing somehow a source of inspiration, or at least a source of engaging discussion, for the idea of non-incarnate fairies. The En-keladim are also discussed in relation to the eldila, and Tolkien seemed to be unsure about their ontological affinities; in a a first draft, Ramer says that the En-keladim are "Eldilic", but, in a later correction, he affirms that they "are of a kind other than Lewis's Eldila (even of lesser rank)" (221). Why did Tolkien feel the need to make this emendation? Possibly because the eldila are more 'angelic' in nature, and act as emissaries of Maleldil (i.e. the Divine Son of God in *The Space Trilogy*).[3] The En-keladim, in the brief descriptions provided, do not manifest any 'divine' association or connotation. And still, their name 'En-keladim' is very reminiscent of the Finnish word for Angel, 'Enkeli'. This could be just a coincidence, but Tolkien was well versed in Finnish and characterised Ramer as a Professor of Finno-Ugric, which could justify a Finnic source[4] for the name of these creatures.

The En-keladim make one more apparition, very brief, in three sketches written before 'The Drowning of Anadûnê', an account of the Downfall of Númenor composed in close association with 'The Notion Club Papers'. At the beginning of the second of the three sketches, Tolkien wrote: "There were 'Enkeladim' once on earth, but that was not their name in this world: it was *Eledâi* (in Númenórean *Eldar*)" (397). In this passage, the Eldar from Tolkien's Secondary World, until that moment conceived as incarnate, were posited as beings of the same kind as the (allegedly non-incarnate) Enkeladim. Was this underlying a major revolution in the metaphysics of Tolkien's Secondary World? Possibly, given that in the first version of 'The Drowning' Tolkien merged Valar (spiritual beings) and Eldar (embodied beings) into a single class of beings, called Balai/Avalai (341-53). Even if he pondered such a radical change, this was never brought to completion. In the subsequent versions of 'The Drowning of Anadûnê, the Enkeladim/Eledâi, now called Nimrî or Nimîr, resemble much more the incarnate Eldar we are familiar with and are again a separate class of beings from the Valar (now called Avalôi or Avalôim), though it is suggested that the former might be their Children or offspring of the latter (358).

'The Notion Club Papers' was never completed, while 'The Drowning of Anadûnê''s metaphysical changes were afterwards discarded. Tolkien's idea of non-incarnate Elvish beings never surfaced again in his writings. Why? Possibly it was just a temporary idea, or maybe he considered daemonic spirits too close to the occult to be a safe subject for stories written by a practicing Catholic like him. A more mundane reason might be that incorporeal beings are not a good subject for stories that must be read by humans made of flesh and blood; the Eldar, who are 'biologically' similar to us, are far more suited

3. It must be noted that the eldila seem to possess a 'subtle' body similar to the one of daemons as described by Calcidius and fairies as described by Kirk. Tolkien somehow stresses that his En-keladim, as well as his "daemonic" fairies from 'Manuscript B' drafts, do not possess a body at all, though they can assume one.

4. *Enkeli* is not a genuine Finnish word, however, but a borrowing probably from Old Swedish *ängil, engil*, which in turn took it from Latin *angelus*.

to the task. However, these minor drafts and passages of Tolkien's work evidence how some ideas were constantly evolving in the Professor's (sub)creative mind, offering to his scholars a slew of fascinating topics to explore.

6 – A final note on the Fays of 'The Book of Lost Tales'

In the 'The Book of Lost Tales', written almost twenty years before the essay 'On Fairy-stories', Tolkien describes a different class of spirits, of smaller stature and power than the Valar, often named 'sprites' or 'fays'. They come in a tripartite host thus mirroring the three hosts of the Eldar, also with respect to their association with three great Valar. In the 'The Book of Lost Tales' there are mentions of (1) the sylphs of the air and the winds devoted to Manwë, (2) the sprites of trees and woods following Aulë and Palurien, and (3) the spirits of the foam and the surf of the ocean, the troops of Falman-Ossë, vassal of Ulmo (*Lost Tales I*, 65-6). Despite the term 'Fay' and 'Fairy' being synonymous in English, Tolkien draws a strong distinction between the two classes of beings in 'The Book of Lost Tales' and in 'The Creatures of the Earth', a hierarchy of the seven categories of beings where Fays are placed just one step below the Valar and above the Fairies (Gilson et al 2003, 9-10). Of Fays, Tolkien writes that they

> must they not be confused with the Eldar, for they were born before the world and are older than its oldest, and are not of it, but laugh at it much, for had they not somewhat to do with its making, so that it is for the most part a play for them; but the Eldar are of the world and love it with a great and burning love, and are wistful in all their happiness for that reason (*Lost Tales I*, 66).

They do not seem to either possess (sub)creative powers or to have a relationship of love towards their creations or the created world. For this reason, I do not consider them as a good candidate for Tolkien's daemonic faeries as postulated in 'Manuscript B' despite that both classes of beings are not incarnate, but purely made of spirit. In later stages of the legendarium, sylphs and Fays were reframed within the class of beings named Maiar, beings of the same order as the Valar but of lesser rank. Even though the Mariar appear loftier and more serious than the playful Fays of the 'The Book of Lost Tales', in the later stages of the legendarium Tolkien still wrote:

> Many lesser spirits of their own kind they [i.e. the Valar] brought in their train, both great and small; and some of these Men have confused with the Elves, but wrongfully [*read* wrongly] for they were made before the World, whereas Elves and Men awoke first on Earth, after the coming of the Valar (*Morgoth*, 144).

In conclusion, in Tolkien's Secondary World, with the only exception of 'The Notion Club Papers' and 'The Drowning of Anadûnê', the association of Elves and non-incarnate spirits seems only to arise as a consequence of confusion and wrong beliefs in the mythological tradition of Men.

Bibliography

Calcidius, *On Plato's Timaeus*, trans. by J. Magee, (Cambridge: Harvard University Press, 2016).

Chaucer, G., 'The House of Fame: Book 2', *Genius*, 27 August 2009, <https://genius.com/Geoffrey-chaucer-the- house-of-fame-book-2-annotated>
De Rosario Martinez, H., 'Fairy and Elves in Tolkien and Traditional Literature.' *Mythlore*, 3.109/110, (2010) 65-84.

Fimi, D., *Tolkien, Race and Cultural History: From Fairies to Hobbits*, (London: Palgrave Macmillan, 2010).

Flieger, V., *There Would Always Be a Fairy Tale*, (Kent: Kent State University Press, 2017).

Gilson, C., C.F. Hostetter, P. Wynne, and A. Smith, eds. *Parma Eldalamberon*, 11 (1995).
— eds. *Parma Eldalamberon*, 12 (1998).

Gilson, C., C.F. Hostetter, P. Wynne, B. Welden, and A. Smith, eds. *Parma Eldalamberon*, 14 (2003).

Green, R.F., *Elf Queens and Holy Friars: Fairy Beliefs and the Medieval Church*, (Philadelphia: University of Pennsylvania Press, 2016).

Grimm, J., *Fairy Legends and Traditions of the South of Ireland: Volume III*, ed. and trans. by Croker, T.C., (London: Thomas Davison, Whitefriars, 1838).
— *Teutonic Mythology*, trans. by J.S. Stallybrass, (London: George Bell & Sons, 1883).

Hall, A., *Elves in Anglo-Saxon England: Matters of Belief, Health, Gender, and Identity*, Anglo-Saxon Studies Series, viii (Woodbridge: Boydell, 2007).

Kirk, R., *The Secret Commonwealth of Elves, Fauns and Fairies*, ed. by W. Scott. (London: David Nutt, 1893).

Lewis, C.S., *Out of the Silent Planet*, (London: HarperCollins, 2005).
— *The Discarded Image: An Introduction to Medieval and Renaissance Literature*, (Cambridge: Cambridge University Press, 1964).

Russell, J., 'Spenser's Sprites: Platonic Daemons in *The Faerie Queene*', *Renaissance and Reformation*, 43.1 (2020), 105-134.

Scull, C. and W.G. Hammond, *The J.R.R. Tolkien Companion and Guide: Chronology*, (London: HarperCollins, 2006).

Shakespeare, W., *The Tempest*, ed. by F. Kermode (London: Methuen, 1975).

Shippey, T.A., 'Light-elves, Dark-elves, and Others: Tolkien's Elvish Problem', *Tolkien Studies*, 1.1 (2004), 1-15
– 'Alias Oves Habeo: The Elves as a Category Problem', *The Shadow-Walkers: Jacob Grimm's Mythology of the Monstrous*, (Turnhout: Brepols Publishers, 2005).
Sick, D.H., 'The Daimones of C. S. Lewis', *Literature and Theology*, 22.2 (2008), 151–161 <https://doi.org/ 10.1093/litthe/frm051>

Stafford, J., *The Register of John Stafford, Bishop of Bath and Wells 1425-1443*, ed. by T.S. Holmes, Somerset Record Society, xxxi, (London: Harrison and Sons, 1915). <https://archive.org/details/somersetpub32someuoft/mode/2up>

Timotin, A., *La Démonologie Platonicienne: Histoire de la Notion de Daimōn de Platon aux Derniers Néoplatoniciens*, Philosophia Antiqua Series, cxxviii (Leiden: Brill, 2012).

Tolkien, J.R.R., *The Letters of J.R.R. Tolkien*, ed. by H. Carpenter with the assistance of C. Tolkien (London: George Allen & Unwin, 1981).
— *The Book of Lost Tales Part I*, ed. by C. Tolkien (London: George Allen & Unwin, 1983).
— *The Shaping of Middle-earth*, ed. by C. Tolkien (London: George Allen & Unwin, 1986).
— *Sauron Defeated*, ed. by C. Tolkien. (London: HarperCollins, 1992).
— *Morgoth's Ring*, ed. by C. Tolkien (London: HarperCollins, 1993).
— *Smith of Wootton Major*, ed. V. Flieger. (London: HarperCollins, 2005).
— *Tolkien On Fairy-stories*, ed. by V. Flieger and D.A. Anderson (London: HarperCollins, 2008).

"I Met a Lot of Things on the Way That Astonished Me": Natural Growth in Writing *The Lord of the Rings*

Christina Scull

In response to pressure from his publisher George Allen & Unwin, J.R.R. Tolkien embarked in December 1937 on a sequel to *The Hobbit* without much idea of how the story might or should proceed, and was as surprised at some of its unexpected turns as his future readers would come to be. He was not a methodical author who would or could write a synopsis for himself or his publisher and then stick to it, nor one able to apply himself to producing a regular amount of text per day, or per year. But then, writing was not his main line of work. He was primarily an Oxford professor, with many demands on his time during term, and sometimes even out of term. He did much of his writing during vacations. But when he was fully absorbed and time allowed, he could write quite quickly – he wrote the first versions of the four chapters of *The Lord of the Rings* from 'The Old Forest' to 'At the Sign of the Prancing Pony' in only a few days at the end of August 1938, and by the end of Michaelmas Term that year had reached Rivendell in 'Many Meetings', and had revised and expanded the existing text and rewritten the whole, filling 300 pages in careful manuscript.

He did foresee a few basic facts quite early: that Frodo would not be able to destroy the Ring, that Gollum would somehow intervene, and that the hobbits would find trouble in the Shire on their return. But often Tolkien had a clear picture only a chapter or so ahead, and sometimes not even that. New ideas and developments arose as he wrote. His work took on a life of its own and expanded in length and scope beyond all expectations. Sometimes new characters appeared, seemingly of their own accord, some fully formed, others only gradually taking on their final form, and the story, already written or planned, would have to be adjusted to assimilate them, though this was not always done immediately. On other occasions Tolkien would introduce a puzzle or a problem without already knowing the answer.

In a letter to W.H. Auden, written on 7 June 1955, Tolkien described writing *The Lord of the Rings*:

> I met a lot of things on the way that astonished me. Tom Bombadil I knew already; but I had never been to Bree. Strider sitting in the corner at the inn was a shock, and I had no more idea who he was than had Frodo. The Mines of Moria had been a mere name; and of Lothlórien no word had reached my mortal ears till I came there. [...] Most disquieting of all, Saruman had never been revealed to me, and I was as mystified as Frodo at Gandalf's failure to appear on September 22. (*Letters*, Letter 163, 216–7)

Christopher Tolkien's minutely detailed account in *The Return of the Shadow*, *The Treason of Isengard*, *The War of the Ring*, and relevant sections of *Sauron Defeated* and *The Peoples of Middle-earth* provides readers, scholars, and critics with a wealth of information about his father's processes of creation. Using these volumes, I will be discussing a few of the changes Tolkien made during the writing of *The Lord of the Rings*, not just for the changes themselves, but to consider how they affected the later narrative and also enriched the story as a whole.

In the first phase of writing, begun in December 1937, there were four accounts of the 'Long-expected Party' before Bingo Bolger-Baggins set out on a journey east with two young cousins as his companions. Tolkien later dropped the 'Bolger', and fortunately replaced 'Bingo' with 'Frodo' – *The Lord of the Rings* was first published in the 1950s, just as bingo, a form of social gambling, was becoming popular. Tolkien had hesitated as to whether the party was given by Bilbo (first and second versions) or, many years after Bilbo had quietly departed from the Shire, by his son Bingo (third version) or his adopted nephew Bingo Bolger-Baggins (fourth version). In each case, the giver of the party made a speech and, using the Ring, vanished before quietly leaving Bag End.

The chapter with Bingo's departure from Bag End in the company of two hobbits followed immediately on the Party. Tolkien wrote to Allen & Unwin on the seventeenth of February 1938 that he had done nothing beyond the first chapter, and had only vague ideas of how to continue. But on the fourth of March he told his publisher that now he had reached the end of the third chapter, the story had gotten out of hand and "taken an unpremeditated turn" (*Letters*, Letter 26, 34). In a draft, apparently written between these two letters, the story did indeed take such a turn. In the first version of 'Three Is Company', as Bingo and his companions walk east through the Shire they hear the sound of hoofs and hide.

> Round a turn came a white horse, and on it sat a bundle — or that is what it looked like: a small man wrapped entirely in a great cloak and hood so that only his eyes peered out, and his boots in the stirrups below.
> The horse stopped when it came level with Bingo. The figure uncovered its nose and sniffed; and then sat silent as if listening. Suddenly a laugh came from inside the hood.
> 'Bingo my boy!' said Gandalf, throwing aside his wrappings. 'You and your lads are somewhere about. Come along now and show up, I want a word with you!' (*Shadow*, 47–8)

Tolkien amended the draft, and in the following typescript replaced Gandalf with a Black Rider who seems to be sniffing to get the hobbits' scent. Notes suggest that Tolkien was considering a series of separate adventures for Bingo and his companions on the lines of those Bilbo experienced in *The Hobbit*, but from this point, except when in refuges such as Rivendell or Lothlórien, the hobbits were in constant fear of the Black Riders. The story became darker, more adult, closer to a thriller like John Buchan's *The Thirty-Nine Steps* than the children's book Tolkien had written about Bilbo. It would be some time before the hobbits learned exactly who the Black Riders were, and why they were pursuing them. Although Bilbo and the dwarves encountered many dangers in *The Hobbit*, the only time they were pursued, only briefly, was after they escaped from the goblins' caves.

In *The Hobbit* Gandalf accompanies Bilbo and company from Bag End as far as the western edge of Mirkwood, and his departure there is to encourage others, especially Bilbo, to take a more active role in their quest. Indeed, it is only in the absence of Gandalf that Bilbo becomes, as Tolkien in the voice of the narrator comments, "the real leader in their adventure. He had begun to have ideas and plans of his own" (*Hobbit*, 'Inside Information', 203). It seems that an early idea for the *Hobbit* sequel was that Gandalf should join the hobbits unexpectedly near the start of the journey, and probably accompany them for at least part of the way, but he had hardly appeared before Tolkien decided to leave the hobbits to manage alone from the beginning, but without forming any idea of what Gandalf might be doing in the meantime. In his 'Introductory Note' to *Tree and Leaf* (1964) Tolkien commented that during 1938–1939, as *The Lord of the Rings* was beginning to grow, he had brought the hobbits to Bree without yet having found a solution for Gandalf's absence, and he had no idea who Strider (or rather, Trotter) was (at this point Trotter was a hobbit wearing wooden shoes). In the next section I will be concentrating on the evolution of Tolkien's successive ideas of Gandalf's actions during the time period covered by Book One of *The Lord of the Rings*, and what (if anything) was to be revealed contemporaneously in the narrative to the other characters and to the reader.

In the first phase of writing Gandalf provided fireworks at the Party and, as noted above, appeared only briefly before being transformed into a Black Rider. On the evening of the same day as the latter event, Bingo told the elf, Gildor, that Gandalf had told him nothing about the Riders but *had* advised him not to delay his departure later than autumn; and that Gandalf had come to help with the Party, and as soon as the fireworks were over left with the dwarves and the elves from Rivendell. Gandalf and his companions were later seen by Marmaduke Brandybuck in Buckland, and by Trotter near Bree. Gandalf, however, knew that Bingo would be following behind, and left a letter for him at the Prancing Pony: "Have learned some news on the way. Pursuit is getting close. [...] Try and catch me up"; and he promised to wait at Weathertop for a while (*Shadow*, 154). There, he left another message that he had waited three days and then left to seek help in Rivendell.

There is no mystery concerning Gandalf's whereabouts. He was not expected to join Bingo and was known to be well ahead. When Bingo reaches Rivendell, Gandalf comments that he was "delighted to have you all here safe. I am really rather to blame. I knew there were some risks – but if I had known more before I left the Shire I should have arranged matters differently" (210). It is clear that the story was evolving, and earlier writing would have to be revised and a suitable background invented (or discovered) to explain the actions of the Black Riders.

In the second phase of composition, in early autumn 1938, there is a gap of many years between the 'Long-expected Party' given by Bilbo, and Gandalf's revelation of the history of the Ring to Bingo. Gandalf leaves Bag End while Bingo makes his plans to leave, but tells him not to leave before he returns. He may have some useful information about the Road, and may want to accompany the hobbit. When he fails to turn up, Bingo and his friends set out without him. This phase extends only as far as the first night with Tom Bombadil, but introduces a new idea: Odo Bolger stayed behind in Bingo's new house at Crickhollow to give a message to Gandalf, if and when he turned up.

As the hobbits sleep in Bombadil's house, a man wrapped in a grey cloak comes quietly and hastily up the path at Crickhollow, knocks softly, waits, passes by the windows and disappears around the corner of the house. After some time, hoofs can be heard coming swiftly down the lane and stopping at the gate. Three hooded figures robed in black enter, bending low over the ground, and place themselves at the door and the corners of the house and stand silent for a while. Suddenly, a blade gleaming with a chill light is drawn, two blows are aimed at the door, and a voice orders it to open to the servants of the Lord. As the door falls back, a horn rings out behind the house. The grey man comes round the corner of the house, no longer hidden under cloak and hat and holding a horn and wand. There are sounds of alarm and fell cries, and along the northward road "there galloped a white horse. On it sat an old man with long silver hair and flowing beard. His horn sounded over hill and dale. In his hand his wand flared and flickered like a sheaf of lightning. [*Added*: Behind clung a small figure with flying cloak. Odo.] Gandalf was riding to the North Gate with the speed of thunder" (303–4). Here the second phase petered out.

Tolkien developed this idea further in the third phase, in which Frodo Baggins replaces Bingo. As Gandalf explains to Frodo in Rivendell: "I was caught in Fangorn and spent many weary days as a prisoner of the Giant Treebeard. It was a desperately anxious time, for I was hurrying back to the Shire to help you. I had just learned that the horsemen had been sent out" (363). He arrived at Crickhollow in time to save Odo from the Black Riders and rode with him towards Bree. A little east from Bree, he met Trotter, to whom he gave a letter for Frodo, telling him to trust Trotter, who would lead Frodo to a place where Gandalf would wait. Gandalf and Odo stayed a night at the Prancing Pony, where Gandalf told Butterbur that if anyone asked for "Baggins" he should say that Baggins had ridden east with Gandalf – a ruse, using Odo to distract the Black Riders. At Weathertop the company, led by Trotter, found a message from Gandalf: "Wednesday Oct. 5. Bad news. We arrived late Monday. Odo vanished last night. I must go at once to Rivendell. Make for Ford beyond Trollshaw with all speed" (355). Later Glorfindel confirms that Gandalf arrived at Rivendell with a hobbit. Sadly, Tolkien never wrote an account of what happened to Odo, nor of Gandalf's escape from Giant Treebeard.

Nothing is said of Gandalf's adventures or imprisonment in the first version of 'The Council of Elrond', nor in the first account of the journey south as far as Balin's tomb written towards the end of 1939, and while Odo was included in the first list of those to accompany Frodo south, he was not among those who set out. At that point, the progress of the story came to a halt, probably for a year. But at the same time as he was writing this first version of the beginning of Book Two, Tolkien was, as Christopher Tolkien notes at the beginning of *The Treason of Isengard*, "also engaged in substantial further revision [...] arising primarily from a changed story of Gandalf's movements, and an explanation of his delay" (5). He tried the idea that the plan to leave was entirely Frodo's, as a result of Gandalf's long absence. But in notes headed "New Plot, Autumn 1939" Gandalf knew of Frodo's planned departure on the twenty-second of September, and intended to return, but was pursued by Black Riders:

> Gandalf has insufficient magic to cope with Black Riders unaided, whose king is a wizard. They pursue him over Sarn Ford and he cannot (or dare not) go back to Shire.
> Eventually he is besieged in the *Western Tower*. He cannot get away while they guard it with five Riders. But when Black Riders have located Frodo and found that he has gone off without Gandalf they ride away. Three are ahead. Three follow Frodo, but miss him and get ahead at Bree. Three come behind. Gandalf follows after. (9)

Tolkien worked out various chronologies to align the movements of Gandalf and the Black Riders with the established account of Frodo's journey to Rivendell.

Apparently in late 1939 Tolkien began on the fourth phase of writing *The Lord of the Rings*, taking up these new ideas, but writing anew only when emendation and cannibalization of earlier manuscripts was not possible. In this phase Gandalf, fearing that he might not be able to get to Bag End, left a letter with Butterbur dated variously 30 August or 12 September, to be given to Frodo should he pass through Bree: "I am starting back tomorrow, & should reach you in a day or two. But things have become very dangerous, and I may not get through in time. (He has found the Shire: the borders are watched, and so am I.) If I fail to come, I hope that will be sufficient warning to you, & you will have sense to leave Shire at once" (49). Tolkien decided that Frodo should dream of Gandalf's escape: he saw Black Riders watching a tower surrounded by a wall, and when they left, summoned away by their leader, he saw a grey-mantled figure on a white horse leaping the wall towards him.

After some hesitation, Tolkien placed Frodo's dream during the night at Crickhollow. He wrote a new version of the Riders' attack on Crickhollow, now taking place during the night the hobbits slept at Bree. Gandalf arrived at Crickhollow and was admitted by Hamilcar (Ham) Bolger who had remained behind, replacing Odo (and to be succeeded by Fredegar, or Fatty, in the published text). Gandalf and Ham escape on a white horse (as in the earlier version) just as the Black Riders break open the door. This was rejected in favour of a version in which Gandalf arrives just as the Riders speed away with Ham as a captive, with Gandalf following in pursuit. Both the Riders and Gandalf think that Ham is Frodo.

At Rivendell, in a text written after the fourth phase, on the fifth of August 1940 or later, Gandalf tells Frodo that he rescued Ham ten miles beyond the Brandywine Bridge. Ham comments that Gandalf "bowled the Rider that was carrying me clean over", but "did not know whether he was relieved or disgusted" when he found it was Ham he had rescued and not Frodo (68–9). When Gandalf hears from Ham that Frodo has gone into the Old Forest, they visit Tom Bombadil before continuing west, staying a night at the Prancing Pony after the hobbits and Trotter have left. Gandalf reports:

> We found two Riders already watching Weathertop. [...] Others soon gathered round, returning from the pursuit further east along the Road. Ham and I passed a very bad night besieged on the top of Weathertop. [...] In the morning we slipped away northwards into the wilds [...] but not too secretly — I wanted to draw them off. But the Chief Rider was too cunning: only four came after us, and only two pursued us far. [...] Still, that is why they did not immediately hunt for you in the wilderness, or observe your arrival at Weathertop; and why they were not in full force for the attack on you. (69–70)

In the fourth phase, the hobbits and Trotter discover on Weathertop, as in the published text, some scratches on a stone. Trotter interprets these as indicating Gandalf's presence there on certain dates. The two stories fit quite well, but Tolkien was not yet finished. On a sheet headed "*New Plot*, Aug. 26–27, 1940" a new and very significant character makes an appearance:

> The wizard Saramond the White [...] or Grey Saruman sends out a message that there is important news: Trotter hears that Black Riders are out and moving towards the Shire [...] He sends word to Gandalf, who leaves Hobbiton at the end of June. [...]
> Gandalf knows that 9 Black Riders (and especially their king) are too much for him alone. He wants the help of Saramund. So he goes to him where he lived on the borders of Rohan at Angrobel (or Irongarth).
> Saramund betrays him — having gone over to Sauron: (either) he tells Gandalf false news of the Black Riders, and they pursue him to the top of a mountain; there he is left standing alone with a guard (wolves, orcs, etc. all about) while they ride off with mocking laugh; (or else) he is handed over to a giant Fangorn (Treebeard) who imprisons him? (70–1)

The plot follows the Riders north to the Shire and then east, kidnapping Ham on the way. Gandalf escapes (no account given) and reaches Bag End and then Bree after Frodo has left, continues east, and rescues Ham. Gandalf and Ham ride to Weathertop and then north, drawing some of the Riders away from the Road.

Tolkien saw in this various weak points, especially Gandalf's failure to send an urgent message to Frodo. He also abandoned the capture of Ham, realizing that the Black Riders would probably kill him, and removed most traces of this story and of Gandalf's various rescues. All that survives in the text is that when Fatty sees the dark shapes creeping into the front garden, he runs out of the back door in terror and raises the alarm. When the black figures find the house empty they flee, one of them dropping on the step a cloak belonging to Frodo. Tolkien also thought that it would spoil the surprise to show Gandalf's actions in parallel with those of Frodo and company, and postponed explanations to the Council of Elrond. Only at the Council do Frodo, and the reader, learn that when Gandalf arrived a little later and found the cloak, he thought that Frodo had been taken prisoner, and his fears were relieved only by the news he received at Bree from Butterbur – that Frodo had spent the previous night there, and left that morning with Strider.

In the published text, Gandalf advises Frodo to leave the Shire with some companions and make for Rivendell. He comments that, although the Road was less easy than it had once been, the journey should not be too dangerous for Frodo. At the end of June, Gandalf hears some news that he finds concerning and tells Frodo: "If I think it necessary after all for you to get off at once, I shall come back immediately, or at least send word" (*FR*, 'Three is Company', 67); and as he leaves, he says that he will be back in time for the farewell party at the latest, as he thinks that Frodo might need his company on the road. Gandalf in person does not enter the published narrative again until Frodo recovers consciousness in Rivendell, and not until 'The Council of Elrond' does Frodo or the reader hear a full explanation of what detained Gandalf and his subsequent actions. On September the twenty-second, the day of the farewell party, Frodo lingers till the last possible moment before leaving. He is already worried about Gandalf when the Black Rider adds to his fears.

Tolkien continued to build up suspense. At Woody End, Gildor comments: "That Gandalf should be late, does not bode well" (84). In Bree, the letter from Gandalf to Frodo written on Midyear's Day and which Butterbur fails to send, urges Frodo to leave by the end of July at the latest; when Frodo asks Strider if he thinks Black Riders had anything to do with Gandalf's absence, Strider replies that he does not know what could have hindered him, save the enemy himself. While revising 'The Council of Elrond', Tolkien's first idea for Gandalf's escape was that Elrond, hearing that Gandalf was missing, sent eagles to look for him. It was not until the fifth version of the chapter that Gandalf told his story: when he left Hobbiton to seek news, he had no definite knowledge of the Riders, and was lured to Isengard by a message from Saruman, conveyed by the unsuspecting Radagast. When he refused to submit to Saruman, he was imprisoned on the pinnacle of Orthanc in Isengard, and was rescued by the eagle sent by Radagast with news gathered at Gandalf's request. In the published text, Tolkien allows Frodo to dream of Gandalf's escape during the first night with Bombadil, but Frodo recognizes its meaning only when he hears Gandalf's story in Rivendell.

Christopher Tolkien's account of the development of *The Lord of the Rings* in *The History of Middle-earth* confirms his father's memory that he himself did not know why Gandalf had failed to come to Frodo's farewell party as promised. Tolkien did not reach the final answer to this question for some time. As the story proceeded, he tried out various explanations, and eventually deliberately removed any contemporaneous accounts of Gandalf's actions to enhance tension in the primary thread. His ultimate solution immediately expanded the scope of the story and the landscape in which it is set, opening a second "front", with the treachery of Saruman predominant in Book Three, beginning with the kidnapping of Merry and Pippin by orcs from Isengard and their encounter with Treebeard, followed by the chase of the Three Hunters and their unexpected meeting with Gandalf, the march of Treebeard and the Ents and their attack on Isengard, Gandalf's overthrow of Saruman's agent in Edoras and his healing of Théoden, the battle at Helm's Deep, and the dramatic parley on the steps of Orthanc with the defeated Saruman.

The final composition of the Company of the Ring to go with Frodo was not achieved immediately. All of its members play a significant part in the story, but two contribute in a rather unexpected way. In a note written before the first version of 'The Council of Elrond', Tolkien stated that the Company should consist of six hobbits (including Trotter, the precursor of Strider), Gandalf, an elf, Glorfindel, and a dwarf, Frâr (changed to Burin), son of Balin. The seed of the later inclusion of Gimli and Legolas was present here. In the earliest versions of 'The Council of Elrond', written in Autumn 1939, those present included two dwarves – Glóin from *The Hobbit* and Burin, later replaced by Glóin's son Gimli – and an elf, Galdor, a messenger from the king of the Wood-elves in Mirkwood. Although Glorfindel, an elf of Rivendell, was among those chosen for the Company in the earliest version of the 'Council', in the first version of 'The Ring Goes South', which reached only as far as Balin's tomb, the Company consisted of five hobbits plus Boromir and Gandalf.

In the following version of the 'Council', Elrond says that the Company should represent the free folk of the world, and chooses Galdor for the Elves and Gimli for the Dwarves. In the third version, when Galdor reports Gollum's escape, made possible because the Elves treated him with too much kindness, Glóin reacts with the comment that the Elves were less tender with him when he was their prisoner. Not until the second version of 'The Ring Goes South' was Galdor renamed Legolas. On several occasions in the published work, on the journey south and through Moria and as they approach Lothlórien, Legolas and Gimli display awareness of the ancient antagonism between their peoples, each declaring that it was not the fault of *his* people that friendship between the two races waned.

The Company is received graciously at Caras Galadhon by Celeborn and Galadriel. But the former, on hearing that the Dwarves had again stirred up evil in Moria, regrets that he allowed the company to enter Lórien. Galadriel intervenes: she smiles at the glowering Gimli and praises the beauty of the former Dwarf kingdom, and he,

> hearing the names given in his own ancient tongue, looked up and met her eyes; and it seemed to him that he looked suddenly into the heart of an enemy and saw there love and understanding. Wonder came into his face, and then he smiled in answer.
>
> He rose clumsily and bowed in dwarf-fashion, saying: "Yet more fair is the living land of Lórien, and the Lady Galadriel is above all the jewels that lie beneath the earth!" (*FR*, 'Farewell to Lórien', 356)

From that moment, Gimli becomes her champion, challenging Éomer when he speaks disparagingly of her, treasuring her gift of three golden hairs, hoping that if he ever returns home to treat the gift as an heirloom, "a pledge of good will between the Mountain and the Wood until the end of days" (376); and from that time, he and Legolas are firm friends despite the history of hostility between their races. This is perhaps the prime example of one of the themes running through *The Lord of the Rings*: abandoning preconceived opinions and learning to appreciate other points of view.

The inclusion of Legolas and Gimli also provides Tolkien's readers with their closest contact with a representative of each race. Yes, there were thirteen dwarves in *The Hobbit*, but mainly seen en masse and sometimes treated as figures of fun. Gimli is a brave fighter and a loyal companion. In his description of the beauty of the Caves of Helm's Deep, he waxes lyrical and contradicts a common picture of Dwarves as mainly seekers of treasure: "No dwarf could be unmoved by such loveliness. None of Durin's race would mine those caves for stones or ore, not if diamonds and gold could be got there" (*TT*, 'The Road to Isengard', 548). Because of their friendship, Legolas agrees to visit the Glittering Caves with Gimli, and Gimli agrees to explore Fangorn Forest with Legolas. When eventually Legolas leaves Middle-earth, Gimli sails West with him.

Elves *are* in the forefront of action in *The Silmarillion*, but there they are larger than life and painted with broad strokes. We learn quite a lot about the Elves from the example of Legolas: he can run on snow; he can see great distances; he is a superb bowman; he needs little sleep or rest; he rides without saddle or reins. Of particular interest is his explanation of how the Elves, immortal within Arda, experience time: "For the Elves the world moves, and it moves both very swift and very slow. Swift, because they themselves change little, and all else fleets by: it is a grief to them. Slow, because they need not count the running years, not for themselves. The passing seasons are but ripples ever repeated in the long long stream" (*FR*, 'The Great River', 388).

But what about Galadriel and Lothlórien? Earlier I quoted Tolkien, writing in 1955, that he had had no thought of Lothlórien until he came there. In the second version of 'The Ring Goes South' Gandalf does say that their journey will lead them down the river Morthond (an earlier name of the Silverlode) and into the woods of Lothlórien; this is apparently where Lothlórien first appears, but possibly it was just a name Tolkien invented when he felt that one was needed (though its Sindarin form suggests at least some connection with Elves). Otherwise, there is nothing to indicate that either Tolkien or the Company had any idea of what lay before them on the other side of the mountains beyond going down the river variously called Redway, Blackroot, Morthond, or Silverlode, to reach the Great River.

Even the 'Sketch of the Plot', written just before Tolkien embarked on the first Lothlórien chapter, gives no hint of the Golden Wood or of Celeborn and Galadriel, only:

> Reach Lothlórien Dec. 15. Take refuge up Trees. Elves befriend them. Dec 15, 16, 17 they journey to Angle between Anduin and Blackroot. There they remain long. (While they are up trees orcs go by — also Gollum.)
> At Angle they debate what is to be done. (*Treason*, 207)

And it is at the Angle that Boromir tries to take the Ring from Frodo. In the event, Tolkien devoted three chapters to the Company's visit to the Golden Wood: 'Lothlórien', 'The Mirror of Galadriel', and 'Farewell to Lórien'. But a synopsis he wrote before he began the chapter 'Lothlorien' included a precursor of Legolas's description of the woods, close to the published text. Lothlórien is one of the most memorable of all the landscapes Tolkien created, a believable and desirable Eden, its beauty all the more poignant because it will soon cease to exist. Tolkien's use of the phrase "mortal ears" in his letter to W.H. Auden suggests that he too felt he had created something rare and extraordinary.

'The Mirror of Galadriel' needed much development to reach its final form. Galadriel's comment in the published text that "the Lord of the Galadhrim is accounted the wisest of the Elves of Middle-earth, and a giver of gifts beyond the power of kings" has puzzled some readers, in light of Celeborn's previously mentioned impulsive reaction against Dwarves, compared with Galadriel's diplomatic intervention to pacify Gimli (*FR*, 'The Mirror of Galadriel', 357). And although Celeborn does give them good advice for their onward journey, it is *she* who mind-reads the members of the Company, who summoned the White Council, who has the visionary Mirror, and who wears one of the Elven Rings, and although she gives her parting gifts ostensibly from herself and Celeborn together, those given to Frodo, Sam, and Gimli are clearly from Galadriel personally.

It did not start out like that. In the first draft of the chapter, Celeborn thought that the Balrog had been sent by Sauron, so there was no offence, and no need for an intervention by Galadriel. Also, Galadriel says there that "the lord *and lady* of Lothlórien are accounted wise beyond the measure of the Elves of Middle-earth" (*Treason*, 248; emphasis mine). In the draft, the meeting ends with Celeborn giving the Company advice for their journey, which they intend to continue immediately.

Almost at once, Tolkien changed his mind, deciding that the Company should stay a while in Lothlórien. A synopsis suggests that they would remain fifteen days in Caras Galadon, and King Galdaron would show Frodo his silver mirror filled with water which shows the past, the present, and the future, though it is not easy to determine which one sees. About this, Christopher Tolkien comments: "It is seen that it was while my father was writing the 'Lothlórien' story *ab initio* that the Lady of Lothlórien emerged [...] and it is also to be seen that the figure of Galadriel [...] as a great power in Middle-earth was deepened and extended as he wrote" (250). And, of course, this deepening would continue even after the completion of *The Lord of the Rings*, and was ended only by Tolkien's death. In the draft of the latter part of the chapter, it is Galadriel who has the Mirror; and as first written, when Frodo offers her the One Ring, she rejects it immediately, because it is evil. Then the fair copy introduces her temptation and rejection, accepting that she must diminish and Lórien fade.

Galadriel's gift-giving in the drafts of 'Farewell to Lórien' is in great part close to the published text – significantly, for some of her gifts will play important parts later, most notably the phial with the light of Eärendil's star, which aids Frodo and Sam in Shelob's lair and in Cirith Ungol, and the box of earth with which Sam will restore the devastated Shire. Even more personal are the strands of hair she gives to Gimli at his request.

While writing in spring 1944 of Frodo and Sam's journey east of the River Anduin to Cirith Ungol, Tolkien reported on his progress regularly in letters written to his son Christopher, then in South Africa. Christopher was later able to use information in these letters to supplement his father's manuscripts when tracing the history of Book Four of *The Lord of the Rings*. On the sixth of May 1944, Tolkien wrote to his son: "A new character has come on the scene (I am sure I did not invent him, I did not even want him, though I like him, but there he came walking into the woods of Ithilien): Faramir, the brother of Boromir – and he is holding up the 'catastrophe' by a lot of stuff about the history of Gondor and Rohan (with some very sound reflections no doubt about martial glory and true glory)" (*Letters*, Letter 66, 79).

The manuscripts do indeed show that Tolkien had not planned that Frodo, Sam, and Gollum encounter anyone on their way south to the Cross-roads, and in the earliest drafts the leader of the Ithilien Rangers was Falborn son of Anborn, a kinsman of Boromir. After the battle, as he questions Frodo about Boromir, Falborn describes his vision of the boat bearing his brother Boromir's body down the river Anduin. In the next draft, "Falborn" gave way to "Faramir". Christopher Tolkien comments: "It is as if he slipped without conscious decision into the rôle that had been preparing for him" (*War*, 147). The encounter in Ithilien added more than two chapters to the story. Notable moments include Sam's poignant feeling of empathy with the slain Southron, the description of the waterfall of Henneth Annûn at sunset, Frodo forced to betray Gollum to save Gollum's life at the Forbidden Pool, and the last ray of the sun on the floral crown on the fallen head of the statue at the cross-roads.

Faramir provides an interesting contrast with his brother and his father. He resists the lure of the Ring, he uses his judgement to choose the right course rather than blindly obey orders, he is a brave leader who wins the hearts of his men and fights only to protect his city, not for personal glory, and he willingly relinquishes power to the rightful king; he is a man who values the arts of peace and is interested in tradition and lore. He played a major part in the rest of the story, in the councils and defence of Minas Tirith and, most significantly, the strategy adopted in the Last Debate depends on his knowledge of Frodo's chosen route.

That Tolkien, while writing Book Three, briefly envisioned Aragorn marrying Éowyn is shown first by Galadriel's message to Aragorn delivered by Gandalf, and by a note written at this time, that Aragorn would wed Éowyn. But in a later, undated note Tolkien pondered whether Aragorn might be too old and lordly, and considered whether Éowyn might be the twin sister of Éomer's father and an Amazon woman. She might die avenging or saving Théoden. This would mean that the message given to Aragorn from Galadriel would need to be altered. But then perhaps Aragorn *did* love Éowyn, and remained unmarried after her death.

Some two years after Tolkien wrote these notes, Faramir walked into the story as described above, and eventually provided a new idea and an important role for Éowyn when Tolkien came to write the account of the ride of the Rohirrim and the Battle of the Pelennor Fields. Éowyn would seek Aragorn's love, but he would gently reject her. In response, she would disguise herself and seek death in battle. She would indeed avenge Théoden's death, when with the aid of Merry Brandybuck she destroys the chief of the Nazgûl. This leads to the chapter in which Aragorn heals the physical wounds of Faramir, Éowyn, and Merry, and subsequently Faramir is able to heal Éowyn's mind with his gentle courtship in the Houses of Healing.

When did the idea of Arwen as a more fitting bride for Aragorn first come to Tolkien? She entered the written text only when Tolkien returned to Book Five in summer 1946, and Halbarad the Ranger brought Aragorn Arwen's message and the standard she had made for him. She was later back-written into the earlier text. Was this decision in any way influenced by the emergence of Faramir? In retrospect, the conditions imposed by Elrond on marriage with Arwen give an added dimension to Aragorn's character and the choices he had to make, and led Tolkien to extend the victory celebrations after Sauron's defeat to include a wedding and, ultimately, to the bittersweet 'Tale of Aragorn and Arwen' in the *The Lord of the Rings* Appendices.

I will conclude briefly with the most startling of the transformations: Trotter the hobbit ranger – wearing wooden shoes because he had been tortured by Sauron, and who might actually be a young relative of Bilbo, Peregrin Boffin, who had run away seeking adventure – was transformed at last into a Man, Aragorn son of Arathorn, the rightful King of Arnor and Gondor by descent from Elendil, who had established the Realms in Exile after the destruction of Númenor at the end of the Second Age. Aragorn's coronation as King Elessar and his marriage to Arwen, daughter of Elrond, his cousin many times removed, provide climactic points in the story. And yet it was not until the hobbits reached Bree on their return journey that "Trotter" would give way to the more impressive nickname "Strider". Further, the transformation of Trotter into Elessar Telcontar with strong links to the First and Second Ages (not just a few reused names) transformed *The Lord of the Rings* into a sequel to '*The Silmarillion*', dragging *The Hobbit* along with it.

Bibliography

Tolkien, J.R.R., *The Letters of J.R.R. Tolkien*, ed. by H. Carpenter with the assistance of C. Tolkien (London: George Allen & Unwin, 1981).

— *The Return of the Shadow*, ed. by C. Tolkien (London: Unwin Hyman, 1988).

— *Tree and Leaf*, (London: Unwin Hyman, 1988).

— *The Treason of Isengard*, ed. by C. Tolkien (London: Unwin Hyman, 1989).

— *The War of the Ring*, ed. by C. Tolkien (London: Unwin Hyman, 1990).

— *The Lord of the Rings*, (London: HarperCollins, 2004).

— *The Hobbit*, (London: HarperCollins, 2007).

Allegory and Story:
Poetic Time Travel in Tolkien's Typological Fictions

Anna Smol

Tolkien liked patterns, as is abundantly evident in his artwork, from newspaper doodles to published illustrations, and also in his literary work, where he often presents us with recurring patterns of characters or events: for example, Lúthien and Beren can be seen as a pattern for Arwen and Aragorn; Ungoliant and Morgoth for Shelob and Sauron. Eärendil is a pattern for mariners who come after him or for saviour figures like Frodo. In the Verlyn Flieger festschrift, *A Wilderness of Dragons: Essays in Honor of Verlyn Flieger*, I have written about a pattern of seers and singers who combine forces to collaborate creatively (2018, 258-79). Why did Tolkien repeat such patterns? In a lesser writer, you might think that he simply didn't have enough imagination to invent new characters and stories, but in the creator of the vast canvas of Middle-earth's ages, cultures, languages, this seems an absurd conclusion. Of course, we certainly do not feel that Arwen's story is exactly the same as Lúthien's, for example. Yes, they're both incredibly beautiful Elvish women of high status who choose to marry mortal men who must prove themselves, but the details of when and where they lived, their specific deeds, their relationships with others, are different. They each have their individual stories, and yet they are connected by some analogous characteristics so that we can discern a pattern, some repeated meaningful elements. This kind of historical patterning, I would suggest, is a feature of Tolkien's typological imagination, which connects stories in different times and places and imbues them with – dare I say it – allegorical significance, but not the domineering kind that Tolkien objected to.

Allow me to explain. I'll talk first about how typology works, then examine some patterns created by Tolkien in which he represents a typological connection with the past and future through the vehicle of poetry, and finally I will consider what Tolkien has to say about allegory, story, and patterns.

Typology is a term used in different disciplines basically meaning a system of classification, a pattern of repeated elements. Typological interpretation occurs in religious writings as well as in secular works. It is, for example, a pervasive feature of Christian biblical exegesis, a hermeneutic which was then extended to other literary works in the Middle Ages and later. The Christian version can be termed "orthodox typology," according to Laurence Coupe, who has contrasted it with "radical typology," a form of myth-making that is not constrained by doctrinal interpretations of the Christian Bible (1997, 64-9). I am not arguing that Tolkien is writing a biblical allegory, but as a medievalist and a Christian, he was well aware of typological interpretations of the Bible, and Tolkien's patterns share some of the characteristics of biblical typology even though he was not usually attempting an explicit connection to scriptural history in his works.

Erich Auerbach's essay 'Figura' offers probably the best-known account of a basic form of typology. The conventional Christian typology that he describes involves making a connection between a person, thing, or event, usually called the 'type' or the 'figure' from one period of time, and another person, things, or event, the 'anti-type' or the 'fulfillment' of the figure, from a later period of time. (The term 'anti-type' does not necessarily mean that it is the opposite of the type). In a way, the type predicts or looks forward in time to the anti-type, which shares some characteristics with the earlier type and is thought to fulfill the spiritual significance promised by the type. That spiritual significance, however, does not override the literal, historical uniqueness of both type and anti-type, at least not in a basic form of biblical typology as described by Auerbach. However, typology can become quite fluid and flexible and shade into various types of allegory. Nevertheless, typology basically works through the selection of congruous elements in the type and antitype. One of the best teachers for the typological mode of interpretation is the late tenth-century, early-eleventh-century monk Ælfric, who wrote a series of homilies in Old English that amount to an introductory course in Christian typological thinking. Here are a few examples from his 'Treatise on the Old and New Testament': Ælfric explains that Adam, who was created on the sixth day, is a type of Christ, who was born in the Sixth Age of the world. Or that the Old Testament Abraham's offer to sacrifice Isaac is a type or prefiguration of God's offer to sacrifice Christ. We can keep going: Joshua, who led his people into the promised land in the Old Testament is a type of Christ in the New Testament, who leads his people into the kingdom of heaven. Medieval interpreters, however, did not constrain themselves only to types of Christ. Christian exegetes could find both types and antitypes in the New Testament era as well. Sometimes, their historical connections relied on etymologies. For example, Ælfric explains that the name of the governor Cyrenius means 'heir,' and so he prefigures Christ, the heir of the Father (1997, 2); because Solomon means 'peaceful,' he is a type of Christ who restored peace (1979, 40).

While both the type and its later 'fulfillment' or 'antitype' retain their literal significance in their own time and place, they also draw attention to a further meaning, an allegorical significance, if you will, that explains the meaning of their connection. But wait, you might be saying to yourself, we all know that Tolkien disliked allegory, as he clearly states in the foreword to the second edition of *The Lord of the Rings*: "But I cordially dislike allegory in all its manifestations. […] I think that many confuse 'applicability' with 'allegory'; but the one resides in the freedom of the reader, and the other in the purposed domination of the author" (*FR*, 'Foreword', X). In a certain kind of allegory, the author dominates the reader by telling the reader exactly what the literal level of the story means – as Tolkien explains: "Allegory of the sort 'five wizards = five senses' is wholly foreign to my way of thinking" (*Letters*, Letter 202, 203). Although a typological imagination might be called allegorical, it is not this kind of domineering allegory that constricts the meaning of its literal details by equating them with a narrowly defined allegorical meaning.

For Tolkien, a typological pattern can offer a vision of the past and can create a coherent and meaningful view of history. Tolkien often achieves this backward look along the lost road of the past through poetic or literary art, which is experienced in a distinctive way as a dream, or an enchanted trance or vision, a 'faërian drama' you could call it, that transports someone to a different time and place, dramatizing the typological connections between past and present (or possibly the future) through the vehicle of poetry.

Take Eärendil as a type for Frodo, for example, in *The Lord of the Rings*. Tolkien prepares us for the typological connection by representing Frodo listening to a song in Rivendell about Eärendil the mariner. The focus is on Frodo's perception of the poem; first it "held him in a spell" (*FR*, 'Many Meetings', 233). Then, "Almost it seemed that the words took shape, and visions of far lands and bright things that he had never yet imagined opened out before him" (233). "Then the enchantment became more and more dreamlike, until he felt that an endless river of swelling gold and silver was flowing over him, too multitudinous for its pattern to be comprehended" (233). And finally, he sinks "into a deep realm of sleep" (233) – not the usual reaction you'd like for your audience if you're performing a song, but in Tolkien's world, that realm of sleep and dream is where the most intense poetic experiences occur, and in this state Frodo eventually hears the voice of Bilbo and can make out the words of the story of Eärendil's wanderings, his arrival in Valinor, and his fate never to return to Middle-earth. This scene helps to associate Frodo with Eärendil, and that connection will strengthen when Galadriel gives him the phial with the light of Eärendil. Finally, in Shelob's lair, their typological connection becomes marked and quite dramatic when Frodo holds up the Phial of Galadriel and the light grows: "as though Eärendil had himself come down from the high sunset paths with the last Silmaril upon his brow" (*TT*, 'Shelob's Lair', 704). And then Frodo cries out, "*Aiya Eärendil Elenion Ancalima!*" (704) which Tolkien translates in Letter 297 as "hail Eärendil brightest of Stars" (*Letters*, Letter 297, 385), and we read that Frodo "knew not what he had spoken; for it seemed that another voice spoke through his, clear, untroubled by the foul air of the pit" (*TT*, 'Shelob's Lair', 704).

I would say that in this instance, Eärendil serves as a type and Frodo an antitype. Eärendil has his story and Frodo has his own. But in some ways they share analogous features. We can formulate their allegorical significance for ourselves in our own individual ways. For example, I would say that Eärendil takes on the burden of trying to save the peoples of Middle-earth against Morgoth's evil, forsaking his home in the process, and that pattern will be reenacted in Frodo's quest against Sauron's evil. The type of Eärendil also has a predictive quality: just as he sailed into the West (in his case, without permission), we might look ahead in time to realize that Frodo will sail as well. The past infuses the present; the present is filled with the meaning of the past.

Another instance of a strange dream-like vision in which a voice seems to speak through the dreamer occurs in Tolkien's alliterative verse drama, 'The Homecoming of Beorhtnoth Beorhthelm's Son.' In this play, Tolkien imagines two characters, one an older experienced and practical farmer named Tída and a younger poet named Totta. The play is set in the night after the defeat described in the Old English poem *The Battle of Maldon*, in which the leader of the English, Beorhtnoth, is killed by Viking invaders but his followers fight on, presumably to the death. The Old English poem is also known for what can be seen as its traditional or proverbial saying uttered by one of the warriors, which Tolkien called the "finest expression of the northern heroic spirit" (*TL*, 143); adapted from the Old English in Tolkien's play as "Heart shall be bolder, harder be purpose, / more proud the spirit as our power lessens!" (141). (Tolkien also adds another couple of lines of his own).

In Tolkien's play, Tída and Totta are sent out by the local abbot to retrieve the leader Beorhtnoth's body from the battlefield. As they are returning with the corpse, the poet

Totta lies down in the wagon and starts to speak "drowsily and half dreaming" (140). He is seeing a scene that appears to be in the present or near future: "There are candles in the dark and cold voices. / I hear mass chanted for master's soul" but then the vision becomes general and apocalyptic: "The world withers and the wind rises" (140). As his vision intensifies, he seems to participate in past – or is it future – events: "It's dark! It's dark, and doom coming!" (141). He sees men gathering and hears them in the hall: "stern words they sing with strong voices" (141). Then he chants the words that come to him in this vision: "Heart shall be bolder, harder be purpose, / more proud the spirit as our power lessens!" (141). It's as if the words are spoken *through* Totta, just as the words are spoken through Frodo in the previous scene I've just described. The doomed heroic men who sing the proverbial verses on heroism become a type that Totta will use in the poem that he is going to compose, which as I've argued elsewhere, will be, according to Tolkien's fiction, the Old English *Battle of Maldon* (2019, 278-80). We see Totta perceiving in this visionary moment the typological pattern that will inform his composition of *The Battle of Maldon*. We are given a glimpse of a pattern of heroic doom, which might even prefigure the future, and we are free to read its allegorical significance as we wish: possibly as an ennoblement of the Maldon warriors by placing them in the context of a heroic tradition or, alternatively, as a critique of how men are doomed to destroy themselves through traditional ideals and a quest for glory.

Perhaps the most concentrated use of typological patterns occurs first in Tolkien's 'The Lost Road' and then in 'The Notion Club Papers', in which a group of men discuss how to craft a time-travel story before moving on to experiment with time travel through dreaming, thus entering into a story, as it were, as if it were being lived firsthand. There is much that I could discuss in this story, but let's turn once again to the always productive type of Eärendil the mariner. In the section of 'The Notion Club Papers' where two club members, Wilfrid Jeremy and Arry Lowdham collaborate in dreaming some visions of the past, they get together with their friends to tell the story of what happened to them as they went on their adventures. Repeatedly in this section of 'The Notion Club Papers' we are reminded of a pattern of seafarers that returns to explicit reference or implied allusions to Eärendil as the foundation, the type, with other seafarers adapted and gathered into Tolkien's typological patterning.

Lowdham introduces the Old English poem 'The Seafarer' into the discussions, calling it "that strange old poem of longing" and quoting a revised version of one passage in both Old English and modern (*Sauron*, 244). Instead of the Old English Seafarer who considers a journey to "*elþeodigra eard*" ('Seafarer', 144; 38), which can suggest a range of meanings: land, country, home of foreigners/ aliens/ pilgrims (my translation), Lowdham's version has a seafarer seeking "Elf-friends' island in the Outer-World" (*Sauron*, 244). As a philologist, Lowdham believes that he has found an older source, and we can identify it as an asterisk poem, to use Tom Shippey's term, a reconstruction by Tolkien of a fictional earlier composition based on the later one that all students of Old English would know.

One of the odd things about the 'The Seafarer' is that the poet speaks of the hardships of seafaring compared to the joys of a life on land, but then perhaps unexpectedly declares in lines 58 to 64: "And so now my thought flies out from my breast, / my spirit moves with the sea-flood, / [...] incites my heart irresistibly to the whale's path / over the open sea" (Liuzza 2014, 34; 58-64). Later in the poem, those cares that surge "*hat ymb heortan*" ('Seafarer', 143; 11) / "hot around my heart" (Liuzza 2014, 32; 11) are associated with *dryhtnes dreamas* ('Seafarer', 145, 65) / "the joys of the Lord" in the following lines: "because hotter to me / are the joys of the Lord than this dead life" (Liuzza 2014, 34; 64-5). Lowdham's version, which replaces "foreigners' land" (*elþeodigra eard*) with "Elf-friends' island," offers a fictional earlier text that has not yet been adapted to Christian early medieval England, creating in his earlier version a type – applicable to Eärendil – which is then re-enacted in different ways later in time: by the Old English Seafarer, by a poem on St. Brendan, by Lowdham's father, by Lowdham himself, and finally by the story of King Sheave, the last seafaring story that is told in this series of seafaring scenes.

In fact, Lowdham *becomes* the Seafarer in the story that he tells the club members. This narrative begins with Lowdham, very like Frodo in Rivendell, saying that "The voices seemed to pour over me like a stream. I felt that I had been dreaming" (*Sauron*, 269). As Lowdham proceeds, we barely notice when he leaves his twentieth-century persona behind and becomes a tenth-century man in King Eadweard's hall. The faces of the men around him have a dreamlike quality in the dim light. As in the vision in 'The Homecoming,' the candles are "guttering" and the wind is "surging" around the hall (270). Lowdham says that he felt tired, not only because he had just come from coastguard duty but also because he was discouraged by the decaying state of his world, a view much like the Old English Seafarer's. This feeling gives rise to feelings that are called "sea-longing" (271). He remembers his father, a seafarer, who had told him tales of distant, paradisal lands across the sea. Significantly, his father, who never returned from his last deep-sea voyage, sailed in a ship named The Éarendel. He wanted to name his son Ælfwine Éarendel, translated as "Elf-friend" Éarendel (234). The Notion Club discussions make clear that Old English Éarendel, with its origins in the Old English poem Crist, does not have the same etymology as Tolkien's mythical Eärendil, lover of the sea, but the two meanings, of a herald or messenger who is also a seafarer, do coalesce.

Even aside from these associations of names and details and the fact that Lowdham quotes the adapted passage from the Old English 'The Seafarer,' in addition, Lowdham's narration of himself as an early English poet and coastguard in King Eadweard's realm merges his twentieth-century identity with the Old English speaker of 'The Seafarer.' Below are passages from Lowdham's narration, which can be compared to the Old English (marked as OE), accompanied by R.M. Liuzza's translation:

> **Lowdham**: "And the sound of the winds and seas on the west beaches was ever a restless music to me, at once a pain and a desire; and the pain was keener in Spring, and the desire stronger in Autumn" (*Sauron*, 271).
> **OE**: *Bearwas blostmum nimað, byrig fægriað, / wongas wlitigiað, woruld onetteð; ealle þa gemoniað modes fusne / sefan to siþe* ('Seafarer', 144; 48-51). "The groves take blossom, the cities grow fair, / the fields brighten, the world rushes on: / all these urge the eager-hearted / spirit to travel" (Liuzza 2014, 33; 48-51).

Lowdham: "I heard the crash of waves on the black cliffs, and sea-birds wailing; snow fell" (*Sauron*, 271).
OE: *Þær ic ne gehyrde butan hlimman sæ , / iscaldne wæg. Hwilum ylfete song / dyde ic me to gomene,* [...] */ Stormas þær stanclifu beotan* ('Seafarer', 143-44; 18-23). "I heard nothing there but the noise of the sea, / the ice-cold waves; the wild swan's song / sometimes served for music/ [...] Storms beat the stone cliffs (Liuzza 2014, 32; 18-32).

Lowdham: "And the longing in my heart drew me on against my fear and land-bound will" (*Sauron*, 271).
OE: *Forþon nu min hyge hweorfeð ofer hreþerlocan, / min modsefa mid mereflode / ofer hwæles eþel hweorfeð wide* ('Seafarer', 145; 58-60). "And so now my thought flies out from my breast, / my spirit moves with the sea-flood" (Liuzza 2014, 34; 58-60).

Lowdham: "But my mouth did not speak the words that I had purposed: [...] in the night watches or pacing on the cold cliffs" (*Sauron*, 271).
OE: *ic geswincdagum / earfoðhwile oft þrowade,/ bitre breostceare gebiden hæbbe, / gecunnad in ceole cearselda fela, / atol yþa gewealc, þær mec oft bigeat / nearo nihtwaco æt nacan stefnan, / þonne he be clifum cnossað* ('Seafarer', 143; 2-8). I've often suffered troubled times, / endured hard heartache, come to know / many of care's dwellings on the keel of a ship, / terrible tossing of the waves, where the anxious / night-watch often held me at the ship's stem / when it crashes against the cliffs (Liuzza 2014, 32; 2-8).

In these examples, we have a Primary World text, the Old English poem 'The Seafarer,' absorbed in Tolkien's mythical and historical Secondary World, all part of a typological pattern of re-enactment. Eärendil is the type, re-enacted by the Old English Seafarer, re-enacted by Lowdham. His description of his experience offers an even more extended and integrated association of type than we have seen in Frodo's moment of becoming Eärendil or Totta's visionary recapitulation of heroic verses. Like them, however, Lowdham is participating in another time and place, dramatically re-enacting a typological connection. As with all of these examples, we are free to articulate the allegorical significance or the applicability of the pattern in our own way.

Finally I would like to turn to some things that Tolkien has said about patterns and allegory and stories. In Letter 163 written to W.H. Auden in 1955, Tolkien explains: "In a larger sense, it is I suppose impossible to write any 'story' that is not allegorical in proportion as it 'comes to life'; since each of us is an allegory, embodying in a particular tale and clothed in the garments of time and place, universal truth and everlasting life" (*Letters*, Letter 163, 212). 'Story' is historically specific, "clothed in the garments of time and place," as Tolkien puts it; it is individual, infinitely variable, we can immerse ourselves in the details. 'Allegory' is consistent and intelligible, pointing to a significance beyond the historically particular. An allegorical meaning, indicating something universal or everlasting, shows us a significant pattern whose interpretation goes beyond the specific and particular story.

Tolkien puts it yet another way in his essay 'On Fairy-stories'. When he writes there about the "countless foliage of the Tree of Tales" (*OFS*, 66), he's suggesting the infinite potential of stories. When Tolkien points out that "The seed of the tree can be replanted in almost any soil" (66), he is revealing a typological imagination which can see each story in a pattern of recurrence, transplanted, as it were, in another place and time. But still, each element of the story is respected for its unique qualities: "Each leaf, of oak and ash and thorn, is a unique embodiment of the pattern" (66).

It's in Tolkien's epilogue to 'On Fairy-stories' that he identifies what to him is, I think, not *a* pattern but *The Pattern*. In identifying what Tolkien calls the "far-off gleam or echo of *evangelium* in the real world" (77) in a story's eucatastrophe, Tolkien brings his ideas on myth and fantasy within view of the Christian Gospels, which he calls "a story of a larger kind which embraces all the essence of fairy-stories" (78). But, as Tolkien says, these are 'far-off gleams' in his stories, to be sure. I contend that Tolkien's typological imagination prefers the infinite proliferation of details of story over the interpretive constraints of allegory. Typological patterns often deal with literal, historical, fictional specificity rather than general allegorical representations. Re-enactments of types can connect past and present and can have diverse meanings. Those of you who might be participating in the masquerade, for example, will be, in a sense, re-enacting certain types because of some significance in them that you find appealing and I suspect, applicable. And maybe you'll even think of yourselves the way Sam does, who in approaching Shelob's Lair, realizes that he's a character in a continuing story with a typological pattern: "and the Silmaril went on and came to Eärendil. And why, sir, I never thought of that before! We've got – you've got some of the light of it in that star-glass the Lady gave you! Why, to think of it, we're in the same tale still! It's going on. Don't the great tales never end?" (*TT*, 'The Stairs of Cirith Ungol', 696-7).

Acknowledgements
I would like to acknowledge the support of Mount Saint Vincent University in the form of conference travel and research grants that enabled me to complete this essay.

Bibliography

Ælfric, *Ælfric's Catholic Homilies: The First Series*, ed. by P. Clemoes, EETS Supplementary Series 17, (Oxford: Oxford UP, 1997).
— *Ælfric's Catholic Homilies: The Second Series*, ed. by M. Godden, EETS Supplementary Series 5, (Oxford: Oxford UP, 1979).
— *The Old English Version of the Heptateuch, Ælfric's Treatise on the Old and New Testament and his Preface to Genesis*, ed. by S.J. Crawford, EETS 160, (Oxford: Oxford UP, 1922)

Auerbach, E., "Figura." 1938. in *Scenes from the Drama of European Literature*, trans. R. Manheim, (University of Minnesota Press, 1984), pp. 11-76.

Coupe, L., *Myth. The New Critical Idiom series*, (New York: Routledge, 1997).

Old English Poetry: An Anthology, ed. and trans. Liuzza, R.M., (Ontario: Broadview Press, 2014).

"The Seafarer." *The Exeter Book. The Anglo-Saxon Poetic Records*, ed. G. P. Krapp and E. Van Kirk Dobbie, vol. 3, (Columbia UP, 1936), pp. 143-47.

Smol, A., 'Bodies in War: Medieval and Modern Tensions in "The Homecoming"', in *"Something Has Gone Crack": New Perspectives on J.R.R. Tolkien in the Great War*, ed. by J. Brennan Croft and A. Röttinger, Cormarë Series 41, (Zurich: Walking Tree, 2019), pp. 263-83.

— 'Seers and Singers: Tolkien's Typology of Sub-creators,' in *A Wilderness of Dragons: Essays in Honor of Verlyn Flieger*, ed. by J. D. Rateliff, (Wayzata, Minnesota: The Gabbro Head, 2018), pp. 258-79.

Tolkien, J.R.R., *Tree and Leaf, including Mythopoeia* (London: HarperCollins, 2001).
— "The Notion Club Papers," in *Sauron Defeated*, ed. by C. Tolkien (London: HarperCollins, 1992), pp. 145-327.
— *The Letters of J.R.R. Tolkien*, ed. by H. Carpenter with the assistance of C. Tolkien, (London: HarperCollins, 1995).
— *The Lord of the Rings*, 50th Anniversary Edition, (London: HarperCollins, 2004).
— *Tolkien On Fairy-Stories*, Expanded edition with commentary and notes, ed. by V. Flieger and D. A. Anderson, (London: HarperCollins, 2008).

To the origins of fairy-tales

Enrico Spadaro

The conception of fairy-tales is undoubtedly a fundamental element in the understanding of the development of Tolkien's legendarium: in the essay 'On Fairy-stories', the author expresses an explicit declaration of poetics. His theories on fantasy and on the development of fairy-tales find their practical application in the tales Tolkien wrote all over his literary career, and in his contemporary English transpositions of some legends and tales of the Old English tradition, such as *Sir Gawain and the Green Knight* or *Pearl*. *Smith of Wootton Major* represents a perfect example of what Tolkien states in 'On Fairy-stories'; even *The Lord of the Rings* was defined as a great fairy-tale, although it could be considered as a collection of several fairy-tales, symbolically identified in the different episodes that constitute the novel narrative structure. Frodo and his friends get out of their familiar environment, the Shire, and they progressively discover many worlds, from the Old Forest, Lothlórien, which is an exemplification of *Faërie* as explained by Verlyn Flieger up to the dark lands of Mordor (2001, 90-115). In all these passages, Tolkien shows how the *inner consistency of reality* he theorised in his essay may be effectively achieved.

The creation of fairy-tales may be then considered as the aim as well as the means of Tolkien's literary production. The cultural and the anthropological context of the years when he was born, the end of the nineteenth century, shows a national resurgence in Europe: Finnish Elias Lönnrot's *Kalevala* or German brothers Grimm's collection of tales contributed to the political independence and unity of these two countries. The works we are mentioning consist of stories where the fantastic element prevails and are based on popular heritages passed down from one generation to another. Grimm's tales are partially an adapted rewriting of Charles Perrault's folk tales published in the seventeenth century. Thus, the fairy mood could be said to belong to a long literary and folk tradition, which could be traced back to its origins: this is why, an author who truly introduced fairy stories in Europe is going to be presented. In this paper, the Neapolitan writer Giambattista Basile (Naples, 1566 or 1575 – Giugliano in Campania, 23rd February 1632) and his most known work, *Lo Cunto de li cunti* (*The Tale of Tales*)[1] are going to be focused on. Although no sources testify to the fact that Tolkien read or knew Basile, the contribution this Italian author gave to the widespread of the fairy genre and to its evolution remains essential, as is going to be shown.

1 – From the court to the popular matter

Giambattista Basile was born in Naples between 1566 and 1575 and enlisted in the Venice army in 1603-1604: his regiment was sent to the island of Crete, where he had the first chances to discover some of the exotic environments which would characterise his tales.

1. Basile, G., *Lo cunto de li cunti*, ed. by M. Rak, (Milano: Garzanti, 1999).

He entered the contemporary literary Venetian society thanks to his participation in the *Accademia degli Stravaganti*, a learned society, which recalled the Neapolitan context where he was born. This composite, multifaceted and multilinguistic border milieu constituted his literary formation and education, within which an antinomy between the Neapolitan literary language and the common Tuscan tradition was developed.

One of his first compositions was *Smorza Crudel Amore*, a *villanella* – a form of mockery part-song in rustic style with a vigorous rhythm, which foreran *canzonetta* and *madrigal*. In 1608, he could return to Naples where he published a poem mostly composed in Crete, *Il pianto della Vergine* and some *Canzonette* (1610), which his brother Donato put to music. From this moment on, he committed to the drafting of theatrical or musical texts such as the play *Le avventurose disavventure* (1611), a sea fable where he exalted pastoral drama with a progressive intensification of the tragic element which ended in a comic way. In 1612 he moved to Mantua, where he attended Gonzaga's court: they gave him some administrative missions. He published some collections of madrigals and odes, such as Ecloghe amorose (1613) or *Venere addolorata*, a musical five-act drama. His continuous participation in literary circles in Mantua and in Naples let him focus on philological themes concerning classical authors and on Petrarchism, with a particular attention on late-sixteenth century mannerist authors like Pietro Bembo. In these years, he started to recollect all the literary matter and the models of lyrical and popular tradition which let him write the first drafts of *Lo Cunto de li cunti*, which was published posthumously. In 1631, he was appointed governor in San Giugliano in Campania where he died the following year: *Lo Cunto de li cunti* was finally released between 1634 and 1636 thanks to his sister Adriana. It is a collection of forty-nine popular tales plus one that gathers all together, in five volumes. It spread half a century before Perrault's tales and two centuries before Grimm's stories: thus, it is the very first Italian collection entirely composed of tales, many of which represent the eldest existing version. All the tales are written in the Neapolitan language, which at first prevented it from a great diffusion, but which is one of its most remarkable and main qualities, even as far as the comparison with Tolkien is concerned, as we are going to show. The entire title is *Lo cunto de li cunti overo lo Trattenemiento de peccerille* (*The Tale of Tales, or Entertainment for Little Ones*), and it is commonly known as Pentamerone, clearly referring to Boccaccio's *Decameron*, whose main frame of division into days of telling – five in our case – is exploited. This work clearly represents the first collection whose tales all may be ascribed to the genre of fairy-tales, which became popular especially in the nineteenth century. Wilhem Grimm, in the preface to the third edition of his *Children's and Household Tales* (1837), wrote that Basile's work was his main point of reference, the best and the richest collection of stories a nation could find. He highlighted the author's natural talent in telling, his cultural background, his intimate knowledge of dialect and the extreme contribution he gave to the widespread of the fantastic matter.[2]

The emergence of a fairy register in the romantic literary research, as well as a greater attention on national and popular tradition in the nineteenth century are some

2. Belmont, N., 'Contes pour les enfants et la maison, collectés par les frères Grimm, édités et traduits par Natacha Rimasson-Fertin', *Cahiers de Littérature Orale*, 65 (2009), http://journals.openedition.org/clo/1162. [accessed 28 January 2021].

of the causes that made European culture identify a source of the fantastic in *Lo Cunto de li cunti*. It was translated into German in 1846 and between 1834 and 1848 some of the tales started to be read in England, where a complete translation was made in 1893, when most of stories where adapted to children according to a bourgeois point view that Tolkien harshly criticised in 'On Fairy-stories'. Basile's work then received more and more attention and renown in Europe as the first literary monument in the history of popular tales. However, in Italy, because of his focus on folklore, *Lo Cunto* was marginalized in the hierarchies of the local literary society after 1861 under the Savoy dynasty, who privileged a kind of unified national literature.

2 – The structure

In 1891 the Italian critic and philosopher Benedetto Croce (1866-1952) firstly showed interest in the publication of *Lo Cunto* in Italy, and in 1925 he completed the first translation into Italian. In 1974, Italo Calvino wrote a preface to the collection and many studies and researches have then been conducted on the fantastic genre, which testify to the popularity the work has now finally gained. In 2015, the director Matteo Garrone adapted three of the tales to make a film, entitled *The Tale of Tales*.

The work is structured around a frame story, in which forty-nine tales are told during five days, hence the name *Pentamerone*. This story regards the life of a princess whose father is unable to make her laugh. The king summons an old sorceress who makes a spell on the girl and a fairy-tale starts: this is the beginning of the other pieces of narrative, among which we should remember *La Gatta Cenerentola* that firstly introduces the figure of Cinderella, *La Schiavotella* that is the source of *Sleeping Beauty*, or *Nennillo e Nennella* that inspires Grimm's *Brother and Sister*.

Lo Cunto de li cunti was written between the third and the fourth decade of the seventeenth century and was initially conceived to be read in the small Neapolitan courts. In his madrigals, Basile used the literary language of his age, whereas in *Lo Cunto* vulgar language is exploited, after a long period the author spent in popular environments. Here he could collect all the common sayings and the models of popular folklore. Typical baroque literature modes were then combined with different narrative techniques. Basile's sources were tales told around the fire, the Greek romance, Middle Ages *exempla*, farces or Boccaccio-style novellas or popular street theatre. Although the work shows a great literary wisdom, the author never completed it, as he continuously preferred to refine his tales and his style (qtd. in Basile 1999, XXXII). This is what happened to Tolkien, who never saw the publication of his entire legendarium, since he had a tendency of perfectionism.

Basile's tales have the same aim as that which Tolkien considered as one of the main functions of fairy-tales, that is to say, escapism and evasion: *Lo Cunto* was conceived to be read in courts so that its members might have fun and relax through moments of diversion based on the modes of the rules of court conversation. The tales could also be part of bigger plays or of a show, where songs, mockeries, puns were performed, hence their character of perfectibility and of flexibility in front of an audience who was always invited to join in these pleasant moments (XXXIII).

As long as we read the text, we may appreciate a fixed structure which could be adapted to particular circumstances such as those aforementioned: by mixing and combining different traditions, Basile sketches the model of a new genre, the fairy-tale. If Tolkien has been generally acknowledged as the father of high-fantasy, Basile may be considered as the father of the modern fairy-tale, as we know it today.

In his work, the Neapolitan author draws a counterfeited epic of the popular matter and of its peculiarities: a kind of farcical epic, since it is clear, despite the complicity between the different narrators and the popular characters, that they have a tendency of mocking the humblest environments of their society (XXXIII).

Lo Cunto has to be read as a text belonging to the oral tradition: many tales show the typical features of those stories that were told around the fire, as the great legends of the past that Bilbo or Aragorn tell the other Hobbits, in moments of relief during their travels (*FR*,'A Knife in the Dark', 250).

However, unlike the epical tales uttered by Aragorn or Bilbo, *Lo Cunto* aimed at making people laugh, throughout entertainment and amusement, and at giving an impression of tranquillity and easing of tensions. This laughter was the beginning of an unceasing desire to hear more and more tales: conflicts ended and people just wanted to have fun and listen to other fantastic tales.

All this used to happen in the court, which then became part of this fairy universe, thanks to the oral and theatrical exposition of the tales. As a matter of fact, *Lo Cunto* was conceived as a piece of comedy, hence its subtitle *Tratteniemento*, where the roots of "entertainment" could be easily remarked. It had to entertain spectators, and on this point of view, language played an essential role: the Neapolitan dialect was ideal as a traditional language of farce and drama, an element that is still recognisable when we walk through the streets of Naples. This is one of the main qualities Tolkien saw in Chaucer's 'The Reeve's Tale', as he explained in his essay 'Chaucer as a Philologist', published in 1934. Tolkien underlines Chaucer's skills in using different English dialects in relation to his characters and to the environments he describes: it is an evident philological interest which gives the story a truly sophisticated image of realism. Tolkien wrote:

> the by-product of a private philological curiosity, used with a secret smile to give some life and individuality to a fabliau of trite sort, [...] a private philological interest, and a knowledge, too, of "dialect" spoken and written, greater than was usual in his day. (Tolkien 2008, 110-1)

This quality – that may be seen in Tolkien's novels referring to his characters' multiple linguistic registers – is also present in Basile's tales, where the Neapolitan language, in opposition to the literary Tuscan language used in the rest of Italy, distinguishes his most remarkable characters. As a consequence, dialect entered narrative by means of literary conventions and figures of speech and rhetoric. This is a subtle and excellent work that reaches a superior level of parody. Dialect was rarely written, thus Basile tried to combine a spoken language with narrative and writing rules and modes: this mixing is one of the best innovations of *Lo Cunto de li cunti*. It is the first great literary work where the popular matter was at the centre of narration, where the outskirts of the world were listened to for the first time. In spite of the comical and parodic spirit characterising the tales, their protagonists are able to overtake obstacles and succeed in their missions, thanks to chance or to their unexpected qualities. As far as this popular and peripheral aspect regarding characters is concerned, another common point with Tolkien can be seen: the English author, in his novels and in some tales such as *Leaf* or *Smith of Wootton Major*, praises the humblest and the most anonymous characters in the world. A hobbit is able to carry the Ring to the Cracks of Doom (*RK*, 'Mount Doom', 1220), moreover a humble smith receives the star that lets him enter the fairy world in the last story Tolkien wrote. In the same way, Basile focuses on the simplest people and he exploits the refined literary experience of the baroque language so as to create a new literary genre and a perfect model of register, the fairy one. A new literary tradition emerged thanks to *Lo Cunto,* where the popular matter was the main subject with the implication of synchronic convergences between literary, theatrical, scientific and philosophical researches (qtd. in Basile 1999, xxxiv).

Basile was the first who could conciliate a great number of simple elements, from a narrative point of view, which turned to be the main features of fairy-tales. He seemed to follow the pattern Tolkien describes in 'On Fairy-stories', when he talks about the great cauldron containing the soup of history, where every author may pick the necessary elements to achieve his or her work. As a matter of fact, Basile was inspired by myths and legends, *exempla* and proverbs, where he collected the structural and thematic unities that form his modern tales. All these sources are assembled thanks to a sophisticated work of literary engineering, which consists of several traditions belonging to different cultural levels with multiple communicative functions.

The fairy logic establishes new rules of spatial and temporal dispositions: the plot does not follow actual time, but a stylized conception of rituals. Moreover, from a spatial point of view, the narration takes place in two different kinds of geography that are constantly intertwined, that is to say known places such as the contemporary reality and unknown and mysterious environments, a new world that the author creates. The factual is the departure to the fictional: the real world is the implicit basis where the Secondary world stems from, the hidden source that allows Tolkien's *inner consistency of reality*, as stated in 'On Fairy-stories' (*Monsters*, 126). This paradigm of plausibility, which most critics consider as the essential condition of fairy-tales and which Tolkien requires in the development of fantasy, is already present in Basile and it confirms his role as a pioneer in the European evolution of the fairy genre.

However, beyond the impression of reality every story gives at the beginning, events do not follow one another according to a cause-effect progression; but it is magic that leads them. Every change looks like a metamorphosis, where words and their power are able to transform actions, deeds, moments and finally the entire world. The passage from the real to the unreal, to the impossible, to the unbelievable characterizes all the narrative development and implies every gesture and every character. The fairy society Basile depicted is not anthropocentric; as a matter of fact, all the living creatures can speak, fight, walk, take part in every event in the same secondary world where humans, beasts and nature live together without any difference, in a constant dialogue between their respective subjective realities (qtd. in Basile 1999, xl).

This textual practice supports all the structure of the collection, from a communicative situation of the pleasure of all that is known to another form of pleasure, the variety and the enthusiasm for the exotic, throughout those traditions that were then considered as marginal: dialects, magic, fantasy and its fabulous beings, some features of comic theatre. Basile relied on this marginal society, from children to old people, who are but the result of that folklore where the unwritten laws of fairy derive from. Humble people, like Tolkien's hobbits, transmit in their narrations around the fire a great set of legends, myths and traditions that form the common background of European culture.

Basile's model soon started to spread in all the old continent, although he wrote in a dialect such as the Neapolitan. It was its structure, more powerful than elementary, presenting events in a comic and transgressive way, that allowed the creation of such a fortunate literary genre. Basile understood that fairy-tales could be addressed to every social class and might be easily exploited in every literary situation, both oral and written. In these stories, different kinds of heroes and mythologies could be matched, hence the multitude of sources of his collection, from Classical legends to contemporary poetry, up to the artistic elaboration of popular stories. A new group of characters that had been in the shadow so far was unveiled to European literature: fairies, orcs, or magicians. The universe of fantasy, of the untold, of the forbidden began its rise in the literary setting and, almost two centuries later, it would become one of the most popular genres in world literature, as Tolkien stated in 'On Fairy-stories' (*Monsters*, 132).

Basile's fairies are ambivalent beings: one of the first we meet while reading *Lo Cunto* is described according to the canons of absolute beauty. In *La Mortella*, the prince sees the fairy coming to his bed at night: he praises her physical appearance by using adjectives usually referred to Venus or to courtly love, such as "golden hair", "a bright face", etc. (Basile 1999, 52-73). Nevertheless, not all fairies are beautiful, but they can give the gift of beauty to the characters they meet: this is what happens to Peruonto, in the eponymous tale, who meets some youth, fairy's children, who offer him the chance of asking what he wishes (74-92).

All these beautiful and bright creatures are often on the brim of darkness that leads to underground worlds. The splendid figure of fairies stands opposite to the ugly and wicked orcs, representing the abyss that only awaits to capture the naïve protagonists. Basile describes orcs as terrible beings, an image of counterfeiting human nature: they all live in a sort of waste, solitary and unliveable lands. They may be compared to Tolkien's monsters, orcs and trolls. The former are introduced as *mockeries of the creatures of Ilúvatar* (*Lost Tales I*, 130). while the latter come from mountains or inhospitable places and are turned into stone when they see the sunlight (*Hobbit*, 'Roast Mutton', 41). In spite of the temporal, linguistic and conceptual differences between Basile and Tolkien, their negative characters all act in a violent way and they represent the total reversal of positive characters, good that is turned into evil.

As far as Basile's topography is concerned, all the adventures take place in continuous travels to and from what Tolkien would define *the perilous realm* of Faërie. On the one hand, the author describes known places, on the other hand, unknown lands are introduced. Little by little, the protagonists explore new areas and new worlds are unveiled to them and to our eyes: they get to know them and they gradually become familiar. This is what actually happens to Smith during his long walks to the fairy lands in *Smith of Wootton Major*. Thus, the fairy genre reduces the distance between ordinary things and what is new, extraordinary and marvellous. Thanks to this progressive approach, conceived both from a material and a metaphysical point of view, the fairy-tale finds one of his most remarkable features that let it emerge within the European literary universe. Grimm's stories, or Carrol's *Alice in Wonderland*, and finally Tolkien's novels are but a few examples of such emergence.

All the locations Basile depicts acquire an attractive *grandeur*, which leads readers or spectators outside the simple imagery of Naples towards the fairy imagery: fantastic places in Italy, or a fabulous East or West are accurately displayed. The fantastic geography parallels the real geography: as well as in Tolkien – just think about Alboin Errol in *The Lost Road* – characters continuously travel between these two levels, between the known and the fantastic and vice versa. These topographical aspects also affect the temporal axis: time is maybe one of the feeblest points of the fairy narration, because of the three following temporal levels:

1. Time beyond time: this is what appears when the tale starts in a temporal segment which is unknown from a determinate chronological point of view. It is what will become the classic 'once upon a time'.
2. This is a clear heritage of the old transparency of myths and it will constantly be repeated in all the Western narrative history, until the famous "Once upon a time, in a galaxy far far away" which introduces every *Star Wars* episode.
3. Time of narrative practice: time may be amplified or reduced without any limitation, insofar that time order is given by the narrative actions and the events composing them. This occurs in the second and in the third tales of the third day, *La Penta Mano-mozza* (*Penta of the Chopped-off Hands*, a variant of *The Girl Without Hands*) and *Lo Viso* (*Face*). This order does not depend on any chronological rule and might even be forgotten by narrators and spectators.
4. Ritual time: the time of the tale is determined upon ritual unities, such as the passage from day to night, producing a contrast between light and darkness. An example may be the seven days *Fioravante* (*Cannetella*, first tale of the third day) needs to get back home. Another ritual is the passage from a place to another, or from an initial negative condition to a final positive one (qtd. in Basile 1999, XLIX).

In the latter case, the plot reveals a change in the status of protagonists, who are initially in a low social position and then turn, as if they were experiencing a metamorphosis, into higher-class characters. This is what happens in *La Gatta Cenerentola*, which is the most famous tale as it is the first emergence of the figure of Cinderella, or in *Petrosinella*, *Lisa* and *Renza*. All the protagonists of these tales evolve thanks to their virtues and they acquire extraordinary qualities. However, these qualities are not destined to everybody, they are unique and inimitable, and those who try to appropriate them are strictly punished, as it occurs in *Renza*, whose protagonist is bound to die. As well as in Tolkien, where the perilous realm of Faërie is not accessible to everyone, but to some privileged beings, with some space and temporal constraints (see *Smith of Wootton Major*), in Basile magical powers are limited to some particular characters (qtd. in Basile 1999, LI).

Beyond the temporal organisation, love and family relationships are other elements which contribute to the evolution of stories: *Cenerentola, Renzolla, Penta, Marchetta, Marziella, Cinziella, Talia* are all married to a king or a prince, and male protagonists, such as *Cienzo*, or *Nardiello*, follow the same pattern. Most of the girls get married to someone belonging to the same social class, whereas men belong to different social groups: a change in their lives and in the progression of the story occurs. The fairy-tale becomes the privileged form of the family matter and love is the bond that builds or destroys stable family relationships (qtd. in Basile 1999, lvi).

3 – Conclusion

The frame of composition of the collection deserves to be shown. All the tales are built in precise sequences which gather them in a series of mini stories. They follow a specific order: the first tales deal with the topic of day and night, the second group stems from proverbs and mottos, thirdly stories about a metaphorical discourse are composed and the last group has its origins in popular traditions and folklore. These elements of the narrative discourse assume their autonomy, indeed a literary density that plots and characters contribute to define. Narrative unities are arranged on a degressive scale from the point of view of the verbal matter and of the true narrative force. In tales about day and night, as long as we read them, proverbs or other figures of speech, such as metaphor, gradually start to define the actual progression of the story. Rhetorical techniques are not only a simple ornament, but the real source of the tale. Rhetoric alters what is told and leads the plot to precise literary directions, where what was once unspeakable is finally unveiled to the great audience of the court.

Every tale is opened by a series of moral or ideological reflections, which get the form of proverbs. As a matter of fact, proverbs contain this capacity of synthesis which characterizes stories told around the fire in popular communities. The textual project of tales is highlighted again: it is a narration whose goals are conversation and entertainment. The segmentation into narrative unities is made possible thanks to this communicative project, which makes *Lo Cunto* a text which may generate other texts. This is really what allows the progressive and endless diffusion of the tradition of fairy-tales in Europe. Every narration might become the original shape of an infinite potentiality of expressions, whose sources may be found in what Tolkien defines as "the cauldron of stories", in his essay 'On Fairy-stories'.

Tolkien may never have read *Lo Cunto de li cunti*, but without Basile's work fairy-tales would not have spread all over Europe, and Tolkien would never have composed and theorised what he wrote about Faërie. The two authors show some convergent points of view on the framing of fairy-tales and Basile, as he wrote at the beginning of the modern age, is undoubtedly the forerunner of the development of popular fantastic literature in our continent.

Bibliography

Alighieri, D., *Vita Nuova*, ed. C. Manuela, (Milano: Feltrinelli, 2010).

— *Divina Commedia*, (Milano: Mondadori, 2010).

— *Vita Nuova, Rime*, ed. P. Donato and G. Marco, (Roma: Salerno Editrice, 2015).

Arduini, R. et al., *Tolkien e i classici*, (Roma: Effatà Editrice, 2015).

Bakhtin, M., "Toward a Methodology for the Human Science." *Professing the New Rhetorics: A Sourcebook*, ed. T. Enos and S. C. Brown, (Englewood Cliffs, NJ: Prentice Hall, 1994), 63–74.

Basile, G., *Lo Cunto de li cunti*, ed. M. Rak, (Milano: Garzanti, 1999).

Belmont, N., 'Contes pour les enfants et la maison, collectés par les frères Grimm, édités et traduits par Natacha Rimasson-Fertin', *Cahiers de Littérature Orale*, 65 (2009), http://journals.openedition.org/clo/1162. [accessed 28 January 2021].

Brékilien, Y., *La mythologie celtique*, (Monaco: Éditions du Rocher, 1993).

Carpenter, H., *J. R. R. Tolkien: A Biography*, (London: George Allen and Unwin, 1977).

Carruthers, L., *Tolkien et le Moyen Âge*, (Paris: CNRS Éditions, 2007).

Ceserani, Remo, et al., *La Narrazione Fantastica*, (Pisa: Nistri-Lischi, 1983).

Chrétien de Troyes, *I Romanzi Cortesi*, ed. G. Agrati, M.L. Magini, (Milano: Mondadori, 1997).

Curry, P., *Defending Middle-Earth. Tolkien: Myth and Modernity*, (New York: Houghton Mifflin, 2004).

Drout, M.D.C., *J.R.R. Tolkien Encyclopedia. Scholarship and critical assessment*, (New York: Taylor & Francis, 2007).

Dumézil, G., *L'ideologia Tripartita degli Indoeuropei*, (Rimini: Il Cerchio, 2003).

Eliade, M., *Aspects du Mythe*, (Paris: Gallimard, 1962).

Ferré, V., *Tolkien: Sur les Rivages de la Terre du Milieu*, (Paris: Christian Bourgois Éditeur, 2001).

Flieger, V., *A Question of Time. J.R.R. Tolkien's Road to Faërie*, (Kent: Kent State University Press, 2001).

Garth, J., *Tolkien and the Great War: The Threshold of Middle-earth*, (London: Harper Collins, 2003).

Gulisano, P., *Tolkien. Il Mito e la Grazia*, (Milano: Ancora, 2001).

Giuliano, S., *J.R.R. Tolkien. Tradizione e Modernità nel* Signore degli Anelli, (Milano: Bietti, 2013).

Hammond, W. G., *J.R.R. Tolkien: A Descriptive Bibliography*, (Winchester: Oak Knoll Books, 1993).

Morris, W., *The House of the Wolfings*, (London: Longman, 1904).

Pantin, I., *Tolkien et ses Legendes*, (Paris: CNRS Éditions, 2013).

Passaro, E. and M. Respinti, *Paganesimo e Cristianesimo in Tolkien. Le due Tesi a Confronto*, (Frascati: Il Minotauro, 2004).

Patch, H.R., *The Other World According to Descriptions in Medieval Literature*, Studies in Modern Languages NS1 (Cambridge, MA: Smith College, 1950).

Pirovano, D., *Poeti del Dolce Stil Novo,* (Roma: Salerno Editrice, 2012).

Santagata, M., "La Moglie di Dante", in *Dante. Il Romanzo della Sua Vita*, (Milano: Mondadori, 2012).

Tolkien, J.R.R., *Beowulf, A Translation and Commentary, Together with Sellic Spell*, ed. C. Tolkien, (London: Harper Collins, 2014).
— 'Chaucer as a Philologist: The Reeve's Tale', *Tolkien Studies*, 5.4 (2008), 109-171.
— *Tales from the Perilous Realm*, (London: Harper Collins, 2008).
— *The Fall of Arthur*, ed. C. Tolkien (New York: Houghton Mifflin Harcourt, 2013).
— *The History of Middle-earth*, vol. 1–12, ed. C. Tolkien (London: Harper Collins, 1983–1996).
— *The Hobbit*, (London: Allen and Unwin, 1937).
— *The Letters of J.R.R. Tolkien*, ed. H. Carpenter with the assistance of C. Tolkien (London: Allen and Unwin, 1981).
— *The Lord of the Rings*, (London: Allen and Unwin, 1955).
— *The Monster and the Critics and Other Essays*, (London: Allen and Unwin, 1983).
— *The Silmarillion*, ed. C. Tolkien (London: Allen and Unwin, 1977).

‘On Fairy-stories’ or the birth of Tolkien’s semiotic theory

Laura Iseut Lafrance St-Martin

‘On Fairy-stories’ is an essay based on a conference talk that Tolkien gave in 1939 at the Andrew Lang Conferences and published in 1947. It marks an important moment in Tolkien’s relation to stories and creative work. Indeed, he was just beginning to work on a sequel to *The Hobbit*, not yet knowing what it would become (i.e. *The Lord of the Rings*). Before working on this conference, Tolkien had not yet questioned the “special relation” between fairy-stories and children: “I had not then given any serious thought to the matter: I had not freed myself from the contemporary delusions about ‘fairy-stories’ and children” (*Letters*, Letter 234, 255). This essay is Tolkien’s meditation on the importance of stories and language. The outcome of this meditation strongly informed Tolkien’s subsequent creation.

‘On Fairy-stories’ is among the most discussed of Tolkien’s texts. A large number of Tolkien scholars have already explored many of the themes present in the essay or have interpreted the text in various ways. It is not a dense text, in the way we usually use this term (meaning a difficult text), but it can be interpreted in various manners and from very different perspectives. For some the essay is a literary manifesto that explains some of Tolkien’s aesthetic choices (Flieger 1983; Curry 1997; Nauman 2019; Izzo 2019 etc.), or a theoretical text about fantasy as a literary genre (Hume 1984; Swinfen 1984; Northrup 2004; Williamson 2015 etc.). For others, it is a theological text (Mende 1986; Fernande 2003; Moulin 2009; Garbowski 2014 etc.) or even a philosophical essay (Smith 2007).

In this paper, we will argue that among all these interpretations there is still one fundamental aspect that has not really been explored yet: ‘On Fairy-stories’ is above all a text that introduces a semiotic theory. But before we go any further, a simple definition of semiotics seems necessary. Semiotics is the study of signs in their different forms, and the study of the signification process. It has roots in the history of philosophy. Philosophers like Plato, Aristotle, St. Augustine, Spinoza and others have had semiotic thoughts on the human relation to the world through signs. Contemporary semiotics is mostly based on Charles Sanders Peirce’s theory and typology of signs (1867, 1868, 1878, 1902). It is based on the idea that semiosis (i.e. the signification process) is informed by the active (and creative) contribution of the interpreter. Therefore, his sign is not a fixed and only conventional one.

To elaborate the argument that ‘On Fairy-stories’ is an essay presenting a semiotic theory, we will present two of the essay’s features that make it difficult to frame. Those problems can be solved by reading it through a semiotic lens. After that, we will present key semiotic concepts at the core of Tolkien’s theory of signification. We will demonstrate that a semiotic interpretation of the essay ‘On Fairy-stories’ can help illuminate parts of Tolkien’s thought.

1 – What is 'On Fairy-stories' really about?

In 'On Fairy-stories', Tolkien obviously talks about fairytales. If it is possible to argue that it is essentially Tolkien's only aim with the essay, it is also possible to find much more than that, as many scholars have already shown (Flieger 1983; Hume 1984; Smith 2007 etc.).

The first 'problem' that makes the essay an elusive one is Tolkien's research questions and what he does with them. At the very beginning of his essay, Tolkien asks three questions: 1) "What are fairy-stories"; 2) "What is their origin?"; 3) "What is the use of them?" (*OFS*, 27). Following these questions, the reader rightfully expects to find three things: 1) a definition of fairy-stories, 2) what their conditions of possibility are and 3) their functions. This is already an impressive proposition, but his discussion goes even deeper than that. He goes into a more fundamental and theoretical discussion, which is where we can find the basis of his semiotic theory.

When we read Tolkien's essay closely in search of semiotic concepts, we get the impression that his discussion progresses on two different levels. First, the essay is explicitly concerned with the three research questions, all the way to the end. But a second level comes through in his discussion of the nature of language and becomes more and more visible as the discussion progresses. For example, it is highlighted by the way he links together the origins of language, mind and stories: "To ask what is the origin of stories (however qualified) is to ask what is the origin of language and of the mind" (38). This kind of vague remarks cannot be discarded or ignored, since it has some very profound consequences on Tolkien's view on the processes of signification. Even though Tolkien does not explain explicitly the reasons why he says that, we can see that his argument is going toward a more philosophical and semiotic one.

This brings us to our paper's second 'problem'. It seems that the essay's core has eluded scholars, even if it has been discussed by many, using various theoretical frameworks and methods. A very famous scholar has gone as far as saying that 'On Fairy-stories' lacks a core:

> However [On Fairy-Stories] is Tolkien's least successful if most discussed piece of argumentative prose. The main reason for its comparative failure, almost certainly, is its lack of a philological core or kernel; Tolkien was talking to, later writing for, an unspecialised audience, and there is some sign that he tried to 'talk down' to them. (Shippey 1982, 66)

To that very serious accusation, Verlyn Flieger and Douglas A. Anderson in their commented edition Tolkien 'On Fairy-stories' have answered that "while 'On Fairy-stories' is packed with information and erudition, it casts so wide a net as to appear at first glance lacking a core, philological or otherwise" (*OFS*, 10). This, combined with the various ways the essay has been interpreted (which we have shown earlier), could show that the heart of the essay, its essential meaning, remained mysterious despite the many scholars who have studied it.

Within this debate, I would like to propose that the core of the essay could, perhaps be semiotic. This means that the essay may not really be about fairytales or the history of fairytales, but rather about the importance of meaningful stories to organize the world and create worldviews, a process which may empower us (or not).[1]

2 – What is the semiotic theory implicit in On Fairy-Stories?

The first insight we have as to Tolkien's semiotic theory is about his concept of applicability (an idea also discussed in 'On Fairy-stories' without using this term). One of Tolkien's most quoted sentences concerns it. It can be found in the foreword of the second edition of *The Lord of the Rings*:

> I much prefer history, true or feigned, with its varied applicability to the thought and experience of readers. I think that many confuse 'applicability' with 'allegory'; but the one resides in the freedom of the reader, and the other in the purposed domination of the author. (*FR*, 'Foreword', 23)

Usually, this passage is used to explain why Tolkien never explicitly commented on the meaning of his fictional works: readers should find their own meaning. While this explanation is, of course, true, it has a more profound implication. To say that 'readers should find their own meaning', you need to have a specific understanding of the various processes of signification.

For C.S. Peirce, father to contemporary semiotics, the signs are composed of three elements: the representamen, the object and the interpretant. The representamen is the physical element of the sign. It is the sound waves of a spoken word as well as the colourful pigment of a picture. The object is what will be signified by the representamen through the process of semiosis. It is the idea (mental part of the sign) which is associated with the representamen, such as the idea of a tree following the perception of green pigment organized in a particular way. The relation between the representamen and the object is not fixed, it is constructed by the interpretant. The interpretant is not the interpreter, it is rather the effect of the sign. The interpretant is a complex entity which embodies various elements such as the context, the semiotic habits of the interpreter, his/her affects and emotions, etc. The semiosis, or the making of meaning, is precisely the construction of the relation between the representation and its object. This process can be synthesized by the Saint-Augustinian *maxim aliquid stat pro aliquo* ('something stands for something else to someone'), meaning that semiosis is both an active and a dynamic process. This is illustrated by the following scheme:

1. Of course, I am not saying that Tolkien had the explicit goal of writing a semiotic theory or that he knew the major theoreticians of semiotic, but rather that his essay presents elements of a semiotic theory and that, using a hermeneutic method (Gadamer 1960), we can make it explicit.

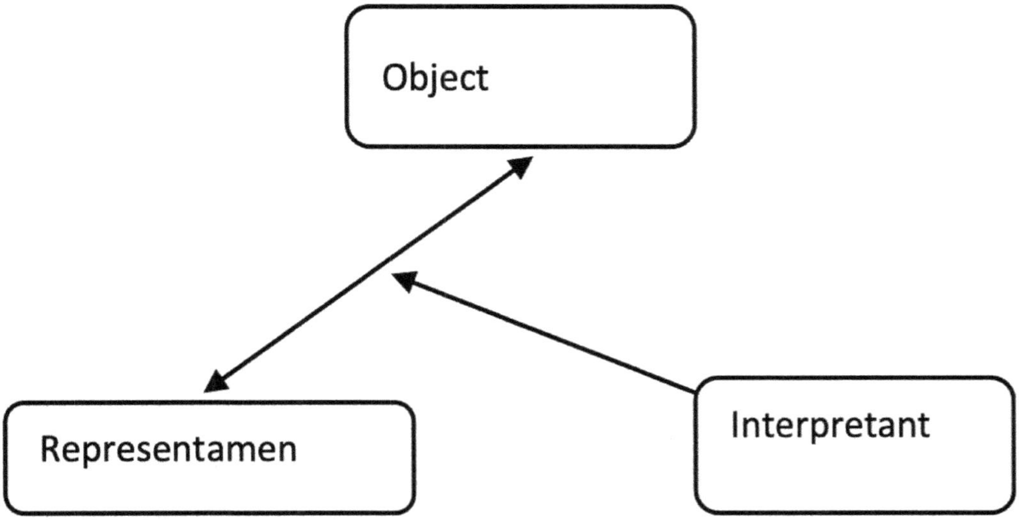

This has many very interesting consequences, one of them being the refinement of the conventional nature of signs. Convention is important (especially for linguistic signs), it is a vital condition for interpersonal communication, but it is not absolute.[2] Signs can mean different things to different people and their meaning is informed by many aspects of life: for example, affects, emotions, and semiotic habits.

The idea of semiosis as a complex nexus influenced by many factors (some being almost untouchable) is also present in Tolkien's linguistic aesthetics. As Ross Smith said, the linguistic aesthetics is Tolkien's attempt to understand "the fickle relationship between the sound of words, their meaning and our emotional responses to them" (2007, 64). This reflection can be linked with a few semiotic theories, but since it is an attempt to bring out the affective part of the signification process, the theory of affects seems to be the most relevant. Affect theory, dating back to Spinoza's *Ethics* (1677), is a philosophical explanation of how we relate to the world based on the idea that bodies are affected by each other in ways that are not predictable, therefore there are many ways to affect and to be affected by the world.

Being affected in different ways means that we relate differently to the world, that we see different things as being possible. Tolkien uses the expression "personal philosophy" in the sense of allowing something to be true or real: "the critic's philosophy does not allow to be possible in 'real life,' so that he would actually disbelieve the tale" (*OFS*, 45). This, from a semiotic point of view, is very interesting. What are we allowing reality to be? This expression implies some active contribution in the making of reality, it gives the individual (and possibly society) the semiotic power to construct the world. In other words, to 'decide' or to 'negotiate' what is true and what is not through a process of valuation (an idea at the foundation of the affect theory).

2. It is worth noting that the Peircean semiotic model contrasts with the semiology based on the works of Ferdinand de Saussure. For Saussure, the sign is a binary entity composed of the 'signifier' (material) and the 'signified' (conceptual), the gap between them is filled by fixed conventional correspondence (de Saussure, 1916). For Peirce, the sign is not a determined entity, it is the sum of its effects of signification.

The question of truth is central in the history of philosophy, but also in semiotics. William James, an important figure in semiotics, developed a philosophy of experience in which certain signs are successfully building relations of meaning and understanding between experiences and objects of experience (1907, 1909, 1912). When a sign or an idea can make an experience repetitively understandable – when the flux of percept is successfully organized into objects and relations between objects – the sign is called a truth for the subject of the experience. This definition can seem unusual at first glance, in fact, James struggled with people attacking and misinterpreting his definitions of truths his entire life, but it is based on a profound understanding of the way ideas are constructed by the human mind. To summarize, a truth is a sign or an idea which has proven through experience to be reliable to make sense of the world. It is a sign in which we trust. This idea can help clarify Tolkien's remarks on the truth of myths and stories in general.

What is important for the analysis of 'On Fairy-stories' is that there is not only a true/false dichotomy. The process of making sense of the world is more complicated than that. There is more than one way to be true and different degrees of truth. It is possible to know that something does not physically exist, and still use it to help organize and to make sense of the world.

This quick overview of some of Tolkien's semiotic concepts can help us sketch his way of understanding semiosis or how we make sense of the world. The first important thing is the occult vocabulary that we find in 'On Fairy-stories'. Concepts like magic and enchantment are very important in Tolkien's thought and certainly have a great importance in Tolkien's semiotic theory. They illustrate different ways to be affected by Primary and Secondary Worlds. Enchantment, understood as a process producing "a Secondary World into which both designer and spectator can enter" (*OFS*, 52), characterize the moment when one worldview (used in the Primary World) is being replaced by another one (constructed with experience in the Secondary World and Secondary Beliefs). It is a moment of semiotic shift, when habits and horizons change.

Magic is a more complicated term, since Tolkien used it in different ways. However, if it is understood as something "produc[ing], or pretend[ing] to produce, an alteration in the Primary World" (52), then it can be linked to the 'actively constructed world' postulate. One of the ideas at the foundation of semiotics is that the world is constructed through the various signs we use to organize it. According to this idea, the 'objective' world is not directly accessible to us, we need to organize it first in order to perceive it. Tolkien's concept of magic can, in part, be associated with that. Using a magic 'idea' in itself produces an alteration in the way we relate to the Primary World. This could be positive or negative, but Tolkien also uses the term 'magic' to talk about the 'scientific domination' of the world. Within the framework of the positive appreciation of over-rationality, a new meaning of 'magic' emerges: the 'magic truths' of scientific thought aim to disenchant the world, hence reducing the possibilities of meaning and altering not only the direct interpreter's world, but also everyone's world.

His theory also highlights the affective part of the signification process, which means that it will consider how bodies are affected by experience and how parts of our relation to the constructed reality is not entirely rational. The affective part of semiosis is something that always eludes the rational comprehension of experience, but still influences how we see the world. Philosophers like Gilles Deleuze (1981) and, more recently, Brian Massumi (1995, 2002) have shown that if we want to understand human experience, we need to look closely into affects and affective experience.

Following this idea, Tolkien's semiotic theory also draws attention to the multiplicity of ways to be affected by primary and secondary worlds, which in time will produce a very complex vision of reality (or realities). It will show how there is way more than casual effects and prior determinations in the many ways we relate to these worlds. Tolkien's refusal to comment explicitly on the meaning of his fictions and his 'cordial dislike' for allegory can be linked to this idea. He knew that whatever he would say would act as an 'authority argument', and thus greatly reduce the range of possible ways to relate to his stories. Therefore, he simply refused to comment. Allegory, as he understood it, is basically a univocal story (i.e. having only one possible meaning). According to his views on processes of signification, he would evidently not like them.

Considering all those remarks together, Tolkien's semiotic theory will present a certain typology of truths and beliefs (there is more than just true/false binary categories). This is perhaps the more important aspect of Tolkien's semiotic theory because it influences all the others. Tolkien said on many occasions that stories should contain 'some kind of truth', which he opposed to scientific truth characterized by domination over the mind. Also, he developed a typology of Primary and Secondary Beliefs, relating to the Primary and Secondary Worlds. All those types of truths and beliefs have different semiotic values, and a more precise typology would highlight not only how they influence us in our experience of Secondary Worlds, but also how they transfer into the Primary World to make it meaningful.

3 – Why study Tolkien's semiotic theory now?

To conclude, I would like to say a few words about the necessity of this analysis. Semiotics is all about worldviews, and it matters because the way we look at the world influences how we act towards it, what we deem important or not. Semiotics aims to understand the importance (good or bad) of the signs and to explore the possibilities we have regarding the organization of the world. If we consider our current global crisis, perhaps there is a problem with the way we inform the world, how we organize it, what we deem important or not. It is about time we rethink how we relate to the world, and Tolkien's thoughts can be a way of doing that. Powerful stories contain truths. Those truths influence us, and thus they change the world. Diving into Tolkien's semiotic theory can be a step toward, as Curry said, re-enchanting the primary world (1997, 59).

Disclaimer

The project presented in this paper was a work in progress. It is the author's PhD. thesis project. There is still much work to do to make this semiotic theory explicit. She would like to thank the *Fond de recherche du Québec* for the financial support, as well as her research supervisor, Maude Bonenfant, for her infallible support. The paper was written in 2019 and the author has since finished her thesis (available in French on the website of University of Québec in Montréal).

Bibliography

Curry, P., *Defending Middle-earth. Tolkien: Myth and Modernity*, (New York: Houghton Mifflin Harcourt, 1997).

de Saussure, F., *Cours de Linguistique Générale*, (Paris: Payot, 1916).

Deleuze, G., *Spinoza-philosophie Pratique*, (Paris: Les Éditions de minuit, 1981).

Fernandez, I., 'La Vérité du Mythe chez Tolkien: Imagination et Gnose', in *La Feuille de la Compagnie Vol. 2: Tolkien, les Racines du Légendaire*, ed. by M. Devaux (Genève: Ad Solem, 2003) 247-272.

Flieger, V., *Splintered Light: Logos and Language in Tolkien's World*, (Kent: Kent State University Press, 1983).

Gadamer, H.G., *Vérité et Méthode: Les Grandes Lignes d'une Herméneutique Philosophique*, (Paris: Seuil, 1960).

Garbowski, C., 'Tolkien's Philosophy and Theology of Death', in *Tolkien and Philosophy*, ed. by A. Arduini & C. A. Testi (Zurich et Jena: Walking Tree Publishers, 2014).

Hume, K., *Fantasy and Mimesis: Responses to Reality in Western Literature*, (Routledge, 1984).

Izzo, M., 'Worldbuilding and Mythopoeia in Tolkien and post-Tolkienian Fantasy Literature' in *Sub-creating Arda: World-building in JRR Tolkien's Works, its Precursors, and Legacies*, ed. by D. Fimi and T. Honegger (Zurich et Jena: Walking Tree Publishers, 2019).

James, W., *Pragmatism, A New Name for Some Old Ways of Thinking*, (Project Gutenberg EBook, 1907) https://www.gutenberg.org/ebooks/5116 [Accessed 17 January 2024].
— *The Meaning of Truth*, (Project Gutenberg, 1909) https://www.gutenberg.org/ebooks/5117 [Accessed 17 January 2024].
— *Essays in Radical Empiricism*, (Project Gutenberg EBook, 1912) https://www.gutenberg.org/ebooks/32547 [Accessed 17 January 2024].

Massumi, B., 'The Autonomy of Affect', *Cultural Critique*, 31 (1995) 83–109.
— *Parables for the Virtual*, (Durham: Duke University Press, 2002).

Mende, L., 'Gondolin, Minas Tirith and the Eucatastrophe', *Mythlore*, 13.2 (1986).

Moulin, J., 'J.R.R. Tolkien's "Eucatastrophe," or Fantasy as a Modern Recovery of Faith' in *Re-Embroidering the Robe: Faith, Myth and Literary Creation since 1850*, ed. by S. Bray, A.E. Gavin, and P. Merchant (Cambridge Scholars Publishing, 2009) 77.

Nauman, J., 'Composition as Exploration: Fictional Development in J.R.R. Tolkien's *The Lord of the Rings*' in *Sub-creating Arda: World-building in JRR Tolkien's Works, its Precursors, and Legacies*, ed. by D. Fimi & T. Honegger (Zurich et Jena: Walking Tree Publishers, 2019).

Northrup, C.B., 'The Qualities of a Tolkienian Fairy-Story', *MFS Modern Fiction Studies*, 50.4 (2004), 814-837 <https://doi.org/10.1353/mfs.2005.0007>.
Peirce, C.S., 'On a New List of Categories', *American Academy of Arts and Sciences*, VII (1867).
— 'Some Consequences of Four Incapacities', *Journal of Speculative Philosophy*, 2 (1868) 140-157.

— 'How to Make Our Idea Clear', *Popular Science Monthly*, 12 (1878) 286-302.
— 'Logic as Semiotic: The Theory of Signs' in *Philosophical Writings,* (Dover: 1902). <https://philpapers.org/rec/PEILAS> [Accessed 17 January 2024].

Shippey, T., *The Road to Middle-earth*, (London: Allen & Unwin, 1982).

Smith, R., *Inside Language: Linguistic and Aesthetic Theory in Tolkien*, (Zurich et Jena: Walking Tree Publishers, 2007).

Spinoza, B., *L'Éthique*, (Paris: Folio, 1677).

Swinfen, A., *In Defence of Fantasy: A Study of the Genre in English and American Literature since 1945*, (Routledge, 1984).

Tolkien, J.R.R., *The Lord of The Rings*, (London: Harper Collins E-Books, 2005).
— *Tolkien On Fairy-stories*, ed. by V. Flieger and D. A. Anderson (London: HarperCollins, 2008).
— *The Letters of J.R.R. Tolkien*, ed. by H. Carpenter with the assistance of C. Tolkien. (New York: Houghton Mifflin Harcourt, 2013).

Williamson, J., *The Evolution of Modern Fantasy – From Antiquarianism to the Ballantine Adult Fantasy Series,* (Basingstoke: Palgrave Macmillan, 2015).

“You have grown, Halfling!” – The Scouring of the Shire

Constance G.J. Wagner

In the roiling maelstrom of war, with every plodding step into the hellmouth of Mordor, one vision sustained the hobbits – that of an Eden untouched, a Shire sleepy but secure. Though the nightmare of war had blanketed the far-flung corners of Middle-earth, the idyllic dream of home and hearth that the Shire represented for the hobbits never quite dimmed. A normal life surely awaited them after so many months of madness.

The surrealness of the Quest and all their adventures is certainly noted by Merry, who as the four hobbits prepare to enter the Shire, observes, “‘It seems almost like a dream that has slowly faded’.” “‘Not to me,’” Frodo responds. “‘To me it feels more like falling asleep again’” (*RK*, ‘Homeward Bound’, 974). This telling contrast of reactions reveals something of the true wages of war for these returning veterans. Though knighted and feted and even grown tall from drinking the Ent-draught, Merry is quite ready to resume his life in the Shire. He is a hobbit, after all. One schooled and elevated by circumstance, but a hobbit all the same.

Frodo, however, is something else. Something *Other*, and his response to Merry tells the careful reader that this has ever been so for the Ringbearer. His true purpose in life has been the Quest, it suggests, and Frodo’s own comment of the return being less real, indeed the stuff of dreams, hints he has a longer road to travel yet. He is now and has always been *Other*. And as such, his homecoming is merely a return to a place he once knew and not a welcome end to the nightmare of war.

Tellingly, Gandalf has already hinted that things in the Shire are not as they remember (973-4). What those differences may be becomes more and more evident with each mile travelled deeper into the hobbits’ homeland. Frodo and his companions ride through a ruined Shire, weary warriors inspecting the ravages of war. This is not the world they remember, not the land they held in memory yet green. Indeed, little green remains to be found, for so many of the trees have been felled to make room for a skewed vision of ‘progress’. Where once there was beauty, now there is blight.

Fewer folks walk abroad, and those they do meet seem nervous, suspicious, and even frightened. And a particular kind of foreboding is found in the fact that even the friendly inns are gone, pulled down and replaced with grim and dreary guard houses. No longer an unneighbourly rustic haven, the Shire now seems a land pocked with self-important Sheriffs set on imposing a vast array of most un-hobbit-like rules.

At the Bridge gate at the Brandywine, an exasperated Sam sums up the situation with the eye of a seasoned soldier: “‘I hoped to have a rest, but I can see there’s work and trouble ahead’” (*RK*, ‘The Scouring of the Shire’, 977). Trouble indeed, for this new and disturbing Shire needs to recall and reclaim all that was bright and good about it before the Shadow drew a shroud of despair across its green fields. These four veterans of “foreign” wars have arrived when they are most needed – and with what is needed most: battle field-honed martial skills; clear-headed judgment under fire; and, most importantly, in the person of Frodo – a deep vein of mercy. All of these will be needed in the home-based conflict to come.

Jackson's film presents the Scouring of the Shire as a nightmarish vision Frodo sees in Galadriel's Mirror, here offered only as a horrific possibility should the Quest fail. In images that ripple across the glass-like water, the Shire is overrun by Orcs, and any resistance to its enslavement is met with bloodshed and flame. Frodo watches the rape of his homeland in growing terror, gripped by the sheer horror of Bag End reduced to burning embers, and Rosie and Sam flinching under the crack of an overseer's whip. The Shire he perceives therein is no longer an idyllic haven but rather an industrial hellhole. It is a vision of such compelling awfulness, he cannot look away. The Eye of Sauron then appears, so searing an image, the very water in the basin begins to smoke, and the Ring around his neck dangles in a kind of fierce longing, dragging Frodo closer to the boiling liquid as if It would join with Its maker through this conduit of Elven magic. In a sheer act of will, Frodo rips himself away, tearing the Ring from his neck.

And yet, Galadriel shows no surprise. Rather, she stands still as stone -- patient, impassive, *immortal* – awaiting *his* reaction. There in the stillness of the star-drenched wood, she seems to Frodo the very essence of ancient wisdom and strength. He offers her the Ring, perhaps in tribute, perhaps in hope that such a one as she could relieve him of his Burden and yet have the Quest succeed. This moment, cloaked in desire, hope, and fear, is a challenge of conscience for them both. Witnessing Galadriel's transmogrification as she contemplates having ultimate power, coupled with the raw visions of war and ruin thrust upon him by the Mirror, shakes Frodo to his very core. The Lady of Lórien has been offered *everything*, only to reject it to follow, instead, the clarion call of conscience (Jackson 2001, Scene 39).

If Tolkien's scenes of Frodo dealing with the Shire's shocking desolation upon his return allow the reader of the novel to experience the Ringbearer's evolution as the Conscience of the Shire, his transcendent experience at the Mirror of Galadriel in the film shimmers with the same intention. Supreme power will not save the Shire, he sees clearly. Only in heeding a higher morality and its demands will there be salvation, not only for the Shire, but for all of Middle-earth.

On the printed page, the weight of this higher morality can be seen to sit heavily upon Frodo's shoulders in his return to a despoiled Shire. While the four hobbits view the wretchedness before them with deepening dismay and even righteous anger, it is Frodo who observes each new shock in a thoughtful and sad silence, assessing and absorbing the changes as they hurt his own soul. "'This is worse than Mordor!'" Sam exclaims at one point in surveying a ruined Bag End, and Frodo agrees, noting, "'Yes, this is Mordor. Just one of its works'" (*RK*, 'The Scouring of the Shire', 994). A moment of shock, and even disgust, for all the hobbits, it is, even more importantly, a stark moment of insight for Frodo who sees the insidious effect the desire for power and control has wrought even here in the haven of home.

Though his companions are appalled by what has happened, Frodo alone is meditative, pondering what it *means*. And although Merry, Knight of the Mark and now the rising voice of action, tells Frodo that the Shire will not be rescued "'just by being shocked and sad'", (983), the Ringbearer even then calls for restraint in any battle to come and also insists that the misguided "Boss" Lotho Sackville-Baggins be rescued, rather than run through, much to the astonishment of Pippin, proud Guard of the Citadel (983).

However, bowed and broken by forces they do not understand, the people of the Shire *do* need a call to action. Such is immediately evident to the returning hobbits, particularly to Sam, who sees Frodo as the obvious one to put things right. When one of the Shirrifs tells the four that the Chief of the Shire wants to see them "'at once,'" Sam is certain that said Chief "'won't be so eager when Mr. Frodo has finished with him'" (979). And Sam is correct, although not in the way that he and especially martially trained Merry and Pippin expect. Frodo, it is clear, is the soul, indeed the conscience, of the Shire, for it is only upon his return that its citizens rally and reclaim their humanity. Merry may in fact be right in stating that the Shirefolk, unsure what to do in their own defence, "'just want a match [...] and they'll go up in fire'" (983). But the igniting spark is Frodo, with Sam, Merry, and Pippin the rustling flames of action.

Immediate action, even combat, is crucial, true, but Frodo sees that any fighting must be tempered with reason and mercy if the future is to be secure. The defence of the Shire, its very reclamation, must not disintegrate into a battle of brother against brother. There is to "'be no slaying of hobbits,'" he insists, reminding his companions that "'no hobbit has ever killed another on purpose in the Shire, and it is not to begin now'" (983). With this, he is clearly reminding his companions of the goodness at the core of Shire life that could so easily be destroyed through acts of vengeful fury that come with civil war. There is no point in fighting, he is subtly suggesting, if by doing so, they become the very thing they are warring against.

This enlightened conscience is further revealed when he empathetically wishes "'for no killing, not even of the ruffians, unless it must be done, to prevent them from hurting hobbits'" (986-7). While some may interpret these remarks as the desire of a weary veteran who has seen too much of war, it also reflects the astute thinking of a leader who would have his people act on their better instincts – and so escape nightmarish flashbacks to what they did in battle for all the long nights yet to come. He is, in effect, a commander-in-chief, who knows he must weigh every element of every possibility before issuing any directive.

And Frodo's companions of the Quest understand this, even if only unconsciously. Merry may be brimming over with plans for defense, and Pippin may be game to lead the Took clan's resistance cohort, but they still look to Frodo. After Merry announces that he does indeed have a plan, Frodo's response is very much in the mode of a general to a trusted commander. "'Very good,'" he tells his cousin, "'You make the arrangements'" (987).

He is not hiding from the horrors of war with this statement. Rather, he has clearly taken on the role of mentor, as Gandalf did for him, guiding the other hobbits into assuming deeper responsibility. Before leaving them at the Shire's borders, Gandalf had told the four hobbits that they must now settle the affairs of their homeland themselves, that such challenges were what they had been trained for (*RK*, 'Homeward Bound', 974). In stepping back to assume a less obviously active role in the fighting and planning, Frodo is thus allowing the others to find their own maturity and strength. Just as his willingness to take the Ring to Mordor inspired the then-future members of the Fellowship to step forward and join the Quest, so too does his hard-won gravitas and measured reasoning prompt others to grow fully into what they were meant to be.

He is a subtle agent of change, the action *behind* the action, setting things in motion by quiet example, offering empathy and compassion, hallmarks of a loving spirit, to the Shire in its hour of need. Even Sam's aged Gaffer, in voicing his complaints about how the ruffians have "'ruined his taters'", acknowledges, albeit unconsciously, Frodo's unique position (*RK*, 'The Scouring of the Shire', 990). The Gaffer's world has always been simple: his home, his hearth, his garden. And now the wider world has crept in and stolen these tranquil joys from him.

Frodo, in listening with patience and respect to Mr. Gamgee's problems and then promising to do his best to make amends, is lauded by the Gaffer as "'a real gentlehobbit'", someone who will see that all wrongs are set right (990). And while the Gaffer's outrage over the fate of his "taters" when battle is brewing at his very door sparks wry amusement in the reader, upon closer reflection, this exchange between Sam's father and Frodo provides something more than a small chuckle at the elderly hobbit's provincialism. It instead confirms that the Ringbearer is not to be viewed as an incipient war lord, but rather an inchoate peace leader, one who knows that the small concerns of daily life share equal, if not greater, importance with the strategies of war.

The praise Frodo then affords Sam's efforts, not just as a servant who has given "'perfect satisfaction'" (as he readily assures the Gaffer), but also as a hero now celebrated in story and song, reflects this insight as well, "for Rosie's eyes were shining and she was smiling at" Sam to hear him so extolled. Frodo, in this way, hopes to help his faithful Sam gain his heart's desire – a homely wish for a wedding in a hoped-for time of peace (991).

This moment of friendship and simple domesticity lingers on the page like the calm before the storm. It is an idyll, an expectation of what the Shirefolk will fight to reclaim with the rising of the sun. Frodo's kindness here has given the hobbit "council of war" a respite of normalcy and simple dreams for the future. It is both a welcome stillness and a reflection of a gentle and caring soul.

Certainly his neighbours see how much these qualities resonate in the returned Ringbearer, even in these troubled times. "'There's got to be some fighting before this is settled, Mr. Frodo,'" Farmer Cotton, in terse acknowledgement of the Ringbearer's obvious pacifism, warns as plans for the coming fighting swirl around all present (991). Frodo voices no objection. Indeed, as a survivor of the unspeakable torments imposed by the Ring, he is no stranger to battle in many forms. He knows – and accepts – what is necessary. But he is still, in this small scene, the heart and soul of the Shire as it is meant to be. However, nowhere in the chapter is Frodo's role as the embodied conscience of the community more evident than in the Battle of Bywater. Merry and Pippin, as whirlwinds of war, figure prominently in the Rolls of Honour recorded after. But Frodo's deeds that day are not martial, Tolkien tells us, but merciful: "Frodo had been in the battle, but he had not drawn sword, and his chief part had been to prevent the hobbits in their wrath at their losses, from slaying those of their enemies who threw down their weapons" (993). Though a single sentence, it is singularly significant, for it resonates with purity. Here Frodo, Knight of the Quest, displays the highest chivalric value: mercy – and here also, the highest spiritual values: forgiveness, acceptance, even unconditional love. And if he is mentioned less in the annals of battle recorded in the Red Book of Westmarch, his impact is somehow more, demonstrating a quiet heroism and guiding grace. For the true lesson of the Quest *is* mercy – and Frodo as Ringbearer has learned it well.

Indeed, even in the aftermath of battle, Frodo remains resolute, steeling himself to finally confront the Chief and call him to account for all the many hurts inflicted upon the Shire. "'Don't be too gentle,'" Merry advises him as they set out, echoing the hopes of many (993). But with this suggestion, a musing Frodo cannot comply. Mercy is now his métier. He will wait and see. And what is seen is near overwhelming, for there is even more devastation on the road to Bag End. A once tree-lined lane has been ripped raw and naked. Nothing of beauty remains standing, including the Party Tree, which lies "lopped and dead in the field" (993). The scarred landscape is Sam's vision in Galadriel's Mirror come to sorrowful life (*FR*, 'The Mirror of Galadriel', 353-4).

This final indignity is too much for gardener Sam, who bursts into angry tears. But his release of frustration is stoppered by the derisive laughter of Ted Sandyman, a layabout hobbit puffed up with self-importance over his place in the new order. And it is this that Frodo finds even more disturbing than the blighted landscape, for he sees in Ted Sandyman a blight of the soul that signifies deeper damage to the Shire than a forest of felled trees. Voicing pain, concern, and frustration of his own, he tells Sam:

> 'Don't waste any more words on the fool, Sam!' said Frodo.
> 'I hope there are not many hobbits that have become like this. It would be a worse trouble than all the damage the Men have done.' (*RK*, 'The Scouring of the Shire', 994)

Frodo's comment about Ted Sandyman reveals mature reflection – something a thoughtful and insightful leader must have and what Frodo has shown with every decision and comment he has made since his return to the Shire. In this pensive observation, it is clear he is making an assessment of what potentially needs to be done to restore order, indeed to return to normalcy. It is not enough, he knows better than most, to win a battle. The aftermath of a conflict can have fierce challenges as well – some obvious, such as damaged property; some subtle, such as damaged souls.

And it is the subtle damage that concerns him most. In surveying the despoiled Bag End, he sees beyond the filth and disorder, even beyond the stench of abandonment, to understand that the real destructive agents lingering in his old home are deception and despair, the most powerful weapons wielded by Mordor.

"'Saruman was doing its work all the time,'" Frodo notes amid the wreck and rubble Mordor's grasp has made of his home, "'even when he thought he was working for himself. And the same with those that Saruman tricked, like Lotho'" (994).

Standing in the shambles of the once fine *smial*, Merry is the embodiment of outrage and Sam, sadness. But Frodo has true insight in this most disturbing of moments, particularly when Saruman suddenly arrives at the door, looking inordinately pleased at the hobbits' dismay over Bag End's ruin. Here Frodo alone has the perspicacity to connect the fallen wizard Saruman and the Shire's new boss, Sharkey, as being one and the same.

As "one who has seen the Eye" (Jackson 2001, Scene 38), one who has looked into the heart of darkness and so knows corruption for the corrosion of the soul it truly is, Frodo here identifies the catalyst of the Shire's ills, labelling Saruman's actions as "'a little mischief in a mean way'" (*RK*, 'The Scouring of the Shire', 995). With these words he confronts the Wizard with the self-possession of a true leader. He is poised and assured, speaking matter-of-factly, as though Saruman's presence, though a surprise, were just one more element to be dealt with in the business of reconstruction. Saruman tries mightily to rattle his confidence, casting slurs on the hobbits' relationship with Gandalf. "'When his tools have done their task,'" he states with a dismissive sneer, "'he drops them'" (995). Insult is followed with mention of injury to the Shire done under his direction, injury that will be near impossible to repair – and therefore pleasant for him to ponder.

The chortling boastfulness Saruman employs here marks him as petty, even churlish. His dark deeds have truly transformed him from the lordly entity he once was. He has shed his wisdom and reacts to confrontation as a petulant underling might. If he can no longer wield power, he will, instead, hurl vile insults, the mean-spirited revenge of one who knows he is bested – and justly so. Frodo, however, faces him with an inherent calmness rooted in deep perception of the wizard's now-debased inner nature. He has weighed all the facts and found Saruman wanting and so responds, not just as commander-in-chief, but as the meditative conscience of the community: "'Well, if that is what you find pleasure in,' said Frodo, 'I pity you. It will be a pleasure of memory only, I fear. Go at once and never return!'" (995).

Frodo's command, strong and just though it is, does not resonate well with some of the now gathering hobbits who, in grief over their own losses, would not see judgment tempered with mercy. And yet, though hostile and hungry for death, they make no move to deliver the telling blow themselves. Their grumbling outrage both amuses and energizes Saruman, who first mocks the crowd and then threatens to lay an undying curse on them and the land should his own potent blood be spilled. The drama of his delivery makes the hobbits recoil, but Frodo alone knows the curse Saruman pronounces to be a hollow threat fuelled only by the power of the fear its hearers may lend it. Understanding only too well the illusion – the lie! – of such "power," he is once again the voice of reason, exhorting the crowd, "'Do not believe him! He has lost all power, save his voice that can still daunt you and deceive you, if you let it'" (995).

Even more compelling, however, is the voice of mercy he adds to his appeal, echoing in spirit lessons Gandalf had taught him when the Quest was new: "'But I will not have him slain. It is useless to meet revenge with revenge; it will heal nothing'" (995). And he repeats the words of banishment to Saruman, who seemingly bows to the inevitable with ill grace and turns to go – but not before attempting to silence one whose power of Voice has supplanted his own. With shocking speed, he draws a knife and stabs Frodo where he stands. Saved by the *mithril* shirt beneath his clothes (so obviously a mark of grace and therefore a symbol of what he has become), Frodo is no more than startled. However, a dozen hobbits, led by Sam, rush to his defense, like foot soldiers defending their captain, like knights defending their king. A true leader motivated by a Higher Good, Frodo stays the hand of his loyal companion, who has drawn their sword against Saruman, pinning him to the ground. Here Frodo's vision becomes more expansive, for he seems to see not just the adversary Saruman has become, but the totality of the Istar's existence on Middle-earth. With the measured reasoning of one who has learned well the lessons of the Very Wise, he grants Saruman clemency, stating:

> 'No, Sam! Do not kill him even now. For he has not hurt me. And in any case, I do not wish him to be slain in this evil mood. He was great once, of a noble kind that we should not dare to raise our hands against. He is fallen, and his cure is beyond us; but I would still spare him, in the hope that he may find it.' (996)

With this striking act of mercy, Frodo shows a dimension of soul beyond what his opponent now possesses. His elevated conscience is here revealed not just in the sparing of Saruman's life but in the proffered hope of redemption. And it is this reminder of the extent of his fall from grace that bestirs in the vengeful wizard an angry awareness of the consequences of his own actions. For he hears Frodo's compassionate words not as a reprieve, but a reprimand.

"'You have grown, Halfling!'" he tells Frodo in a sardonic statement deceptive in its simplicity. Saruman, now reduced to a baser incarnation as "Sharkey", the disreputable boss of the Shire, intends the comment to demean the Ringbearer, who has indeed grown beyond his days of innocence before the Quest (996). The words are meant to be dismissive, to belittle one who has grown too large and "robbed his revenge of its sweetness" (996). The compassion shown to him has put the debased Istar in Frodo's debt – a debt, as Saruman sees it, to a lesser being. He will have none of it and means his words to wound.

But even as they leave the lips of the wizard, they transform from embittered observation to startled pronouncement, a Seeing by one who in Brighter Days was one of the Wise and who, though wrapped now only in a few remaining rags of power, can still see True. For he studies the Ringbearer, Tolkien tells us, with "a strange look [...] of mingled wonder and respect and hatred" (996). Saruman addresses Frodo as "Halfling" with a capital "H", making of the noun a title, as in *the* Halfling, creating echoes of kingly address (much as Aragorn is called the *Dúnadan*). Coming from one who had the power of Voice, it is a near anointing, an acknowledgement of who – and what – Frodo truly is.

Here, in a moment both raw and yet miraculous, Tolkien allows Saruman to be the conduit through which revelation can flow. Frodo, the wizard perceives, has evolved beyond the mundane, becoming now an exemplar of mercy, a champion of Light. And despite Saruman's hasty addition of a dark foretelling of a short and broken life for the Ringbearer, indeed presented almost as a negation of the inadvertently offered ennoblement, it is too late. This fallen angel has named Frodo as numinous for the Ages.

This last moment of Sight, of Power, of Voice is rendered doubly memorable as it is hard followed by Saruman's own shocking demise at the hands of his browbeaten minion Gríma Wormtongue, who has been offered by Frodo a chance to part from his manipulative master and start anew. When a sneering Saruman reveals that "Worm" has done away with Lotho Sackville-Baggins in a particularly grisly fashion, the worm literally turns and slices the wizard's throat, ending his power of Voice in an aptly ironic fashion.

A hail of hobbit arrows then snuffs out Wormtongue's twisted existence, but what yet remains for Saruman's end is something more chilling than the hungry bite of cold steel. His spiritual death is what lingers in the mind, for it is an image most mournful – his grey and soiled soul rising up from the body, yearning for forgiveness from a greater

Unseen Power in the West. But judgment blasts forth in the form of a cold wind, and smoke and sorrow – all that is left of a once noble spirit – dissolves into "nothing" (997).

Though a small mirror of the end of his master Sauron at the Black Gate, the demise of the White Wizard is no less gripping and even profound. In the unnatural silence that settles on those gathered at Bag End, it falls to Frodo to cover the withered remains of an ancient being, once a radiant Maia, who died to goodness long ago. Readers of this passage hang suspended in this meditative moment, Frodo's pity and horror becoming their own as the debris of death that was Saruman is shrouded not with a robe resplendent with many colours, but a cloak dirty with the dust of war. Frodo turns away, sighing and reflective. The War of the Ring has ended at his very doorstep with doleful whispers on the wind. A great enemy of the Shire has been felled, not by his hand, but rather by the hand of an unseen Providence determined that justice be served. It is fitting that Frodo is seen throughout this portion of the tale as an advocate for peace, even a fount of mercy, rather than a returning warrior, shield and sword blazing in the sun. Here he is most definitely the conscience of the Shire, scarred of body and soul, but so better able to offer wisdom born of war's travails.

This quiet yet compelling resolution carries its own kind of power, markedly different from what Tolkien originally considered for Frodo's return to the Shire. In *The End of the Third Age*, Tolkien's early draft for 'The Scouring of the Shire' presents Frodo as an active combatant, dispatching ruffians at swordpoint with the aplomb of a seasoned soldier (1998, 86). But the most striking 'might have been' moment comes when Frodo himself lands what all hope is the last blow of the War of the Ring in a one-to-one sword fight with boss Sharkey, first conceived of, not as an embittered Saruman, but instead as an orc-like man doing the work of Isengard. Frodo answers the ruffian's taunts and aggression with knightly composure and the fixed resolve of a veteran who responds to need:

> The orc-man looked at them with such a leer of hatred as they had not seen even in all their adventures: 'you're liars like all your kind. Elf-friends and [...] Four to one, which makes you so bold':
> 'Very well,' said Frodo, 'one to one.' He took off his cloak. Suddenly he shone, a small gallant figure clad in mithril like an elf-prince. Sting was in his hand; but he was not much more than half Sharkey's stature. Sharkey had a sword [...] and hewed double-handed at Frodo. But Frodo [...] ran in close [...] and slashed his leg above the knee. And then, as with a groan and a curse the orc-man toppled over him, he stabbed upwards and Sting passed clean through his body. So died Sharkey the Boss. (91-2)

Although Sam, ever the loyal squire, here deems the justice of Frodo achieving the final victory of the war as "'Very right and proper,'" such a resolution is only "proper" if Frodo's story – indeed, his very purpose – is conventionally heroic (92). That is, if order is restored, and all the fine young warriors – with Frodo at the forefront – return home, happy, healthy, and ready to resume a quiet life. But such is not Frodo's fate, nor his ultimate purpose, as Tolkien himself learned in doggedly revising and revising this portion of the tale. In The End of the Third Age, Christopher Tolkien notes that his father eventually "perceived that Frodo's experience had so changed him, so withdrawn him, as to render him incapable" of assuming the role of determined war chieftain that the initial draft portrayed (93, 103).

Still, it is a tantalizing "what if," not without its appeal. Indeed, to the orc-like Sharkey of this alternate approach, the *mithril*-clad Frodo seems princely, shining with power and purpose, resolute and ready for physical battle. This image of a returning Ringbearer burnished with a warrior's luster, fired to fighting readiness in the crucible of Mount Doom, fulfils many an expectation for the "appropriate" end to an epic hero's journey. And yet such a picture, however traditionally gratifying it might be, truly does not satisfy the soul.

The hand-to-hand combat that would ensue would be just one more act of aggression, one more thrust of steel. It is war resolved with war, and despite the conventional sense of justice it provides, it lacks *illumination*, the feeling of perfect *rightness* that resonates in the essentially spiritual confrontation with Saruman/Sharkey depicted in *The Return of the King*. The embittered reactions of the once powerful and now diminished entity that is Saruman provide a marked contrast with the elevated quality of mercy Frodo displays in his dealings with the corrupted Maia. The Ringbearer is here obviously evolving spiritually with every word and gesture. Frodo is indeed princely, but not as the initially imagined ending would have it, for there are here no battle cries and banners. No blades bright-red with blood. Rather, cloaked in a mantle of mercy, he is, instead, a Prince of Peace.

Bibliography

The Lord of the Rings: The Fellowship of the Ring, dir. by Peter Jackson, Extended Ed. on DVD (New Line Home Entertainment, 2002).

Tolkien, J.R.R. *The End of the Third Age: The History of the Lord of the Rings*, Part Four. ed. by C. Tolkien (New York: Houghton Mifflin, 1998).

— *The Lord of the Rings: The Fellowship of the Ring,* (New York: Houghton Mifflin, 2003).

— *The Lord of the Rings: The Return of the King,* (New York, Houghton Mifflin, 2003).

Five or Six Ponies?[1]

Jessica Yates

In the 2004-5 revision of the text of *The Lord of the Rings*, the editors changed Merry's line: "There are six ponies in a stable across the fields" to "There are five ponies" on the grounds that the original six ponies were for five travelling hobbits and a pack-pony, and when Tolkien reduced the number of questers to four, he forgot to alter the number from six to five (*FR*, 'A Conspiracy Unmasked', 117). At least one critic took exception to this, as, he said, there must have been a sixth pony in the stable so that Fatty Bolger could accompany the hobbits to the Old Forest and then ride back alone.

As I could see both sides of this argument, I went back to the drafts in *The Return of the Shadow* (1988) to see if I could find a further convincing reason for one or the other reading. And so I did, one neither in the text nor contradicted by it. I handed out a suggested floor plan of the house at Crickhollow, and invited my audience to consider how Merry acquired those six ponies without arousing suspicion; and furthermore what might the Master of Buckland have said and done when he heard that Crickhollow had been raided. From time to time I will indicate moments where I stopped to invite my audience to suggest the next step in my tale.

In this investigation I take my cue from a letter the Professor wrote to Miss A.P. Northey about whether Shadowfax went with Gandalf over Sea. Tolkien wrote "indeed it is more realistic, since in chronicles and accounts of 'real' history, many facts that some enquirer would like to know are omitted, and the truth has to be discovered or guessed from such evidence as there is" (*Letters*, Letter 268, 364). And this prompt came just in time for Shadowfax to appear on the quay at the Grey Havens in the Second Edition.

In my reconstruction of the events at Crickhollow I claim that I am not composing "fan fiction", but rather resemble a professional geologist writing on the geology of Middle-earth, attempting to fit what we are given, into the real world's natural laws. In this case, laws governing human biology and behaviour, house – construction and the provision of personal transport, as observed by me, a housekeeper and house-owner. I am therefore trying to ascertain the facts behind the fiction, and I suggest that if somebody had asked Tolkien a similar question about the ponies, as was asked about Shadowfax, he might have agreed with me.

In their 2005 revision of the text of *The Lord of the Rings* Hammond and Scull, after some consultation, emended Merry's statement that "There are six ponies in a stable across the fields; stores and tackle are all packed, except for a few extra clothes and the perishable food" to "There are five ponies" The six ponies date from the first edition, but there is a note in *The Return of the Shadow* to say that the "six ponies" were a survival from the time when Tolkien planned a quest for five hobbits, so with the pack-pony that made six:

1. Appendix 1 includes my plan of Crickhollow.

> A curious trace of this stage survives in the published text. Since Odo's staying behind had not formed part of the 'conspiracy', Merry had prepared six ponies, five for the five hobbits and one for the baggage When the story changed, and Fredegar Bolger's task 'according to the original plans of the conspirators' [(*FR*, p. 118) was expressly to stay behind, this detail was overlooked, and the six ponies remained at this point (*FR*, 117)] (*Shadow*, 326-7).

In preparing their 2004 edition of *The Lord of the Rings*, Hammond and Scull decided to change "six ponies" to "five", giving their reasoning in *A Reader's Companion*:

> Although some readers have tried to explain the reading 'six ponies' by suggesting that one was for Fredegar to ride as far as the hedge, Merry is here answering Frodo's questions about preparations, with details of transport and provisions specifically for the four hobbits who are to make the journey – excluding Fredegar. (2004, 118)

This change did not go unnoticed by the leading Tolkien scholar John Rateliff, who in an article for *Tolkien Studies* vol. VI, 'A Kind of Elvish Craft' took issue with this decision. He pointed out that there must have been six ponies in the stable, as Fredegar rode with the four questers to the Old Forest, and he could hardly have walked or jogged alongside them: "Five ponies entering the Forest, plus one pony ridden back to Crickhollow by Fatty Bolger, equals six. Tolkien's original count was precisely right, and the new revised text introduces an error by changing it to five" (Rateliff 2009, 13).

Rateliff concluded by warning against altering the original text, without knowing Tolkien's mind. However, obtaining Christopher's authorisation to change "six" to "five" is as near as you'll get. Moreover, we know well that Tolkien made many changes for the Second Edition, such as removing Aragorn's brusque remark to Gimli after he had looked in the *palantír*, and adding the reference to Shadowfax mentioned above. (Many of these changes are noted in *A Reader's Companion*, plus a separate list of changes made in the 2004-2005 editions.)

I now intend to solve this slight academic feud by indulging in a reconstruction of the events at Crickhollow which will ultimately prove that there were only five ponies in the stable – but not the ponies that we think were there. I could certainly see both sides of the argument, and every time I went back to it, I oscillated between them. On hearing that another revision of the text was going forward in 2014, I decided to settle the matter to my own satisfaction at least, go back to *The Return of the Shadow*, and compare the drafts of the early chapters with the published version. Firstly, all the material covering Bree and the pursuit by the Black Riders is consistent. "Beds for four and stabling for five ponies" (*Shadow*, 134); "he wanted news; of four hobbits with five ponies" (152); and in a later chapter "he was asking for news of *four hobbits* riding east out of the Shire" (340); "There is a reward offered for anyone who can report that four hobbits are here" (341); and Gandalf is looking for four hobbits with "five ponies" and by this time he has a fifth hobbit (Odo-Hamilcar) with him (345); and the black riders are looking for "four hobbits" (347-8) and the gate-keeper counts them up to be four, and presumably connects it with the Riders' orders (349). In a footnote Christopher asks the question: "How did the Riders know that there were *four* hobbits?" and notes that this specific enquiry has been dropped from the published version: all the Riders ask for in Bree is "a hobbit called Baggins".

Reading *The Return of the Shadow* and the opening of *The Treason of Isengard* (1989), we find that Tolkien took a lot of time deciding on the names, personalities and clans of the questers. Frodo was originally Bingo, for example. It is obviously much easier to write for four hobbits than five, to create conversations between them and develop their distinct personalities, but it took several drafts to decide to remove the fifth hobbit from the quest. First he was called Odo, then Hamilcar and finally Fredegar (a good Frankish name) shortened to Fatty.

I now move to the journey from Maggot's Farm to Crickhollow and then to the Old Forest, to expound my somewhat left-field theory, which none of the disputing scholars, nor anyone else, has thought of. In the first draft 'To Maggot's Farm and Buckland', the three hobbits Odo, Frodo and Bingo (who has been invisible and playing tricks on Maggot) leave Farmer Maggot's Farm for the river, and walk past Marmaduke without noticing him. He catches them up and they warn him of danger, he laughs at them, and they go to the river where they embark in a rowing-boat. Looking back "they seemed to see a dark black bundle sitting in the gloom; it seemed to be peering, or sniffing, this way and that at the ground they had trodden" (*Treason*, 100).

Marmaduke takes them to "a nice little house on the far side of Bucklebury. It's a mile more, I am afraid, but it is quite cosy and out of the way [...] Not a bad little place. We often use it for guests [...] I have got it quietly ready in the last day or two" (101). As in the published version the house is secluded, surrounded by a lawn, "round which close bushes grew". There is nobody else in the house, but Marmaduke has left a copper which is "nearly on the boil" and three tubs to bathe in. After supper they discuss their plans and Marmaduke says that as they are being pursued, they should leave really early, and to avoid the Riders going across the bridges, they should go through the Old Forest. He has "five good ponies waiting [...] They're stabled in a shed out in the fields behind the house" (104). There are further rewritings of 'A Conspiracy Unmasked' getting closer to the final version, and the role of Fatty, first staying behind in Crickhollow but then rescued by Gandalf from the Riders, brought in an earlier version to Bree, and then all the way to Rivendell. Finally Fatty is left behind and stays in Buckland.

Now here are the major changes in the published version. Merry comes to meet the three hobbits on pony-back, and they think he is a Black Rider, which is an excellent dramatic touch. They go to the ferry, to "a large flat ferry-boat" (such as they have on the Cherwell east of Lady Margaret Hall), Merry leads the pony on to the ferry, and then the others go aboard and Merry ferries them across. On the other side they look back and see something moving, "like a dark black bundle left behind", and hint to Merry that it's dangerous. Frodo comments that it's lucky that the Bucklanders don't keep any boats on the west bank,and asks if the horses could swim across. Merry replies that he never heard of a horse swimming the Brandywine before, and that they would have to go twenty miles to Brandywine Bridge (corrected to "ten miles" in 2004-2005). Barbara Strachey noted this ambiguity when she drew the map showing the Brandywine Bridge, stating that it must have been "10 miles north to the Bridge and 10 miles south on the other side" (1981).[2]

2. There are no page numbers in Strachey.

Now Merry rides ahead, and the others follow for a distance of over two miles to "a narrow gate in a thick hedge", inside which is the house which Frodo has bought with Merry's help. They would have needed a pony and trap to ferry Frodo about from Bag End to Buckland and back to Brandy Hall to settle the affair, for the house belonged to the Brandybucks and was used as an overflow accommodation for guests. I suggest that Frodo actually bought a five-year lease, as he knew he wouldn't stay there long, and could therefore hide the rest of Lobelia's money somewhere on the premises, known to the trusted Merry – in the back garden perhaps or under the floorboards. The Master also wouldn't want to sign his special guest-house away forever.

By the way, as far as I know Tolkien doesn't tell us that the Master is Merry's father, although Christopher has found a rejected version where Merry refers to the guards trying to get a message through to the Master of the Hall if Black Riders appeared at the North Gate by day. In the draft Merry refers to "my father the Master of the Hall" but in the published text he just says "the Master of the Hall" (117) and we have to wait until the Appendices to find that he is the Master's son and heir. We find out that Pippin is the Thain's son when Farmer Cotton tells them that "your dad. Mr Peregrin, he's never had no truck with this Lotho" (*RK*, 'The Scouring of the Shire', 289).

I now want to focus on Merry riding ahead while the other three walk the journey of over two miles behind him. Tolkien does not follow Merry on this journey, but I shall. I suggest that he tethers his pony at the front door and goes in to tell Fatty to finish heating the bath water and cooking the supper. And what then? To recap: Merry was on pony-back when they crossed by ferry-boat; the house was built as a guest annexe to Brandy Hall. Does anything suggest itself? It's dark and foggy, Merry knows that they are being pursued, he saw the dark bundle on the west bank, and although he doesn't realise that the riders are supernatural, he knows that the Ring is magical and sought by the pursuers.

Up to now all readers have assumed that Merry would go on to ride the pony across the fields to the stable where the other five ponies are, added it to the five, unsaddled it, locked the stable and walked back across the fields to the house, but may I suggest that this would have been stupid, when Merry is the most sensible of the questers, formed the conspiracy and collected the ponies together. If he was caught by a Rider on the way to the stable, he might have been killed, the stable ponies dispersed, and then Crickhollow would be at the Riders' mercy. Luckily the Riders had no accomplices in Buckland, and took several days to reach Crickhollow as they planned to attack Bree as well.

So what is Merry going to do with his pony? He won't leave it unsheltered at the front of the house. I always pause here for my audience to tell me that there must be some kind of shed at the back of the house. Thank you very much, but what's better than a shed, given that this house has been built for families of guests? A stable! This house is isolated two miles from Brandy Hall, and remember that through human history people with enough wealth have always made provision for their personal transport at home. People with horses or ponies would have kept them at the back of their houses or stabled them at communal stables. Once the car was invented, houses began to be built with garages, and even terraced houses have parking permits outside, or built over the front garden. Maisonettes and flats have a separate block of lock-up garages nearby.

Tolkien of course had a garage in every house he owned, and probably a bicycle shed at Northmoor Road as well. Once he gave up driving he used his garage as his study!

So I propose that it is inconceivable that a house built for guest and family use would not have its own stable with room for at least two ponies plus a small cart, probably a trap, as families would have luggage and you couldn't expect women and children to ride ponies. Lobelia had a trap: it is a very small cart with only two wheels, the smallest one could have. This implies that the S-B household had at least two servants, one as a cook/lady's maid and one as a groom/handyman/gardener – unless Lotho was given the task of caring for Lobelia's pony, which I don't think he'd be too handy at! One could therefore accommodate up to three ponies, with the trap parked in the paddock.

Soon we shall examine the plan of Crickhollow, but first, how does my theory fit the published text? In the morning Merry woke Frodo at half past four and told him that "I am just going to saddle the ponies, and fetch the one that is to be the baggage-carrier." So Merry has to go to the stable across the fields anyway, but now, according to my theory, he can ride his pony there, saving time and energy. So he unlocks the stable, brings his pony inside, saddles four more ponies, leaves his pony there and brings back the unsaddled pack pony. Then the five hobbits leave the house. "Merry went in front leading a laden pony" and off they go to the stable where they find "the ponies" with no number specified (*FR*, 'The Old Forest', 120)! Barbara Strachey suggests that if they rode for an hour to reach the Tunnel Gate, it was a distance of four to five miles (1981). Here Fatty leaves them and rides back alone.

My theory is thus consistent with the narrative, and now we will look at my suggested plan of Crickhollow, designed to include all the rooms which Tolkien mentioned, as well as one he didn't, but which would be part of a typical house, then and now.[3]

Having decided on the approximate location of the house, there is one essential task the builder must carry out before starting to dig the foundations. The answer is: a water supply. So, how do we find the nearest spring, to provide pure drinking water? Well. Middle-earth is a magical place, so of course somebody would dowse for the spring (and even today there are farmers who believe in the skill). We will therefore place the well centrally in front of the door. And there is another facility which would also have to be provided outside the house... I posed the question and received the answer: a privy, which I have put slightly downhill to the left of the house, as I have put the side footpath on the right-hand side, leading to the paddock and stable, and the back gate used by the questers. Of course, it is a convention among fantasy authors not to refer to natural waste functions, and of those I have read, only Diana Wynne Jones, Terry Pratchett and George R.R. Martin are realistic.

Now we go into the house, which has a wide hall, like the one in 20 Northmoor Road, large enough for some pictures and a small table and chair, as Frodo notices his favourite things arranged in the hall. We know that the kitchen and bathroom are on opposite sides at the back of the house, so the bedrooms would be at the front. However, I have created a living-room, sitting-room, common room or parlour on the left to balance the two twin bedrooms on the right. It's normal for homes to have such a room, which today is often named 'the TV lounge' but traditionally it would be used for

3. See appendix 1 for the layout plan of Crickhollow.

formal dining, out of the heat and smell of the kitchen, and for card and board games, family games and singing. Being on the ground floor, it could also be used for dancing, and a sofa would be an extra bed – used this time for Fatty.

Thinking also of the time after the War, when Merry and Pippin moved into Crickhollow and started socialising with other young people as a prelude to courtship, it would be far more decent for them to entertain their sweethearts in the sitting-room than in their bedrooms, so I made the bedrooms smaller to create a large common room on the other side of the passage. The text also says that Merry and Pippin held "wonderful parties" which proves the existence of a party room: there would be large parties at Brandy Hall and smaller gatherings at Crickhollow, perhaps with sleepovers as young people have today, as I cannot see Estella and Fredegar Bolger going back home over the ferry late at night to Budgeford (*RK*, 'The Grey Havens', 305). No, most likely there would be weekend parties. Should a chaperone be required, they could borrow a cook from Brandy Hall to do the catering and then sleep in one of the bedrooms, put two or three girls in the bedrooms as well, and everyone else kips on the sitting-room floor.

Based on my instinct that the path to the stables was to the east, or slightly south of east, borne out by Strachey, I have located the bathroom, leading into the stable, on the right-hand side, with the kitchen on the left, leading into the back garden. The garden is divided into two oblongs with a fence and gate between them. As the garden must be used to grow fruit and vegetables, we must not allow the ponies to help themselves to our food and fruit from the trees. We therefore have a kitchen garden on the left, equipped with a washing-line, outside larder and tool shed, and a paddock on the right, with a water-trough and wheel-barrow.

Water must come into the house from the well, so I suggest they have a small upright trolley with a frame in which to fit a bucket. Thus women and children may easily fetch water down the passage to the kitchen. Wastewater is collected in a bucket under the sink, to be emptied onto the vegetable beds. The kitchen is furnished with cupboards and drawers for crockery and utensils, and of course has a wood-burning stove, and also a fire, Tolkien says. Both the kitchen and bathroom have stone floors, while the front rooms are carpeted. In the bathroom we have three free-standing metal tubs, and a hearth over which to boil the water. I think Tolkien underestimated the amount of water to be laboriously fetched and heated in order to half-fill three tubs! Normally households without the privilege of internal water supply, taps and drainage would use the same water in a single tub, and bathe the family one after the other, father first. Nevertheless, three tubs would be useful, one for bathing, the other two for washing and rinsing clothes. There would be a mangle, and a pulley to draw up clothes to dry near the ceiling. I think they could also have a flat trolley on which to put the tubs so that they could pull them into the stable and then empty the water on the paddock.

In the stable you have a water trough, a manger for hay, a hayloft for storage, and a straw stack. When a family with a pony is in residence, soiled straw has to be swept up and put into the wheel-barrow, then heaped outside the back gate, from where the farmer will collect it, replacing it with clean straw. Further away I have drawn a small stream running towards the Brandywine, not to provide drinking water for humans, but to refill the water troughs. As there are two gardens, there are two gates. The one on the left is the one Fatty fled through, along a path to a farmer's house "more than a mile away"

(*FR*, 'A Knife in the Dark', 188). The one on the right, leading out of the paddock, is the one the questers took, heading slightly south of east to the stable, and then back on track towards the Old Forest, where the Tunnel Gate is shown both by Tolkien and Strachey as due east of Crickhollow.

We will now follow Fatty on his way back to Crickhollow after leaving the others. He rides back to the stable across the fields, unlocks it, and tidies up, sweeping the soiled straw outside for the farmer to collect. He does not, however, return the key to the farmer yet, in order to carry on with the pretence that the questers are still at home, and so he brings any clean straw from outside into the stable, locks it and returns to Crickhollow, where he stables his pony at the back of the house. There are now several days before the joint attack on Crickhollow and Bree.

I now move to speculating where all the six ponies came from, which Tolkien did not explore. Buying six ponies at once would be too expensive for Merry, and if he begged them from his father's Master of the Stables, who would run a breeding programme, the request would be referred to his father, and he would have to explain why: ponies are not disposable, they are expensive. So that route is ruled out, as the Master of Buckland must not know of the plan, or he would forbid it.

Now, Merry and Pippin were their fathers' heirs, and would have tasks to do around the estates, as well as riding to see one another and to Bag End, an especially long journey for Merry. Thus their fathers would have given them their own ponies and instruction on grooming and feeding them. So that takes care of two of the ponies; they had belonged to Merry and Pippin for several years. Frodo didn't have a pony. Bilbo rode one back from his adventure, but I dare say that when that pony died he did not replace it, preferring to walk everywhere and save himself the work of caring for it. We may remember that Tolkien started his army training in the cavalry while at Oxford, but a few months after a rainy camping expedition he resigned no doubt disliking the sheer work involved in feeding, grooming and mucking out (Garth 2004, 24-5). However, he had acquired first-hand experience invaluable for a writer of medieval fantasy!

Although Frodo relied on Shanks's pony while living at Bag End, once he had moved to Buckland he would be assumed to need a pony so as to go back to see friends, and of course it would be essential for Sam to go and see the Gaffer, and if Sam had a pony, so must Frodo. I suggest, then, that when dealing with the Master over the lease, Merry asked for two ponies from the Buckland stables to be added to the deal. They would then be stabled behind the house until Merry moved them over to the larger stable under cover of dark, the night before his final visit to Bag End to help Frodo pack.

We have now acquired four ponies without suspicion, and the fifth must be Fatty's. Keeping company with Frodo, Merry and Pippin, it would be necessary for Fatty to have a pony as well, so this would be begged by Merry from his father as a long-term loan. Fatty would promise to care for the pony in every way. This could have happened over a year before, well before the quest was mooted. Now for the final pony, the pack-pony. I suggest that Merry begged yet another pony from the Master of the Stable this time, in order to help with the removal, with the pretence that it was for Folco Boffin to ride, though in fact it wasn't necessary, and this was the only pony to be acquired just before the expedition.

On the day of departure "they were busy packing another cart with the remainder of the luggage. Merry took charge of this, and drove off with Fatty" (*FR*, 'Three is Company' 77). The narrator doesn't tell us how the cart moved along the road. But there must have been at least two ponies, easily found, as both Merry and Pippin would have ridden their ponies to Bag End from their homes, and as Pippin was going to walk with Frodo and Sam, Merry would have to take charge of his pony as well as his own. Fatty also rode his pony to Bag End, and there was one more already there, the one supposedly for Folco Boffin, to make up the six. I suggest then that the cart was drawn by Merry's and Pippin's ponies, with Fatty's and Folco's tethered behind. This convoy would need a careful driver, but Fatty was riding with Merry, and would help control the ponies. This manoeuvre gets all six ponies to Crickhollow, and as they were all acquired at different times, Merry avoided suspicion.

I have developed quite a soft spot for Fredegar while writing this. He bore the name of the chronicler of the Franks, which connects him to frankincense, and the Magus who bore it: Melchior. Charlemagne's chief knights were Paladins, as was the name of Pippin's father, and another spelling of Pippin is Pepin. Pepin the Short, a great Frankish king had a nephew Drogo, who rebelled against him, and his son was Charlemagne. Another Paladin was Renaud, the name of the knight in the French ballads related to Lord Nann and the Corrigan, and a name which resonated with Tolkien, being related to Ronald.

I continue to imagine what happened to Fredegar after the raid on Crickhollow. He ran "out of the back door, through the garden, and over the fields. When he reached the nearest house, more than a mile away, he collapsed on the doorstep" (*FR*, 'A Knife in the Dark', 188). I take it that he ran to the left, or north by east, until he reached the farmer's house, thus in the direction of Brandy Hall, and he went by footpaths, so he was less likely to be chased and ridden down. And afterwards, when he went back, he would find a broken front door, but to be kind to him, I say that the Riders did not have time to find and drive away his pony, which was still there.

I expect that after the great alarm had been raised, the Master of Buckland would ride over in person to investigate. This was, after all, the house he had leased to Frodo, and in which he expected his own son had been sleeping, along with the Thain's son, as well as Frodo and Sam. He would demand an answer from Fatty; what would he reply? Again, I expect that Merry had left a story for Fatty to tell, when his father asked where he was: 'Well, they all had ponies, and they decided to make a little journey through the Old Forest to Bree, before the weather turned cold.' 'So,' replied the Master, 'my son didn't see fit to tell me of this. To test the truth of your story, I will send a posse of my best men also through the Old Forest to Bree, and we'll see what they will find.' I would expect nothing less of the Master, than that he should do his best to find out where the bandits came from and what had become of his son.

The Bucklanders would have had a quiet journey: Bombadil would not revisit the Forest until spring; and the barrow-wight had been banished; and they reached Bree shortly after Gandalf had departed in pursuit of the Black Riders. They would therefore have learned from Butterbur of the two attacks on Bree, that the questers had gone off with Strider, and Gandalf had gone after them. And if they asked where the questers had gone, they might have been told of Rivendell, to the east anyway.

The Master returned to Fatty, having already sent a carpenter to repair the front door, and gave him a choice; either to go back home, without the pony, and get his living there, or to look after the house which had been entrusted to him, keep the pony, and work in the Master's Stables; and from time to time take a confidential message by word or note from the Master to the Thain, as Fatty could be trusted, it would seem. So Fatty accepted this arrangement, and the first note he carried was to tell the Thain what had apparently happened to his son Pippin. However, when the Ruffians invaded the Shire, Fredegar went to the Master to ask leave to go back and fight them, which was granted, with maybe a few Bucklanders to help. He could not take his pony, though; if he were captured it would have been eaten! Sadly, he was captured, though I would have preferred to see Fredegar still in charge of his partisans, joining in the fight when the questers returned, when he heard the horn blow. However, he was held in high honour after the war, and became Merry's brother-in-law.

Two scenes which I have amused myself by imagining, which could become fan fiction or even a comedy sketch in other hands, are the reunions of Pippin and Merry with their fathers. Pippin has to quickly explain what happened down south, to his father, and then get his permission for a company of fighting Tooks. The Thain also joined in the fighting in his territory. Merry did not have time to go and see his father before the battle, so I expect he took Pippin along with him to back up his amazing story of battles down south and the liberation of the Shire.

To conclude, if you think some of my theories are too far-fetched, how else could you explain the acquisition of six ponies without suspicion, and wouldn't it be normal for the house at Crickhollow to have its own stable? I am going to cite an example from Tolkien's essay '*Ancrene Wisse* and *Hali Meiðhad*'. He had come across several irregular spellings in the manuscripts which didn't conform to the consistent rules he had so far discerned. Rather than adjust the grammatical rules yet again to explain these forms, he suggested that they were scribal errors or as we would say typoes with no grammatical relevance, and he ruled out recopying by a scribe familiar with another dialect, as that would introduce even more variants, whereas these two manuscripts have a high level of regularity and must have been written, he claimed, by a scribe whose "mother-dialect" it was (Tolkien 1929, 121). Thus he wrote:

> Personally I have no doubt that if we could call the scribes of A and B before us and silently point to these forms, they would thank us, pick up a pen, and immediately substitute the in forms, as certainly one of the present day would amend a minor aberration from standard spelling or accidence if one were pointed to. (122)

I therefore suggest that if somebody had asked him if Crickhollow had a stable, he would have said "of course", and he may also have liked my explanation of how the six ponies were acquired without arousing suspicion. Thus the answer to the question: Five or Six Ponies? is five, but not the ponies you think were there. Fatty's pony was in that stable, but Merry's was at Crickhollow.

Bibliography

Breckon & Breckon [estate agents] Oxford Summertown. 20 Northmoor Road. Listed on Rightmove, 2 July 2019.

Garth, J., *Tolkien and the Great War,* (London: HarperCollins, 2004).

Hammond, W.G. and C. Scull, *The Lord of the Rings: A Reader's Companion,* (London: HarperCollins, 2005).

Rateliff, J., 'A Kind of Elvish Craft', *Tolkien Studies*, 7 (2009) 1-21.

Strachey, B., *Journeys of Frodo,* (London: Unwin Paperbacks, 1981).

Tolkien, J.R.R '*Ancrene Wisse* and *Hali Meiðhad*', in *Essays and Studies, XIV* (The English Association. Oxford: The Clarendon Press, 1929).
— *The Letters of J. R. R. Tolkien*, ed. H. Carpenter with the assistance of C.Tolkien (London: George Allen & Unwin, 1981).
— *The Lord of the Rings*, 2nd ed. (London: George Allen & Unwin, 1966).
— *The Return of the Shadow*, ed. by C. Tolkien (London: Unwin Hyman, 1988).
— *The Treason of Isengard*, ed. by C. Tolkien (London: Unwin Hyman, 1989).

Appendix 1: Crickhollow plan.

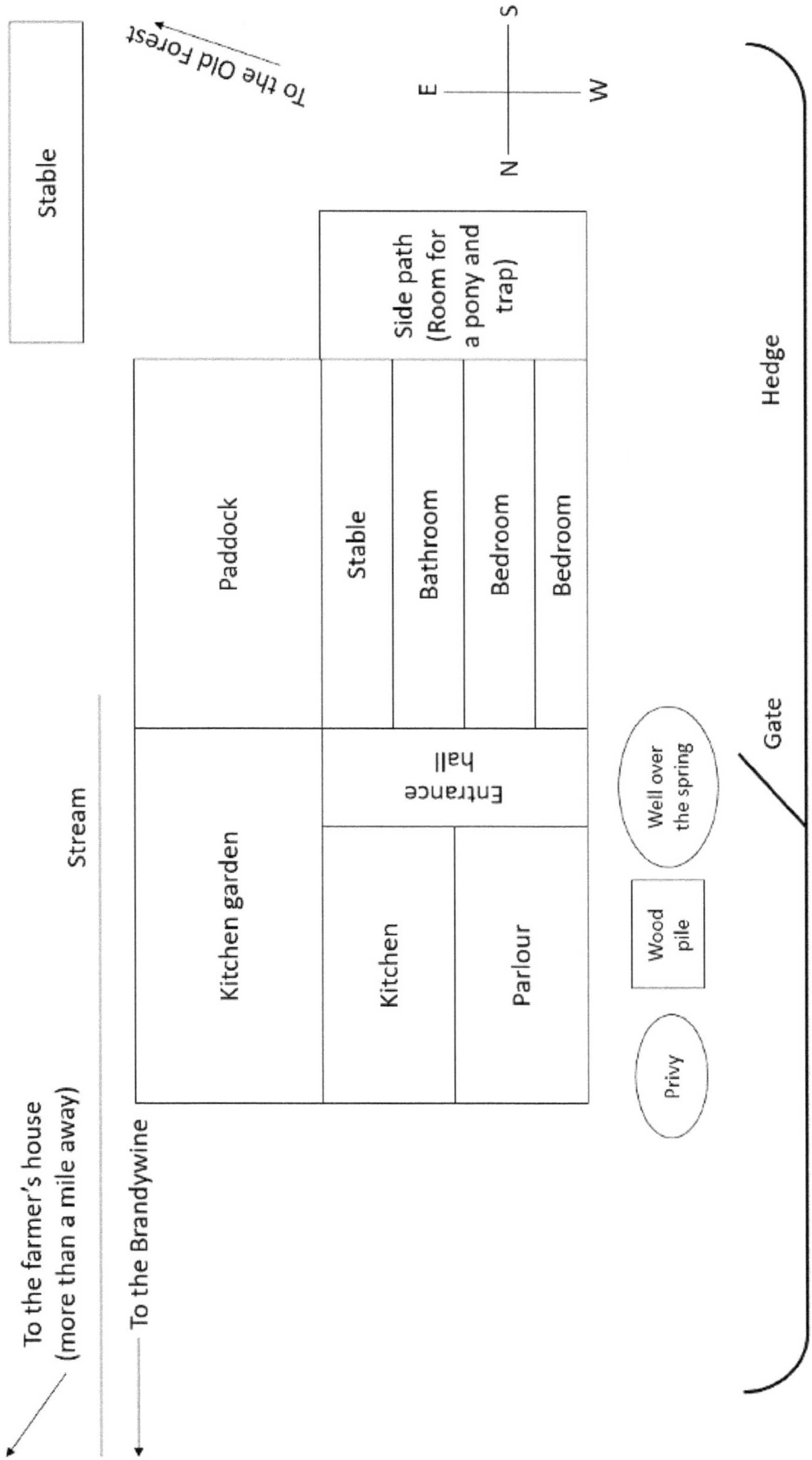
To the farmer's house (more than a mile away)
To the Brandywine
Stream
Stable
To the Old Forest
E
W
N
S
Kitchen garden
Paddock
Kitchen
Parlour
Entrance hall
Stable
Bathroom
Bedroom
Bedroom
Side path (Room for a pony and trap)
Privy
Wood pile
Well over the spring
Gate
Hedge

MYTHICAL, FOLKLORIC, AND LITERARY TRADITIONS

The Dim Echo of the Catcher

Nils Ivar Agøy

In 1928 and 1929, excavations led by the famous archaeologist Mortimer Wheeler and his wife Tessa (less famous both because she was a woman in a traditionally male profession and because she died at the age of 43) were conducted at Lydney in Gloucestershire, at a site where an iron age hill fort had once stood and where the Romans had later mined for iron. An unusual temple dedicated to an obscure Celtic god named Nodens was built there in the fourth century, but abandoned after a few generations. Variants of 'Nodens' were found in three Latin inscriptions at Lydney, but the god was otherwise quite unknown. Based, among other things, on a number of dog figures found at the site, it was assumed that he was ascribed healing powers. The presence of a guesthouse indicated that the site had been a pilgrimage centre, and the Wheelers believed that the temple could "be regarded as the consecrated meeting-place of a college or brotherhood [...] devoted to a cult which [...] had developed along the lines of mystery-cults everywhere popular under the later empire", representing "the ultimate achievement of some one of these lost rivals to Christianity" (Wheeler & Wheeler 1932, 38, 39). The Wheelers asked Tolkien to contribute a note on the god's name to the excavation report, and this the professor did.[1] It is not known exactly when he wrote it, but he received the proofs in December 1931 and returned them by early January 1932. The report was then published in July 1932 (Hammond & Scull 2006, 148, 160f, 164).[2]

Mathew Lyons has claimed that Tolkien actually travelled to Lydney several times while the excavations were in progress, but I have not been able to confirm this from other sources, and it is flatly rejected by Tolkien biographer Raymond Edwards (Lyons 2004, 50, 63, 74).[3] It is not certain that Tolkien ever met any of the Wheelers.

Several attempts have been made to connect Tolkien's peripheral involvement with the Lydney excavations with his Middle-earth writings. There is the fact that the hill where the temple stood was called Dwarfs' Hill in Anglo-Saxon times, and the Roman mining cavities in it have reminded some people of hobbit holes. Then there is the intriguing Lydney ring curse. In 1817 or just before, a so-called 'curse tablet' was found at Lydney, stating that Silvianus has lost a ring and cursing Senicianus with ill-health if he does not bring it to the temple of Nodens. This is thought-provoking. Tolkien, as we know, makes Gollum curse Bilbo by (sur)name for the theft of a ring in the

1. It is highly probable that it was Tolkien's colleague at Pembroke College, R.G. Collingwood, who suggested to the Wheelers that Tolkien could contribute, see Forest-Hill, 2016, 3f., and Phelpstead 2011, 57. Collingwood wrote the section on inscriptions in the excavation report.
2. Tolkien also did work on the name Lydney, but this was not included in the report, possibly because it was finished too late; see Phelpstead 2011, 55f.; Hammond & Scull 2006, 'Reader's Guide', 623.
3. Lyons' assertion seems to be made on the basis of information from a curator at Lydney Park. See Edwards 2014, 159; cf. Sabo 2007, 93.

revised *Hobbit*. The most famous alleged connection, however, easily found on the Internet and clearly regarded by many almost as fact, is the notion that Tolkien's One Ring was in some way inspired by a large, inscribed Roman-era gold ring found in Silchester in Hampshire in the mid-1780s. According to the inscription, it belonged to one Senicianus, and the irresistibly alluring idea is that this is the ring-thief cursed on the tablet.[4] The chances that the Silchester ring is actually the one mentioned at Lydney are microscopical, to say the least,[5] and it has never been established that Tolkien actually knew about the ring found at Silchester.

I am going to talk about quite another possible connection, one which is not found on the Internet at all,[6] but which I believe to be stronger.

In his five and a half-page note on the name Nodens, Tolkien attempted to unravel its roots, parallels and ramifications. He assumed that the Irish mythological hero Nuada ('of the Silver Hand', for he had lost his right hand and had it replaced with a metal one) was a memory of an older and mightier deity who had been worshipped at least in Britain. "Although it is perhaps vain to try and disentangle from the things told of Nuada any of the features of Nodens of the Silures in Gloucestershire, it is at least highly probable that the two were originally the same", he asserted (Tolkien 1932, 133). "Linguistic considerations unaided by other data can do little, usually, to recall forgotten gods from their twilight", he later wrote, but found that "Nodens" might be an exception because its form made it likely that it was a *description*, "a title of a god whose remoter proper name is lost" (135). He deduced that the word was Indo-European, and by going back to Germanic word-stems, illuminated by Gothic, Old English, Old Saxon, Old High German and Old Norse examples (although not Celtic ones; Tolkien thought the cognate form had not survived), he arrived at the conclusion that the name had probably meant "the 'snarer' or the 'catcher' or the 'hunter'". Whether the god had borne such a name in "some sinister sense, or merely as being a lord of venery", i.e. hunting, he could not establish, but he found it "suggestive" that it was, in Celtic mythology, Nuada's *hand* that was remembered. "Even in the dimmed memories of Welsh legend in *llaw ereint* [a reference to the cognate figure, Lludd of the silver hand, in Wales] we hear still an echo of the ancient fame of the magic hand of Nodens the Catcher" (137).

This last sentence is extremely Tolkienian. It illustrates his tendency to evoke, coax and call forth conceptions and figures from long-forgotten eras on the basis of single words and their roots. He loved the dark and misty borderlands between history and mythology, and used comparative philology to try and illuminate them. As we know, this tendency played an important role in the creation of his legendarium. The inspiration he derived from two lines of Cynewulf's ninth century poem 'Crist', and especially the word "Éarendel", is a famous example. Another is Tom Shippey's brilliant demonstration of how Tolkien, on the basis of Old English *silhearwan*, tentatively reconstructed an ancient notion of fire-demons, and used them in his legendarium under the name of Balrogs.

4. The number of articles on the subject is enormous. Lynn Forest-Hill's 2016 article is one of the better treatments. See also Edwards 2014, 159f.

5. Cf. https://romaninscriptionsofbritain.org/inscriptions/306, visited on July 27, 2019. Here the verdicts of Tolkien's above-mentioned colleague R.G. Collingwood and his fellow expert R.P. Wright is that the connection is "unlikely".

6. Do, however, see Agøy 2003, 110; and cf. 9 note below.

Both Shippey and Tolkien's younger colleague Arne Zettersten have often mentioned how Tolkien's professional work and his fiction are deeply intertwined. Indeed, a main theme in Zettersten's 2011 book, *Tolkien's Double Worlds and Creative Process*, is how the professor did not seem to make any clear distinction between his legendarium and his philological work.[7] Referring to Tolkien's last years, Zettersten wrote that he himself

> learnt more and more to follow his [i.e. Tolkien's] switches from research and facts into fictional literature and understood better and better how he could dwell in both worlds at the same time or enjoy interplay between them. These tracks between the two worlds ran very closely together and Tolkien could rush along them simultaneously. (2011, 25)

In another context, he mentions how Tolkien "could suddenly flit between the primary and the secondary world without the slightest difficulty or doubt" (113).

You will no doubt have gathered by now that I think Tolkien's note on the name "Nodens" is in some way reflected in his legendarium. But where and how? There is no entry for "snarer" or "catcher" or "hunter" in the indices of *The Silmarillion* or *The History of Middle-earth*. But wait; there is indeed a Hunter, who intriguingly is said to be mythological.

In chapter 3 of *The Silmarillion*, 'Of the Coming of the Elves', we learn how the Elves woke by the starlit mere of Cuiviénen and how Oromë the Vala, riding on his white horse Nahar, came upon them, and loved them, and named them Eldar, the people of the stars. And I quote:

> Yet many of the Quendi were filled with dread at his coming; and this was the doing of Melkor. For by after-knowledge the wise declare that Melkor, ever watchful, was first aware of the awakening of the Quendi, and sent shadows and evil spirits to spy upon them and waylay them. So it came to pass, some years ere the coming of Oromë, that if any of the Elves strayed far abroad, alone or few together, they would often vanish, and never return; and the Quendi said that the Hunter had caught them, and they were afraid. And indeed the most ancient songs of the Elves, of which echoes are remembered still in the West, tell of the shadow-shapes that walked in the hills above Cuiviénen, or would pass suddenly over the stars; and of the dark Rider upon his wild horse that pursued those that wandered to take them and devour them. Now Melkor greatly hated and feared the riding of Oromë, and either he sent indeed his dark servants as riders, or he set lying whispers abroad, for the purpose that the Quendi should shun Oromë, if ever they should meet. (*Silmarillion*, 49f.)

The hypothesis, then, is that the shadowy and terrible figure of the Hunter is partly, maybe largely, derived from, or inspired by, the equally shadowy figure of Nodens the Hunter (or Catcher or Snarer, but Tolkien would have had to choose one), in a decidedly sinister sense.

A principle that is too often ignored, in Tolkien scholarship as elsewhere, is that if you have a theory, you should do your best to disprove it. So, what are the counterindications?

The main thing to check is of course when the concept of the Hunter appears in the legendarium. If it was present before Tolkien worked on the Lydney inscriptions, the

7. See Zettersten 2011 chapters 4 and 14, cf. 7, 46, 112-114, 123, 151, 211.

hypothesis is dead. There are several texts dating from before 1931 that refer directly or indirectly to the coming of the Elves and their long march westwards. Cuiviénen as the starting-point of the "long marches" is mentioned once in the earliest version of 'The Lay of the Children of Húrin', written when Tolkien taught at Leeds, and the 'Sketch of the Mythology', usually dated to c. 1926, tells how Oromë discovered the Elves by Cuiviénen, and that Melkor is captured before they start their march. "The Eldalië (people of the Elves) are invited to Valinor for fear of the evil things of Morgoth that still wandered in the dark" (*Lays*, 18; *Shaping*, 13). In the relevant part of the 'Quenta', dated by Christopher Tolkien to 1930, Morgoth is also captive when the Elves set out for the West, although there is again reference to many of his evil things who dared "to roam in the secret pathways of the world" (*Shaping*, 84).

The 'Quenta' was developed into the 'Quenta Silmarillion' that Tolkien sent to his publisher in late 1937, and intermediate versions are not known for the parts covering the earliest history of the Elves (*Lost Road*, 199f.). The 'Quenta Silmarillion' is very similar to the 'Quenta' where the awakening of the Elves and their march is concerned, in substance if not in wording (212f.). No mention is made of any Hunter or other sinister figure harassing the marching Elves, but unfortunately it is impossible to say exactly when the relevant part of the 'Quenta Silmarillion' was written. Tolkien did write both the earliest and later Annals of Valinor in the early and mid-1930s, but here Oromë's discovery of the Elves and their march is only mentioned summarily, without details (*Shaping*, 264; *Lost Road*, 112). Then, after starting a revision of the 'Quenta Silmarillion' in 1937-1938, *The Lord of the Rings* took over, and the Silmarillion was put on the shelf for many years.

It is in the major reworking Tolkien attempted after the publication of *The Lord of the Rings* that the Hunter makes his appearance. It happens first in a marginal addition to 'The Annals of Aman', dating perhaps from 1958; an addition later expanded and typewritten to replace the earlier page. The context is Oromë's finding the Elves, and the marginal passage tells that:

> Melkor's lies were soon abroad, so that whispers were heard among the Quendi, warning them that if any of their kindred passed away into the shadows and were seen no more, they must beware of a fell huntsman on a great horse, for he it was that carried them off to devour them. Hence it was that at the approach of Oromë many of the Quendi fled and hid themselves. (Morgoth, 73)

In the replacement text, this is expanded:

> Yet many of the Quendi were adread at his coming. This was the doing of Melkor. For by after-knowledge the masters of lore say that Melkor, ever watchful, was first aware of the awakening of the Quendi, and sent shadows and evil some years ere the coming of Oromë, that if any of the Elves strayed far abroad, alone or few together, they would often vanish and never return; and the Quendi said that the Hunter had caught them, and they were afraid. Even so, in the most ancient songs of our people, of which some echoes are remembered still in the West, we hear of the shadow-shapes that walked in the hills about Kuiviénen, or would pass suddenly over the stars; and of the dark Rider upon his wild horse that pursued those that wandered to take them and devour them. Now Melkor

> greatly hated and feared the riding of Oromé, and either verily he sent his dark servants as riders, or he set lying whispers abroad, for the purpose that the Quendi should shun Oromë, if ever haply they met. (73)

This is the text we find in the published *Silmarillion*, only with some minute language-modernising and perspective-altering changes. It concerns the situation *before* the war in which Melkor is taken captive, but later in the annals there is reference to "the lies of Melkor concerning Oromë and Nahar" which make some Elves fear Oromë "as a demon that would devour them" (82).[8]

Tolkien also worked on the 'Quenta Silmarillion' from about 1950. In a text probably written in the late 1950s, Aulë sends weapons to the Quendi, because it had become "known to the Valar that the Quendi were beset by prowling evils that had discovered the places of their dwelling beside Cuiviénen" (276f.). This fits very well with the just-quoted passage from 'The Annals of Aman'. Finally, in the 'Grey Annals', begun c. 1950, the spies of Melkor discover the Quendi in Valian Year 1080, "and afflicted them", five years before Oromë arrives at the scene (*War*, 5). This was actually a later addition to the manuscript, and it is clear that it stems from the same time that Tolkien wrote the Hunter and the Rider into 'The Annals of Aman', after considering placing it in 'The Grey Annals' instead (105; cf. 117).

So far, the hypothesis survives. There is no mention of the dreadful Hunter in legendarium texts until after Tolkien's work on the Lydney inscriptions.

Is it an argument against the connection that the legendarium presents the Hunter as being also a Rider? I do not think so. As we have just seen, 'The Annals of Aman' and the published *Silmarillion* use both appellations in the same context, and there is no reason to believe that Nodens the Catcher, as imagined by Tolkien in 1931, could not have been a rider as well. Some of you will, when the talk is of frightening riders, probably have considered the Black Riders of *The Fellowship if the Ring* or recalled the one mentioned by Boromir when he told the Council of Elrond about Gondor's war in the east:

> A power was there that we have not felt before.
> 'Some said that it could be seen, like a great black horseman, a dark shadow under the moon. Wherever he came a madness filled our foes, but fear fell on our boldest, so that horse and man gave way and fled.' (*FR*, 'The Council of Elrond', 245)

Although it would be rash to rule them out completely, these tentative Nazgûl links are in my estimation too tenuous to support a claim of inspiration from Nodens like the one I make for the Hunter in *The Silmarillion.*

My argument is admittedly circumstantial.[9] The thing that originally made me think of the connection, is that Nodens the Catcher, remembered by his hand, and the

8. This was also an addition to the first typescript.

9. The present paper was written in early 2019. After it had been presented at Tolkien 2019, I discovered that John D. Rateliff had made a similar argument towards the end of his most interesting article about Tolkien's 'The Name "Nodens"' in *A Wilderness of Dragons: Essays in Honor of Verlyn Flieger*, published in 2018. I take this as a welcome independent confirmation of the idea that I originally propounded in 2003.

legendarium Hunter, both inhabit a half-lit mythological borderland. They are unclear figures, remembered only vaguely, but are therefore more terrifying. They represent that which we fear to meet at night in the dark, unknown places, outside the light of the campfire. Tolkien found the memory of Nuada's hand "suggestive". I think it is suggestive also how the figures of Nodens and the dark Hunter are described by him in strikingly similar ways. "Even in the dimmed memories of Welsh legend in *llaw ereint* we hear still an echo of the ancient fame of the magic hand of Nodens the Catcher" (Tolkien 1932, 137), he wrote; while the Hunter figures in "the most ancient songs of our people [the Elves], of which some echoes are remembered still in the West" (*Morgoth*, 73). My tentative contention is that in the dark and terrible Hunter, we hear an even dimmer echo of the ancient Nodens, and that this is yet another instance of how Tolkien's philological calling informed and inspired his legendarium.

Bibliography

Agøy, N. I., *Mytenes Mann: J.R.R. Tolkien og Hans Forfatterskap,* (Oslo: Tiden, 2003).

Edwards, R., *Tolkien,* (London: Robert Hale, 2014).

Forest-Hill, L., 'Tolkien, Lydney and the Vyne: Patterns of Loss and Discovery', online paper (2016) <https://www.academia.edu/26869694/Tolkien_Lydney_and_the_Vyne.doc> [accessed 23 July 23 2019].

Hammond, W.G. & C. Scull, *The J.R.R. Tolkien Companion and Guide*, 2 Vols (London: HarperCollins, 2006).

Lyons, M., *There and Back Again in the Footsteps of J.R.R. Tolkien,* (London: Cadogan Guides, 2004).

Phelpstead, C., *Tolkien and Wales: Language, Literature and Identity,* (Cardiff: University of Wales Press, 2011).

Rateliff, J. D.: '"To Recall Forgotten Gods from their Twilight": J. R. R. Tolkien's 'The Name *Nodens*', in *A Wilderness of Dragons: Essays in Honor of Verlyn Flieger*, ed. by J. D. Rateliff (Wayzata: Gabbro Head, 2018), pp. 196–224.

Sabo, D., 'Archaeology and the Sense of History in J.R.R. Tolkien's Middle-earth', *Mythlore*, 99/100 (2007), 91–112.

Shippey, T. A., *The Road to Middle-earth*, (London: Allen & Unwin, 1981).

Tolkien, J.R.R., *The Lord of the Rings*, (Boston: Houghton Mifflin, 2004).
— *The Lays of Beleriand*, ed. by C. Tolkien (London: Allen & Unwin, 1985).
— *The Lost Road and Other Writings*, ed. by C. Tolkien (London: Allen & Unwin, 1987).
— *Morgoth's Ring*, ed. by C. Tolkien (London: HarperCollins, 1993).
— 'The Name "Nodens"', in *Report on the Excavation of the Prehistoric, Roman and Post-Roman Site in Lydney Park, Gloucestershire*, Reports of the Research Committee of the Society of Antiquaries of London, IX (London: Oxford University Press, 1932) 132-137. Reprinted in *Tolkien Studies*, 2007.
— *The Shaping of Middle-earth*, ed. by C. Tolkien (London: Allen & Unwin, 1986).
— *The War of the Jewels*, ed. by C. Tolkien (London: HarperCollins, 1994).
— *The Silmarillion*, ed. by C. Tolkien (London: Allen & Unwin, 1977).

Wheeler, R.E.M., and T.V. Wheeler, *Report on the Excavation of the Prehistoric, Roman and Post-Roman*

Site in Lydney Park, Gloucestershire, Reports of the Research Committee of the Society of Antiquaries of London, IX (London: Oxford University Press, 1932).

Zettersten, A., *J.R.R. Tolkien's Double Worlds and Creative Process: Language and Life,* (Basingstoke: Palgrave Macmillan, 2011).

Tolkien, Folklore, and Foxes: a thoroughly vulpine paper (with optional singing)

Professor Dimitra Fimi

In *The Fellowship of the Ring*, specifically the last chapter of Book I, chapter 12, 'Flight to the Ford', the hobbits and Aragorn chance upon the trolls from Bilbo's very first adventure in *The Hobbit*. Despite some initial alarm, they soon realize that the trolls are, of course, safely petrified, and a moment of relieved gaiety occurs. Merry asks for a song, and Sam obliges by singing an eight-stanza narrative song about a troll who has stolen a bone and is munching it happily, before being confronted by the nephew of the bone's owner, who demands it back. Up until this point in the plot, the reader has encountered a good few songs by hobbits, but only a handful more will appear in the remainder of *The Lord of the Rings*. Frodo has already been wounded at Weathertop, the hobbits are well out of the Shire, and things are getting darker and more serious. The dreaded Black Riders will appear again very soon after this scene, more dangerous than ever. And yet, Samwise Gamgee has the gusto and creative spirit to invent impromptu (and very funny) lyrics for what he explains is 'an old tune', adapting the subject-matter for the occasion, the spot of Bilbo's earlier adventure, in the shade of the three trolls.

Tolkien students and fans will know that Tolkien did not invent this song just for Sam, and only when he got to that point of writing *The Lord of the Rings*. Tolkien was a great recycler. He first wrote what became 'The Stone Troll' in the 1920s. The earliest version was called 'Pēro & Pōdex' (Latin 'Boot and Bottom', i.e. the human's boot that kicked the troll's very hard bottom!), later revised as 'The Root of the Boot' (*Bombadil*, 193). It was under this latter title that it was included (with other poems by Tolkien and E.V. Gordon) in *Songs for the Philologists,* originally composed when both of them were at Leeds (Tolkien 1936, 20-1). Tolkien actually was recorded singing this version of the poem by George Sayer in 1952. This recording was included in the 1975 Caedmon Records LP titled *J.R.R. Tolkien Reads and Sings His The Hobbit and The Fellowship of the Ring* and has been reproduced in later collections of Tolkien audio material.[1]

'The Root of the Boot' is very close to Sam's song, though with more regional dialect words, and more religious references, notably to heaven and hell, as in the following two verses:

> 'Young man', says the troll, 'that bone I stole;
> But what be bones, when mayhap the soul
> In heaven on high hath an aureole
> As big and as bright as a bonfire?
> On fire, yon fire.'
> (*Bombadil*, 194)

1. Tolkien, *J.R.R. Tolkien Reads and Sings His The Hobbit and The Lord of the Rings* (1975); later also included in J.R.R. Tolkien, *The J.R.R. Tolkien Audio Collection* (2001).

So the troll seems to be saying, in a very Christian-spirited fashion, that Tom shouldn't worry about the body of his dead uncle – what really matters is the soul which is now up in heaven surrounded by a bright halo – so munching old John's old bone is neither here nor there.

However:

> Says Tom: 'Oddsteeth! 'tis my belief,
> If bonfire there be, 'tis underneath;
> For old man John was as proper a thief
> As ever wore black on a Sunday –
> Grundy, Monday!
> (194)

So clearly old man John was no saint with a halo – the only bright thing about him are the flames of hell roasting him! Christopher Tolkien mentioned that his father was 'extremely fond' of the troll song and that he remembered his father singing it, adding that his delight in the line "If bonfire there be, 'tis underneath" was among his very early recollections from his father (*Shadow*, 142).

Sam, therefore, is not just singing words to an 'old tune'. He is literally reusing an old song by Tolkien. But the 'old tune' itself is also recycled. It is a real old tune from an old folk song. Most people know it as 'The Fox Went Out', or 'The Fox and the Goose', or just 'The Fox'. Typically, it begins with:

> The fox went out on a chilly night,
> he prayed to the Moon to give him light,
> for he'd many a mile to go that night
> before he reached the town-o, town-o, town-o,
> he had many a mile to go that night
> before he reached the town-o.
> (Lewis-Stempel 2020, 79)

The story it tells is that of a fox out at night to steal his dinner from the nearby town. The fox reaches the farmer's yard, and seizes a goose (or in some versions a duck) by the neck, the quacking of which wakes the old woman in the farm, who alerts the farmer. But too late! By the time the farmer has blown his horn, the fox is far away and comfortably reaches his 'cozy den' where his ten little ones are waiting. And then the fox, his wife, and the little cubs have the meal of their lives at the expense of the farmer. If that story reminds you a bit of Roald Dahl's *Fantastic Mr Fox* (1970), this is because they are part of the same tradition.

'The Fox' is a very popular folk song indeed, collected widely in England (often Devonshire and Cornwall) but with versions also well known in Scotland, and a long history of transmission in North America, in the North from New England to Iowa and in the South from North Carolina to Missouri (Perkins 1961, 237, 239). There are variations on the lyrics, but the main story, certain descriptive terms, the metre and repetitions, and some specific turns of phrasing remain the same (1961). There are also variations of the tune. Tolkien seems to have favoured a particular version, which comes from the collection *What the Children Sing* (1915), by Alfred Moffat, illustrated by H. Willebeek Le Mair.[2]

But how old is this 'old' folk song? Why did it attract Tolkien's attention? Is it just its addictively memorable tune? Is it its subject matter? Or is it its age and provenance? The latter possibility is a strong one. In 1952, two scholars published their respective editions of a 15th-century Middle English poem, found in a manuscript in the British Museum, conventionally called 'The Fox and the Goose'. The first scholar was Rossell Hope Robbins in his *Secular Lyrics of the XIVth and XVth Centuries* (1952, 43). The second one was R. H. Bowers in the *Journal of English and German Philology* (1952, 393-4). The poem begins like this:

> 'Pax uobis,' quod the ffox,
> 'for I am comyn to toowne.'
>
> It fell ageyns the next nyght
> the fox yede to with all his myghte,
> with-outen cole or candelight,
> whan that he cam vnto the toowne.
> (Perkins 1961, 245)

The story is very similar, and the meter is the same. If one tries, one could actually sing this exactly the same way as Tolkien sings 'The Stone Troll', and one can sing the modern folk song 'The Fox'. Bowers himself pointed to the similarity of the Middle-English poem with the 'The Fox Went Out', while in 1961 George Perkins wrote the definitive article that proved that the ME poem is indeed the ancestor of the modern folk song.

The Middle-English poem is written in the dialect of the East Midlands, with perhaps some Northern influences, and the manuscript is dated to within twenty-five years either way of 1500, but there is good reason to believe the song was in existence for some time before that (Kurath and Kuhn 1954, 94). Robbins included it in his edition of popular songs, which "would be sung at popular gatherings in the hall, in the inn, on the green, on the road" (1952, xxxiv). It is clearly incomplete (it is missing the beginning), it contains a number of irregularities and archaisms, and therefore it seems to have been remembered, with some omissions, from oral tradition; it could well be 100 years older than the manuscript (Perkins 1961, 236).

Now, all three of these publications are too late for 'The Root of the Boot', which, as mentioned above, Tolkien first composed in the 1920s. But Tolkien may well have known the manuscript (which was listed in earlier publications) (Brown and Robbins 1943, no. 1622) and in any case could have suspected that 'The Fox' was way older than 19th-century folklore collecting efforts. Versions or extracts were actually printed a good few times in the earlier 19th century, before the big rise of the folklore movement,

2. Jessica Yates, who owns her mother's copy of this collection, first detected the many parallels between the rhymes with their piano accompaniment in this book and those in *Songs for the Philologists* written by Tolkien. Tolkien's grandson Michael confirmed in 1998 that he owned the book, passed down from his grandparents to his father (Jessica Yates, personal communication).

and I give below a small selection. First, from an extract in 1801 in *Gammar Gurton's Garland: or The Nursery Parnassus*, by Joseph Ritson:

> Old Mother Widdle Waddle jumpt out of bed,
> And out at the casement she popt out her head:
> Crying the house is on fire, the grey goose is dead,
> And the fox he is come to the town, oh!
> (Riston 1810, 41)

And in 1826 Sir Walter Scott also knew a version which began:

> 'Eh,' quo' the tod, 'it's a braw licht nicht,
> The win's i' the wast, and the mune shines bricht.
> The win's i' the wast, and the mune shines bricht,
> And I'll awa' to the toun, O.
> (qtd. in Opie 1977, 175)

There is also evidence to suggest that 'The Fox' was popular in North America at least since the Civil War (Perkins 1961, 239).

Tolkien may well have known the manuscript of the Middle-English poem, but he must have also recognized the resonances of the later folk song with the medieval *tradition* of the cunning fox as a folk-song and folktale character. As far as medieval foxes go, the familiar figure is Reynard the Fox, the anthropomorphic trickster fox who became so popular in medieval Europe (there are versions of his stories in Dutch, English, French and German), that 'renard' became the standard French word for 'fox', replacing the old French *goupil* (Terry 1992, 3). Reynard's adventures involve him deceiving other anthropomorphic animals for his own benefit or trying to avoid their attempts at retaliation. He eludes capture and justice, he always manages to turn every situation to his own advantage, and he survives against all odds through sheer cleverness and cunning. He is a typical popular culture subversive hero – not at all heroic or noble, but most certainly triumphant at the end of every story.

Reynard is mentioned in 'On Fairy-stories', at the point where Tolkien deals with beast-fables, a genre which – he argues – has some connection to fairy stories, but is not fairy-story proper, because, Tolkien explains, "the animal form is only a mask upon a human face" (*OFS*, 36). Two names from the Reynard cycle (both of them antagonists or rivals of the clever fox) crop up elsewhere in the legendarium. In *The Book of Lost Tales*, Tevildo, the Prince of Cats, a character who later evolved to become Sauron, also bears the name Tiberth, clearly an allusion to Tibert the Cat in the Reynard stories (*Lost Tales II*, 45, 47-9, 51). Also, three Thains of the Shire, Isengrim Took the first, second, and third (Isengrim the second was the most notable one!) bear the name of Isengrim/ Ysengrim the Wolf, the main enemy (and victim!) of Reynard (*FR*, 'Prologue', 2, 3; *RK*, 'Appendix B'). Tolkien himself explained: "The name is an old Germanic one perhaps best known now as the name (Isegrim) adopted for the Wolf as a character in the romance of Reynard the Fox" (Tolkien 1975, 168-9).

We also know – though it remains unpublished – that in the 1920s Tolkien wrote a poem titled: 'Reginhardus the Fox' (Reginhardus is the Germanic cognate of 'Reynard')

(Scull and Hammond 2017, 118). This was sitting alongside three other poems inspired by medieval bestiaries: 'Oliphaunt' (which is well known, because it ended up in *The Lord of the Rings* – another case of recycling), 'Fastitocalon' (which was included in *The Adventures of Tom Bombadil*), and 'Monoceros the Unicorn' (which is also unpublished).

Tolkien was also aware of other medieval foxes. In the 1950s Tolkien was appointed to supervise G.M.G. Evans of St Hugh's College as a B.Litt. student, working on a thesis on 'an edition of the fable of 'The Fox and the Wolf' from MS Digby 86' (394). This is the 13th-century story of a fox (called Reynard at least once in the MS) who fails to outwit a rooster, but manages to fool a wolf. Tolkien would have also been familiar with the fox in the *Ancrene Wisse* (a text he edited). In the *Ancrene Wisse* each of the seven deadly sins is represented by an animal and the fox stands for covetousness (Wada 2003, 3). Also, *Sir Gawain and the Green Knight* includes a famous fox hunt scene. (In this case the fox doesn't fare that well, I am afraid!) Tolkien actually wrote in a letter to Naomi Mitchinson (about an overdue lecture he had to write) that: 'I composed it with "all the woe in the world", as the Gawain-poet says of the wretched fox with the hounds on his tail' (*Letters*, Letter 176, 228). He also used another medieval fox as an analogy when writing to his publishers regarding the Ace paperbacks controversy in the USA. He compared Donald A. Wollheim of Ace Books to 'Dan Russell', the wily fox in 'The Nun's Priest's Tale' in Chaucer's *Canterbury Tales*:

> I trust that I do not sound too cordial in my final reply to Wollheim. I had agreed to be 'amicable' – but not juicy.... His letter is so comically reminiscent of Dan Russel to Chanteclere: com doun and I vil telle thee what I mente. (He could, of course, have approached me from the beginning with his flatter, but he is not quite as clever as the Fox). (Scull and Hammond 2017, 691)

The fox, actually has had a long legendary career in literary and popular culture, from antiquity to modern folklore. For Aristotle the fox is associated with the primordial (and threatening) powers of the earth. It hides itself in burrows and eludes empirical observation. It is wicked through and through. For Lucretius, the fox is deceitful and beguiling – combining wickedness with cunning. Christian texts and iconography condemned the fox as evil: the 2nd-century Physiologus compares the Fox with the devil (Wallen 2006, 11-3, 15).

But by the time the Reynard cycle of stories was developing in the later Middle-Ages the tradition had diverged into two separate strands. First, thee 'canonical' Christian interpretation of the fox as devilish, corrupting and evil (there are numerous medieval depictions of the fox dressed as a priest, luring an innocent congregation of ducks or geese to their death – a clear warning for the faithful of the devil's wiles!); and, second, the secular (and far more popular) celebration of the fox as a survivor via pure cleverness, which, yes, may cross into deceit, theft, being economical with the truth, or different degrees of criminal activity, but which at the end acknowledges subversion and breaking the rules as a way to get by in a largely unjust society (45-51).

This ambivalent position of the fox (both wicked and praiseworthy) is actually very much mirrored in the bafflement this creature has caused to later scientific observation.

The fox is a between-and-betwixt creature that has eluded easy and neat scientific classification. It is something in-between a cat and a dog: while it belongs to the canidae family, it has evolved catlike morphological features (e.g. its whiskers that have tactile receptors, foot pads, semi-retractile claws, and sort-of-luminous eyes) and feline hunting strategies (e.g. it pounces on its victims) (23-4, 36-7). It is significant that J.D. Henry's scientific study on red foxes is subtitled: 'The Catlike Canine',[3] while Martin Wallen's influential book on all aspects of foxes (from nature to literature and culture) repeats in different wording that statement: "of all creatures, the fox seems to be the one whose most defining characteristic is ambiguity" (32).

And ambiguity, rather than consistency is what we get from Tolkien's treatment of foxes. In his engagement with medieval foxes I discussed above, we see Tolkien pitying the hunted fox in *Sir Gawain* (or rather himself via the hunted fox in *Sir Gawain*!), and simultaneously critiquing but also admiring the 'cunning' of the fox in 'The Nun's Priest's Tale'. This same ambivalent attitude continues in other uses of the fox in Tolkien's work. Gollum is twice compared to a fox in *The Lord of the Rings*, first by Aragorn in *The Fellowship of the Ring*, when Frodo tells him that he thinks he's seen Gollum:

> 'Ah!' said Aragorn. 'So you know about our little footpad, do you? He padded after us all through Moria and right down to Nimrodel. Since we took to boats, he has been lying on a log and paddling with hands and feet. I have tried to catch him once or twice at night; *but he is slier than a fox*, and as slippery as a fish. I hoped the river-voyage would beat him, but he is too clever a waterman. (*FR*, 'The Great River', 384; emphasis mine)

Much later, Faramir uses the same comparison when he demands to know the aim of Frodo and Sam's journey:

> 'Where is the third of your company? '
> 'The third?'
> 'Yes, the skulking fellow that we saw with his nose in the pool down yonder. He had an ill-favoured look. Some spying breed of Orc, I guess, or a creature of theirs. *But he gave us the slip by some fox-trick.*' (*TT*, 'Of Herbs and Stewed Rabbit', 657; emphasis mine)

In both of these cases the fox analogy points to a creature that smacks of evil and deceit but is also to be rather admired for his skillful elusiveness.

We also know that Tolkien used the figure of the fox in one of his earliest linguistic documents, the Book of the Foxrook, a small notebook in which he outlined a secret code composed in 1909, inspired by his involvement in the Scouting Movement and his interest in linguistic invention (Smith and Wynne 2000, 27-46). In this notebook Tolkien seems to be using elements of Animalic (a language he learned from his cousins Mary and Marjorie Incledon) in that he equates a scout with a fox. Smith and Wynne have speculated that the choice of the fox to signify a scout may be referring "to the fox's reputation as a woodland creature of proverbial cunning" (32). The fox analogy here is positive, pointing to skill with signs and communication, but it also allows for a hint of something that can potentially go wrong: stealthiness and secretiveness.

3. Henry 1996.

I think that this long literary and folklore tradition of the fox as an ambiguous creature is also part of the reason why the folk tune of 'The Fox' attracted new lyrics about a troll from Tolkien. One may well say, of course, that a troll is evil through and through. But is that a fair judgment? The trolls in *The Hobbit* certainly have cannibalistic desires and plan to cook the dwarves and Bilbo, but one has to accept that they are not typical villains. They are rather stupid and the sources of a humorous note at that point in the text. At the same time, the Stone Troll in Sam's song is not that evil either. He just wants to gnaw on a dead man's bone, who – let's face it – doesn't really need that bone anymore! From our modern point of view the Stone Troll is very much in the hipster tradition of using leftovers and discarded ingredients to create a sustainable meal! It is only when Tom tries to poke him (or rather kick his bottom) and is morally pedantic (his logic is that theft is theft, whether the owner needs his bone or not!) that the Troll threatens Tom (but still doesn't quite action his threat!) And it is important to remember that Tolkien has at least one wholly sympathetic troll in his corpus: the troll in 'The Bumpus', a poem later revised and included in *The Adventures of Tom Bombadil* as 'Perry-the-Winkle', which features a lonely troll with exceptional baking skills, looking for a friend (*Bombadil*, 201-9).

So, if we think of both the Fox in the folksong, and the Troll in Sam's song as creatures in ambivalent positions (whose side are we on in the folksong? I suspect most of us are with the fox who has ten little cubs to feed), then the resonances between the tune Sam uses and the lyrics he invents are even stronger. If this is 'an old tune' even in the Shire, then I suspect Tolkien means that old Shire tune to actually be 'The Fox'. Which makes things complicated if we now turn to yet one more occasion on which Tolkien used the same tune, 'The Fox Went Out'. Because this time we have no mere troll. This time, the lyrics are about Grendel.

When Christopher Tolkien published his edition of his father's translation of *Beowulf*, he also gave us a lot of supplementary materials which are relevant to this discussion. First of all, we now have Tolkien's teaching notes on *Beowulf* and in this extensive commentary on the poem Tolkien is preoccupied with a number of thematic strands, one of which is how the poem combines historical elements with folkloric motifs and traditions. Christopher, in his usual generosity, gave us one more text: 'Sellic Spell', Tolkien's attempt to 'reconstruct' a folktale that could have been the folkloric source in the composition of *Beowulf* as we know it. Most importantly for this paper, the last 'extra' that Christopher offered us were two 'Lays' which attempt to re-cast the story of Beowulf as traditional folk ballads (i.e. narrative folk songs). And, what a surprise, these two lays are also intended to be sung in the tune of 'The Fox Went Out'.

Both lays are compact and memorable summaries of *Beowulf*. If we focus on the first (and shorter) lay, we can see immediately that the opening stanza is structurally very close to 'The Fox':

> Grendel came forth in the dead of night;
> the moon in his eyes shone glassy bright,
> as over the moors he strode in might,
> until he came to Heorot.
> (*Beowulf*, 417)

Like the fox, Grendel appears at night and has a distance to cover, while the moon is referenced in the second line of both texts. In the lay, instead of the triple repetition of 'town-o' we have the metrically compatible 'Heorot'. The last two stanzas of the lay allude (very briefly and rather cryptically if one does not know the story) to the eventual destruction of Heorot in the distant future of the storyline, and the death of Beowulf. In the last stanza, "one hoar of head" refers to the now old, white-haired Beowulf, who is lying dying from the dragon's venom, and brings to mind the light of Heorot (419).

Using 'The Fox' as a tune for a humorous troll song is one thing, but using it for a retelling of one of the most venerable texts in the history of English literature is quite another. One could argue that Tolkien had grown too fond of the tune of 'The Fox' and that he just re-used it out of habit: it is catchy, it has a meter that had worked for him before, and it has the credentials of a folksong that has survived over many generations. So if one wants to compose a hypothetical folk ballad about Beowulf, one can't go too wrong by using it. Or can one? Wouldn't we expect a more somber and melancholy tune for a ballad that ends with the final destruction of Heorot and Beowulf's death? On the other hand, isn't the repetition of 'Heorot' three times in every stanza a glorious way to celebrate this famous mead hall, and perhaps make its destruction feel more poignant at the very end? It is all rather complicated. But, I guess, that is what the folk tradition is too: complicated. Folk songs sung in the 19th century can be shown to go back to the Middle Ages, creatures that are condemned in ecclesiastical sources can be celebrated in the folk tradition, monstrous beings such as Trolls and even Grendel, can be treated in a comic or sympathetic way – one can certainly crack a bit of a smile at the line: "but Grendel gnaws the flesh and bone/of the thirty thanes of Heorot", which brings vividly to mind the scene of the Troll and the old bone (417).

Grendel of course is not Tolkien's troll. He is not usually considered as ambiguous, though there is some scholarship claiming that Grendel is to be pitied: he's an exile, he is a loner, he is jealous of the happiness of Heorot – perhaps he is a bit misunderstood?[4] And Grendel has luminous eyes. As per above, the lay opens with:

> Grendel came forth in the dead of night;
> *the moon in his eyes shone glassy bright*,
> (417; emphasis mine)

In his translation Tolkien writes that 'from his eyes stood forth most like to flame unholy light' (33). It is very tempting, therefore, to link this to the luminous eyes of the fox as perhaps an unconscious chiming note between the subject matter of Grendel and the tune of 'The Fox'.

What is fascinating is that in all three sets of lyrics, 'The Fox', 'The Stone Troll' and 'The Lay of Beowulf', the antagonist (the fox, the troll, and Grendel) sort of all win eventually! The fox gets the goose and escapes unscathed; the troll manages to make Tom's leg lame and continues to munch his bone rather defiantly; and Grendel's curse seems to work in the end, as the poem ends with the destruction of Heorot and Beowulf.

4. See, for example, Robert L. Chapman, 'Alas, Poor Grendel', *College English*, 17.6 (1956), 334-337 and Joseph L. Baird, 'Grendel the Exile', *Neuphilologische Mitteilungen*, 67 (1966), 375-81.

But let's return to the Shire, as this paper comes to a close. I have promised a 'thoroughly vulpine paper', and vulpine might as well mean 'labyrinthine' – foxes' burrows are underground labyrinths with multiple exits and dead ends, and so far I have taken you through the turns (and some of the dead ends) of a metaphorical fox's burrow. But readers will legitimately protest that so far I have not mentioned *the* fox, i.e. the fox we encounter (and whose inner thoughts we hear) in *The Lord of the Rings*. Bear with me a little longer, we're coming to this point.

I have discussed in my previous work how Book I of *The Fellowship of the Ring* is particularly concerned with folklore – hobbit folklore specifically.[5] Indeed, the conception of the hobbits is very close indeed to the 19th-century perception of the sort of people that usually transmit oral folklore: they are rustic and naïve, mostly uneducated and simple-minded, and revel in telling amusing stories and singing traditional rhyming songs. These songs are not about heroic legend, but rather associated with everyday activities. For example, in the beginning of *The Fellowship of the Rings*, when Frodo, Sam and Pippin are on the way to Buckland, they start singing a drinking song ("Ho! Ho! Ho! to the bottle I go/To heal my heart and drown my woe", *FR*, 'A Shortcut to Mushrooms', 90). Later on, while taking a bath after arriving at Crickhollow, Pippin sings "one of Bilbo's favourite bath-songs" praising the delights of hot water (*FR*, 'A Conspiracy Unmasked', 101).

In addition, some of the songs the hobbits sing are good examples of how folklore really works: by every singer changing and modifying traditional material for their own purposes. For instance, consider the 'walking song' that Frodo, Sam and Pippin sing, again on the way to Buckland ("Upon the hearth the fire is red,/Beneath the roof there is a bed", *FR*, 'Three is Company', 77). We are told that "Bilbo Baggins had made the words, to a tune that was as old as the hills, and taught it to Frodo" (77). Similarly, when Merry and Pippin have convinced Frodo that they will go with him in his great adventure, they sing a farewell song which "they had apparently got ready for the occasion. It was made on the model of the dwarf-song that started Bilbo on his adventure long ago, and went to the same tune: Farewell we call to hearth and hall!/Though wind may blow and rain may fall" (*FR*, 'A Conspiracy Unmasked', 106).

And, of course, even more impressively, we saw at the very beginning of this paper how Sam seems perfectly capable of creating an entire new set of lyrics for an 'old tune' on the spot. Impressed by the funny and metrically intricate troll song, Pippin inquiries:

> 'Where did you come by that, Sam?' asked Pippin. 'I've never heard those words before.' Sam muttered something inaudible. 'It's out of his own head, of course,' said Frodo. (*FR*, 'Flight to the Ford', 208)

If we keep in mind how all of this first part of *The Lord of the Rings* is steeped in folkloric concepts and examples, if we recall Sam's use of 'The Fox' (which may well have been a Shire folk song), and if we also bring to mind Tolkien's lifelong engagement with medieval foxes and the tradition of Reynard the Fox, then the presence of one of

5. Dimitra Fimi, 'Hobbit Songs and Rhymes: Tolkien and the Folklore of Middle-earth', *LOTR Plaza*, 2009, available at: http://dimitrafimi.com/articlesandessays/hobbit-songs-and-rhymes-tolkien-and-the-folklore-of-middle-earth/ (accessed 8 Nov 2020).

the most baffling characters in that same opening section of *The Lord of the Rings* may become a bit less inexplicable.

As Frodo, Sam, and Pippin walk out of the Shire and towards Crickhollow, we find this much-discussed scene:

> Just over the top of the hill they came on the patch of fir-wood. Leaving the road they went into the deep resin-scented darkness of the trees, and gathered dead sticks and cones to make a fire. Soon they had a merry crackle of flame at the foot of a large fir-tree and they sat round it for a while, until they began to nod. Then, each in an angle of the great tree's roots, they curled up in their cloaks and blankets, and were soon fast asleep. They set no watch; even Frodo feared no danger yet, for they were still in the heart of the Shire. A few creatures came and looked at them when the fire had died away. *A fox passing through the wood on business of his own stopped several minutes and sniffed.*
>
> *'Hobbits!' he thought.* 'Well, what next? I have heard of strange doings in this land, but I have seldom heard of a hobbit sleeping out of doors under a tree. Three of them! There's something mighty queer behind this.' He was quite right, but he never found out any more about it. (*FR*, 'Three is Company', 72; emphasis mine)

Critics have tried to accommodate the thinking (perhaps also talking?) fox in various ways. Surely it's remnant of the whimsy of *The Hobbit* (which does include a talking thrush) or a remnant of the tradition of beast fables and talking animals in children's literature (which *The Hobbit* was, but *The Lord of the Rings* isn't really, so Tolkien just didn't take the fox out when he should have). That may be a solution, but Tolkien revised this part of *The Lord of the Rings* numerous times, and the fox remained in the story. Why?

I would argue that this fox, who is on its way to sort out 'business of his own', is actually fitting perfectly with this part of the story. Here is a representation of the fox who is off to steal a goose for his little ones (the same fox of the folk song Sam uses – perhaps that's the 'business of his own'), or he is a representation of Reynard the Fox, off to deceive one of his usual victims, or the fox of the Gawain poet, who may not survive too long if he isn't careful, or the fox of one of the other medieval texts Tolkien knew. A folkloric character with a long pedigree in British tradition, a creature of ambivalent credentials, both clever but also tricksy, a liminal animal which crosses boundaries of natural classification, just as the three hobbits are crossing the boundaries of the Shire and are heading towards the great unknown, off to meet another 'foxy' character soon, Gollum.

In this thinking fox, Tolkien creates a meeting point between his own world of Middle-earth and an entire folkloric tradition, and bridges the songs the hobbits have been singing so far with the real-world-folk tune of 'The Stone Troll' that Sam will sing in a couple of chapters. Folk poetry, folk singing, and a hint of something half-familiar, half-threatening at the thresholds of the Shire, just as the hobbits are heading towards the biggest adventure of their lives: the fox may have 'never found out any more about it', but, fortunately, we do!

Bibliography

Baird, J. L., 'Grendel the Exile', *Neuphilologische Mitteilungen*, 67 (1966), 375-81.

Bowers, R. H., 'The Middle English "The Fox and the Goose"', *Journal of English and Germanic Philology*, 51 (1952), 393-394.

Brown, C. and Robbins, R.H., *The Index to Mddle-English Verse,* (New York: Columbia University Press for the Index Society, 1943).

Chapman, R. L., 'Alas, Poor Grendel', *College English*, 17.6 (1956), 334-337.

Fimi, D., 'Hobbit Songs and Rhymes: Tolkien and the Folklore of Middle-earth', *LOTR Plaza* (2009) <http://dimitrafimi.com/articlesandessays/hobbit-songs-and-rhymes-tolkien-and-the-folklore-of-middle-earth/> [Accessed 8 November 2020].

Henry, J. D., *Red Fox: The Catlike Canine,* (Washington, DC: Smithsonian Books, 1996).

Kurath, H. and S.M. Kuhn, *Middle English Dictionary: Plan and Bibliography,* (Ann Arbor: University of Michigan Press, 1954).

Lewis-Stempel, J., *The Wild Life of the Fox,* (London: Doubleday, 2020).

Opie, I. and P., *The Oxford Dictionary of Nursery Rhymes,* (Oxford: Clarendon Press, 1977).

Perkins, G., 'A Medieval Carol Survival: "The Fox and the Goose"', *The Journal of American Folklore*, 74.293 (1961) 235-244

Riston, J., *Gammar Gurton's Garland: or The Nursery Parnassus,* (London, repr. Glasgow: Hugh Hopkins, 1810).

Robbins, R.H., ed., *Secular Lyrics of the XIVth and XVth Centuries,* (Oxford: Clarendon Press, 1952).

Scull, C. and Hammond, W.G., *The J.R.R. Tolkien Companion and Guide, Volume I: Chronology*, rev. and expanded edn. (London: HarperCollins, 2017).

Smith, A.R. and Wynne, P., 'Tolkien and Esperanto', *Seven: An Anglo-American Literary Review*, 17 (2000) 27-46.

Terry, P., ed. and trans., *Renard the Fox,* (Berkley: University of California Press, 1992).

Tolkien, J.R.R., 'The Root of the Boot', in *Songs for the Philologists,* (London: privately printed in the Department of English at University College, 1936) 20-1
— 'Guide to the Names in *The Lord of the Rings*', in *A Tolkien Compass*, ed. by J. Lobdell (La Salle, IL: Open Court, 1975) 153-201.
— *The Adventures of Tom Bombadil and Other Verses from the Red Book*, ed. by C. Scull and W. Hammond (London: HarperCollins, 2014).

Wada, Y.,, 'What is Ancrene Wisse?', in *A Companion to Ancrene Wisse*, ed. by Y. Wada (Woodbridge : Boydell & Brewer, 2003) 1-28.

Wallen, M., *Fox,* (London: Reaktion Books, 2006).

“It cries for such curses”: Tolkien and Laȝamon

Nelson Goering

Not everyone reading this may have heard of Laȝamon. He is easy enough to introduce, and nearly every point on his resume will make him look like an ideal candidate for one of Tolkien’s greatest sources. Yet in many ways, he is the source that never was. To find out why, we will need to take a closer look both at Laȝamon himself, and at what Tolkien made of his medieval predecessor.

Laȝamon was a medieval poet from the West Midlands of England, specifically from a small place he called *Erneleȝe*, now Areley Kings, where he was a priest at the parish church.[1] He tells us this in the opening to his poem, where he also gives his name (and, of course, his father’s name, *Leovenað*). The more archaic manuscript spells this *Laȝamon*, with the funny Middle English letter ‘yogh’, *ȝ*, used to represent a sound no longer used in English.[2] You will more often find his named spelled as Layamon – this is not quite accurate (*ȝ* could be pronounced like ‘y’ in some words, but was not in this name), but certainly less off-putting. Others write *Lazamon*, which is simply inept. His name is literally a compound of older forms of the words law and man, so some people today modernize it to Lawman.[3]

Laȝamon’s poem is a hefty work, well over twice the length of *Beowulf* and *Sir Gawain and the Green Knight* combined. Like a number of other medieval works on British history, it is usually called the Brut,[4] and is essentially a historical narrative. Laȝamon traces the many rulers of Britain from their supposed ancestry in Troy, through such figures as King Lear and King Arthur, going on down to Cadwalader who, in this version of history, cedes the kingdom of England to the German Athelstan. For both Lear and Arthur, this is their first treatment in the English language, while old standbys of English and British tradition, such as Hengest, Horsa, and Vortigern, play prominent roles as well.

---

1. The church has, unsurprisingly, been altered in various ways since Laȝamon’s day, but is still sanding. It has a very nice prospect over the surrounding valleys: as Laȝamon puts it, *sel þar him þuhte* ‘it seemed wonderful to him’ (he is speaking of himself, introduced in the third person). In 1898 an old Norman window was reopened and filled with a stained-glass depiction of Laȝamon at work. If one finds oneself in or near Birmingham, I recommend a visit to Areley Kings – this is easiest by car, but possible by rail and bus (just bring a book, since the connections are a little indirect).

2. Specifically a voiced velar fricative, [ɣ] in the International Phonetic Alphabet. The sound was a bit like the German *ach*-sound, as in Ba<u>ch</u>, but pronounced with the vocal folds vibrating to create a sort of buzz.

3. The more modernizing manuscript gives his name as *Laweman*, or once as *Loweman*.

4. In much medieval historical literature, it was told that <u>*Brit*</u>*ain* had been settled by <u>*Brut*</u>*us* of Troy, a descendant of Aeneas. This idea was part of the general mythologizing that gave various European places a Trojan pedigree, modelled after the *Aeneid*. Despite this common appellation, however, the only names given in the manuscripts themselves are *Hystoria Brutonum* or (in Otho) *Liber Brutonum*.

This is not to say that Laȝamon was a real pioneer in terms of narrative. Like many medieval authors he was reworking older sources. In this case, his primary source, which he followed fairly closely but not strictly, was the Anglo-Norman poem *Geste des Bretons* (or *Roman de Brut*), composed half a century earlier by a man from Jersey named Wace. Wace himself drew heavily on the famous, or infamous, *Historia regum Britanniae* by Geoffrey of Monmouth, which was so influential in kicking off the Arthurian craze of the later Middle Ages.[5]

Laȝamon stands out less for his narrative innovation than for his language, poetic form, and rather antiquarian approach to including curious notes and details. His *Brut* is one of the earliest examples we have of the period we now call Middle English, probably written around the year 1200, though as so often the surviving manuscripts were written somewhat later. His West Midlands dialect was very close in time and space to the 'AB' variety of Middle English that Tolkien spent so much time and scholarly effort recovering,[6] and makes much use of archaic and poetic language continuing the Old English alliterative tradition. The poem can be seen as standing at the pivot between two traditional periods. On the one hand, it draws on Old English poetic vocabulary,[7] and retains much more of the inflectional system than even other Middle English texts of the same period; on the other, it is based (for almost the first time) on a work in French, heralding a new orientation in English literature, and showing some traces of linguistic influence from both French (though not yet very strongly) and Norse (though not so much as dialects from more strongly Norse-settled areas; see Dance 2003).

The form of the poem reflects a similar kind of balancing point between the worlds of Old and Middle English. Laȝamon's lines are sometimes held together by alliteration, in the Old English style, and sometimes by rhyme, in the French style. The following passage, an extended simile comparing Arthur's foe Childric to a hunted fox, gives a taste of Laȝamon's poetic style:[8]

5. For an overview of both Wace and Laȝamon, and their wider place in the historiography of Britain, see Matheson (2009) and especially Marvin (2009, 223-9).

6. Though perhaps with more 'southerly' features. It is often hard to distinguish what comes from the scribes and what from the poet, but 'southern' characteristics such as the voicing of initial *f*- to *v*- (as in vox for fox, seen below) are common. Tolkien also speculates at one point that where the manuscript reads *neode*, as if for phonetic [nøːdə], Laȝamon *might* have had **nyde*, or [nyːdə], a southern development. This is uncertain, because the reason for positing the sound value [y] is for the sake of rhyme, and (as Tolkien readily acknowledges) Laȝamon's rhymes are 'rocky' (1926, 64).

7. To take an example from the upcoming passage, the word *segges*, meaning 'warriors' or, by poetic imprecision, 'men', is almost entirely restricted to Middle English alliterative verse.

8. Citations of the poem draw on Madden (1847) and Brook & Leslie (1963, 1978); both editions are discussed below. I provide line references to each edition to help readers find cited passages in whatever edition they prefer. I have modified the manuscript text by providing punctuation, and somewhat smoothing out the orthography, which is notoriously irregular, even by the standards of the day. In particular, I have regularized the use of *u* and *v* (which were regarded as variants of the same letter during this period) to make the reader's life a little easier – though note that Laȝamon's dialect often has *v* where other varieties of English might have *f* (*vox* for *fox*, etc.). I have left *þ*, *ð*, and *ȝ* alone. The first two should be read as *th*, the latter is variably *y* (*ȝeond* was pronounced much the same as modern *yond*) or the strange velar fricative sound discussed above

He weneð to beon of duȝeðe baldest alre deoren.
Þenne siȝeð him to segges under beorȝen
mid hornen mid hunden, mid haȝere stefenen,
Hunten þar talieð, hundes þer galieð,
þene vox driueð ȝeond dales and ȝeond dunes.
He vlih to þan holme and his hol isecheð
i þan virste ænde, i þan holle wendeð.
Þenne is þe balde vox blissen al bideled
and mon him todelveð on ælchere helven.
Þenne beoð þer forcuðest deoren alre pruttest.
Swa wes Childriche.
(*Brut*, lines 20851-20871 in Madden 1847, 10404-10414 in Brook & Leslie 1978)

He [the fox] believes himself to be, for his power, the boldest of all creatures.
Then men come after him under the hills
with horns and hounds, with raised voices,
hunters there shout, hounds there bay,
when they drive the fox across valleys and across hills.
He flees to the cliff and seeks out his hole
into the furthest end, turns within the hole.
Then is the bold fox deprived of all joy
and men dig him out on every side.
Then is the proudest of animals the most despised.
Thus was Childric.

Six of these lines show alliteration, though not always in accordance with the old rules of a poem like *Beowulf*, half a millennium before. For example, *þene vox Driueð ȝeond Dales and ȝeond Dunes* has heavy *d*-based alliteration, including on the last stressed syllable of the line, in *dunes* 'hills'. This kind of final alliteration is strictly forbidden in Old English metrical practice, and Laȝamon's poetics show a distinctively new kind of alliterative verse, approaching in some ways the later alliterative style of poems like *Sir Gawain and the Green Knight*.[9]

---

with respect Laȝamon's name. Of course, even if you can roughly sound out Laȝamon's words, the overall language, now some eight centuries old and in a dialect far removed from most later 'standards', is hardly comprehensible without some special study. The translations of Laȝamon's text are my own.

9. The best study to date of Laȝamon's extremely difficult metre is Yakovlev (2008, ch. 3). Yakovlev presents Laȝamon as a kind of middle stage, halfway between *Beowulf* and *Gawain* (2-14, 267-82). Pascual (2017, 2018) pushes back against this idea, especially as elaborated by Weiskott (2016) and Cornelius (2017). Pascual accepts the continuity between Old English verse and the poetry of the 'alliterative revival', including *Gawain* (Russom 2004, Fulk 2004), but sees Laȝamon (and the few similar works that survive) as an outlier: 'Laȝamon and his contemporaries are best understood as literate innovators working outside the oral tradition of classical alliterative verse and relying on some of its most characteristic features, like alliteration, only occasionally' (2018, 226). I do not think either view can be correct. Pascual overstates Laȝamon's departures from Old English tradition: alliteration is not used only 'occasionally', but in very many lines, and there are elements of vocabulary and phraseology that can hardly have come from anywhere but Old English verse (and in forms that strongly suggest oral, not written,

There are numerous further peculiarities in the rhythmic details of his lines, not all of which are at all well understood.

Laȝamon's notion of rhyme is also not simply lifted from French practice, but interpreted in his own rather loose way. The rhymes *talieð* and *galieð* in the third line are very exact, but to a modern reader *delveth* and *helven* might raise an eyebrow, as might *cuðest* and *pruttest*. Yet these are not even close to the loosest rhymes we find in the *Brut*.

Stylistically, the *Brut* in general does not show the density of apposition and enjambment that give Old English poetry much of its peculiar flavour. At the same time, Laȝamon does not represent a radical break, and the fox-hunt simile shows a large number of parallelisms and repetitions-with-variation that may be fairly regarded as the outgrowth of the Beowulfian style of half a millennium earlier. In general, Laȝamon is more straightforward, less stylistically intricate, and more willing to compose line by line. The overall effect is once again of something between the more classic expressions of 'Old' and 'Middle' English alliterative styles (in this case, at least partly explainable as the normal result of syntactic changes in the language more generally).

All told, we might expect this poem to have held considerable interest for Tolkien.[10] Narratively, the prominence of King Arthur, on whose reign and deeds Laȝamon lingers for much longer than those of any other ruler, surely caught his attention. While Arthur may not have held quite the appeal for Tolkien of the Danish legends of *Beowulf*, we can hardly deny that Tolkien felt the charm of the Rex quondam, Rexque futurus. Linguistically, Tolkien was deeply invested in dialects of the West Midlands, and spent an immense amount of scholarly energy unravelling fine details of texts such as *Ancrene Wisse* and the various texts of MS Bodley 34, all produced within a few decades of the *Brut* and in very closely related (though broadly slightly more innovative) dialects.

But despite all these credentials, Laȝamon's influence would appear to be rather minimal, and he is not much discussed in the scholarship on Tolkien. He has no entry in Scull & Hammond's monumental *Companion and Guide* (2017), and only a rather brief précis by Carl Phelpstead appears in the *Tolkien Encyclopedia* (2007). As far as I can tell, the only real discussions of Laȝamon as a possible source for Tolkien's narratives are a few keen observations by Tom Shippey, two brief mentions by Christopher Tolkien in *The Fall of Arthur*, and a useful recapitulation of the known points by Phelpstead, which goes somewhat beyond his *Encyclopedia* entry (2011, 75-6). If there has been any more extensive investigation, I have overlooked it.

---

transmission; *eotand* 'giant' for *eoten*, with its folk-etymological ending, is a ready example). But Yakovlev (as well as Weiskott and Cornelius) are too ready to discount Laȝamon's use of rhyme (which is found in more lines than alliteration is), and it remains at least unclear whether all of Laȝamon's rhythmic innovations are ancestral to the *Gawain*-metre. Pascual would see Laȝamon as unrelated to the mainline alliterative tradition; Yakovlev sees him as, effectively, the direct child of the *Beowulf*-tradition, and the father of the *Gawain*-tradition. It might be more accurate to see Laȝamon as indeed the son of Old English poesy, but more of an uncle than a father to the alliterative revival.

10. In passing, I might note that Tolkien is not the only author of fantasy who had read Laȝamon. K.V. Johansen, author of *Blackdog* and related books, which draw on inspirations from across Eurasia, wrote a masters thesis on Laȝamon's *Brut*, according to her online biography: http://kvj.ca/bio2018.html

Most of the proposed resonances are concerned with particular words or short, distinctive passages of description.[11] Shippey has pointed out that Tolkien probably got the memorable word *dwimmerlaik* from Laȝamon's *dweomerlake* specifically (2007, 48, 169-72). Forms of the word do appear in other Middle English texts – including *Cleanness*, a poem closely related to, and likely by the same poet as, *Sir Gawain* – but usually with *dw-* simplified to *d-*: Cleanness has (plural) *demorlaykes* (also see Gilliver, Marshall, & Weiner 2006, 108-10). Christopher Tolkien has drawn attention to the place name *Romeril* in *The Fall of Arthur* (*Arthur*, 117; cf. 47; IV, 41), referring to the site where Arthur lands on his invasion of Britain against the usurper Mordred. Many Arthurian works place this somewhere in Kent, but only Laȝamon names the specific location *Romerel*, a corruption of Wace's *Romenel* (modern *Romney*):

And Arður him to scipe fusde mid alle his verde,
and hehte þat his scip-men brohten hine to Romerel,
þer he þohte up wende in to þissen londe.
Þæ he to þere havene com, Mordred him wes avornon;
ase þe dæi gon lihte heo bigunnen to fihten...
Þer weore al þat fiht idon, ah þat niht to raðe com;
ȝif þa niht neore, islaȝen hi weoren alle
(*Brut*, lines 28306-28315, 28360-28363 in Madden 1847, 14128-14132, 14155-14156 in Brook & Leslie 1978)

and Arthur hastened to ship with all his army,
and ordered that his sailors brought him to *Romerel*
where he thought to come up into this land.
When he came to the haven, Mordred was before him;
as the day began to lighten, they began to fight…
There the fight was all done, but night came too quickly;
if it had not been night then, they [Mordred's host] would have all been slain

It is easy to see why the 'Elvish' ring of *Romerel* would have caught Tolkien's eye (or ear).

Shippey (2003, 60fn.), Christopher (*Arthur*, 146-8), and Phelpstead have all made note of the striking detail that Arthur is ferried off to Avalon by a group of Elves – this is, indeed, one of the most famous details in the entire poem, and has attracted interested well beyond its Tolkienian relevance:

'And ich wulle varen to Avalun, to vairest alre maidene,
to Argante þere quene, *alven* swiðe sceone,
and heo scal mine wunden makien alle isunde,
al hal me makien mid *haleweiȝe drenchen*.
And seoðe ich cumen wulle to mine kineriche
and wunien mid Brutten mid muchelere wunne.'
(*Brut*, lines 28610-28621 in Madden 1847, 14278-14282 in Brook & Leslie 1978)

And I wish to fare to Avalon, to the fairest of all maidens,
to Argant the queen, an *elf* exceedingly beautiful,

11. For a further example, see Shippey (2000, 24-5), picked up by Phelpstead (2011, 75-6).

and she shall make my wounds all better,
and make me whole with *balsam drinks*.
And truly I will come to my kingdom
and dwell with the Britons in great joy.

The 'holy drinks' mentioned here might also put us in mind of the drink *limpë* that Eriol Ælfwine receives in Tol Eressëa in *The Book of Lost Tales* – Eressëa being, at least later on, explicitly identified with Avalon by Tolkien – or with the Elvish healing cordial *miruvórë* (formally adapted from Gothic elements, but there is nothing in Gothic that would suggest the substance) (*Lost Road*, 24).

Perhaps there are more resonances and echoes of this sort to be found, but as it stands, the characterization of Phelpstead seems apt: 'the harvest is more meagre than one might have expected' (2011, 75). The question remains of just *why* this is so, and the extent to the relatively poor haul of investigations of the *Brut* so far fairly reflect Tolkien's interest, or lack thereof, in his early Middle English predecessor.

Part of the answer surely lies with investigators, and the difficulties faced by any modern critic in dealing with Laȝamon. His poem is very long, in a language far more archaic and 'dialectal' (from the perspective of modern standards) than Chaucer's or even the *Gawain*-poet's. The major editions of the *Brut* do not do much to make the situation easier. There are only two complete editions of the poem, and neither introduces the kinds of punctuation, easily digestible notes, and other apparatus that would open the poem up to students. There is no 'Tolkien-Gordon' for the *Brut* as there is for *Sir Gawain*.[12]

Beyond this, source criticism loves to find narrative parallels, and this is exceptionally hard in the case of the Brut, where the story consists entirely of historical, or pseudo-historical material that is found widely across later medieval literature. The Arthurian sections in particular – among the parts that Tolkien might be expected to have read with the keenest narrative eye – were of course reworked so often through the Middle Ages, even just in later English sources, that we can usually only definitively pick out Laȝamonian resonances in focused passages, like the Elves of Avalon, or peculiar names, like Romerel.

Nonetheless, despite these obstacles it is clear that Tolkien had some familiarity with the *Brut*, and at least one or two direct echoes from it may be seen in his own fiction. The larger question remains, however, of just what Tolkien's engagement with the *Brut* was like – a question that might help us better appreciate how much more we should look at Laȝamon as a 'source' for Tolkien, and to evaluate the resonances that we do see.

Tolkien's relationship to Laȝamon was, if nothing else, long-lasting. Tolkien's first exposure to the *Brut* came at the latest as an undergraduate, when he was examined on a number of texts from Morris's *Specimens of Early English* (1887), including a 600-line extract from the *Brut*.[13] This section was one continuous episode, dealing with

12. There are partial exceptions, where portions of the *Brut* have been published in more accessible formats. The most substantial is Barron & Weinberg (2001), which covers the entire Arthurian section.

13. The same selection (or one two lines shorter, to be precise) also represents the 'Laȝamon' selection in Hall (1920), an important anthology which Tolkien acquired very soon after its

the arrival of Hengest and Hors (sic) in Britain, and culminating in the courtship and marriage of King Vortimer and Hengest's daughter Rowenne. This episode is well told, engaging in its own right, and provides an evocative, though hardly historical, portrayal of the first 'Sæxes' arrival in Britain.[14]

Before long, Tolkien probably turned to the only full edition of the poem available in his day, *Layamon's Brut, or Chronicle of Britain*, edited by Frederic Madden in 1847. This monumental edition consists of three hefty volumes, and remains the best edition of the poem to date. Madden very carefully reproduced the full text of both of the two surviving manuscripts of the *Brut*, down to fine details of spelling, punctuation, and abbreviation. It is a wonderful edition for textual scholars, but not the most readable text that a philologist has ever made. Madden did help his readers along by providing a running translation into modern English in smaller type at the foot of each page, though this is a strictly philological and very literal translation, noting every small variation between the two manuscripts, and has no pretensions to literary quality. In many ways Madden's text is an astounding scholarly achievement, and a very valuable foundation for future philologists to work from. Unfortunately, this foundation has been rather neglected in the century-and-a-half-plus since. Ideally later scholars would have produced both more accessible editions and critical texts. No full edition has adopted any of the features we might expect to eventually see in a pedagogically minded work: normalized spelling for students, introduction of modern punctuation, friendly notes for students (or hurried scholars), or a synthetic critical text based on comparison of the two surviving manuscripts.

One halting step towards this goal was taken by Joseph Hall, who in 1924 published *Selections from Layamon's Brut*. This is a reasonably good and student-friendly text, with a very handy philological introduction to the language. Tolkien owned this book: Cilli notes that he acquired it the year it came out, during his time at Leeds, and that it is inscribed as "from the delegates" (2019, 159).

The only other full edition that has appeared, from the Early English Text Society, is rather deficient. It consists of two volumes of text (Brook & Leslie 1963, 1978), which hardly represent much of an advance over Madden's despite being published well over a century later. The promised third volume with a glossary and full notes, which might have represented a more material contribution, never materialized. In any case, the first volume of the EETS edition only appeared after Tolkien had retired, and the second after his death. For all of his professional life, Madden's edition was the *Brut*, for all intents and purposes.

Tolkien would have had access to this edition in university libraries, and Christopher Tolkien tells us that: 'My father acquired a very fine copy of this rare and costly work in 1927' (*Arthur*, 147). It is almost certainly this edition that Tolkien used when he taught the *Brut*. Exactly when and how often he did so is unfortunately not entirely clear. He had produced duplicated pages on 'Phonology, and the Grammar of *Layamon's Brut*'

publication (Cilli 2019, 114). Hall's notes and philological overview in the second volume are particularly full and remain worth consulting.

14. Laȝamon also shows a certain linguistic awareness. At the wedding of Vortimer to Rowenne, their inability to communicate directly is noted: 'Fortimer spæc Bruttisc, and Rouuenne Saxisc' (lines 14978-14979 in Madden).

in November 1920, and may have lectured on 'Middle English Texts (*Layamon's Brut*: Selections)' in the academic year 1924-1925 (Hammond & Scull 2017, 122, 135-6). How often Laȝamon appeared in his more general lectures on Middle English and in tutorials remains uncertain. Minor references to Laȝamon also about throughout his Middle English scholarship, including in the notes for *Sir Gawain* and in 'Chaucer as a Philologist'.[15] The bulk of these notes are focused on lexicology and alliterative formulas – potentially interesting in aggregate, if you are interested in the history of Middle English verse, but not very revealing about Tolkien's views on Laȝamon.

For a clearer view on Tolkien and Laȝamon, we have to turn to his more technical philological writings. One of his most important, though less famous achievements was the untangling of the so-called 'AB' dialect, a specific variety of Middle English of the early thirteenth century in the West Midlands. In the paper where he presents these findings, '*Ancrene Wisse* and *Hali Meiðhad*', Tolkien notes that Laȝamon's *Brut* does not belong to the 'AB' language because it is too archaic: it predates the development of the distinctive verbal forms that define the AB language:

> But if we come west, we discover that as we approach the date 1200 we get not *fondin/þolien* [i.e. with a distinction between monosyllabic *-in* and disyllabic *-ien* endings] but fondien/þolien [i.e. both with disyllabic endings]. This latter is substantially the state of the language of the longer Layamon text, and one of the points in which that confused document shows analysable regularity. (Tolkien 1929, 119)

Perhaps the most revealing comment here is the phrase 'one of the points in which that confused document shows analysable regularity', which hints at the tantalizing frustration of being a philologist working on the *Brut*. Large and archaic as Laȝamon's corpus is, the manuscript transmission is rather difficult. There are only two surviving texts, known as Caligula and Otho,[16] both held in the Cotton collection. Caligula is longer and notably more archaic in language (this is the 'longer Layamon text' that Tolkien refers to), and is generally the more highly valued by philologists. Otho, for its part, has two strikes against it. First, it is the product of a revision that replaced many of the more difficult and obscure words (so interesting to philologists) with newer and less interesting ones, 'modernized' the grammar somewhat to a slightly later style (though still overall 'early') form of Middle English, and trimmed the text considerably to streamline Laȝamon's rather wordy narrative.[17] Secondly, it was trimmed down further when long sections of it were charred by fire.

Nonetheless, even the Caligula text presents significant difficulties, and it is easy to see why Tolkien would call it 'confused'. While many medieval scribes in no way aimed for a standard orthography, the spellings used in Caligula are exceptionally chaotic and

15. See Cilli for a non-exhaustive list (2019, 159).

16. These are both from the Cotton collection, where Roman busts were used to mark out various shelves of manuscripts. This bust-based system remains in use for labelling the various documents even today.

17. This process of revision is of course very interesting in itself, and raises a number of questions about the overall history of the text and its transmission. Tolkien, however, never to my knowledge commented much on the Otho text.

diverse, and many of the forms found look bizarre to anyone thinking about historical phonology or dialectology. This situation is really not comparable to the variations found in works such as *Beowulf* or *Pearl*. For Tolkien, with such a chaotically written poem on the one hand, and the remarkably consistent AB writings on the other, abounding in 'analysable regularity', it is hardly any wonder that the latter attracted his scientific interest so much more. Tolkien was not afraid of hard work – the thousands of verbal forms he assembled for his *Ancrene Wisse* paper were not collected in an afternoon – but the mess of the *Brut* may have prompted Tolkien to turn his philological energies in more obviously rewarding directions.

Tolkien's frustration with the state of the surviving Laȝamon manuscripts seems to have extended beyond its language. In the 'Year's Work in English Studies' for 1924 (published in 1926), Tolkien pauses during a discussion of vowel changes in Middle English to lament:

> some person or persons unknown have obviously badly damaged *Layamon*, so that its present form falters in its literary and linguistic evidence, though it cries for such curses as Chaucer pronounced upon Adam the Scrivener – curses that cannot be too often called to mind. It is at least arguable that we should sooner cry the mange upon the scalps of scribes than build too loftily upon their laziness. (1926, 64)

This suggestion of tampering on a literary, and not just linguistic level is intriguing, but Tolkien does not explain himself any further, either in terms of the extent or nature of these literary alterations. Certainly this lament, even as it castigates the scribes, suggests Tolkien held the 'real' Laȝamon (or at least his imagination of him) in some regard, even if once again Tolkien then quickly moves on and leaves us to wonder about the details.

That said, any regard for the 'real' Laȝamon may still have been somewhat tempered. Michael D.C. Drout has quoted a snippet of a lecture – apparently primarily on *Beowulf* – that claims that the '*Brut* illustrates a "breach" that had occurred in English cultural continuity':

> The breach was precisely in kinship, dynasties and politics, largely in language, but not in religion. It is as if far off rumours of Celtic lore, the Roman invasions and conquest, the Roman imperial troubles and abandonment of Britain, the invasions and conquests of the English and the Saxons, their resistance under Æthelwulfing kings to the Norse invaders, had all become jumbled in a vast haze of battle, in which the only constant is the land, Britain, without even an imaginative poetic sense of chronology or sequence. (Drout 2011, 15)

Tolkien really does hit on Laȝamon's weakest points. His poem is encyclopaedic, cataloguing a long history, but with little sense of motion across the work as a whole.[18] Many of the reigns are repetitive, especially the shorter ones, and the battles in particular can be very hard to distinguish from one another. This is not to say that some episodes, such as King Lear's story, are not well told, and certain sections, such as the several

18. In fairness to Laȝamon, religious shifts are presented as epochal changes – unsurprising given his profession. This, however, does relatively little to give much structure to the work as a whole, or to mitigate the repetitious nature of many passages.

thousand lines that relate the events from the departure of the Romans through King Arthur's reign, do have a definite shape to them. Many of the battles are individually vivid and memorable, with a real energy to them. But however energetically told, Laȝamon did not have the skill to make the many dozens of large battles all interesting and engaging, and the overall effect can indeed be one of haze. These failings, I suspect, Tolkien attributed to Laȝamon himself, not to scribes, and probably justly.

The criticism that the *Brut* was 'without even an imaginative poetic sense of chronology or sequence' may be particularly damning from Tolkien. As a writer and a critic, from his own annals and calendrical systems, to his praise of the *Beowulf*-poet's coherency of chronology, Tolkien was a stickler for precise and logical time schemes. Laȝamon certainly would not win Tolkien's goodwill by his apparent disinterest in such things.

Still, 'engagement with' is not quite the same thing as 'positive appreciation for', and this passage betrays a thought-out and critical reading of Laȝamon. It is also by now a commonplace that frustration with a work could spur Tolkien on, and his dissatisfaction with it may have led him to do better in his fiction. In particular, his lively criticism of the chronological flatness of the *Brut* contrasts sharply with the dominating effect of Time in his own Arthurian poem, *The Fall of Arthur* – here, if anywhere, we might suspect the *Brut* to be a major point of reference, something on Tolkien's mind during composition.

In Tolkien's Arthurian tale, chronology is everything. Events across large distances are linked in time by the great storm that sweeps across Europe from East to West. Dawn and dusk mark the rapid pace of the plot, giving real meaning and urgency to Lancelot's brief hesitation over whether to help Arthur, and the disastrous consequences that follow from this slight delay. In the grand scheme of things, the opening lines of the work tell us that Arthur intended 'thus the tides of time to turn backward' – a running refrain echoed later on in increasingly tragic terms (*Arthur*, 17; I. 5).[19] Tolkien had always had some interest in time in his fiction before the 1930s, but *The Fall of Arthur* is concerned with both detailed close chronology and the great turn of history in a much deeper way than any of Tolkien's earlier narratives.[20] These concerns find themselves folded directly into *The Lord of the Rings*, again ranging from the detailed synchronization of the phases of the moon and the spread of Sauron's dark cloud over the land – things which tie together the dispersed members of the Fellowship and lend coherence to a potentially highly fragmented storyline – to the larger shifts of history marked in melancholy terms by the passing of the Third Age and the departure of the Elves.

19. I, 179; II, 213; III, 218, 224, 227.

20. Perhaps others would dispute this point, but in general *The Lost Tales* gain a large part of their 'fairy tale' feel precisely from their relatively non-chronological orientation, and neither of Tolkien's great *Lays* of the 1920s show as developed an interest in time or Time as *Arthur*. The reckoning of Time, and the shift from the era of the Trees to that of the Sun and Moon is indeed old in Tolkien, as is the idea that an ancient mythological age has faded away, but it takes many years for Tolkien to really integrate these concerns into his close narratives. This strict chronological approach to storytelling is, perhaps, a more 'in solution' expression of the same impulses that led Tolkien to explore questions of Time more experimentally and explicitly in works such as *The Lost Road* and *The Notion Club Papers* (cf. Flieger 1997).

If any of this concern for time really is even partly a backlash to Laȝamon – and I do not claim that this was the only factor at work – then we have here a poem that made a major contribution to Tolkien's creative work, but in a rather negative way. As with *Macbeth*, Tolkien may have found more in the *Brut* that needed, in his mind, correction than things that inspired emulation.

So much, then, for the negative. That Tolkien saw Laȝamon as a flawed writer, whose work had been further damaged by scribes and circumstances, should not necessarily lead us to think he found no value in his West Midlands predecessor. If nothing else, Tolkien may have had real sympathy with Laȝamon's attempts to reach back across a cultural 'breach' (precisely the situation he felt himself to be in), and surely appreciated the elves and dwimmerlaiks and other old stones in Laȝamon's new tower.

Laȝamon also has genuine literary qualities which, though he never comments directly on them in the published materials, we might guess were not wholly unappealing to Tolkien. The *Brut* makes very effective use of speeches, often (like *Beowulf*) telling the same event both in direct narration and again in a speech, or (unlike *Beowulf*) via letter. His battle scenes are, as I said, far too numerous, but many have something of the compact power, and not infrequently the precise phraseology, of Old English poetry. It is difficult to place Tolkien's own battle scenes as specifically derivative of this or that particular source, but passages such as the following might well be in the soup, as it were:

Þa þiderward gon ride Arður þe riche
mid unimete folke, væie þah hit weore.
Uppe þere Tambre heo tuhte tosomne,
heven here-marken, halden togadere,
luken sweord longe, leiden o þe helmen:
fur ut sprengen, speren brastlien,
sceldes gonnen scanen, scaftes to-breken.
Þer faht al tosomne folc unimete.
(*Brut*, lines 28540-28555 in Madden, 14242-14249 in Brook & Leslie 1978)

Then Arthur the mighty began to ride to that place
with an uncountable host, fated (to die) though it was.
Upon the Tamber they drew together,
raised up war-standards, held together (in company),
unsheathed long swords, smote on the helms:
fire (began) to spring forth, spears to bristle,
shields began to shatter, shafts to break apart.
There that countless host fought all together.

Laȝamon's antiquarian commitment to relating everything he knew about British history led him to include much material he had no way to make really interesting, but when he hit his stride he was a poet to be reckoned with.

All this is my own judgement, but not *just* my own. Laȝamon has received high praise from a few critics over the years. Most relevantly, C.S. Lewis wrote a vigorous introduction to another book of extracts, edited by G.L. Brook (1963). Lewis is almost breathless in his praise of Laȝamon, hitting all the points I have raised and more – apparently a striking contrast with Tolkien's 'jumbled' and 'confused', but then, any general literary judgement Tolkien might have ever made (commenting on the poet in general, and not a contextual remark on his cultural circumstances), any real 'potting a poet in a paragraph', has not yet been published. For the purposes of this essay, it certainly would have been rather more helpful if Tolkien had written this preface rather than Lewis. As it stands, I can only suspect that at least some of what Lewis found so engaging about the *Brut* goes for Tolkien too, and may even have come from him – but it is hard to be sure.

But even without such a pot with a pickled poet in, I think one thing is clear: Laȝamon mattered to Tolkien. In his possible appreciation of the *Brut*'s many strengths, in his certain irritation at its flaws, and in his much-expressed frustration and perhaps despair at the philological mess presented by the surviving manuscripts, he had a long and complex history with the poem. He studied it, read it, and taught it. When Tolkien was working on AB texts or *Sir Gawain* or *Sir Beowulf*, it was lurking in the background, and the same may be said of *The Fall of Arthur* – and perhaps of other works.[21]

Bibliography

Barron, W.R.J. & S.C. Weinberg (eds.). 2001. *Layamon's Arthur: The Arthurian section of Layamon's Brut*, 2nd edn. Exeter: University of Exeter Press.

Brook, G. L. (ed.). 1963. *Selections from Laȝamon's Brut,* Oxford: Clarendon Press.

Brook, G. L. & R. F. Leslie (eds.). 1963. *Laȝamon: Brut*, Vol. 1 (The Early English Text Society No. 250). Oxford: Oxford University Press.
— (eds.). 1978. *Laȝamon: Brut*, Vol. 2 (The Early English Text Society No. 277). Oxford: Oxford University Press.

Cilli, O., *Tolkien's Library: An Annotated Checklist,* (Edinburgh: Luna Press Publishing, 2019).

Cornelius, I., *Reconstructing Alliterative Verse: The Pursuit of a Medieval Meter,* (Cambridge: Cambridge University Press, 2017).

Dance, R., *Words Derived from Old Norse in Early Middle English: Studies in the Vocabulary of the South-West Midland Texts,* (Temple: Arizona Center for Medieval & Renaissance Studies, 2003).

Flieger, V., *A Question of Time: J.R.R. Tolkien's Road to Faërie*, (Kent: The Kent State University Press, 1997).

Fulk, R. D. 'Old English poetry and the Alliterative Revival: On Geoffrey Russom's "The Evolution of Middle English alliterative Meter"', in *Studies in the History of the English Language II: Unfolding Conversations*, ed. by A. Curzan and K. Emmons (Berlin: Mouton de Gruyter, 2004) 305–312.

21. I have left Tolkien's only long, wholly original narrative alliterative poem untouched in this discussion. A comparison of the *Brut* with *The Lay of the Children of Húrin* would likely be productive, though perhaps more in the realm of metrical practice and alliterative phraseology than in narrative detail.

Gilliver, P., J. Marshall and E. Weiner. *The Ring of Words: Tolkien and the Oxford English Dictionary,* (Oxford: Oxford University Press, 2006).

Madden, Frederic (ed.). 1847. *Laȝamon's Brut, or Chronicle of Britain*, 3 vols. London: Society of the Antiquaries of London.

Marvin, J., 'The English Brut Tradition', in *A companion to Arthurian literature*, ed. by H. Fulton (Oxford: Wiley-Blackwell, 2009) 221–234.

Matheson, L.M., 'The Chronicle Tradition', in *A companion to Arthurian Literature*, ed. by H. Fulton (Oxford: Wiley-Blackwell, 2009) 58–69.

Pascual, R.J., 'Oral Tradition and the History of English Alliterative Verse', *Studia Neophilologica*, 89 (2017), 250–260.
— 'Alliterative Metre and Medieval English Literary History', *Journal of the Spanish Association of Anglo-American Studies*, 40 (2018), 221–230.

Phelpstead, C., '*Brut* by Layamon', in *J.R.R. Tolkien Encyclopedia: Scholarship and Critical Assessment*, ed. by M.D.C. Drout (London: Routledge, 2007) 76–77.
— *Tolkien and Wales,* (Cardiff: University of Wales Press, 2011).

Russom, G., 'The Evolution of Middle English Alliterative Meter', in *Studies in the History of the English Language II: Unfolding Conversations*, ed. by A. Curzan and K. Emmons (Berlin: Mouton de Gruyter, 2004) 279–304.
— 'A Brief Response', in *Studies in the History of the English Language II: Unfolding Conversations*, ed. by A. Curzan and K. Emmons (Berlin: Mouton de Gruyter, 2004) 313–314.

Scull, C. & Hammond, W. G., *The J.R.R. Tolkien Companion and Guide*, 2nd edn. (London: HarperCollins, 2017).

Selections from Early Middle English: 1130-1250, ed. by J. Hall (Oxford: Clarendon Press, 1920).

Selections from Laȝamon's Brut, ed. by G.L. Brook (Oxford: Clarendon Press, 1963).

Shippey, T., *J.R.R. Tolkien: Author of the Century,* (Boston: Houghton Mifflin, 2000).
— *The Road to Middle-earth*, Rev. and expanded edn. (Boston: Houghton Mifflin, 2003).
— *Roots and Branches: Selected Papers on Tolkien by Tom Shippey,* (Zollikofen: Walking Tree Publishers, 2007).

Specimens of Early English. Part I: From 'Old English Homilies' to 'King Horn', ed. by R. Morris (Oxford: Clarendon Press, 1887).

Tolkien, J.R.R. 'Philology: General works', *The Year's Work in English Studies* 5 (1926), 26–65.
— 'Ancrene Wisse and Hali Meiðhad', *Essays and Studies* 14 (1929), 104– 26.
— *Beowulf and the Critics*, ed. by M.D.C. Drout, 2nd edn. (Tempe: Arizona Center for Medieval & Renaissance Studies, 2011).
Weiskott, E., *English Alliterative Verse: Poetic Tradition and Literary History,* (Cambridge: Cambridge University Press, 2016).

Yakovlev, N., 'The Development of Alliterative Metre from Old to Middle English' (unpublished thesis, University of Oxford, 2008) <https://ora.ox.ac.uk/objects/uuid:02e46bb4-0abb-479d-9c50-64be689e013e>

The Worm and the Ring:
The Ouroboros as a Pattern in Tolkien's Legendarium

Michaela Hausmann

Eric Rücker Eddison and John Ronald Reuel Tolkien are both regarded as important writers of literary fantasy (cf. Clute 1999, 338; Williamson 2015, 132), and Ursula K. Le Guin even considers Eddison and Tolkien among the "three master stylists" of fantasy literature (Le Guin 2004, 149). Moreover, both authors studied at Oxford, both loved and show influences of Icelandic sagas, both included poems in their tales and both created secondary worlds. Tolkien himself acknowledged to have read every book by Eddison (*Letters*, Letter 294, 377) and the authors met at an Inklings gathering in Oxford in 1944 (*Letters*, Letter 73, 84; Carpenter 2006, 190-1).[1] Yet with regard to the question of influence, one of Tolkien's letters from 1957 immediately comes to mind, in which he famously concludes his review of Eddison's works as follows: "I still think of him as the greatest and most convincing writer of 'invented worlds' that I have read. But he was certainly not an 'influence'" (*Letters*, Letter 199, 258).

Literary influence is difficult to assess and even harder to prove. Yet I would like to argue that both authors make use of an ancient symbol, namely that of the Ouroboros, the snake or dragon that devours itself. There are a few striking parallels between Eddison's *The Worm Ouroboros* and Tolkien's legendarium. While it may not appear as an explicit symbol in Tolkien's works, I hope to show that the Ouroboros – along with its connotations – serves as an implicit pattern in his legendarium in several ways. The aim of this paper is ultimately not to prove an influence but to suggest a certain literary or imaginative kinship between Eddison and Tolkien that made both writers play with similar ideas albeit to different ends.

At first, there will be a short overview of the Ouroboros symbol and some concepts that have been attached to it over time. Subsequently, I would like to explore the One Ring as an abstract version of the Ouroboros and compare Eddison's King Gorice and Tolkien's Sauron in more detail. The third part of this paper is concerned with the Ouroboros as an underlying pattern of the physical and metaphysical design of Arda, and of Eddison's and Tolkien's story structures. In the end, I would like to conclude with a short résumé about Eddison's and Tolkien's use of the Ouroboros symbol in their literary works.

The Ouroboros can be translated as "tail-eater" and it is usually depicted as a serpent or dragon that bites its own tail, thereby forming a circle (Pesch 1985, 92). As a symbol, it is widespread in many cultures across the globe:

1. Although Eddison had met C.S. Lewis already in Oxford in February 1943, it is not entirely clear whether he also met Tolkien on this occasion. Whereas Carpenter as well as Scull/Hammond believe this to be the case (cf. Carpenter 2006, 190; cf. Scull and Hammond 2017, 276), Tolkien himself only mentions the 1944 meeting in his letters and claims in another letter to have met Eddison only once – at the 1944 meeting of the Inklings (cf. *Letters*, Letter 73, 84; Letter 199, 258).

> Combined evidence from anthropology, archaeology and the history of literature, art and religion shows that the image was once known on all inhabited continents, enjoying particular popularity at latitudes between the equator and 30° north. (van der Sluijs 2012, 148)

Due to its longevity and wide geographical dissemination, the Ouroboros has attracted a variety of diverse meanings. For the purpose of the ensuing analysis, I would like to concentrate on three in particular: (a) the Ouroboros as the unity of opposites; (b) the Ouroboros as the shape of the world; and (c) the Ouroboros as a symbol of time. The meaning of the Ouroboros as the "unity of opposing forces" (Mathews 2002, 25). It derives from "its joining of the yin-yang's earthly, or dark, and heavenly, or light, principles [...] and its frequent depiction as a winged serpent or dragon" (25). As such, it connects the antithetical spheres of earth and sky. But the serpent is itself an ambivalent image as it denotes deadly poison but also healing, it stands for the treacherous snake of Eden but also for wisdom (cf. de Groot 1969, 557).

In the art of alchemy, the Ouroboros symbolises the mutation of all things into one another (cf. Haage 1993, 559) and the ultimate interrelatedness of all matter – it is therefore "both philosophers' stone and *prima materia*l" (de Groot 1969, 557). This idea of the unity of all things is encapsulated in the famous Greek formula that often accompanies the Ouroboros: "hen to pan" meaning "the One, the all" – one is all and all is one (Mathews 2002, 24).

This interconnectedness of all matter is related to the use of the Ouroboros as a symbol of the entire world and the cosmos. In his research of the symbol, Marinus van der Sluijs argues that "certain bright phenomena in the sky," such as "the Milky Way, rainbows, comets, lightning flashes and polar lights have often attracted ophidian metaphors" (van der Sluijs 2012, 148). At the same time, "[t]raditional cosmologies situated the ouroboros as frequently in the underworld as in a circular ocean surrounding the earth, sometimes defining its boundary or supporting the earth and causing occasional earthquakes" (149). In many cultures, the ocean surrounding the inhabited lands of the world is personified as a huge dragon or coiled snake, as in the Babylonian Tiamat, the primeval sea goddess whose dead body is cut to create heaven and earth (cf. Browning 2009, 45), or as in the Biblical sea monster Leviathan, "literally meaning the coiling one," (van der Sluijs / Peratt 2009, 10). The Book of Isaiah relates how "the Lord with his sore and great and strong sword shall punish leviathan the piercing serpent, even leviathan that crooked serpent; and he shall slay the dragon that is in the sea" (Isaiah 27:1; emphasis original). Not only does this passage present Leviathan as the dragon-shaped epitome of the sea but it also casts it as a cosmic enemy of God. A similar constellation can be found in Norse Mythology, in which the Midgard serpent is explicitly envisioned as an Ouroboros. *The Prose Edda* gives an account of how Odin "threw the serpent into the deep sea that surrounds all lands. But the serpent grew so large that now, out in the middle ocean, it lies coiled around all lands, biting its tail" (Sturluson and Byock 2005, 39).

Apart from its use as a symbol of the cosmos and the shape of the world, the Ouroboros may also be used as a symbol of time, most notably of temporal cycles. It "symbolizes time as a process of eternal return, the steady movement and cyclic rebirth of the sun in the pre-Copernican world" (Pesch 1985, 93). An early example of this idea can be traced to ancient Egyptian belief where the Ouroboros is associated with the god Apophis, the incarnation of evil, darkness and the ocean, and the cosmic enemy of the sun god Ra (cf. Haage 1993, 558). At the same time, however, it represents Mehen – "an immense coiled serpent" that "encompasses Ra in his many coils, and protects him from all outside evil" as he journeys through the underworld at night before he is reborn as the light of the new day (Piccione 1990, 43). Based on this cycle of day and night, the Ouroboros came to be associated with other temporal cycles, especially the year and the annual cycle of the seasons: "through its ability to shed its skin, the serpent itself symbolizes the process of renewal in nature: unlike other creatures, the snake is revitalized every spring" (de Groot 1969, 554). Some medieval and Renaissance depictions of Saturn, or other personifications of Time, show the Ouroboros as one of his emblems. Such depictions hark back to classical antiquity, when the Ouroboros

> was associated [...] with cyclic renewal, restoration, and rebirth, and was depicted with Aion (personification of eternal temporal renewal), Asclepius (resurrecting god of medicine), and deities, such as Demeter, Serapis, and Mithras, whose mysteries connected the cyclic death and rebirth of nature to that of man. (Cohen 2000, 323)

In some illustrations, Saturn, Time, or even Death, hold both an Ouroboros as well as a scythe, thereby juxtaposing seemingly contrary notions of cyclical and linear time. Cohen argues that such contrasting attributes of time "served to visually differentiate between time's perpetuity as opposed to the discontinuity of temporal existence" (2000, 323). This endless cyclical motion and the impression that the Ouroboros simultaneously devours itself and gives birth to itself make it an emblem of infinite renewal, cyclical time, death and rebirth and thus eternity. However, it is important to distinguish between eternity in the sense of endlessness and perpetual cycles as represented by the Ouroboros on the one hand and eternity in a Christian theological sense on the other (cf. Uhlig 1969, 15). The latter is a state of perfection beyond time: "Time walks and flies but never stands still. Eternity by contrast appears as the three parts of time combined, immobile and unchangeable. [...] All hope and beauty awaited man above the temporal world, in heaven" (303). This differentiation between eternity in the theological sense and the endless cycle of time is echoed in Northrop Frye's study of the mysticism of William Blake:

> There are in Blake, as in Swedenborg, two suns, one alive and unfallen, the source of life and light, and one dead [...] The latter is the zodiacal sun, symbolizing the fallen conception of eternity as indefinite or endless recurrence. The image for this is the circle; and the serpent in a circular form with its tail in its mouth is therefore a perfect symbol of the zodiac (1990, 140-1)

The two suns accordingly stand for a divine and living eternity and for the fallen world that is subject to time and which is symbolized by the Ouroboros. Having explored the complex interpretations of the Ouroboros symbol as the unity of opposites and consequent interrelatedness of all things, as an image for the circular shape of the world and as a symbol of the perpetual cycle of time, I now wish to turn to the analysis of E. R. Eddison's and J. R. R. Tolkien's use of this symbol.

The round shape of the Ouroboros leads quickly to the most famous round object in Tolkien's works – the One Ring. Like the Ouroboros, the One Ring also represents a unity of opposites. It grants power to its wearers while at the same time enslaving them; it enhances wisdom, but it also narrows the mind to a singular desire. Thus, Galadriel observes that under the influence of the Ring Frodo "begin[s] to see with a keen eye" and has "perceived [her] thought more clearly than many that are accounted wise" (*FR*, 'The Mirror of Galadriel', 475-6, 477). But towards the end of his journey to Mount Doom, he eventually succumbs to the desire for the Ring. This unity of opposing forces which the One Ring signifies is also embodied by Gollum who as Gandalf remarks "'hated [the Ring] and loved it, as he hated and loved himself'" (*FR*, 'The Shadow of the Past', 73). Gollum's body also visualises how the Ring may grant a longer life but physically and mentally reduces its wearer to a shadow of himself.

Moreover, the Ring inscription "One Ring to rule them all" eerily recalls but essentially perverts the "hen to pan" – the One the all – formula. Whereas the latter suggests that one is all and all is one – a mutually symbiotic interdependence – the One Ring unilaterally exerts power over all: "[The One Ring] contained the powers of all the others, and controlled them, so that its wearer could see the thoughts of all those that used the lesser rings, could govern all they did, and in the end could utterly enslave them" (*Letters*, Letter 131, 152).

When thinking about rings, it is worthwhile to have a closer look at their owners since rings look back to a long history as symbols of power and authority. Eddison and Tolkien both exploit these connotations of rings in their fiction. Just as the One Ring belongs to Sauron and forms an inextricable part of his identity, there is a ring in Eddison's *The Worm Ouroboros* that also serves to characterise its wearer. It belongs to King Gorice and it is described as "his great signet ring fashioned in gold in the semblance of the worm Ouroboros that eateth his own tail" (Eddison 2014, 91). In his study of the symbolism of the Ouroboros, de Groot mentions an illustration in a sixteenth-century edition of Horapollo's *Hieroglyphica*, which shows the Ouroboros "with the name of a particular king inscribed in the middle of it, representing a bad ruler" (de Groot 1969, 455). As it happens, Gorice and Sauron are presented as the owners of Ouroboric rings and both are bad rulers. Yet there are even more parallels between them.

For one, King Gorice XII and Sauron are the central antagonists of *The Worm Ouroboros* and *The Lord of the Rings* respectively. They are both sorcerers (cf. Eddison 2014, 61, 404; *Silmarillion*, 181) who lead their wars mostly from a black fortress with an iron tower (cf. Eddison 2014, 51-2; *FR*, 'The Breaking of the Fellowship', 523; *RK*, 'Mount Doom', 1233). A far more curious parallel, however, concerns their recurrent incarnations. Gorice XII is not only the twelfth of his name, but he is the twelfth version of one and the same entity. As Lord Gro muses in *The Worm Ouroboros*: "'the soul endureth, albeit the body perish'" (Eddison 2014, 54). These incarnations all have different skills and forms, but they are essentially the same being. Once a version of Gorice ceases to exist, a new manifestation of Gorice appears and takes its place. An ancient prophecy cited by Lord Gro conveys this concept very clearly: "'Ten, eleven, twelf I see / In sequent varietie'" (Eddison 2014, 55). The phrase "in sequent variety" curiously resembles what Tolkien later came to call "[t]he Enemy in successive forms" in his letters (*Letters*, Letter 131, 146). Similar to Gorice, Sauron "could assume many forms," and although his bodies are repeatedly destroyed – at the downfall of Númenor and after Isildur had cut off his Ring at the end of the Second Age – his spirit endures (*Silmarillion*, 341). As Gandalf describes it: "Always after a defeat and a respite, the Shadow takes another shape and grows again" (*FR*, 'The Shadow of the Past', 67). Later in the story, Gandalf clearly connects this incessant recycling of the Enemy to the existence of the One Ring. Not only will Sauron always return as long as the One Ring exists, but "[i]f any of the Wise should with this Ring overthrow the Lord of Mordor, [...] he would then set himself on Sauron's throne, and yet another Dark Lord would appear" (*FR*, 'The Council of Elrond', 348-9). Hence, in *The Worm Ouroboros* and in *The Lord of the Rings*, Gorice's Ouroboros ring and Sauron's more abstract Ruling Ring represent the everlasting recycling of evil. Both stories thereby make use of the symbol of the Ouroboros as an image of the endless cycle of destruction and renewal.

The enemy in successive forms is an inextricable part of the overall storyworld design of Arda in Tolkien's legendarium, or, more precisely, of Arda Marred, for Arda is not the image of perfection the Valar had originally had in mind. Arda became corrupted by Melkor and "the seeds that he had planted still grew and sprouted, bearing evil fruit, if any would tend them" (*Silmarillion*, 310). The metaphors of seeds and fruit echo the meaning of the Ouroboros as an image of the seasonal and agricultural cycle. It may appear somewhat ironic that these metaphors of nature and nurturing are applied to the recycling of evil here, yet they demonstrate that through the actions of Melkor evil has become ingrained in the texture of Arda. It is therefore a fallen world and the product of the ceaseless struggle between Morgoth and the Valar: "naught might have peace or come to lasting growth, for as surely as the Valar began a labour so would Melkor undo it or corrupt it. […] slowly nonetheless the Earth was fashioned and made firm" (12). Even after the war of the Valar and Morgoth, Arda continues to be the platform for the endless wars between the children of Ilúvatar and the corruptions of Morgoth. In that sense, Arda Marred also embodies the meaning of the Ouroboros as the unity of opposing forces.

More revealing with regard to the Ouroboros as a pattern are the descriptions of Arda's physical shape. The very first glimpse of Arda describes it as "globed amid the Void" (6). Moreover, Arda is enclosed by two girdles: Ekkaia, "the Outer Sea" that "encircl[es] the Kingdom of Arda" and "the Walls of the Night" (30). These circles are reminiscent of the two Ouroboros patterns of Norse mythology that define the boundaries of the world – the circular wall around Midgard and the oceanic Midgard serpent. After the Akallabêth Arda is changed into a full globe so that sailors who attempt to find the West are said to "set but a girdle about the Earth and returned weary at last to the place of their beginning" (337). Hence, the notion of a circular world even becomes reinforced. In this context, Marjorie Burns sees the Straight Road to Valinor as an escape route from this "pattern of circles held within circles" as it "leads beyond the confines of Middle-earth and on to Valinor" (Burns 2005, 80). While this is true in the strictly physical sense, the Straight Road does not offer escape from the metaphysical circles of the world – from Arda's fate and existential laws, which leads us to the aspects of temporal and existential cycles in Arda.

Just as the shape of Arda resembles that of the world in Norse mythology, day and night's rotation in Tolkien's story cosmos seems modelled on Egyptian mythology in which the sun vessel travels on the subterranean ocean at night in order to rise to the sky the following morning (cf. *Silmarillion*, 109-13). In addition to the sun, the moon's cycle is also used to measure time in the form of night and months. Apart from the cycle of day and night, Arda also has seasonal cycles and the different ages of the world are often conceived of as "cycles" (*Letters*, Letter 131, 145, 146, 150) or "circles" (*Silmarillion*, 9). Tolkien's Arda is therefore a zodiacal world of dynamic temporal cycles – heavenly and earthly, natural and historical.

Whereas the cyclical destruction and rise of the Enemy has been discussed above as a strong feature in Tolkien's legendarium, the cycle of death and rebirth is most poignantly portrayed by Tolkien's Elves: "When 'killed', by the injury or destruction of their incarnate form, they do not escape from time, but remain in the world, either discarnate, or being re-born" (*Letters*, Letter 181, 236). Hence, the Elves' cyclical existence is also connected to the Ouroboros as an image of constant death and renewal, or immortality. Besides the concept of cyclical time, however, there is also the notion of linear time, or, to borrow the images used by Michael Drout, "Time's Cycle" and "Time's Arrow" (Drout 2007, 50-1). In her landmark study *A Question of Time*, Verlyn Flieger observes that these "contrasting concepts of time" coexist in Tolkien's legendarium so that time appears "as both fluid and static, linear and circular, mortal and immortal" (Flieger 2000, 22). While the Elves represent Time's Cycle, Men represent Time's Arrow for "the sons of Men die indeed, and leave the world;" (*Silmarillion*, 36). Men have a relatively short life-span but Ilúvatar's gift grants them the unique capacity to transcend the physical as well as existential circles of Arda. The Elves, on the other hand, are invariably tied to the history of the world which – and that is their tragedy – rather resembles an arrow. It has a clear beginning and it is said that it will end at some point (cf. *Silmarillion*, 15, 4). Time in Arda can thus perhaps be visualised as a series of successive cycles but with a clear Alpha and an Omega – a combination of cyclicality and linearity. The same also applies to the fate of the Elves which Tolkien described as "serial longevity" (*Letters*, Letter 212, 284). He further explains that the Elves "are therefore immortal. Not 'eternally', but to endure with and within the created world, while its story lasts" (*Letters*, Letter 181, 236). This is the reason why the Straight Road is not really an escape route for the Elves. It may be an escape from the physical boundaries of the globed world, but the Elves are nevertheless tied to the world's fate. Arda Marred is a fallen world and the Elves' cyclical existence echoes Frye's argument about "the fallen conception of eternity" which is symbolised by the Ouroboros (see above). Whereas Men have the gift of death – "a hope without assurance" (*Silmarillion*, 316), the Elves are imprisoned in an Ouroboric world and in an Ouroboric form of life, and although the world is said to come to an end at some point, "Ilúvatar has not revealed what he purposes for the Elves after the World's end" (36).

It may therefore be hardly surprising that the Elves are "'embalmers'", that they desire to arrest time altogether (*Letters*, Letter 154, 197). Tolkien used a beautiful metaphor to illustrate their plight. The Elves' weakness is "to become unwilling to face change: as if a man were to hate a very long book still going on, and wished to settle down in a favourite chapter" (*Letters*, Letter 181, 236). This desire is granted to the heroic Demons in Eddison's *The Worm Ouroboros*. After the ultimate defeat of the Witches, the Demons hate to face a peaceful but boring world without their opponents. Upon their request, the tale returns to its beginning, creating a temporal loop, in which the events of the Demons' war against the Witches can be endlessly repeated (Eddison 2014, 453-9). They are in fact allowed to settle down in their favourite chapter. Yet Tolkien's Elves are not as lucky. Although Galadriel achieves the desire to arrest time in measure when she creates Lothlórien as an earthly paradise seemingly immune to the effects of time, it must eventually fade "and the tides of Time will sweep it away" (*FR*, 'The Mirror of Galadriel', 475). Flieger brilliantly interprets Lothlórien as a source of temptation to both the Elves and the readers: "It is a cautionary picture, closer in kind to the Ring than we'd like to think, shown to us in all its beauty to test if we can let it go" (Flieger 2000, 112). In a sense, the Elves try to create unfallen and timeless eternity in a fallen world – an act of subcreative hubris that cannot last because only the Ainur and Ilúvatar are eternal and outside time.[2] The Elves must eventually accept change because in Arda time and tales must invariably progress and follow a linear course, and to resist or deny "the unfolding of the story" is "against the design of God" (*Letters*, Letter 181, 236). In their treatment of story structures, Eddison and Tolkien therefore differ decisively. Whereas Eddison uses the dragon that eats its own tail as an image for his entire story in order to create an endless loop, Tolkien rejects the idea of a circular story although he too uses Ouroboric patterns of unity, space and time in his legendarium.

In conclusion, the question remains whether Eddison was an influence on Tolkien or not. There are similarities between both writers. Their antagonists Gorice and Sauron share a number of parallels, both writers use the concept of recurrent incarnations, and employ a ring as a symbol for the recycling of evil. Apart from the One Ring which serves as an abstract version of the Ouroboros, the tail-eater appears as an underlying pattern for the physical shape and fallen state of Arda, for the Elvish cycle of death and rebirth, and for other temporal cycles in Arda Marred. Yet unlike Eddison, whose story becomes itself an Ouroboros, Tolkien's legendarium demands that this dragon must eventually be slain in order to gain true freedom: the One Ring must be unmade, the physical circles and existential cycles of the world must be transcended through death; time must progress and stories must eventually lead to new chapters. After all, it seems fair to say that Eddison and Tolkien are connected by an imaginative kinship because they engaged with similar ideas and concepts. Although Tolkien came to a different solution than Eddison with regard to their story structures, the Ouroboros, along with its manifold associations, also crawls through Tolkien's legendarium.

Bibliography

Browning, W.R.F. (ed.) *A Dictionary of the Bible,* (Oxford: Oxford University Press, 2009).

Burns, M., 'Containment and Progression in J. R. R. Tolkien's World', in *The Rings Goes Ever On: Proceedings of the Tolkien 2005 Conference*, ed. By S. Wells (Coventry: The Tolkien Society, 2005) 78-86.

2. In *The Silmarillion* it is stated that Ilúvatar and the Ainur are in the "Timeless Halls" and that the Ainur that came into the world "had entered at the beginning of Time" (*Silmarillion*, 10). There is also hope for a future eternal paradise in the Christian sense: "Never since have the Ainur made any music like to this music, though it has been said that a greater still shall be made before Ilúvatar by the choirs of the Ainur and the Children of Ilúvatar after the end of days. Then the themes of Ilúvatar shall be played aright" (4).

Carpenter, H., *The Inklings: C.S. Lewis, J.R.R. Tolkien, Charles Williams and Their Friends,* (London: Harper Collins, 2006).

Clute, J., 'Fantasy' in *The Encyclopedia of Fantasy*, ed. J. Clute and J. Grant (New York: St. Martin's Griffin, 1999) 337-9.

Cohen, S., 'The Early Renaissance Personification of Time and Changing Concepts of Temporality', *Renaissance Studies*, 14.3 (2000) 301-328.

de Groot, H.B., 'The Ouroboros and the Romantic Poets', *English Studies*, 50.1-6 (1969) 553-64.

Drout, M.D.C., 'Reflections on Thirty Years of Reading *The Silmarillion*', in *The Silmarillion: Thirty Years On*, ed. By A. Turner. (Zolligkofen: Walking Tree Publishers, 2007) 33-57.

Eddison, E.R., *The Worm Ouroboros,* (London: Harper Collins, 2014).

Flieger, V., *A Question of Time: Tolkien's Road to Faërie,* (Kent: The Kent State University Press, 2000).

Frye, N., *Fearful Symmetry: A Study of William Blake,* (Princeton: Princeton University Press, 1990).

Haage, B.D., 'Der Ouroboros in Hartmanns "Erec" Vers 7669 – 7679', in *Kommentar zur Artusepik Hartmanns von Aue,* by L. Okken (Amsterdam: Rodopi, 1993) 555-564.

Le Guin, U., 'Extract from From Elfland to Poughkeepsie [1973]', in *Fantastic Literature: A Critical Reader*, ed. By D. Sandner (Westport: Praeger Publishers, 2004) 144–155.

Mathews, R., *Fantasy: The Liberation of Imagination,* (New York/London: Routledge, 2002).

Pesch, H.W., 'The Sign of the Worm: Images of Death and Immortality in the Fiction of E. R. Eddison', in *Death and the Serpent: Immortality in Science Fiction and Fantasy,* ed. by C.B. Yoke and D.M. Hassler (Westport: Greenwood Press, 1985) 91-101.

Piccione, P.A., 'Mehen, Mysterie, and Resurrection from the Coiled Serpent', *Journal of the American Research Center in Egypt*, 27 (1990) 43-52.

Scull, C. and W.G. Hammond, *The J.R.R. Tolkien Companion and Guide: Chronology,* (London: Harper Collins, 2017).

Sluijs, M.A.v.d and Peratt, A.L., "The Ourobóros as an Auroral Phenomenon." *Journal of Folklore Research* 46.1 (2009), pp. 3-41.

— "The Ouroboros and the Aurora." Wouter Welling (ed.). *Dangerous and Divine: The Secret of the Serpent*. Amsterdam: KIT, 2012, pp. 148-153.

Sturluson, S., *The Prose Edda*, Transl. Jesse L. Byock. (London/New York: Penguin, 2005).

The Bible: Authorized King James Version with Apocrypha, Introd. and Notes by Robert Carroll Stephen Prickett. (Oxford: Oxford University Press, 2008).

Tolkien, J. R. R. *The Letters of J. R. R. Tolkien*, ed. by Humphrey Carpenter with the assistance of Christopher Tolkien. (Boston: Houghton Mifflin, 1981).
— *The Silmarillion*. London: Harper Collins, 1999.
— *The Lord of the Rings*. (London: Harper Collins, 2007).

Uhlig, Claus. "Ouroboros-Symbolik bei Spenser, The Farie Queene, IV, x, 40-41." *Germanisch-Romanische Monatsschrift* 50, (1969), pp. 1-23.

Williamson, Jamie. *The Evolution of Modern Fantasy: From Antiquarianism to the Ballantine Adult Fantasy Series*, (New York: Palgrave Macmillan, 2015).

Failed Quests and Faithlessness in Tolkien

Dr. Danko Kamčevski

1 – Introduction: quest, anti-quest, failed quest

Resonances between the works of J.R.R. Tolkien and the medieval romances are quite prominent and obvious even in the author's own literary preoccupations, such as editing *Sir Gawain and the Green Knight.* Quests hold a central place in medieval romances as well as in Tolkien's works. A paradigmatic statement could be that "*The Lord of the Rings* is the story of a quest, and of a world in which the quest takes place, a world in which it can be meaningful" (Basney 2004, 184). On the other hand, *The Lord of the Rings* was also characterized as something like a reversed quest, or 'anti-quest', when compared to classical stories: "Thus the paradigm of the Golden Fleece is both imitated and reversed, as that myth had itself altered the typical narrative framework of the quest. Something golden has been taken from a serpent, with evil consequences (imitation), but it must be and is given back (reversal)" (Newman 2005, 241-2). Tolkien himself considered the phenomenon of quest not such a rare and exclusive occurrence, limited neither to 'rich', 'those on vacation', or heroes:

> Most men make some journeys. Whether long or short, with an errand or to simply go 'there and back again', is not of primary importance. As I tried to express it in Bilbo's Walking Song, even an afternoon-to-evening walk may have important effects. When Sam had got no further than the Woody End he had already had an 'eye-opener'. For if there is anything in a journey of any length, for me it is this: a deliverance from the plantlike state of helpless passive sufferer, an exercise however small of will, and mobility – and of curiosity, without which a rational mind becomes stultified. (*Letters*, Letter 183, 239)

Thus, 'quest' can be understood in at least two ways. From a structural point of view, it is a journey undertaken for the sake of an achievement: acquiring a 'boon' or slaying a dragon. In the case of *The Lord of the Rings*, the structure of a journey and achievement remains while changing the whole point to losing something, such as tossing the Ring into Mount Doom. The other meaning of 'quest' is less literary and more philosophical: the quest belongs to the essence of being human. The meaning is more existential and closer to Tolkien's own words cited here.

In this paper I am more interested in the second interpretation of a quest. Besides containing quests and 'anti-quests' alike, Tolkien's works also contain stories in which protagonists *fail* to actually go on quests. The 'there and back again' structure is practically missing or at best incomplete, it is difficult to approach it from a strictly structural point of view. However, if we approach such stories from the existential point of view, we can talk meaningfully about these *failed quests*. In this case, protagonists first fail as human beings and this is then mirrored in the stories of their lives.

Given that quests were at the centre of medieval chivalric romances and that these flourished in a thoroughly Christian era, it can be argued that success in a quest depended on success in being a Christian (knight). Having in mind that Tolkien was a devout Catholic who claimed his own works were deeply Christian, we can also surmise that Tolkien's failed quests are also built on the basis of heroes failing in what are essentially Christian values.

Here I propose to base the argument on the three greatest Christian values, according to Saint Paul the Apostle, as stated in one of his epistles: "As it is, these remain: faith, hope and love, the three of them; and the greatest of them is love" (Anon. 1999, 1300). Faith is related to things unseen, the only ones truly eternal. We are asked to open our spiritual eyes, lest we be tricked by the shifting world of phenomena. However, the other two Christian values also play a role in explaining why some of Tolkien's protagonists fail.

2 – Mordred, the man of surfaces

Let us begin with Tolkien's sadly unfinished masterpiece, *The Fall of Arthur*. As is well known from the Arthurian tradition, the breaking of the Round Table and Arthur's kingdom was initiated by the affair between Guinevere and Sir Lancelot, in the unveiling of which Mordred played a pivotal role. Mordred finished the destruction of the kingdom by proclaiming himself the king and trying to abduct Guinevere. However, even though both Lancelot and Mordred are to blame for the breakup of the kingdom, we see that there is an apparent difference between them. Lancelot *does not* want to seize the kingdom; which seems to be Mordred's main preoccupation. Lancelot and Guinevere follow their hearts:

> To Lancelot her love gave she
> In his great glory gladness finding. (*Arthur*, 36)

Their love is not instrumental. Surely, they could not avoid falling in love; the main sin is acting on desire and being unable to control their passions. Their love is not mixed with envy, hate or urge for power; as such it is (ironically) pure. Hence it is possible for both of them to repent. Thus we read of Lancelot:

> For the love longing of his lord Arthur
> He would heal yet honour with his heart's anguish (39)

Arthur is moved by his own heart as well:

> Grief knew Arthur
> In his heart's secret (40)

The key word is *heart*. Lancelot, Guinevere, and Arthur are, with all their mistakes, imperfections, transgressions and sins, still personalities in whom heart plays an important role. In Arthurian tradition, Lancelot and Guinevere become a hermit and a nun, respectively. Arthur ends up as an almost saintly figure, the national symbol of Britain. The whole Grail chapter of both Malory and French *Vulgate* testifies to a very close relationship between knighthood and Christian spirituality. A failed knight is not yet a failed human being. They have sinned, yes; but they have not lost their faith. They still have heart. And it is exactly what is missing from Mordred's actions:

> His bed was barren; there black phantoms
> Of desire unsated and savage fury
> In his brain had brooded till bleak morning. (27-8)

Mordred is ruled by unsatisfied passions that are far from being romantic. They are only carnal affairs. Phantoms are delusions that one might have when hallucinating from fever. Tolkien psychologizes Mordred's betrayal. Mordred is *frustrated* and this leads to a distorted view of reality and unhealthy, aggressive urges. Furthermore, these are nested within his brain, the seat of rational mind. Mordred is most irrational where he should be most rational.

What Mordred feels is not love but *lust*. Lancelot and Guinevere's affair is preceded by mutual attraction. There is nothing of a sort in Mordred's case. Never does he try to seduce Guinevere or impress her at a tourney. He does not behave like a knight. Mordred simply wants to snatch Guinevere away from Arthur; thus desire for Guinevere might even be mixed with envy towards the king. There is a world of difference between wanting something because we want it for ourselves and wanting something because we do not want someone else to have it.

Furthermore, Mordred's lust is mixed with another quite worldly urge – the desire for power. Guinevere is to be used in at least two ways: to satisfy lust and achieve power. Neither Lancelot nor Guinevere ever dreamed of killing Arthur or usurping the kingdom, which is all Mordred seems to think about. All Mordred sees are not persons, but *opportunities*:

> Time is changing;
> The West waning, a wind rising
> In the Waxing East. The world falters.
> New tides are running in the narrow waters.
> False or faithful, only fearless man
> Shall ride the rapids from ruin snatching (32)

Mordred is a calculating person, quite unlike Lancelot and Guinevere whose love is truly blind as love is often said to be: they do not see or refuse to see the consequences of their actions. Lancelot and Guinevere are not future-oriented; they could more accurately be called selfish and foolish. The heart lives in the moment; but the brain is concerned with creating plans and strategies. Mordred does not see Guinevere as a beloved woman, but as a means to an end: a sexual object, a queen. Guinevere is reduced to a complex of interpretations within a discourse of power. She exists and is a possibility insofar as she can be *used and abused*. In Mordred's mind, Arthur's kingdom began with the marriage of Arthur and Guinevere. It could be quite possible that Mordred is not able to imagine a Round Table without Guinevere as a queen. Thus we have analogy such as:

dissolution of the Round Table ↔ dissolution of Arthur and Guinevere's marriage

In this case, if he takes Arthur's place, Guinevere comes within the 'same package', as it were. Like everything else he wants, Guinevere is treasure:

This treasure take I, ere towers crumble,
And thrones are o'erturned, thirst first will I slake. (32)

"Mordred reduces the queen to a commodity and mocks the idea that she might exercise any choice in the matter as he conflates her possible roles as 'slave or lady'" (Downs 2014, 60). Mordred goes beyond good and evil into strictly utilitarian behaviour.[1] Guinevere and Lancelot could feel the sin; it was attractive because sin is always sweet. For Mordred, sin is not sweet as it is no longer sin; Mordred does not feel his behaviour is sinful. Therefore, while Guinevere and Lancelot can repent, for Mordred this is not a possibility.

The transcendence into the spirit goes by overcoming basic bodily existence and we see that Mordred is wholly enslaved to his own body. Mordred's path to the Kingdom of Heaven, to repentance, is blocked. In a mental atmosphere close to his own, Mordred would be called a 'man of facts', 'objective', 'realistic', 'resourceful'. He lacks faith in the unseen, replaced with fear forcing him to cling to what he can see, touch, taste, hold. He is a man of surfaces, dominated and moved only by forces outside, perhaps unconscious and unable to control himself. As such he is unable to go on a quest in which he would find a meaning of his own. In fact, he destroys the society built on quests and spiritual maturation.

In *The Fall of Arthur*, almost everybody fails: Arthur, Lancelot, Guinevere, Mordred. However, even failures can be differentiated between those in which the path to redemption is still open and those, such as Mordred's, that seem to be beyond redemption.

3 – Aotrou, simulation of faith

The Lay of Aotrou and Itroun illustrates the faithlessness of its main character – Aotrou – on a more private level. The variation of the motif of failure through lack of hope and faith is here shown within a family drama.

1. However, it would be unfair to put all the blame on Mordred and identify him as the sole representative of the age in which to have becomes more important than *to be* (to use Erich Fromm's insightful parallel). Arthur's kingdom endured and progressed as long as it had chivalric adventures that kept introducing dialectic and dynamic. A good example can be found in *Sir Gawain and the Green Knight*. The text includes oath-breaking in a feeble society that cannot measure up to the Green Knight, with knights compared to 'beardless boys' – and yet, Gawain's adventure reforms the whole chivalric society that starts wearing the Green Girdle. However, in Tolkien, and also in *Alliterative Morte Arthure*, we see Arthur fall when he adopts the role of a war-leader, a conqueror. Arthur too goes beyond the measure and there is no dynamic person such as Gawain to reinvigorate the failing society. Instead of the optimistic, faithful Gawain, in *The Fall of Arthur* we witness a nihilist and pragmatist, Mordred. Arthur's army marches into nightmarish ambience of continental Europe which simply does not feel as home. Both in Arthur's kingdom and in Mordred, we see an example of not being able to create new value and going with redistribution, changing of hands, instead. Mordred's appearance is thus logical.

As in the case of Mordred, let us first look at Aotrou's motivation. Does he want a child for love of family or for giving birth to beauty by the act of love, to use the Platonic dictum? Far from it. One could say that Aotrou is conquered by fears. He is afraid of not having children and has given up hope that he will have them naturally. His fear is actually related to the future of his castle. One could almost claim there is a so-called *self-fulfilling prophecy*, for the very beginning of the lay states that of Aotrou's castle there remains only "a ruined toft now green" (*A&I*, 19). Aotrou has nightmares which portend a dark future:

> Thus pondering oft at night awake
> His darkened mind would visions make
> Of lonely age and death; his tomb
> Unkept, while strangers in his room
> With other names and other shields
> Were masters of his halls and fields. (21-2)

A few lines before he is described as a man filled with vanity: "his pride was empty, vain his hoard" (17). Children are viewed as his extended hand that would keep hold of his wealth even after he has died. "Everything is futile" it was said in *Ecclesiastes* 1:2 (Anon. 1999, 727). Vanity is exactly clinging to the worldly. Hoarding is a modern phenomenon of clinging to material things even when they are quite useless. In mythology and Tolkien's works, dragons are notorious hoarders. In Tolkien's poem 'Hoard' we witness a succession of characters who try to keep the hoard, but in the end the hoard outlives them all, showing the pointlessness of their actions:

> The old hoard the Night shall keep,
> While earth waits and the Elves sleep. (*Perilous Realm*, 231)

Therefore, "vain his hoard" is a damnation of Aotrou's materialism. Aotrou clearly identifies himself with his wealth. From Christian point of view, this is a pagan tendency as pagans often rely on heroic acts or material objects (grand palaces, monuments) to survive in collective memory. The motif of cursed hoard is quite frequent in Tolkien: the dragon and his hoard in *The Hobbit* which he practically does not use, as well as the Arkenstone; the Silmarils. Each of these precious things caused endless strife.

Aotrou is being more rational than it might seem. It is said that Aotrou did not make his decision abruptly. It had been brewing in his mind for some time: "thus council he took *at last*" (*A&I*, 23). All the while, however, Aotrou tries to convince himself that he has made a good decision:

> At last he slept in weary sleep
> Beside his wife, and dreaming deep,
> He walked with children yet unborn
> In gardens fair (35-7)

He has practically *bought* peaceful sleep. When he later talks with Itroun, he speaks of a new beginning: they are still young and should make merry – the days of joys are coming:

> A merry feast we'll make this year,
> And there shall come no sigh no tear;
> And we will feign our love begun
> In joy anew (41)

As if all this deception were not enough, Aotrou starts convincing Itroun that they are rewarded for their hope and faith:

> we'll pray that this year we may see
> Our heart's desire more quickly draw nigh
> Than yet we have seen it, thou and I;
> For virtue is in hope and prayer. (41-3)

In his dreams he fantasizes about his two children to come, but cannot escape the

> On lawns of sunlight without hedge
> Save a dark shadow on the edge. (47)

When the dream comes true and the children are born, Aotrou keeps claiming that all was due to hope and prayer:

> 'Now full' he said, 'is granted me
> Both hope and prayer' (55)

In other words, Aotrou simulates faith and in the end it seems he has convinced himself that he had been nothing but a good Christian thus far. He refuses to pay Corrigan for her services in a manner that shows his conviction – or self-delusion:

> I will not stand here turned to stone;
> But I will leave thee cold, alone,
> And I will ride to mine own home
> And the waters blest of Christendom. (79)

It is difficult to see what was particularly Christian in his behaviour. Surely, succumbing to despair was not. *The Book of Job* is a clear example of losing everything – family as well as wealth – but not losing faith. Another example is Abraham who was ready to sacrifice his own son, Isaac, based purely on his faith in God. In contrast to these, Aotrou, who could not have children as inheritors of his wealth, makes a deal with the witch, which is exactly the opposite of accepting God's 'mysterious ways'.

Hence, Aotrou fails in multiple ways as he has lied to Itroun, God, to himself, and finally Corrigan. Corrigan is the reality that he has to face: nothing in this world comes without a price:

> 'Now it is earned, come bring to me
> My fee,' a voice said, 'bring my fee!' (85)

Trying to trick and lie to everyone, Aotrou brings about his own doom. He dies, without having enjoyed his wealth or his children. Itroun dies too. Possibly even the children, as the initial lines speak of ruins where the castle once was. The lay finishes in a moralistic tone that reinforces the message that Aotrou fails exactly due to faithlessness on practically all levels:

> God keep us all in hope and prayer
> From evil rede and from despair,
> By waters blest of Christendom
> To dwell, until at last we come
> To joy of Heaven where is Queen
> The maiden Mary pure and clean. (111)

Tolkien juxtaposes maiden Mary to Corrigan: faith to magic, mother of God to a witch Comparing Tolkien's lay with its source, Tom Shippey draws a parallel with *Sir Gawain and the Green Knight*:

> The refusal, the curse, and the death of Aotrou are there in the Breton ballad; but in Tolkien alone the death is deserved, or at least prompted by Aotrou's attempt to sway Providence by supernatural forces. Tolkien's moral is clear and unequivocal. Aotrou's sin lay not in submitting to the Corrigan – he defied her as successfully as Sir Gawain warded off the Green Knight's lady, and with a firm profession of Christian faith – it lay in having any dealings with her at all. (2002, 293-4)

However, Gawain feels the pang of conscience. Aotrou has almost no self-reflection. Even though Corrigan is clearly an evil temptress, Aotrou's moral demise is indisputable. He goes from failure to failure, leaving out any chance that he might have been tricked. Faithlessness comes in the form of easy solutions, something to be especially aware of in our age of technology and the ease it brings into our lives.

4 – Túrin Turambar, seeing with Morgoth's eyes

The aforementioned theme of faithlessness is studied in greater detail and with more depth in *The Children of Húrin*. Besides obvious associations such as Kullervo from *Kalevala* as well as King Oedipus, an antecedent could also be the story of Balin from Malory's *Le Morte D'arthur*: cursed by a mysterious woman, Balin is followed by death wherever he goes. The final catastrophe occurs when he participates at a tournament and, due to heavy knight's armour hiding both his and his opponent's faces, slays and is slain by his own brother.

Túrin's story has been called this "tragic irony [...] closely related to the main motif of the whole novel – the motif of doom or destiny" (Марчетић 1985, 255). The tragic irony is noticed in another Serbian reception of Tolkien's work: ""The immanent mythical", admittedly as a material, is structured in *Silmarillion* with epic codes containing essentially tragic connotation (Oedipal variation in the episode 'Of Túrin Turambar'; syntagms of Orestes and Antigone in a story that, like an arc, connects the episodes 'Of Maeglin' and 'Of Tuor and the Fall of Gondolin'); in *The Hobbit*, however, the humorous leitmotifs point at the initial phase of desacralization of Tolkien's worlds, and the trilogy of the Ring of evil faces us with the ambiguity, the code of *tragic irony*" (Јованов 1985, 263).

Túrin's story is set during a time when the Valar are all but gone and the peoples of Middle-earth feel abandoned. A conversation between Turin and Sador about destiny reveals that humans are in the dark over the destiny of their souls. Túrin is not even sure whether death is natural: "'Has it always been so? Or do we suffer some curse of the wicked King, perhaps, like the Evil Breath?'" Morgoth has grown to a stature of doom itself (*CoH*, 43). This is, however, exactly what Morgoth's intention was. In the conversation between Húrin and Morgoth, we can see that Morgoth presents himself as the one true ruler of the entire world.

> I am the Elder King: Melkor, first and mightiest of all the Valar, who was before the world, and made it. The shadow of my purpose lies upon Arda, and all that is in it bends slowly and surely to my will. But upon all whom you love my thought shall weigh as a cloud of Doom, and it shall bring them down into darkness and despair. Wherever they go, evil shall arise. Whenever they speak, their words shall bring ill counsel. Whatsoever they do shall turn against them. They shall die without hope, cursing both life and death. (64)

Morgoth has twisted the meaning of Ilúvatar's 'gift of death' into the 'curse of death'. Morgoth's reinterpretation. When Húrin replies that, even if Morgoth were really the lord of the world, still death would be a release from him, Morgoth replies:

> Beyond the Circles of the World I will not pursue them,' said Morgoth. 'For beyond the Circles of the World there is Nothing. But within them they shall not escape me, until they enter into Nothing. (65)

Morgoth is thus revealed as the originator of the belief that the material world is all that exists. Having been established as the only visible force of great power in the world – the prince of the world. Death is a cessation of life, the destruction of the soul. Therefore, from such a point of view it is possible to imagine that one would rather accept the rule of the devil and live, rather than die and go into the void. Morgoth is indeed a 'diabolus simius Dei' figure. He has twisted the image of death, the idea of the world, and though he is also a creature of the world, he has proclaimed himself an idol to the dwellers of Middle-earth. Morgoth is establishing himself as a gnostic deity, a dark demiurge, standing outside of human history. Only, Morgoth is inside the history and greatly influencing it.

In fact, Morgoth is the personalization of that doom that leads heroes to self-destruction, both in works of Antiquity and in this particular work. The curse of Morgoth overturns almost every decision that Túrin makes. But of greater importance is how Túrin internalises Morgoth's point of view. He scorns the idea of the Valar:

> 'The Valar!' said Túrin. 'They have forsaken you, and they hold Men in scorn. What use to look westward across the endless Sea to a dying sunset in the West? There is but one Vala with whom we have to do, and that is Morgoth; and if in the end we cannot overcome him, at least we can hurt him and hinder him. (160-1)

Túrin cannot, of course, disprove the claims of the Elves which come from their own immediate experience. However, Túrin trusts only his own experience, in which there are no Valar, and not much happiness. From having lost his sister and father in childhood, through exile and the murder of his friend, Túrin has been shaped almost exclusively by negative experience. It is no wonder he believes the world is indeed ruled by a prince of darkness. In fact, he has generalized his own fate. At the same time, he has shut his eyes to the experiences of others, the tradition, history, tales – all the things which would reassure him of the presence of goodness and virtue in the world.

This is the desacralization which is effectively occurring in Túrin's soul. Valar are guardian-spirits of the world, each symbolically related to regions and elements of life on earth: fire, earth, water, air, dreams, stars. "In Tolkien's cosmological design the Valar create, sustain, and are sourced in aspects of nature. Nature in Tolkien's legendarium, in other words, is connected to the divine and is the province of angels" (Campbell 2014, 435). The Noldoli, who know of Valar, thus "see nature as a thing of intrinsic value" (Garth 2004, 219). That is why the absence of Valar from Middle-earth goes along with the loss of sanctity surrounding the material world. When Túrin looks at the stars, hears the wind, or touches the water, he is no longer able to feel (even in imagination) the presences of Varda, Manwë, or Ulmo. "Tolkien's story of Túrin Turambar may appear to come close to the 'disenchanted' mode of literature. The ironies of inescapable circumstance either deprive Túrin of victory or they cheat him of its fruits" (304). The disenchantment is what separates Túrin from Frodo and Sam, among other characters. Frodo knows of Varda, and Sam has a holy experience of hope and faith when he looks at the sky, as witnessed by the oft-quoted paragraph, describing Sam seeing a star:

> The beauty of it smote his heart, as he looked up out of the forsaken land, and hope returned to him. For like a shaft, clear and cold, the thought pierced him that in the end the Shadow was only a small and passing thing: there was light and high beauty for ever beyond its reach. (*RK*, 'The Land of Shadow', 932)

It is exactly this that we cannot imagine with Túrin. His reaction to seeing the star would have been sarcastic. But the hobbits succeed in their quest. They keep going even when things are not looking hopeful at all. On the other hand, Túrin has acquired a very pagan belief in fate. Túrin has, in fact, an ambiguous relation to fate. At one point he calls himself "Agarwaen, the son of Úmarth (which is the Bloodstained, son of Ill-fate), a hunter in the woods", which would mean that he has accepted his share in the world (*CoH*, 159). The killing of his friend is explained by this framework of doom:

> Beleg drew his sword Anglachel, and with it he cut the fetters that bound Túrin; but fate was that day more strong, for the blade of Eöl the Dark Elf slipped in his hand, and pricked Túrin's foot. Then Túrin was roused into a sudden wakefulness of rage and fear, and seeing a form bending over him in the gloom with a naked blade in hand he leapt up with a great cry, believing that Orcs were come again to torment him; and grappling with him in the darkness he seized Anglachel, and slew Beleg Cúthalion thinking him a foe. (154)

In fact, what is here called fate could indeed be Túrin's oversensitive state of mind. Rage, fear, nightmares and paranoia have already been seen in the case of Mordred. Like Mordred, Túrin is thinking with his body, the mechanical, reactive side of his being. No wonder he develops a concept of fate, for fate too is something impersonal, mechanical, like the body. Túrin uses fate to explain to himself that he has lost control of himself. Túrin's relationship to fate becomes ambiguous as at one point he dubs himself Túrin Turambar, the master of fate. "Túrin's dogged struggle against fate sets the seal on the heroic status he achieves in combat. Fate may laugh at his efforts, but he refuses to be humbled" (Garth 2004, 304).

Spiritual alienation from the Valar in favour of Morgoth's propaganda of fate is closely related to his alienation from society: "He keeps changing his name as if he had no real sense of self, taking on a succession of abstract identities, each of which is a marker of his alienation from himself and the world around him" (Flieger 2012, 123-4). The psychology of Túrin is complex and in this regard quite modern as the character has been compared to Joseph Conrad's Lord Jim in this regard: "Soon both characters move to self-exclusion from society, changing their names to remain anonymous, and ultimately resort to violence" (Arul 2019, 178).

Túrin practically adopted Morgoth's point of view. In the foreword to *The Children of Húrin*, Christopher Tolkien relates Tolkien's idea of "seeing with Morgoth's eyes":

> My father gave a definition of what this meant: if one were forced to look into Morgoth's eye he would 'see' (or receive in his mind from Morgoth's mind) a compellingly credible picture of events, distorted by Morgoth's bottomless malice (*CoH*, 19)

Likewise, Túrin believes he has a truthful picture of the world, even though he has left out the transcendental half of it; he is poisoned by anxiety and pride, believing he can defeat or 'outstare' fate. In reality, Túrin is mostly reactive and simply does not have time to stop and reflect. The mastery of fate is an illusion leading to being mastered by fate: "A Túrin Turambar turún' ambartanen: master of doom by doom mastered!" (243). Morgoth's deception and Túrin's self-deception reinforce the feeling that there really is fate, and not merely Morgoth's strong interference and Túrin's pessimism and inability to control himself.

5 – Conclusion, faithlessness and 'the Eye of Sauron'

The three examined characters fail in their inner quests, not having demonstrated the chivalric virtue of faith. Their wishes and intentions can have different directions, and be good and commendable, as in the case of Aotrou or Túrin; or sinister, like Mordred's – but the results are the same nevertheless. All beings of Middle-earth are free to develop themselves, grow, stagnate, or get twisted. The seen, empirical world cannot be the ultimate measure of things. Melkor himself wanted a better, more perfect Arda, from his point of view, and ended up as Morgoth. Tolkien describes Sauron too as "beginning well, at least on the level that while desiring to order all things according to his own wisdom he still at first considered the (economic) well-being of other inhabitants of the Earth" (*Letters*, Letter 183, 243). Sauron abused this desire to make the world a better place by manipulating the Elves during the Second Age, finding "their weak point in suggesting that, helping one another, they could make Western Middle-earth as beautiful as Valinor" (*Letters*, Letter 131, 152). The final clue that the core of Sauron's problem too was a spiritual one is the fact that he could not find strength to repent: "He was given an opportunity of repentance, when Morgoth was overcome, but could not face the humiliation of recantation, and suing for pardon; and so his temporary turn to good and 'benevolence' ended in a greater relapse, until he became the main representative of Evil of later ages" (151). In this context, we can, I believe, better understand Gandalf's words spoken at the Black Gate of Mordor: "We did not come here to waste words in treating with Sauron, faithless and accursed; still less with one of his slaves. Begone!" (*RK*, 'The Land of Shadow', 901).

Faithlessness in the form of Morgoth's eyes – in its significantly named iteration of 'the Eye of Sauron' – occurs with more or less intensity with other characters in *The Lord of the Rings*. The Palantir is an appropriate analogy. The knowledge that Sauron's forces are greater than the forces of all other peoples of Middle-earth has a demoralising effect. Boromir is tempted to use the Ring as an easy solution; Denethor is driven to suicide; Saruman despairs and becomes a traitor; Pippin is almost driven to madness by seeing the world as Sauron intended him to see. Indeed, Gandalf warns that few are able to withstand the eye of Sauron and accept the vision of the world he offers. In a similar way the Mirror of Galadriel with its power to see at distance and at possible futures can similarly be disheartening, and it is no wonder that at one point the Eye of Sauron appears in the Mirror. It is potentially already there.

Too much knowledge may lead us to believe that knowledge is all there is. The key lies in the 'things unseen', that are not subject to knowledge in its ordinary meaning. But if one's idea of the world is materialistic, limited, unethical, lacking transcendence, nihilistic, then faith becomes impossible. And thus acts of faith become non-existent. Fate is not conquered by force. Fate is conquered by faith.

Bibliography

Arul, M.R., 'Il giogo di orgoglio e vergogna. Túrin Turambar e Lord Jim', in *Tolkien e i Classici, volume I*, ed. by R. Arduini, C. Barella, G. Canzonieri, and C.A. Testi (Roma: Eterea Edizioni, 2019) 177-188.

Basney, L., 'Myth History, and Time in *The Lord of the Rings*', in *Understanding The Lord of the Rings: The Best of Tolkien Criticism*, ed. by R.A. Zimbardo and N.D. Isaacs (New York: Houghton Mifflin, 2004), pp. 183-194.

Campbell, L., 'Nature', in *A Companion to J. R. R. Tolkien*, ed. by Stuart D. Lee (Oxford: Wiley Blackwell, 2014), pp. 431-445.

Downs, J.M., '"Radiant and terrible": Tolkien's Heroic Women as Correctives to the Romance and Epic Traditions', in *A Quest of Her Own: Essays on the Female Hero in Modern Fantasy*, ed. by L.M. Campbell (Jefferson, North Carolina: Macfarland, 2014), pp. 55-75.

Flieger, V., 'Tolkien's Wild Men from Medieval to Modern', in *Green Suns and Faërie: Essays on Tolkien*, (Kent: The Kent State University Press, 2012), pp. 115-126.

Garth, J., *Tolkien and the Great War,* (London: HarperCollinsPublishers, 2004).

Jovanov, S., 'Cleansing Utopia: The Trials of Anthropos: Addams, Orwell, Tolkien', *Летопис Матице српске*, 161.436.3 (September 1985) 262-265.

Marčetić, A., 'On Tolkien's myth- making', *Летопис Матице српске*, 161.436.3 (September 1985) 254-261.

The New Jerusalem Bible: Standard Edition, ed. by H. Wansbrough (New York: Doubleday, 1999).

Newman, J.K., 'J.R.R. Tolkien's *The Lord of the Rings*: A Classical Perspective', *Illinois Classical Studies*, 30 (2005), 229-247.

Shippey, T., *J.R.R. Tolkien: Author of the Century,* (New York: Houghton Mifflin Company, 2002).

Tolkien, J.R.R., 'Hoard' in *Tales from the Perilous Realm,* (York: Houghton Mifflin Harcourt, 2008).
— *The Children of Húrin,* (New York: Ballantine Books, 2007).
— *The Fall of Arthur*, ed. by C. Tolkien (London: HarperCollinsPublishers, 2013).
— *The Lay of Aotrou and Itroun*, ed. by A. Mikić (Novi Sad: Snoviđenja, 2015).
— *The Letters of J. R. R. Tolkien*, ed. by H. Carpenter with the assistance of C. Tolkien (London: George Allen & Unwin, 1981).

Bilbo, Ulysses and the Greatness of the Unknown

Gloria Larini

The parallels between *The Lord of the Rings* and *The Odyssey* have often been emphasized, but less so with *The Hobbit*. We know very well that *The Hobbit* was written as a children's book but contained the roots of *The Lord of the Rings*. Tolkien considered that the tale "has escaped from [his …] control" (Tavella 2002, 43) "becoming twisted and boundless" (Larini 2019, 3). This study is a continuation of my article about this comparison between Homer's poems and *The Hobbit*. In this paper I will examine the parallels between Ulysses and Bilbo, exploring the frames of *The Odyssey* and *The Hobbit* and some common themes.[1] The principal concepts analysed are greatness, the unknown, and the greatness of the unknown. The aim is to contribute a new study of *The Hobbit* in parallel with Homeric epic poems linked by *mythopoiesis*, the invention of the myths (cf. Bologna 2002, 77).

The unknown is great in both works, capable of creating situations for characters to overcome. It contributes to the protagonist's heroism, making them defeat their fears. Bilbo is guided by a force that he involuntarily manages and corrects: he is the one that Gandalf chooses for the mission of the conquest of Ring, because he has the right characteristics for this. The instinct for adventure is in Bilbo's Took genes (Chance 2016, 62). In fact, at the beginning of the tale Tolkien points out that Bilbo had inherited "something a bit queer in his make-up from the Took side, something that only waited for a chance to come out" and "still something not entirely hobbitlike about them, and once in a while members of the Took-clan would go and have adventures" (*Hobbit*, 'An Unexpected Party', 10). The adventure begins with the meeting of the unknown in the form of the dwarves. In fact the first dwarf is characterized by the adjective "uninvited" and this unexpected arrival put the protagonist in crisis: Bilbo "liked visitors, but […] he liked to know them before they arrived, and he preferred to ask them himself" (13).

In fact in *The Hobbit* the concept of hospitality is different from the Greek; Greek culture accepts anyone who knocks on the door (Avon-Soletti 2005, 407). For example Ulysses, when he unexpectedly goes into the palace of the Phaeacians, is welcomed. However, Bilbo "knew his duty" and he does everything necessary to accommodate his sudden guests. The day that the dwarves and Gandalf arrived is defined "the most awkward Wednesday he ever remembered" (*Hobbit*, 'An Unexpected Party', 13, 15). The beginning of Bilbo's adventures causes a continuous conflict between his Tookish and Baggins natures. Hearing the dwarves' songs, Bilbo felt that "something Tookish woke up inside him, and he wished to […] hear the pine-trees and the waterfalls, and explore the caves, and wear a sword instead of a walking-stick" (20). But as soon as

---

1. The analysis of the text follows criteria of the structuralism and was carried out on the Greek text of the Odyssey and on the English text of *The Hobbit*. For *The Hobbit* see the 75th Anniversary Edition, Tolkien 2012, and for the Odyssey the Vincenzo Di Benedetto's Italian Edition, 2010. The translation from Greek to English is mine.

Bilbo began to imagine unknown places and dangerous adventures, he also "shuddered; and very quickly he was plain Mr. Baggins of Bag-End, Under-Hill, again" (20).

The dwarves evidently see Bilbo differently from either the way in which he feels about himself or from the way in which Gandalf presents him. Maybe Gandalf's opinion of Bilbo anticipates his transformation. At the beginning Bilbo is characterised by Gandalf as a "friend and fellow conspirator" and also "most excellent and audacious hobbit" (20). Bilbo instead "was wagging his mouth in protest at being called *audacious* and worst of all *fellow conspirator*" (20; emphasis mine). Ulysses, on the other hand, is a hero from before *The Odyssey* begins as he fought in the Trojan War and gained fame – in Greek language *kleos* (Nicosia 2003, 181, 184). He is a fearless, astute character, but static: in *The Odyssey* the characters are usually 'types' that don't change during their travels. On the contrary, Bilbo undergoes significant change thanks to his journey and experiences (Arduini 2011, 35).

Bilbo is guided by his Tookish genes and desires in his heart and soul greatness and the unknown. Ulysses appears to be hindered by the gods or Destiny during his return home yet he is always the master of himself, his adventures, and desire to explore the unknown (Gladstone 2010, 254). He does not fail as a hero as although he struggles, he overcomes every obstacle. Bilbo on the other hand fluctuates between fear and nostalgia. The etymology of nostalgia is *nostos* (return) and *algos* (pain) from Greek. It indicates the pain of distance, of travelling away from home. Although nostalgia prevails in Ulysses he feels no fear, he faces every calamity with courage. For Bilbo, nostalgia doesn't consist of regaining a throne, it's simply Bag End, where everything is known, calm, and repetitive. He is constantly afraid, because everything is terrifying:

> Bilbo had never seen or imagined anything of the kind. They were high up in a narrow place, with a dreadful fall into a dim valley at one side of them. There they were sheltering under a hanging rock for the night, and he lay beneath a blanket and shook from head to toe. (*Hobbit*, 'Over Hill and Under Hill', 52)

He sees "a wind and a rain, and the wind whipped the rain and the hail about in every direction, so that an overhanging rock was no protection at all" and he imagines "the dangerous part about caves" (54). The text is full of references to darkness, danger, mystery, and the monstrous, like in these passages:

> The goblins began to sing, or croak, keeping time with the flap of their flat feet
>
> […]
>
> For goblins eat horses and ponies and donkeys (and other much more dreadful things). There in the shadows. (57-8).
>
> Quite suddenly Dori, now at the back again carrying Bilbo, was grabbed from behind in the dark. (60)

Fear derives from the unknown and Bilbo overcomes his fear for the first time when he points his sword at Gollum and subsequently when he manages to get past the orcs in the tunnels. The door resists but thanks to the Ring, it fails and Bilbo demonstrates his courage despite the fear. The author points out that "Bilbo's heart jumped into his mouth. He gave a terrific squirm. Buttons burst off in all directions. He was through, with a torn coat and waistcoat, leaping down the steps like a goat" (76). But the fear never takes over Bilbo and he thinks "to go back into the horrible, horrible, tunnels and look for his friends. He had just made up his mind that it was his duty, that he must turn back" (78).

The motives for the adventure are different. Although Ulysses is trying to get home, his journey is complicated because of Poseidon's intervention as punishment for Ulysses' *hybris* against Polyphemus (Larini 2019, 10). However, Bilbo's adventure comes from his Tookish desire for adventure and Gandalf's encouragement. It's only Gandalf that finds him suitable for the adventure at the start of the tale.

Ulysses exerts his free will throughout his journey. When he arrives exhausted on Scheria there is nothing left for him, but he must decide whether to give up and die or fight and move on. Fundamentally Ulysses' greatness is also his intelligence and cunning in the face of difficulty.

In *The Hobbit* the greatness of the unknown is represented by the mystery and the danger of the countryside. The description of Mirkwood is one such example: the countryside is hostile and "Their trunks were huge and gnarled, their branches twisted, their leaves were dark and long. Ivy grew on them and trailed along the ground" and Mirkwood is "the greatest of the forests of the Northern world" (*Hobbit*, 'Flies and Spiders', 112). Additionally, for Bilbo open spaces such as mountains and wild lands generate a sense of fear as they "must not miss the road" (*Hobbit*, 'A Short Rest', 43) and the wizard Gandalf warns "Don't leave the path!" (*Hobbit*, 'Queer Lodgings', 115). Mirkwood itself is "as dark in there in the morning as at night, and very secret" with "a sort of watching and waiting feelings" (113). Although his fear of the unknown is perhaps overwhelming, Gandalf, who may represent an agent of Providence, says: "I'm not going to allow you to back out now, Mr. Baggins" (113).

Bilbo's cunning is both active and passive when he overcomes his fear. It is commonly active when he encounters monstrous beings and is passive when he is faced with dangers from the landscape (Sirri 1997, 269). Ulysses' cunning is found when he is trying to survive monsters, magic, and the sea. In his adventures, Ulysses meets living beings that endanger his life and the life of his companions: the Lestrigons, the Cyclops, goddess-enchantresses, goddess-nymphs, other divinities, unknown people, all of whom keep him from his home.

The environment plays a significant role in each text. In *The Odyssey*, water is associated with Poseidon and is dangerous; it's constantly unstable and changing. However, in *The Hobbit* water is often a source of salvation such as during the Company's escape from the Elven-realm or when Smaug falls in the lake. Water is a source of purification, it saves. In contrast to *The Odyssey*, earth is instead the constant threat.

The character's connection to nature in both texts is important. They consistently immerse themselves in nature such as when Bilbo and the dwarves take off their clothes and bathe in the river and when Ulysses and his companions rest and eat near the sea whenever they reach new land and leave the manmade boat.

Time also generates uncertainty and fear of the unknown. Words like "perhaps" or "probably" are used throughout *The Hobbit*, denoting uncertainty of what will happen or if he will even return home alive. However, for Ulysses, time works differently as each island is its own temporal pocket where time moves differently. In *The Odyssey* and *The Hobbit* we can find explicit temporal indications. For example, the beginning of a new day in the former is indicated with a temporal periphrasis like "the next morning, the dawn was again bright beautiful". The passing time is marked by words that express the interruption between night and day and this is a temporal common element. Moreover when Ulysses raises the sails to make the trip as quick as possible, time moves faster. The same happens for Bilbo: "the sun had only just turned west when they started" and "still the next morning dawned bright and fair again" and "they should reach the forest-gate early on the fourth-day, that they rode still forward after dusk and into the night beneath the moon" (*Hobbit*, 'Queer Lodgings', 111).

Bilbo's metamorphosis seems complete during his conflict with the spiders as his cunning, like Ulysses', is highlighted by the author. This episode is a struggle between the monsters and Bilbo's new-found heroism in order to save his friends: "half a dozen [spiders] were killed before the rest drew off and left Bombur to Bilbo" (*Hobbit*, 'Flies and Spiders', 131). When read side by side, Bilbo changes more than Ulysses' because the latter is already a King and a war hero, and the former has to overcome his size, lack of physical strength, and training to survive. The dwarves subsequently recognise Bilbo's transformation: "they really expected him to think of some wonderful plan to help them" (*Hobbit*, 'Flies and Spiders', 133).

In conclusion, fidelity, tenacity, and overcoming weakness are all fundamental characteristics of both characters.

Bibliography

Arduini, R., '*Lo Hobbit*: Stilemi Fiabeschi dell'opposizione tra luce e ombra', in *Tolkien. La Luce e l'Ombra*, ed. by G. Agnoloni (Ascoli Piceno: Senzapatria, 2011) 17-41.

Avon-Soletti, M-T., 'La pérennité des principes régissant des lois de l'hospitalité', in *Le barbare, l'étranger: images de l'autre*, ed. by D. Nourrisson and Y. Perrin (Saint-Etienne: Université de Saint-Etienne PUSE, 2005) 403-419.

Bologna, T., *La compagnia dell'anello, il potere: J.R.R. Tolkien creatore di mondi,* (Rimini: Il Cerchio, 2002).

Chance, J., *Tolkien, Self and Other: 'This Queer Creature'*,(London: Palgrave Mcmillan, 2016).

Gladstone, W.E., *Studies on Homer and the Homeric Age*, III (Cambridge: Cambridge University Press, 2010).

Larini, G., 'Giant, Solitary and Anarchist. The Trolls in *The Hobbit* and Polyphemus in the Odyssey', in *Tolkien and the Classics*, ed. by R. Arduini, G. Canzonieri, and C.A. Testi (Zurich: Walking Tree Publishers, 2019) 3-12.

Tavella, E., *Tolkien dalla fiaba al mito: creazione e significato dell'universo fantastico de Il Signore degli Anelli,* (Florence: Firenze Libri, 2002).

Tolkien, J.R.R., *The Hobbit,* (Boston: Houghton Mifflin Harcourt, 2012).

Travelers in Time: J.R.R. Tolkien and Joseph O'Neill

Kris Swank

Within the space of a couple of years, Irish novelist and playwright Joseph O'Neill in *Wind from the North* (1934) and *Land Under England* (1935), and J.R.R. Tolkien in 'The Lost Road' (written c.1936; published 1987) penned time-travel narratives exploring father-and-son relationships, altered consciousness, ancestral memory, and the poignancy of doomed civilizations. Both authors also encapsulated in these works the twentieth century inter-war period's anxieties over rising totalitarianism and dystopia, religious conflict, and the destruction of the past. The means of time travel in both Tolkien's and O'Neill's novels – travel via the unconscious mind – was based on the contemporary theories of J.W. Dunne's *An Experiment with Time* (1927). Yet, the similarities between their novels extend beyond Dunne's theories to parallel settings, characters, and situations, inviting comparison and even speculation of influence. This speculation is bolstered further when comparing Tolkien's time-travel fiction to that of his friend, C.S. Lewis, as Tolkien's work appears to be closer in harmony with O'Neill's writings than Lewis's. Ultimately, however, regardless of whether or not O'Neill directly influenced Tolkien's 'The Lost Road', the similarities between their works effectively illustrate the *zeitgeist* of intellectual thought on precognitive dreaming and cultural anxieties in the 1930s.

1 – Experiments with Time

During the 1930s and '40s in Britain and Ireland, 'Time' seemed to be on everyone's mind, or, rather, the mystery of Time and human perception was of great interest to the intellectuals and artists of the era, including Tolkien and three Irish-born authors: Dunne, Lewis, and O'Neill. Verlyn Flieger notes, in her ground-breaking study *A Question of Time: J.R.R. Tolkien's Road to Faërie* (1997), that the Victorians had also previously grappled with Time and its relationship to the human mind, particularly the unconscious mind, thus setting the stage for much of what was written about Time in the 1930s and '40s. In George Du Maurier's novel, *Peter Ibbetson* (1891), two lovers meet in their dreams, revisit their childhood haunts, and even travel beyond the boundaries of their own lifetimes into their ancestral pasts. H.G. Wells's *The Time Machine* (1895) concerns a Victorian gentleman-scientist who invents a machine which can move backwards and forwards through time. Sigmund Freud published his non-fiction book, *The Interpretation of Dreams* (1899), and "Einstein's Special Theory of Relativity [in 1905] postulated that time and space, far from being absolute, were relative to the position of the observer" (Flieger 1997, 38). In his 1916 essay, 'The Structure of the Unconscious', Carl Jung first used the term, the 'collective unconscious', to refer to the universal symbols or archetypes he believed were hard-wired into the human brain. In 1929, Jung explained, "In dreams, fantasies, and other exceptional states of mind the most far-fetched mythological motifs and symbols can appear autochthonously at any time" (1975, 111). Flieger notes that as, "the new century loomed, the impulse to inquire into the hidden, unrealized potential of mind and soul gave rise to a proliferation of individual and concerted experiments in the occult whose practitioners included" (among others), W.B. Yeats, A.E. Waite, Aleister Crowley, Madame Blavatsky, Rudolph Steiner, and others (1997, 36). Flieger writes, "These deliberate investigators into occult and mystical disciplines were consciously searching for alternative realities" (36).

And then the Great War (1914-1918) engulfed much of the world. Flieger writes that Tolkien's own time was one of the most turbulent in history, with, "Its wars, its use of technology in its most destructive aspect, its material progress and spiritual confusion, its avowedly 'modern' ethos" (3). After the first World War, and with indications of the second one looming, many in Tolkien's generation became dissatisfied with the present-day, and began dreaming of travelling somewhere else in Time.

In 1927, J.W. [John William] Dunne (1875–1949) published the first edition of *An Experiment with Time* (revised in 1929 and 1934), a widely-read theory of Time and precognitive dreaming which he later referred to as 'Serialism'. Dunne was born on a British Army base in County Kildare, Ireland, to an Irish father and an English mother, though he spent most of his childhood and subsequent career in England. He fought in the Second South African War, or Boer War (1899-1902), and was invalided to Britain, twice: first, with typhoid fever, and second, with heart disease. Dunne then went to work for the British War Office developing gliders and monoplanes. His innovative designs were fired by the imaginative works of Jules Verne and Dunne's friend, H.G. Wells. After noticing that he would sometimes dream of events which occurred weeks or months later, Dunne began keeping a careful journal of his dreams to corroborate his recollections. This led Dunne to propose that Time was not linear, but, rather, a field. Flieger writes, "Dunne's major point was that Time is not, as generally supposed, divided into discrete categories of past, present, and future. Rather, it is, like space, a continuous field that can be perceived and moved into, most often through dreams" (2007c, 648-9). Mark O'Connell explains Dunne's theory with a quote which Jorge Luis Borges attributed to Arthur Schopenhauer: "dreaming and wakefulness are the pages of a single book, and that to read them in order is to live, and to leaf through them at random, to dream" (2009, 224). Dunne described his theory with the image of an artist who attempts to paint a complete picture of the universe. He begins by painting the landscape as he sees it. However, the artist cannot observe himself within that landscape, although he is part of the universe, so a second artist is needed, standing a little way behind the first, to observe and paint both the landscape and the first artist. A third artist standing further back is then needed to paint both of the first two artists, and so on, through an infinite regression of observers until one comes to an Ultimate Observer who can perceive the entire universe and everything in it.[1] Dunne proposed that in our waking state, we are like the first artist with a limited perspective of the present moment, but in impressionable states of mind, such as dreaming, we might be able to perceive the more expanded perspectives of the second observer, et. al., which would appear to us as different moments in Time.

1. See Dunne's description and illustration of infinite regression in *The Serial Universe* (1934, 29-33).

Flieger writes that Dunne's *Experiment with Time*, "had a terrific impact when it appeared, though its influence was perhaps greater on literature than on science" (1997, 46). The wide range of British authors influenced by Dunne's theories in the 1930s and 40s included H.G. Wells, John Buchan, James Hilton, T.S. Eliot, E.R. Eddison, and J.B. Priestly, among others (Flieger 1997, 46; Clute 2018; O'Connell 2009, 224; and Stewart 2008, 69, 70, 73, 76-8).[2] In Ireland, Denis Johnston, James Joyce, W.B. Yeats, and Flann O'Brien, "were all aware of, and to varying degrees influenced by" Dunne's theories (Maxwell 1984, 221, n.7; and O'Connell 2009, 224).[3] O'Connell maintains, "Writers, then, were open to Dunne's theories in a way that physicists and psychologists were not, for the obvious reason that the imaginative possibilities they suggested greatly outweighed their scientific value. In particular, Dunne's ideas had a conspicuous impact on writers of what might loosely be termed the literary fiction of the fantastic" (2009, 224). Victoria Stewart writes, "works such as Buchan's and Priestley's use Dunne's thinking about time as a means of expressing not only the numbed aftermath of the First World War but the anxious apprehension of what may be to come" (2008, 63). For example, "Buchan's novel [*The Gap in the Curtain*], reflects the political and economic uncertainties of the post-First World War and post-Wall Street Crash period [...] J. B. Priestley's *Time and the Conways* [...] had been supplemented by anxieties about a possible future conflict' (Stewart 2008, 73). Stewart asserts, "By the 1940s, Dunne's ideas were well-enough established for authors to assume a familiarity with his work on the part of their readers, and his name often appears as a passing reference point for disturbed perceptions of time" (76). Flieger concurs, "while it lasted, Dunne's theory was so current and popular a topic that *not* to understand it was a mark of singularity" (1997 46; emphasis original).

Like many of their contemporaries, the Oxford friends and colleagues, Tolkien and Lewis, were also intrigued by Dunne's theories of Time. Flieger writes,

> There would be little doubt, even without corroborating evidence, that Tolkien and his Inkling friends had read and discussed Dunne, for it is very much the kind of thing that would have engaged their intellects [...] Both Tolkien and Lewis owned copies of the revised and enlarged third edition of *An Experiment with Time*. (47)

Guy Inchbald agrees, "The nature of space and time featured among their discussions from time to time, and Dunne's Serialism was given a good airing. It came to influence the ideas and fictional writings of them both" (2019, 80).

2. See, for example, H.G. Wells's story, "The Queer Story of Brownlow's Newspaper" (1932) and novel, *The Shape of Things to Come* (1933); John Buchan's *The Gap in the Curtain* (1932); James Hilton's *Lost Horizon* (1933) and *Random Harvest* (1941); T.S. Eliot's "Burnt Norton" (1935); E.R. Eddison's *Zimiamvian Trilogy* (1935-1958); and J.B. Priestley's plays, *Dangerous Corner* (1932), *Time and the Conways* (1937), and *An Inspector Calls* (1947), and his nonfiction *Man and Time* (1964) and *Over the Long High Wall* (1972).
3. See, for example, Denis Johnston's play, *A Bride for the Unicorn* (1933); and Flann O'Brien's *The Third Policeman* (written in 1939 or 1940).

2 – J.R.R. Tolkien & C.S. Lewis: The 'Toss-Up'

Born in Belfast, Northern Ireland, Clive Staples Lewis (1898-1963), known as "Jack" to his friends, is the second Irish-born author in this story. At this time, he was J.R.R. Tolkien's (1892-1973) Oxford colleague and great friend. Lewis was also intrigued by Dunne's *An Experiment with Time*. Five times from 1938 to 1967, Tolkien mentioned in his published letters an agreement the two men had made to write "excursionary 'Thriller[s]': a Space-journey and a Time-journey [...] each discovering Myth" (*Letters*, Letter 24, 29).[4] In 1955, Tolkien wrote, "C.S. Lewis said to me long ago, more or less [...] 'if they won't write the kind of books we want to read, we shall have to write them ourselves'" (*Letters*, Letter 159, 209). John Rateliff argues that Lewis had read both Charles Williams's *The Place of the Lion* (1931) and David Lindsay's *A Voyage to Arcturus* (1920) sometime around February to April of 1936 (2000, 204). The two books "had a tremendous impact on Lewis: they proved to him that contemporary authors could adopt a modern pulp genre, such as science fiction or mystery-thriller, and use it as the vehicle for sophisticated philosophical ideas" (Rateliff 2000, 201). John Garth identifies, "Olaf Stapledon's future histories of human evolution and the supernatural Christian thrillers of Charles Williams" as the sort of genre fiction which "might offer a wider audience for their own ideas" (2016). While the agreement with Tolkien is not mentioned in Lewis's published letters or memoirs, it is confirmed in his brother Warren Lewis's diary over a decade later (in the 24 May 1948 entry). Warren wrote that his brother "made a proposal to Tolkien, 'We shall have to write books of the sort ourselves. Supposing you write a thriller that's a time-journey – you have such a strong sense of time – and I write one that's a space-journey'" (qtd. in Sayer 2005, 254). Rateliff writes, "the hero of each book would undertake a journey through space or time, experiencing a series of adventures along the way, leading to his eventual discovery that some old myth or legend was actual fact – in Lewis's case, the apocryphal legend of Lucifer's rebellion; in Tolkien's, the legend of the fall of Atlantis. Both books would have a contemporary setting" (2000, 202). Although the exact date of this 'toss up' – as it is popularly called – is unknown, Christopher Tolkien, Rateliff, and Garth agree that it most likely occurred in 1936, although Rateliff pegs it early in the year and Garth in December (*Lost Road*, 10; Rateliff 2000, 204; Garth 2016).[5]

In any case, we can see the results of the agreement by late 1937. Lewis wrote to his friend Owen Barfield on 2 September of that year, "The thriller is finished and called 'Out of the Silent Planet'" (Lewis 2004, 218). The book, submitted for publication in October or November, was published a year later, in September 1938 (Rateliff 2000, 204). Eventually, Lewis published three books in the series – his so-called 'Space Trilogy' – also including *Perelandra* (1943) and *That Hideous Strength* (1945).

Lewis mentions Dunne in *That Hideous Strength* when his character Mark Studdock quips he is not able to see into the future, 'not living in Mr. Dunne's sort of time nor in

4. The five references to the agreement with Lewis appear in Tolkien's *Letters* (pp. 29, 209, 342, 347, and 378).

5. In a 1964 letter to Christopher Bretherton, Tolkien wrote, "When C. S. Lewis and I tossed up, and he was to write on space-travel and I on time-travel"; from this quotation their agreement is frequently referred to as the 'toss up' (*Letters*, Letter 257, 347).

looking-glass land' (Lewis 1965, 130). Inchbald discusses several examples of Dunne's theories depicted in Lewis's Narnia novels. For example, Narnian time runs differently from our own in *The Lion, the Witch and the Wardrobe* (1950) and other volumes in the series. The Narnia that readers know is revealed to be just one of several serial worlds at the end of *The Last Battle* (1956) when the friends of Narnia are called to go "further up and [...] further in"; each world is "more real and more beautiful than the Narnia down below" (Lewis 1973, 180).

2.1 – C.S. Lewis & 'The Dark Tower'

Lewis also considers Dunne's Serialism in an unfinished novel related to his Space Trilogy that is commonly called 'The Dark Tower' (1977). Five academic gentlemen, not unlike the Inklings, gather in the college rooms of Cambridge University's Professor Orfieu to observe the events of another timeline – or 'Othertime' – through the 'chronoscope' that Orfieu has invented. Yet, rather than viewing their own past or future, Othertime appears to be a parallel timeline in which mysterious Stingingmen use protuberances growing out of their foreheads to inject poison into their followers and turn them into mindless automata controlled by a single "Big Brain" (Lewis 2017, 85). One of the Stingingmen is the doppelgänger of one of the Cambridge academics, young Scudamore, while one of the Stingingman's followers is the doppelgänger of Scudamore's fiancée, Camilla. When the chronoscope shows the Othertime-Camilla in danger, the Scudamore from our time leaps through the chronoscope in order to save her. In the Othertime world, Scudamore discovers that his consciousness now resides in the body of his doppelgänger, while in our world, the consciousness of the Stingingman takes its place in Scudamore's body. Lewis uses this consciousness swap to avoid the problem of taking a body physically into another time, for, as Orfieu explains, "the same piece of matter can't be in two different places at the same time" (Lewis 2017, 3). The particles composing a body today will, in five hundred years, "be all over the place – some in the earth, some in plants and animals, and some in the bodies of your descendants, if you have any" (2). Thus, "any kind of 'time machine', anything that would take your body to another time, was intrinsically impossible" (5). Later, Elwin Ransom, the character common to all of Lewis's 'Space' novels, contradicts this theory by proposing the two Scudamores do, in fact, share the same particles, but not at the same time. He argues, "But there aren't two bodies. There's only one body existing at two different times" (66; emphasis original). The consciousness exchange turns out to be more of a mind-meld than a mind-swap. The knowledge possessed by the original persona remains with the body to be accessed by the new persona. For example, Scudamore later relates, "as long as he lived in the Othertime, [he] found no difficulty in speaking and understanding a language which was certainly not English" (73).

Walter Hooper estimates that Lewis began writing 'The Dark Tower' in 1938 (Lewis 2017, ix). Rateliff argues for a later date of 1944-1946 (Rateliff 2000, 211-2). Either estimate places its composition after 1936, when Tolkien likely worked on (and abandoned) his half of the 'toss-up' with Lewis. So, while 'The Dark Tower' was not a precursor to Tolkien's 'time-journey' novel, it does illustrate Lewis's idiosyncratic interpretations of Dunne's time-travel theories and, thus, highlights the differences between his and Tolkien's interpretations.

2.2 – Tolkien & 'The Lost Road'

Tolkien's first attempt at fulfilling his half of the agreement with Lewis resulted in 'The Lost Road', an incomplete draft submitted to his publishers, Allen & Unwin, on 15 November 1937, very close to the time that Lewis submitted *Out of the Silent Planet* for publication (Rateliff 2000, 205). Both 'The Lost Road' and Tolkien's later, second, attempt at a time-travel narrative, 'The Notion Club Papers' (written 1945; published 1992), "are stories about twentieth-century men who travel back in time through their dreams" (Flieger 1996, 39). Flieger describes Tolkien's planned storyline for 'The Lost Road':

> Here Alboin and Audoin, a modern English father and son surnamed Errol (cf. Eriol the Mariner from *The Book of Lost Tales*) travel by means of their dreams through recessive ancestral identities. These were to participate in a sequence of episodes from early English history, prehistory, and myth, arriving finally at Númenor in time to witness its destruction in the fictive prehistory of Tolkien's mythology. (2007a, 393)

'The Fall of Númenor,' then, would represent the true history behind the myth of Atlantis.

Tolkien read the third edition of Dunne's *Experiment with Time* around Christmas of 1934 (Flieger 1996, 39). In *A Question of Time*, Flieger writes,

> Tolkien's copy, in the possession of his son, Christopher, contains his interleaved notes and comments, jotted in the course of reading on Dunne's ideas and the theory he derived from them. Tolkien's comments are not always in complete agreement with Dunne; nevertheless, they show a clear relationship between Dunne's *Experiment* and the mechanism Tolkien used in two time-travel stories, *The Lost Road* and *The Notion Club Papers*. In addition, two unattached pieces of paper bearing diagrams remarkably similar to the kind drawn by Dunne are among Tolkien's notes and rough drafts from the early period composition of *The Lord of the Rings* [1954-1955]. (1997, 47)

Elsewhere, she argues,

> Tolkien found in *An Experiment with Time* a principle through whose operation the mind could dream through time in any direction. This psychic principle he combined with Carl Jung's wholly compatible psychological theory of the collective unconscious, the commonly shared, unconscious memories of the human community, and used both to effect a mode of travel through dreamed serial identities. (1996, 39-40)

These serial identities (what Anna Smol referred to at this conference as Tolkien's repeated 'typologies') would take the form, time and again throughout history and pre-history, of a father and son whose names could be translated as "Bliss-friend and Elf-friend" (*Letters*, Letter 257, 347). Like Lewis, Tolkien thought a Wellsian "time machine" was "preposterous and incredible" (*OFS*, 96). And, like Lewis, Tolkien favoured a para-psychological approach to time-travel, although Tolkien's travelling is accomplished via dreams and people connected by ancestral relationships, while Lewis's travelling is accomplished through the proximity of parallel worlds and doppelgängers.

'The Lost Road' never progressed past four chapters (two concerning the present-day Errol family and two concerning their counterparts in the waning days of ancient Númenor), plus some fragments and notes for other proposed chapters, including one set in Anglo-Saxon England. Tolkien's publisher was not optimistic about its commercial potential (*Lost Road*, 98). In fact, the firm's reviewer called it "a hopeless proposition" (Rateliff 2000, 205). Rateliff argues that the combination of this discouraging review, Tolkien's need to ready *The Hobbit* (1937) for publication, his regular academic duties, his desire to greatly enlarge 'The Lost Road' narrative, and the eventual distraction of writing *The Lord of the Rings*, all together doomed any chances of Tolkien's completing 'The Lost Road' (2000, 205). What is extant of the text, however, is indicative of both the agreement with Lewis and the influence of Dunne's time-travel theories. It also reveals a close sympathy with the work of another contemporary author, our third Irishman, O'Neill.

3 – Joseph O'Neill

Biographer, M. Kelly Lynch, writes that when Joseph O'Neill (1878-1953) died he was variously remembered as the Permanent Secretary to the Department of Education for the Irish Free State (1923-1944), the brilliant protégé of Celtic scholar Kuno Meyer, the husband of author Mary Devenport O'Neill, and a celebrated member of the literary and artistic circle which included W.B. Yeats and Æ (i.e. George William Russell), but "within a generation he had nearly been forgotten – a name and a source of an anecdote or two" (1983, 4). Later in his life, O'Neill claimed to have been born in 1884 in the romantic, Gaelic-speaking Aran Islands; in fact, he was born in 1878, in the more mundane town of Tuam, Galway (5).[6] According to his biographer, M. Kelly Lynch, this was not merely a ruse, but a deeply held desire of O'Neill's to be descended from the ancient Gaels. Lynch explains that O'Neill "spent twenty-five years buried in the bureaucracy of the Irish Department of Education, loathing the petty, bourgeois life he lived, longing for the heroic past" (O'Neill 2000, book jacket). At the age of 56, O'Neill finally turned to writing: producing a play, some poems and serialized fiction, and six novels, the first two of which were *Wind from the North* and *Land under England*.

3.1 – O'Neill & Land under England

Land under England is the story of Anthony Julian, the son of an archaeologist. As the protagonist's name indicates, Julian and his father are descendants of the ancient Romans in Britain, a fact that turns to obsession for Julian Sr., who goes missing while exploring Hadrian's Wall for information about the Roman legions once stationed there. In pursuit

6. O'Neill's biography has always been contested, partly because O'Neill wanted it that way. His birthdate is variously given, for example, as 18 December 1878 (Lynch 1979, 535), 1883 (Crossley 1987, 94), and 1886 (Howard 2019, 236). Even his most prolific biographer, Lynch, variously states O'Neill's death date as either May 6, 1952 (1979, 535 & 537) or May 3, 1953 (1983, 59), which may stem from editorial confusion over the date on which O'Neill suffered a cerebral haemorrhage (spring 1952) and the date on which he died (seventeen months later in 1953).

of his missing father, the younger Julian discovers a subterranean entrance beneath the Wall, through which he passes into a nightmarish world of darkness, bioluminescent plants, and giant, predatory insects. Finally, the younger Julian discovers the descendants of a lost Roman legion living far underground, and with them, his father. In the fifteen hundred years since the Roman Empire abandoned Britain, the survivors developed into a totalitarian society ruled by Master Minds who espouse a fear-mongering doctrine that the upper world would invade and destroy their society if its presence were known. In exchange for security, the citizens willingly submit to telepathic mind-control which renders them benumbed automata.

Both Tolkien and Lewis read the novel. Shortly after its publication, Lewis wrote to his friend Arthur Greeves on 23 April 1935, "The most interesting story I have read recently is *Land Under England* by one O'Neill: you should try it" (Lewis 2004, 160). Lewis may have shared his enthusiasm with Tolkien just as he shared it with Greeves. In any case, Tolkien read O'Neill's book by March 1938 at the latest. The previous month, on 18 February 1938, Tolkien had commended Lewis's *Out of the Silent Planet* to his publisher, Stanley Unwin. When Unwin asked for commentary on Lewis' manuscript, Tolkien replied on 4 March 1938,

> I realize of course that to be even moderately marketable such a story must pass muster on its surface value, as a *vera historia* of a journey to a strange land. I am extremely fond of the genre, even having read *Land under England* with some pleasure (though it was a weak example, and distasteful to me in many points). I thought *Out of the Silent Planet* did pass this test very successfully. (*Letters*, Letter 26, 33)

Marijane Osborn found significant influence from *Land under England* in Lewis' *Perelandra* and *The Silver Chair* (1953) in such elements as underground civilizations, mind control, and giant insects. She writes, "In both novels, Lewis makes significant use of Joseph O'Neill's *Land under England*, as he draws on contemporary anxieties, ancient literatures, and his own nightmares in ways that allude to and supplement O'Neill's already allusive story" (Osborn 2001, 115). Osborn's essay does not address 'The Dark Tower', but here, too, can be found echoes of *Land under England*. In 'The Dark Tower', the populace is under the mind-control of a 'Big Brain' just as O'Neill's Roman descendants are under the mind-control of 'Master Minds.' The minions of both civilizations go about their labours as unthinking automata; both groups of peoples having been convinced that such an arrangement would protect them from imminent invasion by hostile forces: in O'Neill, from the world above; in Lewis, from an invading hoard.

Significant similarities may also be detected in *Land under England* and Tolkien's 'The Lost Road'. Both stories revolve around father-son relationships, ancestral heritage, engagement with the distant past, and the poignancy of doomed civilizations. The themes of totalitarian dystopia come to the fore in Sauron's manipulation of Ar-Pharazôn, the disappearances of dissidents, and the stoking of fears over Valar oppression. Similarities with *Land under England* may even be felt later in Tolkien's *The Lord of the Rings* in 'The Paths of the Dead' where both works depict legendary, subterranean civilizations lingering long past their downfall in history.

3.2 – O'Neill & *Wind from the North*

When Lewis and Tolkien read *Land under England*, they would have seen that O'Neill had written another book, for that first 1935 edition published by Victor Gollancz announced on the title page that O'Neill was the 'Author of *Wind from the North*'. Despite Tolkien's estimation that *Land under England* was "weak" and "distasteful [...] in many points", he did report reading it with 'some pleasure' and may have sought out O'Neill's *Wind from the North* as well. Published in October 1934, O'Neill's first won the 1934 Harmsworth Prize of the Irish Academy of Letters for the best work in English prose on Irish subject matter ('Books' 1936, 42; Lynch 1983, 12). In addition to purchasing a copy for himself or borrowing it from a friend, Tolkien could have accessed the Bodleian Library's 1934 copy, although there is no direct evidence from either Lewis's or Tolkien's letters, statements, or personal libraries that either man ever read the book. Nevertheless, *Wind from the North* is a near-contemporary of 'The Lost Road' and engages with Dunne's time-travel theories in a similar fashion. Thus, the two novels may still shed light on one another as representative literature from a certain moment in history.

In *Wind from the North*, a nameless twentieth-century clerk is hit by a tram-car on a busy Dublin street who wake in the mind and body of a Viking in Norse Dublin during the events leading up to Brian Boru's invasion and the battle of Clontarf (1014). In the same way that Lewis's Scudamore inhabits a different body in 'The Dark Tower' but retains some of the original inhabitant's memories, the nameless clerk inhabits the body of Olaf Ulfson, scion of a powerful Viking family, yet retains his memories of the language and customs of Norse Dublin. O'Neill wrote, "The novel, in so far as it is historical, does not so much aim at a re-telling of actual events as at giving a picture of the everyday life of the Norsemen of Dyflin [i.e. Dublin] in the early years of the eleventh century" (O'Neill 1934, 341). Lynch argues, "The theme of the novel is based on Karl Jung's doctrine of man's search for his Ancestral Self and on AE's belief that every man lives through repeated reincarnations" (1979, 536).

The attractions of *Wind from the North* for Tolkien are immediately apparent from the 1934 edition's jacket description of time travel, Norse adventurers, and the tension between Christian and pagan religions:

> It is often forgotten that Dublin, in the early Middle Ages, was a Norse town. And those were stirring times. By strange accident a modern man finds himself thrown back into the midst of that eleventh-century town [...] A story of adventure undoubtedly [...] but the dominating adventures in it are the dark adventures of a man's soul, the shock of opposing creeds, the profound despair of one who has found no solution to the eternal question. (O'Neill 1934, book jacket)

Additionally, the book contains other things of interest to Tolkien: two maps of Norse Dublin, vivid depictions of a Viking-age society, engagement with the issues of colonialism and nationalism, a focus on father-son relationships, and Dunne's theories of serial lives exemplified in historical fiction.

Both O'Neill's *Wind from the North* and Tolkien's 'The Lost Road' are framed by stories of twentieth-century men who travel into the distant past while unconscious.

O'Neill's narrator undergoes "a trans-migratory experience" after his traffic accident (Lynch 1983, 13). Tolkien's Alboin and Audoin Errol travel to the past through their dreams. Both novels concern the conflict of rival religious groups played out as a debate between fathers and sons. In O'Neill, Ulf, the father, wants to preserve Christian Norse power in Dublin, while Olaf, the son, is manipulated by the pagan Gudrun who seeks to return the society to pagan worship. In Tolkien, Elendil, the father, wants to preserve faithfulness to Ilúvatar and the Valar, while Herendil, the son, is manipulated by Sauron who establishes a cult of Morgoth and seeks to subvert loyalty to the Valar. In both works, pending, cataclysmic battles are destined to topple the established civilizations. In 'The Lost Road', the god-like Valar destroy the ships of the unfaithful Númenóreans and inundate the island of Númenor. In O'Neill, the legendary Brian Boru amasses a Gaelic army to push the Norse colonizers off the island of Ireland.[7] Both O'Neill's and Tolkien's works are also conspicuous by the absence of wives and mothers. In *Wind from the North*, Olaf's un-named Gaelic mother died giving birth to him. In 'The Lost Road', Alboin Errol's un-named mother died giving birth to him, and later his own un-named wife died when their son, Audoin, was young. In the ancient Númenórean timeline, Elendil's un-named wife – Herendil's mother – is likewise absent.

O'Neill and Æ were fascinated by Dunne's theories of serial memory. Æ wrote in a review of Dunne's *Experiment with Time*, "Any who dream can, if they read, become fishermen in that Great Deep" (Russell). Upon publication of *Wind from the North*, Æ wrote to O'Neill, "I think your story of the Norse is a personal memory breaking through [...] This is the Ancestral Wisdom Keats said was in every man, and if we wished, we could turn in 'drunk with that old wine of heaven.' [...] You have doubtless killed and gone adventuring with the Vikings, and hunted [...] and worshipped strange gods on the mountains" (qtd. in O'Neill 2000, 12). O'Neill became "convinced that beneath the façade of his own 'modern self' lay several ancient and heroic pre-Christian souls" (11-2). He fantasized about being descended from both the romantic Gaels and the rubicund Hebrideans (11-2). Olaf, with his Gaelic mother and Norse father is just such a person. Lynch writes, "In 1926, after a dinner party with Æ and Jonathan Cape, O'Neill purportedly experienced the first of a series of 'dream visions' that comprised his first novel, *Wind from the North*" (1983, 12). The novel's unnamed modern narrator, that unassuming Dublin clerk, is an avatar of O'Neill himself, propelled backward in time into the body of one of his imagined ancestors.

This is very much like Tolkien's serial father-son pairs repeating certain phrases or situations down through time. For Tolkien, "unconscious memories were specifically ancestral" (Flieger 2007d, 650). His recurring 'Atlantis haunting' is the most famous example, in which Tolkien dreamed of being inundated by a massive wave. He later discovered his son Michael suffered from a similar dream (*Letters*, Letter 163, 213; Letter 257, 347). Flieger writes, Tolkien's "concept of inherited memory [is] as a direct channel to the past, not through song or story or proverb but through the operations of the unconscious mind in dreams. Tolkien uses memory as the psychic or psychological

7. In O'Neill's novel, the Norse colonizers serve as stand-ins for the colonizing English of O'Neill's own time. Tolkien felt that Anglo-Saxon culture – what he considered his 'true culture' – had also been colonized and crushed by the Norman Invasion of 1066 (see Garth 2003, 52).

connection between characters of the narrative present and their inherited or ancestral past" (Flieger 2007b, 413). Thus, his "modern-day Englishmen travel back to Númenor at the time of its downfall via their own ancestral pasts, experiencing or inhabiting the memories of a succession of forebears" (414).

Beyond the similarities in their approaches to Dunne's theories, however, O'Neill's and Tolkien's works also contain some closely reflective scenes. Two passages from each of the two works – O'Neill's *Wind from the North* and Tolkien's 'The Lost Road' – will exemplify their close and specific echoes.

3.2.1 – Waking up in the hall

In both of the first pair of scenes, a twentieth-century man falls unconscious and wakes up in a Viking-Age mead hall. O'Neill's *Wind from the North* begins with a traffic accident in which a twentieth-century Dublin clerk receives a blow on the head and blacks out. He awakes in eleventh-century Norse 'Dyflin' as a man is bending over him. "'How are you feeling, Olaf?'" the other man asks (1934, 10). 'Olaf' recalls,

> I staggered to my feet and looked round me in a sort of stupefaction. I was in a large dimly-lit hall. A crowd of men and women dressed in curious clothes were standing round me, looking at me and talking to me and to one another. I tried to remember what had happened to me but could not, nor could I remember the men nor the hall, for the moment, though both it and the men seemed familiar. (O'Neill 1934, 10)

The great hall is described as long and smoky, a fire runs down its middle, and on each side a line of tables runs along the walls. This is an accurate description of a Viking-Age mead hall. 'Olaf' is told that he was kicked in the head by the mule, Hviti, and he blacked out. He observes, "Even the language they were speaking was strange to my ears, although I understood it. That was the extraordinary thing about it. I understood it" (11). He is soon taken to speak with his father, Ulf, elsewhere in the hall, where they await the arrival of Ragnal, Olaf's cousin who has just arrived on the Dragon-ships from the Orkney Islands (14).

Tolkien's 'The Lost Road' was originally planned with just two timelines – the modern and the Númenórean – but, at some point, Tolkien decided to add a number of intervening timelines with additional father-son pairs. Among "several pages of very rough notes and abandoned beginnings" is the start of 'The Ælfwine Story', featuring a previously developed character, the tenth-century Anglo-Saxon mariner Ælfwine. The fragment begins, like O'Neill's, as a character awakes in a Viking-Age hall. Flieger contends, "It seems probable that the awakening of this Ælfwine was to be coincident with the falling asleep of his Alboin counterpart [in the twentieth century], and that dream, as before, was to be the means of transition from one time to another" (Flieger 1996, 41). Tolkien begins, "Ælfwine awoke with a start – he had been dozing on a bench with his back to a pillar. The voices poured in on him like a torrent. He felt he had been dreaming; and for a moment the English speech about him sounded strange [...] He looked down the hall, looking for his son Eadwine. He was due on leave from the fleet, but had not yet come' (*Lost Road*, 91-2).

The similarities with the passage from O'Neill are remarkable. In both texts, two men – the fictive O'Neill and Alboin – lose consciousness in the twentieth century and wake up in a Viking-age mead hall inhabiting another identity – Olaf and Ælfwine, respectively – both of whom have also just awakened: Olaf from being kicked unconscious by the mule and Ælfwine from dozing. Both men are surrounded by people and are disoriented by their voices. Olaf calls their language "'strange to my ears'" (O'Neill 1934, 11). Ælfwine finds "the English speech about him sounded strange" (*Lost Road*, 91). Nevertheless, both Olaf and Ælfwine can understand the language. As with Scudamore in 'The Dark Tower', language faculties remain with the host body. However, for Tolkien and O'Neill, the relationship between the medieval and modern bodies is ancestral rather than one of doppelgängers from parallel timelines. Both Olaf and Ælfwine are waiting for someone to arrive with the fleet. Both O'Neill's and Tolkien's father-and-son pairs even have reflexive names: Ulf and Olaf, Ælfwine and Eadwine, respectively. These two brief scenes are remarkably similar in several key aspects.

3.2.2 – Walking down to the sea

In the second pair of passages, the two protagonists – here, O'Neill's Olaf and Tolkien's Númenórean, Elendil – each take a walk from their hilltop gardens down to the waterside. Waking up the next morning, Olaf decides to take a look around at his father's hall and *tún*.[8] He recounts, "I went down the hall and out into a porch. The porch opened into a sort of garden yard surrounded by a tall thickset hedge [...] From the porch door I could see the sky flecked with hard brilliant scales of red" (O'Neill 1934, 25). Later, he returns to explore some more,

> When I looked round me outside I found that I was in a town, on a hill, surrounded by wooden walls. On my right, over the quick-set hedge that separated our dwelling from the street, I could see a high tower [...] From the height on which I was standing the garden sloped steeply down to the east. The eastern wall of the town rose over the lower hedge at the bottom of the garden, but not so high that I couldn't see beyond it a bay that lay shining under the frosty morning light [...] I went slowly down the garden [...] When I went out through the hedge-gate I found myself in a narrow lane that ran between the hedge and a high wooden wall, which I knew was the outer wall of the town. A low door was open in this wall, and, when I went through this, I found myself in a sort of wooden quay. (O'Neill 1934, *passim* 27-8)[9]

Tolkien's Elendil also walks in his hilltop garden, but in the beauty of the evening, rather than the morning. The white tower and golden roof of his house glow in the rays

8. O'Neill uses the Old Norse tún, from the Proto-Germanic **tūnq*, referring to a hedged plot, enclosure, courtyard, homestead, or a field or meadow around such a dwelling. Tolkien's *Túna* (Q, pron. [ˈtuːna]) was the green hill in Aman [i.e. Valinor] upon which was founded the city of Tirion. In early versions of the legendarium, it was known as *Tûn* (see *Shaping*, 9, for example).
9. This scene is interspersed in O'Neill's novel with observations on the many out-buildings and laborers in Ulf's *tún*. Olaf's observations of the landscape are presented here significantly elided to form a more continuous narrative.

of the setting sun. Elendil approaches, "the great hedge of *lavaralda* that fenced the garden at its lower, western end" (*Lost Road*, 63). Tolkien writes,

> He passed under an arch of shining leaves, and walked swiftly down rock-hewn steps to a white beach [...] Elendil stood and surveyed the cove and its rocky walls once more; and as he looked, his eyes rose by chance to his own house among trees and flowers upon the slopes above the shore, white and golden, shining in the sunset. (*Lost Road*, 64)

The two scenes reverberate with similar settings, imagery, and mood. In fact, they operate like mirror images of one another. One scene is at sunrise, the other at sunset, but both focus on the quality of the light. One garden faces east, the other west, but both are situated on hilltops that slope down to great encircling hedges. Openings in the hedges run along high walls – one wooden, the other rocky – which lead down to the waterside. Both men spy high towers on the hilltops. Both speakers also experience a peculiar sense of duality, a mental fog, at once familiar and strange: the result of possessing two sets of memories simultaneously. Olaf finds that Ulf's *tún* "looked strange to me, yet extraordinarily familiar"; the twentieth century recedes like "some strange nightmare" (O'Neill 1934, 25). Elendil's house in Númenor appears as both a real thing and a vision. He thinks, "as a thing in some other time and story, beautiful, beloved, but strange" (*Lost Road*, 64). Olaf finds his father, Ulf, along the quay. Elendil finds his son, Herendil, on a spur of rock by the cove. The descriptions of both scenes evoke similar feelings of beauty and melancholy, as something precious will soon pass away.

Both novels recount the beginning of the end-times for two powerful civilizations. The Battle of Clontarf (A.D. 1014), depicted at the end of O'Neill's novel, marks the end of Norse power in Ireland. In Tolkien's story, Ar-Pharazôn's forthcoming battle with the Valar will mark the end of Númenor. In O'Neill, Ulf and Olaf reconcile, but are overwhelmed by Gudrun's pagan liegemen. At the moment of Olaf's death, the modern-day narrator wakes up in a Dublin hospital, in possession of both sets of memories: his own and Olaf's. 'The Lost Road' was never finished, although Tolkien wrote some text and notes for possible endings: Elendil and Herendil remain divided, or they reconcile; Elendil survives, or he is captured by Sauron, or he drowns. At the moment of Elendil's death, would Alboin Errol wake up in his twentieth-century armchair possessing both his own and Elendil's memories? That seems a likely ending, but one which Tolkien never wrote.

4 – Conclusion

The numerous similarities between these two novels invite comparison and speculation of influence. Both Tolkien and O'Neill focus on the father-son bond, and its fracturing. Anticipated wars (analogous to the impending war with Germany) loom on the horizon in both novels, and both are concerned with the dangers of pagan backsliding, missing wives/mothers, the destruction of the past, and doomed civilizations. There are also very similar depictions of Dunne's Serialism as a succession of historically-connected lives, with time travel between those lives possible via the unconscious mind. 'The Dark Tower' also illustrates Serialism, but rather through parallel-world doppelgängers who leap (fully awake) through a 'magic mirror'. In theory and numerous details, Tolkien's 'The Lost Road' is closer to O'Neill's *Wind from the North* than it is to Lewis's 'The Dark Tower'. Yet, we lack direct evidence that Tolkien ever read O'Neill's first novel. At best, for now, we can call *Wind from the North* an 'inferred source' (a category Tom Shippey discussed at this conference in his presentation of Oronzo Cilli's book, *Tolkien' Library*, 2019).

At the very least, both authors were breathing the same intellectual air of the 1930s when Jungian concepts of collective memory and Dunne's theories of precognition and Serialism held sway in literary circles. Both Tolkien and O'Neill address similar anxieties, such as rising totalitarianism in Europe, religious conflict, and the destruction of the romantic heritage of their respective ancestral cultures. They were far from the only authors who chose to travel imaginatively in time once they had encountered Dunne's theories. However, they are among the few who chose to relive the past rather than speculate about the future. Moreover, their interpretations of Dunne are particularly in harmony. Perhaps because O'Neill's works are either out-of-print or hard-to-find, this thematic kinship between Tolkien and O'Neill has not been better explored. Perhaps it is because O'Neill is not well-remembered in literary circles today. Yet, further analysis may yield additional examples of the common theoretical underpinnings expressed in their artistic output, particularly in their dreams of Time.[10]

Bibliography

'Books', *Detroit Free Press*, (23 February 1936) 42 <https://www.newspapers.com/newspage/97538484/> [accessed 25 February 2021].

Buchan, J., *The Gap in the Curtain,* (London: Hodder & Stoughton, 1932).

Clute, J., 'Dunne, J W.', *SFE: The Encyclopedia of Science Fiction,* (11 August 2018) <http://www.sf-encyclopedia. com/entry/dunne_j_w> [accessed 25 February 2021].

Crossley, R.. 'Review: Dystopian Nights', *Science Fiction Studies*, 14.1 (March 1987) 93-98 <https://www. jstor .org/stable /4239798> [accessed 26 February 2021].

Du Maurier, G., *Peter Ibbetson,* Kindle ed. ([New York: Harper & Brothers, 1891]).

Dunne, J.W., *An Experiment with Time*, 2nd ed. (London: A & C Black Ltd., 1929) <https://archive.org/ details/ AnExperimentWithTime> [accessed 09 August 2019].
— *The Serial Universe*, (London: Faber And Faber Ltd., 1934) <https://archive.org/details/serialuniverse 032783mbp/page/n9> [accessed 25 February 2021].

Eddison, E.R., *Styrbjörn the Strong,* (Minneapolis: University of Minnesota Press, 2011).

Flieger, V., 'Lost Road, The', in *J.R.R. Tolkien Encyclopedia: Scholarship and Critical Assessment*, ed. by M.D.C. Drout (New York: Routledge, 2007a) 392–394.

10. The author is indebted to the work of Dr. Verlyn Flieger, as well as her feedback on an earlier draft of this paper. Any errors representing Dr. Flieger's theories or publications are the responsibility of this author. The author is also grateful for the support and feedback of her thesis supervisors, Professor Dimitra Fimi and Dr. Geraldine Parsons.

— 'Memory', in *J.R.R. Tolkien Encyclopedia: Scholarship and Critical Assessment*, ed. by M.D.C. Drout (New York: Routledge, 2007b) 413-414.
— *A Question of Time: J.R.R. Tolkien's Road to Faërie,* (Kent: The Kent State University Press, 1997).
— 'Time', in *J.R.R. Tolkien Encyclopedia: Scholarship and Critical Assessment*, ed. by M.D.C. Drout (New York: Routledge, 2007c) 647-650.
— 'Time Travel', in *J.R.R. Tolkien Encyclopedia: Scholarship and Critical Assessment*, ed. by M.D.C. Drout (New York: Routledge, 2007d) 650-651.
— 'Tolkien's Experiment with Time: *The Lost Road*, "The Notion Club Papers" and J.W. Dunne', *Mythlore*, 21.2 (Winter 1996) 39-44 <https://dc.swosu.edu/mythlore/vol21/iss2/9>.

Freud, S., *The Interpretation of Dreams*, trans. by A.A. Brill, 3rd ed. (New York: Macmillan, 1913) <https://archive. org/details/interpretationof1913freu> [accessed 25 February 2021].

Garth, J., *Tolkien and the Great War: The Threshold of Middle-earth*, (Boston: Houghton Mifflin, 2003).
— 'When JRR Tolkien bet CS Lewis: the wager that gave birth to *The Lord of the Rings*', *The Telegraph (London)* (8 December 2016) <http://www.telegraph.co.uk/books/what-to-read/jrr-tolkien-bet-cs-lewis-wager-gave-birth- lord-rings/> [accessed 25 February 2021].

Howard, R.J., 'Estranging Ireland: The underground self of the Irish free state in Joseph O'Neill's *Land Under England*', *Irish Studies Review*, 27.2 (2019) 235–252 <https://doi.org/10.1080/09670882.2019.1600640>.

Inchbald, G., 'The Last Serialist: C.S. Lewis and J.W. Dunne', *Mythlore*, 37.2 (Spring/Summer 2019) 75-88 <https://dc.swosu.edu/mythlore/vol37/iss2/5>.

Jung, C.G., *The Structure and Dynamics of the Psyche*, trans. by R.F.C. Hull, in *The Collected Works of C. G. Jung: Complete Digital Edition*, VIII, ed. and trans. by Gerhard Adler and R.F.C. Hull (Princeton: Princeton University Press, 3rd printing with corrections, 1975), 111 <https://www.jungiananalysts.org.uk/wp-content/uploads/2018/07/ C.-G.-Jung-Collected-Works-Volume-8_-The-Structure-and-Dynamics-of-the-Psyche.pdf>

Lewis, C. S., *The Collected Letters of C.S. Lewis, Volume 2: Books, Broadcasts and the War, 1931-1949*, ed. by W. Hooper, Kindle ed. (London: HarperCollins, 2004).
— *The Dark Tower and Other Stories*, ed. by W. Hooper (New York: HarperOne, 2017).
— *The Last Battle,* (New York: Collier, 1973).
— *The Lion, the Witch and the Wardrobe,* (New York: Collier, 1973).
— *The Silver Chair,* (New York: Collier, 1973).
— *That Hideous Strength,* (New York: Collier / Macmillan, 1965).

Lindsay, D., *A Voyage to Arcturus*, (London: Methuen, 1920) Kindle ed.

Lynch, M.K., 'O'Neill, Joseph [James] (1878-1852)', in *The Macmillan Dictionary of Irish Literature*, ed. by R. Hogan (London: Macmillan Press, 1979) 535-537 <https://doi.org/10.1007/978-1-349-07795-3>.
— 'The Smiling Public Man: Joseph O'Neill and His Works,' *The Journal of Irish Literature*, 12 (1983) 3–72.
Maxwell, D.E.S., *A Critical History of Modern Irish Drama 1891-1980,* (Cambridge: Cambridge University Press, 1984) <https://archive.org/details/criticalhistoryo00maxw> [accessed 25 February 2021].

O'Connell, M., '"How to Handle Eternity": Infinity and the Theories of J.W. Dunne in the Fiction of Jorge Luis Borges and Flann O'Brien's *The Third Policeman*', *Irish Studies Review*, 17.2 (2009), 223-237 <doi: 10.1080/ 09670880902885412>.

O'Neill, J., *Land Under England,* (London: Gollancz/Orion, 2018).
— *Wind from the North,* (London: Jonathan Cape, 1934).
— (as Michael Malía), *The Black Shore*, ed. by M. Kelly Lynch, (Lewisburg, PA: Bucknell University Press, 2000).

Osborn, M., 'Deeper realms: C.S. Lewis' re-visions of Joseph O'Neill's *Land Under England*', *Journal of Modern Literature*, 25.1 (2001) 115-120 <doi:10.1353/jml.2001.0021>.

Priestley, J.B., 'Dunne and Serialism', *Man and Time,* ([London]: Crescent Books, 1964) 242-261.
— *Time and the Conways,* (London: William Heinemann, 1950) <https://archive.org/details/in.ernet.dli.2015.531481 /page/n5> [accessed 25 February 2021].

Rateliff, J.D., '*The Lost Road, The Dark Tower*, and *The Notion Club Papers*: Tolkien and Lewis's Time Travel Triad', in *Tolkien's Legendarium: Essays on the History of Middle-earth*, ed. by V. Flieger and C.F. Hostetter (Westport: Greenwood, 2000) 199-218.

Russell, G.W. [i.e. Æ], '*An Experiment with Time* [review]', *The Living Torch*, ed. by M. Gibbon, (New York: Macmillan, 1938) 131-133.

Sayer, G., *Jack: A Life of C.S. Lewis*, 2nd ed. (Wheaton, IL: Crossway Book, 2005).

Stapledon, O., *Last and First Men & Star Maker: Two Science-Fiction Novels*, (New York: Dover, 1968) <https://archive.org/details/lastfirstmenst00olaf> [accessed 25 February 2021].

Stewart, V., 'J. W. Dunne and Literary Culture in the 1930s and 1940s,' *Literature & History*, 17.2 (2008), 62–81 <doi:10.7227/lh.17.2.5>.

Wells, H.G., *The Time Machine: An Invention*, Kindle ed. (New York: Henry Holt, 1895).

Williams, C., *The Place of the Lion*, (Grand Rapids: William B. Eerdmans, 1950) <https://archive.org/details/ placeoflion00will> [accessed 25 February 2021].

CITIES AND ENVIRONMENTS

A Tale of Two Cities (or perhaps more)[1]

Denis Bridoux

This paper began as I was studying Tolkien's drawing of Taniquetil or, to give it its full name, *Halls of Manwë and Varda on the Mountains of the World Above Faerie*,[2] as part of a document to support the Aubusson Tisse Tolkien project. For best viewing, I heartily recommend looking at the enlargement of the central section of the illustration in Catherine McIlwaine's *Tolkien Treasures* (2018).

In 'The Sketch of the Mythology',[3] dated 1925, Tolkien carried out a radical contraction and reorientation of the content of *The Book of Lost Tales* (1916-1919), his first major writing. Condensing into thirty pages, including notes, what took two volumes to publish posthumously sixty years later, and withdrawing the narrative connecting the tales, he achieved a text in which he substantially altered the geography of Aman and created the overarching narrative framework of the legendarium, which would guide his writing for the remainder of his life. The watercolour painting dates from this intermediary period between the writing of 'The Book of Lost Tales' and that of the first proper version of 'The Silmarillion', the 'Quenta Noldorinwa'[4] (1930-1931).

In order to interpret correctly what we see in the painting, we need to be aware of the date of its origins, as its geography gives the impression to correspond more to the texts which precede it than to the one which follows it, the latter being much less precise than the former. It can be confusing to seek to see 'accurate' representations of locations in the published *Silmarillion*, as what we see may not tie in properly with what we read in the final text.

The painting appears drawn from the shores of Eressëa, probably from a low cliff. In its middle, nestled at the foot of the mountain, facing the sea, sits a city. It occupies a tiny section, – 2.4cm x 0.81cm (0.9 in x 0.3 in) – of the whole watercolour, itself slightly larger than an A4 sheet, and this includes the swanship with a furled sail in front of it. Yet, when one looks at it closely, it contains a surprising number of details. Tolkien probably painted it with the help of a magnifying glass. He may have learnt to do this from his grandfather Suffield who could write the Lord's Prayer on a circle the size of a penny coin. Even though he may have been initially limited by the size of the paper he used, he was used to this format which he used throughout his life. We cannot exclude that he might have carried out preliminary sketches of it to be clear about what he was

1. The original presentation at Tolkien 2019 was supported with pictures.

2. In Hammond W.G. and C. Scull *J.R.R. Tolkien, Artist & Illustrator*, (London: HarperCollins, 1995), p. 56, Fig. 52. An enlargement of the section discussed in this paper appears in C. McIlwaine, *Tolkien Treasures,* (Oxford: The Bodleian Library, 2018), pp. 66-67. I recommend viewing this enlargement while reading this essay.

3. In *The Shaping of Middle-earth*..

4. In *The Shaping of Middle-earth*.

showing, but we do not know of any. It is also likely that he used pencil to sketch the drawing before painting it. Several other, uncoloured, pencil sketches dating from the same period already exist, illustrating respectively one of several views of *Nargothrond, The Vale of Sirion and Gondolin and the Vale of Tumladin from the Cristhorn*. Although these remain uncoloured, they may show us the state of *Halls of Manwë* had it remained uncoloured. At this stage, he could also have chosen to reproduce the sketch in China ink, another medium he favoured and had used for *Roverandom*.

First: are we seeing one city, or two cities side by side? To all appearances, we appear to be looking at a single city, tinted mainly white, gold and very pale grey, set on a relatively low grey hill, the top of which might have been levelled, divided into two sections which mirror one another, set about 120 degrees from each other and separated by a wide white slope, which could be a stair with low steps. It may be that the two sections are identical, but that we see the left one front up and the right one more from the side.

If we start at the bottom then we notice that both lower sections of the hill show tiers or terraces which seem to have been carved out of its body. On the left-hand side, what appears to be a stair rises from the ground to city level on the left. Its shadow falls on the carved area of the left section, which indicates that it receives the light of the lowering Sun in the West passing through the gap between the front mountain and Taniquetil, as the angles of Sun and shadow match. The stair may be guarded by a decorated balustrade, as there appear to be distinct finials and pinnacles on its ledge, but these could also be the summit of individual buildings that we cannot see because hidden by the city wall on the left.

The two parts of the city are on a level with the top of the white slope which separates them. They seem tiered also and what may be buildings or perhaps blocks of buildings, tinted gold, appear to rise from the levelled area of the hill on each side. One can distinguish five or more of them on the left section and three or more on the right. The white and grey areas may be buildings too, but if so, no feature can be determined. The top of each section appears to terminate in points, as if they were miniature mountains. They look more like natural features than buildings. No distinguishable towers can be seen, which is significant, as we will see later.

The city, and the hill on which it is situated, stands quite close to the shore. There seems to be an embayment just in front of the white central stair, presumably to allow the berthing of a ship and the alighting of passengers and cargo, but it could never be called a harbour, or accommodate a flotilla. To the left of the city, we see what appears to be some vegetation, probably trees. It would have begun to grow where the light of the Trees fell at the time of their shining. It stretches before the left-hand side of the city and the balustraded stair. It surrounds another, wider, embayment. A port area? If this is the case, there is no obvious 'sea-carved arch of living rock'[5] to be seen, which is also significant, as it is a distinguishing feature of one of the cities of the Elves in Elvenhome presented in *The Silmarillion*.

5. In the description of Kópas the 'mighty arch of living stone' survived into the '*arch of living rock sea-carved*' in the much briefer description of Alqualondë in *The Silmarillion* (61), also in 'The Flight of the Noldoli', *The Book of Lost Tales: Part I*, (136).

Which city is it? Is it Tirion on Túna, or could it be Alqualondë, the Haven of the Swans?[6] At this stage, the jury is still out. Details do not fully match either of the cities evoked or described in the text. The city we behold is not in a cleft but by the sea. It appears not on a high hill but a low one. It is made in two sections. It appears to have several stairs and terraces, but no high tower. Its walls are white, gold and grey, as of pearl. There is no visible high arch or what would clearly appear to be a harbour area. Vegetation appears to grow on its left.

In *The Book of Lost Tales: Part I* the cities which concern us are called Kôr and Cópas Alqaluntë, also known as Swanhaven.[7] They appear again in the Tale of Earendel in *The Book of Lost Tales: Part II.*[8] In addition to *Halls of Manwë* (July 1928), we can also look at the matching illustrations that Tolkien has left us, *Tanaqui* (Easter 1915, April 4), *The Shores of Faerie* (May 10, 1915) and *Gondolin and the Vale of Tumladin, as seen from Cristhorn* (September 1928). The details we read in *Lost Tales* are more persuasive. The illustration seems to match Kôr much more closely than Cópas Alqaluntë, even though there does not seem to be a white tower. It appears on be settled on two hills instead of one.

Finally, in 'The Sketch of the Mythology',[9] the information is too cursory to draw conclusions, but Swanhaven appears to have shifted geographically closer to Tûn.

The watercolour entitled *Tanaqui*[10] (Easter 1915, April 4th), represents the earliest version of the city of the Elves, Kôr. Highly stylised, it depicts a white city built on top of a tall sable hill (*sable* is the heraldic term for black). It is built on several tiers and light shines from the topmost level of the tiered section. A tall and slender tower stands erect on the right of the city. What looks like a path rises up the front of the hill, ending by a narrow aperture into the city. The poem entitled 'Kôr, in a City Lost and Dead',[11] written a few weeks later, is its companion piece.

Just a few weeks later, in a drawing entitled, *The Shores of Faery* (May 10, 1915),[12] Tolkien would depict another city and write a poem about it.[13] As seems to be common for Tolkien, the painting of the subject may well have preceded the writing, and one would have led to the other. It could be a later version of the same city, which would have ripened in his mind in the intervening period. As the *Tale of Eärendel* in *Lost Tales II* is only barely outlined and its structure was never finalised, it is uncertain however whether this is Kôr itself, as Christopher Tolkien thinks, or another city, situated on the Western shore of Valinor, where Eärendil comes to rest, as the poem's wording is ambiguous. Features similar to Kôr appear, but the light now shines from the top of the slender tower. Individual buildings can be seen, their front lit by the light of the Fruit of Laurelin, the future Sun. To the left of the city, or behind it, what could be interpreted

6. Descriptions can be found in chapters 5, 9 and 24 of *The Silmarillion.*
7. Descriptions can be found in chapters 5 and 7.
8. Descriptions can be found in chapters 5.
9. Published in *The Shaping of Middle-earth.* The matching artwork is viewable in Hammond, W.G. and C. Scull, *J.R.R. Tolkien, Artist & Illustrator* (47, fig. 43).
10. In Hammond, W.G. and C. Scull, *J.R.R. Tolkien, Artist & Illustrator* (47, fig. 43).
11. In *The Book of Lost Tales: Part I* (136).
12. In Hammond, W.G. and C. Scull, *J.R.R. Tolkien, Artist & Illustrator* (50, fig. 46).
13. In *The Book of Lost Tales, Part II.*

as the shore of a sea appears, hence the name of the drawing, bordered by some green which could be trees.

If we compare the city that we see in *Halls of Manwë* to the other two, it appears to be a hybrid, not quite Kôr or even Tûn anymore, and not yet Tirion or Alqualondë. It does not correspond anymore to the earlier representations of the city/cities that we have just seen, but nor does it either to another city which is supposed to have been built in memory of Tirion by Turgon, the fabled Gondolin, most famous among the cities of the Elder Days on Middle-earth. Indeed, Tolkien drew Gondolin during the same period he drew *Halls of Manwë* (September 1928), and the city built by Turgon resembles Kôr more closely than the city below Taniquetil than he had drawn only a few weeks before.[14]

Furthermore, the Minas Tirith of *The Lord of the Rings*, with its tiers, towers and pinnacles and, more especially, a great white tower, also appears to have been built on the same model. We can clearly see the filiation first between Kôr and Gondolin, then between Gondolin and Minas Tirith on his early drawings of the Gondorian city.[15] The towers and buildings on the drawing of Steinborg could just as well have been of a view of Gondolin. At the time of writing about the siege of Minas Tirith, Tolkien would draw much inspiration from his Fall of Gondolin, written 30 years before. Just as today we see many features echoing Greek and Roman buildings in towns and cities round the world, Tirion was the archetypal city on Middle-earth.

So, the city below Taniquetil is not really the Tirion of the *Silmarillion* that we know. Despite some similar features, such as its stairs and terraces, which may be characteristic of Noldorin architecture, it looks different from the chief city of the Eldalië. It is in the wrong location and the key feature from which it owes its name, Mindon Eldaliéva, the Tower of the Elves, is lacking, which gives its name to the city (Tirion means 'Great Watch Tower').[16] It is set on a low hill, not a high one, and is built in two sections instead of one.

Is the city on the way to becoming Alqualondë? This seems to be the case. In *Lost Tales*, its dwellers are called Solosimpi. Referring to the third tribe of the Elves, the term means 'Shore-pipers'. It is likely that this nickname was given to them by the Noldor, and that it carried derogatory connotations in their mouths. The tales of the Elder Days are mainly the story of the Noldor and was transmitted by them. The first version of 'The Silmarillion', dating from the end of the 1920s, was called 'Quenta Noldorinwa, The Tale of the Noldor'.[17]

The Noldor condescendingly said of the Solosimpi that they had once inhabited "strange dwellings among shoreland rocks" as, from the earliest of times, they already dwelt in caves (*Lost Tales I*, 121-2). Whether on Eressëa or on the shores of Middle-earth, caves are referred to many times in relation to them in *Lost Tales I*. Their attraction to caves would also manifest in Middle-earth, where many of the dwellings of the later Sindar and Nandor (Sylvan Elves) are located underground.

---

14. In Hammond, W.G. and C. Scull, *J.R.R. Tolkien, Artist & Illustrator* (61, fig. 58).
15. In Hammond, W.G. and C. Scull, *The Art of The Lord of the Rings* (114-115, fig. 105, 106).
16. In 'Index' in *The Silmarillion*.
17. Published in *The Shaping of Middle-earth*.

In Cornwall, Tolkien visited and drew the cliffs of the Lizard Peninsula in July 1914.[18] The power of the sea carves deep caves into the serpentine cliffs. Most of them ultimately collapse, creating embayments and coves. The description of the western coast of Tol Eressëa closely matches the Cornish coastline he described in a letter to Edith.[19] The seagreen colour is clearly visible at the bottom of the *Halls of Manwë* drawing.

It is also highly probable that this notion of Solosimpi dwelling in caves would have been inspired by the Tolkiens visiting the Cheddar Caves during their honeymoon at Clevedon, Somerset, nearly two years later in March 1916. A seaside resort in the county of Somerset in South-west England, Clevedon, north and east of Weston-Super-Mare, is situated just a few miles away from the famous Cheddar Gorge and Caves, a site of worldwide geological and archaeological importance since the discovery at the beginning of the twentieth century of remains of human habitation dating from the Upper Paleolithic era (circa 7,000 BC) inside the caves. About ten years after this discovery, the newlyweds had the opportunity of visiting the site during their stay, and it made a deep impression on Tolkien, inspiring among others the Glittering Caves in *The Lord of the Rings*. Most probably, it also inspired Menegroth and Nargothrond, the underground mansions of Kings Thingol and Finrod, which he had written about twenty years before, and probably also the Elvenking's Palace in *The Hobbit*, which is inspired by Menegroth.

As the legendarium progressed, the Third Kindred of the Elves gradually underwent a significant change in status, reflected in the evolution of their habitation. This was accompanied or, more probably, knowing Tolkien, preceded by a change of name. Their somewhat derogatory epithet of Solosimpi, or 'Shoreland Pipers' with which they began their existence, had been applied to them since the beginning of their long journey from the distant Palisor, in the East of Middle-earth. Although they might have piped away along the shores of Coivienéni, their name actually only became relevant when they reached the sea on the margins of Hisilómë, and once they had reached Aman. The name was probably given to them by the Gnomes (the Noldor) whose industrious temper contrasted markedly from that of the somewhat simple-minded carefree Elves. They gradually became called the 'Teleri', which was initially the epithet for the noblest of all the Elves, the First Kindred. As applied to the former Solosimpi, the term Teleri still retained some derogatory connotations, as it meant 'the Tarriers' (*Silmarillion*) at this stage of the evolution of High-Elven Quenya. Echoes of the Noldor's contempt toward the Teleri linger still in the published Silmarillion.[20] Immediately prior to the Kinslaying,

18. See Hammond, W.G. and C. Scull, *J.R.R. Tolkien, Artist & Illustrator* (London HarperCollins, 1995), pp. 24-5.

19. See *Biography*, 100. For a view of the area, see: https://www.google.com/maps/@49.9734158,-5.2698476,526a,35y,56.72h, 73.95t/data=!3m1!1e3. Best seen in 3D and rotated to be viewed from the sea.)

20. 'The name *Teleri*, the Last-comers, the Hindmost, was given to them by those before them on the march', in 'Index' in *The Silmarillion.*

'**TELES-** elf, sea-elf, third tribe of the Eldar. Q *Teler*, pl. *Teleri*; *Telerin Telerian*; general pl. *Telelli*, *Telellie* 'Teler-folk'. Originally the sense was 'hindmost, tarrier'; cf. Q *tella* hindmost, last, *telle* rear (*télesā); N *tele* end, rear, hindmost part (pl. *telei*)'. In 'The Etymologies', *The* addressing Olwë to convince him to surrender his ships to him, he sneeringly and insultingly states argues that, without the help of the Noldor, who carved, dug and built their haven, the Teleri would still be dwelling in "huts on the beach" (*Silmarillion*).[21] The Solosimpi's upgrade in status was repeated a second time later as the name 'Lindar', another name for the First Tribe, also became attached to them. Meaning 'the Singers', it finally removed any negative taint from their name. The first kindred then acquired its final name, the Vanyar, or Fair-Elves, which is how we know them.

The Solosimpian society, which began somewhat anarchically, evolved also. Their leader, Ellu Telemno, who was mentioned earlier in the text at the time of their Sea crossing, does not even appear in the argument with the Noldor who are seeking to steal their ships, which led to the Kinslaying. It is an anonymous voice among the Sea-Elves which stirs them to resist the Noldorin attempt.

However, with the newly expanded importance bestowed in the legendarium upon the Teleri, they acquired a King, Olwë, whose daughter Eärwen would marry Finarfin, one of the children of Finwë, the King of the Noldor. She would be the mother of Finrod Felagund and of Galadriel, the noblest of the Elves in Middle-earth at the end of the Third Ages, a singular rise from such humble beginnings.

To reflect their change in status, the main dwelling place of the Solosimpi evolved also. From the humble beginnings in Lost Tales described above, qualified by haughty Gnomes fond of tall towers of "strange dwellings among the shoreland rocks" or "mere huts on the beach" it became a port town, built in the northern confines of Elvenhome, Cópas Alqaluntë, or Swanhaven, set in a natural harbour in a cliff area (*Silmarillion*).

A critical feature of Swanhaven was its natural "arch of living rock, sea-carved" (*Silmarillion*). This would have been a realistic feature in a cliff area. Many 'stacks' we see today on cliff shores are the end stage of caves and arches carved into the stone by the action of the sea. Swanhaven may have originally been inspired by Lyme Regis in Dorset county, or by Whitby in Yorkshire (or perhaps by a combination of the two), both of which are set on cliff shores. Cópas Alqaluntë shares some features with these ports and seaside resorts, and Tolkien had visited both before writing Lost Tales. He had stayed in Lyme, the larger of the two, endowed with a substantial port area, with his brother and their tutor Father Francis Morgan "every summer after his mother's death"[22] and two of his early holiday visits there are documented (1906-1907). He stayed there again for his summer holidays of 1927 and 1928, and this is where he painted *Halls of Manwë* in July 1928. Durdle Door, one of the better known cliff arches in the UK, is situated on the Dorset coast to the east of Lyme Regis and Tolkien may have visited it. Tolkien visited Whitby in 1910 and again much later in 1945. The "winding stairs in the rock leading down to the harbour's edge" mentioned in *Lost Tales* may have been inspired by the "199 steps leading to the remains of Whitby Abbey, on top of the cliff." He sketched and painted both locations a number of times (*Lost Tales* I, 121-2)

Lost Road.

21. 'In huts on the beaches would you be dwelling still, had not the Noldor carved out your haven and toiled upon your walls.' In *The Silmarillion*, chapter 9.

22. 'Every summer he had taken them on holiday to Lyme Regis, where they stayed at the Three Cups Hotel and paid visits to his friends in the neighbourhood.' In *Biography*, chapter 3.

However, with the reorganisation of the geography of Aman, the cliff shores disappeared, and Swanhaven moved much closer to the Calacirya, northwards of the Pass of Côr, so close in fact that "Elwing, wandering along the margin of the Sea, came near to Alqualondë" where "Eärendil returning [from Tirion] found her." (*Silmarillion*) Yet the arch, which was the most distinguishing feature of the harbour, was apparently preserved. So, instead of a natural haven protected by cliffs from the sea with a natural living rock arch as its sole point of entry and egress, the harbour area would need to be dug and the arch to be built, albeit of 'living rock', i.e. unadorned stone.

And this seems to be precisely what happened. Under King Olwë, the humble port of the 'shore-pipers' became a noble city, Alqualondë, built for the Teleri by the Noldor who: "carved out their harbour and toiled upon their walls" and "their halls were of pearl, and of pearl were the mansions of Olwë." (*Silmarillion*). They may well have been the same architects who designed Tirion, which would explain the echoes of the previous city we see before us.

As the Teleri were more populous than both the Vanyar and the Noldor from the time of their awakening in Palisor/Cuiviénen, perhaps a large city in two sections may have been judged necessary. But why make the two bodies of the city identical? The answer to the question might lie in the fact that the Third Tribe had been led on the long journey westward by two brothers who perhaps were twins. Only one of the twain, Olwë, had been forced to leave his vanished brother behind to guide a part of their tribe across the Sea. In the meantime, the rest of the tribe continued to search for the other brother, Elwë, who had disappeared in the forests of Beleriand, entranced by love for Melian the Maia. He later became King of the Sindar – the Teleri who remained in Middle-earth – and the father of Lúthien Tinúviel. Although this is nowhere stated in words, it is highly probable that Elwë and Olwë were indeed twin brothers, as gemellity is a common trait among the Teleri and their descent. Although it is nowhere stated in the texts, the pictorial representation of the city in *Halls of Manwë* seems to provide the necessary evidence for this. Many Indo-European cultures, which we know inspired Tolkien, share similar elements in their mythology dating from their common origin. One of these myths is of the 'Divine Twins', one of whom is immortal and the other dies.

It is therefore highly probable that Olwë had the city built this way in the expectation of welcoming his brother and co-leader Elwë and his people, who had remained in Middle-earth, when they would cross the Sea at last. But this would not happen for a long time, at the end of the First Age of the Sun only, and Elwë would make his own journey westward in a different fashion, via the Halls of Mandos. This explains why Alqualondë is a twin city, built by a twin for himself and his twin who never came, as they became sundered by seas and much more.

So, if an arch there still is, where is it located? No longer having to search in vain for a natural arch which is nowhere to be seen, let us revisit the drawing. We saw earlier what seemed to be an embayment located between the two sections of the city in front of the wide white slope. But is it? On closer range and with the help of the latest and most detailed version of the drawing in *Tolkien Treasures* by Catherine McIlwaine, we can see that, delineating this embayment, there appears to be a built arch of unadorned white stone. Individual stones appear, their edges showing some sort of arched vault in gold colour. In fact, the whole white area just behind the sea and in front of the city may be a harbour wall sheltering the port. The strong foreshortening of the perspective and the wall hide the port area behind, dwarfed by the city. This is a much more satisfactory interpretation than my earlier embayment hypothesis, which appeared poorly drawn anyway, something which would have been unusual for Tolkien at this stage of his experience as an artist. In addition, based on our reflection above, it is much more logical to place the arch in the central part, just between the two bodies of the city, so as not to favour one section of the city at the expense of the other, as one twin would not want to appear superior to the other.

To round-up this reflection, an intriguing aside is provided by Scull and Hammond in their *Reader's Guide: Volume 1*, in their entry on 'Clevedon', where the Tolkiens stayed for their honeymoon. In September 1952, the Tolkiens returned to Clevedon for a second honeymoon and, in a letter addressed to his son Christopher (25th September 1952), Tolkien sent a sketch with the accompanying note: "Not a vision of Tirion, but an attempt to catch Cardiff caught in a rainbow across the Severn Sea." (Scull & Hammond 2017, p. 246). Why did Tolkien feel the need to say this? Could it really be that the view of the city seen from the shore of Tol Eressëa across the Bay of Eldamar was originally inspired by a view of distant Cardiff across the Bristol Channel from Clevedon during the Tolkiens' honeymoon in 1916?

In the changing geography of Aman post 'Sketch of the Mythology', Tirion was moved further inland, right inside the Calacirya which had been newly cut through the Pelóri. It left behind an empty space below Taniquetil which required filling, as it was much more strategically located for the purpose of the story than Swanhaven ever had been. The island of Eressëa was moved much closer to the coast of Eldamar, close enough that the *Halls of Manwë* illustration is painted from the perspective of a low Eressëan shore cliff, and Númenor was set in its location later for the same reason. Alqualondë, the Swan-Haven, was put in Tirion's place and acquired some of the features of the former, but not all of them, which explains the ambiguity and uncertainty we feel when seeing it on the July 1928 illustration of *Halls of Manwë*. But Tolkien had already resolved this ambiguity in his mind, perhaps thanks to his drawing. A month later, he would draw how Tirion would look like in his mind, not by representing it directly, but by drawing its mirror in Middle-earth instead, the fabled Gondolin. He was about to start working on the 'Quenta Noldorinwa', which would put into words what he had already seen with his mind's eye. A fitting act of sub-creation.

Does it ultimately matter which city we see nestled below Taniquetil? Perhaps not. Each one of us will have an opinion. What remains most amazing are the consummate skill and considerable care Tolkien used to paint it, managing to fit so much information into such a small space, more like a 16th century limner than a painter, and his ability to evoke so much with so little.

Bibliography

Carpenter, H., *J.R.R. Tolkien: A Biography*, (London: George Allen & Unwin, 1977).

Hammond, W.G. and C. Scull, *The Art of The Lord of the Rings*, (London, HarperCollins, 2015).
— J.R.R. Tolkien, *Artist & Illustrator* (London, HarperCollins, 1995).

McIlwaine, C., *Tolkien Treasures,* (Oxford, The Bodleian Library, 2018).

Priestman, J., *J.R.R. Tolkien, Life & Legend,* (Oxford, The Bodleian Library, 1992).

Scull, C. and W.G. Hammond, *The J.R.R. Tolkien Companion, Reader's guide, Vol 1,* rev. edn. (London, HarperCollins, 2017).

Tolkien, J.R.R., *The Silmarillion*, ed. by C. Tolkien (London, George Allen & Unwin, 1977). Ebook.
— *The Book of Lost Tales I*, ed. by C. Tolkien (London, George Allen & Unwin, 1983).
— *The Book of Lost Tales II*, ed. by C. Tolkien (London, George Allen & Unwin, 1984).
— *The Shaping of Middle-earth*, ed. by C. Tolkien (London, Unwin Hyman, 1986).
— *The Lost Road*, ed. by C. Tolkien (London, Unwin Hyman, 1987).

Negotiating Dichotomies in Landscapes

Elise McKenna

The Silmarillion and *Unfinished Tales* provide the history of Middle-earth's landscapes and the background for the events in *The Lord of the Rings* and *The Hobbit.* Three of the most complete narratives that will be explored are 'Of the Ruin of Beleriand and the Fall of Fingolfin,' 'Of Beren and Lúthien,' and 'Of Túrin Turambar.' Through these stories, the reader can experience immense landscapes essential to the narratives. The main characters within the above stories are affected by the different topographies and events that happen on them.

Tolkien's landscapes: Hithlum, Beleriand, Dorthonion, and Nan Dungortheb reflect classic dichotomies such as good and evil, sanity and insanity, and life and death. To discover these, one need only look to what appears in the landscapes. Mountains, rivers, fields, and forests delineate the regions, acting as liminal borders. The word liminality, derived from the Latin word *limen*, means threshold, and will be the basis for my discussion here.

A liminal space is a transitional space, which when crossed, affects the one who crosses it. It is the 'between' place and is all at once ambiguous, duplicitous and/or binary. In the three stories, 'between' places are pivotal because they are where decisions must be made and where characters change in mind and raiment. I use Tolkien's definition of raiment as not only the clothing, but also the physical form. The characters in the three narratives, Fingolfin, Beren, Lúthien, and Túrin negotiate not only the topographies but also the dichotomies within the lands and themselves.

Landscape is very organic for Tolkien, as has been pointed out by many Tolkien scholars over the decades. In a BBC History Extra article, Tolkien is quoted as saying, "One writes [...] not out of the leaves of trees still to be observed [...] but [...] out of the leaf-mould of the mind" (Wilkes 2019). This is like a forest floor, where the decaying matter of previous growths feeds the creation of new ones. Aptly noted by Wilkes and as clear as Tolkien's love of trees. Further, Tolkien's descriptions of the landscapes can be seen in anthropomorphic terms, not surprisingly. Owing to time, this paper will not discuss this at length, but further additions will be added to more fully explore this idea. I include it here because it is integral to how Tolkien devotes his language and description to land as a living being and a character that affects the other characters who interact with it.

In 'J.R.R. Tolkien: The British and the Norse in Tension,' Marjorie Burns discussed the dichotomies in regards to the author's depiction of landscapes both of external (earth) and internal (mind), as in "forest and garden, home and wayside, comradeship and solitude," (1990, 51). While her article looks at the author's ability to hold duplicitous ideas in regards to his intent, I plan to expand that idea in terms of the dichotomies in landscapes, as well as within the main characters. I will specifically focus on stories from *The Silmarillion* 1977 version, as I feel it is worthy of cannon in its own right. These three stories, 'Of the Ruin of Beleriand and the Fall of Fingolfin,' 'Of Beren and Lúthien,' and 'Of Túrin Turambar' and how the four characters become transformed as they negotiate the changes to landscapes within those narratives speaks to the author's duplicitousness.

1 – 'Ruin of Beleriand and Fall of Fingolfin'

Let's examine Chapter 18, 'the Ruin of Beleriand and the Fall of Fingolfin.' Fingolfin, second High King of the Noldor, is profoundly affected by the hardships and changes in landscapes, both through his travels and by events outside of his control. To begin with, Fingolfin was born in Valinor, in the undying lands. He lived there while the Two Trees, Telperion and Laurelin, were still living. Tolkien said this land is "a kind of Paradise" (*Letters*, Letter 131, 148). In Valinor were the most beautiful gardens, verdant mounds, fountains, and "opals, and diamonds, and pale crystals, [were] strewed upon the shores and scattered in the pools; marvelous were the beaches in Elendë in those days." (*Silmarillion*, 65). There could be no more ideal land in which to live.

This is the land Fingolfin left, taking the larger host of the Noldor with him, as per the oath of his half-brother, Fëanor. Unfortunately, Fingolfin and his host of the Noldor were then betrayed by Fëanor after the kinslaying of Alqualondë. Fingolfin was left in a quandary: how to get to Middle-earth. The only way left to him is the furthermost north: cross the Helcaraxë, known as the Grinding Ice, a thin stretch of pack ice between the Undying Lands and Middle-earth, his final destination.

The Helcaraxë is a liminal space. It is the threshold separating paradise and the earthly lands. It is described as, "a narrow strait" with "vast fogs and mists of deathly cold, and sea-streams […] filled with clashing hills of ice and the grinding of ice deep-sunken" (*Silmarillion*, 100). The mutability of this shifting land is important. The inherent dichotomy of the Helcaraxë is the water, as it is both a liquid and a solid, a stream and ice. It is also both moving and still. The landscape is mutable, ever changing as it grinds from top to bottom, and it is difficult to see due to fog and difficult to endure due to the cold. Also, it is imbued with life. "Terror […] and cruel hills" are part of this landscape (102). While uninhabitable, it is still alive in a sense, if only to instill terror and cruelly kill with deathly cold. It is not easy to traverse this space, and actually causes a great loss of the host of the Noldor, including Fingolfin's wife, Anairë. Fingolfin must transition here from threat of death, to general death, and now, personal death. This is a change from the place he came from, the Undying lands, to the harsh reality of a landscape where elves can die, and being so new to the banishment, it might be forever.

When they arrive in Middle-earth, Fingolfin settles the host of the surviving Noldor in Hithlum. From where they were in Hithlum, some of the dichotomies in the landscape can be seen. In the story, "the land [of the Noldor] was fair and their kingdoms were wide" yet Thangorodrim, smaller in comparison to the vast lands, and Morgoth's stronghold, could be seen (180). Maps show Ard-galen as a large green field to the south. The forces of the Noldor keep constant watch of it, since its placement is in the direct line of Thangorodrim (Fonstad 1991, 12-5).

Slowly, Fingolfin's people and resources grow, even in the shadow of Thangorodrim. In this area of Middle-earth, the dichotomy of the fertile and the foul are seen where mountain ranges act as protective barriers. More of this appears in the next section of this paper: 'Of Beren and Lúthien.' However, the field of Ard-galen will soon be marred and become a liminal space that Fingolfin crosses.

The forces of the Noldor besieged Morgoth in his northern fortress of Angband, holding the northern mountain fences of Beleriand and their passes against his forces. In 455, Morgoth broke the Siege of Angband (*Jewels*, 52). As events unfurl in the battle known as the Dagor Bragollach, the Battle of Sudden Flame, rivers of fire consume the green plain of Ard-galen, the vast grassland. The land is utterly barren and lifeless. The choking dust bowl that it becomes is named Anfauglith (*Silmarillion*, 181).

Also destroyed by Glaurung, balrogs, and orcs are Lothlann, Maglor's Gap, all lands between the arms of Gelion to the slope of Mount Rerir, Thargelion, and Lake Helevorn. East Beleriand and Dorthonion are lost. Fingolfin was caught up in the fourth Great Battle, witnessing all the beauty and green of his lands and those of the Noldor destroyed. "Fingolfin beheld (as it seemed to him) the utter ruin of the Noldor, and the defeat beyond redress" and was filled with "wrath and despair" (184). Maddened by the massive destruction of the lands and the obliteration of a great host of Elves and Elf-friends, the race of Men who were honored and fought alongside the Elves, Fingolfin rode out on Rochallor, his steed, and the image was like to Oromë, one of the Valar. "He passed over Dor-nu-Fauglith like the wind amidst the dust [...] for a great madness of rage was upon him, so that his eyes shone like the eyes of the Valar" (184).

This crossing further affects Fingolfin. Not only is he likened to Oromë riding Nahar, but Fingolfin is also like the wind, which is attributed to Manwë. Finally, while battling Morgoth at the gates of Angband, he "gleamed beneath [Morgoth's shadow] as a star, for his mail was overlaid with silver, and his blue shield was set with crystals" (185). At each stroke of Grond, Morgoth's great hammer, "Fingolfin leapt away, as lightning shoots from under a dark cloud." (185). This is the realm of Varda, Lady of the Stars. His sword Ringil "glittered like ice", which is the mingling of both Manwë and Ulmo (185). The description of Fingolfin alludes to no less than four of the Vala in his transformation as High Elf from Aman. This certainly would be necessary for an elf to have any hopes of prolonged combat with a Maiar.

Fingolfin was said to be "the strongest, most steadfast, and most valiant" of Finwë's sons (63). These admirable qualities do serve him, in what can be considered Tolkien's view of the theory of courage. Tom Shippey sums this up with, "its great statement was that defeat is no refutation. The right side remains right even if it has no ultimate hope at all" (2003, 156). Tolkien exemplifies this theory in the description of Fingolfin's battle with Morgoth outside the gates of Angband.

The scene unfolds as Morgoth slamming down Grond, rending the earth and creating great pits in what was a smooth landscape. This dichotomy puts the very earth at odds with itself. However, Fingolfin always springs aside, as the earth is pitted around him. They fought a great duel, and although in heightened 'Vala-esque' transformation Fingolfin wounded Morgoth seven times, in the end Fingolfin faltered, unable to physically negotiate the landscape around him. Tragically, "he stumbled and fell backward" into one of the great pits, "and Morgoth set his foot upon Fingolfin's neck [...] and the weight of it was like a fallen hill" (*Silmarillion*, 186). If there is a doubt that the land has affected Fingolfin, it is now undeniable that it has transformed him from this description. Landscape is now figuratively on top of Fingolfin and his final transformation will be from life to death.

In 'The Ruin of Beleriand and the Fall of Fingolfin,' Fingolfin went from a happy care-free life among the Valar to hardship. He experienced the betrayal of kin, and the bereaving crossing of the Helcaraxë, to his own death. Each happened in a liminal space. On the shores of Valinor, on the Helcaraxë, and in the pitted earth outside of Angband. He'd witnessed the marring of his lands due to evil, and it was the proverbial straw. He transformed. In Hithlum, he had once again found prosperity, only to have it destroyed by Morgoth. It was after this, that he became grim, though no less valiant. The changes to the lands affected Fingolfin to the point of rage, which increased his strength. He alone met Morgoth, valiantly in single combat, brave but hopeless. Fingolfin – transitions from the undying lands to the land where he can 'die,' and this is mutable, as his spirit will eventually find its home in the Halls of Mandos.

2 – 'Of Beren and Lúthien'

Next, let's examine Chapter 19, 'Of Beren and Lúthien' and some of the areas of Middle-earth that are described. Tolkien, in the famous letter to Waldman in 1951, said that this story was the most fully treated. One of the most recognizable quotes from Tolkien's letters is his telling of what he wanted to achieve by writing *The Silmarillion*. The cosmogonic would be founded on the fairy-story "in contact with the earth" (*Letters*, Letter 131, 144). He continued to further reference what type of land with "soil of the North West," and this was "to England, to my country" literally, the very soil (144). Looking at the stories through the lens that Tolkien supplied here, the land itself is quite significant. It is a living entity, rather than mere platform for the goings-on of the characters, and as such, the landscape can influence the characters. Movement from Middle-earth out of Gondolin to Angband – this is the transitional: terror is a physical force that can be manipulated to change an ordinary landscape of Middle-earth. From within The Girdle of Melian to outside that protected woodland, darkness, madness, etc. is outside waiting and actively trying to affect the characters.

Beren, a mortal man, lived with his father and eleven loyal followers in the highlands of Dorthonion. The land where they dwelt was populated with hills and forests that helped them hide from foes and helped them fight foes. The delineation of where is safe and where is unsafe was outlined in a sense with these landmarks. It allowed Beren and companions to initially disappear and remain hidden from Morgoth, while still inflicting damage to Morgoth's troupes. These borders are actively protected. After Beren's father and companions were betrayed and slain, Beren wandered there for four more years. It is then that a change comes about. Beren, "became the friend of birds and beasts, and [...] from that time forth he ate no flesh nor slew and living thing that was not in the service of Morgoth" (*Silmarillion*, 197). This came from within and shows his communion with the other inhabitants of Dorthonion. After a while, "all that land was [becoming] filled with evil" and "all clean things were departing from it", so Beren had to make a decision (198).

To do so, he climbed, "into the high regions of Gorgoroth, the Mountains of Terror, [and] he descried afar the land of Doriath" (198). To get there, he travelled across the wilderness of Dungortheb, described as "where horror and madness walked" (198). Beren had to then negotiate how to get into Doriath and avoid the evil. He did, but was not unscathed by the wilderness. He "came stumbling into Doriath, grey and bowed as with many years of woe, so great had been the torment on the road" (198-9). The land's dichotomy was a mix of sorcery meant to get into the headspace and drive one mad, and the protective Girdle of Melian meant to keep the land and people safe in that area from outside people through hiding magically. Both seductive and protective powers were at odds; the evil invited and the good shielded away – opposite to what makes sense. The effects on Beren, who wandered between these liminal spaces, were that of hair turning grey and a loss of strength and virility.

Once he crosses into the protective land, breaking the threshold of Melian, he spies Lúthien and becomes enchanted. In this, he reflects the "abyss of shadow" with a "barren and forsaken heart" (200). The directness of the object correlative is very clear. Beren reflects his surroundings, physically. When he travels the Narog to the Falls of Ivrin with Felagund, and continues on the North road to the Western Pass between Ered Wethil and Taur-nu-Fuin, Beren mirrors the evil roaming that land for "by the arts of Felagund their own forms and faces were changed into the likeness of orc" (206). It is Felagund who makes those changes, but Beren is reflecting what is already in the area, instead of changing himself. When Felagund dies just before Lúthien arrives, Beren is in Tol-in-Gaurhoth's dungeon described as a "deep pit, dark and silent" (207). After the death of Felagund Beren is alone and forsaken, reflecting the dungeon where he was imprisoned by Sauron, and he falls "down into darkness" (211).

In Dorthonion, Beren becomes one with the landscape and animals there. At most times, he reflects the land and space around him, and although reflecting it, does not ultimately change it or become changed because of it. This goes for all of the liminal spaces he crosses from the mountains to the forests and glades to the pits of Isle of Sauron.

Looking at the relationship between Lúthien and the liminal spaces in the story, it is clear that she does not reflect the changes in landscape; she alters the landscape and herself for example when she "danced upon a green hill," singing and sprouting flowers "from the cold earth where her feet had passed" (199). Lúthien lived in Eglador, a forested realm, and when she no longer sang due to Beren's hopeless quest, it caused a "brooding silence" (203), which affected Thingol's entire realm. When Lúthien is imprisoned in Hírilorn, the three trunked great tree, there are several dichotomies. The space is both home and not home; it is a safe place and a prison; it is a house and a living tree. In this dichotomous space, she grows her hair to extreme length and weaves a cloak that "wrapped her beauty like a shadow" (208). The change in her description is both visible and invisible, much like her imprisonment is still within the realm but no longer a visual part of it.

She continues on her quest to save Beren and reaches the next landscape – the bridge leading to Sauron's Isle. When she sang, "the Isle trembled" (211). She sings a song of power, "which no wall or stone could hinder," and the "gates were thrown down," "the walls opened," and the "pits laid bare" (211-2). All of this space was changed by Lúthien as well. It should be noted here that the quest is far greater and thus more land is altered. It should be noted that she is half-Maiar.

Lúthien again is reunited with Beren, yet he leaves her to continue the quest for the Silmaril. He wanders the Pass of Sirion to Taur-nu-Fuin, and spies Angband and Thangorodrim. He stands "alone upon the threshold" (216). Tolkien once again has a character looking out from a liminal space with dichotomies. Lúthien follows Beren with Huan, and once they reach Taur-nu-Fuin, she transforms both – Huan into "the ghastly wolf-hame of Draugulin [and herself] into the bat-fell of Thuringwethil" (216). They reach Beren and meet, as expected, in a liminal place, "between the desert and the wood," whereupon the guises are now Beren as Draugulin and Lúthien once again as the bat-fell (217).

There is another dichotomy presented here as well. While both Beren and Lúthien took the forms of evil creatures, in their eyes shone a clean spirit. They are both evil on the outside and good on the inside. Once they make it to the very Seat of Morgoth, Lúthien's voice is even more powerfully transformed into an elemental sound of water in deep pools, causing all the host of Angband to fall into a slumber. Morgoth, as during the battle with Fingolfin, is likened "as a hill sliding in avalanche" (219). Lúthien has the ability to alter landscapes, and quite large ones at that, so equating Morgoth with a hill, the land, allows her to have power over a former Vala. The power she is imbued with harkens back to the beginning formation of the very foundation of Middle-earth.

Final changes to a landscape due to Beren and Lúthien is the land of Ossiriand and Tol Galen. After the miraculous return of the two to Middle-earth, those lands were renamed, Dor Firn-i-Guinar, the Land of the Dead that Live. For the story of Beren and Lúthien, Beren reflects the landscape and makes decisions on the borders & liminal spaces, where changes are needed or required. Lúthien has more power than Beren, a mortal, or Fingolfin, a High King of the Noldor. Where Fingolfin changes in description, Beren reflects the landscape, and Lúthien alters the different topographies, as well as herself and Beren.

3 – 'Of Túrin Turambar'

The final story I want to explore through the lenses of liminal landscape and dichotomy in character is Chapter 21, 'Of Túrin Turambar.' Of all the tales, this one is the most poignant because of its theme – that fate is inescapable. It ties into Tolkien's idea of northern courage, as well, which further drives the heartbreaking events within. Each time I read this story, I find myself trying to counsel Túrin – if you only go left instead of right, if you trust the right people and not the wrong ones, if you just listened to your best friend. The effect on me as a reader is duplicitous. And sadly, like Túrin's fate in the story, I cannot change the tragic outcome.

Túrin was the son of Húrin and Morwen of Dor-lómin. His wanderings cover much of the areas previously discussed. So extreme are the effects of these events in the different landscapes that Túrin's identity is altered, although not his fate. Túrin was born in the year that Beren came upon Lúthien in Neldoreth (*UT*, 76). Due to the spreading evil in the land, Túrin was sent to foster with Thingol in Doriath. However, Túrin and his companions managed to get lost in the Girdle of Melian, but lucky for them, Beleg Strongbow came along and led them to Menegroth.

This is the first of numerous thresholds that Túrin crosses. He grows to be sullen and ever-worried for his mother Nienor. Although he is fostered for nine years and favored in Thingol's halls, he still wanders to the borders of that land, being held back and yearning to go. Thus the first dichotomy is set up. Túrin asked for mail and a sword, and he went to battle on the marches of Doriath, fighting alongside Beleg. After three years, Túrin returns to Menegroth, only to accidentally kill Saeros, an elf of the court of King Thingol, who joked scathingly, "If the Men of Hithlum are so wild and fell, of what sort are the women of that land? Do they run like deer clad only in their hair?" (*Silmarillion*, 244). While this does indeed foreshadow the coming of Nienor, it insults Túrin to the heart, and when further incidents occur, Túrin metes out a Dante-esque punishment, leading to the death of Saeros when he falls "into the chasm of a stream" (244). Túrin swiftly leaves and passes through the "Girdle of Melian [and] into the woods west of Sirion" (244). Thus he moves too quickly, and unlike Beren who paused at the liminal landscapes to make the right crucial decisions, Túrin marches on without heeding. He joins outlaws and "their hands turned against all, Elves, and Men, and Orcs" (244). At this point, Túrin not only changes in turning away from fighting the good fight, he renames himself to account for it: he is now Neithan, the Wronged.

Once in the wooded lands south of Teiglin, he finds Beleg has been captured by his men. He is urged to come fight again on the Pass of Anach, which "lies between" (245) the Crissaegrim and the walls of Gorgoroth. The great wind lords and land of Morgoth are described here as the dichotomy. The different areas of land are becoming inundated with evil. If this sounds familiar, it should. The same thing was happening when Beren's father was slain. However, instead of going to a safer place, Túrin decides to continue on to Amon Rudh, a "hill [that] stood upon the edge of the moor-lands", thus a liminal space (245). Unfortunately, good counsel and decisions are not made. In response to Mîm's son's death, Túrin seconds the name of Mîm's home and assumes its debt: Bar-en-Danwedh, the house of ransom. This place had the vantage point of many different landscapes from "the forests of Brethil [... to] the Mountains of Shadow" (249). Yet Túrin stays and does not move to cross any threshold, still broodingly Neithan the Wronged.

When Beleg returns once again, he and Túrin fight together and the region between Teiglin and the west march of Doriath is renamed, "the Land of Bow and Helm," and "Túrin named himself anew, Gorthol, the Dread Helm" (252). Túrin was finally happy, a changed disposition. It is short-lived. Due to more betrayal, Túrin is captured, tortured, and in a fit of madness, accidentally kills Beleg. Another elf called Gwindor leads Túrin, mute and unseeing, to Eithel Ivrin, the starting point for the Narog, and Túrin drinks from the water, and is healed of his madness. This area was still clean, and its goodness helped change Túrin, and they continued on to Nargothrond. Túrin again renames himself, "Agarwaen the son of Umarth" and rightly so-called "the Bloodstained, son of Ill-fate" (257). This unfortunately is not the end of the names. He now wields Gurthang, the reforged sword of Beleg. While fighting only on the Guarded Plain, he calls himself 'The Mormegil,' (258) believing his own hype for the most part, and becomes fearless while wearing the mask.

It would be remiss not to move on to the meeting and subsequent tragedy of the coming of Glaurung. The bridge that Túrin helped to construct and keep intact against advice, allows a way for the dragon to cross into the stronghold and wreck lives. It becomes a threshold where Túrin is mesmerized and deceived by the direct stare of the Glaurung. While on the bridge of Nargothrond, taken by Glaurung, Túrin stood as one graven of stone" (262). He makes the wrong decision. The quest is put forth by Glaurung to save Finduilas or find his mother and sister. Unable to complete both simultaneously, he fails both. Túrin calls himself "Wildman of the Woods" as a way to channel that strength without acknowledging his real name and hopefully find Finduilas (266). He has Haudh-en-Elleth, a mounded grave for Finduilas, created and he changes falling "down into a darkness of grief" (266).

Yet, he is again healed and changes his name once more to become Turambar, Master of Doom. However, this hubris is a fatal flaw. More woes come and when he meets up with Glaurung for the final time, it is at Cabed-en-Aras, near a deep river and leap-able gorge. Glaurung's words echo what has been Túrin's fears all along and it was in calling Túrin names, "Evil have been all thy ways, son of Húrin. Thankless fosterling, outlaw, slayer of thy friend, thief of love, usurper of Nargothrond, captain foolhardy, and deserter of thy kin" (262).

Each time Túrin crosses a liminal space, whether forests, plains, roads, bridges, or waterways, he changes his name and remakes himself to become a different person. Túrin's changes are significant in that he continues to fall into darkness and bring himself out of it seemingly stronger. Yet, it all proves vain as can be seen in the *Narn i Chin Húrin*. Túrin continuously misreads his situations, and when given the chance for a decision between options, he chooses the wrong one. His names reflect his self-pity when he actually has better options, and when he is headed for disaster, his chosen name reflects the opposite. This is one more instance of changes in a character as they traverse liminal spaces, and dichotomies are brought forth.

For all of this, to recap a bit might be worthy. High Elf king Fingolfin transforms into the likes of the Vala. Beren, son of Barahir of the line of Men, reflects the changing landscape and spaces he occupies. There is an Elf-Maiar maiden, Lúthien who becomes more than that, drawing on both lineages in attempts of a defeat that Fingolfin was unable to accomplish. Finally, Túrin of the race of Men attempts to overcome his fate to no avail, no matter the thresholds he crosses and names he assumes. Each of these characters struggle to fulfill their quest in the Long Defeat of Morgoth as they interact on and with the different topographies. These landscapes, as living thresholds with liminal borders, reinforce the dichotomies of life and death, love and loss, death and rebirth, haven and horror, and sanity and insanity as they affect and are affected by those aforementioned characters.

Bibliography

Burns, M., 'J.R.R. Tolkien: The British and the Norse in Tension', *Pacific Coast Philology,* 25.1/2 (1990) 49-59.

Fonstad, K.W., *The Atlas of Middle-Earth*, rev. edn. (Boston: Houghton Mifflin Company, 1991).

Shippey, T., *The Road to Middle-earth: How J.R.R. Tolkien Created a New Mythology,* (Boston: Houghton Mifflin Company, 2003).

Tolkien, J.R.R., *The Silmarillion*, ed. by C. Tolkien (New York: Houghton Mifflin, 1977).
— *The Letters of J. R. R. Tolkien*, ed. by H. Carpenter with the assistance of C. Tolkien (London: George Allen & Unwin, 1981).
— *The War of the Jewels*, ed. by C. Tolkien (London: Harper Collins, 1994).
— *Unfinished Tales of Númenor and Middle-earth*, ed. by C. Tolkien (London: Harper Collins, 1998).

Wilkes, J., *Tolkien: the Mastermind of Middle-earth*, online video recording, HistoryExtra.com, 2019, <https://www.historyextra.com/period/20th-century/tolkien-writer-mastermind-middle-earth-hobbit-lord-rings-writing/> [accessed 15 June 2019].

"Rivers of flame and a great reek rising": volcanoes and the horror of the sublime in J.R.R. Tolkien's Legendarium

Sian J. Pehrsson

Humanity has an enduring fascination with the volcanism that shapes our planet's surface. It both nurtures and despoils the niches in which we live (Sheets 2015). It forms a graphic reminder that we are but travelers on an Earth that churns away indifferent to our fate; and Art, with its search to enlighten, explore, and entertain, has turned again and again to these terrifyingly capricious natural features.

Since the time Empedocles was said to have leapt into Etna fires, volcanoes have fascinated scientists, poets and authors alike (Ziolkowski 2017). They have frequently been the subject of historical and fantasy literature or film, featuring in such famous novels as Dante's *Inferno*, Malcolm Lowry's *Under the Volcano*, Jules Verne's *Journey to the Center of the Earth*, and, most recently, N.K. Jemisin's Hugo-award winning *The Broken Earth* trilogy, which imagines a world riven cyclically by catastrophic eruption. A review of volcano films finds that such features as Mike Myer's *Austin Powers*, Ingrid Bergman's *Stromboli*, *The Last Days of Pompeii* and *Dante's Peak* all share a common thread: passion and peril. From literature to theatre or film, three themes bind the representation of volcanoes: 1) volcanism as an unpredictable hazard, 2) volcanic edifices as entrances to the underworld, and 3) volcanoes as home to evil doers (Sigurdsson and Lopes 2015). In this last aspect in particular, J.R.R. Tolkien's works are in a familiar vein. From the moment in 'The Shadow of the Past' when Frodo sees wells of flame in the embers of Bag End's fire, to his ultimate struggle at Sammath Naur, Mount Doom looms literally and metaphorically over Tolkien's epic as a symbol of dread and horror.

Analysis of the geology of Arda in Tolkien's Legendarium is a fertile but less oft-tilled field of study. A number of excellent contributions consider it in general (Mason 1975; McIntosh 1973; Sarjeant 1992; Gee 2005; Hynes 2012) and specific aspects, including glaciation (Howes 1967), geomorphology (Reynolds 1974), and geophysics (Coombs and Read 1995). Despite, however, the wealth of detail Tolkien included in his works, the majority of these articles treat volcanism only obliquely, with its edifices and products being assessed for their indications of broader geodynamic or orogenic process.

This contribution seeks to consider Tolkien's volcanoes in their own right. It will review historical representations of volcanism in myth and literature; outline Tolkien's fiery mountains and the narrative devices he used to portray them; and postulate natural geologic influences from their geomythology. It will be shown that a parallelism is evident between the evolution of geologic thought and volcanic process in mid-Twentieth century and the increasing sophistication of Tolkien's own volcanic description. Lastly, a link between Icelandic eruption and imagery of Melkor is proposed.

1 – Volcanism's Depiction in Literature

Prior to the modern era, volcanism entered literary works predominantly in one of two spheres: Romanticism and myth. Romanticism, the late eighteenth century movement in arts and literature is most closely linked to volcanism through Edmund Burke's definition of the sublime (Ariel 2010). It seems fitting to our subject that Burke sought to apply scientific method to his enquiry on the nature of our human passions: the 'Beautiful', appreciation of the well-formed and aesthetically pleasing, and the 'Sublime', our strongest passion, underpinned by terror or fear, and having the foundational power to impel and destroy us.

> In volcanism we have these two passions intertwined. Brady notes that 'the natural sublime (is) linked to […] vastness, enormity and power; the dark, powerful, towering, raging and tumultuous' (2012, 187). Volcanoes embody the very definition of this concept: at once vast and beautiful, incomprehensible in their violence after ages of quietude. Paulson argues that they are 'an aestheticizing of evil and its various forms: chaos, disorder, obscurity, and sin' (2007, 118)

This Romantic conception of one of nature's most powerful forces proved influential for several generations of artists and writers, and also tourists undertaking the Grand Tour to Vesuvius. Although most famous for its 79 A.D. destruction of the Roman city of Pompeii, the latter-day Vesuvius is a gentler giant, immortalized by D. H. Lawrence in 'Peace':

> Brilliant, intolerable lava,
> Brilliant as a powerful burning-glass,
> Walking like a royal snake down the mountain towards the sea (2013, 553)

Lawrence's words capture our instinctual response to such unchained natural power – awe, wonder, fear. This primal force capable of generating the strongest of sensations in their beholders is at once capricious and compelling, for danger can also spur delight. And although studies on the sublime in Tolkien's often focus on his landscapes (Sandner 1997) or the dreadful and majestic Valar, his volcanoes in and of themselves are equally representative.

There is no doubt that both humans, and hobbits, are insignificantly small in comparison to their might.

2 – Classical history and Norse mythology

The Romantic perspective endures but it is the earlier world of myth and legend, and our long uneasy cohabitation (Sheets 2015), that have most shaped our present instinctual horror of volcanism. With the dominant influence of Mediterranean and Norse mythology on the West (Frierson 1991; Johnston 2005) volcanoes have become places of punishment, sources of unlimited power, or passageways to the Underworld.

Hephaestus, the Greek god of fire and metal-working, kept his forge below ever restless Etna, having chained the Titan Typhoeus in its bowels. Typhoeus' subterranean struggles and stirrings were thought to trigger the volcano to erupt (Sigurdsson 2015). Talos, a bronze giant fashioned by Hephaestus, attacked Jason and his Argonauts with rocks and blazing heat and is considered by some to be an embodiment of Thera, the ancient volcano of the isle of Santorini. Vulcan, the Roman God of Fire, is linked to many of Hepaestus' qualities (including being cuckolded by a beautiful wife) and similarly uses the unquenchable fires of Etna on Sicily as his forge. In contrast to Hephaestus however, Vulcan has a stronger association with the destructive capabilities of fire and volcanism. His worshippers believed that suitable sacrifices could avert or ameliorate eruption. Some scholars consider parts of the Icelandic sagas celebrating the god *Þórr* (Thor) are emblematic of historical eruptions, particularly in his wielding of thunder and leaving quaking earth in his wake (Taggart 2017), although this is an ongoing subject of debate.

Links between volcanoes and representations of the underworld have a long history, with one of the most elegantly depicted being Kircher's 1665 *Systema Ideale Pyrophylaciorum Suberraneorum* showing regular spaced summits about the globe crowning a tree root-like maze of magma channels leading to a molten core. The postulated link between Etna herself and the underworld was so robust that 'sailing to Sicily' in medieval times was a euphemism for going to Hell (Sheets 1995, 119). For the Norse peoples, this symbolic association was also significant: the summit of the shield volcano Hekla on the island of Iceland was described in the Völuspá of the *Poetic Edda* (Larrington 2014) as a portal to a hellacious underworld, traversed by flocks of birds embodying the poor souls coming and going through its maw. Indeed, this belief was so strong in local folklore that aspects of it persisted to the early nineteenth century (Thorarinsson 2017).

Not all those who suffered below volcanoes were titans or demi-gods. Virgil, the Roman poet who interpreted Greek mythos, proposed that Etna's rumblings, flaming magma and tremors were the hero Enceladus' tormented cries, desperate breath, and railing against his prison, having been buried there by the goddess Athena as punishment for disobedience (Kozák and Čermák 2010). Enceladus' brother Mimas was also held to have been buried beneath Etna's neighbour Vesuvius by Hephaestus, and the blood of defeated giants could be seen in the upwelling of the Phlegraean Fields at its feet.

In contrast to the fungible material of the West, the Circum-Pacific peoples, who inhabit the very active Pacific Ring of Fire, came to view volcanoes as living edifices; literally embodying them as the gods themselves, torn by those most intense of human emotions – jealousy, rage and love – that battle and burst forth when these emotions become uncontainable. From the very earthly love triangle of Hawaiian Kīlauea's Pele and her sister Hi'iaka battling over the handsome Lohiahu (Westervelt 1963; Vitaliano 1976), to the steadfast Smoking Mountain Popocétepl and his White Lady Iztaccihuatl, lovers side by side in the Valley of Mexico who could not bear to be out of each other's sight (Vitaliano 1973), or Mount Fuji's Sengen, the goddess of fire who would throw from the mountain any pilgrims that were impure of heart (Davis 1992) Pacific legend imbues volcanic edifices with personal and potent cares and jealousies. The Itelmen and Koryak peoples of Kamchatka depicted that isthmus's highly restive spine (precarious home to fifty periodically active volcanoes) to be inhabited by jealous gods inflamed by rage or holding hearts that still burnt with fiery love for a woman (Downing 1956). Maori legends tell of the volcano Taranaki fighting his rival Tongariro for the love of

Pihanga and, in grief and defeat, fleeing west across the north island of New Zealand, leaving a huge scar on the landscape and three isolated, angry, slumbering mountains (Anderson 1969).

A common feature of these all myths is that they are held by peoples occupying the deadly and dangerous slopes or environs of young, very active, often Holocene or more recent stratovolcanoes that have formed through the geodynamic process of subduction wherein a downgoing tectonic plate releases water into the overlying plate's mantle wedge, triggering melting and volcanism. The products of this process are highly volatile and silica-rich, and consequently explosive, magmas, far more destructive on average than *most* Mediterranean or Icelandic volcanoes, especially when paired with the Pacific's predilection for tsunami.

Viewed in this lens, a link between extreme and dangerous emotion seems natural. As does a poignant and piercing need to appease these raging gods through the ultimate offering: sacrifice. Thus, the ancient Mayans, Aztecs, and Incas, and more recent indigenous people of central Africa, Nicaragua and Indonesia, offered livestock and humans (often warriors or young women) to their volcanoes (Kozák and Čermák 2010). The practice has mercifully lapsed, replaced by modern continuous monitoring of those considered most dangerous and proximal to populated regions (Global Volcanism Program 2019).

3 – Tolkien's Fiery Mountains

In Tolkien's legendarium we have half a dozen fiery mountains, edifices which either erupt or are products of former eruption.

Orodruin in Mordor, arguably the most famous volcano in fantasy literature, is literally glossed as 'burning mountain' but is also known as Amon Amarth and Mount Doom. Orthanc, which was "riven from the bones of the earth in the ancient torment of the hills" is made of gleaming obsidian, a volcanic neck with a 'bubbling cauldron' below (*TT*, 'The Road to Isengard', 140). Thangorodrim, the Oppressive Peaks, and Ered Engrin, the Iron mountains, erupt in the earlier Ages of Middle-earth but are most likely extinct by the Third Age. Meneltarma, with its prominent radial ridges and classical conical stratovolcano profile, complete with a summit crater is, given Númenor's Atlantean associations, perhaps a nod to Thera on Santorini, similarly linked to a doomed ancient civilization. Erebor of the Hobbit, rich in metal and jewels, forming the star shape of an incised extinct volcano with ridge fissures, is arguably a volcano (Sarjeant 1992), and Dol Guldur, a high lone mountain caused to belch fire and flame, has been proposed to be one, but if so it would be considered monogenetic, not continuously active like its brethren.

In fantasy, adventure and romantic literature alike, volcanoes are inherently sinister features, associated with personal and political revolution (Ariel 2010), quests and seeking (Ziolkowski 2017), but above all, horror (Sigurdsson and Lopes 2015). Volcanoes are said to loom but mountains soar. They are dark and dangerous; deadly below oftimes beautiful and temptingly fertile cloaks. Tolkien used this subtle unsettledness in the Hobbit but most successfully applied it in *The Return of the King* where the Fellowship's quest and its perils are inexorably drawing to a point – the summit of Mount Doom.

Drawing on his deep understanding of Northern and European myth (St. Clair 1992; Shippey 2000), Tolkien imbued Arda's fiery mountains with many of the common elements of volcanic horror: random eruption instigated by capricious gods; forges and seats of power for evil-doers; fell cauldrons, cracks of doom, into which beings or artifacts are flung and sacrificed, or both, in Gollum's tragic case. The inherent dichotomy of an erupting mafic volcanic landscape: bright red, molten incandescence and chill black hardened lava flow, moreover fit his theme of light and dark, being a natural phenomena with at once a terrible darkness and a searing brightness.

As Sarjeant (1992) has pointed out, each of the key malevolent figures in his works, Melkor, Sauron, and Saruman, made homes, fortresses, and forges in fiery mountains. Of Melkor it was said he "ruled both fires and the cruellest frost, both the uttermost colds and the deepest furnaces beneath the hills of flame" (*Lost Tales I*, 3, 68). Fire is unquestionably a primal fear to humans when uncontrolled, and lava, a volcano's fiery vomit, is named from the Latin or Italian 'lavare'; to wash away the fruits of human labour (Sigurdsson 2015). Thus the power that Melkor harnessed was "The Secret Fire [...] sent to burn at the heart of the world", a clear allusion to subterranean mythos and volcanism (*Silmarillion*, 2, 25).

Tolkien's volcanoes are dark, black, sinister edifices; isolated, lone, lofty mountains subject to sudden eruption, pouring out rivers of flame at the will of their capricious lords. The result is a natural feature of Arda infected by evil, described with his prevalent motif of dire mechanization: "all the while far below there was a rumour and a trouble as of great engines throbbing and labouring" was said of Mount Doom by Sam, exhausted and thirsty, on its slopes (*RK*, 'Mount Doom', 196).

He also successfully used Pacific-style personification to augment terror. A review of the syntax used throughout *The Lord of the Rings* shows Orodruin is "tormented" by eruption; "tongues" of fire "vomit" and "belch"; the landscape is "pockmarked" by ejecta like a disease. Reeking fume mantles the slopes like a "cloak" (196). Common descriptors applied to beings abound: Tolkien's volcanoes "awake", they "glare" and "throb", lie in "smoldering slumber", as threatening and dangerous as a sleeping beast (196). They have mouths and feet and faces. They are most assuredly angry.

Although there has been limited direct treatment of Tolkien's depiction of volcanism in scholarship, one of the more interesting is the interpretation of William Sarjeant. There is no doubt that in the Legendarium allusions to the geologically sinister appear, but went further. He posited from his analysis of possible Middle-earth plate tectonic geometry that Tolkien's fire mountains are intraplate hotspot volcanoes associated inherently with evil. Intraplate volcanism occurs where there is active deep mantle upwelling and impingement of this hot source on an overriding thick crustal or oceanic plate (Francis and Oppenheimer 2004). Under the force of adiabatic decompression, a focused plume of magma pierces the crust, and a key facet of this manifestation is a voluminous outpouring of basaltic lava, seemingly without cause. With Sarjeant's interpreted plate geometry Erebor, Dol Guldur, Orthanc and Orodruin all appear as lone, lofty volcanic features, each hosting a denizen of Shadow and triggering a subliminal response to their randomness.

Although intriguing hints of classical hotspot chains occur in Erik Mueller-Harder's map analysis (2019), close examination of the descriptions of Tolkienian eruption highlights that instead of hosting inherent evil (that the material as shaped by Aulë has been corrupted), the stuff of Arda is exploited for its power by Melkor and Sauron: Thangorodrim and the Iron Mountains, Amon Amarth and Dol Guldur, all spout flame or 'smoke' under their new masters' influence. For example, of Morgoth it is said: "Now Morgoth [...] caused vast smokes and vapours to be made, and they came forth from the reeking tops of the Iron Mountains, and afar off they could be seen in Mithrim" (*Silmarillion*, 3, 109); and of Sauron: "(he) used the fire that welled there from the heart of the earth in his sorceries and in his forging" (292).

His choice of using personification to add depth to the description of eruptions is also instructive in this regard. The erupting mountains are said to be in "turmoil" and "torment", they clearly suffer by their misuse, and do not revel, as they might if turned willingly to the forces of evil (Filipovic 2018, 4).

4 – The Geology of Arda's volcanoes

What was Tolkien's inspiration for his fiery mountains? The broad literary influences are clear: Pliny the Younger on Vesuvius and the Völuspá of the Poetic Edda, considered to depict the medieval eruption of Eldgjá in Iceland. There is direct corroboration that he was familiar with these sources as he quoted the former (Shippey 2000) and owned the later (Cilli 2019). Although Peter Jackson used New Zealand's Ngauruhoe as the literal stand-in for Mount Doom, conventional wisdom has held that Stromboli is Mount Doom. This opinion, from Clyde Kilby (Kilby in Plotz 1968), seems doubtful, because, as John Garth has pointed out, Tolkien did not visit Italy until the summer of 1955, just before *The Return of the King* was published (Garth 2020). Furthermore, though in profile the upper part of Mount Doom was sketched to look like a lonely Stromboli with a stratovolcano's soaring conical shape, its eruptive products are not those of Strombolian eruption. Known as the 'Lighthouse of the Mediterranean' (Oppenheimer 2011), Stromboli erupts with frequent, mild blasts of Volcanic Explosivity Index 1-3 out of a possible 8. It ejects incandescent cinder, lapilli and bombs, tens to a few hundred meters down its flanks, so regularly that it gives its name to this eruptive style (Francis and Oppenheimer 2004).

Other somewhat problematic geologic manifestations have been proposed. Sarjeant suggested that much of the entire topology of Mordor – the Ephel Duath, Mount Doom, the Morannon and Gorgoroth, be included in a single Krakatoa-esque, supervolcano (Sarjeant 1992). The evidence for this is thin: the Ephel Duath are not known to be of volcanic origin, nor is the plateau or its surrounding northern fence. An additional curious interpretation is that of Ingles and Orthia (2016) who surmise a link to extraterrestrial volcanic and geodynamic processes, although publicisation of such was almost non-existent in the 1930s-50s when Tolkien was writing. The volcanic features of Mars were not confirmed until the Mariner 9 mission in 1972 and the volcanism of Io, a moon of Jupiter, was not discovered until 1979, during Voyager 1's fly past.

If not Mediterranean or Martian, what then are Tolkien's volcanoes? Many authors have documented Tolkien's interest and delight in geology: Henry Gee (2005), Gerard Hynes (2012), and Kristine Larsen (2005) are particularly notable examples. In a letter to Cotton Minchen, Tolkien once explained that "having geological interests, and a very little knowledge, I have not wholly neglected this aspect, but its indication is rather more difficult – and perilous!" (*Letters*, Letter 187, 264). Gee has rightly observed that it is unsurprising Tolkien was interested in the Earth Sciences given his own view of his profession: "I am primarily a scientific philologist. My interests were, and remain, largely scientific" (Gee 2005, 34). The synergy is obvious: both geology and philology are concerned with classifying sometimes subtle variations, and the consequent understanding gleaned through reconstruction of secular change. While this is most obvious with paleontology, it is true of most aspects in geology, including volcanology that is concerned with landscapes that are fundamentally ephemeral and periodically developed over millions of years, events that are fleeting at least as far as geologic time is concerned.

Tolkien's timing for his interest was excellent. Flieger and Anderson note in their commentary of *Tolkien On Fairy-stories* that "The geologic comparison here is both timely and intentional: geology and mythology being coeval disciplines arising in roughly the same period and out of the same human impulse to dig into origins" (*OFS*, 106). He was serendipitously proximal to a new Earth Sciences department at Oxford that was at the forefront of a rapidly evolving science. Although we do not have direct knowledge that he attended lectures, public or otherwise, Hynes details Tolkien's own growing interest. It cannot have been superficial. Gee correctly notes that Tolkien's use of the word 'Gondwanaland' proves he was aware of Wegener's radical new theory of continental drift and its exotic terminology (Gee 2005, 59; *Letters*, Letter 296, 409-10).

The author's stated concern was that Middle-earth's geology be scientifically possible rather than historically accurate. Hynes suggests that as a reader of science fiction, he was well aware of the expectations it engendered in readers in terms of coherent world building (see Gee 2005, 23-41), and that Tolkien strove to show Middle-earth as a part of our Earth (*Letters,* Letters 220, 239, 283, 376). How well did he succeed? To assess this we must turn to Geomythology.

5 – Geomythology

Geomythology is a term coined by Dorothy Vitaliano to describe the study of mythologized and/or catastrophized accounts of real geological events in mythology or more broadly etiological explanations for the present environment of our world (Piccardi 2007).

Currently we view Earth's evolution as consistent with plate tectonic theory (at least as far back as the Neoarchean) and, in practice, this explains observational geology tolerably well. Superimposed on an almost imperceptible rate of change (in which on the modern plate circuit India gets a speeding ticket for going 10 cm/yr!), are catastrophic, geologically immediate events such as bolide impacts. Both processes, the uniformitarian and the catastrophic, can be discerned in etiological myth, those fables invented to explain environmental features, the very ones that Tolkien, in his desire to create an ancestral mythology for England (Larsen 2005; Behrooz 2019), drew on.

A close reading of his texts intriguingly shows, however, there was much more of modern geologic science underpinning his narration of his volcanic world than one would surmise at first. Several examples of Tolkien's descriptions of Orodruin and how they mirror volcanic process will serve to illustrate this geomythology. In *RK* he describes the 'great smoke and steam' from the mountain and the 'sharp grit of it [...] like lashing whips fell a torrent of black rain' (*RK*, 'Mount Doom', 198, 201). Sharp grit and lashing whips are exactly the characterization one would use for air fall lapilli – the ash sized glassy ejecta, ballistic bombs and wind modified drops of lava that are known as Pelee's hair and tears that produce an incomparably sharp dark rain that falls out of an eruption column. The scene of Sam and Frodo at the pinnacle of their journey when "there came a flash of red that leaped upward, and smote the high black roof" beautifully captures the leaping, sometimes hundreds of metres high, jet-like sprays of molten magma that form 'fire fountains', the result of gas release from low viscosity basalt during sustained eruption (196).

A number of Tolkien's descriptions are very specific, such as lightning crackling during the eruption, a result of dense ash particles rubbing together, or the noxious halide and dioxide gases released making the Hobbits dizzy and inconveniently hugging lows in Gorgoroth's topography due to their density (191). A number are more general, like the "low ashen hill piled at the Mountain's foot", a cinder cone formed over a flank fissure vent, or the extreme hotness of the basaltic magma that gets compared to Ancalagon the Black's most fearsome hot flame (201). Along with the image of a secondary summit cone built above a flatter shield, these details paint a remarkably evocative picture of an open conduit shield volcano.

One of the most delightful and informative depictions comes from plate 165 in Catherine McIlwaine's gorgeous catalog *Tolkien: Maker of Middle-earth* (2018). In the lower left corner of a painting by Tolkien largely depicting the base of the Tower of Barad-dûr, he has sketched great snaking rivers of red, incandescent lava, flowing outward from Orodruin and widening as they traverse the low landscape. This illustration is remarkably accurate as to this particular style of eruption. Rapid, fast spreading, channelized effusive basaltic eruptions form highly sinuous, snaking, channelized flows that spread out and widen on flatter topography under the influence of gravity and hydraulic head. These are not the stickier trachytic, sodium-enriched short lava flows of Stromboli or Etna, nor is the overall eruption style. If not these famous edifices, then what has Tolkien created? Arguably, a volcano all his own.

6 – Styles of eruption

Symbolically, Tolkien mixed the elements of Eastern and Western myth to narrate and shape his volcanoes but evidently he also literally mixed styles of eruption to animate them.

In his depiction of a high temperature, fluid, moderately volatile and low viscosity effusive basaltic eruption on an initially low profile shield we have the typical Hawaiian eruption style, characteristic of intraplate volcanism and notably Iceland (Francis and Oppenheimer 2004). These volcanoes are some of the largest on Earth and have significant eruption rates, repeated summit and flank eruptions, fire fountaining and complex reservoirs. Stromboli and Etna's trachytic lavas are many times more viscous than Mauna Loa's, hence the formation of great snaking rivers of lava. His depiction of the flows in particular are remarkably detailed. He described the irregular surfaces of cooled upper flows, including their remarkable twisting and turning into statues and spires of solid rock: "Rivers (of fire) wind their way [...] until they cooled and lay like twisted dragon-shapes vomited from the tormented earth" (*RK*, 'The Tower of Cirith Ungol', 153). Whether it was his own fancy to bring the dragon theme in, dragon head shapes on top of mafic lava flows have actually been literally photographed from Cinder Butte, Montana (Donnelly-Nolan 2010) as the fantastical shapes that form on top of the immediately and violently cooled lava-air interface are justifiably famous. He even beautifully described the iridescent surface of recently cooled lava (*RK*, 'Mount Doom', 192). The great snaking rivers of highly fluid lava typical of Hawaiian effusive eruption painted in his images of Orodruin's paroxysm, as are the long, fire-fountaining fissures of Iceland. He applied this style also to multi-coned Thangorodrim from which "Then suddenly Morgoth sent forth great rivers of flame that ran down swifter than Balrogs from Thangorodrim, and poured over all the plain" (*Silmarillion*, 3,151).

Tolkien also employed the very recognizable elements of a Plinian eruption which is characterized by powerful, continuous, gas-driven explosions producing columns of volcanic debris and hot gases ejected high into the stratosphere. The towering, spreading anvil-like ash cloud of such an event is perfectly described, but this is not the short, umbrella pine-like shape of the eruption column familiar to most from Pliny's letter to his father. Rather it is the subsequent, climactic column that reaches sufficient height to attain neutral bouyancy and spread laterally: "a great fume that, beaten upwards by the opposing airs, mounted higher and higher, until it reached a region above the wind and spread in an immeasurable roof, whose central pillar rose out of the shadows beyond their view" (*RK*, 'The Land of Shadow', 173). Vesuvius's eruption in 79 AD released 100,000 times the thermal energy of the atomic bomb and produced widespread, 10's to 100 km distant, ashfall (Oppenheimer 2011; Ziolowski 2017). This latter process can be seen in Tolkien's description of Mordor's Ashen Mountains that "stood like somber grey ghosts" (*RK*, 'Mount Doom', 185).

Most incredibly, the characteristic floating clouds of pyroclastic flow or surge from the collapse of a Plinian eruption column are also depicted. Tolkien writes: "Smokes were pouring from it and while those that rose into the upper air trailed away eastward, great rolling clouds floated down its sides and spread over the land" (*RK*, 'Mount Doom', 185). These deadly but beautiful phenomena were first observed during the 1902 eruption of Mount Pelée in the Caribbean volcanic chain. The eruption clouds that float over the land at high speed, faster than a man can run, are a churning, boiling mass of superheated gas, steam and fragmented rock, and are some of the deadliest features of an eruption (Oppenheimer 2011). The aftermath of a hydrovolcanic or Plinian eruption is also excruciatingly encountered as Sam and Frodo traverse the near hundred mile wide region of fuming, barren, ash-ridden land that is the plain of Gorgoroth. Sam says of it that the "flats were [...] all tumbled, pocked with great holes, as if [...] still a waste of soft mud, it had been smitten with a shower of bolts and huge slingstones. The largest of these holes were rimmed with ridges of broken rock, and broad fissures ran out from them in all directions" (*RK*, 'Mount Doom', 186). This eerily evokes the first pictures of National Geographic's expedition to the Valley of 10,000 Smokes near Katmai, Alaska in 1916 and also photographs from 1924 of the hydrovolcanic eruption of Halema'uma'u crater on Kīlauea, Hawaii.

7 – Volcanology and world-building: a parallel evolution

As discussed above, Tolkien had an avowed keen interest in science and specifically geology, one that he obviously drew on to describe his many fiery mountains as realistically, (and terribly!), as possible. Just as Tolkien's own view of his world evolved, scientific understanding of geology changed, and the emergence of modern observational volcanology can be seen across his writings in parallel with a shift in literary mode from the 'mythological' to the 'historical' as described by Dimitra Fimi (2009).

Immediately after the First World War, ca. 1920, the Shape of Arda was yet uncertain, but following Tolkien's arrival at his new post at Oxford in the mid 1920s, Hynes postulates that details of geologic time and dynamic process begin to emerge. The chaining of Melkor and Flight of the Noldi after the Battle Sudden Flame in the earlier works are barely sketched in detail, the effusions of the Iron Mountains were briefly said to "stain [...] the bright airs in the first mornings of the world" (*Silmarillion*, 3, 109), whereas Orodruin's demeanor and eruption is given much of a pivotal chapter in *Return of the King*. The first mention of the Cracks of Doom appears in the late 1930s and the final chapters of *Return of the King* were being written following the Second World War, with the central chapter for our purposes, 'Mount Doom', being finished in 1946.

This time period overlapped with foundational changes in the science, during which it evolved from one of primarily 'knowledge in aftermath', noting features long since formed, to one of real-time process observation with the advent of active observatories and gas, temperature, and volcanic earthquake monitoring (Figure 1; Sigurdsson 2015). Prior to 1900 volcanology had been part of a 'divine science' and 'armchair geology' practice. With the rise of 19th-century naturalism, it became an empirical field study. Sigurdsson describes how 19th and 20th-century research in thermodynamics, petrology, geochemistry and plate tectonics contributed to the current understanding of volcanic activity as a partially predictable process linked to the planet's heat engine. At the outset of Tolkien's writing, following his experiences in World War One, conceptions of volcanology were still primitive. The fact that basaltic magma was generated by partial melting of periodotite had only just become recognized; fanciful notions of the Neptunists and Plutonists who debated the quantity and role of heat in the planet's interior had at long last given way to an image of basalt as formed from magma sourced below a surficial crust, but the process of its extraction and emplacement into the upper crust was lacking. Notwithstanding the still common present day error to refer to ash in a volcanic eruption column as 'smoke', first hand accounts of eruptions prior to the 1940s were rare and had a tendency to be spectacularized, often conflating multiple eruptive modes to one event, more based on what the writer knew of volcanoes than any particular observation at the site. Isabella Bird's descriptions of the summit of Kīlauea in 1873 are a lovely exception (Woolf 2018).

Some of the features that Tolkien described, such as fire fountaining, pyroclastic flows, ballistic ejecta on Gorgoroth, density and health effects of volcanic gasses were not widely recognized until as late as the 1930s and 1940s (Sutton and Elias 2014; Sigurdsson 2015). It seems probable that he would have availed himself of talks and lectures given at the newly reinvigorated geology department at Oxford, particularly (given his knowledge of Wegener's radical new continental drift theories) Arthur Holmes' framing of convection and petrologic (i.e. magma and thereby lava) process as linked to what would ultimately be called plate tectonics. Holmes did much to popularize the new theory and set England at the forefront of the nascent science.

About this time, other facets of volcanologic theory changed. An early influential treatise on Italian ashfall deposits by Dolomieu was translated and through it recognized that what looked like normal stratified sediments were in fact consolidated volcanic ash, the product of fallout from explosive eruptions, as correctly described by Tolkien. Additionally, the global scale of volcanic eruptions had caught the attention of the public following the late 1890's accounts of Krakatoa in Indonesia and Tarawera in New Zealand. Mount Pelée in Martinique, Mauna Loa and Kīlauea all had major eruptions through the time of Tolkien's earliest writings, but perhaps more importantly specific features he described, like the contemporaneous satellite cones on Cerro Azul or fire fountains in Hekla, were first observed and highlighted to the public with the advent of modern media, around the time that the chapter on Mount Doom was being created (Figure 1). The first widely circulated footage of an active volcanic eruption in progress was filmed during the American occupation of Italy in 1944 when the 340th Bombardment squadron had the questionable luck to have been stationed on Vesuvius's flanks. As soon as the eruption started planes were scrambled to capture the event, producing a mesmerizing public record although unhappily a number of them were damaged or destroyed in the weeks to come when a new flank of the eruption opened far too close to their scenic perch.

John Garth explains that we do know that Tolkien paid attention to these accounts, as he showed an interviewer in 1961 newspaper clippings describing Hekla's latest eruption. This was done to provide an example of the way in which Tolkien worked and gathered material and information relevant to his world-building (Garth 2020, 5, 94). The sheer number and wealth of features he gives to Orodruin in particular, exemplifies his desire to carefully portray the outward, physical challenges of Frodo's climactic struggle, alongside the inner. In this, he creates a fictional eruption of a volcano that is fittingly awe-inspiring and fearsome, sublime in all ways.

As Ursula Le Guin once noted "Science describes accurately from outside, poetry describes accurately from inside. Science explicates, poetry implicates. Both celebrate what they describe" (2015, 9).

One particular passage of Tolkien's from the *Ainulindalë* I think reflects both aspects, the scientific and poetic, creating a whole that captures a terrible beauty. Of Melkor he wrote that the Ainu appeared "as a mountain that wades in the sea and has its head above the clouds and is clad in ice and crowned with smoke and fire" (*Silmarillion*, 1, 22). In this, we have an almost perfect personification of the ever active, glaciated Icelandic volcanoes Hekla, Grimsvotin and Laki, a part of the Atlantic mid-ocean ridge lifted up and exposed on rocky shores. They, too, ride the sea, wreathed in billowing cloud, and crowned in ice and fire.

Acknowledgements

I have made an effort in this paper to cite volcanology sources that are accessible to non-specialists and have listed only primary scientific sources for some documentation of scientific timelines. The field is as vast and broad as the features it considers, but for those interested, Maurice Krafft's book is very approachable (see Bibliography), the undergraduate texts by Peter Francis and Clive Oppenheimer are particularly good, and Haraldur Sigurdsson's Encyclopedia of Volcanoes is amazingly detailed in all aspects of the field. I am indebted to Chris Vaccaro for originally making someone outside literary academia welcome at Tolkien-in-Vermont; to John Garth and Mitchell Riddell for their encouragement and many discussions of Arda and Middle-earth geology. The enthusiasm and support of Dawn Walls-Thumma, Lisa Grundy and Una McCormack have been instrumental in this endeavor, and Neil Rogers of the Geological Survey of Canada kindly provided the time to complete this project. And lastly, this is for my late father who bought me, in the same year, my first copies of *Fellowship of the Ring* and Francis's *Volcanoes*.

Bibliography

Anderson, J., *Myths and Legends of the Polynesians,* (Tokyo: Charles E. Tuttle Co., 1969).

Ariel, J., 'Volcanoes and The Unconscious Mind: A Case Study' (unpublished thesis, Brown University, 2010).

Behrooz, A.,'Temporal Topographies: Mapping the Geological and Anthropological Effects of Time in J.R.R. Tolkien's Legendarium', in *Sub-creating Arda: World-building in J.R.R. Tolkien's Works, Its Precursors and Legacies*, ed. by D. Fimi and T. Honegger (Zurich: Walking Tree, 2019) 217-236.

Brady, E., *The Sublime in Modern Philosophy: Aesthetics, Ethics, and Nature,* (Cambridge: Cambridge University Press, 2012).

Burke, E., *A Philosophical Enquiry into the Origin of Our Ideas of the Sublime and Beautiful,* (New York: Harper and Brothers, 1757).

Cilli, O., *Tolkien's Library: An Annotated Checklist,* (Edinburgh: Luna Press Publishing, 2019).

Coombs, J., and M. Read, 'A Physics of Middle-Earth', in *Proceedings of the Tolkien Centenary Conference* 1992, ed. by P. Reynolds and G. GoodKnight, *Mallorn*, 33 (1995) 323-329.

Donnelly-Nolan, J., 'Geologic Map of Medicine Lake Volcano, Northern California', *U.S. Geological Survey*, 25 August 2011 <https://pubs.usgs.gov/sim/2927/> [Accessed 18 January 2024].

Downing, C., *Russian Tales and Legends,* (New York: H.Z. Walck, 1956).

Fimi, D., *Tolkien, Race and Cultural History: From Fairies to Hobbits,* (London: Palgrave Macmillan, 2009).

Filipovic, J., 'Representations of Evil in J.R.R. Tolkien's Middle-Earth' (unpublished thesis, University of Dusseldorf, 2018).

Francis, P., and C. Oppenheimer, *Volcanoes*, 2nd edn. (Oxford: Oxford University Press, 2004).

Frierson, P., *The Burning Island: A Journey through Myth and History in Volcano Country, Hawaii,* (San Francisco: Sierra Club Books, 1991).

Garth, J., *The Worlds of J.R.R. Tolkien,* (Princeton: Princeton University Press, 2020).

Gee, H., *The Science of Middle-earth,* (London: Souvenir, 2005).

Global Volcanism Program, *Smithsonian Institution National Museum of Natural History Databases*, online database, <https://volcano.si.edu/> [accessed 10 December, 2019].

Davis, F.H., *Myths and Legends of Japan,* (New York: Dover Publications, 1992).

Howes, M., 'The Elder Ages and the later glaciations of the Pleistocene Epoch', *Tolkien Journal*, 3.2 (1967) 3-15.

Hynes, G., 'Beneath the Earth's dark keel: Tolkien and Geology', *Tolkien Studies*, 91.1 (2012) 21-36.

Ingles C., and L.A. Orthia, 'A New Synthesis on the Geology of Middle-earth: Genesis, Orogeny and Tectonics'(2016) <http://sandpaw.weblogs.anu.edu.au/files/2016/06/Ingles-Orthia-2016-Middle-earth-geology.pdf> [Accessed 18 January 2024].

Johnston, P., *Cultural Responses to Volcanic Landscapes: The Mediterranean and Beyond,* (Havertown: David Brown, 2005).

Kilby, C. and Dick Plotz, 'Many Meetings with Tolkien: An Edited Transcript of Remarks at the December 1966 TSA Meeting', *Niekas*, 19 (1968) 39–40.

Kircher, A., 'Systema Ideale Pyrophylaciorum Suberraneorum, quorum montes Vulcanii, veluti spiracula quaedam existant', online map, original drafting 1665, <https://www.geographicus.com/P/AntiqueMap / Pyrophylaciorum-kircher-1665> [accessed 15 April, 2019].

Kozák, J., and V. Čermák. *The Illustrated History of Natural Disasters, Volcanoes, Earthquakes, and Tsunamis* (Dordrecht: Springer, 2010).

Krafft, M., *Volcanoes: Fire from the Earth,* (London: Thames and Huston, 1991).

Larrington, C., *The Poetic Edda,* (Oxford: Oxford University Press, 2014).

Larsen, K., 'Shadow and Flame: Myth, Monsters and Mother Nature in Middle-Earth', in *The Mirror Crack'd: Fear and Horror in J.R.R. Tolkien's The Lord of the Rings and its Sources*, ed. by L. Forest-Hill (Newcastle: Cambridge Scholars Publishing, 2008) 169-196.
— 'A Little Earth of His Own: Tolkien's Lunar Creation Myths', in *The Ring Goes Ever On: Proceedings of the Tolkien 2005 Conference*, II, ed. by S. Wells (Coventry: The Tolkien Society, 2008) 394-403.
Lawrence, D.H., *Complete Poetry,* (Pickering: Blackthorn Press, 2013).

Le Guin, U., *Late in the Day: Poems 2010–2014,* (Oakland: PM Press, 2015).

Lowry, M., *Under the Volcano,* (New York: Harper Perennial Modern Classics, 2007).

Mason, R., 'The Geology of Middle-Earth', *Mallorn*, 9 (1975) 12-15.

McIlwaine, C., *Tolkien: Maker of Middle-earth,* (Oxford: Bodleian Library, University of Oxford, 2018).

Mueller-Harder, E., 'The "lost connections" of Tolkien's first map of *The Lord of the Rings*: Part I, Deconstruction', online presentation, 6 April 2019, <https://sam.tolkienists.org/00x7/> [accessed 18 January 2024].

McIntosh, P., 'The geology of Middle-Earth', *Mallorn*, 7 (1973) 3-7.

Oppenheimer, C., *Eruptions that Shook the World,* (Cambridge: Cambridge University Press, 2011).

Paulson, R., *Sin and Evil: Moral values in Literature,* (New Haven: Yale University Press, 2007).

Piccardi, L., 'Preface', in *Myth and Geology*, ed. by L. Piccardi and W.B. Masse (London: Geological Society of London, Special Publications, 2007).

Reynolds, R. C., 'The Geomorphology of Middle-earth', *The Swansea Geographer*, 12 (1974) 67-71.

Sandner, D., 'The Fantastic Sublime: Tolkien's "On Fairy-Stories" and the Romantic Sublime', *Mythlore*, 22.1 (1997) 4-7.

Sarjeant, W.A.S., 'The Geology of Middle-earth', *Mythlore*, 21.2 (1996) 334-339.

Sheets, P., 'Volcanoes, Ancient Peoples, and Their Societies', in *Encyclopedia of Volcanoes*, ed. by Haraldur Sigurdsson, 2nd edn. (Cambridge: Academic Press, 2015) 1313-1319.

Shippey, T., *J.R.R. Tolkien: Author of the Century*, (London: Harper Collins, 2000).

Sigurdsson, H., 'History of Volcanology', in *Encyclopedia of Volcanoes*, ed. by Haraldur Sigurdsson, 2nd edn. (Cambridge: Academic Press, 2015) 15-41.

Sigurdsson, H. and R.M.C Lopes, 'Volcanoes in Literature and Film', in *Encyclopedia of Volcanoes*, ed. by Haraldur Sigurdsson, 2nd edn. (Cambridge: Academic Press, 2015) 1345-1361.

St Clair, G., 'An Overview of the Northern Influences on Tolkien's Works', *Mythlore*, 21.2 (1992) 63-67.

Sutton, A.J., and T. Elias, 'One Hundred Volatile Years of Volcanic Gas Studies at the Hawaiian Volcano Observatory', in *Characteristics of Hawaiian Volcanoes: United States Geological Survey Professional Paper 1801*, ed. by M. Poland, T.J. Takahaski and C.M. Landowski (2014) <https://pubs.er.usgs.gov/publication/pp18017>.

Taggart, D., 'All the Mountains Shake: Seismic and Volcanic Imagery in the Old Norse Literature of Þórr', *Scripta Islandica*, 86 (2017) 99-122.

Thorarinsson, S., *Hekla, A Notorious Volcano*, trans. by J. Hannesson and P. Karlsson, (Reykjavík: Almenna Bókafélagið, 1970).

Tolkien On Fairy-Stories, ed. by V. Fleiger and D.A. Anderson, expanded edn. with commentary and notes (London: Harper Collins, 2014).

Tolkien, J.R.R., *The Fellowship of the Ring*, (London: George Allen and Unwin, 1974).
— *The Two Towers*, (London: George Allen and Unwin, 1974).
— *The Return of the King*, (London: George Allen and Unwin, 1974).
— *The Silmarillion*, ed. by C. Tolkien (London: George Allen and Unwin, 1977).
— *The Book of Lost Tales, part I*, ed. by C. Tolkien (London: George Allen and Unwin, 1983).
— *The Lost Road and Other Writings*, ed. by C. Tolkien (London: George Allen and Unwin, 1987).
— *The War of the Ring*, ed. by C. Tolkien (London: George Allen and Unwin, 1990).
— *The Letters of J.R.R. Tolkien*, ed. by H. Carpenter with the assistance of C. Tolkien (London: George Allen & Unwin, 1981).

Vitaliano, D., *Legends of the Earth: Their Geologic Origins*, (Bloomington: Indiana University Press, 1973).

Westervelt, W., *Hawaiian Legends of Volcanoes*, (Rutland: Charles Tuttle Company, 1963).

Woolf, J., *Isabella Bird: Playing with Hawaiian Fire*, online blogpost, 11 May 2018 <https://www.rsgs.org/blog/isabella-bird-playing-with-hawaiian-fire> [accessed December 15, 2019].

Ziolkowski, T., 'Volcanic Eruptions and their literary reverberations', *The Modern Language Review*, 112 (2017) 793-821.

The Beauty of the Horrendous and the Eerie: The Fantastic, the Marvellous, and the Sublime in *The Lord of the Rings*

Michaela Schneider-Wettstein

J.R.R. Tolkien's *The Lord of the Rings* is a story of pain and misery, and yet it has been a success for many decades capturing the hearts and minds of thousands of people around the globe. The question is how a story of hardship and privation attracts so many readers. I attempt to seek the answer to one of the aspects – credibility – and the mechanisms used to establish it. In 1777 Clara Reeve stated that "We can conceive, and allow of, the appearance of a ghost; we can even dispense with an enchanted sword and helmet: but then they must keep within certain limits of credibility" (qtd. in Roberts 2012, 27). And indeed, Tolkien establishes an otherworld with all kinds of creatures and inhabitants that are so different from the ones in our world, but if we allow to be enchanted, as Tolkien would put it, we, perhaps, also allow ourselves to faintly believe in a world that is home to Middle-earth. Tolkien argues that when we enter the otherworld is constructed by Sub-creation, and that we perceive the content as "true" within this world but that we are banned, when "the spell is broken" (*TL*, 12). In other words: if credibility is lost, the Secondary World is lost, and the reader is drawn back into the Primary World. This tension relies on the relationship between reader and literature. Wolfgang Iser states that "the literary work has two poles, which we might call the artistic and the aesthetic: the artistic pole is the author's text, and the aesthetic is the realization accomplished by the reader", and, moreover, that the text sends a message which the reader is "composing" (2010, 1524). My argument aims to bring together Tolkien's *The Lord of the Rings* with Edmund Burke's notion of the sublime and Tzvetan Todorov's theory of the fantastic. First, both theoretical concepts are introduced and examined, and then follows a detailed analysis of the examples of Minas Tirith and Khazad-dûm as well as The Old Forest and Lothlórien. In *The Lord of the Rings*, Tolkien utilises the effects of sublimity and aspects of what Todorov defines as the fantastic to create what he calls 'Secondary Belief' and therefore intensifies immersion as well as the credibility of Middle-earth, although it is an otherworld.

Edmund Burke's notion of the sublime is that it is an aesthetic experience which is touching and grounded in physiology rather than an intellectual matter (Guyer 2015, ix). He further argues that pain and fear cause an unnatural tension of the nerves, which causes the sublime, and, consequently, everything that causes this tension then eventually is sublime (Burke 2015, 107). Moreover, Burke distinguishes actual pain that affects the mind through physical impact and terror that he calls "pain suggested", which affects the body through mental impact (33-4, 105-6). Thus, the sublime is a matter of self-preservation because danger, pain, sickness, or death result in emotions of horror and are provoked by terrible objects and terror (33; 71). However, we are not looking for real danger but a modified and distanced version (34). This distanced danger may occur in literature, in which we are not physically involved but only mentally and hence deal with pain suggested. The formula for literature then is relative pleasure combined with sympathy result in the sublime. For Burke relative Pleasure means that pleasure needs relation to pain and danger (31), and its removal then causes delight (32), whereas sympathy means that we are put in place of another and are affected like them (44). Moreover, we feel delight in their misfortune and pain but also feel an urge to relieve them (39; 40). Tolkien associates the fairy-story with what he calls enchantment and peril: with joy and sorrow (*TL*, 3), which is a concept that suits the sublime well because it entwines the tension between delight and pain as in Burke's argument. In this sense, Tolkien's concept of the fairy-story is one realisation of Burke's sublime. *The Lord of the Rings* combines both concepts continually in many ways. One obvious example would be Galadriel, who is a combination of beauty and terror: admired and feared, which will become clear in the discussion of the examples. Fear, for Burke, is the most effective of all emotions that sets the mind into a stasis because it is directly linked to pain, death, and danger (2015, 46). This state of stasis he calls "astonishment", which provokes the sublime "by an irresistible force" (46).

One of the major themes of Burke's sublime is infinity, which is only achieved by a very limited number of concepts (52). The other is obscurity as in lack of knowledge, limited understanding, and flawed or impaired perception, e.g., in darkness (48), which ends with the acquisition of knowledge (50-1). In this sense, infinity is also obscurity because it has no perceivable end or beginning and therefore exceeds knowledge, which will become clear with the concept of the artificial infinite used to explain the examples later. First, a closer look at obscurity itself within the literary concept is necessary. Burke claims words as superior means of communication to transport "*affections* of the mind from one to another" (49). But how is obscurity created in communication? This question leads back to Iser, who says that communication in literature happens "between the explicit and the implicit, between revelation and concealment", where the explicit acts as "a reference to what is not said" and therefore provokes the reader to make meaning of it (2010, 1527). In other words: the reader fills the gaps with content they find the most likely to fit the purpose. While Iser's discussion happened roughly two centuries after Burke's, the latter drew from contemporary ideas of imagination. Burke says that "man possesses a sort of creative power of its own", and, moreover, that the human mind would process it by recalling and recombining the "images of things", which is "the most extensive province of pleasure and pain" (2015, 18). In summary, obscurity is the dominant factor in the process of causing fear or terror, which results in the sublime. It will become clear how Burke's other causes of sublimity also subsume into obscurity. What does this mean in the context of Tolkien? According to his essay 'On Fairy-stories', Tolkien locates the imagination and its provoking forces within the power of Faërie (*TL*, 23). To understand how the Faërie and obscurity spark sublimity, it is necessary to understand Todorov's concept of the fantastic.

Todorov's fantastic is an elusive and ephemeral occurrence based on the duration of uncertainty which is triggered by an inexplicable event; in summary, an individual in the real world encounters an event that is instantaneously inexplicable by the laws of nature. Consequently, there are two possibilities: either the event is a product of illusion or imagination and therefore not true or it is true but follows different laws of nature. The fantastic then covers the duration of hesitation before it is clear which possibility is applicable (Todorov 1975, 25). Moreover, it is obligatory that the reader must hesitate, but the character may or may not, and, additionally, the reader must not interpret allegorical or poetic meaning into the text, and, finally, they must think that the world is a real one with living individuals (33). Especially the latter is a problem with Middle-earth as an otherworld and needs careful consideration after the theoretical framework has been established. The duration of hesitation then ends once the reader decides for one possibility or the other: if they discover a natural explanation for the event, the fantastic concludes into the uncanny, and if they realise that the event needs new laws of nature unknown to the real world, the fantastic concludes into the "marvellous" (41). These two terms are also referred to as "supernatural explained" and "supernatural accepted" (41). However, the fantastic is rarely realised in its pure form, but rather expands throughout the entire story and concludes either in the uncanny or the marvellous. Todorov calls these fantastic-uncanny and fantastic-marvellous (44). The decision or clue is then left until the end of the story. There are innumerable examples in *The Lord of the Rings* for both occurrences. The examples I use include Gollum and the Balrog, but first the formal requirements of the marvellous need explanation.

While both bordering genres are of interest here, the marvellous is of greater importance because, by Todorov's and Tolkien's definition, Middle-earth is itself a prime example of the marvellous and the Faërie respectively. For Tolkien says that the Faërie is an otherworld with living beings and landscapes (*TL*, 3, 9) where fairies live (9). Moreover, the very "nature" of Faërie for Tolkien is "the Perilous Realm itself, and the air that blows in that country" (10). In other words, the lands with new laws of nature that are needed to explain the fantastic event. Todorov's marvellous, then, is Tolkien's Faërie. However, Todorov does not limit the marvellous to the land of fairies but argues that the "state of the supernatural" shifts to "a 'formal' element" (1975, 54). This definition includes narratives from various genres and unites them as marvellous whether it be a fairy-tale or a fantasy story. The obligatory and therefore unifying property is that state of the supernatural, which must be set in an otherworld with other-worldly laws of nature. Todorov then categorises different types of narratives, of which three are applicable to *The Lord of the Rings*, but not all will be discussed in detail: the hyperbolic marvellous, the exotic marvellous, and the instrumental marvellous. The hyperbolic marvellous comes emerges with size, enormous size, as you will (54). In *The Lord of the Rings* certainly the Eagles and Mûmakil match this criterion. However, this exaggeration in size is not necessarily bound to creatures. Middle-earth affords superlatives in size especially in architecture, as the examples of Minas Tirith and Khazad-dûm will show. The exotic marvellous on the other hand is a supernatural occurrence that is not presented as such and not questioned (55). This is true for only a few examples and only in certain aspects. The Elves may be an example because they are not presented as supernatural and they do not know what the concept of magic is supposed to mean. A good example is when the Hobbits are given Elvish cloaks for their journey and Pippin asks whether these are magic cloaks, but then is told that "'I do not know what you mean by that,' answered the leader of the Elves", and "'They are elvish robes certainly, if that is what you mean.'" (*FR*, 'Farewell to Lórien', 204). Finally, the instrumental marvellous refers to technologies that are not available in the contemporary context, but which are not altogether impossible (Todorov 1975, 56). While this sounds very abstract, the principle is quite simple: Middle-earth resembles a mediaeval society but several technologies are available that would not have been present in mediaeval reality in our world. Athelas is one example because it functions rather like an antibiotic than a simple herbal remedy to cure Frodo's wound after he was stabbed by a Ringwraith (*FR*, 'Flight to the Ford', 261). Another example is the Palantír that allows one to look at far-away places, which is today realised as binoculars and telescopes, and, perhaps, video calls.

Todorov then distinguishes three properties: utterance, act of uttering, and a syntactical aspect (1975, 76). First, utterance refers to figurative language taken literally as in the hyperbolic marvellous and exaggeration, or the realisation of a figurative utterance (77-9). A third aspect means that the "figure and the supernatural are on the same level, and their relation is functional", which means that everyday figurative and idiomatic language foreshadow a supernatural event (79). The expressions Todorov introduces produce uncertainty by using words of uncertainty like "seem", "as if", and other conditional grammatical structures or constructions hinting to tropes. Second, the act of uttering relates to the authenticity of the narrative voice because a character can lie but a narrator cannot (86). Additionally, Todorov says that while a homodiegetic narrator contributes to uncertainty, a heterodiegetic narrator instantly indicates the marvellous (83). Todorov's explanations would make it impossible to locate *The Lord of the Rings* anywhere within the scope of the fantastic, but his argument is flawed insofar as it does not consider other narrative situations that utilise an unreliable narrator together with formal elements of conditional grammatical structures or hinting to tropes, which create a credible uncertainty when the reader identifies with the character. The solution is that an unreliable narrator must be established with narrative structures like psychonarration, where the heterodiegetic narrator is in the foreground of the narrative but adds general observations. This could then combine with interior monologue to create a free indirect discourse. The inner thoughts of the character are then communicated through the narrator: narrator and character become one. There are several occasions where the relationship between narrator and character(s) becomes unclear in *The Lord of the Rings*. One example is when the Hobbits encounter Old Man Willow in the Old Forest and the narrator states that "Frodo did not like the sound of this" (*FR*, 'The Old Forest', 153) The narrator adds a general observation of Frodo's emotional reaction, which they could not possibly have access to if they were simply a third person. Passages like this occur multiple times, like when the Fellowship travels through Khazad-dûm, the narrator says that "Frodo's spirits had risen", that "now a deep uneasiness, growing to dread, crept over him", also that "his senses were sharper and more aware of things that could not be seen", or that "he felt the certainty of evil ahead" (*FR*, 'A Journey in the Dark', 27). Tolkien uses this technique and adds conditional grammatical structures to foreshadow possible supernatural events as described above, when Frodo encounters dread "As if it were a breath that came in through unseen doors out of deep places, dread came over him. His hand were cold and his brow damp" (136). The dread moves as if it was a breath to foreshadow Gollum's approach to follow the Fellowship unnoticed into Khazad-dûm, which will be discussed in more detail later. Conditional grammatical structures to denote the fantastic also appear in direct speech, which is an unreliable narrator by definition. For example, when Sam describes being in Lothlórien as "if I was inside a song, if you take my meaning" (*FR*, 'Lothlórien', 178). It emphasizes the unreality of the land and its enchanting powers. This enchantment, Tolkien argues, emerges when we enter the Faërie (*TL*, 9) and create a "Secondary Belief" (38). The reader then enters the Faërie of Middle-earth as Sam enters the Faërie of Lothlórien. The fundament of this enchantment is credibility. Tolkien argues that "it is at any rate essential" for the Faërie to "be presented as 'true'" and not be embedded into anything that compromises the conscience, e.g., an illusion or a dream (14). As James Edward argues that it was "Tolkien's greatest achievement" that he established the otherworld as normality (2012, 65) and hence as credible option. Finally, the fact that the characters themselves may not be familiar with all laws of nature of Middle-earth contributes tremendously to the credibility of uncertainty. When the Hobbits leave the Shire, they are naïve people who know nothing of the world beyond the borders of their homeland or further than Bree at best.

The first examples are the two cities of Khazad-dûm and Minas Tirith, of which the first is an edifice and the second is like a hybrid of an edifice and an urban jungle. Khazad-dûm is built inside, or rather under, a mountain, and Minas Tirith is built around Mount Mindolluin, reaching far inside the rock. One city is deserted and in ruins, infested with dark powers (*FR*, 'The Bridge of Khazad-dûm', 147) and the other befallen with depression and despair because of a thinning population (*RK*, 'Minas Tirith', 12). Minas Tirith has seven walls of stone that are very strong and old and it "seems" that they were not built but carven by giants of "bones of the earth" (10). The city is of a grand structure: the battlement thrones 700 feet above the plains, and the pinnacle of the Tower of Ecthelion is 1,000 feet above them (12). Tolkien again uses the conditional to create uncertainty as to which the origins of the walls are. The walls seem to have not been built but carven by giants. The giants here may hint to mythical creatures or simply to very tall men, but no matter which category the reader decides to side with, it is obvious that these walls would be a difficult and troublesome work for average-sized men, perhaps even impossible to build. The sheer exaggeration then hints to the uncertainty whether otherworldly powers were involved, especially because Middle-earth is inspired by mediaeval societies with little technological development. Mediaeval churches on Earth had a similar effect on people like Minas Tirith has on Pippin, for he "gazed in wonder" and "cried aloud" (10). Inextricably entwined with this exaggeration is the difficulty that was required to build the structure, which makes the idea grand, and, hence sublime (Burke 2015, 63). Thus, the sheer size and height that constitute the exaggeration are another source for the sublime. Burke states that "Greatness of dimension, is a powerful cause of the sublime" (59). Another source for the sublime is magnificence, which means "A great profusion of things which are splendid or valuable in themselves" (63). There are two exceptional examples in Minas Tirith: the Tower of Ecthelion and the great hall: "the Tower of Ecthelion, standing high within the topmost wall, shone out against the sky, glimmering like a spike of pearl and silver, tall and fair and shapely, and its pinnacle glittered as if it were wrought of crystals;" (10) and in the hall "Monoliths of black marble, they rose to great capitals carved in many strange figures of beasts and leaves; and far above the shadow the wide vaulting gleamed with dull gold, inset with flowing traceries of many colours" (14). Moreover, "Suddenly Pippin was reminded of the hewn rocks of Argonath, and awe fell upon him, as he looked down that avenue of kings long dead" (15). Three aspects are combined by Tolkien here: exaggeration in size, exaggeration in grandeur, and exaggeration in durability or period. All three aspects dissolve into obscurity. It is beyond the capacity of our brain to understand how this greatness came into existence as it is far beyond our scope to understand time spans that reach outside our own lifetime. In other words: lives and events that rely solely on remembrance by hearsay, folktales, myths, etc. and are not transmitted by witnesses are outside our own lifetime and therefore demonstrate our own finiteness opposing a chronology that seems to have no beginning and no end. Burke refers to this phenomenon as "artificial infinite" and explains that the artificial infinite is a deception of the mind because we cannot perceive beginning and ending of an entity and therefore perceive it as infinite, and, hence, this infinity leads to the sublime (2015, 60). Furthermore, Burke also argues that "the imagination cannot rise to any idea of infinity" (62). Burke's limitation of the artificial infinite to visual perception is flawed because the mind is also capable of perceiving abstract ideas of the artificial infinite as has been shown with time spans. Nevertheless, not perceiving a beginning and an ending makes them obscure and therefore not only sublime but may also cause an uncertainty whether the entity is supernatural or not and therefore spark the fantastic.

One important example of the artificial infinite is the architecture of Minas Tirith. While the city is an urban jungle of seven levels, it is also "delved into the hill" and each level has "an arched tunnel, piercing a vast pier of rock whose huge out-thrust bulk divided in two all the circles of the City save the first" (*RK*, 'Minas Tirith', 11). The Citadel on the topmost level "also looked eastward, but was divided in the heart of the rock" (12). The city, then, is not perceivable in its entirety because large parts are inside the mountain. Therefore, its architecture could be classified as artificial infinite, but also as an edifice. John Clute defines an edifice as something in between a house and a city which looks smaller from the outside, but its inside could span so far that its limits are not perceivable spatially and temporally, and that it is "dominating the landscape" (2019). Edifices, then, are an artificial infinite and therefore also sublime. Other examples for edifices are Hobbit holes, especially the Great Smials, also the Hornburg/Helm's Deep in Rohan, the Last Homely House in Rivendell, and, of course, Khazad-dûm. Burke says that edifices spark sublimity and connects them with darkness because darkness creates obscurity and turns the familiar into something unfamiliar (2015, 66). Khazad-dûm is pitch-dark, and the darkness provides a perfect surrounding for the fantastic (*FR*, 'A Journey in the Dark', 123). Moreover, Khazad-dûm is constituted of stairs, arches, passages, and tunnels going into all directions (126). Additionally, the mines stretch at least over 40 miles from the West-door to the East-gate (125). Thus, the borders of the city are not perceivable for the Fellowship, which makes Khazad-dûm an edifice and an artificial infinite. The mines spark such a terror that only Gimli has courage but most of the fellowship are troubled by the darkness (126). Even more so: "The wildest imaginings that dark rumour had ever suggested to the hobbits fell altogether short of the actual dread and wonder of Moria" (132). Finally, Burke argues that "All general privations are great, because they are all terrible; Vacuity, Darkness, Solitude and Silence" (2015, 58). Khazad-dûm is not only dark, wide, and empty but also silent (*FR*, 'A Journey in the Dark', 127-8).

Two fantastic elements are remarkable inside the mines: first, Gollum follows the Fellowship, but Frodo does not know yet. In parts of the narrative, he becomes the focaliser. When he discovers that they are being followed, the fantastic is established because he is unsure about it. He *imagines* that he hears something, he almost feels certain that he heard it. However, he is not sure whether the sounds are real or not: "Yet Frodo began to hear, or to imagine that he heard, something else: like the faint fall of soft bare feet. It was never loud enough, or near enough, for him to feel certain that he heard it" (128). Again, Tolkien uses everyday language to create uncertainty in an ambiguous environment. There is a chance that Frodo's mind plays tricks on him because he is tired. Within the marvellous environment of Middle-earth, Tolkien not only creates fantastic encounters but a sort of meta-fantastic by hinting to sleepiness and dreaming that compromise Frodo's conscience: "His head had nodded. 'I must have nearly fallen asleep on guard,' he thought. 'I was on the edge of a dream.'" and later "When he lay down he quickly went to sleep, but it seemed to him that the dream went on" but then finds the rest of the fellowship whispering when he wakes up (136). It is particularly interesting that this fantastic occurrence within the frame of the marvellous world then concludes into the uncanny or offers an uncanny solution to the pale points of real voices that sneak into Frodo's dream. The second element is when the Balrog appears. The foreshadowing creates an uncertainty as to what it is that makes its way toward the fellowship. Gandalf encounters something unfamiliar of great power he cannot name or categorise. The uncertainty is even deepened during the first moments of the direct encounter with the entity because "What it was could not be seen", the entity is described to be "like a great shadow, in the middle of which was a dark form, of man-shape maybe, yet greater", and "a power and terror seemed to be in it and to go before it" diminishing the light (150). The Balrog then fits both: the fantastic and the sublime because the uncertainty whether there is a real supernatural event only concludes into the marvellous when Legolas calls the Balrog out (150). Furthermore, the Balrog sparks terror because it wields a power strong enough to sweep the fellowship away. Burke argues that power is the threat of pain and therefore it creates terror, or, in other words the sublime (2015, 53-4). Khazad-dûm, then, is an edifice: dark, obscure, vast and of greatness, silent, an artificial infinite, and it hosts fantastic encounters. It is a sublime manifestation in all its essential properties.

As there are two cities, there are two forests: one dark and the other fair but both dangerous in their own way. Forests are part of Nature or wilderness, and in the 18th century the concept of wilderness was different to that we know today. Wilderness back then was associated as deserted, savage, a waste that caused bewilderment and terror (Cronon 1996, 8). This association was biblical and taken from the St. James Bible and referred to the "margins of civilization", where people could get lost and deviate from their path, which leads to "moral confusion and despair" (9). Thence, the forest is at the margins of civilisation with the danger of leading people from their (moral) path into despair. One biblical example of this concept is Christ's encounter with the devil in the desert, where he withstood the temptation (8). William Cronon then argues that wilderness was a scary place where people did not go unless they had to, and that its only worth was by transforming it from its "uncivilized state" fit for human needs (9). Wilderness, however, also had a supernatural aspect. When biblical characters like Satan, Christ, and angels were in the wilderness, "the boundaries between human and nonhuman, between natural and supernatural" must be blurry, and that is where the sublime filled in as a "far from being a pleasurable experience" (10). Tolkien takes the reader back into that past where the wilderness was a scary and dangerous place at the margins of civilisation.

The first example, The Old Forest, resembles this image of wilderness neatly: it is a dark and silent place, where the boundaries of the natural and supernatural dissolve because "The forest is queer", the trees "do not like strangers", and observe and interfere with passers-by (*FR*, 'The Old Forest', 145). Moreover, the forest is not in a familiar state compared with the forests we know. While trees and other plants are alive and moving their branches, they certainly cannot watch passers-by or move their branches deliberately to affect them. The trees of The Old Forest, however, have human like properties, which unfold in darkness and Merry reports that they are "whispering to each other, passing news and plots along in an unintelligible language", and the branches and trunks move on their own so much that they could capture people (145-6). Under the cover of darkness, and hence in obscurity, they are said to move like animate individuals with a will and conscious. Merry does not use any language that hints to uncertainty: there are no conditional constructions or everyday idioms in his report, but, however, the direct speech combined with hearsay make him an unreliable narrator, which establishes uncertainty. What starts out as a factual report, evolves into a vague folktale because "They do say" and "or so I am told" (145-6) that indicate that Merry cannot vouch for the authenticity of the reports. Nevertheless, the foundations for foreshadowing a supernatural event are laid. Thence, sublimity and the fantastic once again converge and it is uncertain whether the fear the Hobbits feel is a product of their imagination or substantiated. In another example the narrative situation becomes blurry again with a collection of feelings, conditional structures and idioms creating uncertainty: "it seemed that the trees become taller", the Hobbits's feelings are described as "uncomfortable", they act as *if* they expect something when they look around and behind their backs, and the trees "seemed" to hinder their passing until Pippin shouts out and provokes, perhaps, a reaction. All the feelings may simply originate in the minds of the Hobbits creating the illusion of a supernatural encounter (147).

The hobbits' encounter with Old Man Willow is even more fantastic: "Sleepiness seemed to be creeping out of the ground and up their legs, and falling softly out of the air upon their heads and eyes" (153). The sleepiness here acts as the subject of the sentence as if it was an animate object. The metaphor maps verbs of motion onto sleep, more precisely a verb of motion associated with critters like insects, snakes, or supernatural creatures. The metaphor SLEEP IS A CREATURE adds another dimension of uncertainty to this encounter because sleep is not an animate object and certainly has no individual will or willpower. The sleepiness, however, evolves to function as possibly impacting the clear vision and perception of the Hobbit's minds, for they fall asleep or into a twilight state of mind between being awake and sleeping, and when the fantastic events occur they hear "a soft fluttering as of a song half whispered" and "The leaves fluttering against the bright sky dazzled him", when finally they "they could almost hear words, cool words, saying something about water and sleep. They gave themselves up to the spell and fell fast asleep" (154). The narrative situation is again unclear: inner thoughts are mixed with conditional structures and idioms to create uncertainty. The tree talk is almost slipping, but Frodo still perceives it. However, it may be the whistling of leaves in the wind that his compromised mind turns into talking, which turns into a lullaby. Frodo is "half in a dream" when he moves to the stream, where he meets Sam, who eventually breaks the 'spell' and does not believe Frodo's idea of a living tree that would physically interfere with the Hobbits (154-5). However, Sam is proven wrong and Old Man Willow turns out to be real. The fantastic concludes into the marvellous and they discover that the Old Man Willow has captured Merry and Pippin (155). Wide awake, they find Pippin and Merry enclosed into the trunk of the willow. There is no doubting, no uncertainty now: when Frodo and Sam try to free their friends, the tree mocks them with laughter and it reacts with violence to any attempts that may hurt it (156). The Old Forest then is dark, obscure, and dangerous. At the margins of civilisation, the boundaries between the natural and supernatural dissolve, and the forest tempts passers-by to sleep and linger on and therefore lose their path and remain in despair within the forest's borders. Sublimity and fantastic merge here and create a land of terror.

Unlike The Old Forest, Lothlórien is light, airy, and bright. However, it is a dangerous forest either. Lothlórien seems to be a land from another time or world. Time itself progresses differently within its borders, and the Fellowship cannot remember how long they have stayed there (*FR*, 'The Mirror of Galadriel', 188). There is a feeling of infinity entrenched into the lands because "Frodo felt that he was in a timeless land that did not fade or change or fall into forgetfulness" and his impression was that he was himself eternalised in Lothlórien (178). The land itself is infinite and immortal, opposed to human memory that will eventually fade as has been explained earlier. Time loses its meaning within the borders of Lothlórien, which makes the lands sublime but also incredible. For Frodo "it seemed to him that he had stepped over a bridge of time into a corner of the Elder Days and was now walking in a world that was no more" (176). The difference of time progression is made explicit when Celeborn welcomes Aragorn, recalling that "'It is eight and thirty years of the world outside since you came to this land'" (183). Lothlórien is under the power of Galadriel, who lives in Caras Galadhon within the forest. However, her power is limited geographically to the area within the border of Lothlórien: Frodo looks at the "green city" from a distance and "it seemed to him that the power and light came that held all the land in sway", but "Beyond the river the land appeared flat and empty, formless and vague, until far away it rose again like a wall, dark and drear" (*FR*, 'Lothlórien', 179). He makes these observations before he meets Galadriel, so he does not yet know if there is a real power or if his imagination plays tricks on him: it seems only that the city emits light to influence the country around it. After the Fellowship met Galadriel, a conversation between Frodo and Sam reveals that they believe that something magical might be happening even though magic cannot be detected, but that Galadriel must be the source of this magic (*FR*, 'The Mirror of Galadriel', 191). The power is omnipresent, but nobody seems to actively use it. It is unclear what the Hobbits expect the Elves to do. Whether they had hoped for the chanting of spells, ritual gestures, or light flashes remains unsaid, although Sam seems to classify fireworks as magic doings by Gandalf (191). This example is similar to the scene where the Fellowship is presented with the Elvish cloaks mentioned earlier in context of the exotic marvellous. Indeed, the Elves use their powers naturally, but never present them as magic or supernatural. On the contrary, Elves do not understand what the Hobbits mean by 'magic' and are astonished that 'magic' is also applied to "the decits of the Enemy" (193). This is an example for what Tolkien means when he argues that magic must "be taken seriously, neither laughed at nor explained away" (*OFS*, 11). The credibility of enchantment relies on the seriousness of the magic and the Faërie/ marvellous respectively.

Galadriel's power is also dangerous, and Gondor fears the Lady. Boromir refers to Lothlórien as "that perilous land we have heard in Gondor, and it is said that few come out who once go in" (*FR*, 'Lothlórien', 161). The perilous land, the land of the Faërie, the marvellous, and yet a Gondorian folktale mixed with myths and hearsay. A land that causes terror and hence sparks sublimity. Boromir's fears are met when Galadriel 'questions' each member of the Fellowship, when she "held them with her eyes, and in silence looked searchingly at each of them in turn" (*FR*, 'The Mirror of Galadriel', 186-7). While no words are spoken, Galadriel's gaze has the power to look into the minds of the Fellowship and search them. Later that night, when the company retires into their tent, they talk about the meeting with Galadriel. Most of the company agree that they felt "naked" and had been offered a tempting option to leave the quest, but only Boromir raises the question whether it was a test to tempt them into deserting the Fellowship (187-8). Indeed, the Fellowship is tested by Galadriel just like Christ is tested in the desert. Lothlórien is a dangerous land that threatens to lead people astray from their moral path. Galadriel's power is so great that it resembles a godlike entity, and, as Burke puts it that "we shrink into the minuteness of our own nature, and are, in a manner, annihilated" when we encounter omnipresent powers, and even the prospect of mercy cannot diminish the terror of the possibility to be powerless and destroyed (2015, 56). In other words: Galadriel's power and omnipresence are so overwhelming that the threat of pain and death dominate her reception, even though she shows predominantly friendly behaviour and gestures. The terror can never be entirely overcome in her presence. Galadriel and Lothlórien are one: both terrifying and beautiful and both omnipresent. The Elf queen and the forest are immortals but new-born in every instant, fantastic and sublime. For when Frodo is "lost in wonder" at Cerin Amroth "All that he saw was shapely, but her shapes seemed at once clear cut, as if they had been first conceived and drawn at the uncovering of his eyes, and ancient as if they had endured for ever" in a tension of new creation with every new perception (*FR*, 'Lothlórien', 177-8).

I aimed to unite Tolkien's *The Lord of the Rings* with Burke's sublime and Todorov's fantastic to prove how Tolkien achieves to create a credible otherworld. The argument has shown that enchantment is Burke's sublime, that the Faërie, or otherworld, is an element of Todorov's marvellous and that the fantastic offers gaps for the reader to fill with their imagination just as Iser explains in his reception theory. Substantial examples taken from close reading the novel prove that Tolkien creates an otherworld by implementing unreliable narrators and choosing naïve protagonists that are unfamiliar with the laws of the world outside the Shire. The enchantment/sublimity relies on the credibility of the Faërie/marvellous to make the elements of the fantastic effective. Tolkien uses distinct elements to create uncertainty, which prove to be closely related to Burke's idea of obscurity. The argument further proves that obscurity is the main concept behind sublimity and includes all other concepts Burke introduces, most importantly the artificial infinite. The latter is found throughout *The Lord of the Rings* repeatedly in various concepts such as architecture or time. A story of privation, then, is a story of relative pleasure, where the reader sympathises with the protagonist(s) to follow them through encounters of distanced danger and wishes to relieve their pain and fear. The degree of immersion is dependent on the degree of sublimity the text affords. Therefore, immersion and sublimity, or enchantment respectively, are inextricably entwined. *The Lord of the Rings* manages to create a very high degree of sublimity and therefore enchantment and immersion because Tolkien crafts a credible otherworld with the help of unreliable narrators within a marvellous environment that effectively use formal elements of the fantastic, which afford uncertainty for the reader repeatedly throughout the story.

Bibliography

Burke, E., *A Philosophical Enquiry into the Sublime and Beautiful*, ed. by P. Guyer, 2nd ed. (Oxford: Oxford University Press, 2015) 3-140.

Clute, J., 'Edifice', in *SFE. Encyclopedia of Fantasy,* (1997) <http://sf-encyclopedia.uk/ fe.php?nm=edifice> [Accessed 1 September 2019].

Cronon, W., 'The Trouble with Wilderness: Or, Getting Back to the Wrong Nature', in *Environmental History*, 1.1 (1996) 7-28.

Guyer, P., 'Introduction', in *A Philosophical Enquiry into the Sublime and Beautiful*, ed. Paul Guyer, 2nd ed. (Oxford: Oxford University Press) vii-xxxvii.

Iser, W., 'Interaction Between Text and Reader', in The Norton Anthology of Theory and Criticism, ed. V. B. Leitch, 2nd ed. (New York: Norton & Company, 2010) 1524-1532.

James, E., 'Tolkien, Lewis and the Explosion of Genre Fantasy', in *The Cambridge Companion to Fantasy Literature*, ed. E. James and F. Mendlesohn (Cambridge: Cambridge UP, 2012) 62-78.

Todorov, T., *The Fantastic: A Structural Approach to a Literary Genre,* (New York: Cornell University Press, 1975).

Tolkien, J.R.R. 'On Fairy Stories', in *Tree and Leaf*, ed. C. Tolkien (London: Harper Collins, 2001) 1-82.
— *The Lord of the Rings,* (London: Harper Collins, 2001).

Roberts, A., 'Gothic and Horror Fiction', in *The Cambridge Companion to Fantasy Literature,* ed. E. James and F. Mendlesohn (Cambridge: Cambridge University Press, 2012) 21-35.

RELIGION, SPIRITUALITY, AND FAITH

Leaf by Niggle by *Northwest*: J. R. R. Tolkien and Alfred Hitchcock as Catholic Artists

Revd. Dr. Justin Anthony

1 – Implicit Theology and Catholic Art

People tend to make a basic mistake when it comes to understanding religion. They think it is all about *believing* stuff: and, if you are a hostile critic of religion, believing stuff that is impossible to believe. This is what we might call 'orthodoxy' – sound opinions. However, as sociologists of religion for at least a hundred years have realised, religious practice tends to precede religious belief. This is what we might call 'orthopraxis' – sound (or otherwise!) actions. These actions will have an implicit motivating force behind them, an ideology, or even a theology, even if the motivating force is not acknowledged or recognised. As Claude Lévi-Strauss argued and demonstrated: "myths operate in men's minds without their being aware of the fact" (1970, 12). This is, when it comes to Christian cultural and religious expression, known as 'implicit theology'. It is the recognition that people inhabit a world in which signs, symbols, assumptions, stories, taboos, and those parts of life that are never to be mentioned, are in a way more powerful and more significant, than the explicitly stated upfront 'values' of a person and the organisation in which she works or lives.[1] Implicit theology is the insight that "practices shape belief and religious beliefs also shape practice" (Percy 2010, 11). Or, more formally, implicit theology tells us that "the primary materials of theology are often not so much the formal statements of ecclesial bodies, but rather their operant practices, beliefs and interpretations" (314).

Is this a helpful way to approach, comparing and contrasting, J.R.R. Tolkien and Alfred Hitchcock as Catholic Artists of the twentieth century? We can see this implicit/explicit, formal/informal, action/belief dynamic at play in the consequent task facing us. How do we define a 'Catholic Artist'? How do we define a 'Catholic Work of art'? Is it simply the career, or the artistic work, of someone who attends a Catholic church on Sundays, or was baptised a Catholic? To adopt this strategy is the methodology that beset Film and Religion studies twenty years ago, when examinations on whether or not

1. Think of the times you have been served in a shop by a glowering and angry worker who, nevertheless, wears an officially produced name-badge printed with 'Happy To Help!'

I attended a conference recently in which this was the methodology adopted in examining the theology of the films of Roland Emmerich: all those imprecations, solemnly and futilely tabulated as evidence of Emmerich's engagement with religion. It is part of the problem of the methodology in a paper such as LeiLani Hinds's, where Catholic visual designs in the Jackson films are enumerated but never defined. Why is Pippin kissing the ring of Denethor *necessarily* evocative of a Catholic kissing the ring of the Pope, and why do designs based on Charlemagne's church in Aachen *necessarily* act as Catholic subtexts? There is a problem in distinguishing between cultural and confessional allusions here (LeiLani Hinds 2008).

a film was 'religious' would be predicated on the number of mentions given to "God!" or "Jesus Christ!" in the script.[2]

Alternatively, is it the career, or the artistic work, of someone who intends her work to bring people into fellowship with the Universal Church and the See of Rome? In this way, John the Evangelist would be the first, and prototypical, Catholic artist: "Many other signs also did Jesus in the sight of his disciples, which are not written in this book. But these are written, that you may believe that Jesus is the Christ, the Son of God: and that believing, you may have life in his name" (John 20:30-1).[3] Furthermore, in this mode one could assert that a truly 'Catholic' artist should reflect in their 'Catholic Art' the values of Vincentian Canon, a test set by Vincent of Lérins, that the true Catholic faith is that which has been *quod ubique, quod semper, quod ab omnibus creditum est* ('what has been believed everywhere, always, and by all') (Vincent of Lérins 1915). Is Catholic Art subject to a similar test of "ecumenicity, antiquity, and consent" (Cross and Livingstone 2005)?

Alternatively, and thirdly, we may follow the (D.H.) Lawrentian school of criticism and interpretation: "Never trust the artist. Trust the tale" (Lawrence 1923, 3). This strategy was wholly supported by C.S. Lewis, who once agreed with an early critic of his Space Trilogy: "I have an idea that a critic and a book are company, but that the author is *de trop*. Wd. my Milton book have been improved or ruined by a meeting with Milton? […] you may reply 'Well, that is what the books mean to an intelligent reader and what does it matter what you meant them to mean?'–a point of view I wholly agree with" (Lewis 2006, 162; emphasis original).

Even so, whichever of the three strategies we adopt, it is necessary to define some form, at least, of what makes a Catholic artist *Catholic*, if we are to examine what is in common and what is different between two such, otherwise very different, artists as Tolkien and Hitchcock. One made films, one wrote books; one consorted with starlets, one gave lectures; one lived in Beverly Hills and one lived in Headington. Other than the fact that their lives, largely, overlapped (Tolkien, 3 January 1892–2 September 1973; Hitchcock, 13 August 1899–29 April 1980), is there nothing else we can say?[4]

2 – Catholic Worldview

This is where Pedro Ángeles-Ruiz in his paper for the 2005 Tolkien Society Conference is unintentionally useful (2008). While examining the possibility that Tolkien utilized a literary technique of contrafactura in treating his implicit Catholicism, Ángeles-Ruiz introduces the idea of the worldview. A Catholic artist is one who possesses a Catholic world view, a *Weltanschauung*. However, this passes the definitional problem down the line, as we must now define a Catholic worldview. Ángeles-Ruiz paraphrases Romano Guardini's definition: "Being Catholic means accepting with absolute gravity the supernatural revelations in its whole gist and in all of its domains and complexities of

2. And I want to avoid the mistake of insisting that everything has to be defined from first principles, even including 'what do we mean by "Tolkien"?' – paper deliberately left uncited!
3. Anon. 'John 20:30-1' in *Douay-Rheims 1899 American Edition*, BibleGateway.com. Available at: https://www.biblegateway.com/passage/?search=John%2020&version=DRA.
4. He does so in a footnote, which diminishes some of the impact of his interesting insight.

daily life. Catholicism embraces basically all the typical possibilities" (2008, 52). So, a Catholic worldview is a position adopted implicitly or explicitly by an artist, which indicates her participation in the "organic articulation" of spiritual, psychological and ethnological typologies (52).[5]

Here Guardini is challenging two mistaken ideas about the Church and human nature, that is, ecclesiology and anthropology. On the one hand he challenges older, Catholic, and neo-scholastic ideas that the Church consists of a hierarchical organisation which was set up, in *toto* and completely, at the time of Christ and the Apostles, in order to guard and sanctify the 'rank and file' faithful. On the other hand, and against liberal Protestantism and the wider German culture, he is challenging the ideal of individualism, which erodes the sense in which the Church is a mystical body of Christians bound together in a spiritual mutuality: "the living Christ stands at the center of the believing community and that the source of unity is the Holy Spirit" (Krieg 1997, 58).[6] In this worldview, "God does not remain an empty word or a mere fiction but is the all-encompassing reality which defines the world and human existence" (Schilson 1995, 34).

Romano Guardini might sound like a fairly obscure theologian upon which to base a methodology, but his early work on recovering the nature of the Church from the depredations of both authoritarianism and individualism were hugely influential on the development of thinking that was expressed in the Second Vatican Council (1962-1965), and in recent years his importance to contemporary Catholic thinking has been emphasised by the use made of him by two of his greatest fans: Popes Benedict XVI and Francis. Benedict quoted Guardini in his farewell discourse to the College of Cardinals, and Francis quoted repeatedly from Guardini in his encyclical *Laudato Si'* (Benedict XVI 2013; Francis 2015).

This is all important material to consider when we think about the constitutive elements of, especially, Hitchcock's Catholicism.[7] Catholic ecclesiologists and anthropologists working after Vatican II demonstrated Guardini's sense of the mystical, unitive and spiritual nature of being a Catholic Christian. Gerald O'Collins gives three characteristics of the Catholic worldview: "a desire to incorporate all material reality into their sacramental and devotional life, a willingness to practise the principle of 'both/and',[8] and a deep concern for unity" (O'Collins 2017, 101). Furthermore, in a deepening of the first principle, "Catholicism at its best and truest focuses its heart on Jesus, who came to live, die, and rise for our salvation" (O'Collins and Farrugia 2015, 388). The sacramental life is based upon an encounter with another, *the* Other, an encounter that

5. We have a problem here in that Ángeles-Ruiz is translating into English a Spanish translation of a book originally written in German by an Italian born priest! As far as I can tell this Spanish language book is a version of Guardini's inaugural lecture at the University of Berlin in 1923, which has never been translated into English (Guardini 1923).

6. Krieg is summarising Guardini's work in *Vom Sinn der Kirche*, which was later published in English translation as *The Church and the Catholic and The Spirit of the Liturgy* (Guardini 1940).

7. Quotations from Guardini are on pp. 77, 81, 86, 149, 150, and 160. For a survey of Guardini's influence on, among others, Hannah Arendt, Thomas Merton, Pope Paul VI, and Flannery O'Connor, see Krieg, *Romano Guardini: a precursor of Vatican II* (1997, 192–201).

8. Otherwise known as 'paradox: the contradiction you like.'

Martin Buber described as "I/Thou" (Buber 1970). O'Collins and Farrugia go on to describe how these essential doctrinal and existential characteristics are manifested through the artistic imagination and skill of Catholic artists, everyone from Warhol to Leonardo to Haydn.

This cultural manifestation was explored further by Andrew Greeley, who talks about how "Catholics live in an enchanted world, a world of statues and holy water, stained glass and votive candles, saints and religious medals, rosary beads and holy pictures" (Greeley 2000, 1). But the paraphernalia are signifiers for the Catholic sensibility which sees "the Holy lurking in creation" (1). Catholics, together and severally, are "haunted by a sense that the objects, events, and persons of daily life are revelations of grace" (1). The technical word for this is sacramental. Greeley's thesis is that this attitude, neither modern, nor post-modern, but properly and empirically pre-modern, is the means by which "the sensibility expressed in Catholic high culture continues to influence Catholic popular culture and artists who are not known for their explicit piety" (3).

This is where we can return, with renewed insight, to the implicit theology work of someone like Martyn Percy. He demonstrates that the implicit part of the formula is as important as the theology part: implicit implies ideas of "entanglement, of being entwined, and in the overlapping of involvement;" furthermore, statements of authority are often those not "plainly expressed" (Percy 2009, 314). Ideas, attitudes, and epistemological impulses and imperatives (i.e., *where* it is we think we might be going and what it is we think we might *know* when we get there), are at work without being questioned, and are protected from questioning because they are *operational* rather than *propositional*. In other words, the way we do things has a different level of scrutiny than the *arguments* we make about the way we do things. Its very authority comes from its implicit mode: "it does not *need* to make itself explicit" (314; emphasis mine).

If such an authority derives from performance rather than argument, operants rather than propositions, then it follows that implicit theology is more easily seen in the mode of story rather than philosophy. We make arguments to demonstrate explicit theologies or ideologies; we tell stories to have implicit theologies or ideologies. Stories are, says Don Cupitt, "interpretative resources, models and scenarios through which we make sense of what is happening to us and frame our own action" (Cupitt 1991, ix). Furthermore, it is "through stories that our social selves, which are our real selves, are actually produced." This is an imperative, which goes with the (human) territory: "Because we use language and live in time, we must tell stories" (79; emphasis original).[9]

Hitchcock agreed. He saw his role as a storyteller. As he said in a series of interviews with the French director François Truffaut:

> I always feel comfortable about a project when I can tell the story in a very simple way, from beginning to end, in a fairly abbreviated version. I like to imagine a young woman who has been to see the movie and goes home very satisfied with what she's seen. Her mother asks her, 'How was the movie?' And she answers, 'It was very good.' The mother says, 'What was it about?' And the girl replies, 'Well, it was about a young woman who

9. Of course, Cupitt would deny a reality to God outside the creation and experience of humanity, and this implies the social and narrative construction of what we call "reality". This would not be, certainly, Tolkien's belief.

> so and so and so' Well, I feel that before undertaking to shoot a movie, one should be able to do just that, to satisfy oneself that it can be narrated just as clearly, the whole cycle. (Truffaut 2017, 315)

And Truffaut concurred: "In any film there comes a moment when the story must have the priority" (315). So, we can say, in a preliminary summary, that a Catholic Artist produces a work of Catholic Art which sacralises life, that is, demonstrating that everything we see is not everything that there is. Furthermore, this sacralised life (and creation) contains a moral and ethical imperative laid upon us, as human beings, in our relationship with the rest of the cosmos, nature and other humans. The imperative comes because the best way to understand the cosmos is to think of it as Creation, and our place within it in relation to a Creator. This reality is better expressed through story, than propositional bullet points, and that there is always need for 'both/and', or 'Yes, but'.

3 – Tolkien as a Catholic Artist

It has been said that among the very few incontrovertible things that could be said of Tolkien is his status as a Catholic artist, and his legendarium as a Catholic mythos: "Tolkien's Christianity and Roman Catholicism are an integral element of his fiction and, therefore, a necessary element to account for in any fair and reasonable interpretation of his work" (Mitchell). Tolkien's biographer agreed: "His commitment to Christianity and in particular to the Catholic Church was total. [...] His religion was [...] one of the deepest and strongest elements in his personality" (Carpenter 2002, 133). However, both Ronald Hutton and Verlyn Flieger have pointed out that much of the intensity of Tolkien's claimed status as a Catholic creator of Catholic art was an *ex post facto* reaction to his critics when *The Lord of the Rings* was published (Hutton 2008, 33; Flieger 2002, 1–5).[10] In this respect Hutton and Flieger are agreeing with Lawrence, when he wrote: "The proper function of a critic is to save the tale from the artist who created it" (Lawrence 1923, 3).

Tolkien once said in a letter to a Jesuit friend that "*The Lord of the Rings* is of course a fundamentally religious and Catholic work; unconsciously so at first, but consciously in the revision" (*Letters*, Letter 142, 172). Perhaps the reason he did not include anything that he thought could be construed as religious practice in the book, was from the exercise of similar sensibility as that espoused by Guardini. Guardini's worldview:

> did not permit Guardini to speak directly about the primary datum of theology, namely, God. Instead his rigorous theological reflection was directed toward the world, because this is the concrete realm and context of human life. Given this orientation, Guardini provided clear perceptions of the world from the standpoint of faith and offered insights on living as a Christian in the modern age. (Schilson 1995, 34)

10. Reportedly, Flieger has made further comments in this vein in her guest of honour address at MythCon50 in the summer of 2019, although my only access to those comments has been via a third-party's tweets, rather than anything more reliable or scholarly: (Flieger 2019).

It was something of this process that led to the creation of *Leaf by Niggle* (1945). The story came to Tolkien, complete and without an unseemly striving for allegorical meaning, in a dream (*Letters*, Letter 98, 113). The complexities of its writing and publication aside, it is clear that the story meant a lot to Tolkien, as teased out by D. Thomas Hanks (Hanks 2012). He tells his aunt Jane Neave something of the autobiographical roots of the story,[11] his love of a lost poplar, the felled trees of the Broad Walk of Christ Church, and the tangles he had found himself in at the time in writing *The Lord of the Rings*. But even though the story had, if not unhappy, then at least anxious roots, he still asks "If it has any virtues, they remain as such, whether you know all this or do not. I hope you think it has some virtue" (*Letters*, Letter 241, 322). Niggle is a small man, and an obsessive man, who resents the demands of those around him, and even as he responds to those demands, learns nothing of his unity with the demanders. It is only when he realises that his art was recognised in his vocation to service that he finally sees the beatific vision of his longed-for Tree:

> He gazed at the Tree, and slowly he lifted his arms and opened them wide. 'It's a gift!' he said. He was referring to his art, and also to the result; but he was using the word quite literally. (*TL*, 110)

The allegory, despite himself, could not have been clearer. Tolkien described, in a long letter to his son, the challenges of living as a Christian in the modern age, his disappointments in his Catholic faith, the challenge it exercised on him, even into his seventies, and the existential and salvific commitment it required of him.

> Our love may be chilled and our will eroded by the spectacle of the shortcomings, folly, and even sins of the Church and its ministers, but I do not think that one who has once had faith goes back over the line for these reasons (least of all anyone with any historical knowledge). 'Scandal' at most is an occasion of temptation – as indecency is to lust, which it does not make but arouses. It is convenient because it tends to turn our eyes away from ourselves and our own faults to find a scape-goat. (*Letters*, Letter 250, 337–8)

Faith is not contrasted with doubt here. Faith is both sourced within doubt and the means of overcoming doubt: "I now know enough about myself to be aware that I should not leave the Church (which for me would mean leaving the allegiance of Our Lord) for any such reasons" (338).

We see then that Tolkien's faith was not a caricatured settled thing, a possession to be treasured or jealously guarded. As Flieger has pointed out he was a man of "polarities", building his work, and his life, "on contrasts–between hope and despair, between good and evil, between enlightenment and ignorance–and these contrasts are embodied in the polarities of light and dark that are the creative outgrowth of his contrary moods, the 'antitheses' of his nature" (Flieger 2002, 2). Carpenter agreed: Tolkien's character, in

11. Even though he, as a point of principle, disliked all autobiographical explications of an author's work almost as much as he disliked allegorical interpretations of the same: "so obsessively interesting to modern critics that they often value a piece of 'literature' solely in so far as it reveals the author, and especially if that is in a discreditable light" (*Letters*, Letter 241, 321).

which his Catholicism was situated, and through which it was expressed, was "never moderate: love, intellectual enthusiasm, distaste, anger, self-doubt, guilt, laughter, each was in his mind exclusively and in full force when he experienced it" (Carpenter 2002, 133).

Even so, we can stipulate, for the sake of this paper that the predominant themes of grace, communion, sacrament, veneration, mediation, eschatological vision, a tragic vision of history, pity, and mercy all act as strong Catholic Christian themes and motifs within Tolkien's fiction.

4 – Hitchcock as a Catholic Artist

> "there is not one of Hitchcock's films that is not more or less marked by Christian ideas and symbols" (Rohmer and Chabrol 1992, 113)

Alfred Hitchcock was born to a Catholic family, and received the sacraments of the Catholic Church at the various rites of passage of a man's life: his wife converted to Catholicism on their marriage (Truffaut 2017, 316). On the other hand, he once admitted to Truffaut "I don't think I can be labelled a Catholic artist, but it may be that one's early upbringing influences a man's life and guides his instinct" (316). His Catholicism, with many years' hindsight, set him apart from the rest of English society: to be a Catholic family in England was "in itself is an eccentricity" (25). He described his schooldays in a fairly generic Catholic-trauma manner: he was educated with the Jesuits at St Ignatius College in north London, and it was at this time, he later told Truffaut, "that a strong sense of fear developed – moral fear – the fear of being involved in anything evil. I always tried to avoid it." Part of the reason to avoid moral evil was a simple fear of physical punishment: "In those days they used a cane made of very hard rubber. I believe the Jesuits still use it. It wasn't done casually, you know; it was rather like the execution of a sentence. They would tell you to step in to see the father when classes were over. He would then solemnly inscribe your name in the register together with the indication of the punishment to be inflicted, and you spent the whole day waiting for the sentence to be carried out" (26). Interestingly enough, some of Hitchcock's contemporaries do not remember such cruel chastisement, nor that Hitchcock was especially singled out for attention (Spoto 1994, 25–7). The story is more powerful than the reality.

Hitchcock's eccentric religious affiliation, along with his cultural and social placing in London's society, explains his emotional development or repression to his (American) biographer: he was part of groups and sub-groups that "rigorously avoided the articulation of feelings", and furthermore, "his Catholic-Cockney avoidance of emotional display made him shun demonstrations of any strong feeling" (21).[12]

Demonstrations of feelings might be absent, but that doesn't mean experience of emotions were equally absent. For Hitchcock, and his students, the predominating emotion of his life, emerging from his cultural Catholicism, was guilt, the "predominant theme of Hitchcock's films" (17). Hitchcock's experience, and depiction, of guilt came from "the complexities of his own inner life" but also from the great themes of

12. Which does not sound like the emotional and/or social behaviour of either subgroup to me!

"contemporary art and literature" (17). Spoto argues that when the artistic theme of guilt is "connected to some experience of a religious tradition," the work of art is "informed with a rare human intensity" (17). For Spoto this is a moral strategy. A freedom from corruption can only come with guilt, the process by which acceptance of one's "standing condemned and accepting forgiveness and redemption freely or enduring punishment and hoping for a second chance" (17). A struggle with, and then an acceptance of guilt, whence it may come, is the sign of a true artist in the twentieth century, in which moral responsibility is reduced to an experience along the spectrum from "an infraction of manners" to psychosis (17).

But, if the dominant theme of Hitchcock's work is guilt, it is not just the "guilt of the guilty" but also "the guilt of the apparently innocent" (Giles 1992, 326). He repeatedly examines what happens when a protagonist is mistaken for an outlaw, either by society's mechanisms of discipline and punishment or by those already living outside the law. How would you defend your innocence, when, in fact, there is a lot for you to feel guilty about?[13] This was enough for Rohmer and Chabrol to describe him as a "Catholic auteur," because he explored allegories of original sin, the Fall, its consequences, and the "interchangeable guilt of all mankind" (Rohmer and Chabrol 1992, 25, 149). We see the latter in his films with the recurring trope of a blameless bystander who comes to be regarded as a more likely criminal than any person who might actually have committed the unlawful act.

So, for example, *Shadow of a Doubt* (1943), *Spellbound* (1945), and *North by Northwest* (1959), although any Hitchcock aficionado could choose any three of his more than fifty films. In *Shadow* Joseph Cotton plays Uncle Charlie, a man who makes a living from seducing and killing widows. The villain's sister is given the name "Emma", Hitchcock's own mother's name, who at the time was living with him in Hollywood and was mortally ill. Uncle Charlie, as well as villain, is the protective realist to his niece, also called Charlie, telling her: "Do you know the world is a foul sty? Do you know if you ripped the fronts of houses, you'd find swine? The world's a hell! What does it matter what happens in it?" (Hitchcock 1943). The world is *massa damnata*.[14]

In *Spellbound*, in which there is "a sense of brooding guilt" (Spoto 1994, 274) as a result of a long-repressed psychologically damaged childhood, Gregory Peck (as the

13. This was the theme of the introduction to Dr. Rowan Williams's sermon at his enthronement as Archbishop of Canterbury: "It's sometimes been said that if someone came up to you in the street and whispered, 'They've found out! Run!', nine out of ten of us would. We nearly all have secrets that we don't want exposed – even if they are quite trivial in the cold light of day – and that phrase tell us a lot, the cold light: we don't want to be under the kind of detached scrutiny that threatens and diminishes us, sitting under a bare light bulb and being interrogated. So when it looks as though our secrets are about to be revealed, we easily panic and run" (Williams 2003).

14. The Original Sin of Adam is transmitted, via concupiscence, to the whole of humanity, resulting in each individual person participating in the "damned lump" of human nature. This was defined by Augustine in his anti-Pelagian writings of the late fourth century, and first used in his 'Miscellany of Eighty-Three Questions'. Interestingly, even though later schoolmen like Anselm separated the transmission of Original Sin from concupiscence by the thirteenth century, it has remained indelibly associated with sex, and the guilt that comes from sex, in the popular mind ever since. The devil has all the best theology. (Augustine of Hippo 2008, Qn. LXVIII.3, 117 in this edition)

damaged hero) complains: "I'm haunted, but I can't see by what" (Hitchcock 1945). It is only Ingrid Bergman's unorthodox treatment of her patient that allows him to be free when she tells him: "People often feel guilt over something they never did. It usually goes back to their childhood. The child often wishes something terrible would happen to someone, and if something does happen to that person, the child believes he has caused it. And he grows up with a guilt complex over a sin that was only a child's bad dream" (Hitchcock 1945).

Hitchcock shows us in *Spellbound* that sin has real effects, and the first step to relieve the sufferer from the consequences of sin is to see if the sin was real in the first place. For Hitchcock, Spellbound examined "guilt incapacitating the reach toward love, and in every film to come he would affirm this mutual, tragic connection" (Spoto 1994, 274).

Cary Grant plays Roger Thorncliff, the hero of *North by Northwest*, with his customary skill in negotiating suavity and slapstick. He begins as a complacent advertising man, driven across the United States by secret agents who believe he is George Kaplan, an agent with access to a microfilm. As the pursuit goes on, Hitchcock and Grant together manage to show how "Thorncliff gradually comes to believe that he might in fact be guilty after all; indeed, in an ontological sense, perhaps Thorncliff's former beliefs about his own sanctimonious innocence were a form of naivete and self-delusion" (Giles 1992, 326). Hitchcock shows us that the verities of any man's sense of himself are as illusory as the stories peddled by Madison Avenue. And the power of (self-) delusion is emphasized by the microfilm. We are never given a clear description of its contents or significance; no 'The Shadow Of The Past' exposition here. The microfilm is Hitchcock's important "MacGuffin" trope. As he told Truffaut, in many of his films the "MacGuffin" is the catalyst of the plot: "it's the device, the gimmick, if you will, or the papers the spies are after. [...] The only thing that really matters is that in the picture the plans, documents, or secrets must seem to be of vital importance to the characters. To me, the narrator, they're of no importance whatever" (Truffaut 2017, 138). It is as if Hitchcock is saying that the matters we care so much about, that cause us so much pain, are in themselves transitory and worthless. They are only significant in as much as they do cause us pain and trial, which we, no matter what our delusory ideas about our deserts might be, most justly do deserve. Here Hitchcock deviates from Tolkien's more modest judgement: "Many that live deserve death. And some that die deserve life. Can you give it to them? Then do not be too eager to deal out death in judgement" (*FR*, 'The Shadow Of The Past', 59). For both Hitchcock and Tolkien, there is judgement. For Hitchcock, the universe, providence, will provide that judgement, for Tolkien it ill-behoves humanity or hobbits to take on the role themselves.

In Hitchcock's sensibility just deserts and judgement apply as much to love, as they do to crime: "lover and beloved never find liberation from the shackles of their past, can never rise from the chains of resentment and remorse." His work, emerging from his experience and his sensibility, became "tortured, guilt-ridden fantasies" (Spoto 1994, 274).

Perhaps this is inevitable, as Spoto praises his subject, in the preface to his impressively thorough biography, as having:

> an uncanny ability to locate and diagnose much of the psychological suffering of the world, much of the delusion and sickness just below the surface of polite society. He spoke to us out of the twentieth century's sense of guilt, angst, and obsession with violence, sex, and the detached machinery of death. (viii)

Whereas Tolkien lived and died as a faithful, if struggling, Catholic, Spoto tells of a different end for Hitchcock. "I was born a Catholic," he said in an interview with a pupil from St Ignatius College in 1973: "I went to a Catholic school, and now I have a conscience with lots of trials over beliefs." But as his mental and physical faculties declined, he ceased in any public observance of religion: "he rejected the suggestion that he allow a priest, a friend of the O'Connell family, to come for a visit, or to celebrate a quiet, informal ritual at the house for his comfort. [...] 'Don't let any priests on the lot,' he had whispered to his office staff in the last year. 'They're all after me; they all hate me.' There was no way of convincing him to see a clergyman at home, either, although he imagined their presences there, too." As Spoto sadly says: "Hitchcock could find no path to confront the trials, nor means to work out the struggle, in doubt and faith, and so to bring peace to his troubled spirit." (Spoto 1994, 551–2).

5 – *Leaf by Niggle* By Northwest?

Both Hitchcock and Tolkien acknowledged, if nothing else, the influence of their Catholic upbringing and culture on their work: Tolkien went one step further than Hitchcock, and claimed, explicitly, a Catholic sensibility expressed in and through his work. Even if one wants to take a full Lawrentian position and distrust Tolkien's own witness to his motivations and achievements (both wanting to, and succeeding, in placing a Catholic imagination in his work), then there are enough critics, not all of them co-opting Tolkien for political or polemical purposes, who recognise that Catholic imagination at play in the Legendarium for it to be a useful critical and hermeneutical tool. Although Hitchcock denied an explicit Catholic sensibility in his life, he admitted the possibility of it in his work, and external critics, who might not necessarily have been very sympathetic to the veridical and moral claims of Catholicism, have seen the aesthetic and ethic evidence of its presence in Hitchcock's *oeuvre*. Hitchcock admitted, within bounds of his general playfulness/untrustworthiness with interviewers, that some of what he considered to be the great Catholic themes of morality and existential status were of concern to him in how he approached stories, their content and their themes. So, there is some validity in seeing a commonality to Tolkien and Hitchcock.

What about the differences? Summarizing wildly, I would say that Hitchcock was much more interested in social isolation, and the effects of social isolation on his protagonists, and Tolkien in the responsibilities and benefits of social integration; Hitchcock in selfishness, and Tolkien in duty; Hitchcock in the Fall and Tolkien in Creation; Hitchcock in guilt and Tolkien in salvation. All these themes and tropes, on both sides, can be seen as Catholic Imagination.

And yet, of course, to say that Tolkien is interested in community and mutual responsibility does not mean that he is not interested in exploring the consequences of the alternative: Sméagol/Gollum, Saruman, Fëanor, Túrin, Denethor, are all characters in stories, in which to lesser or greater extents, pride and consequential isolation are explored. Similarly, Tolkien does not neglect the idea of original sin, the moral, and often fatal, flaw in every conscious creature which means that none is without sin in *The Lord of the Rings*: even Frodo 'falls' at the last, and it is only Gollum's greater greed for the Ring that 'saves' the quest and 'saves' Frodo – saves him if only for a slightly longer and troubled life in Arda.

When examining these similarities, I tried the thought-experiment of imagining 'Alfred Hitchcock Presents *The Lord of The Rings*': what would a Hitchcockian version of the war of the Third Age look like? To begin with I thought that it would be very, comically, different to Tolkien's. If Hitchcock applied his usual method, he would begin with an innocent, who through accident, unknowingly comes into possession of the MacGuffin, wanted by faceless and impersonal forces of evil, who pursue him from his comfortable life and society into the wastelands of Indiana, whereupon he – and then I stopped, and wondered how that was very different from Frodo, the One Ring, the Black Riders, and fleeing the Shire.

Perhaps Tolkien and Hitchcock are closer in their imagination than might be apparent on first thought and first sight: and wouldn't that be a particularly appropriate expression of a Catholic Imagination?

Bibliography

Ángeles-Ruiz, P., 'Catholic "contrafactura" of Myth in Some J.R.R. Tolkien's Writings', in *The Ring Goes Ever On: Proceedings of the Tolkien 2005 Conference: 50 Years of 'The Lord of the Rings'*, edited by S. Wells, II (Coventry: The Tolkien Society, 2008) 51-64.

Augustine of Hippo, 'De Diversis Quaestionibus Octoginta Tribus (Miscellany of Eighty-Three Questions)', in *Responses to Miscellaneous Questions: Miscellany of Eighty-Three Questions; Miscellany of Questions in Response to Simplician; and, Eight Questions of Dulcitius*, ed. by R.F. Canning, The Works of Saint Augustine, XII (Hyde Park: New City Press, 2008) 13–157.

Benedict XVI, 'Farewell Address to the Eminent Cardinals Present in Rome', *Vatican Website*, 28 February 2013, <https://w2.vatican.va/content/benedict-xvi/en/speeches/2013/february/documents/hf_ben-xvi_spe_20130228_congedo-cardinali.html> [Accessed 18 January 2024].

Buber, M., *I and Thou*, trans. by R.G. Smith, 2nd edn. (Edinburgh: T & T Clark, 1970).

Carpenter, H., *J. R. R. Tolkien: A Biography,* (London: HarperCollins, 2002).

Cross, F. L., and E. A. Livingstone, 'Vincentian Canon', in *The Oxford Dictionary of the Christian Church*, 3rd edn. (Oxford: Oxford University Press, 2005).

Cupitt, D., *What Is a Story?,* (London: SCM, 1991).

Flieger, V., *Splintered Light: Logos and Language in Tolkien's World,* (Kent: Kent State University Press, 2002).

— 'The Arch and the Keystone', *Mythlore*, 38.1 (2019) 5-17 <www.mythsoc.org/mythcon/mc50-sked.htm> [Accessed 18 January 2024].

Francis, 'Encyclical Letter Laudato Si' of the Holy Father Francis on Care for Our Common Home', *Vatican Website*, 24 May 2015 <http://w2.vatican.va/content/francesco/en/encyclicals/documents/papa-francesco_20150524_ enciclica-laudato-si.html> [Accessed 19 January 2024].

Giles, P., 'Guilt and Salvation: Alfred Hitchcock and Martin Scorsese', *In American Catholic Arts and Fictions: Culture, Ideology, Aesthetics,* (Cambridge: Cambridge University Press, 1992) 325–53.

Greeley, A., *The Catholic Imagination,* (Berkeley: University of California Press, 2000).

Guardini, R., 'Vom Wesen katholischer Weltanschauung', *Die Schildgenossen*, 4. (1923) 66–79.
— *The Church and the Catholic and The Spirit of the Liturgy*, tran. by A. Lane (London: Sheed & Ward, 1940).
— *La Esencia de La Concepción Católica Del Mundo*, trans. by A. Gómez Robledo (Mexico City: Universidad Nacional Autónoma de México, 1957).
— 'Vom Wesen Katholischer Weltanschauung', in *Unterscheidung Des Christlichen: Gesammelte Studien*, 1923-1963, ed. by H. Waltmann, 2nd edn. (Mainz: Matthias Grünewald, 1963) 1–22.

Hanks, D.T., 'Tolkien's "Leaf by Niggle": A Blossom on the Tree of Tales', *Journal of Inklings Studies*, 2.1 (2012) 23–48.

Hitchcock, A. dir, *Shadow of a Doubt*, (Universal Pictures, 1943).
— *Spellbound*, (United Artists, 1945).
— *North by Northwest*, (Metro-Goldwyn-Mayer, 1959).

Hopkins, G.M. 'God's Grandeur (1877)', in *Poems and Prose*, ed. by W.H. Gardner (London: Penguin Classics, 1985) 27.

Hutton, R., 'The Pagan Tolkien', in *The Ring Goes Ever On: Proceedings of the Tolkien 2005 Conference: 50 Years of 'The Lord of the Rings'*, ed. by S. Wells, II (Coventry: The Tolkien Society, 2008) 32–39.

'John 20:30-1' in *The Douay-Rheims 1899 American Edition Bible*, BibleGateway.com. Available at: https://www. biblegateway.com/passage/?search=John%2020&version=DRA [Accessed 24 January 2024].

Krieg, R.A., *Romano Guardini: A Precursor of Vatican II,* (Notre Dame: University of Notre Dame Press, 1997).

Lawrence, D.H., *Studies in Classic American Literature,* (New York: Thomas Seltzer, 1923).

LeiLani H., 'Peter Jackson and Tolkien's Catholicism', in *The Ring Goes Ever On: Proceedings of the Tolkien 2005 Conference: 50 Years of 'The Lord of the Rings'*, ed. by S. Wells, II (Coventry: The Tolkien Society, 2008) 221–27.

Lévi-Strauss, C., *The Raw and the Cooked*, trans. by J. Weightman and D. Weightman, Mythologiques, I (London: Cape, 1970).

Lewis, C.S. 'To Wayland Hilton Young, Jan 31, 1952', in *The Collected Letters of C.S. Lewis*, ed. by W. Hooper, III (London: HarperCollins, 2006) 161–62.
Mitchell, P., 'Some "Certainties" in Tolkien and Tolkien Studies', *Dallas Baptist University* [n.d.] <www3. dbu.edu/mitchell/tolkiencertainities.htm> [Accessed 19 January 2024].

North by Northwest, dir. By A. Hitchcock (Metro-Goldwyn-Mayer, 1959).

O'Collins, G., *Catholicism: A Very Short Introduction*, 2nd edn. (Oxford: Oxford University Press, 2017).

O'Collins, G., and M. Farrugia, *Catholicism: The Story of Catholic Christianity*, 2nd edn. (Oxford: Oxford University Press, 2015).

Percy, M., '"Fresh Expressions": A Journey into Implicit Theology', *Implicit Religion*, 12.3 (2009) 313–32.
— *Shaping the Church: The Promise of Implicit Theology*, Explorations in Practical, Pastoral, and Empirical Theology (Surrey: Ashgate, 2010).

Rohmer, É. and C. Chabrol, *Hitchcock: The First Forty-Four Films*, trans. by S. Hochman (Oxford: Roundhouse, 1992).

Schilson, A., 'The Major Theological Themes of Romano Guardini', in *Romano Guardini: Proclaiming the Sacred in a Modern World*, ed. by R.A. Krieg (Chicago: Liturgy Training Publications, 1995) 31–42.

Shadow of a Doubt, dir. By A. Hitchcock (Universal Pictures, 1943).

Spellbound, dir. By A. Hitchcock (United Artists, 1945).

Spoto, D., *The Dark Side of Genius: The Life of Alfred Hitchcock*, new edn. (London: Plexus, 1994).

Tolkien, J.R.R.,.'Leaf by Niggle', *The Dublin Review*, 216.432 (1945) 46–61.
— *The Letters of J. R. R. Tolkien: A Selection*, ed. by H. Carpenter with the assistance of C. Tolkien (Boston: Houghton Mifflin, 2000).
— 'Leaf by Niggle' in *Tree and Leaf: Including Mythopoeia and The Homecoming of Beorhtnoth,* (London: HarperCollins, 2001).
— *The Lord of the Rings,* (London: HarperCollins, 2002).

Truffaut, F., *Hitchcock*, ed. by H. Scott (London: Faber & Faber, 2017).

Vincent of Lérins, *The Commonitorium of Vincentius of Lerins*, ed. by R.S. Moxon (Cambridge: Cambridge University Press, 1915).

Williams, R., 'Enthronement Sermon', *Rowan Williams: 104th Archbishop of Canterbury*, 27 February 2003 <http://rowanwilliams.archbishopofcanterbury.org/articles.php/1624/enthronement-sermon.html> [Accessed 19 January 2024].

The tale of the Children of Húrin and the Fall of Men

Zoya Metlitskaya

Even those who are skeptical about J.R.R. Tolkien's books cannot deny that his legendarium impressed readers profoundly, and that it was not the short-lived effect produced by a bestseller. Many stories I have heard or read[1] might be summed up in one phrase: 'I read *The Lord of the Rings* and it changed my life'. Tom Shippey reported that four readers' polls commissioned in Britain at the end of the 1990s and addressed to very different groups of society produced the one and the same result. In the list of "five books you consider the greatest of the century" *The Lord of the Rings* took first place. One poll produced a different result: *The Lord of the Rings* came in second place, in first was the Bible (2000, xx-xxi). It seems that Tolkien perceived the impression his book made, though did not understand clearly why that was taking place. In the draft letter to Carole Batten-Phelps he wrote:

> Looking back on the wholly unexpected things that have followed its [*The Lord of the Rings*] publication [...] I feel as if an ever darkening sky over our present world had been suddenly pierced, the clouds rolled back, and an almost forgotten sunlight had poured down again. As if indeed the horns of Hope had been heard again [...] *But How?* and *Why?* (*Letters*, Letter 328, 412-3)

In my research, a small part of which is presented in this paper, I try to answer these questions which Tolkien posed. I attempt to hear what the 'horns of Hope' blowing in Arda proclaim, and to look more thoroughly at the brightest light poured down therefrom.

Tolkien's statements about his adherence to Catholicism give rise to the temptation to answer these questions in the simplest way: the light we are speaking of comes from the Christian religion. Many scholars scrutinized Tolkien's works looking for the Christian (Catholic) ideas and practices. Such an attitude surely makes sense. Though Tolkien insisted that the world of his legendarium is not Christian he himself often used Christian terms to describe his ideas about certain images or plots of his books.[2] But the circle of people who had seen the light from Arda and were profoundly affected by it is much broader than the Christian audience of Tolkien's books. Meanwhile attempts to present Arda as a pagan (in the usual meaning of the term) world[3] or to create a kind of new religion based on Tolkien's legendarium also does not seem to me convincing.

---

1. See, for example, the answers of readers of *Beyond Bree* about how they first discovered the works of J.R.R. Tolkien published in *Beyond Bree* in 2007. I also had a brief talk with William Fliss, who collected interviews on this topic, and he confirmed my opinion.
2. See, for example, Tolkien's letter to Milton Waldman (*Letters*, Letter 131, 146-7), and to Major R. Bowen (*Letters*, Letter 200, 259-60).
3. See, for example, the Tolkien Society publication *Tolkien the Pagan? Reading Middle-earth through a Spiritual Lens*, ed. by Anna Milon (Edinburgh: Luna Press Publishing, 2019).

An attentive reader cannot be unaware that in some key aspects (for example, the Cosmology) Arda theologically differs from the world that Christian teaching describes, as well as from the pagan world of classical or Germanic mythology. In my opinion, to reveal and analyze theological particularities of Arda is critically important if we want to more clearly understand this World and in the long run to answer the question I posed above.

The approach I am using in my work implies that the 'natural theology' of Arda reflected in the legendarium might and *should* be analyzed as a *complete* and *self-sufficient* system of historical facts and inner beliefs, without attempting to fill the gaps by references to Tolkien's personal religious ideas or those of the researcher (*Letters*, Letter 165, 220). In this paper I am going to illustrate this thesis by discussing one important question: the falling (or not falling) state of Man in Arda. But first I want to pose two questions, which, I hope, will be answered at the end of the discussion. The first of them touches upon Tolkien's idea of the three Great Tales of Men of Númenor, which were later remembered and handed on by the Dúnedain in Middle-earth. These are:

> (1) *Narn Beren ion Barahir* also called *Narn e-Tinúviel* (Tale of the Nightingale);
> (2) *Narn e-mbar Hador* containing
> (a) *Narn i-Chîn Húrin* (or *Narn e-'Rach Morgoth*, Tale of the Curse of Morgoth);
> (b) *Narn en-Êl* (or *Narn e-Dant Gondolin ar Orthad en-Êl*, [Tale of the Fall of Gondolin and the Rising of the Star]) (*Morgoth*, 373).

Surely, the first and the third of the Tales narrate the beginning and the conclusion of the story of the Rising of the Star, very important for the Dúnedain; they are also relevant to the genealogy and the history of the royal dynasty of Númenor and, later, the kings of Arnor and Gondor.[4] But what about the *Tale of the Children of Húrin*? It is surely one of the gravest tales in the history of Middle-earth, but is this the only reason for remembering it for many thousand years? I suppose that there must be something else in it, but we return to that matter later.

The second question is plainer and clearer. In the brief outline of the history of the First and Second Ages Tolkien describes the events in Númenor after Sauron's coming there as the *Second* Fall of Man:

> *The Downfall of Númenor*, the Second Fall of Man (or Man rehabilitated but still mortal), brings on the catastrophic end [...] *The Downfall* is partly the result of an inner weakness in Men – consequent, if you will, upon the first Fall (unrecorded in these tales), repented but not finally healed. (*Letters*, Letter 131, 154)

Really, this Fall might be called 'second' only if the 'first' was not actual in that time. Tolkien does not clarify what he means when speaking of "Man rehabilitated but still mortal". He obviously had some difficulties with the idea of the Fall of Man. Even

4. "But the son of Barahir was Beren One-hand, who won the love of Lúthien Thingol's daughter, and returned from the Dead; from them came Elwing the wife of Eärendil, and all the Kings of Númenor after" (*Silmarillion*, 178).

more dubious was his conception of the mortality of Men. Much has been written on the topic,[5] but I am not going to discuss the problem from this point of view here. The only thing I want to highlight is that Tolkien himself, as it seems, did not have a clear understanding of these issues.

Nevertheless, looking thoughtfully through Tolkien's texts one can discover that they contain not only the explanation of the Fall, but also the description of the Redemption. And the Redemption has nothing in common with Tolkien's idea of the 'Old Hope',[6] which he himself named elsewhere "the parody (inevitable) on Christianity" (*Morgoth*, 354).

So, the only detailed description of the Fall of Man is the *Tale of Adanel*, that remained unknown to the Eldar, but was put down in writing in Númenor in the later Second Age (344). In this tale the Fall is described so.

Morgoth deceived and frightened men, and then demanded from them the submission to him as their lord. And then as Adanel narrates:

> we spoke as he commanded saying: "*Thou art the Lord*"; Thee only we will serve. The Voice [really, the Voice of Eru] we abjure and will not hearken to it again. (347)

As a result of this deed, men cease to hear the Voice of Eru. Only once it spoke to them, saying:

> Ye have abjured Me, but ye remain Mine. I gave you life. Now it shall be shortened, and each of you in a little while shall come to Me,[7] to learn who is your Lord: the one ye worship, or I who made him. (347)

Thus, the event called the Fall of Man involved two key acts:

1) The change of allegiance from Eru to Morgoth, the Enemy. It is very well known that an oath of loyalty is a kind of ritual act that creates an indispensable (as one may say, partly mystical) connection between the person, who brings it forth and his lord. Oaths were treated in such a way in the Middle Ages, and in Middle-earth too.

2) Men ceased to hear the Voice of Eru. This needs additional explanation. It is worth noting that in the *Tale of Adanel* it was said that "the first Voice we never heard again" (347), not that "he ceased to speak with us". What really happened? What did the "abjuration" mean? It is told in the *Ósanwe-kenta* that every *fëa* (mind)[8] has absolute power to make the barrier of Unwill, and close itself from any other mind, however powerful it may be (*Ósanwe-kenta*, 23-4). The only exception is Eru, who can penetrate

5. For a detailed review of Tolkien's opinions on the topic and latter scholarship see article 'Mortality and immortality' in *The J.R.R. Tolkien Companion & Guide: Reader's Guide* (Scull and Hammond 2006, 604-11).

6. "They [people of the Old Hope] say that the One will himself enter into Arda, and heal Men and all the Marring from the beginning to the end" (*Morgoth*, 321).

7. It may also be concluded from this statement that life of men was shortened not to punish them for their abjuration but to reduce their sufferings in the dominion of Morgoth. But it is not of concern with our topic now.

8. Tolkien in *Ósanwe-kenta* used the word *sáma* because he spoke not only of Men and the Eldar, but also of Ainur, which have no *fëa* and *hröa*.

the barrier of Unwill, but for the sake of the Free Will of any *fëa* (as we may assume) almost never do that (*Ósanwe-kenta*, 30).

So, Adanel's statement that after the Fall Men ceased to hear the Voice, might mean that their *fëar* (i.e. *sámar* of the Incarnates) being aware and ashamed of their abjuration, did not perceive it. It is this case Adanel speaks of: not that Eru rejected Men, but they refused to hear Him.

Now we have to turn our attention to another well-known text, the part of *Narn i-Chîn Húrin* named *The words of Húrin and Morgoth.* It is worth outlining very briefly the sequence of events. Morgoth tried to daunt Húrin, but did not succeed. Then he cursed him, his wife Morwen and their offspring. But Húrin remained unbend. He continued debate with the Enemy and at last said:

> This last then I will say to you, thrall Morgoth […] and it comes not from the lore of the Eldar, but is put into my heart in this hour. *You are not the Lord of Men*, and shall not be, though all Arda and Menel fall in your dominion. (*CoH*, 65)

Húrin explicitly rejected Men's allegiance to Morgoth and so "unmade", *annulled the oath*, which from this time lost its force. Moreover, he declared that the words were "put into his heart". By whom? It seems unlikely that it was one of the Valar for two reasons. The first is that the Valar (with one significant exception)[9] at the time were not concerned with the affairs of Middle-earth. The second, even more essential, is that a Vala cannot penetrate the barrier of Unwill, posed by a Man, and it seems very unlikely that Húrin would have addressed somebody he knew not. It is much more likely that he, feeling unendurable fear and despair, in a last effort to withstand the tremendous power of the Enemy unconsciously communicated with the Voice he, hypothetically at least, knew. So, the second act of the Fall, the refusal of Men to hear the Voice, was annulled too. And it was really after these words that Morgoth (who, unlike Húrin, was well aware what had been done) "cursed Húrin again" – this time not for threat or for mocking, but in great wrath – "and set his power upon him" (*CoH*, 65). The incredible sufferings of Húrin, his wife, his children and everyone he meets during his wanderings was the result of his great deed. One may say that it was the *Redemption of the Fall*, performed not by God, but by men. So, from the time of Húrin Men have not fallen (as well as the Eldar), though fallible, due to genuine fallibility of all nature in Arda Marred. They may be served or deceived by the Enemy, but they hear the Voice and might (and must) make the right choice.

In the latter history of Middle-earth we can discover events and practices, which would be impossible, if Men were fallen, and did not hear the Voice. Firstly, we know that Ulmo spoke with Tuor and made him the tool for the fulfillment of his plans (*UT*, 22-3); it seems improbable that any of the Valar decided to communicate with the Men and sought the cooperation with one of them, if they did not communicate with Eru.

Then, we know that the people of Númenor could depart by their own will (*UT*, 235; *Letters*, Letter 156, 205; *RK*, 'Appendix A'); that hardly would have been possible if

9. As we know, Ulmo addressed Tuor, son of Huor, by inner thought, by signs and then in person, but it was in "the year twenty and three since the Nirnaeth" (*UT*, 22), that is *after* Húrin's heroic deed.

they did not hear the Voice. Moreover the kings of Númenor thrice in the year spoke to Eru from the summit of Meneltarma (*UT*, 174).

Now, in conclusion I want to return to the questions posed at the beginning of the paper. The answers, I hope, are obvious. The *Tale of the Children of Húrin* (along with the text known as the *Wanderings of Húrin*) was kept and handed on by the Dúnedain as one of the Great Tales because it narrates the critically important tale – the story of the Redemption of the Fall of Man.

The Downfall of Númenor, though it had been called (presumably by the Dúnedain) "the Second Fall of Man", was not the Fall in the strict sense, because it affected only the men of Númenor, and no other people, in whatever condition they might be.

Bibliography

Scull, C. and Hammond, W.G., *The J.R.R. Tolkien Companion & Guide: Reader's Guide,* (London: HarperCollins, 2006).

Shippey, T., *J.R.R. Tolkien: Author of the Century,* (London: HarperCollins, 2000).

Tolkien, J.R.R., *The Children of Húrin*, ed. by C Tolkien (London: HarperCollins, 2007).
— *The Letters of J.R.R. Tolkien*, ed. by H. Carpenter with the assistance of C. Tolkien (London: George Allen & Unwin, 1981).
— *The Lord of the Rings,* (London: George Allen & Unwin, 1983).
— *Morgoth's Ring*, ed. by C. Tolkien (London: HarperCollins, 1993).
— 'Ósanwe-kenta', ed. by C.F. Hostetter, *Vinyar Tengwar*, 39 (July 1998) 21-34.
— *The Silmarillion*, ed. by C. Tolkien (London: George Allen & Unwin, 1977).
— *Unfinished Tales of Númenor and Middle-earth*, ed. by C. Tolkien (London: George Allen & Unwin, 1980).

A Ray of Light: The Theological Vision of Letter 89

Guglielmo Spirito

"When he saw them he knew that he had always known them
and realized what part each one of them had played at many an hour in his life
when he had supposed himself alone, so that now he could say to them,
one by one, not 'Who *are* you?' but 'So it was you all the time'"
(Lewis 2008, 219)

1 – A ray of light through the very chinks of the universe

At the end of the year 1944, Christopher Tolkien was sent to South Africa to train as a pilot. His father began a series of long letters (numbering at least eighty) that were sent to his son by airmail. He was desperately worried about Christopher's safety (fatal crashes were common amongst trainee pilots) – "my heart is gnawed out with anxiety" – and freely admitted to spending much small, free time as he had writing not *The Lord of the Rings*, but writing letters to Christopher (*Letters*, Letter 89, 99).

Despite his anxiety over the war, Tolkien managed to send his son some words of hope. The uncertainties of the war encouraged Tolkien to focus on some key points that accordingly would offer to his troubled son inner stability and resilience in the face of his everyday challenges. This would include in particular a repeated invitation to *remember your Guardian Angel.*

In this paper's discussion of Tolkien's peculiar angelology I will focus in particular on Letter 89 To Christopher Tolkien, 7-8 November 1944), a letter "as notable for its sentiments of fatherly concern as for its creative theological speculation", as Jonathan S. McIntosh remarks (2017, 62). Letter 89 has in fact a peculiar quality and richness, which is related to the concrete circumstances of its writing, the uncovering of his own personal spiritual experience (which reveals a deep and perceptive inner world), the variety of threads (ancient and new, past and present) that are intertwined in a single design (with a certain suggestive overlap between the Primary world in which the author lives, and the Secondary world of the sub-creator who lives in him).

At the center of Letter 89 there is the mysterious presence of the Guardian Angel, which Tolkien evokes with the desire to comfort his son. Tolkien's fondness for, and interest in guardian angels had already emerged in another letter, sent earlier in the year, in which he again mentioned to Christopher the Guardian Angel, here described as a *bright point of power* – supporting us, as it were *from behind*, giving us the strength to face God freely for ourselves, like a spiritual umbilical cord or life-line.

The perception of the Angel as a *spiritual umbilical cord* (so that it gives us life, as in the womb) – or at least, to his being there, in the umbilical cord, a *bright point of power* – is original and powerfully expressive. An interesting element of this description is Tolkien's emphasis that he perceives a look of benevolence fixed on him, but at the same time he does not see the other Face (which the angel sees) behind him, which supports him at all times. It seems that in Letter 89 Tolkien is speaking not only of a 'notion and feeling' (for how accurate and truthful they were), it is rather the description of a lived experience, real, corroborated by a sort of delicate personal illumination ('*apperception*').

This seminal description of this experience is expanded in Letter 89, in which Tolkien offers a rich and original account of the discreet but powerful presence of the Guardian Angel. This is described by Tolkien as one small mote, suspended in the Light of God, and "glittering white because of the individual ray from the Light which both held and lit it [...] not a thing interposed between God and the creature, but God's very attention itself, personalized" (*Letters*, Letter 89, 99).

By personalized love, Tolkien stresses, he is not simply referring to a figure of speech, but rather as a real (finite) person. This is accordingly what gives him a great sense of joy and the realization that the shining poised mote was himself (or any other human person that he might think of with love): "I have with me now a definite awareness of you poised and shining in the Light" (99).

The phrasing used in this powerful description, with its emphasis on the suddenness and the great sense of joy, in the midst of the darkness, evokes that kind of refreshment and consolation for which Tolkien forged the neologism *eucatastrophe*,[1] which he describes in very similar terms in the final section of 'On Fairy-stories'.

The correlation between these two texts is confirmed by the synthetic description at the end of the letter. His momentous experience of his Guardian Angel was "a sudden glimpse of the truth behind the apparent *Anankê* of our world, but a glimpse that is actually a ray of light through the very chinks of the universe about us" (100). A sentence which closely recalls the final wording of 'On Fairy-stories'.[2] Tolkien's advice to Christopher to remember his Guardian Angel can be thus related to Tolkien's eucatastrophe-infused-certainty that his son is not alone in battle, a certainty in which father and son may feel reassured.

2 – The multiple roots and lifeblood of this wisdom

Here I will trace the possible origin of Tolkien's belief in the Guardian Angel, and the prominence given to them in his literary and personal experience, especially as expressed in the letters I have discussed above. In fact, his wide familiarity with the Classics, his great passion for the Nordic Sagas, and his deep personal spiritual convictions, rooted in the biblical-patristic and medieval heritage, flow together like a karst river, as it were, without dispersing any tributary of living water. This irrigated and nourished his imagination; shaping images; enhancing his resources of perception and vision. Because of this, we can take a look at some threads behind Letter 89 in particular, incorporated into Tolkien's inner world. Perhaps in this way we will be able to perceive the letter's suggestiveness and versatility of perspective.

I will briefly start my study of Tolkien's angelology with ancient Greece. Hermes is a liminal being that shifts between the everyday world of humanity and the realm of gods

1. cf. *OFS*, 119.
2. cf. *OFS*, 77.

ranging from *psychopomp* to messenger (*anghelos*). In this context, we may remember that in his last day at school at King Edward's School, Birmingham in 1911, Tolkien performed as Hermes in a production of Aristophanes' *Peace*.

In Plato's *Apology of Socrates*, Socrates claimed, referring to popular beliefs of this time, to have a *daimonion* (literally, a "divine something") that frequently warned him (in the form of a 'voice') against mistakes but never told him what to do. "It is impossible that two things only should be joined together without a third. There must be some bond in between both to bring them together" (*Timaeus* 31 b-c). The principle is not stated but assumed in the assertion of the *Symposium* that god does not meet man, they can only encounter one another indirectly: there must be some wire, medium, introducer, or bridge in between them.

On this point St. Thomas Aquinas, centuries later, quotes pseudo-Dionysius and confirms him: "the pattern whereby divine things reach us through the mediation of angels might be unbroken".[3] Thus the dazzling, celestial luminescence of the Trinity reverberates and bounces through the nine-rung angelical ladder (whose purpose was to channel illumination from the divine world to humanity) and reaches men through their Guardian Angels (the rank closest to humans).[4]

If we then pass from Late Antiquity to the Middle Ages, the intuitions are enriched and blended, integrating data also from other origins (Semitic and Nordic). *Angele Dei*, also known as the Prayer to one's Guardian Angel, was in the past attributed to St. Anselm (c1033-1109), for it appears in medieval collections of St. Anselm's works. However, it is clear that this prayer was added to Anselm's works sometime after his death. As best can be determined, this prayer is an interpolation of Reginald of Canterbury's (c 1109) Life of St. Malchus. The fifteenth-century poem "To the gud angell" comes from *Oxford, Balliol College* MS. 354. It is interesting that the poem does not actually use the phrase "Guardian Angel", although it is clearly the relationship envisaged: a single angel whose office is to guide and guard one particular individual. So the medieval name seems to have been also "good angel", as this poem's heading suggests – though the Middle English Dictionary also offers "familiar angel" as a medieval expression. Further, the Old Norse word for a Guardian Angel seems to be exactly the same as the word for a familiar spirit (in the pagan sense) – *fylgja*.

In this regard, it is legitimate to ask whether there was still 'an English Angel' in Tolkien's time. Through the centuries, despite the iconoclastic storm of the Reformation, the variegated richness of reflection and creative imagination on Angels reaches up to the Oxford movement, and particularly to John Henry Cardinal Newman.[5] The *Birmingham Oratory* was founded by Newman in 1848. As wards of Father Francis Morgan, Tolkien and his brother spent much of their time between 1904 and 1911 at the Oratory.[6] Probably a good part of his initial knowledge about Angels came through osmosis during these years.

Inklings members C.S. Lewis and Charles Williams were additionally fond of angels. Lewis's perspective is apparent in *The Discarded Image*, his scholarly work

3. qtd. in Lewis's *Discarded Image*, 73.
4. cf. Stanford 2019, 165; Muehlberger 2013, 205; Daniélou 2009, 96-8.
5. cf. Caldecott 2005, 78.
6. cf. Scull & Hammond 2006, 117-8.

on medieval and Renaissance literature. His preface to *The Screwtape Letters* reveals the seriousness with which he approaches the subject: it proposes that a mistaken view of angelic beings is more dangerous than ignorance of them. *The Space Trilogy* seeks to avert that danger. In it we are confronted by angelic *eldila* – inscrutable and luminous beings inhabiting deep space.[7] Lewis considered writing a *Companion Novel* to *The Screwtape Letters* from an Angel's perspective. At first, the concept of some new messages detailing "archangelical advice to the patient's guardian angel" delighted Lewis (Lewis 2008, 253). But his standards were too high and that project never took off. "Mere advice would be no good," Lewis lamented, "every sentence would have to smell of Heaven" (254).

We can also note that angels inspired the beginning of Tolkien's writing during the Great War. He was haunted by the single line from Crist: "*Éalá Éarendel engla Beorhtast / ofer middangeard monnum sended*" ("Hail Earendel, brightest of angels, / above the middle-earth sent unto men"). Tolkien said that on reading these lines he "felt a curious thrill, as if something had stirred in me, half wakened from sleep". Thus began his mythology.[8] Equally we find 'angels appearing in his later mythological work – we may remember that the *Istari* or Wizards were *angeloi*, *messengers*, emissaries from the Lords of the West, the "angelic powers" who rule Arda.[9]

As Tolkien wrote to Deborah Webster on 25 October 1958 "only one's Guardian Angel, or indeed God Himself, could unravel the real relationship between personal facts and an author's works" (*Letters*, Letter 213, 288). These examples of probable influences on Letter 89 demonstrate Tolkien's familiarity with Angels throughout his life. The realistic intuitions that great men and cultures of the past had about these mysterious beings converge in this refined theological text. Tolkien's deep reflection discretely reveals to us his personal degree of extraordinary spiritual maturity.

3 – Original traits of the guardian angel according to Tolkien

Tolkien's vision on the nature and role of angelic beings can be thus traced back to a number of sources, which directly or indirectly influenced his intellectual and spiritual development. And yet, there are some elements in his angelology which are peculiar and original, which I will briefly outline.

The emphasis on the individuality and personalization of the Guardian Angel, indeed described as "One small mote […] glittering white because of the individual ray from the Light which both held and lit it", and "God's very attention itself" (*Letters*, Letter 89, 101). According to Tolkien, God's personalized love takes the form of the guardian angel, a sort of twin of man, inseparable from him, the bright point of power where that life-line, that spiritual umbilical cord touches: there is our angel. Sergius Bulgakov words perfectly illustrate Tolkien's original views: μέτρον ἀνθρώπου, ὅ ἐστιν ἀγγέλου[10]

7. The name *eldila* probably comes from "The Eidola and the Angels" in *The Place of the Lion*, by Charles Williams, where he speaks about angels in Dionysius the Areopagite.
8. cf. Hammond and Scull 2006, 233-4.
9. cf. Letters 131, 153, 156, 200, 257, 320.
10. The Angel's measurement is Man's measurement.

(Rev. 21:17; Bulgakov 36).[11] This emphasis on the individuality of the Guardian Angel, intertwined with the individuality of the human, was quite original for Tolkien's time.

There is a second element in the letter which deserves attention, whose originality was clearly perceived by Tolkien and suggested his caution and wondering whether it was legitimate. His statement: "it is a finite parallel to the Infinite [...] as the love of the Father and Son (who are infinite and equal) is a Person (the Holy Spirit), so the love and attention of the Light to the Mote is a person (that is both with us and in Heaven): finite but divine: i.e. angelic" (101). Tolkien is here boldly suggesting that, analogically speaking, the relationship (the "attention") between the Creator and his human creature corresponds to the relationship between Father and Son within the Divinity: between God and man there is the Angel as a bond of love, while between the Father and the Son, there is the Holy Spirit who is the love that unites them both. This implies that in some mysterious way, the Guardian Angel fulfills a task, analogous to and derived from that of the Holy Spirit, being and acting as a luminous reflection of uncreated love in the created world.

The boldness, subtlety and theological solidity of the reflection reaches its highest point: a sort of ingenious exegesis of Mat. 18:10, in the light of Trinitarian relations, but without clear parallels in the history of Western angelology. Although there could be much more to say about the affinity between St. Bonaventure and Tolkien's thought regarding the relationship of the Holy Spirit with the Angels, I dare say not even St. Bonaventure nor St. Thomas (the culmination of philosophical and theological reflection on angels in the history of Western thought) had come to that point.

In conclusion, it must be recognized that Tolkien's intuition remains plainly original, undoubtedly audacious, and unheard of in the field of Philosophy and Theology. Yet it is transparently delimited within the canons of the best theological thought, without ambiguity, inaccuracies or heterodoxies of any kind. Fully traditional yet totally new. The Professor demonstrates that to grasp the piercing light of a disruptive, gentle and peaceful living intuition is to express it with creative boldness, humility and transparency.

Through Tolkien we know that, beyond borders and shadows, we are not alone: a ray of personal light, which is a real (finite) person, though invisible, accompanies us in every step and every moment. And (using the words that Gandalf once said to Frodo), we also "were meant to have it. And that may be an encouraging thought" (*FR*, 'A Long-expected Party', 2). "I wd. venture to say that he was – strictly– an 'ἄγγελος: that is, with the other *Istari*, wizards, 'those who know', an emissary from the Lords of the West", wrote Tolkien in a Letter to Fr. Robert Murray (*Letters*, Letter 156, 206). And this also may be an encouraging thought.

Bibliography

Anon., 'Rev. 21:17' in Douay-Rheims 1899 American Edition, BibleGateway.com. Available at: https://www.biblegateway.com/passage/?search=Revelation%2021&version=DRA

11. Anon. 'Rev. 21:17' in Douay-Rheims 1899 American Edition, BibleGateway.com. Available at: https://www.biblegateway.com/passage/?search=Revelation%2021&version=DRA.

Bulgakov, S., *Jacob's Ladder. On Angels,* (Cambridge: William B. Eermans Publishing Company, 2010).

Caldecott, S., *The Power of the Ring. The Spiritual Vision Behind the Lord of the Rings,* (New York: The Crossroad Publishing Company, 2005).

Daniélou, J., *The Angels & Their Mission,* (Manchester: Sophia Institute Press, 2009).

Lewis, C.S., *The Screwtape Letters,* (London: HarperCollins, 2008).

McIntosh, J.S., *The Flame Imperishable: Tolkien, St. Thomas, and the Metaphysics of Faërie,* (Kettering: Angelico Press, 2017).

Muehlberger, E., *Angels in Late Ancient Christianity,* (Oxford: Oxford University Press, 2013).

Scull, C. and W.G. Hammond, *The J.R.R. Tolkien Companion and Guide: Reader's Guide,* (London: HarperCollins, 2006).

Stanford, P., *Angels. A Visible and Invisible History,* (London: Hodder & Stoughton, 2019).

Tolkien, J.R.R., *The Letters of J.R.R Tolkien*, ed. by H. Carpenter with the assistance of C. Tolkien (New York: Houghton Mifflin Company, 2000).
— *Tolkien On Fairy-stories*, ed. by V. Flieger and D.A. Anderson, (London: HarperCollins, 2008).

Tolkien and Aquinas on Death

Claudio A. Testi

In this contribution I will propose a comparison between J.R.R. Tolkien and Thomas Aquinas on the problem of human death. This comparison is extremely important because death and immortality are fundamental themes in Tolkien's works[1] and the similarities and differences between Tolkien and Aquinas with regards to this problem better elucidates the complex relationship between Tolkien, his works, and Catholic religion. By focusing on these aspects, I will make my exposition as simple and clear as possible.[2]

1 – Death in Tolkien: Basic Concepts

Tolkien distinguishes two meanings of death:

1 – *Death as the severance of fëa and hröa* (*soul and body*): this kind of death affected both men and Elves, but for men it was inevitable, while for elves it was merely possible (for example, if an Elf was killed by a weapon).

> Elves are destined to know 'death' in their mode, being sent into a world which contains 'death', and having a form for which 'death' is possible. For though by their prime nature, unmarred, they rightly dwell as *spirit and body* coherent, yet these are two things, not the same, and *their severance* (*which is "death"*) is a possibility inherent in their union. (*Morgoth*, 244-5; emphasis mine)[3]

> '*death*' [is] *the severing of these two* [*fëa* and *hröa*]. (316-7)

2 – *Death as a departure from this living world, without redress*: this is inevitable for humans but impossible for Elves because, through reincarnation, they would usually return to this living world, or otherwise remain in the Halls of Mandos within the circle of the world.

> *There are two deaths: the one is a harm and a loss but not an end* [departure with return], *the other is an end without redress* [death as departure without return]: and the Quendi suffer only the first. (311; emphasis mine)

---

1. "The real theme for me is about something much more permanent and difficult: Death and Immortality" (*Letters*, Letter 186, 246).
2. For a more complex exposition, see Testi 2012a-2012b.
3. Further abbreviations:
- Athrabeth: Amanuensis typescripts of 'Athrabeth Finrod ah Andreth' (1959-1960);
- Commentary: 'Commentary to Athrabeth' (1959-1960);
- LawsA: 'Laws and Customs among the Eldar' (late 1950s);
- NOO: '*Notes on Óre*' (1968).

We will see that, for Tolkien and Aquinas, each kind of death could be qualified as:

a – *Natural or not natural*: death is natural if it occurs as a result of the internal and physical structure of the person who dies, otherwise it is not natural

b – *in conformity with, or contrary to, the design* of the Creator (Eru, God): death is in conformity with the design if it occurs because of the conditions originally surrounding a created person, otherwise it is contrary to the design.

Below, I will examine human death according to these distinctions, asking the same four questions (two for each kind of death) of Tolkien's legendarium and Aquinas:

- Question 1: Is death as severance natural?
- Question 2: Is death as severance in conformity with the design?
- Question 3: Is death as departure without redress natural?
- Question 4: Is death as departure without redress in conformity with the design?

2 – Death as severance

Question 1: Is death as severance natural?

Concerning the legendarium, the answer is yes, then no. In fact, up to 1958, death was seen as Eru's gift to humankind, so death was *natural* for them:

> The point of view of this mythology is that 'mortality' or a short span, and 'immortality' or an indefinite span was part of what we might call the biological and spiritual nature of the Children of God, Men and Elves (*Letters*, Letter 156, 204)

> Mortality, that is a short life-span having no relation to the life of Arda, is spoken of as the given nature of Men: the Elves called it the Gift of Ilúvatar (*Letters*, Letter 212, 285; emphasis mine)

Later in the *Athrabeth* this idea was judged by Andreth to be an Elvish error, so death as severance was considered *not natural* for humans:

> 'Yet, – asks Finrod – if we consider the briefness of life in all Middle-earth, must we not believe that your brevity is also *part of your nature*?'
> 'I think that *you err*, and all who think likewise,'- answers Andreth [...] '*Men are not by nature short-lived.*' (*Morgoth*, 308-9; emphasis mine)

> But the Elves were on their part generally ignorant of the persistent tradition among men,[4] that *Men were also by nature immortal*. (332; emphasis mine)[5]

4. In fact, in *Athrabeth*, Tolkien attributes to Elven traditions (known by Finrod) the idea of death as a gift to humanity (indeed, that death is tied to human nature), something that he supported until 1958-1960: I have further explained this theme in Testi 2012a.

5. The concepts expressed in *Athrabeth*, the apex of Tolkien's thought on the theme of death, will be reaffirmed, unchanged, in various successive writings, as attested to, for example, in the *Notes on Óre* of 1968 and in an interview given to the BBC that same year, where Tolkien, quoting Simone de Beauvoir, said that "there is no such thing such as a natural death" (see De Beauvoir 2001, 102; Vink 2004 and 2008; Lee 2018, 156).

In Aquinas, death as severance is *natural for humans* (as death was the gift of Ilúvatar in Tolkien up to 1958) because, following Aristotle's anthropology, soul and body (being the form and the matter of humans) are not necessarily linked, so severance is natural, and incorruptibility (here meaning immortality) is not by nature:

> *death of man is natural* (Aquinas, 1985, II-II q. 164 a. 1 co, 440; emphasis mine)[6]

> Now *this incorruptibility* [in the primitive and paradisiac state] was man's, *not by nature,* but by a supernatural gift of God. Therefore this might be attributed to God, and *not to human nature.* (I, q. 102, art. 4, 332; emphasis mine)

It is important to note that this position is explicitly accepted in official Catholic theology:

> *man's nature is mortal* (*Catechism of Catholic Church,* no. 1008; emphasis mine)

As a consequence the immortal nature of Man (as affirmed by Andreth) has been refuted by the Catholic Church, who explicitly *condemned* the following thesis:

> The *immortality* of the first man was not a benefit of grace, but a *natural condition* (Denzinger 1985, n. 1978/ 1078, 772; emphasis mine)

> 'regard *death no longer as a natural condition of man,* but truly as a just penalty for original guilt' since, [...] it insinuates that *death,* which in the present state has been inflicted as a just punishment for sin by the just withdrawal of immortality, *was not a natural condition of man,* as if immortality had not been a gratuitous gift, but a natural condition. (Denzinger 1985 n. 2617/1517, 924)

Question 2 – Is death as severance in conformity with the design?

In the legendarium, death as severance was considered *in conformity with the design* up to 1958, being Eru's gift inevitable for humans since their creation. Later death as severance was considered *contrary to the design,* in fact in the *Athrabeth* we find the new idea that if men had not followed Morgoth they would have been assumed as both soul and body by Eru out of this living world, so in this design *they would not have* suffered the severance of soul-body:

> Then basing his argument on the axiom that *severance of hröa and fëa is unnatural and contrary to design,* he [Finrod] comes (or if you like jumps) to the conclusion that the fëa of unfallen Man would have taken with it its hröa into the new mode of existence (free from Time) In other words, *that 'assumption' was the natural end of each human life,* though as far as we know it has been the end of the only 'unfallen' member of Mankind. (*Morgoth,* 333; emphasis mine)[7]

6. See also Aquinas 1992 ch. 10 lect. 4 n. 1425, 215. See also 1985, I-II q. 85 a. 5, 333; 1965a q.5 a. 5, 554; 1965b ch. 4 n. 500, 33; 2005 c. 5 lect.3 n. 416, 352. All references to Aquinas are structured by date, part, question, article, chapter.
7. Here Tolkien refers to the Virgin Mary (*Morgoth,* 357, n6) since, in letter 212, dated 1958, he states that "The Assumption of Mary, the only unfallen person, may be regarded as in some ways a simple regaining of unfallen grace and liberty" (286).

According to Aquinas, death as severance is *not in conformity* with the design because, in the original plan, God created man mortal by nature (see above) but also gave him the *gift of immortality* which, if it had not been lost (as happens as a result of the original sin), would have permitted human beings to *avoid* this severance:

> For man's body was indissoluble not by reason of any intrinsic vigor of immortality, but by reason of a supernatural force *given by God to the soul, whereby it was enabled to preserve the body from all corruption* so long as it remained itself subject to God. (Aquinas, 1985, I q. 97 art. 1, 285; emphasis mine)

This position is also accepted by the official Catholic theology:

> Adam and Eve, were constituted in an original 'state of holiness and justice'. This grace of original holiness was 'to share in [...] divine life'. By the radiance of this grace all dimensions of man's life were confirmed. *As long as he remained in the divine intimacy, man would not have to suffer or die.* (*Catechism of Catholic Church*, no. 375-6; emphasis mine)

> *Death was therefore contrary to the plans of God* the Creator and entered the world as a consequence of sin (*Catechism of Catholic Church*, no. 1008; emphasis mine)

In conclusion, concerning death as severance, we have discovered that Tolkien's legendarium never fits with official Catholic ideas which consider death as severance to be *natural and not in conformity* with the design, while in the legendarium it is considered natural and *in conformity* with the design (Elvish conception), or *not natural* and not in conformity with the design (Andreth's position).

3 – Death as departure without redress

Question 3: Is death as departure without redress natural?

Yes, at each stage of the evolution of Tolkien's mythology death as departure is natural, because the soul of man is at each stage intrinsically oriented out of this living world:

> It should be regarded as an Elvish perception of what *death — not being tied to the 'circles of the world'* – should now become for Men, however it arose. (*Letters*, Letter 212, 286; emphasis mine)

Both Aragorn (before 1958) and Andreth (later) affirm the same position:

> *We are not bound forever to the circles of the world*, and beyond them is more than memory. (*RK*, 'Appendix A', 1394; emphasis mine)

> Dying we *die*, and *we go out* to no return. (*Morgoth*, 311; emphasis mine)

This position fits with Aquinas. For him, in God's Design, if Adam and Eve had not sinned, they would not have known death as severance, because of the gift of immortality (see question 2) *and* the design which allowed humans to be transferred to Heaven with both soul and body (as happens in the original assumption which is understood through the *Athrabeth*, quoted above), so avoiding the severance between the two:

> God made man outside of paradise, and afterwards placed him there to live there during the whole of his animal life; and, having attained to the spiritual life, *to be transferred thence to heaven.* (Aquinas, 1985, I, q. 102, art. 4, 332; emphasis mine)

Question 4: Is death as departure without redress in conformity with the design?

In the legendarium death as departure *is in conformity* with the design because this is the mode in which Eru created humans, Arda and Eä. In fact, if death is a gift, then human departure happens by necessity, in conformity with the design. But this would also happen from Andreth's perspective; in fact, as we have seen, it is explained that, if man had not followed Morgoth, he would have been assumed as being out of the circle of the world.

For Aquinas also, death as departure is *in conformity with* the design. In fact, from a Christian perspective, the problem is: if Adam had not sinned, would he have lived forever in Earthly Paradise? Aquinas' answer, as we have seen, is no because he would have been transferred to Heaven with soul and body (as Finrod and Andreth surmised), so his departure is in conformity with the design of the Creator.

4 – Tolkien and his knowledge of Catholic ideas of death as severance

I would like to complete this exposition with a final question: was Tolkien aware of the true Catholic position regarding death as severance? The answer lies in this text dated 1958:

> This [death as the *Gift of Ilúvatar*] is therefore an 'Elvish' view, and does not necessarily have anything to say for or against such beliefs as the *Christian that 'death' is not part of human nature*, but a punishment for sin (rebellion), a result of the 'Fall'. (*Letters*, Letter 212, 285-6; emphasis mine)

As we can see, Tolkien erroneously thought that, in Christian belief, death as severance was not part of human nature (see 2, Question 1 and correctly thought that it occurs as a result of the 'Fall' (so death as severance is not in conformity with the design). This means that Tolkien *erroneously thought* that Andreth's position on death as severance fits perfectly with Christian and Catholic ideas.[8]

---

8. It must be said that this separation keeps Tolkien in a certain ambiguity, in the sense that not always does he make a clear distinction between *separation as an act* in which spirit and body tear away and separation as a state in which the *fëa* lives far away from its *hröa*. This ambiguity may be found also inside the *Athrabeth* where he talks about, without distinguishing between them apparently, «*serving*» (separation-act *Morgoth*, 316-7, 308-9 and «*severance*» meant as state (*Morgoth*, 333). From the examined Tolkien texts it is, however, very clear that both are not natural, whereas according to Aquinas and Catholic theology the first one is 'natural' and the second one 'unnatural' (such that there is the dogma of the resurrection of the body; see also 1985, I. q. 89 art.1, 137: "but [for the soul] to be separated from the body is not in accordance with its nature").

Concerning death as departure, I have no cause to doubt Tolkien was aware that, from a Christian perspective, humans have been destined for paradise ever since their origins.

5 – Conclusion

The contents of this analysis can be summed up with the below table:

Tolkien, Aquinas and Death in Men	In the legendarium		In Aquinas and Catholic theology	From a Christian perspective according to Tolkien
	Up to 1958 (Elvish tradition)	Later (Andreth's position)		
1: Is death as severance natural?	Y	N	Y	N
2: Is death as severance in conformity with the design?	Y	N	N	N
3: Is death as departure without redress natural?	Y	Y	Y	Y
4: Is death as departure without redress in conformity with the design?	Y	Y	Y	Y

The table demonstrates that with regards to human death as departure, Tolkien's legendarium and his knowledge of Catholic Theology completely fits with the ideas of Aquinas and Catholicism (rows 3 and 4).

However, where human death as a severance of soul-body is concerned the Elvish tradition of death as a gift and Andreth's ideas contradict this Elvish tradition, Aquinas's, and Catholic theology (see row 1 column 2). Tolkien seems to have had erroneous ideas about the Catholic position about death as severance as natural (see row 1, column 4).

Each tradition within the legendarium, however, does share some elements with the Aquinas (and Catholic views): Elvish tradition agreed with Aquinas with regards to death-severance as being natural for humans (row 1, column 1); Andreth's ideas agreed in relation to death-severance conforming with the design (row 2, column 2).

This is further proof that Tolkien's legendarium exists in a Pagan universe (because at every stage it never completely fits with Christian ideas). It is, however, in harmony with Christian Revelation because each tradition (Elvish and Andreth's one) shares 3/4 of the answers with Catholic theology and appears as a smaller part of a wider truth (see Testi 2018).

Bibliography

Aquinas, T., *De Malo*, II, Quaestiones Disputatae (Turin, Marietti, 1965a).
— *Expositio Super Job ad litteram*, ed. by Leonina (Rome: Sanctae Sabina, 1965b).
— *Somma Teologica*, (Bologna: Edizioni Studio Domenicano, 1985), Available at: http://www.documentacatholicaomnia.eu/03d/1225-1274,_Thomas_Aquinas,_Summa_Theologiae_%5B1%5D,_EN.pdf [Accessed 19 January 2024]
— *Commento al Vangelo di S. Giovanni VI-XII,* (Rome: Città Nuova, 1992).
— *Commento all'Epistola al Corpus Pulinim: Lettera ai Romani,* (Bologna: Edizioni Studio Domenicano, 2005)

'Catechism of the Catholic Church', *Vatican Website* (Vatican City: Vatican Publishing, 1993) <https://www.vatican.va/archive/ ENG0015/_INDEX.HTM> [Accessed 19 January 2024].

De Beauvoir, S., *Una morte dolcissima,* (Turin: Einaudi, 2001).

Denzinger, H., *Enchiridion Symbolorum,* (Bologna: EDB, 1985). <English version: http://patristica.net/denzinger/> [Accessed 1 August 2019]

Lee S.D., 'Tolkien in Oxford" (BBC, 1968): A reconstruction', *Tolkien Studies*, 15 (2018) 115-176.

Testi C.A., 'Tolkien's Legendarium as a *meditatio mortis*', in *The Broken Scythe. Death and Immortality in the Works of J.R.R.Tolkien*, ed. by R. Arduini and C.A. Testi (Zurich and Jena: Walking Tree Publishers, 2012a) 39-68.
— 'Logic and Theology in Tolkien's Thanatology', in *The Broken Scythe. Death and Immortality in the Works of J.R.R.Tolkien*, ed. by R. Arduini and C.A. Testi (Zurich and Jena: Walking Tree Publishers, 2012b) 175-192.
— *Pagan Saints in Middle-earth,* (Zurich-Jena: Walking Tree Publishers, 2018).
— 'Tolkien and Aquinas', in *Tolkien and the Classics*, ed. by R. Arduini, G. Canzonieri, and C.A. Testi (Zurich-Jena: Walking Tree Publishers, 2019) 57-72.

Tolkien J.R.R., *The Letters of J.R.R. Tolkien*, ed. by H. Carpenter with the assistance of C. Tolkien (London: George Allen & Unwin, 1981)
— *Morgoth's Ring*, ed. by C. Tolkien (London: HarperCollins, 1993)
— *The Lord of the Rings,* (London: HarperCollins, 2014)
— 'Notes on Óre', *Vinyar Tenwar*, 41 (July 2000) 11-19.

Vink, R., 'The Wise Woman's Gospel', *Lembas Extra,* (2004) 15-40.
— 'Immortality and the Death of Love: J.R.R. Tolkien and Simone de Beauvoir', in *Tolkien 2005. The Ring Goes Ever On. Proceedings*, ed. by S. Wells (Coventry: The Tolkien Society, 2008) 117-127.

A Journey through Workhouse Infirmary and Niggle's Parish. Problems with a Tolkienian Eschatology in *Leaf by Niggle*

Christian Trenk

"[I]t conveys a sudden sense of endless *untold* stories: mountains seen far away, never to be climbed, distant trees (like Niggle's) never to be approached – or if so only to become 'near trees' (unless in Paradise or N's Parish)" (*Letters*, Letter 96, 110f; emphasis original), Professor Tolkien wrote to his son Christopher in early 1945, using his short story *Leaf by Niggle* to illustrate the wonder of untold stories.

Tolkien's *Leaf by Niggle* is a story about a painter who neglects and forgets his other duties in life in favour of attempting to finish an ever-growing painting of a tree. When Niggle is finally called on a long-expected and dreaded journey, he leaves behind too many unfinished tasks, including the painted tree, and is taken to a Workhouse Infirmary where he undergoes a painful but ultimately healthy reform. He is judged fit to be dismissed from the workhouse and moves on to a pleasant green country where he is reunited not only with his old neighbour, who was a constant distraction back home, but also with a completed version of his painted tree that has come to life as a real tree. He and his neighbour tend the tree and countryside together for a while before Niggle embarks on another journey towards the mountains in the distance.

Leaf by Niggle is what the author himself calls a "purgatorial" story about a painter whose life's work comes to completion beyond all hope (*Letters*, Letter 153, 195). The Christian theology of purgatory and paradise, death and existence beyond, is called 'eschatology' from the Greek τα ἔσχατα, 'the last things'. An eschatological reading of *Leaf by Niggle* is neither a necessary, nor the only possible way to interpret this story, but Tolkien's own way of referring to and using the story makes it a plausible interpretation.

If Tolkien attributed eschatological significance to his story, it is then reasonable to assume that it expresses some of Tolkien's very own thoughts on what comes after death, from which we can gain glimpses into a Tolkienian Eschatology. This paper will point out some key characteristics of this eschatology as presented in *Leaf by Niggle*, and highlight some of those by briefly comparing them to examples of current Catholic doctrine as expressed in the *Catechism of the Catholic Church*. This comparison will unsurprisingly show similarities but also draw attention to where full compatibility seems impossible. Some obstacles to a seamless eschatological reading according to Catholic theology will be discussed in greater detail. Whether Tolkien ever intended his ideas to be compatible with Catholic teaching is in this context less relevant than the observation that these obstacles and problems exist.

A complete picture of Tolkien's eschatological worldview could only be attained by looking at the whole body of his writings – published and unpublished – and even such a picture would be inconclusive at times. The narrower focus, necessitated by the shortness of this paper, instead allows a more detailed look at some of the characteristics and problems of an eschatology in *Leaf by Niggle*. This paper will therefore have a much narrower focus than the more comprehensive observations by Thomas Fornet-Ponse in his paper on Tolkien's theology of death (Fornet-Ponse 2005), and also be able to delve deeper than that paper into some of the finer points of a Tolkienian Eschatology in *Leaf by Niggle*.

A brief exploration of why the story can be called autobiographical and eschatological will be followed by a retelling of its important elements and relevant details. The ensuing analysis will focus on three key locations from the story respectively, and raise questions about the compatibility with Catholic doctrine because of the chronological order and some defining characteristics of the different stages.

Why then is the story called autobiographical and eschatological? In his letters, Tolkien often alluded to the story, which he uncharacteristically wrote to near completion in one sitting, in a way that beautifully illustrates how well it corresponded to his own situation. Despite his insistence that none of the "biographical terms (so obsessively interesting to modern critics [...]) really illuminates 'Leaf by Niggle' much" (*Letters*, Letter 241, 321f.), what preoccupied him at the time of writing does indeed seem to offer a clue to what the story could have meant to Tolkien – and squares with how he referred to it later.

When Tolkien wrote *Leaf by Niggle* in the late 1930ies, he was also diverting time from his duties as an Oxford professor to work on the sequel to his recently published *The Hobbit* (*TL*, vi). *Or There and Back Again*. In later letters, he repeatedly used the image of a tree to describe his own work, calling *The Lord of the Rings* "my own internal tree [...] growing out of hand, and revealing endless new vistas" (*Letters*, Letter 241, 321), as well as referring to other stories he could have written as "mere budding leaves like so many of silly Niggle's" (*Letters*, Letter 98, 113). He also confessed: "Like Niggle I want a 'public pension', and am equally unlikely to get one" (114). Just like Niggle, he was labouring tirelessly to complete an ever-growing work of art, and just like Niggle, the constant distractions of daily life seemingly kept him from finishing it. These examples show: the parallels between his own and Niggle's situation are apparent, and Tolkien was aware of them, using the story of Niggle to illustrate his own predicaments.

He does, however, also use the story to illustrate thoughts that are concerned with things beyond his immediate circumstances: He calls *Leaf by Niggle* a "purgatorial" (*Letters*, Letter 153, 195) story, as mentioned before, and uses it to allude to some kind of paradise (*Letters*, Letter 96, 111). A closer look at the story itself will show how easy it is to draw parallels between the story's stages and widespread ideas on death and life thereafter. It seems helpful therefore to recapitulate some of the story's key elements before then exploring their possible eschatological significance.

In the story's opening sentence, even before learning that Niggle was a painter, the reader is told that he was a man "who had a long journey to make" and that he "knew he would have to start sometime'" on that journey even though he "did not want to go"(*TL*, 9). When the time had finally come to start the journey, the departure came unexpected (20f.) with Niggle being "not even finished" (21) with his painting or his preparations. He had to go nonetheless and could only manage to grab "a paint-box and a small book of his own sketches" (21): a fitting summary for what had kept him occupied all along instead of packing.

He was then – without retaining even these meagre belongings – shuttled to a Workhouse Infirmary for extensive treatment, work and "to do some thinking" (22). Slowly forgetting what had occupied his time before the journey (23), he eventually "began to have a feeling of – well satisfaction [... and] was quieter inside" (24) and even "took it fairly well" (24) when his whole routine was forcibly changed. Niggle was then finally put before a Court of Inquiry where two voices adjudicated his case by contemplating "the Records" (26) which revealed "the time he wasted, not even amusing himself" (25) but also his "genuine sacrifice" (27) to help his neighbour, Mr. Parish. After enquiring about Parish, Niggle was sent "on to the next stage" (29) by the two voices' joint judgement.

Niggle then came to a place where he was reacquainted with his past: he rode "his bicycle" (30) towards what he eventually understood to be "his Tree, finished. If you could say that of a Tree that was alive" (31) and he recognized it all as "a gift" (31) for him to now continue working on (33). For this continuation though, he soon realized that "I need help and advice: I ought to have got it sooner" (34), and also that it had all "been produced in collaboration with Mr Parish" (32) who at this moment arrived to join Niggle's efforts at continuation.

When their work was almost complete, and they went for a walk through the country, they met a shepherd (37) who led Niggle away into another country, towards the Mountains in the distance (39). Parish, recognizing the Tree as Niggle's only at the moment the latter was about to leave, set out to further continue the work with his wife whose arrival seemed imminent (37f.). The tale ends with a jump to the Two Voices from the Court of Inquiry reminiscing about how useful Niggle's Parish is proving "[a]s a holiday, and a refreshment. It is splendid for convalescence; and not only for that, for many it is the best introduction to the Mountains" (42).

This summary – invariably a gross simplification – leaves us with different stages of the story to be analysed in greater detail. The story takes place in three locations or areas: Niggle's home country, the Workhouse Infirmary next to the station, and finally the region which will become known as Niggle's Parish. A fourth place, one which the story never reaches though, are the Mountains. The four locations can be – and often are – seen to correspond with different stages of death and life thereafter, which will form the basis of the following considerations. The limits of such a straightforward equation will become apparent straight away.

The least contentious interpretation seems to be the identification of Niggle's departure with the act of dying itself. Niggle's home is then life before dying, and Tolkien's representation of death leads to a twofold observation: Firstly, dying is – and although this might seem trivial at first glance, it certainly is not – an unavoidable part of human existence and its inevitability is known to everyone. Niggle, from the outset, is characterized as someone who has a journey to make – even before being identified as a painter: someone who has to die, and he and everyone else know the fact, just as everyone in our Primary World knows that they will have to die eventually. It is his status as someone expecting a journey that defines him more than the occupation which gains him his (limited) fame.

Secondly, it is usually[1] not up to humans to choose their own time or circumstances of death. Death often comes as a surprise or shock, especially to those who have not taken the time and effort to prepare themselves for it, just as Niggle finds himself being whisked away at just the moment when he is about to put in a final effort to complete his picture (19). Death is inevitable and its precise circumstances are beyond one's control, *Leaf by Niggle* reminds the reader: another seemingly obvious but nonetheless crucial observation.

The centrality of death as an integral part of human existence in Tolkien's writings has been compared by Thomas Fornet-Ponse to the centrality of death in the teachings of Karl Rahner (Fornet-Ponse 2005, 183f.). The Jesuit professor can serve as a point of comparison "not only because he played a key role in reenvisioning Roman Catholic eschatology, but also because most, though by no means all, of his theories and suggestions, albeit controversial when first proposed, have now been widely accepted, and in this sense they may be regarded as representative of contemporary Catholic eschatology" (Phan 2008, 225). In Tolkien's case as well as in Rahner's, human existence is best understood as a temporal reality in this realm which gains its meaning and importance through being oriented towards life in the other realm.[2] As it is, the centrality of death in *Leaf by Niggle* as the first thing we learn about the protagonist serves as a powerful Tolkienian statement to underline the centrality of death and life thereafter for everyone's existence.

Moving beyond the departure from his home country, as Niggle did, the story reaches the Workhouse Infirmary with its Court of Inquiry. The Workhouse Infirmary is ultimately a place of healing and preparation but is not without its toils and hardships. Niggle slowly lets go of what kept him occupied in life, seemingly being stripped of even the little he took from his home in the first place, when he "left his little bag behind" on the train (*TL*, 22).

He is given time, forced even, to contemplate his life when ordered to "do some thinking" (22). And he is taught to abandon his bad habits, he is taught to concentrate on the task at hand during his work shifts. He becomes more balanced and calm in the process but also becomes resigned to his fate. He seems to relinquish all care for his own interests.

He is then finally judged by the Two Voices, one severe, the other "gentle, though it was not soft" (25). They do not seem to judge him primarily on the progress he has made in the Workhouse Infirmary but instead undertake an honest appraisal of his life records with all its wasted time, taking into account Niggle's motivations and sacrifices (26f.).

The Second Voice is not making excuses for him, merely pointing out redeeming features just as the First Voice is not sadistically looking for reasons to condemn him. Remarkably, the alternative to being sent on towards the Tree is not to be condemned to some other place but merely to "stay some time yet," which would "not do him any harm,

1. The question of self-determined death cannot be considered in the context of these brief considerations. The case of Denethor in *The Lord of the Rings*, and especially Gandalf's judgement of him, might offer a glimpse into Professor Tolkien's thoughts on the matter.
2. The similarities become even more striking when considering the *legendarium* and Tolkien's idea of the 'gift of Illuvatar' which does however go beyond the scope of this paper.

perhaps" (26). The decision is ultimately that of the Second Voice, the reader learns – "you have the last word" – but is eventually taken with the First Voice's approval (27).

Tolkien presents a stage after death which offers room for painful reflection and correction, at the end of which an unremittingly honest yet fair appraisal of a person's whole life and desires judges the patient fit to move on.

Parallels to the idea of Purgatory as a cleansing state before Paradise are not far-fetched. At first glance there are many similarities to the teaching of such a preparatory place of "self-integration and self-transformation required by a person's sins themselves, which fracture the unity of his or her personality" (Phan 2008, 223) where "whatever impurities you suffer are removed" (*Catechism of the Catholic Church*, no. 1022). However, an important Catholic prerequisite for entering purgatory is absent – or misplaced? – in Niggle's story:

The Catholic Church asserts a judgement of the "immortal soul at the very moment of death" (no. 1022) which will lead to damnation or salvation. Purgatory, according to this teaching, is not at all a punishment or limbo-state before judgement, but a place for cleansing and preparation after being judged fit for Paradise. Purgatory is supposed to be the first step onwards into Paradise – as it is for Niggle – but, importantly, the first step *after* the initial judgement of worthiness.

The weighing of Niggle's life, as it happens at the Court of Inquiry, should have taken place before his entry into the Workhouse according to Catholic doctrine. There is plenty of judgement passed on Niggle before he arrives in the Infirmary: The Inspector (*TL*, 19-21), the Driver (21), and certainly the Porter (22) all judge Niggle on the state of his affairs and preparations, but they do not pass a formal sentence. No deliberated and fair verdict that weighs all the evidence is reached before Niggle is taken to the Workhouse Infirmary. That multi-faceted judgement is reserved for the Court of Inquiry, which in turn does not explicitly fall back on any of the previous judgements even though it judges Niggle primarily based on his life's merits instead of his progress within the Infirmary. If the Infirmary is understood to be purgatory, elements of Tolkien's depiction of Purgatory seem to be at odds with the 'proper order of things' according to Church doctrine insofar as linear time can be considered relevant in an afterlife.

Keeping in mind the observed discrepancies, one can nonetheless point towards the compatibilities between *Leaf*'s ideas and Catholic teaching: The personal judgement is one of clement but honest appraisal, and the cleansing place is a place where the acquired imperfections are painfully de-learned and the groundwork for a fulfilling life in Paradise is laid. This fits well with current Catholic theological ideas on purgatory (*Catechism of the Catholic Church*, nos. 1030-32). The main issue preventing a straightforward equation of the Workhouse Infirmary and purgatory is the order of events.

Niggle is sent on from this reformative stage to a reunion with aspects of his former life in the green country which will later become known as Niggle's Parish. The first reunion occurs right at the platform: Niggle is reunited with "his bike" – his bike, not just any bike, Tolkien writes, and he puts special emphasis on that meaning by continuing "at least it looked like his" (30). Niggle experiences a second reunion when he suddenly recognizes ahead of him "the Tree, his Tree, finished'" (31). Once again, the object is clearly identified as having a relation to him by the possessive pronoun in an additional clause. And yet, even more explicitly stated this time, it is not wholly the same but changed: "finished" (31). A similar pattern emerges regarding Niggle's reunion with his former neighbour Parish: It clearly seems to be Parish, and yet things have changed: the limp has lessened, they understand each other silently, and their skills and interests seem slightly altered (34f.).

In fact, they, as well as the Tree, are not just changed, they seem made whole. Parish eventually even "lost his limp" (36). And as Parish's leg is healed, so is Niggle's strained relationship with Parish: Whereas his neighbour had often seemed an annoyance in life, he is now recognized as a vital part of what – through their combined efforts – will become Niggle's Parish. And yet again, the strained relationship of the past has not been merely wiped away. Instead, Niggle realizes how that relationship had all the while shaped his Tree, so that he can acknowledge: "Some of the most beautiful [... parts had] been produced in collaboration with Mr Parish" (32).

As the tree has been completed and made whole, as Parish's leg has been made whole again, so has Niggle and his relationship with Parish been finally completed, made whole, 'finished.' Tolkien presents us with a vision of a place where this world's realities are being freed from the shackles of imperfection and set free, so to speak, to become what they were always meant to be. Set free, though, to then interact with other improved realities to form yet another reality beyond what had previously seemed possible.

The result of this, of Niggle and his talents, Parish and his talents and their interrelationship is what will be revealed in the end as Niggle's Parish. Niggle's Parish truly is a place where life in all its imperfections has been transformed; it is also a place, where life in all its splendour has been preserved. And it has, by the end of the story, become a place where life has been elevated to something beyond all previous imagination: a gateway to the Mountains.

At first glance, Niggle's Parish might seem comparable to Paradise, where humans "retain, or rather find, their true identity, their own name" (*Catechism of the Catholic Church*, no. 1025), a place, which the "anthropocentric view sees [...] as very much like an idealized of life as we presently know it. The focus is on family reunions, human relationships, and the full range of activities that make this life interesting and meaningful"(Walls 2008, 402). Tolkien himself might be seen to equate the two, when he writes of "Paradise or N's Parish" in one of his letters (*Letters*, Letter 96, 111). However, the "or" is not necessarily equating them ("Paradise, or in other words Niggle's Parish") but could rather be meant to introduce Niggle's Parish as a second option for approaching the distant trees that Tolkien writes about in this context ("either Paradise or Niggle's Parish").

Equating the lands surrounding the Tree with Paradise also overlooks another major problem with regards to the compatibility with Catholic doctrine: the Mountains. Paradise is usually understood as the final destination of the saved souls in afterlife, yet Niggle's Parish clearly serves as a mere staging post for a further destination. There is the Catholic doctrine of a day of Final Judgement for all creation that comes at the end of times (*Catechism of the Catholic Church*, nos. 1038-41) but one could hardly argue that what little Tolkien lets us know of the Mountains can be reconciled with this particular doctrine. The staggered departure by Niggle and Parish, as well as the on-going arrival of even more people to the region seem to be at odds with the idea of one final common step further for all of creation. Once again, the order of events seems to pose a problem.

One could of course question the importance of time and the validity of linear time in particular for a world *post mortem* – as one could also have done regarding the timing of the judgement earlier on. Discrepancies remain nonetheless: The extensive character development in Niggle and certainly in Parish (who expects the same of his wife) while in the region clearly attests to the provisional quality of the place. No one arrives in Niggle's Parish as a perfect being; they still need to learn and de-learn essential qualities. Niggle's Parish is essentially a place of development, it is at its core a place of further preparation for the Mountains.

In light of these observations, it seems indeed more fitting to speak of the Mountains as Paradise – glimpsed only from afar in *Leaf by Niggle* – and of Niggle's Parish as another purgatory. This approach seems compatible with Tolkien's own implicitly expressed ideas as well, since he called the story purgatorial, not paradisiacal. If agreeing to this interpretation, *Leaf by Niggle* presents to us two functions of purgatory: de-learning properties and habits that hinder our progress towards a wholesome life, as well as re-learning qualities that further it.

In this reading, some insights into the state of being we hope for in Paradise are still to be gained. The story expresses them by showing the necessary preparations and hinting at the final 'product' that will enter Paradise: one which has been transformed and yet preserved – its weaknesses annulled, its strengths preserved and its whole existence elevated to heights unforeseen. This would seem reconcilable with current Catholic doctrine and theology. More importantly though, it might be perceived by many as a consoling vision of an existence after death in which our distinctive qualities (and quirks) retain some importance; a moving vision of paradise, and, as Tolkien remarked just before the quote which stood at the beginning of this paper: "it is the untold stories that are most moving" (*Letters*, Letter 96, 110).

Such a reading is not without its difficulties for the compatibility with Catholic teaching either though: It devalues the importance of the Court of Inquiry, relegating it to a mere judgement of the patient's readiness for another step. This interpretation seems to be at odds with the arguments we hear the Court make: the two voices debate the merits of Niggle's life, its shortcomings and successes rather than just the progress he has made in the Workhouse. While the Court does judge the readiness to move on, it does so by taking great care to weigh the life before the Workhouse: It seems to be more than just an appraisal of readiness. The Court of Inquiry with its placement on the one hand, and its seeming importance on the other therefore appears as the largest obstacle to fully reconciling Tolkien's eschatological vision in *Leaf by Niggle* with Catholic doctrine. What the Court says seems more in line with Catholic teaching of particular judgement at the time of death, the point in time when the Court happens seems incompatible with that teaching. What happens in the Workhouse Infirmary seems compatible with Catholic teaching of purgatory, as does what happens in Niggle's Parish.

In the end, the matter must be left open to the reader's interpretation. A definitive answer which stage represents what and what importance the Court has is not possible – neither is it necessary. *Leaf by Niggle* may be an allegorical story with autobiographical and eschatological elements, but whosoever tries to postulate a strictly symbolic eschatological reading would have to explain who or what is signified by such puzzling characters as the Inspector, the Driver, the Porter, the officials and attendants and the severe doctor in the Workhouse Infirmary, and the shepherd – no capital letters for some of them, it should be noted – (*TL*, 22, 37f.) or, for instance, the mysterious tonic Niggle and Parish are given (29, 36). The story is not an enigma to be 'solved' completely, it is not a riddle with only one answer like those exchanged by Bilbo and Gollum.

Tolkien's aim was not to write a concise and conclusive treatise on eschatology; therefore, his story must not be subjected to the same theological scrutiny that academic theologians must expect. His story does seem to offer glimpses of Tolkien's hope for an afterlife though which would merit further reflection and even closer inspection. These glimpses echo elements of Catholic eschatology which will come as no surprise given Tolkien's well-documented religious beliefs and background. It would be absurd to propose that Tolkien was trying to make his story compatible with the 1992 Catechism of the Catholic Church (or other magisterial documents from that decade). And while any discussion on the author's intended compatibility with today's Catholicism is therefore moot, the comparison does hint at the spiritual value an eschatological reading of *Leaf by Niggle* might have to today's Catholics and other Christians, as well as all those who might be inclined to accept it as such – but also its limitations.

In the end, it is Niggle's own words, used "quite literally'" (*TL*, 31), that best describe the curious little story: "It's a gift!" (31). And all we have to decide is what to do with the gift that is given us (*FR*, 'The Shadow of the Past', 51).

Bibliography

Anon., *Catechism of the Catholic Church,* (Vatican City: Libreria Editrice Vaticana, 1997).

Fornet-Ponse, T., 'Tolkiens Theologie des Todes', in *Hither Shore*, 2 (2005) 157-186.

Griffiths, P. J., 'Purgatory', in *The Oxford Handbook of Eschatology*, ed. by J.L. Walls (Oxford: Oxford University Press, 2008) 427-445.

Phan, P.C., 'Roman Catholic Theology', in *The Oxford Handbook of Eschatology*, ed. by J.L. Walls (Oxford: Oxford University Press, 2008) 215-232.

Tolkien, C., 'Preface', in *Tree and Leaf,* by J.R.R. Tolkien (London: HarperCollinsPublishers, 2001) v-ix.

Tolkien, J.R.R., *The Letters of J.R.R. Tolkien*, ed. by H. Carpenter with the assistance of C. Tolkien (London: HarperCollinsPublishers, 2006).
— *The Lord of the Rings,* (London: HarperCollinsPublishers, 2007).
— *Leaf by Niggle,* (London: HarperCollinsPublishers, 2016).

Walls, J.L., 'Heaven', in Walls, Jerry L. (ed), in *The Oxford Handbook of Eschatology*, ed. by J.L. Walls (Oxford: Oxford University Press, 2008) 399-412.

Tolkien's War Gods: Studying Tolkien's View of War through the Characterization of Makar and Tulkas

Charlie Trimm

As might be expected for someone who fought in World War One, war played a dominant role in Tolkien's writings. Since my research area in my day job as an Old Testament scholar is warfare, I have become interested not only in how Tolkien portrays the topic in his books but also how the voluminous *History of Middle-earth* series might provide further details about his views of warfare. This paper will look at the characterization of Tolkien's two main war gods, Makar and Tulkas. The characterization of Tulkas remains constant throughout the entire evolution of Tolkien's world, but Makar appears only in *The Book of Lost Tales.* At the end of the paper I will examine three possible reasons for his disappearance.

1 – *The Silmarillion*: Tulkas

We will begin with what is most familiar: the character of Tulkas in the published *Silmarillion*. Since much of the material is well known, I will provide only the highlights. We will begin with the longest description of Tulkas. "Greatest in strength and deeds of prowess is Tulkas, who is surnamed Astaldo, the Valiant. He came last to Arda, to aid the Valar in the first battles with Melkor. He delights in wrestling and in contests of strength; and he rides no steed, for he can outrun all things that go on feet, and he is tireless. His hair and beard are golden, and his flesh ruddy; his weapons are his hands. He has little heed for either the past or the future, and is of no avail as a counsellor, but is a hardy friend" (*Silmarillion*, 28–9).[1]

The *Silmarillion* describes Tulkas' involvement in a variety of events early in the story, mostly involving various conflicts with Melkor.

1. The first chapter of the Quenta Silmarillion recounts how Melkor initially had the upper hand until Tulkas arrived and caused Melkor to flee to the outer darkness. In the resulting time of peace, Tulkas married Nessa and slept. His nap might be a reflection of his lack of attention to the future because while he slept Melkor infiltrated Middle-earth without the knowledge of the Valar and began constructing the fortress Utumno in the far north of Middle-earth (35–6).
2. After strengthening Utumno, Melkor decided to attack the Valar and destroy the two lights. While his attack was successful and resulted in the marring of Arda, he immediately fled back to his fortress because of the wrath of Tulkas (36–7).
3. When the time approached for the coming of the elves, Tulkas recommended that

1. Interestingly, John Garth suggests a connection between Tulkas and a friend of Tolkien. "Tulkas, with his laughter, yellow hair, and sporting prowess, may catch aspects of Christopher Wiseman" (Garth 2003, 257).

the Valar attack Melkor to protect them (though his advice was not followed). However, when the Valar discovered the elves, Manwë decided the time had come to attack Melkor, which pleased Tulkas greatly. After the siege of Utumno, Tulkas wrestled Melkor and bound him with the chain named Angainor (48–51).

4. After Melkor finished his time of imprisonment, he bowed before the Valar and asked for pardon. He received that pardon, but Tulkas "clenched his hands whenever he saw Melkor his foe go by; for if Tulkas is slow to wrath he is slow also to forget" (66). When Melkor is revealed to be unfaithful, Tulkas quickly went to arrest him. However, Tulkas could not find him because he was protected by the spider Ungoliant (70–3, 77).
5. Tulkas' final involvement in the story is his demand that Fëanor return the silmarils to Yavanna so that she could heal the marred trees (78).

In summary, Tulkas is a strong and loyal friend who frequently uses his strength to defeat Melkor. However, Tulkas is so strongly committed to defeating Melkor that he is rather impulsive and not much use as a counselor because he does not think about the future. Tolkien even includes stories about how his desires are sometimes opposed by the other Valar, who reign in Tulkas' enthusiasm to defeat Melkor.

2 – *The Book of Lost Tales*: Tulkas

We will now turn to the less familiar version of Tulkas found in *The Book of Lost Tales*. *The Book of Lost Tales* are Tolkien's original version of his created world, written during the late 1910s and early 1920s. Since the characterization of Tulkas in *The Book of Lost Tales* is relatively similar to that of the published *Silmarillion*, I will summarize here only the differences.

1. A few events involving Tulkas were included in the *The Book of Lost Tales* but not in the *Silmarillion*. For example, Tulkas assisted Aulë with his craftsmanship of a variety of items (*Lost Tales I*, 71–4). He also helped with the hiding of Valinor (235–7).
2. Tulkas has a son named Telimektar (107).
3. Tulkas' house is described in some detail: "His was a house of mirth and revelry; and it sprang high into the air with many storeys, and had a tower of bronze and pillars of copper in a wide arcade. In its court men played and rivalled one another in doughty feats, and there at times would that fair maiden Nessa wife of Tulkas bear goblets of the goodliest wine and cooling drinks among the players" (75–6).
4. The most significant additions about Tulkas are the extra details about Tulkas' struggle with Melkor (called Melko in *The Book of Lost Tales*).
    - In the earliest defeat of Melko (before the founding of the two lights), Tulkas "gave him a blow with his fist" (67).
    - The gods invited Melko to live in the house of Makar until a house could be built for him, reassuring him that only Tulkas would object to Melko returning. Melko agreed if the gods bowed down to him without their

weapons; however, he refused to see Tulkas. When he heard this, Tulkas was very upset. Manwë said that Tulkas would come, but he would come chained in Angaino for Melko's sake. Melko wanted Tulkas to come kiss his foot so that he could kick him in revenge for previous treatment. The final events of the battle when Tulkas saw the Valar about to bow before Melkor proceed as follows:

> So fiercely did wrath blaze up in the hearts of Tulkas and Aulë at that sight that Tulkas leapt across the hall at a bound despite Angaino, and Aulë was behind him and Oromë followed his father and the hall was full of tumult. Then Melko sprang to his feet shouting in a loud voice and his folk came through all those dismal passages to his aid. Then lashed he at Manwë with an iron flail he bore, but Manwë breathed gently upon it and its iron tassels were blown backward, and thereupon Tulkas smote Melko full in his teeth with his fist of iron, and he and Aulë grappled with him, and straight he was wrapped thirty times in the fathoms of Angaino. (110)

After the battle Tulkas destroyed the gates of the fortress. Melko's doom was to spend three ages in a vault of Mando and afterwards for "four ages yet dwell as a servant in the house of Tulkas, and obey him in requital of his ancient malice" (112).

- After Melko's escape, Tulkas did not respond positively to a messenger sent by Melko. "Tulkas would have hurled stones at him from the walls and slain him, but the others as yet suffered him not to be mishandled." After listening to the herald Tulkas again desires to silence the herald, and eventually the gods killed the herald by throwing him off a cliff (162–4).

5. Finally, the second volume of *The Book of Lost Tales* includes a brief note about the eschatological battle involving Tulkas and Melkor (*Lost Tales II*, 282). While some later accounts of this last battle do not include Tulkas (*Shaping*, 44–6), most of the versions feature him in this battle (198).

In sum, while we learn more details about Tulkas' fighting ability and his hatred of Melko in *The Book of Lost Tales*, his character is largely the same as what we see in the later *Silmarillion*. The main features of Tulkas lost in later versions are details about his house and the existence of his son as well as specifics of some of his battles against Melko.

3 – *The Book of Lost Tales*: Makar

Much less well known than Tulkas is the other major war god in *The Book of Lost Tales*, Makar. Since Makar is not present in the published *Silmarillion*, I will go through the texts about him in more detail.

We are introduced to Makar in negative terms. When the Valar arrive, Makar is said to be among the last. "There came still hurrying late Makar and his fierce sister Meássë and it had been better had they not found the world but remained for ever with the Ainur beyond Vaitya and the stars, for both were spirits of quarrelsome mood, and with some other lesser ones who came now with them had been the first and chief to join in the discords of Melko and to aid in the spreading of his music" (*Lost Tales I*, 66). Makar's first action confirms this negative introduction: he is the only one of the Valar to oppose Manwë's anger against Melko. In contrast, Tulkas is one of the two Valar chosen to hunt down Melko and force him to appear before Manwë (67). The difference between the two warriors is described elsewhere in terms of *casus belli*: "Nonetheless is he [Tulkas] no wrangler or striker of blows unprovoked as is Makar" (75). A few pages later Tolkien provides us with the longest description of Makar and his sister (79).

However, this does not mean that Makar only supported Melko: he also supplied the Valar with armor in their battle against Melko (107).[2] In spite of this, after the capture of Melko, during the trial Makar continued to defend him. "Yet Makar still spake for him, although not warmly, for said he: ''Twere an ill thing if peace were for always; already no blow echoes ever in the eternal quietude of Valinor, wherefore, if one might neither see deed of battle nor riotous joy even in the world without, then 'twoud be irksome indeed, and I for one long not for such times!'" But when Melko was sentenced to spend three ages in the vault of Mandos, it seemed good even to Makar (111–2). The final reference to Makar in *The Book of Lost Tales* comes after Melko's escape, when Makar and Tulkas worked together to track him. However, neither were able to capture Melko (170–1).

In sum, Tolkien portrays Makar as quite a different kind of war god than Tulkas. While Tulkas fights mainly alone and with his hands, Makar has a massive armoury and minions who practise their fighting in his presence. Tulkas fights for justice, while Makar fights for the sake of fighting and is described as being the most appreciative of Melko among those who dwell in Valinor. He even seems to view peace as a bad status because without fighting life would be boring.

4 – Reason for the Changes

As noted earlier, texts after *The Book of Lost Tales* largely preserve the characterization of Tulkas, cutting out only the references to his house, his son, and some specific details about his battles with Melkor. In contrast, Tolkien completely removed Makar and his sister from the later versions. Unfortunately, Tolkien did not leave any notes about the reason for this omission. We will now turn briefly to examine three possible reasons why he executed these changes.

The simplest reason for the change is that Tolkien never intended to actually cut Makar and the background of Tulkas. *The Book of Lost Tales* are among the fullest accounts of many of Tolkien's stories as the later versions are often summaries. Since by their very nature summaries leave material out, Tolkien might not have been cutting Makar but rather pushing him into the background. Perhaps as part of these summaries Tolkien wanted to spend less time on the Valar and more on the elves, which would require some cutting of the Valar material. If this is the case, then nothing ideological can be read into the changes.

2. Another reference to this is found in an early prose fragment (*Shaping*, 6). However, Makar's armour was also stolen by Melkor and his troops from Makar's house and used in battle against the Valar (*Lost Tales I*, 159).

The second possible reason we can examine is that it is connected to a change in tone relating to the Valar. In his commentary on *The Book of Lost Tales*, Christopher Tolkien simply notes that Makar was "a 'Melko-faction' in Valinor that was bound to prove an embarrassment" (*Lost Tales I*, 93). In line with this argument, Elizabeth Whittingham has argued that Tolkien desired to convert the Valar from a Norse-influence group in *The Book of Lost Tales* to a more biblical idea of spirit beings in the later versions of his world (Whittingham 2007, 64–99). While the word "angel" never appears in the *Silmarillion*, Tolkien refers to the Valar as angels in a few of his letters, most prominently in his very long letter to Milton Waldman (*Letters*, Letter 133, 146).[3] Makar is an anomaly among the Valar and his house partially corresponds to Valhalla in Norse mythology, where warriors fight before Odin (Garth 2003, 257). The removal of the houses of the Valar (including those of Tulkas and Makar) would then be part of a trend to reduce the corporality of the Valar, making them less like humans and more like angels. Likewise, the removal of a "wild card" like Makar makes the lines between good and evil more strongly drawn, like in the biblical worldview. Other evidence includes the removal of children of the Valar (such as the child of Tulkas). If this theory is correct, the changes to Makar (and secondarily to Tulkas) are part of a change in tone from a Norse-inspired pantheon to a biblical view of angels.

However, this theory is not iron-clad. For example, Tolkien does not remove the houses entirely because he continues to refer to various halls of the Valar (he merely removed the elaborate descriptions of their houses). Indeed, Christopher Tolkien argues that his father did not intend to deny the elaborate descriptions of these houses, but merely assumes them in later summaries (*Lost Tales I*, 92–4). Tolkien has also not made a uniform good and evil distinction among the spirit beings, because the Maier continue to show ambiguity: Ossë has to repent from some of his actions and many Maiar turn evil (Silmarillion, 30–2). Indeed, in Letter 156 Tolkien emphasizes that "all the 'angelic' powers concerned with this world were capable of many degrees of error and failing between the absolute Satanic rebellion and evil of Morgoth and his satellite Sauron, and the faineance of some of the other higher power or 'gods'" (*Letters*, Letter 156, 202). From the other direction, the angels in the Bible are not as monolithically good and evil as Whittingham portrays them (though of course the issue more concerns Tolkien's personal view of angels in the Bible rather than necessarily the correct biblical view of angels).

Another major point against this view is that Tolkien cut other of the Valar without any apparent ideological significance. The most prominent of these is Ómar, the Valar associated with music, who is also cut after *The Book of Lost Tales* (*Lost Tales I*, 76, 81). Surely his removal does not mean that Tolkien was now opposed to music! The removal of Ómar is good evidence for merely pushing characters into the background rather than rejecting them.

The third possibility for the change is that it reflects a change in view of warfare for Tolkien. John Garth notes that Makar originally was more prominent in the mythology because he was one of the first named Valar in Middle-earth, even before Tolkien went

3. The idea also is in a draft of a letter to Peter Hastings (letter 153), a letter to Robert Murray, S. J. (letter 156), a letter to Christopher Bretherton (letter 257), and several other letters.

off to war in France (2003, 125–8). Indeed, as early as 1910, Tolkien had participated in a debate with his friends about the necessity of war. Rob Gilson led the arguments for abolishing war, while Tolkien "insisted that war was both a necessary and a productive aspect of human affairs" (21–2). In addition, in the summer of 1912 Tolkien voluntarily joined the King Edward's Horse, which was a territorial cavalry regiment (though he resigned after only a few months) (Carpenter 1977, 66). Garth writes that "the presence of Makar and Meássë and their brutalist iron hall in Valinor suggests an ambivalent view of war as a necessary evil" (Garth 2003, 257). This early view of Tolkien could be portrayed as one more open to the necessity of warfare, even when it involves characters like Makar.

However, the later attitude of Tolkien towards war could be understood as much more negative. The poignant scene in *The Lord of the Rings* of Sam pondering the background of the slain warrior of Harad (from the chapter 'Of Herbs and Stewed Rabbit') illustrates this scepticism about war.[4] This same attitude would be seen particularly in the letters he wrote to his son Christopher during World War Two. Here are two of the strongest examples of this dislike of war.

> How stupid everything is!, and war multiplies the stupidity by 3 and its power by itself: so one's precious days are ruled by (3x)2 when x=normal human crassitude (and that's bad enough) (*Letters*, Letter 61, 73).

> The utter stupid waste of war, not only material but moral and spiritual, is so staggering to those who have to endure it. And always was (despite the poets), and always will be (despite the propagandists) – not of course that it has not is [sic] and will be necessary to face it in an evil world. But so short is human memory and so evanescent are its generations that in only about 30 years there will be few or no people with that direct experience which alone goes really to the heart. The burnt hand teaches most about fire (*Letters*, Letter 64, 75–6).

This anti-war trajectory could provide an answer for the removal of Makar. As Tolkien matured and watched war ravage his entire world for a second time, he became cynical about war and its beneficial effects. Therefore, he changed his mythic world to match his new view of warfare by removing the ambiguous character of Makar.

However, such a reconstruction seems unlikely. First, he left Tulkas virtually untouched in his world. If he wanted to remove approval of war, then it would seem like a good opportunity to also remove Tulkas. Second, the removal of Makar happened in his earliest drafts of the *Silmarillion* in the early 1930s, long before World War Two. It might be possible that seeing what was happening in post-war Germany caused him to become more cynical about the beneficial effects of warfare, but that also seems unlikely. Third, the vast majority of *The Book of Lost Tales* were written after Tolkien's participation in World War One. If his experience in the trenches made him cynical about the benefits of warfare, then surely he would not have written Makar from the beginning, especially when he was in the hospital recovering from the war. Fourth, part of Tolkien's later musings about Tulkas make such a trajectory unlikely because it

4. See reflections on this episode in Flieger 2017, 55–8.

appears that Tolkien's thoughts on war remain largely consistent. We now turn to this latest reference to Tulkas to address this point.

5 – Later Musings

Tolkien's final musings about Middle-earth late in his life do not change the characterization of Tulkas, but add to his commentary on Tulkas. One final text from the late 1950's deals with Tulkas. The text, entitled 'Melkor Morgoth' and published as part of *Morgoth's Ring*, describes how Tolkien wanted to make Melkor more powerful even than Manwë. However, his desire to have creatures under his power disperses his power such that the Valar are able to defeat him. Melkor nearly repents (similar to Gollum's moment in *Lord of the Rings*), but does not and eventually fakes repentance. He delights in "desecrating" repentance this way and then seeks to also desecrate Valinor by sneaking in through his feigned repentance (though he also really wants to avoid being bound with the chain Angainor, which he still fears) (*Morgoth*, 391). He offers to help the Valar heal Valinor, which Manwë accepts. However, Tolkien sees this offer negatively. Tolkien says "It is this offer which seduces or deludes Manwë – Manwë must be shown to have his own inherent fault (though not sin)" (392).

At this point Tolkien begins to discuss Tulkas. "Against the advice of some Valar (such as Tulkas) he grants Melkor's prayer." However, not surprisingly Tulkas is not one to simply accept this decision without complaint. Tolkien continues: "Melkor is taken back to Valinor last (save for Tulkas who follows bearing Angainor and clinking it to remind Melkor)." Tolkien includes a footnote at this point in the text providing further explanation of his view of Tulkas. "Tulkas represents the good side of 'violence' in the war against evil. This is an absence of all compromise which will even face apparent evils (such as war) rather than parley; and does not (in any kind of pride) think that any one less than Eru can redress this, or rewrite the tale of Arda" (392).

The rest of the story largely proceeds as originally written. In sum, the major difference is that Melkor now faked his repentance already at Utumno rather than after the three ages of imprisonment, removing the need for Tulkas to wrestle him and bind him with a chain. However, Tolkien never wrote these changes into any version of the Silmarillion. But these musings helpfully show us Tolkien's views on warfare near the end of his life: some violence is needed in the war against evil and it is possible to call this violence good. Tolkien also emphasizes that ultimately only God can fix the problem of evil.

6 – Conclusion

In conclusion, the war gods of Middle-earth provide us an interesting window into Tolkien's view of warfare. The original version of his world included both Tulkas and Makar, one a respectable and just warrior who consistently opposed the evil Melko, the other a character of armor and weapons who loves to fight for the sake of fighting and does not seem that concerned about injustice. However, Makar is quickly written completely out of the story, while Tulkas remains virtually unchanged. It is unlikely that these changes reflect a change of view by Tolkien because his views on warfare do not seem to change much over the years. Tolkien retains a view of war that recognizes both its necessity for the sake of justice but also its cost. Perhaps the changes are part of a larger plan to put the Valar more into biblical categories, but this seems somewhat overly neat and tidy. If forced to choose, I would lean slightly towards the possibility that Tolkien did not actively cut out Makar, but merely relegated him to the background as part of the summarizing of his tales because this would make it parallel to other things that he relegated to the background (like the house of the Valar) and other parts that are removed are not done for ideological reasons (like the removal of Omar).

Bibliography

Carpenter, H., *J.R.R. Tolkien: A Biography,* (London: HarperCollins, 1977).

Flieger, V., *There Would Always Be a Fairy Tale: More Essays on Tolkien,* (Kent, OH: Kent State University Press, 2017).

Garth, J., *Tolkien and the Great War: The Threshold of Middle-Earth,* (Houghton Mifflin, 2003).

Tolkien, J.R.R., *The Letters of J.R.R. Tolkien*, ed. by H.Carpenter with the assistance of C. Tolkien. (Houghton Mifflin, 1981).
— *The Book of Lost Tales: Part One*, ed. by Christopher Tolkien (Houghton Mifflin, 1983).
— *The Book of Lost Tales: Part Two*, ed. by Christopher Tolkien (Houghton Mifflin, 1984).
— *The Shaping of Middle-Earth: The Quenta, the Ambarkanta, and the Annals*, ed. by Christopher Tolkien (Houghton Mifflin, 1986).
— *Morgoth's Ring*, ed. by Christopher Tolkien (London: HarperCollins, 1993).
— *The Silmarillion*, ed. by Christopher Tolkien, 2nd edn. (Houghton Mifflin, 2001).

Whittingham, E.A., *The Evolution of Tolkien's Mythology: A Study of the History of Middle-Earth*, Critical Explorations in Science Fiction and Fantasy Series, 7 (Jefferson, NC: McFarland, 2007).

POLITICS AND LAW

Law in Tolkien

José María Miranda Boto[1]

1 – Tolkien and Law?

It is a truth universally acknowledged, that any researcher who wants to deal with J.R.R. Tolkien's works will find a subject fitting their own academic background. This delightful situation derives, certainly, from the richness and coherence of Tolkien's sub-creation. There is no doubt that the immensity of the field is the essential ingredient of the Tolkienian Universe and a source of pleasure for his readers.

Nowhere does it appear that Tolkien had the least professional or academic link with the world of Law, neither in his real life nor in his literary life. Evidently, in the course of his years he was under the legal tutorship of Father Morgan,[2] got married,[3] paid taxes,[4] became part of the faculty of several colleges and universities,[5] participated in the tedious task of reviewing a course syllabus (Scull and Hammond 2017, 952-3), made purchases,[6] paid traffic fines,[7] served in the British Army,[8] and negotiated publishing contracts.[9] However, none of the above actions goes beyond the usual relation of an

---

1. I would like to thank Silvia Gutiérrez Bregón for the kind proofreading of this paper. This essay draws heavily on the author's own book, *El Derecho en Tolkien*, Ediciones Cinca, Madrid, 2017. It is highly recommended to read it in Spanish, since it is much more entertaining. The materials from *The History of Middle-earth* (*Laws and Customs among the Eldar*, especially) have not been incorporated into this paper. Lawyers should not deal with Parliament bills until they have been passed into formal law. The same happens with those wonderful books: drafts are not a safe ground of research for a lawyer.

2. An essential work on Father Morgan Ferrández Bru, 2018. On the legal aspects of this choice, 84.

3. Since the *Marriage Act* 1836, within the framework of the emancipation of Catholics in the United Kingdom, the marriage celebrated by a Catholic priest was legal.

4. On the bulky taxes derived from the royalties generated by *The Lord of the Rings*, (Carpenter 1990, 248). This was a recurring theme in his correspondence, as a matter of fact.

5. His letter of June 27, 1925, requesting the Rawlinson and Bosworth Professorship of Anglo Saxon in Oxford, is a perfect model of summary CV and self-assessment, with which the academic evaluation authorities, the modern *Four Wise Clerks of Oxenford*, are very pleased today.

6. On his years as student in Oxford: "After a year Tolkien wrote that he had 'a good few bills unaccounted for', and added: 'Money matters are not very cheerful'." (Carpenter 2000, 61).

7. "Tolkien's driving was daring rather than skilful" (Carpenter 2000, 162).

8. In the King Edward's Horse, before the Great War, and in the Lancashire Fusiliers in 1915, after concluding his studies.

9. "In fact, it was because Houghton Mifflin has violated a legal provision limiting the number of proof sheets that could be brought into the country that Ace had issued its unauthorized edition; according to Kilby it was this unauthorized edition by Ace that made Tolkien famous" (Chance 2001, 34). A synthesis in Scull and Hammond (2017, 1-8).

average person with the field of Law, where no professional links are established.[10]

In the elaboration of the Arda fresco, he gave life to a background of landscapes, towns and kingdoms of a depth hitherto unknown. In no way am I implying that he was the first author to incorporate these elements into his narrative.[11] The fact I would like to point out is the key importance of Tolkien's writings in the establishment of a new paradigm, in Kuhnian terms, for the fantastic narrative as a literary genre. Tom Shippey, in a moment of reasoned enthusiasm, referred to Tolkien as "Author of the Century", as the "Chrétien de Troyes of the twentieth century" (2001, xviii).

In a letter to his friend Lord Halsbury, Tolkien shares his view on this topic: "I do not think that anything is referred to in The L. of the R. which does not actually exist in legends written before it was begun" (*Letters*, Letter 174, 228). Again, resorting to his own thinking, this time in a letter to Naomi Mitchison, Tolkien's task in his work could be characterized as "an elaborate form of the game of inventing a country – an endless one, because even a committee of experts in different branches could not complete the overall picture" (*Letters*, Letter 154, 196).

By relying on the elements that Tolkien listed above, the reader would be able to acquire an in-depth knowledge of the dimension of Arda. Yet, Tolkien left out the field of Law in his subcreation. This paper aims to adopt the legal point of view in the analysis of his work, and its author has taken the liberty of including himself, without a hint of shame or a useful letter of recommendation, in the committee of specialists referred to by Tolkien in the aforementioned letter. There is nothing original about this. The author of this paper is a humble follower of the path that great masters of the Law have already transited before him: the path that takes us to the role of Law in Literature.

This is possible because, as the classic quote goes, *ubi societas, ibi ius*. Where there is society, there is Law. And nobody can question the exceptional ability of Tolkien as a builder of societies. When writing the History of Númenor, Tolkien, most likely unintendedly, was developing another subcreation, that is, the History of Law in Númenor. As Francisco Tomás y Valiente pointed out, Law is a historical reality, something that exists and transforms through time (Tomás y Valiente 1983, 23). Thus, it could be said that Law might be one of the "green suns", using Tolkien's own idea present in 'On Fairy-stories', that will test Arda's coherence.

2 – The role of Law in Tolkien's works

Law will be analysed in this paper from different approaches, with a strong focus on Middle-earth studies but aiming to provide as well as some hints from Tolkien criticism, with the final goal of enriching the perception of his work (Scull and Hammond 2017, 282).

First of all, we will start with an introduction of some transversal issues, such as the presence of Law in some episodes or its different meanings and goals. Secondly, Law will be addressed as an element for comedy, mainly through some episodes from

10. "It was one of his strongest-held opinions that the investigation of an author's life reveals very little of the workings of his mind" (Carpenter 2000, 127).

11. William Morris, among others, may have influenced him in this respect (Carpenter 1990, 84).

The Hobbit. In the following section of this paper, our goal will be to find the legal translation of some essential pillars of society. After such 'formal' approach to legal matters, Hobbit-Lore will appear in the guise of a case study on the rules of succession of the Queens of Númenor. The final part, focused on *The Lord of the Rings* as a teaching tool at Law Faculties, will deal with the employment relationship between Frodo and Sam.

The first finding of this research is the predominance of Natural Law over Positive Law in Tolkien's works. Law, as a rule, is nearly indistinguishable from Morality and Justice, all of them emanating from a series of eternal, immutable principles that derive from a common source. This common source is, most certainly, Eru Ilúvatar who, despite not being mentioned in *The Lord of the Rings*, is the clear origin of all good things in the world. Eru would take the place of the Christian God as the primal source of society's ordination.

Valinor is the perfect scenario to develop this statement. Among the Ainur, it cannot be said that there is Law, but we are sure that the notion of Justice exists, and the perception of the Law inseparable from Morality remains intact (Fernández Higgs 2003, 80). There has not been any codification of norms, or any foundational pact of the society. The world of the Ainur has been ordained by Eru and only Melkor and those who have followed him to the Darkness dare to challenge him. Thus, Manwë "was appointed to be, in the fullness of time, the first of all Kings" (*Silmarillion*, 16). No one questioned this power, except the Dark Enemy of the World. Even Ulmo and Tulkas assumed the coexistence with Melkor, once liberated, since "for those who will defend authority against rebellion must not themselves rebel" (66).

The idea of a pre-existing Justice appears in the first dialogue between Melkor, when he claims the lordship of Arda, and Manwë. The latter opposes the former's claim affirming that "this kingdom thou shalt not take for thine own, wrongfully, for many others have laboured here do less than thou" (10). The idea of *suum quique tribuere*, central in Ulpian's idea of Justice, can be easily extracted from the words of the Vala.[12]

The character of Mandos is, in itself, a confirmation of this theory. He is the Judge without rules, the Adjudicator on his Conscience, the Mouth that utters the words of Eternal Law. He is, indeed, not the Judge, but the Doomsman of the Valar. Nonetheless, he condemns and prosecutes only by order of Manwë, which means that he does not seem to have any capacity to act *ex officio*. Although this Judge evidently has theological resonances, none of them is related to the Constitutional Reform Act, 2005. He does not apply any legislation but decides purely in equity. We could even refer to him as an arbitrator. In this task his terrible and implacable memory helps him. Throughout the 'Quenta Silmarillion', Mandos appears to exercise his fearsome function on several occasions.

The idea of Law being a covenant between individuals to build up society does not fit in Tolkien's works. Legal positivism fits better in science-fiction, indeed, where Law is seen mainly as a tool of oppression. The complete absence of Justice is a usual trait in the grim, dark future that awaits Humanity. In Tolkien's days, by the way, that perspective was already into force in Germany or the USSR.

12. "Irresponsible lordship most troubles Tolkien" (Chance 2001, 6).

In Tolkien's narrative, this situation also leads to the predominance of customary law over written law. There are no charters, no *Corpus Iuris Civilis* of any type, there is not even a Magna Carta. In a certain way, it is normal, because only a lawyer writing a novel could take care of devising legal codes as a literary background. Perhaps Owen Barfield, as a solicitor, could have developed this kind of subcreation, extending his professional background to Literature, such as Tolkien did with Philology.

All pieces of Law mentioned in Middle-earth lack written support and even regarding the laws of Númenor, one can find several flaws in their planning. No one knows where the rules concerning the government of Minas Tirith were established, nor the exact location of the disciplinary regime of the members of the Guard. The same can be said about any legal disposition ever adopted by Thingol as king of Doriath.

The best example of an unwritten legal system within Tolkien's world, in any case, is the one devised for the Shire: "they attributed to the king of old all their essential laws; and usually they kept the laws of free will, because they were The Rules (as they said), both ancient and just" (*FR*, 'Prologue', 9). This is a remote precedent in time, whose authority is undisputed, and over which there is a consensus that nobody defies.

Tolkien himself tried to explain this idea of the ancient rules: "A Númenórean King was monarch, with the power of unquestioned decision in debate; but he governed the realm with the frame of ancient law, of which he was administrator (and interpreter) but not the maker" (*Letters*, Letter 244, 324). For any lawyer, the obvious question here would be *Quis*, that is, who is, then, the legislator? Still, this question remains unanswered.

In any case, traces of the English Common Law can be detected in Tolkien's writings, in opposition to the written Roman Law and its derivatives during the Middle Ages in Europe. It is remarkable that Tolkien declared his hate for the Roman Empire. Law being the central element of Roman civilization, it is clear that part of that hate filtered itself into the legal characterization of Middle-earth, even if the Reunited Kingdom was conceived as "far more like the reestablishment of an effective Holy Roman Empire with its seat in Rome than anything that would be devised by a 'Nordic'" (*Letters*, Letter 294, 276).

In a certain way, the legal culture in Tolkien's works takes a clear influence from the English system in its rejection of Civil Law, both in the Anglo-Saxon period and after the Norman Conquest. The absence of Parliaments and priests, on the other hand, is another factor that leads to the inexistence of Civil Law.

The beauty of the Shire, from the legal point of view, lies in defying this well established fact in two moments. The first one takes place during Sharkey / Lotho's regime, when a new set of Rules was established. These new rules are indeed written, as the Hobbits will find them in the Guard-House in the Brandywine Bridge: "On every wall there was a notice and a list of Rules" (*RK*, 'The Scouring of the Shire', 1000).

They are perfectly codified and most excellently written in capital letters, which shows anything but scorn on the formalities of Law. It is clear that, for Tolkien, written Law (and even capital letters) can become a tool of tyranny.[13]

The second text-*aficionado* where Tolkien makes use of written Law is the complete opposite of what has been described: Samwise Gamgee. The text in letter 214 is Law

13. On the Scouring of the Shire and politics, see Shippey (2001, 167).

in all its splendour: awful wording, lots of ambiguity, even a first attempt of gender-inclusive language.

One last issue that must be dealt with, before moving on to the next sections of this paper, is the place of Law as Philology. Nearly every reader of Tolkien's works finds an extreme pleasure in the choice of words he made regarding legal issues. Nothing is casual. In three cases at least words were chosen that bring into the narration old legal institutions that are usually lost in translation.

The word "weregild" ("man price") appears on two occasions. First of all, in Elrond's narration of the events of 3441 S.A about Isildur and the "weregild for my father, and my brother" (*FR*, 'The Council of Elrond', 243). The second appearance can be located in the less glamorous *Appendices*: "Turin II of Gondor sent to Folcwine a rich weregild of gold" (RK, 'Appendix A', 1403).

Weregild "under ancient Teutonic and English Law was payment in compensation or fine for murder and other crimes" (Hammond and Scull 2014, 231).

The second word is the apparently innocent "folklands", used to describe the territorial divisions in the Shire (*FR*, 'Prologue', 9). Again, according to Hammond and Scull, it "is a term of Old English Law, denoting land of a folk or people, as opposed to bookland, held by charter or deed" (2014, 33). This contrast fits perfectly with the abhorrence of written Law detected in the Shire.

3 – Law as a joke

The fun appears when one begins to examine *The Hobbit*.[14] It was conceived as a book for children, and although some of the first reviews, influenced by C.S. Lewis, pointed out that it was a book that could be read and reread by adults, the truth is that the general tone of the work is quite childlike (Carpenter 1990, 202). Tolkien, years after its publication, greatly abhorred the gags and inconsistencies that populated the book, which in time had become a direct vehicle of communication with this audience of little age.[15] Among those gags, we can find many related to Law.

The Hobbit contains the only contract ever collected from the entire History of Middle-earth. No one ever committed the vulgarity of holding a private þusiness and documenting it so literally. Chapter II, 'Roast Mutton', begins with Bilbo's considerable hangover after his meeting with the dwarfs, and so great was his discomfort that he had not yet removed the dust from the clock on the mantelpiece (beautiful anachronism, by the way). If he had, he would have found the document that Gandalf finally gave him, and which had been written by his fellow conspirators.

The document clearly gathered consent, object and form. The dwarves expressed their incontestable and documented acceptance of the offer of "professional assistance",

14. The essential work from a British point of view is Smith, 2016.

15. Some survived, some didn't. "'Pipeweed' shows Tolkien's wish to accept a common feature of English modernity, which he knew could not exist in the ancient world of elves and trolls, and whose anachronism would instantly be betrayed by a word with the foreign feel of 'tobacco'. Actually Bilbo does use 'tobacco' on page 14 of *The Hobbit* and Gandalf mentions 'tomatoes' not much later. In the first edition. The third changes 'cold chicken and tomatoes' to 'cold chicken and pickles.'" (Shippey 2003, 69).

and the conditions collected as a counterpart were pristine (*Hobbit*, 'Roast Mutton', 28). They are pure contemporary language, clashing with the Quest that would soon start (Shippey 2001, 41).[16]

Everything seemed clear, until Smaug the Golden tried to convince Bilbo with his serpentine language of the deception to which the dwarves had subjected him. In his duel of wit, with the poisonous language of the great reptiles,[17] the dragon pointed out the possible loopholes in the deal. Smaug showed himself here not only as the last of the *urulóki* but also as a fine formalist and manipulative pettifogger.

From a technical point of view, the legality of the object of the contract should be taken into consideration. The "professional assistance" referred to by the great Thorin Oakenshield was the euphemistic expression behind the announcement that Gandalf left at Bilbo's door: "Burglar wants a good job, plenty of Excitement and reasonable Reward".[18] Bilbo's contract is, therefore, clearly illegal, since its purpose is contrary to the law. Is it not?

On behalf of Bilbo, we should point out that in his capacity as a service provider, he does not commit any illegality. The only object that he extracted from Smaug's treasure, initially, was a great two-handed cup, as heavy as he could carry. We might add that Thorin, in his capacity as the legitimate Heir of the Kingdom under the Mountain, was the legal owner of the cup, and that Bilbo was doing nothing but stealing from a thief. But it would be self-deception because the truth is, that Bilbo was in fact, a criminal.

This idea is reinforced by the way in which Bilbo freely interpreted the contract that bound him to Thorin & Co.,[19] when he appropriated the most valuable treasure of the Lonely Mountain, the Arkenstone, the heart of the Mountain. Malice could not be defined in a better way: you are well aware of what you are doing and you want to do it anyway. We get knowledge and will together.

The contract reappeared, carefully folded inside a pocket of Bilbo's jacket, shortly before the Battle of the Five Armies.[20] Such a singular situation! A chainmail of mithril under Bilbo's old jacket. In any case, we have excellent teaching here: always keep the documentation at hand, because you do not know when it may be necessary.

A final legal surprise awaits the reader at the end of *The Hobbit*, as well as Bilbo: the auction[21] of his assets. It is worth noting, first of all, that the auction was conducted

16. And adds: "But on the other hand few modern contracts qualify profits with the gloomy phrase "if any" or assume that there will be no funeral expenses, because the contracting party or parties will have been eaten" (41-2).

17. "He speaks in fact with the characteristic aggressive politeness of the British upper class, in which irritation and authority are in direct proportion to apparent deference or uncertainty" (Shippey 2003, 90).

18. "[Bilbo] is admittedly a bourgeois. That is why Gandalf turns him into a Burglar. Both words come from the same root (*burh* = 'town' or 'stockaded house'), and while they are eternal opposites, they are opposites on the same level" (Shippey 2003, 72).

19. "Nothing could be more familiar in modern commerce than the "& Co.". But Thorin's "Co." is not a limited company but a company in the oldest sense – fellow travellers, messmates." (Shippey 2001, 42).

20. On Bilbo's language on this occasion: "It is fair to say that no character from epic or saga could even begin to think or talk like Bilbo" (Shippey 2003, 85).

21. "*The Hobbit* indeed ends with a joke derived from the Glossary just mentioned, for in the

by Messrs. Grubb, Grubb & Burrowes.[22] In a world of customary law, inherited from the Kingdom of Arthedain, it was greatly amusing and clever to be called the same as a traditional English law firm, which dealt with the liquidation of the supposedly deceased Mr. Baggins and was, in turn, the last adversary that he had to defeat to finish his trip.[23]

And all that happened because the hobbit adventurer was 'presumed dead'. One can imagine the huge uncertainty that these two words produce in a lawyer. What circumstances had to concur to reach such conclusion? Some hobbits were known to have departed and never return (at least two Took, Hildifons and Isengar, the youngest of Old Took's children), but we do not know much more.

So, who was supposed to start the auction procedure? We can imply from the text that the Sackville-Bagginses did it, being too willing to move all their furniture to Bag End. After all, Otho was the son of Bilbo's uncle, his first cousin, that is, his fourth degree relative (the kinship with Frodo was far more remote, first and second cousin, once removed either way).

Who benefited from the result of the auction? We know that it was advertised with a white and red sign, a colour particularly important in the legal world of the Shire, and that many of Bilbo's things had already been sold at lunchtime (the auction started at ten o'clock). We also know that the prices were varied, "from next to nothing to old songs (as is not unusual at auctions)", which clearly implies that the compensation system was not exclusively monetary (*Hobbit*, 'The Last Stage', 270). We can ponder that the Sackville-Bagginses, Bilbo's presumed heirs, were not the direct beneficiaries of the auction, since if they had entered into possession of all Bilbo's patrimony, they would not have needed to liquidate it. The question, in short, remains unsolved.

Something of this mocking spirit remains in the first chapters of *The Lord of the Rings*. Bilbo's will is the best example, and the humour is obvious if we compare it with Lobelia Sackville-Baggins' or Frodo's last wills and testaments.

The aforementioned hereditary succession of Mr. Bilbo Baggins offers, indeed, a great interest to the scholar of the Law of the Shire. Firstly, because of the material existence of a will, which was read carefully, with great frustration, by Otho Sackville-Baggins. Secondly, because it informs us about the formalities that gave validity to the document: "according to the legal customs of hobbits, which demand among other things seven signatures of witnesses in red ink" (*FR*, 'A Long-expected Party', 39).

Huddersfield dialect the Word "okshen" meant not "auction" but "mess". [...] And when Bilbo returns home, what he finds is an "okshen" in both senses, mess and auction at once." (Shippey 2001, 8).

22. Gorgo, Gorgo y Borgo in the Spanish translation (Anderson 1990, 329). The translation is not consistent with the guests' list to Bilbo's party, where they are called, more properly, Cavada and Madriguera.

23. "In a sense, the last 'King under the Mountain' is the legal trio introduced at the end of the novel. The tunnelling names of Grubb, Grubb and Burrowes illustrate their literal and figurative positions as "kings" or monsters under the mountain, in this case the comfortable tunnel belonging to Bilbo in Underhill. These dragon like lawyers guard a treasure accurately named Bag End that they intend to auction. They represent a less frightening adversary than the others and therefore, more easily to defeat. Nevertheless, this Hobbit trio forces Bilbo to realize that a "King under the Mountain" may be a neighbour Hobbit – or even oneself" (Chance 2001, 61-2).

The mention of "customs" instead of "law" makes again the point on the importance of customary law. And, thirdly, because of its content, in which we can distinguish between the main mass of the inheritance, which corresponded to Frodo, and various legacies, with better or worse intentions, which corresponded, among others, to Gaffer Gamgee and Rory Brandybuck.

One last piece of writing in which we find the use of legal issues as a comical resource is Tolkien's humorous work, *Farmer Giles of Ham*. I will not deal with the University-mocking paragraphs, so clear to one who comes from the same guild, but with Giles' role as legislator and statesman.

Lord, Earl and King, successively, Giles has all the features of great leaders found in the more formal and sober works of Tolkien, even opposing the legitimacy of origin of Ambrosius Aurelianus[24] to his own origin. He was a legislator, who applied the most severe law against the prophecies of bad omen. He directed international relations, winning a place under the sun for the Little Kingdom. He rewarded merit, with the creation of the order of the cavalry of the Wormwards, and thanked those who helped him,[25] even the petty miller as an obsequious servant of the crown. Garn lived happily and proudly, more boastful than ever, the parson became bishop,[26] and even Agatha became a queen of great size and majesty. The balance achieved by Elessar is not more fruitful, in short, than the one obtained by the redheaded and bearded farmer of Ham (Rodríguez Valls 2007, 196).

4 – Law as an element in society

If Law was used deliberately as a humorous element, the serious approach to it is, apparently, less obvious in Tolkien's writings. Law appears as a part of the tapestry, as one of its many threads, that the scholar must cautiously follow in order to reach a conclusion. Most of these hidden legal elements deal with kingship, the organization of the army, the trespassing of borders. They are typical elements in a para-medieval picture.

Marriage is the most transversal legal issue in Tolkien's works, as it is present in all the described societies, except for Mordor. There is marriage among the Ainur, Elves, Men, Dwarves, Hobbits and even Ents. Marriage can even be defined as the foundation of society. As a matter of fact, this is its very condition, as we will exemplify with the case of the Valar.

It is a manifestation of the aforementioned natural law perspective that the institution of marriage appears in the very first moment of Eä. Angelic creatures as they are, the

24. Or, more accurately put, Augustus Bonifacius Ambrosius Aurelianus Antoninus Pius et Magnificus, dux, rex, tyrannus et Basileus Mediterranearum Partium.

25. "The triumph of commons over aristocracy, however, communicates a singularly unmedieval and very modern idea: it suggests a nineteenth- or twentieth-century revolutionary outlook, except that the leader of the commoners actually becomes king and a new aristocracy is created, presumably with his own new commons. […] The old order is revitalized, but perhaps there is no real change except in the introduction of a bourgeoisie, yet another class." (Chance 2001, 133).

26. "It is very nearly irresistible to conclude that in his mixture of learning, bluff and sense the parson represents and idealised (Christian) philologist" (Shippey 2003, 99).

Valar, in essence, do not have female or male sex, they even lack a corporeal form, which they only assume by their own will. The decision, therefore, to incarnate responds to the creation of a model of society implicit in the family as its fundamental cell. Thus, Tulkas and Nessa were married at the feast of the Spring of Arda, a luminous moment at the beginning of Time, a symbol of what the existence of the Children of Ilúvatar would be in the future. Life as a couple must be the rule, without implying, between the Valar and the Maiar, nothing else beyond formal coexistence. Ulmo assumes in this scenario the qualities of the typical single grumpy cousin and is presented as the sullenest of them, leaving aside the natural circumspection of Mandos and the permanent sadness of Nienna.

The Valar must remain heterosexual and monogamous for life. That was the rule for them, and that would be the rule for the Children of Eru as well. Of how the Elves were married we do not know anything, except that marriage between close relatives was not allowed, as exemplified in the case of Idril and Maeglin. We have, however, the interesting testimony of what Curufin told Eöl. The Dark Elf, with arts not entirely lawful, had taken Aredhel, daughter of Fingolfin, as his wife: "For those who steal the daughters of the Noldor and wed them without gift or leave do not gain kinship with their kin" (*Silmarillion*, 157). From this statement it seems that the Noldor women did not have the capacity to marry for themselves and that they needed a complement of capacity to marry. The law mentioned by Curufin, on the other hand, is an enigma. It seems reasonable, though, to forbid the killing of visitors and in laws.

Who Galadriel asked for authorization to marry Celeborn remains a mystery. The daughter of Finarfin would be, once again, a woman who breaks models and clichés, taking as a husband someone who was not of her own race, this singular Philip of Edinburgh in the shape of a Teleri Elf.

We know, however, that widowhood was not an impediment to a new marriage. The casuistry, however, is very small, unique in fact. We only know of two widowed Elves, Finwë and Turgon. The wife of the first king of the Noldor, Míriel, died as a result of the birth of Fëanor, who consumed all her energies. Turgon's wife, Elenwë, in turn, perished during the terrible crossing of the Helcaraxë. Of these two, it is only clear that Finwë took another woman, Indis of the Vanyar, thus engendering the second royal line, not to everyone's liking.

The second marriage of Finwë is central in the development of the fate of the Noldor and its moral aspects are well developed in *The History of Middle-earth*. As it has been noted at the beginning of this paper, that text will not be used as a source in this paper. Thus, the only conclusion we can draw from the 'Quenta Silmarillion' is that a second marriage was a possibility.

Concerning the Edain of the First Age, the only legal rule that we know from this dark time is linked to marriage. It is legal as well as moral: the prohibition of marriage between siblings, a central issue in the drama of the children of Húrin. Perhaps the father's consent for marriage was necessary, judging by Beren's thoughts: "nor would he withhold Lúthien from Thingol for ever. For he held by the law of Men, deeming it perilous to set at naught the will of the father, save at the last need" (*Silmarillion* 216). The final clause, as it is usual in Law, destroys all the previous considerations, by the way.

The prohibition of marriage between close kin reappears in Númenor. Siblings were not allowed to marry each other, the descent into Darkness was not so intense. But, apparently, marriage between cousins was also forbidden. This rule was respected, until the well-known case in 3255 S.A. of Pharazôn marrying his cousin, Míriel, against her will, “doing evil in this and evil also in that the laws of Númenor did not permit the marriage, even in the royal house, of those more nearly akin than cousins in the second degree” (*Silmarillion*, 322).

Taking that simple statement, we can point out several legal issues. First of all, the previous consent from the bride was necessary (in this case, a disputed issue, depending on the version of the ‘Akallabêth’ that you read). Secondly, the prohibition of marriage between cousins, a measure clearly inherited from the lessons of the First Age. And thirdly, the rule applied also “even in the royal house”.

That exception may point to Aldarion’s rule “that the King’s Heir should not wed save in the Line of Elros, and that any who did so should cease to be eligible for the Heirship” (*UT*, 209). From the legal point of view, there are two interesting aspects concerning Aldarion’s decision. First of all, it is described as an “ordinance”, a full legal term that does not make sense in that context, unless understood in a general sense, such as in the *Cambridge Dictionary*, “a law or rule made by a government or authority”.

This ordinance, in any case, was a consequence of a previous decision: “it was also ordained at the instance of the Council that a female heir must resign, if she remained unwed beyond a certain time” (209). The Council of Númenor appears here, in a single episode, as a legislative instance, in contradiction to all that is said elsewhere. Secondly, later in the text, it is said “but the marriage of the Heir to another member of the Line of Elros remained the custom ever after” (209). We can clearly notice here again, the blurred distinction between statutory law and customary law.

If we take marriage from the perspective of Canon Law, an approach absolutely necessary when dealing with the legal aspects of marriage, marriage in Tolkien’s works is much less complex than what one should expect. It is not, in any culture, a sacrament, and neither is it a contract. It is a mere exchange of consent, as clearly observed in Arwen and Elessar’s wedding, and even more clearly in Éowyn and Faramir’s .

The key word we need to consider is “trothplighted”. Once again, Philology reappears under the mask of Law. According to the *Oxford English Dictionary*, it means “the act of plighting troth; a solemn promise or engagement, especially of marriage; betrothal”, “troth” being a Middle English variant of truth.

All the marriages described share the notes indicated earlier in this paper: heterosexual, monogamous, and for life. Nevertheless, the example of Queen Berúthiel challenges this theory. We read in *Unfinished Tales* that “King Tarannon had her set on a ship alone with her cats and set adrift on the sea before a north wind” (*UT*, 402). It is the only single case of presumed repudiation that we can find in Tolkien’s works. Apparently, this did not cause her much suffering: “Berúthiel went back to live in the inland city, and went to the bad (or returned to it – she was a black Númenórean in origin, I guess)” (Castell 1968, 147).[27]

Aldarion and Erendis had a sad, unfruitful conjugal life, but their marriage was never

27. I am greatly indebted to Joel Merriner for giving me access to the original source.

dissolved. There was no Henry VIII in Númenor. It is certain that Galadriel and Celeborn had a peculiar lifestyle when dealing with family life, but we cannot presume that their marriage was ever in danger. Perhaps Fëanor and Nerdanel's relationship could drive us to some other facts, but it will be left here as a simple hint for future research.

5 – Law vs. Justice

For people who have not received legal training, Law and Justice can mean the same thing. However, after paying the first legal bill, the difference remains forever clear. In the legal world, there are few concepts more beautiful than Ulpian's definition of Justice: *Honeste vivere, neminem laedere, suum cuique tribuere*. Live honestly, harm no one, give to each one what is due. Everybody could subscribe to these ideals.

It is harder to understand Max Weber's idea of the real meaning of Law: "An order will be called [...] law if it is externally guaranteed by the probability that coercion (physical or psychological), to bring about conformity or avenge violation, will be applied by a staff of people holding themselves specially ready for that purpose" (Weber 1978, 34). It is tough, but it is real. Which characters from *The Lord of the Rings* may fit in such definitions? For the purpose of this paper, King Elessar could be linked to Ulpian's concept of Justice and Sauron, in turn, could be linked to Weber's conception of Law. These are just two of many other examples.[28]

There are no professional judges and lawyers in Middle-earth, except Messrs. Grubb, Grubb and Burrowes. The whole judicial task is in the hands of the King, who is not only a healer, but also a judge and legislator. It has been this way since the times of Thingol and Turgon in the long-ago days of the First Age, and it kept going like this during the Fourth Age in Gondor.

One of the first tasks of King Elessar was the judgement of Beregond. The facts were incontestable. From a positivist point of view, Beregond's fate was sealed: he had to die. The way of his death, by the way, would be an interesting issue to deal with, but we will not address it here. It is worth noting though, that Elves used to throw people from a cliff, just as old Romans did to traitors from the Rupe Tarpeia. Whatever the instrument, getting the death penalty as consequence for some of these actions barely fits any proportion between crime and punishment.

But King Elessar was not interested in the strict enforcement of Law. On the other hand, he chose to start his government with an act of mercy,[29] under the name of material Justice. And this time we see how the King ruled in equity rather than in law.[30] He recognised all the faults of that brave man of Gondor, by expelling him from the Guard. The penalty that would have corresponded, as noted, should have been death, but Elessar understood that Faramir's defence was mitigating enough to avoid this

28. "Often Tolkien shows characters having to make decisions not between obvious good and evil but as to what is the right action, even if not taking it is not actually evil" (Scull and Hammond 2017, 462).

29. On the issue of pity and mercy, see Scull and Hammond (2017, 989ss).

30. He had already expressed this preference in his first meeting with Éomer. "This is the first of six instances in *The Lord of the Rings* when someone decides that it is right to disobey an order and, in so doing, aids the eventual success of the Free Peoples" (Hammond and Scull 2014, 372).

punishment. The King's justice was manifested in the appointment he made next, when he ordered Beregond to leave Minas Tirith, although he put him in charge of Faramir's personal guard.

We should remember that Pippin had already anticipated this, in his exchange with Beregond: "'Well, you must choose between orders and the life of Faramir,' said Pippin. 'And as for orders, I think you have a madman to deal with, not a lord" (*RK*, 'The Siege of Gondor', 827). It is impossible to express in a clearer way the idea that unfair orders bring with themselves a personal, natural right to oppose them.[31] And this is one of the clearest expressions of Tolkien's personal ideas about "the system" (*Letters*, Letter 56, 42).

On the other hand, we have the Lord of the Rings himself. In the remarkable letter to Milton Waldman, around 1951, Tolkien pointed out that Sauron "very slowly, beginning with fair motives: the reorganising and rehabilitation of the ruin of Middle-earth, 'neglected by the gods', he becomes a reincarnation of Evil, and a thing lusting for Complete Power" (*Letters*, Letter 131, 151). It is easy to perceive Lord Acton's classic idea about the corruption of power here. Furthermore, in another letter from 1954, he added that the Dark Lord "was not indeed wholly evil, not unless all 'reformers' who want to hurry up with 'reconstruction' and 'reorganization' are wholly evil, even before pride and the lust to exert their will eat them up" (*Letters*, Letter 153, 191).

All these ideas have an unmistakable influence on 20th-century events, and show, perhaps unconsciously, Tolkien's mistrust for the modern State. In this conception, Sauron was perfectly capable of adding Law, as a monopoly of violence, to his arsenal. It is clear that Sauron used it, among other purposes, to prevent his hordes of orcs from destroying each other and to build a sustainable kingdom in the Black Land. What did Sauron do for Mordor? He organized the production of the necessary food for the entire troop, built cisterns to supply the troops in the regions without water, took care of the disposition of the camps of his hosts within the Dark Land, created a maintenance service for roads to clear the way to the Sammath Naur, "repaired and cleared again by the labours of countless orcs". The Romans did much less in Judea.

The Dark Lord, of course, seems to have been a victim of his own bureaucracy, as Gorbag and Shagrat commented, in such a typical depiction of public employees criticizing those above. This gossip reveals chains of command, a sense of discipline, the feeling of punishment, and all that is Law.[32]

The Orcs were, without a doubt, creatures little receptive to justice, but they perfectly embodied the respect for the Law caused by the atrocious fear that engendered its breach in the world of Sauron and also in that of Saruman. The dialogue that Pippin's captors held is a perfect example of the dissuasive function of a legal order supported by an effective sanctioning capacity. The repeated mentions to spies and informers reveal a

31. "This is perhaps Tolkien's clearest expression of the view that obedience to orders should not be absolute, that in some circumstances it is right to disobey and yet fulfil a greater duty." (Hammond and Scull 2014, 551).

32. "Orcs here, and on other occasions, have a clear idea of what is admirable and what is contemptible behaviours, which is exactly the same as ours. They cannot revoke what Lewis calls "the Moral Law" and create a counter-morality based on evil, any more than they can revoke biology and live on poison." (Shippey 2001, 133).

climate of terrified paranoia, where the slightest criticism or disobedience could lead to death. The different loyalties that can be observed (the Dark Tower, Minas Morgul, Saruman, the unknown chieftains of Moria), do not seem to have helped to achieve an easy coexistence.

In effect, the references to the orders are constant and also to what would happen if they were not fulfilled, by will or by negligence. The malevolent voice, later identified with the cunning Grishnákh, even spoke of making a report denouncing his companions, a perfect bureaucrat embodying the banality of evil. Uglúk, in a similar line, warned Merry that "any trouble will be reported at the other end" and to Pippin that "Payment is only put off" (*TT*, 'The Uruk-hai', 449). Gorbag and Shagrat, in Mordor, were installed in the same chant: "Full description of every article, garment, weapon, letter, ring, or trinket is to be sent to Lugbúrz at once, and to Lugbúrz only" (*TT*, 'The Choices of Master Samwise', 740). There is no doubt that these creatures participated in the most painful characteristics of the executioners of evil laws.

Undoubtedly, the punishment *par excellence* that the Orcs knew was death, and Uglúk constantly threatened with it. Sauron even applied it collectively, extending to the entire guard this punishment for the breach of his orders. It should be noted that the execution seemed to have definite ways when time was available for it. It is better not to think about what the procedure was; the end of King Eärnur of Gondor, if it had ever come to be known, would have been the most horrifying of examples. Another of the capital penalties we know of is being sent to Shelob's Lair.

Despite this main position of death in the dark punitive catalogue, the mention that Shagrat made to "the Black Pits" allows to conceive a disciplinary establishment of filthy characteristics, even for the fear of an Orc (*RK*, 'The Tower of Cirith Ungol', 905).

Torture, of course, was one of the tools of Sauron's regime, either as a prelude to execution or as a means of interrogation. We know perfectly well that Gollum went through it, surviving by the twisted design of the Dark Lord. Grishnákh threatened Merry and Pippin, clearly making reference to the procedure: "You'll wish there was more that you could tell to satisfy the Questioner, indeed you will: quite soon. We shan't hurry the enquiry" (*TT*, 'The Uruk-hai', 456). It is difficult not to wonder about the nature of the aforementioned Questioner, Orc or Man, and on the way to access such a position. We only have the testimony of Frodo, clearly inspired in the brutality of the 20th century.

On the other hand, there are two strange mentions to the identification number of the Orcs, something typical of an army with an organized recruitment. No commentator seems to have paid attention to these passages, while the camps of Mordor have been identified with those known to Tolkien in the First World War (Hammond and Scull 2014, 608).

I consider that the presented proof would convince any jury of the existence of someone in Mordor who coordinated the planning of the army, someone who took care of the organization of land and troops, someone who understood the importance of Law. I am referring to Sauron, Lord of the Rings, a lawyer, but definitely far from being just or fair.

6 – Pure 'Hobbit-Lore': a case-study

Little is clear about the succession of women to the Sceptre in Númenor, because the sources come from the *Unfinished Tales* and present contradictions, which is usual given the nature of the Tales. The only sure thing is that Tar-Aldarion had only one daughter from his unhappy marriage to the unbelievably beautiful Erendis.

Until then, the succession had always been resolved by granting superior rights to the male, as happened in the case of Silmariën and Tar-Meneldur, both children of Tar-Elendil. From the firstborn descended the Lords of Andunië who would survive the Fall and establish the Realms in Exile. The second continued the line of Elros to his son Tar-Aldarion, who as previously indicated, had one daughter, Ancalimë, second in beauty only to Míriel. The Appendices tell us, in a quite laconic way, that "she became the first Queen; for it was then made a law of the royal house that the eldest child of the King, whether man or woman, should receive the sceptre". The Line of Elros, on the other hand, tells us that "in her favour Aldarion altered the law of succession, so that the (eldest) daughter of a King should succeed, if he had no sons. This change displeased the descendants of Elros, and especially the heir under the old law, Soronto, Aldarion's nephew, son of his elder sister" (*UT*, 220).

The information of these two texts is not the same in any way. The commentary of the *Unfinished Tales* indicates it: "This is not in agreement with the account of the earlier and later laws of succession" (225). In 'Aldarion and Erendis' the subject is developed more widely, pointing out the contradictions and offering a clearer picture.

The objective of the reform of Aldarion was, by all means, to allow that his daughter Ancalimë wielded the sceptre. He intended, therefore, the elimination of the "Salic law", which forbade a woman becoming Queen in her own right. The reform indicated in the Appendices is meaningless, since Ancalimë was an only child and there was no competition to be resolved in terms of primogeniture. This should lead us to believe that in Númenor during the first eight centuries of the Second Age, women had forbidden access to the throne and not a simple postponement of this right. This conclusion, adapted to what has been said about The Line of Elros, takes ahead, in consequence, the second sentence of what is affirmed right there: Soronto had no cause for complaint, since the old law would have excluded him from the sceptre by basing his title on a female line, while the new law placed him in the position of presumed heir, as indicated in the *Unfinished Tales*: "it is said that she remained unmarried so long that her cousin Soronto, relying on the provision of the new law, called upon her to surrender the Heirship" (211). If Aldarion had died without changing that "Salic law", the next King of Númenor would not have been Soronto, son of the daughter of Tar-Meneldur (the sister of Aldarion), but a male descendant of Eärendur, the younger brother of Tar-Elendil.

Did the exclusion of women from the sceptre of Númenor make sense? The reform of Aldarion allowing women to rule, can be understood as a return of the Edain tradition of the First Age. However, the fact that Haleth was an isolated example does not allow us to consider the Edain as egalitarian. Simply, the succession laws were those of a male military chieftainship in which women had different responsibilities. The fact that the King of Númenor was not a warrior anymore, could justify the repeal of this rule.

'Aldarion and Erendis' also includes other contents of the reform. It was established at that time, at the behest of the Council, that the heiress should resign if she remained unmarried after a certain time, and Tar-Aldarion himself established the need for the King's Heir to marry someone from The Line of Elros, as mentioned earlier, when paradoxically he had not done it. The first of the provisions was repealed shortly (as a result of Ancalimë's rejection of the measure, although he ended up marrying, to his disgrace), and allowed that, after Tar-Súrion, Tar-Telperiën received the sceptre. Her reign oversaw a large number of outstanding events in the History of Númenor. She was the first woman who received the sceptre by the principle of primogeniture (the sisters of his father Súrion had rejected it), she was the only ruler of Númenor who did not marry, and therefore, the only case, leaving aside two usurpations, in which it was necessary to fall back in the Line of Elros to find a successor, in this case the son of his younger brother, who adopted the name of Tar-Minastir.

From the second provision, already commented, "this rule of 'royal marriage' was never a matter of law, but it became a custom of pride: a symptom of the growth of the Shadow, since it only became rigid when the distinction between the Line of Elros and other families, in life-span, vigour, or ability, had diminished or altogether disappeared" (216).

7 – *The Lord of the Rings* as a tool to teach Labour Law

For many readers of Tolkien's work, Sam Gamgee is the true hero of the epic narrative. Tolkien himself shared this opinion to a large extent. In fact, the relationship between Frodo and Sam is inspired by the author's experience during the Great War,[33] where the servant Gunga Din is superior to the master.

Inspiration, however, does not provide food. Frodo and Sam were not enlisted in the British Army, but one of them was a local landowner and the other one, a gardener. In this section, we will proceed to study what would be the legal nature of the relationship between them from the point of view of the Spanish labour legislation. For this, an analysis of the four notes that characterize the employee relationship in Spanish Law will be made. Once this examination is completed, this situation will be subsumed under one of the existing legal categories.

We will start with a previous consideration of salaried work as an activity that only individuals can perform. Animals, legal persons and even replicants cannot have access to an employment contract. In a world like Middle-earth, legal personality should, logically, be recognized to other types of existence. Sam had been born alive and had completely detached himself from his mother's womb, for which he fulfilled the requirements of article 30 of the Spanish Civil Code; he had, thus, acquired legal personality. The elimination of the picturesque requirement of having human form by Law 20/2011 avoids annoying disquisitions on whether the Hobbits fulfilled such a requirement. In any case, we could easily understand that it is achieved in view of the jurisprudence or of the people who appear in certain TV shows. On the part of

33. "My Sam Gamgee is indeed a reflexion of the English soldier, of the privates and batmen I knew in the 1914 war, and recognised as so far superior to myself." (Carpenter 2000, 89).

Frodo, hypothetical employer, there is nothing outstanding to note, given the breadth of assumptions that the Spanish legislation admits in such a position.

Their legal personality recognized, it is necessary to analyse if the contractors have capacity. Although both of them are prone to make some stupid decisions, such as claiming the Ruling Ring as their own or attacking Shelob single-handedly, there is nothing to suggest that Frodo and Sam are not in their right mind and should be disqualified. As the contract is signed in the Shire, there is no relevant element concerning the condition of foreigner. The only aspect to keep in mind, therefore, is age. Well, both contractors fully comply with the requirement at the time of the War of the Ring. Frodo Baggins reached the age of majority on 22nd September 2999 T.A., the day of the celebrated party of Bilbo's 111th birthday.

Sam Gamgee, on the other hand, turned 33 in 3013 T.A. However, before that date, he would have needed the capacity complement provided by Hamfast Gaffer Gamgee, his father, an authentic authority on roots. He would have needed it if he had entered into a contract on his own, but there is a very important fact that should be valued. The Gaffer worked as gardener in Bag End, first as assistant or apprentice of old Holman Greenhand and later as titular gardener. But "now that he was himself growing old and stiff in the joints, the job was mainly carried on by his youngest son" (*FR*, 'A Long-expected Party', 22). From these words, we can make two important assumptions, leaving aside the question of Social Security benefits that the older Gamgee could receive in our days. In the first place, Sam was already a gardener at the time of the famous birthday party at 2999 T.A., when he was just a 19-year-old lad, a very early age among the Hobbits, although already within the period of the 'tweens'. Sam working at such an early age was pure child exploitation, in any case, which would probably be intolerable in Spanish law. The second relevant fact to consider, is the ability of the Gaffer to associate someone to his work, without seeming to mediate any new contract. "Mainly" allows us to conclude, without a doubt, that there was a simultaneity of work between the Gaffer and Sam.

According to Spanish law, this situation could be redirected to two legal institutions. In the first place, if there was a continuity in time of this simultaneous work, Sam could be considered as an associate assistant of his father, a figure that although it is included in Article 10.3 of the Workers' Statute, has a long history, dating back to the Middle Ages. If, on the other hand, it was a sporadic substitution, it would fit in the margin of flexibility that jurisprudence has recognized about certain tasks at the service of urban farms, as exemplified by the judgement of the Supreme Court, Chamber IV, of 25th January 2000. This fact will be evaluated later when trying to venture a definitive theory about the legal relationship that is being discussed.

After bringing these previous aspects of great relevance to light, it is convenient to proceed with the analysis of four characteristic notes. In the first one and less complex to study, voluntariness will be addressed. Sam, no doubt, freely exercised his activity as a gardener. There is no mandatory personal duty in this case that could contradict this situation.

Secondly, does Sam charge Frodo for his services? The remuneration trait is certainly decisive when it comes to qualifying an activity as salaried work. Well, nowhere is it recorded that Sam, or his father, saw any financial compensation for their work. Certainly, the Gaffer receives generous presents from Bilbo when he disappears, but such a general context of gifts, has no transcendence. We will discuss this issue later on.

The third feature is that of *ajenidad*, a word untranslatable into English. It has two different sides: in the fruits (benefits) and in the means. The first dimension is related to the situation in which "the fruits of work are attributed initially and directly to a person other than the person who performs the work" (Alonso Olea, 1994, 50). We have the testimony of Sam himself: "Mr. Baggins now, that I work for" expressing perfectly the characterization of this transfer of benefits to a third party (*FR*, 'The Shadow of the Past', 45). On the "ajenidad" in the fruits, there is no doubt: the direct beneficiary of the good state of the garden and of the tasks of Sam is Frodo.

On the *ajenidad* in the means, the main point to consider would be the ownership of the shears with which Sam carries out his tasks in Bag End, the same treacherous scissors which will reveal the curious Gamgee before Gandalf. Unfortunately, we do not have anything conclusive on this issue.

Finally, regarding subordination, "insertion in the managerial and organizational circle of the employer", the problem we find is that we do not have any written testimony from Frodo giving orders to Sam as gardener (Supreme Court, IV Chamber, 27th May 1992). He is seen working only in the morning of Saturday, 13th April, 3018 T.A., and it was Sam himself who decided on the tasks he would do and when to do them the previous day, at the end of his tavern session. Sam enjoys, apparently, a wide capacity to organize his work schedule, which does not necessarily exclude the existence of an employment relationship.

After the transfer to Crickhollow, it seems possible to detect a substantial change in his working conditions, since Sam, after leaving Hobbiton, will go "to do for Mr. Frodo and look after his bit of garden" (*FR*, 'Three is Company', 69). It is not difficult to conceive that it is a substantial modification of his working conditions, since it meant functional mobility outside the permanent group, having incorporated the new tasks that were hidden under the name of "doing for Mr. Frodo". An example of these tasks would be found in the orders that Pippin gives to Sam when they wake up, somewhat imperatively, after their first night on the field: "Get breakfast ready for half-past nine! Have you got the bath-water hot?" (72). It is clear that Sam would have added to the functions of Angus MacAllister those of the incomparable Jeeves.

At this point, it is convenient to collect all the evidence found. To the voluntariness and the *ajenidad* that would indicate the existence of an employment contract, we could oppose the lack of any news about the remuneration and a flexible subordination. If we opted for a strict interpretation of these elements and remembered the capacity of substitution between the Gaffer and Sam, we could decide that between Frodo and Sam there was no employment relationship before the retirement of his father, but they would fit within the works of friendship, good-neighbourhood and benevolence of article 1.3.d of the Workers' Statute.

However, after the retirement of the Gaffer, if we consider that Sam does not live on thin air (on the contrary, we know that he spends money on alcohol, and not precisely sporadically) and that talking about money is an improper vulgarity within the noblest epic fantasy, we can safely imagine that Frodo regularly paid Sam an amount of which

Tolkien, with the style and elegance of an Oxford Don, would have decided not to tell us about. There would, then, be remuneration.

In that case, the key element to consider would be the subordination or its very absence, because in this second scenario, Sam could be a self-employed worker., He could be even considered a self-employed worker economically dependent, a TRADE, if he fulfilled the requirements of article 11.1 of Law 20/2007, of the Statute of Autonomous Work. Given that we do not know about any other garden in which Sam performs his activity, we can conclude that more than the 75% of his income comes from Frodo and, therefore, the legal requirement would be met.

However, in terms of subordination, it has been recognized that "a very influential factor in the degree [of this] and in the configuration of the provision of work [...] is professional qualification. Highly qualified jobs are often provided under autonomy or free exercise; when they are provided in a subordinate regime, the forms of it are more subtle and relaxed, they do not affect the *lex artis* or technical rules of execution of the contract." (Martín Valverde, Rodríguez-Sañudo Gutiérrez and García Murcia 2012, 41). Nobody doubts Sam's capacity as gardener, the most famous in History, no less. Assuming these postulates and taking for granted the intuitive existence of remuneration, we could conclude that there was an employment relationship between Sam and Frodo.

And then, all papers in order, the Tale of Frodo of the Nine Fingers and the Ring of Doom could start.

Bibliography

Alonso Olea, M., *Introducción al Derecho del Trabajo*, 5th edn. (Madrid: Civitas, 1994).

Anderson, D.A., *El Hobbit anotado*, trans. by M. Figueroa and R. Masera (Barcelona: Minotauro, 1990).

Carpenter, H., *J.R.R. Tolkien. A biography*, (New York: Houghton Mifflin Company, 2000)
— J.R.R. Tolkien. Una biografía, trans. by C. Peralta (Barcelona: Minotauro, 1990).

Castell, D., 'The Realms of Tolkien', *New Worlds*, 50.168, (1968) 143-154.

Chance, J., *Tolkien's Art. A Mythology for England,* (Lexington: The University Press of Kentucky, 2001)

Curry, P., "La modernidad en la Tierra Media", in *J. R. R. Tolkien. Señor de La Tierra Media*, ed. by J. Pearce (Barcelona: Minotauro – Planeta DeAgostini, 2002), 49-55.

Fernández Higgs, B., *Tolkien y el reencantamiento del mundo,* (Santiago: Ediciones Universidad Católica de Chile, 2003).

Ferrández Bru, J.M., *El "Tío Curro": La Conexión Española de J.R.R.Tolkien*, 2nd edn. (Edinburgh: Luna Press Publishing, 2018).

Hammond, W.G. and C. Scull, *The Lord of the Rings. A Reader's Companion,* (London: Harper Collins, 2014).

Martín Valverde, A., F. Rodríguez-Sañudo Gutiérrez, J. García Murcia, *Derecho del Trabajo*, 21st edn. (Madrid: Tecnos, 2012).

Odero, J.M., *J.R.R. Tolkien: Cuentos de Hadas,* (Pamplona: Eunsa, 1987).

Rodríguez Valls, F., 'El relato fantástico como metáfora de la existencia humana: Una referencia a los cuentos de J.R.R. Tolkien', *Thémata. Revista de filosofía*, 39 (2007) 195–202.

Scull, C., and W.G. Hammond, *The J.R.R. Tolkien Companion and Guide*, rev. edn. (London: Collins, 2017).

Shippey, T., *The Road to Middle-earth,* (New York: Houghton Mifflin Company, 2003).
— *J.R.R. Tolkien. Author of the Century,* (London: Harper Collins, 2001).

Smith, M., 'Legal Bother: Law and Related Matters in *The Hobbit*', in *The Return of the Ring. Proceedings of the Tolkien Society Conference 2012*, ed. by L. Forest-Hill (Edinburgh: Luna Press Publishing, 2016) 123-142.

Tolkien, J.R.R., *Unfinished Tales of Númenor and Middle-earth*, ed. by C. Tolkien (London: Harper Collins, 1980).
— *The Silmarillion*, ed. by C. Tolkien (London: Harper Collins, 1998).
— *The Letters of J.R.R. Tolkien*, edited by H. Carpenter, with the assistance of C. Tolkien (London: Harper Collins, 2006).
— *The Lord of the Rings*, (London: HarperCollins, 2010).
— *The Hobbit*, 2nd edn. (London: Harper Collins, 2011).

Tomás y Valiente, F., *Manual de Historia del Derecho Español*, 4th edn. (Madrid: Tecnos, 1983).

Weber, M., *Economy and Society*, ed. by G. Roth and C. Wittich (University of California Press, 1978).

Tolkien's Libertarian Moral Impulse: Domination and the Lust for Power as the Summum Malum

Craig A. Boyd

Tolkien was by no means a political philosopher nor did his writings explicitly engage political issues in any systematic way. But he does offer some interesting insights about freedom and the evils of domination as we see expressed in his scepticism of Churchill "and his gang", in his reflections on why "*Nolo episcopari*" is the one qualification for a bishop, and in his confession that he preferred "anarchy" to other forms of government. But if one does a close reading of *The Lord of the Rings* – especially in light of his *Letters* – we see an approach to society (both in its political and moral aspects) that reveals a distrust of anyone who desires power and its use to dominate others. In *Letter 52*, Tolkien writes that the chief moral problem (and we see this in both his fiction and in the actual world) is the desire of some people to control and dominate others. He says that "The most improper job of any man, even saints (who at any rate were at least unwilling to take it on), is bossing other men. Not one in a million is fit for it, and least of all those who seek the opportunity" (*Letters*, Letter 52, 64). Both the desire to control others and the activity itself are evil. Even though the desire might start with a good intention – a desire to "make things right" – it inevitably degenerates into an unhealthy and immoral need to dominate others. This 'bossing' of others seems to highlight the differences between the two great wizards: Saruman and Gandalf.

Although Saruman feigns collegiality and wisdom, he harbours arrogant and domineering sentiments. He is angered by the fact that some preferred Gandalf as the head of the White Council; and Tolkien frequently describes him as "proud" (*UT*, 390). It is his pride that leads him to believe that he can, and should, dominate others since this will be good for everyone. This deviant desire to dominate others manifests itself in his quest to possess the Ring of Power.

In contrast to Saruman, Gandalf emerges as a particularly illuminating moral exemplar. Although Gandalf has great power, he never uses it to dominate or coerce others. Even when he confronts Saruman after the Battle of Helm's Deep where he offers forgiveness and redemption. But throughout the narrative, Gandalf encourages, persuades, and invariably cautions against harm and the taking of life, as evidenced in his caveat to Frodo not to take life needlessly (*FR*, 'The Shadow of the Past', 59). The reason Gandalf refuses the Ring is because he knows that it would tempt him to dominate others – even if his intentions were initially good. In the end, Gandalf's willingness to provide others with maximal freedom is a sign of the libertarian impulses Tolkien weaves into *The Lord of the Rings* as it also mirrors what he writes in the letters. Yet, Tolkien's libertarianism is not merely freedom for freedom's sake. Rather, it is a response to the evils of domination and control. For Tolkien, freedom must always orient itself to a good beyond itself – to the care and well-being of others. I begin with a brief account of Tolkien's views on freedom and how he describes the lust for power in the context of his brief remarks about politics. I then move on to a consideration of how this plays out in his narratives in the contrast between Saruman and Gandalf.

1 – Libertarian Impulses and the Problem of Power

Before moving any further, I need to define what I mean by 'Tolkien's libertarian impulses' by contrasting it with metaphysical freedom and political freedom. I do not use 'freedom' here in its traditional metaphysical meaning as juxtaposed with determinism as philosophers who would lobby for "genuine freedom of the will" (Augustine 1978). Nor do I employ it as contemporary political philosophers in the analytic tradition do with regard to the freedom to determine what is good for me and the freedom to pursue it (Nozick 1978). Others have commented on the nature of providence and freedom with regard to Tolkien's metaphysical views (Hibbs 2003). And even though there may be resonances in terms of political freedom, since he seems to desire minimal state involvement in an individual's private life, I do not think this is the central issue for him. Certainly, the Hobbits in the Shire do well without a centralized government but this is because there is a kind of general beneficence of one to another that precludes the need for government control and the need to order people to the good.

Tolkien never uses the term 'libertarianism', but he does confess that he prefers "anarchy" as a system to others. In the context of his criticism of Churchill he writes,

> My political opinions lean more and more to Anarchy (philosophically understood, meaning abolition of control not whiskered men with bombs) – or to 'unconstitutional' Monarchy. I would arrest anybody who uses the word State (in any sense other than the inanimate realm of England and its inhabitants, a thing that has neither power, rights nor mind); and after a chance of recantation, execute them if they remained obstinate! [...] Government is an abstract noun meaning the art and process of governing and it should be an offence to write it with a capital G or so as to refer to people. (*Letters*, Letter 52, 63)

The reification or at least the personification of an abstract entity – an abstract entity that seems to desire more and more power – makes Tolkien suspicious, since those who aspire to be in charge invariably have power as their primary motivation. In his comments about those who desire the power to "boss" others he notes that "[t]he mediævals were only too right in taking *nolo episcopari* as the best reason a man could give to others for making him a bishop", since the only one to be trusted with power was the one who did not trust himself (64).

The way Tolkien seems to think of freedom – and what we might call 'Tolkienian Libertarianism' or a kind of 'moral libertarianism' – is that creatures should always be free from domination by others and free to pursue the good. And here we see more clearly the contrast with the kinds of political libertarianism as espoused by people like Nozick (1974) and Ayn Rand (1964) who think that there really is no genuine good for a human being other than that which they conceive of as being good 'for them'. That is, modern political thinkers are sceptical about basic human goods. But Tolkien, the Catholic, rejects this notion emphatically and stands in radical contrast to Rand, for example, who espouses the idea of freedom for selfishness. Without a clear orientation to genuine goods and the morally permissible means to achieve them, the person becomes corrupted. Political libertarianism, therefore, is insufficient for the task of moral integrity. Creatures are not merely amoral entities pursuing their own idiosyncratic goods in a morally neutral cosmos; rather, agents are always embedded in a moral context – one that requires not only good ends but morally good means. Freedom is freedom for the good. Those who would choose a bad end (e.g., the desire to control others) or choose an immoral means (e.g., destroying innocent life for "the greater good") have misused their freedom. And in Saruman's case, we see a character who does both.

2 – Saruman's Lust for Power

The problem with those who lust for power is that the desire for power ends up consuming them. We can see this operative in a variety of Tolkien's characters: Sauron, Saruman, Boromir, and Denethor. And even the latter two, who would use it for good, would end up dominating and controlling others. Domination is a kind of over-reaching beyond what a person should rightfully seek. Tolkien writes that, "The supremely bad motive is (for this tale, since it is specifically about it) domination of other "free" wills. The Enemy's operations are by no means all goetic deceits, but "magic" that produces real effects in the physical world. But his magia he uses to bulldoze people and things, and his goeteia to terrify and subjugate" (*Letters*, Letter 155, 200). The motive here, as moral philosophers have consistently noted (Aquinas 1948), serves as the cause of the agent's actions. And this raises an important point. One must not only intend a good purpose but also use the proper means to accomplish that good purpose. Tolkien himself notes that the magic in the story is neither good nor evil "but only by a motive or purpose or use" (*Letters*, Letter 155, 199).

The end intended may be evil – as in the case of Sauron who feels compelled to control others – or it may be good – as in the case of Denethor who says of the Ring, "Nay, it should have been kept, hidden, hidden dark and deep. Not used, I say, unless at the uttermost end of need, but set beyond his grasp" (*RT*, 'The Siege of Gondor', 813). Denethor would use it for good but fails to see that an individual's intended purpose is merely one of the sufficient conditions for moral goodness , a person must also have to resist the temptation the Ring offers. The use of a thing might be even more critical as one can overlook the manner it is used by justifying the means in terms of the end one intends. But what of Saruman? Did he will an evil end as well as an evil means?

Tolkien sees all creatures as created good – and that it is only through some kind of corruption that they become evil. This basic notion of 'evil as privation' explains his comment that "In my story, I do not deal in Absolute Evil. I do not think there is such a thing, since that is Zero. I do not think that at any rate any "rational being" is wholly evil" (*Letters*, Letter 183, 243). Saruman was one of the Maiar, and so, was created good – very good. But in his pursuit of the good of knowledge for the purpose of defeating Sauron he becomes corrupted.

At some point, Saruman turned from pursuing the good (and being good) to a person who would dominate others – and to seeing this domination of others as something good. Gandalf says of him that, "it seems that he was not content. Further and further abroad he gazed, until he cast his gaze upon Barad-Dûr. Then he was caught!" (*TT*,

'The Palantír', 598). Saruman's fixation with the Ring (and his use of the Palantír) combined with his desire for control corrupts him – and turns even his study and search for knowledge into a corrupt curiosity (Boyd 2020, 228).

Like Sauron, Saruman uses his magic and his power to dominate others for the purpose of gaining more power. "Power-lust", as Tolkien calls it, is the chief temptation of wizards (*Letters*, Letter 203, 262) and this is especially true of Saruman, who uses every power available to him – especially his use of words – to gain even more power. He convinces Radagast to send Gandalf to Orthanc where he believes he can persuade the Grey Wizard to join him in his pursuit of the Ring – but he also knows that Gandalf has hidden from him important facts about the Hobbits, the Shire, and the Ring. When Gandalf arrives at Orthanc, Saruman presents an argument that he hopes will persuade Gandalf.

> He drew himself up then and began to declaim, as if he were making a speech long rehearsed. "The Elder Days are gone. The Middle Days are passing. The Younger Days are beginning. The time of the Elves is over, but our time is at hand: the world of Men, which we must rule. But we must have power, power to order all things as we will, for that good which only the Wise can see." He came and laid his long hand on my arm. "And why not, Gandalf?" he whispered. "Why not? The Ruling Ring? If we could command that, then the Power would pass to us. That is in truth why I brought you here. For I have many eyes in my service, and I believe that you know where this precious thing now lies. Is it not so? Or why do the Nine ask for the Shire, and what is your business there?" As he said this a lust which he could not conceal shone suddenly in his eyes. (*FR*, 'The Council of Elrond', 259)

With reference to the end intended and the means of accomplishing this task, Saruman betrays himself to Gandalf (McInerny 1989).

First, the desire for the Ring is itself corrupt. It is a desire for power and control. And after long years of study, he knows this and Gandalf also knows this – as he too, has studied the Ring and its powers. Saruman's "lust" for the Ring is a desire for an evil end. He no longer intends the good – but has capitulated to his desire. But even in his attempt to hide his perverse intentions, he explicitly expresses his intent to join with Sauron.

> We may join with that Power. It would be wise, Gandalf. There is hope that way. Its victory is at hand; and there will be rich reward for those that aided it. As the Power grows, its proved friends will also grow; and the Wise, such as you and I, may with patience come at last to direct its courses, to control it. We can bide our time, we can keep our thoughts in our hearts, deploring maybe evils done by the way, but approving the high and ultimate purpose: Knowledge, Rule, Order; all the things that we have so far striven in vain to accomplish, hindered rather than helped by our weak or idle friends. There need not be, there would not be, any real change in our designs, only in our means. (*FR*, 'The Council of Elrond', 259)

He now admits his intention but also shows that his end (control and rule) will permit any means necessary. He downplays this, by "deploring evils done by the way" since the end intended – he thinks – will justify it. He has both: (1) an evil intention, and (2) an evil means to that end.

For Saruman, only a select few are wise enough to wield power. In his view, men and elves and other creatures have demonstrated that they are not capable of ruling themselves well. The only remedy is for those who have arrogated control for themselves to govern those who are 'lesser' beings. In light of this 'insight', Saruman thinks he is a better manager of peoples' lives than anyone else; but just as important, Saruman has the power (and will) to rule over others rather than leaving them free to mismanage themselves. An unjust peace, in his mind, is better than a just anarchy. And to this end, Saruman raises an orc army to destroy Rohan.

In his quest for power, Saruman's orc army will attack Rohan but he will also need fuel for his war machine. He instructs his orcs to cut down the trees in Fangorn forest. This is one of those 'necessary evils' that furthers his designs. Of course, like many who calculate in a utilitarian manner, Saruman fails to accurately anticipate the consequences of his behaviour. He both loses the battle of Helm's Deep as well as Orthanc itself as he does not consider the anger of the Ents – nor the seemingly insignificant causal activities of the Hobbits that precipitate the Ent's retaliation. As Gandalf observes to Gimli, Legolas, and Aragorn, "It was not in vain that the young hobbits came with us, if only for Boromir's sake. But that is not the only part they have to play. They were brought to Fangorn, and their coming was like the falling of small stones that starts an avalanche in the mountains" (*TT*, 'The White Rider', 496). The "avalanche" buries Saruman.

He is defeated and retreats to Orthanc and imprisoned but eventually escapes and makes his way to the Shire where he has already established his own domination of the entire region. He has used his power to intimidate, pervert, and control the residents of the Shire and their way of life. When the four heroic hobbits return, they find that Mordor (or rather Isengard) has taken root in the Shire whilst they have been away. The vision in Galadriel's Mirror has come to pass. People are oppressed by the systemic industrialization and bureaucracy couched in the language of paternalism. Saruman, as 'Sharkey', is of course behind it. Saruman's people have subjugated the hobbits. But the hobbits resist and rise up against the oppression freeing themselves and returning the Shire to its bucolic pre-Sharkey conditions.

Over the entire narrative, Saruman places his own desire for power and control over the goods of persons and of friendship. Unlike Gandalf and others who oppose Sauron, Saruman lives alone and seems to dislike the company of others. Tolkien writes that Saruman's "mind was in contrast to Gandalf's always more attracted by artefacts and instruments of power rather than by persons" (*UT*, 406). Jane Chance observes that Tolkien objects to "the deployment of post-Enlightenment technologies in the governance of people" (2001, 21). In wanting to control others, Saruman's focus turns to the means by which he can successfully (and efficiently) accomplish this. His development of the Uruk-hai, the war machines, and the mechanization and industrialization of the Shire are ample evidence.

There is a lack of what the Ignatian tradition calls "cura personalis" – the care of and for persons. Clearly, Saruman cared more for machines than for creatures as he was willing to create an entire army of orcs to do his bidding. In contrast to the callousness of Saruman, Gandalf expresses care even for those orcs in the service of the Enemy. He tells Denethor, "I pity even his slaves" (*RT*, 'The Siege of Gondor', 814). Not only does

Saruman not care he willingly sacrifices anything he needs for his own conquest, since the ends always justify the means – even if it involves sacrificing 'lesser' beings.

There are, then, three kinds of people here. First, there are those like Gandalf who desire good ends and deploy only good means (i.e., refusing to dominate others and respecting the freedom of other agents) to achieve those good ends. Second, there are those like Denethor and Boromir who also desire good ends but succumb to the temptation to use any means available to them in forcing their wills upon others. Although their desires are good, their integrity disintegrates in the desire to dominate others even in the pursuit of the good. Finally, there are those like Saruman who desire evil ends and employ evil means – especially the dominance of other free creatures to achieve their purposes. This last group deserves more attention since Tolkien sees this lust for domination particularly in the character of the ruffian and the boss.

3 – Ruffians and Bosses

A constellation of three terms captures Tolkien's sentiments concerning domination and abuse: ruffian, bully, and boss. But the key term – used especially throughout the last two chapters of *The Return of the King* – is "ruffian". Tolkien employs this term no fewer than 48 times. It is his preferred word of choice for Saruman's minions. But he uses words like "bully" and "boss" in negative ways as well. The first thing, though, is the idea that the ruffian is the one who bullies and cows others by threats and force – and this is exactly what they do in 'The Scouring of the Shire'.

The Oxford English Dictionary notes that a 'ruffian' is "a brutal or lawless villain; a violent criminal, a thug" (1997). It is generally understood as a term of abuse and can also mean a "swaggering bully". The ruffians who take over the Shire use violence – and the threats of violence – to enforce their (and their boss') will.

The bully – a close semantic relative of the ruffian – is a "tyrannical coward who makes himself a terror to the weak" (1997). And this is exactly what the ruffians do to the hapless hobbits in the Shire. The typical activity of the ruffians is to "bully" and "boss" others.

A boss, then, is a ruffian who has either risen through the ranks or has been appointed through some kind of prior status. In this light, Saruman – as a 'boss' – is simply a ruffian with a great deal of power. Like the other ruffians, Saruman uses threats to accomplish his goals – especially after Gandalf strips him of his staff.

This idea of the ruffian as a swaggering bully is how Tolkien uses the word in the last few chapters of *The Lord of the Rings*. The ruffians fit the description of the bully especially as they typically enforce their agenda through verbal threats rather than actual physical force (though physical force may be used if the threats themselves fail to get the desired result). They presume to have a more privileged status than the hobbits in the Shire; and when Frodo, Sam, Merry, and Pippin refuse to wilt under their threats, they take umbrage at the four returning heroes. The ruffians expect that their threats and bullying tactics will bring the hobbits under submission, but these hobbits are different; they can see through the threats and possess a courage that the ruffians cannot comprehend. One passage captures this well. When the hobbits confront one of their leaders, the chief ruffian responds to them:

> 'So that's your tone, is it? Change it, or we'll change it for you. You little folk are getting too uppish. Don't you trust too much in the Boss's kind heart. Sharkey's come now and he'll do what Sharkey says.'
> 'And what may that be? said Frodo quietly.
> 'This country wants waking up and setting to rights,' said the ruffian, 'and Sharkey's going to do it; and make it hard, if you drive him to it. You need a bigger Boss. And you'll get one before the year is out, if there's any more trouble. Then you'll learn a thing or two, you little rat-folk.' (*RT*, 'The Scouring of the Shire', 1005)

Through intimidation and threats, the ruffian thinks he can simply use brutish rhetoric and threats to get the hobbits to submit. But the usual tactics do not work on these hobbits since they possess virtues such as courage and magnanimity that the ruffians do not. As a result, fear does not dissuade them from challenging the ruffians.

The ruffians – and especially the bosses – arrogantly assume that they know best what is good for others and so do not hesitate to grasp power and inflict their views on others, especially for what they call the "rat-folk". This is true not only in the sub-created world of Middle-earth but also in mid-twentieth century England.

Tolkien distrusted those real life characters who strategized and consolidated their own power, especially Churchill, whom he also refers to as a "ruffian" (*Letters*, Letter 53, 65). In the context of making the claim that "*Nolo episcopari*" is the primary qualification for a bishop, he develops the idea that anyone who desires power – regardless of the reason – has already been corrupted, at least *prima facie*. As we saw above, he was convinced that "the most improper job of any man, even saints (who at any rate were at least unwilling to take it on), is bossing other men. Not one in a million is fit for it, and least of all those who seek the opportunity" (*Letters*, Letter 52, 64). Churchill sought the opportunity throughout his life – demonstrating, at least to Tolkien – that he was unfit to hold authority. And so, Tolkien refers to "Winston and his gang" in a way that demonstrates he trusts them less than he would the average person. The similarities between Churchill and Saruman are not simply their rhetorical finesse and domination of others, but also their desire for power and their preference for bombs and machines to accomplish their tasks.

In contrast to the ruffian-like behaviour of Saruman and his minions, both Gandalf and Galadriel see the temptation to power as simultaneously attractive and repellent, especially when Frodo offers the Ring to each. Gandalf tells Frodo, "With that power I should have power too great and terrible. And over me the Ring would gain a power still greater and more deadly. [...] Yet the way of the Ring to my heart is by pity, pity for weakness and the desire of strength to do good. Do not tempt me! I dare not take it, not even to keep it safe, unused" (*FR*, 'The Shadow of the Past', 61). Gandalf knows that power corrupts; but so too, does Galadriel. Her response is similar. She says to Frodo, "You will give me the Ring freely! In place of the Dark Lord you will set up a Queen. And I shall not be dark, but beautiful and terrible as the Morning and the Night! Fair as the Sea and the Sun and the Snow upon the Mountain! Dreadful as the Storm and the Lightning! Stronger than the foundations of the earth. All shall love me and despair!" (*FR*, 'The Mirror of Galadriel', 365-6). But she rejects it as well. Galadriel understands the temptation of The Ring and its inevitable Domination of other selves. As a person who desires the good – but also desires the appropriate means to that good – she knows that controlling others is always to be avoided – even for a good intention. Although Tolkien does not elaborate on her last statement that "All shall love me and despair", one could reasonably interpret this to mean that even the love of Galadriel would be coerced – and, so, a violation of others' freedom.

4 – Freedom for the Good

For Tolkien, freedom from domination and coercion is simply the first necessary condition for acting well. Freedom is not simply an instrumental good, it must be directed to an object or a goal beyond its own self-centred desires. Another way of saying this is to see that freedom is a good as a means, but not the good itself. There are genuine goods that extend beyond my own desires and liberties.

There are, of course, various particular goods like beer, mushrooms, singing, the making of poetry, a good walk, treasure, and a hot bath. However, there are more important goods as well. These goods would include living with integrity, honesty, and in fellowship with one's friends and neighbours. This theme can be seen throughout Tolkien's writings but especially in *The Hobbit* and *The Lord of the Rings*. In *The Hobbit*, for example, Thorin Oakenshield's parting words to Bilbo are: "There is more in you of good than you know, child of the kindly West. Some courage and some wisdom, blended in measure. If more of us valued food and cheer and song above hoarded gold, it would be a merrier world. But sad or merry, I must leave it now. Farewell!" (*Hobbit*, 'The Return Journey', 348). Thorin recognizes too late that friendship is more valuable than treasure.

Like other flawed characters – especially Boromir – Thorin uses his status and position in an attempt to control the outcome of events. That is, these characters think that a good end (whether it might be the restoration of a Kingdom or the defence of one's homeland) justifies any means of securing that good. There is no denying that the goods they desire are genuine goods. Rather, it is in the coercion and use of power in attaining the good in question that vitiates the action. Thorin's ostracization of Bilbo, and Boromir's attempt to take the Ring by force from Frodo, show a character that is already partially corrupted. Boromir reveals this attitude at the Council of Elrond when he says, "Saruman is a traitor, but did he not have a glimpse of wisdom? Why do you speak ever of hiding and destroying? Why should we not think that the Great Ring has come into our hands to serve us in the very hour of need? Wielding it the Free Lords of the Free may surely defeat the Enemy" (*FR*, 'The Council of Elrond', 267). Even though Gandalf and Elrond warn him that it cannot be used in this way, he still thinks that he could use it for good. But the desire for it leads to his own demise.

A good end can only be attained through a good means. The coercion of others, the forced conscription of slaves, or even the taking of the Ring from a hobbit by force cannot be an acceptable means for an otherwise good end since it would mean violating the freedom and dignity of other persons. In fact, Gollum's own acquisition of the Ring was by means of murder. The Ring, perceived as a good, entices those who desire it to use any means available to acquire it. As Tolkien claims, "You can't fight the enemy with his own ring without turning into an enemy" (*Letters*, Letter 81, 94). Tolkien sees here that the desire to possess and control corrupts the one who cannot overcome this desire. Once a person has surrendered to the temptation of power and domination, that person is no longer free in the most important sense but has become bound by the object of desire.

Gandalf, unlike Saruman, is not fettered by his desire for the Ring. He has no desire to control or dominate others. When he asks Bilbo to leave the Ring, he does not coerce him. When asked by Pippin what he will do to Saruman after destroying Saruman's staff, Gandalf replies, "'I? Nothing!' said Gandalf. 'I will do nothing to him. I do not wish for mastery'" (*TT*, 'The Voice of Saruman', 585). Gandalf's vocation is not domination of 'lesser' souls, but the care of persons and those things that require care. He is, in fact, a steward of 'the good'. In one of his heated conversations with Denethor, the real steward (i.e., Gandalf) instructs the titular steward on what it means to fulfil his vocation. He says,

> 'The rule of no realm is mine, neither of Gondor nor any other, great or small. But all worthy things that are in peril as the world now stands, those are my care. And for my part, I shall not wholly fail of my task, though Gondor should perish, if anything passes through this night that can still grow fair or bear fruit and flower again in days to come. For I also am a steward. Did you not know?' (*RT*, 'Minas Tirith', 758)

A particularly striking contrast between Gandalf and Saruman is that Gandalf puts his knowledge and wisdom to serve others; he cares for others no matter how insignificant they may seem. While Saruman calls the hobbits "rag-tags" and diminishes them and tries to dominate them at every opportunity, Gandalf sees their value as persons and cares for them as much as he cares for those deemed 'the most important'. Saruman uses his power and freedom to dominate and pursue his own selfish ends. Gandalf uses his to care and nurture.

For Tolkien, freedom is not a good in itself but an instrumental good to be put in the service of caring for others. The goods of genuine fellowship preclude attempts at dominating others by force or status. Moreover, one's freedom must only be used to persuade, not dominate. In the pursuit of various good ends we must also take care not to employ immoral means to those ends – no matter how honourable or noble those ends might be.

Although Saruman may have started out as a good wizard – desiring the good of the inhabitants of middle-earth – he became corrupted; he desired too much for himself, he lusted after power, and he illicitly dominated those he felt were expedient. Juxtaposed with Saruman, stands Gandalf who consistently rejects coercion for persuasion, dominance for care, and expediency for integrity.

Bibliography

Aquinas, Thomas, *Summa Theologica*, trans. by Fathers of the English Dominican Province (Notre Dame: Christian Classics Publishers, 1948).

Augustine, *On the Problem of Free Choice*, trans. by Dom Mark Pontifex (Mahwah: Paulist Press, 1978).

Boyd, C.A., 'Augustine, Aquinas, and Tolkien: Three Catholic Views on Curiositas' *The Heythrop Journal*, 61.2 (2019) 222-33.

Chance, J., *Lord of the Rings: The Mythology of Power,* (Lexington: University of Kentucky Press, 2001).

Hibbs, T., 'Providence and Dramatic Unity in *The Lord of the Rings*' in *The Lord of the Rings and Philosophy*, ed. by G. Bassham and E. Bronson (2003) 167-78.

McInerny, R., *Ethica Thomistica: The Moral Thought of St Thomas Aquinas,* (Washington, DC: The Catholic University of America Press, 1989).

Nozick, R., *Anarchy, State, and Utopia,* (New York: Basic Books, 1974).

Oxford English Dictionary, (Oxford: Oxford University Press, 1997)

Rand, A., *The Virtue of Selfishness,* (New York: Signet Books, 1964).

Tolkien, J.R.R., 2002, *The Annotated Hobbit*, ed. Douglas A. Anderson. Boston: Houghton Mifflin.
– *The Letters of J.R.R. Tolkien*, ed. by H. Carpenter with the assistance of C. Tolkien (Boston: Houghton Mifflin, 1981).
– *The Lord of the Rings,* (Boston: Houghton Mifflin, 1965).
– *Unfinished Tales*, ed. by C. Tolkien (Boston: Houghton Mifflin, 1980).

The trial of Húrin: justice seen to be done?

Jan van Breda

This paper focuses on the children of Húrin and Morwen. Christopher Tolkien tells us that in his later years, his father J.R.R. Tolkien gave the story a more and more central position, it became "the dominant and absorbing story of the end of the Elder Days, in which complexity of motive and character, trapped in the mysterious workings of Morgoth's curse, sets it altogether apart" (*Jewels*, viii-ix). This observation is borne out by the fact that in the 1950s, Tolkien wrote a long account of Túrin's story in the 'Grey Annals'. So extensive was this version, that it forms the basis of much of the published *The Silmarillion*. But the story of the children of Húrin is also recorded in the 'Narn I Chîn Húrin', posthumously published much later, in 2007. One may note that of the three Great Tales of the First Age published since that year, this is the only one with a coherent, finished story from beginning to end. It is worth noting, also, that the coda of the story of Túrin and Nienor in the 'Narn' is the release of Húrin, his coming to the grave of Túrin and his finding Morwen there. *The Silmarillion* gives us more details as it relates the discussion between Morgoth and Húrin at Húrin's release after having been held captive for 28 years, following the Nirnaeth Arnoediad. An old man of about 60, Húrin wanders southward through Hithlum, his former home, finding it to be occupied by Easterlings. He decides to try and find the hidden city of Gondolin. This search ultimately leads to its downfall. Húrin then turns to Brethil where he finds Morwen at Túrin's grave. Arriving next at Nargothrond, he takes the Nauglamír from the wreck of the city and travels to Doriath to give it to Thingol in scorn, thinking that the king maltreated his children and his wife. The wise words of Melian open his eyes and uncover the curse Morgoth put on him: "it is said that Húrin would not live thereafter, being bereft of all purpose and desire, and cast himself at last into the western sea: and so ended the mightiest of the warriors of mortal Men" (*Silmarillion*, 231-2). The coming of Húrin to Doriath set in motion its tragic ruin.

In *The War of the Jewels*, however, the story of the wanderings of Húrin contains yet another narrative thread: 'The Wanderings of Húrin' (*Jewels*, 251-310). With this storyline Tolkien came to the furthest point in the stories of *The Silmarillion* in all the reworkings and expansions he made on it after World War II. The later stories, about the fall of Doriath and Gondolin and the defeat of Morgoth were not again picked up after the completion of *The Lord of the Rings*.

One might agree that the trial of Húrin in Brethil is a long way off from the dragon killing and the incestuous relationship of the main protagonists of the 'Narn'.

Ultimately it was excluded from *The Silmarillion*. Christopher in retrospect regretted this and blamed it on the attempt to achieve a collated Silmarillion, tampering too far and overstepping on his father's work. What does this mean in relation to this story of Húrin? I think there are several elements that made the story important for Tolkien. First and foremost, with 'The Wanderings of Húrin' he would bring the tragedy of this branch of the house of Hador to a 'fitting' close by providing a tragic ending not only for the children but also for the parents. Secondly, he may have wanted to record the ending of the important house of the Haladin. Thirdly, there is hardly a tale in the legendarium that gives us a more perceptive view on the subtle evil of Morgoth than this story. The published *The Silmarillion* only hints at the influence of Morgoth's curse on Húrin after his release, and it takes this story to become fully aware of not only the power of the curse, but also of the devastating influence it has on others. Finally, justice is used in a negative sense for what I will for now call political gains; and quite consciously so. Thus, this story provides more insight into the views of Tolkien on justice.[1]

I will now focus on three themes in the story. First, I will make some remarks on what I will conveniently but not accurately call 'constitutional law': the formal and informal system of primary principles and laws that regulate the functioning of (in this case) Brethil society. Secondly, I will take a closer look at the way Manthor takes up the defence of Húrin. It will be seen that Tolkien added a moral dimension to the seemingly technical trial of Húrin. That moral dimension constitutes the third theme.

Throughout the story[2] there are references to Brethil law and customs. It starts right after Húrin has attacked Hardang by throwing a stool at him. When Húrin is imprisoned, he is visited by Manthor "wise in the laws and customs of his people" (*Jewels*, 279). Manthor points out that it is good Brethil custom that any prisoner should have a 'friend' (I will return to this term later). He also points out that Húrin's case must be tried by the Folk and not by Hardang, apparently referring to some law or custom. He sweeps the guards even further off their feet by pointing out that, again apparently on the grounds of some law or custom, a prisoner cannot be denied counsel and help. When the guards feebly remark that the order to keep the prisoner isolated came from Avranc, the rebuttal is that Avranc had been given other orders by him, Manthor, Avranc's superior. The final blow is effective: "Choose then between a young runagate, and the laws of the Folk" (279). An easy choice, is it not? Well, in our modern society it is (I hope). And so it is for the guards: "men did not like chieftains who tried to overrule the folk" (279). No absolute monarch (or rather, chieftain) in Brethil, but a leader chosen through the rules of law and bound by the rules of law.

The gathering of the Folk and the subsequent trial at the "Folkmoot for Judgement", as it is called, seem governed too by laws and customs. "already five hundred of the headmen had come in, and that was by custom deemed the least number which might count as a full meeting of the Folk" (281).

The story introduces some procedural rules for trials. The Halad is the accuser; he will present the facts to the Folk and propose a penalty. Then the charged person has the right to deny the facts and/or to offer a defence for what he has done, "by himself or by the mouth of a friend" (283). Witnesses can be summoned. If the accused does not speak (as Húrin will at first not speak) judgement is passed: "then there is no more to do" (285), meaning apparently no more inquiries have to be made into the case. The Folk vote not only on the guilt of the charged person and on the penalty, but apparently also on any points of discussion coming up during the trial. Thus, the Folk are at a

1. On this theme, see also van Breda, J.H., 'The Mercy and Justice of the King', in *Lembas Extra 2015: Unexplored Aspects of Tolkien and Arda*, ed. by C. van Zon and R. Vink (Soest: Boekscout.nl, 2015) 121-66.

2. All quotes, unless otherwise specified, are from this story.

certain point in the story about to vote on whether the fetters should be released from Húrin – until Hardang, the one having the authority to put Húrin in fetters, allows them to be taken off. The voting is said to be done by pebbles, black for nay and white for aye.

It might be noted too, that the Folkmoot was a men's business. I deduce that from the fact that the lines: "it was the custom of the Haladin that in all matters other than war the wives were also summoned to counsel and had equal voices with the husbands" (279), as well as other references to the participation of women in Brethil society, were struck out by Tolkien – although he may have reasoned that the involvement of women in the later fighting was not logical or even improper (in his view).

After Hardang has begun the accusation of Húrin, things take an unexpected turn: Manthor claims: "In our law no man may recite an offence against himself; nor may he sit in the seat of judgement while that charge is heard. Is not this the law?" "It is the law," the assembly answers (284). The whole assembly seems to know this law, so one wonders why Hardang did not – or did he wish to forget it as that was more convenient from a political point of view? Whatever the case, the fact that Hardang is not allowed to judge his own case, is worthy of closer examination. The edition of these laws by F.L. Attenborough in *The laws of the earliest English Kings* (1922) may have aroused Tolkien's interest or even been known to him.[3] I have ploughed through list after list of crimes and their punishments. Mention is made of a Folkmoot or of the fact that, when the interests of the king are damaged, the king himself is no longer allowed to pass judgement.[4] These should be approached carefully as those laws are almost all material and not procedural. I have not found any article which said *who* should judge in cases like these anyway. In this respect Brethil law is a lot more modern than Old-English law. In fact, it might very well be that this piece of Brethil legislation was 'inspired', so to speak, by the famous McCarthy-rule of the divisional court in the case of the King vs. Sussex Justices, *ex parte* McCarthy, of 9 November 1923.[5] McCarthy was, after being involved in an accident with a motorcycle, prosecuted for dangerous driving. But there also was a civil claim for damages against him. A deputy clerk who supported the justices that ruled in the criminal case, was also a member of the firm of solicitors engaged in the civil claim. Was he fit to act as a clerk to the justices in that case? Lord Hewart CJ answered this question negatively: "The answer to that question depends not upon what actually was done but upon what might appear to be done. Nothing is to be done which creates even a suspicion that there has been an improper interference with the course of justice" (1923).

The mere appearance of bias is sufficient to overturn a judicial decision. Or as Lord Hewart put it even more concisely in what has become a much quoted aphorism: "[J]

3. The book is, however, not mentioned in Cilli, O., *Tolkien's Library: An Annotated Checklist* (Edinburgh: Luna Press Publishing, 2019).

4. Quite the opposite, in fact. For instance, there are several decrees which declare what punishment one should get when one robs the king, or kills the smith in the service of the king, or commits an offence in the house where the king is feasting. There is no indication that the king could not be the judge in matters like these.

5. The rule was accessed via <https://www.bailii.org/cgi-bin/format.cgi?doc=/ew/cases/EWHC/KB/1923/1.html> [accessed July 2019].

ustice should not only be done, but should manifestly and undoubtedly be seen to be done" (1923).

So when Hardang steps down from the Doom-Rock, justice is seen to be done in front of all the Folk of Brethil. His successor: Avranc. Although some advocate Manthor to this position, he himself waves that possibility away: as the defender of Húrin, he is essentially just as involved in the case as is Hardang. Avranc takes up the presentation of the case and proposes the penalty: "it could justly be death" (*Jewels*, 285). And although that seems rather too harsh for throwing a stool at someone's head, the handling of this procedure might lead us to the conclusion that justice was indeed seen to be done. But Tolkien was a subtle man and we will soon discover that behind the fair appearance of justice glooms self-interest and lust for power – the evil of Morgoth. To understand this better, it is now time to turn to the second theme: Manthor's tactics.

It is Manthor who takes on the defence of Húrin, and on first appearance he seems to have two reasons for that. When hearing that Húrin has entered Brethil, Manthor expresses his admiration: "What he may do is unknown […] What he has done we know, and our debt is unpaid" (275).[6] Secondly, Manthor is wise in laws and customs and therefore, one might say, naturally inclined to perform this task.

How does he proceed? When arriving at the prison, he tells the guards that it is a good custom that any prisoner should have a friend. The word 'friend' in this context drew my attention, as it did not seem to denote quite the usual meaning we attach to this word. For why should a prisoner need a friend, in the sense of a soulmate or buddy? The word may initially give rise to an association with the term *amicus curiae*, literally 'friend of the court'. This legal concept was known in law as early as Roman law and is used even today in certain legal systems (the English legal system, amongst others). However, the function of the *amicus curiae* cannot be compared to the role Manthor takes on himself. For the *amicus curiae* is appointed by the court to inform the court on certain legal aspects of a case. This often requires specialist, academic knowledge. However, I also came across the English law figure of the *proximus amicus* (or *prochein ami* or next friend or litigation friend) which refers to a person who represents another person who is under disability or otherwise unable to maintain a suit on his or her own behalf.[7] The disability may arise from mental disability or from lack of access to counsel. This fits the role of Manthor much better, even more so if we accept the suggestion that Húrin is presented as one that might suffer from a mental disability. This word 'friend' gives rise to some gentle word-play from Tolkien. When Manthor says Húrin needs a friend for counsel, the guards answer: "the friend is chosen by the prisoner, […] but this wild man has no friends" (279). The first friend is clearly the legal friend, the second friend is the 'friend-friend'. And when Manthor is admitted to Húrin, and tells him: "But now you have need of a friend" (280), Húrin answers: "I have no friends, and wish for none in this land" (280), he is clearly not aware of Brethil laws and customs. To this Manthor replies: "One stands before you" (280), clearly meaning: I am your friend, legal and otherwise.

6. Looking back to these words at the end of the story, they are ever so ironical – as I said, Tolkien was a subtle man.

7. Lemma on 'litigation friend': <https://en.wikipedia.org/wiki/Next_friend> [accessed July 2019].

Let us take a closer look now at how Manthor presents the case of Húrin. One has to realise that there can be no reasonable doubt that Húrin threw a stool at Hardang. There were many witnesses present, Manthor being one of them. Denying the act would be pointless. Manthor therefore openly admits: "My friend does not deny the main charge" (287). So a different line of defence has to be adopted. In such cases, it is not unusual to bring in the difficult personal circumstances of the accused (often cynically rendered as: "Don't blame me; I had a bad childhood"). To be sure, Húrin's circumstances offer plenty of clues. Manthor sums them up: Húrin is "head of a great House, a man whose deeds are sung by Elves and Men. But he is now grown old, dispossessed, grief-laden, travel-worn" (289). Húrin did not spit out the food offered to him, it choked him, not uncommon for a man half-starved swallowing food in haste. So far, an acceptable defence-strategy.

But Manthor takes things a step further. When he starts to accuse Hardang and Avranc of committing unlawful acts he turns things around. He shares with the Folk his suspicions on the food being drugged by Hardang or someone in league with him. He suggests that the violent act of Húrin was provoked by Hardang. Manthor presents the facts from the point of view of Hardang in a masterly, vivid way: there he comes, the "old carl" (289). "You do not rise. You do not speak to him" (289). "O shame and wonder [...] that you so dishonour your chair, that you so dishonour your hall, that you so dishonour the Folk of Brethil. [...] How do you like such manners in this man that we have made Halad of Brethil?" (289). And most of the Folk react as Manthor desires, shouting: "Set him free" but also: "Away with this Halad!" (290) And when the unfettered Húrin adds a false accusation about Morwen, ending with: "How long will you suffer this man called Hardang to sit in your chair?" (291), the day is won. Small wonder "Hardang was aghast at this turn" (291). And then the fighting starts.

Even excluding the part of Húrin in the downfall of Hardang, it should be noted that for the defence of Húrin, it was not necessary to defame Hardang so strongly. Also note that the moment the Folk call upon Hardang to step down from the chair, Manthor does not try to de-escalate the situation, but adds even more oil to the fire. What motive could Manthor have for doing so?

That question brings us to the third and final theme: the moral dimension. Or in more simple words: who is the good and who is the bad guy? Or in more judicial terms: who is the most righteous of them all?

The first character to examine is Húrin. It is the curse of Morgoth that causes Húrin to make more than one fatal decision: trying to find Gondolin and thus furthering the discovery of its hiding place by Morgoth; setting out to Brethil in search of "vengeance for his wrongs, and for the wrongs of his kin", "out of a black deep anger" (274), as it is said; throwing a stool at Hardang for no good reason really; and falsely accusing Hardang for throwing out Morwen. Hardang, seconds before dying, is right when he tells Húrin: "you came to destroy me, and you at least have not denied it" (294), and calling him merciless. Manthor too realises, but too late for also close to death, the evil Húrin has brought onto Brethil: "was not this your true errand, Man of the North: to bring ruin upon us to weigh against thine own? The House of Hador has conquered us" (297). In fact, Húrin is twice associated with orcs: "orc-deeds" (277) and "some [...] set forth Húrin in the likeness of some fell Orc-chieftain" (279). It is also said: "you bring your manners from Angband" (277). The acts of the old warrior, one of the heroes of the Nirnaeth, can only be qualified as immoral and unjustified.

Manthor seems a more likely candidate. As said, he acts as the 'friend' of Húrin; his plea at the trial to honour Húrin appropriately and the way he devotes himself to the acquittal of Húrin, seem unfeigned. Against that background, we, the readers, are quickly won over to his side as he strives, it seems, for justice to be done, not belittling Húrin's act of aggression, but putting that act in the perspective of Húrin's character and the provocations of Hardang and Avranc.

Manthor unhesitatingly admits that he had a hidden motive, even if he is ascribing it to the shadow of Morgoth. Looking back from this perspective at his role at the trial, Manthor *used* the law, not to achieve a fair judgement, but to increase his chances of gaining personal power, a window of opportunity to become the new Halad of Brethil. In that play, Húrin is no more than a seemingly innocent tool to dethrone Hardang. It can safely be said that Tolkien had no sympathy for such men. In *The Lord of the Rings*, the word 'power' (often written with a capital P) almost always has a negative connotation.

Thinking further along these lines, it might even be postulated that Hardang is more righteous than Manthor. He allows Húrin to be judged by the Folk, even if the penalty is uncertain. He allows the fetters to be taken off from Húrin. He admits that he cannot be the judge of Húrin, respecting the laws of Brethil, even when that weakens his position. That he tries to mitigate the consequences of this by appointing Avranc to the chair, is an indication of his failing morality. Indeed, Tolkien tells us that he makes that decision "in black anger and [as] all wisdom failed him" (*Jewels*, 284). Earlier, as Manthor tried to get entrance to Húrin in his prison, the guards tell him: "the Halad forbids us to admit any one save the guards" (279), but soon afterwards they admit this order came from Avranc, not from Hardang. Still, Hardang too, like Manthor, is shown to be preoccupied with power and resentment. There was a line written at the beginning of the story that Hardang in his heart was not sure of his seat in the Master's chair. It was struck out, not, I think, because it was not an adequate characterisation of Hardang, but because Tolkien did not want to give away too much about the man, so early in the story. But at the trial, it is said of Hardang that he tells Avranc he is sorry he hindered him from shooting Manthor. And when the fight is about to break out, people are said to join Hardang's side, "some without love for him or his deeds, who nonetheless held to their loyalty and would at least defend him from violence, until he could answer for the Moot" (291). Seconds before dying, Hardang tells Manthor: "I think that you have always begrudged that the Folk chose me to the chair and not you" (294). The impression Hardang ultimately leaves behind is of an insecure leader who tries to hold on to this throne, even when he has lost the support of the majority of the Folk.

That makes this tale of Húrin's trial ever so dark. The evil that Húrin brings with him from Angband, infests the leadership of Brethil and ultimately causes the end of the valiant House of the Haladin, one of the three houses of the Edain: "and lesser men ruled in Brethil in the time that was left" (297).

The modern views of Tolkien on the role of justice, leadership and power in a community, are clearly visible in 'The Wanderings of Húrin'. He is an advocate for 'justice being seen to be done' and for leadership that is not preoccupied with staying in power but by unselfishly striving for justice and the good of the Folk. Unwise leaders acting in anger, run the risk of causing strife within the community, death and ultimately the end of houses. Not that this point of view should surprise us. This story is not the only in Tolkien's legendarium that reflects on just leadership. It would be interesting to take all these strands together and present them in a coherent study. 'The Wanderings of Húrin' deserves a central place in such a study.

Bibliography

Attenborough, F.L., *The Laws of the Earliest English Kings,* (Cambridge: Cambridge University Press, 2015).

Cilli, O., *Tolkien's Library: An Annotated Checklist,* (Edinburgh: Luna Press Publishing, 2019).
Lord Hewet CJ, The King v. Sussex Justices. Ex parte McCarthy (1923).

Tolkien, J.R.R., *The Silmarillion*, ed. by C. Tolkien (London: George Allen & Unwin, 1977).
— *The War of the Jewels*, ed. by C. Tolkien (London: HarperCollins, 1994).

van Breda, J.H., 'The Mercy and Justice of the King', in *Lembas Extra 2015: Unexplored Aspects of Tolkien and Arda*, ed. by C. van Zon and R. Vink (Soest: Boekscout.nl, 2015) 121-166.

Taking Care of the Land:
Stewardship in Tolkien's Middle-earth

Dr. Sara Brown

The concept of 'stewardship', with its connotations of caring both for a land and its peoples, is a core theme in Tolkien's Middle-earth legendarium. At the heart of this theme of caretaking is the importance of the sense of security and comfort to be found in the simplest of places – the home. The reasons for this lie in Tolkien's own real-world experiences, living through the upheavals and anxieties of the twentieth century, and observing the inevitable changes these wrought in the England of his childhood. It is little wonder, then, that Tolkien chose to place such emphasis on the idea of protecting and preserving that which he held dear.

World War II had been an all-consuming experience for the people of Britain: large numbers of both men and women were drafted into either the armed forces or the Home Guard and industry shifted almost entirely to the provision of war necessities. Jobs previously done almost exclusively by men were taken over by women, many of whom did not wish to revert to their traditional domestic role as the men returned (Brook, 2-3). Post-war austerity measures, imposed to meet the enormous war debt, a national fuel shortage and one of the worst winters on record in 1947 meant that food rationing continued to create hardship until it finally ended on the 4th July 1954. Britain was effectively bankrupt after WW2 and in huge debt to the USA following the 'Lend-Lease' Agreement. No longer the economic powerhouse it had been before the devastation of two world wars hit two successive generations, Britain's empire was all but gone. The bomb damage of the Second World War only worsened the condition of Britain's social housing stock, most of which was in poor condition prior to the outbreak of war, necessitating widespread clearances of slum areas in various cities (Willink, 'Memorandum', 1). Rebuilding took longer than the clearances, leaving many families struggling to find suitable accommodation and, by the end of 1945, it was estimated that "there was an immediate need for over a million homes" in England and Wales (Willink, 'Conclusions', 101). Post-war austerity was characterised by a national fuel shortage, ongoing food rationing, and poorly-heated homes, many of which had outside lavatories and were without running water. The changing landscape of Britain in the mid-twentieth century included extensive rebuilding and the construction of numerous 'new towns', as well as increasing industrialisation and road-building.

It is in this Britain, rebuilding itself after two disastrous wars, constructing a new understanding of society and the importance of home, and beginning to experience the changes that the mass economic immigration of foreign cultures would soon bring, that Tolkien was writing *The Lord of the Rings.* It is little wonder, then, that the concept of 'home' is at the heart of the Middle-earth legendarium. This is particularly so in *The Lord of the Rings*, as the defence and protection of home is one of the main motivations for the Fellowship's quest to destroy the Ring of Power.

One of the fundamental differences between *The Hobbit* and *The Lord of the Rings* lies in the way that Tolkien presents and deals with the idea of 'home' in each. These differences are made all the more apparent by the fact that both narratives begin at the same place – Bag End – home first to Bilbo, then also to Frodo, each a central protagonist. This is significant, as this comfortable, even luxurious home lends a sense of familiarity within this secondary world. There are bedrooms, a kitchen, parlours and pantries, whose functions are recognizable to the reader and thus provide an important link between the reader and Middle-earth. In his *Mythlore* article 'All the Comforts: The Image of Home in *The Hobbit* and *The Lord of the Rings*', Wayne G. Hammond suggests that "Bag End is a bridge between the world of the reader and the world of the story that helps to make the distant and sometimes strange matter of the tale acceptable to someone besides the author" (1987, 30). In addition, Bag End has importance in that it serves as the 'ideal', the home for which both Bilbo and Frodo have feelings of longing and to which they desire to return, as well as epitomising the image of what should be protected and maintained in the face of threat and danger.

In *The Hobbit*, home is a constant. Throughout the narrative, Bilbo refers to his cosy hobbit hole whenever discomfort or dangers threaten, such as the moment in Chapter 4 when he and the Dwarves are captured by the goblins and taken into the "deep, deep dark" of the mountain, or in Chapter 8 when he is alone in Mirkwood and surrounded by the giant spiders (Hobbit, 'Over Hill and Under Hill', 67; 'Flies and Spiders', 151). He is allowed to return to that home, enriched by his experiences on the quest and his portion of Smaug's treasure that he has earned. He comes back to find the Sackville-Bagginses trying to sell all his things and claim Bag End, but this is a pale reflection of the effects of the Scouring of the Shire in *The Return of the King*. Although Bilbo has to act quickly to save Bag End, he still regains his home virtually untouched and certainly undamaged. Tolkien's message here is that some change is always inevitable: it is clear, though, that this event heralds the changes in Bilbo as a person rather than changes in the world as a whole, as the event is both small and personal. Home itself is unchanged; the Shire at the end of *The Hobbit* remains as it was when Bilbo left it.

In contrast, in *The Lord of the Rings* almost all the places encountered by the members of the Fellowship are under constant threat, in a state of change, or newly under threat. As Simon Malpas argues: "If Bilbo's adventures lead him through a series of comparatively stable homelands [...] the journey undertaken by Frodo and his companions is through a world whose peoples exist in states of continual conflict, migration and vagrancy, which even the destruction of the Ring only problematically renders secure" (2005, 85-6). The village of Bree, encountered in *The Fellowship of the Ring*, seems at first to be a traditional, welcoming place in which Hobbits and Men live side-by-side in harmony. It soon becomes apparent that this is not the case as, in a reflection of the post-war influx of foreigners into Britain, the Bree-folk's way of life is now at risk from "the big folk" arriving from the South (*FR*, 'At the Sign of the Prancing Pony', 152).

By the time of *The Lord of the Rings*, Rivendell and Lothlórien are also homes in a state of imminent change. The time of the Elves is over and they are leaving Middle-earth: the power of the three Elven rings is in danger and even Rivendell is no longer safe. Much like Rivendell, Lothlórien is in the autumn of its time. Tolkien unequivocally shows the reader that these may be temporary places of respite but they are no longer the Elven strongholds they had once been. Similarly, Minas Tirith was once a vital and impenetrable fortress of the civilisation of the Men of the West, the blood of Númenor. Now it is weakened by the broken line of kings and vulnerable to attack. Throughout the course of *The Lord of the Rings*, Minas Tirith stands in very real danger of being overrun by Sauron's forces, a threat which becomes all too real in *The Return of the King*. The safety of Rohan is threatened by Sauron, particularly after the weakening of Théoden through the influence of Saruman and Wormtongue. In addition, Saruman encourages the fierce Dunlendings to attack Rohan, to reclaim the land taken from them long ago. Moria, once the Dwarven kingdom of Khazad-dûm, is discovered to have been overrun by Orcs and is unlikely ever to be reoccupied by the Dwarves. This period is a time of great change as well as great danger, and this has an inevitable effect on the Peoples of Middle-earth. In an unmistakable parallel with both twentieth- and twenty-first-century problems, *The Lord of the Rings* "struggles to make sense of the possibility of community during a period where industrialisation, war and rapid transformations of technology threaten to destabilise traditional notions of being in common" (Malpas 2005, 86).

Even before these transformations become fully apparent to either the reader or the characters in *The Lord of the Rings*, it is evident that home itself is not always 'safe', nor a haven of stability as it is initially perceived on first encountering the Shire. Dangers previously unseen, unnoticed, or at least overlooked, may lie within and threaten its people. In Rohan, its king has been weakened by the machinations of Saruman, whose stronghold lies on its borders. Gríma Wormtongue has slowly achieved control over Théoden and, in so doing, helps Saruman to gain power over Rohan. Operating in this insidious and subtle way enables Saruman to gradually exert an increasingly powerful influence, until it is too late for those around him to act. This control fundamentally debilitates Rohan and greatly endangers its entire population; in Rohan, the king is the cornerstone of the security of the land – an enfeebled king necessarily means a less stable and less safe homeland.

Similarly, in Gondor, Denethor is weakened by his struggle with Sauron through the palantír and is losing control. This has a similar effect on Gondor as Théoden's debilitation has on Rohan: although most around him do not realise it, Denethor is placing Gondor in great peril as a result of his failure to properly maintain his stewardship. His over-confidence in believing that he had mastery over the palantír and could pit his own mental strength against that of Sauron, his arrogance in refusing Gandalf's counsel and his eventual slide into madness would have signalled disaster for Minas Tirith, and subsequently for the rest of Gondor, had it not been for the actions of Gandalf, Aragorn and their allies. Once a mighty power, formidable in its opposition to Sauron, Gondor was already lacking its former strength before Denethor's failure; his weakness jeopardises the safety of Gondor and its people.

It is evident, then, that Tolkien is placing the idea of 'home', and the defence of 'home', at the heart of the quest to destroy the Ring. However, Tolkien is foregrounding this idea long before the events of *The Lord of the Rings*. A significant number of characters within the Middle-earth narratives are charged, at different times, in different places and in different ways, with the care of Middle-earth. These 'stewards', as it would be correct to name them, have clearly defined roles and responsibilities to the land and its peoples.

The word 'steward', or 'stigweard' as it was originally, means the 'keeper of the hall' and was the position held by an official in a medieval household who would have been responsible for its management. Under the feudal system, it was the lord who had all of the legal authority; traditionally, he would delegate much of this authority to a trusted steward who would administer the estate and oversee its day-to-day management. This mandate was all-inclusive, from the broadest policies to the most trivial details. For the estate to function properly, the steward had to maintain a comprehensive overview of all the household minutiae, as well as an appreciation of all that the successful husbandry of the estate and its lands would entail. The position was one of enormous responsibility; the best steward would be one who felt the responsibility on the deepest level, who identified with the role and carried it out with devoted industry.

In environmental or ecological terms, stewardship may be defined as the assumption of accountability for the welfare of the world, an acceptance of responsibility for something one does not actually own. Simply put, stewardship is "the concept of responsibly managing all of our resources for the benefit of present and future generations of people, plants, and animals."[1] An important medieval discussion regarding humanity's relationship with Nature was whether it should be dominated, tamed to our use, or if we were meant to be stewards of the land, preserving it for future generations. This was a dispute that, at the time, would have been perceived as being theological rather than ecological; however, it seems clear that both aspects of the argument lie at the heart of the conflicts in Middle-earth.

An initial exploration of this debate as it relates to Tolkien's work may be approached through an examination of the Greek word *oikos*, meaning 'house', which is the root of the modern word 'ecology'. It appears in the New Testament in many forms, including *oikonomos*, which is usually translated as 'steward', or 'house manager', many of whom were actually slaves. The words 'steward' and 'stewardship' appear over twenty times in the King James Version of the Bible; an interesting point as King James I of England was also James VI of Scotland, a country whose monarchy had, like Gondor's, failed of succession and passed into the hands of stewards. Eventually this family adopted the name 'Stuart', the Scottish form of "steward," thus indicating their status. In their work *Ents, Elves and Eriador*, Matthew Dickerson and Jonathan Evans propose that this idea is central to the Christian understanding of stewardship, suggesting "servanthood and upward responsibility rather than lordship" (2006, 281). Their argument regarding a Christian's ecological responsibility therefore follows that: "[b]ased on the etymology of the terms and the statements of scripture, it is possible to state our role in this manner: Christian = Steward = Ecologist" (282). The concept of stewardship as it is presented in the legendarium, central to Tolkien's view of good government in its broadest sense, thus encapsulates both an ecological standpoint and Judeo-Christian notions of responsibility.

Stewards and guardians are an essential construct in Middle-earth from the moment of naissance. Many of the Ainur, who sing the world into being in *The Silmarillion*, choose to descend into Arda to guide and order its growth. Of the fifteen who do so, fourteen become the Valar, all-powerful beings whose responsibility it is to shape and prepare the world for the coming of the Children of Ilúvatar: the Elves and, eventually,

1. See Environmental Stewardship at the University of Michigan.

Men; the fifteenth Ainu being Melkor, later known as Morgoth, who brought discord into the music of the Ainur and desired dominion over Middle-earth. With them into Arda, as it says in the 'Ainulindalë', go the lesser Ainur, known as the Maiar, whose purpose is to aid the Valar in their work. Both the Valar and the Maiar, who choose to enter the world at its beginning, are therefore bound to Middle-earth until its end, even though by the events of the War of the Ring, most have long been physically separated from Middle-earth; the road to Valinor is attainable only by the Elves and those few who are permitted to sail with them.

Some of the Maiar have a greater role in the history of Middle-earth than others; to these few a specific purpose is often assigned, that of guardian and helper through turbulent times. One such is Melian who, alone of the Ainur, marries one of the Children of Ilúvatar, King Elu Thingol of Doriath. For many hundreds of years, she protects the kingdom of Doriath by casting around it a powerful shield known as the Girdle of Melian, which guards and defends it from its enemies:

> Melian put forth her power and fenced all that dominion round about with an unseen wall of shadow and bewilderment: the Girdle of Melian, that none thereafter could pass against her will or the will of King Thingol, unless one should come with a power greater than that of Melian the Maia. [...] Within it there was yet a watchful peace; but without there was peril and great fear. (*Silmarillion*, 114)

The Elves themselves are also, to a certain extent, stewards and guardians of Middle-earth. Immortality brings with it certain responsibilities as, to all intents and purposes, Elves are both the present and future generations of the world. For example, Tolkien discloses to the reader the particularly deep regard the Elves have for the trees, and the obvious affinity felt for such things that would also live for many ages. As Treebeard observes to Merry and Pippin in *The Two Towers*: "The Elves began it, of course, waking trees up and teaching them to speak and learning their tree-talk. They always wished to talk to everything, the old Elves did" (*TT*, 'Treebeard', 457). The Elves are joined in their love for the trees by the Ents, who are undoubtedly central to Tolkien's view of responsibility for the natural world. They are created by the Valar specifically to be stewards and guardians of the trees they care for and are known as Shepherds of the forest. As Dickerson and Evans state: "One of the most significant aspects of Tolkien's environmental vision, and one informing all areas of his ecology, is his clarification of the real role of a steward. In the specific context of environmental stewardship, and especially the stewardship of wilderness and trees, he provides the model of the Ents" (2006, 39).

In *The Lord of the Rings*, it becomes apparent that the more powerful of the Elves carry a heavy burden of responsibility in Middle-earth; using their great power and wisdom, they have the task of protecting and defending large areas of Middle-earth that form the last sanctuaries for those Elves who have not yet sailed into the West. During the course of the narrative, Tolkien reveals that Galadriel and Elrond each bear one of the Elven Rings of Power; forged by Celebrimbor and untouched by Sauron, these rings are not corrupted as were those given to the Dwarves and the Kings of Men. Nenya, the Ring of Adamant, allows Galadriel to keep Lothlórien and all its natural beauty protected from the dark forces of Mordor. Its power lies in preservation, protection and a certain level of concealment from evil; it is "a secret power here that holds evil from the land" (*FR*, 'Lothlórien', 329). Nenya's powers do not entirely prevent attacks by Orcs, who are still able to enter Lothlórien, but it does help to maintain and sustain the land, keeping it veiled from Sauron's gaze. The efficacy of this ring's power to preserve is made evident by what transpires in Lothlórien after Galadriel bears it with her away into the West: the magic and beauty of Lórien fades, the great mallorn trees disappear and the land is gradually depopulated. As Tolkien reveals in 'The Annals of the Kings and Rulers', in Appendix A to *The Lord of the Rings*, only 120 years later, when Arwen comes there to die, Lórien is deserted and "the land was silent" (*RK*, 'Appendix A', 1038).

We discover in *Return of the King* that Elrond is the bearer of Vilya, the Ring of Air, which is the mightiest of the three Elven Rings of Power. Like Nenya, its purpose is also to heal and to preserve, a power utilised by Elrond to maintain the safety of Rivendell. It could also be speculated that Vilya was, in some small way, the source of Elrond's ability to control the elements, as he does when commanding the river Bruinen to flood at the Ford of Rivendell, thus washing away the Nazgûl. As Gandalf explains to Frodo in *Fellowship of the Ring*: "The river of this valley is under his power, and it will rise in anger when he has great need to bar the Ford" (*FR*, 'Many Meetings', 218). Elrond, like Galadriel, is a steward of the land; he preserves and protects it, safeguarding it for future generations, even if these generations are Men rather than Elves. The nature of the Elven Rings of Power, in stark contrast to the One Ring, is defensive rather than offensive: we are told in *Fellowship of the Ring* that, unlike the Ring, they "were not made as weapons of war or conquest: that is not their power. Those who made them did not desire strength or domination or hoarded wealth, but understanding, making, and healing, to preserve all things unstained" (218). In other words, they lend themselves to the role of guardian and are therefore a suitable symbol of the status of steward.

Fittingly the third Elven ring, Narya, is borne by Gandalf, through whose character Tolkien is able to illustrate fully his vision of true stewardship. He achieves this both through Gandalf's own words and actions, but also in the contrast that is depicted between Gandalf and those other characters in the narrative that are in a position of authority. Tolkien uses certain characters to distinguish between different viewpoints of stewardship and power; it is these competing visions that are at the heart of the narrative in *The Lord of the Rings*.

In *Ents, Elves and Eriador*, Dickerson and Evans consider a number of widely divergent ways in which the term 'stewardship' may be used in terms of a Christian world view and apply them to Tolkien's presentation of stewardship in his legendarium. This is justified in two ways – firstly, that Tolkien's work is undoubtedly influenced by his Christian beliefs and secondly, because the gospels record many parables concerning stewards, with all of which Tolkien would assuredly have been familiar. To this end, they draw on the work of Jim Ball, who has conducted research of the use of the term specifically amongst evangelical Protestant communities.[2] One such interpretation

2. See Ball, J 'The Use of Ecology in the Evangelical Protestant Response to the Ecological Crisis' in *Perspectives on Science and Faith: Journal of the American Scientific Affiliation* 50.1 (1998) 32-38. Quoted in Dickerson and Evans (2006) 39 – 43.

relates particularly to the Elves, exploring their relationship with the natural world and their position within it. This is termed “caring management”, which “sees humans in the roles of both lord and servant, as gardeners and managers, with the rest of creation having intrinsic value apart from that bestowed on it by those who tend and nurture it” (Dickerson & Evans 2006, 42).

This interpretation certainly appears to correspond with the way in which Tolkien's Elves interact with nature, seeming to be so much a part of the land around them that even someone as ‘grounded’ as Sam can perceive it, observing in *Fellowship of the Ring*: “Whether they've made the land, or the land's made them, it's hard to say” (*FR*, ‘The Great River’, 469). The food they consume and the beverages they are able to make imply a particular level of both horticulture and viniculture; the Elves apparently live in harmony with the land but work with it both to produce the food that they need and to enhance its beauty. As mentioned above, both Galadriel and Elrond (and Melian before them) are able to exercise a certain amount of control over their surroundings but do so for the benefit of the land, as well as those who live upon it. One illustration of this point is in Silmarillion, when the Valar are debating whether to summon the Elves to come to Valinor, to protect them from Melkor and the destruction that he is causing to the land. Ulmo speaks against this summoning, arguing that the Elves should remain in Middle-earth because they have the ability to restore the world to the way it should be, using “their gifts of skill to order all the lands and heal their hurts” (*Silmarillion*, 60). This implies some authority over the land, or the ability to impose a structure upon it, however caring or nurturing that ordering may be. As Dickerson and Evans argue: “[e] ven when it is undertaken rightly and lovingly, horticulture implies some rule over the land and its products – some aspect of the ruler choosing what the land will produce and how it will be arranged” (42).

The same argument could be made of other characters in the legendarium, including Béorn and Tom Bombadil. Béorn may live in harmony with the land around him but he is certainly a manager of sorts: the animals wait upon him and work for him, although it is clear that he loves them and is concerned for their welfare. Tom Bombadil works with the land and with all living things but makes no claim to ownership, believing that living things each belong to themselves. He is “the Master of wood, water and hill” but not the owner – a guide or mentor within his domain but not a dictator (*FR*, ‘In the House of Tom Bombadil’, 122). Tom may be a benevolent steward, but he does not hesitate to take steps to dominate those living things within his bounds, should it prove necessary. His power to command the obedience of such malevolent entities as Old Man Willow, for example, is a significant indicator of his ability and willingness to order the natural world as he sees fit.

In terms of stewardship and their relationship with Arda, the primary difference between these characters and Gandalf is the fact that they do exercise some level of control over the land. This contrasts sharply with Gandalf's approach; Dickerson and Evans posit that Gandalf could be described as following a model of “servanthood stewardship”, which “sees the intrinsic value of creation but also conceives of humans as servants within it” (2006, 43). In this view of stewardship there is no sense of imposing order, no implication of any kind of authority, merely a willingness to serve the land and those who live upon it, offering help wherever and whenever it is needed. This works on every level of interaction with nature: Gandalf does not treat the horses as beasts of burden but as partners in their enterprise, even fellow soldiers. In *Two Towers* he does not command Shadowfax to bear him – using neither saddle nor bridle, he says "with your leave, my friends, we will ride. We beg you to use all the speed that you can. [...] I will set Gimli before me, and by his leave Shadowfax shall bear us both" (*TT*, 'The White Rider', 493). He addresses the great eagle, Gwaihir the Windlord, as friend and apologises for being his burden (491). All of nature is in Gandalf's care and all is of equal importance.

With this in mind, Gandalf does not measure victory in the war against Sauron as being the survival of the peoples of Middle-earth. Although this is undoubtedly desirable, Gandalf is aware that success might be measured in terms of the continued existence of anything that can "still grow fair or bear fruit and flower again in days to come" (*RK*, 'Minas Tirith', 742). Although Gandalf plays a central role in marshalling forces against Sauron and in helping to direct the course of battle, his main purpose is the preservation and protection of all of Middle-earth. The restoration of the kingship in Gondor is desirable mainly because he perceives that it would have numerous benefits for Middle-earth as a whole. Gandalf is not a king; he evinces no desire to rule or to command either the peoples of Middle-earth or any other living creature. As he makes clear to Denethor in *Return of the King*: "The rule of no realm is mine, neither of Gondor nor any other, great or small. But all worthy things that are in peril as the world now stands, those are my care" (742). Gandalf is fully aware that the ecological consequences of a victory for Sauron's forces would have implications for all living things in Middle-earth, not just its peoples.

It is primarily in the contrast with Denethor that the reader can fully appreciate Gandalf's selfless notion of stewardship. Denethor is the Steward of Gondor; he is not a king, but he is most certainly a ruler. A man of great power and wisdom, in whom "the blood of Westernesse runs nearly true"; he "can perceive, if he bends his will thither, much of what is passing in the minds of men, even of those that dwell far off" (742-3). However, Denethor's perception of what a steward should be differs greatly from Gandalf's. He is a proud man who refers to himself as "the Lord of Gondor" who is "not to be made the tool of other men's purposes, however worthy" (741). He refuses Gandalf's counsel with the declaration that "the rule of Gondor [...] is mine and no other man's, unless the king should come again" (741); however, it is clear that the return of a king to Gondor is now an event unlooked for, and Denethor has no intention of surrendering his authority.

Gandalf reminds Denethor that it is his task, as Steward of Gondor, to "keep some kingdom still against that event" (741), which is one of the three main aspects of stewardship when it is considered in a political sense. A good steward should be responsible for the safety of the kingdom in the king's absence, be accountable to the king for the correct attention to that duty and, finally, be prepared to surrender authority upon the king's return. As Dickerson and Evans point out, "the second and third aspects require explicit acknowledgement of the king's authority over the steward, and the third is central to the title of the final book in *The Lord of the Rings*" (2006, 42). Denethor's attitude to Gandalf would certainly imply a potential reluctance on his part to cede authority to the king upon his return, and this is proved true when Gandalf confronts

Denethor in Rath Dínen. It is at this moment that Denethor reveals one of the ways in which he fails to be a true and loyal steward:

> thou wouldst [...] bring up this Ranger of the North to supplant me. [...] But I say to thee, Gandalf Mithrandir, I will not be thy tool! I am Steward of the House of Anárion. I will not step down to be the dotard chamberlain of an upstart. Even were his claim proved to be true, still he comes but of the line of Isildur. I will not bow to such a one, last of a ragged house long bereft of lordship and dignity. (*RK*, 'The Pyre of Denethor', 836)

Denethor also fails to understand the true meaning of stewardship; instead of existing to serve others, as Gandalf does, Denethor perceives his role to be that of a ruler who should be prepared to do anything he deems necessary to preserve his rule. He repudiates the counsel of Gandalf as he sees this as making him the tool of others; this is something he is not prepared to do. Denethor prefers to control and so rejects the idea of serving, even if it is for a worthy cause – unlike Gandalf who understands that his primary function is that of a servant and undertakes this role gladly. Denethor sees the world as being divided into those who are tools, and those who are prepared to use these tools. "Rulers (including stewards), he explains, are those who use others as tools but are not themselves used" (Dickerson & Evans 2006, 38). Of greatest concern would be the fact that, to a certain extent, he would even go so far as to compare himself with Sauron, who "uses others as his weapons [...] So do all great lords, if they are wise [...] Or why do I sit here in my tower and think, and watch, and wait, spending even my sons?" (*RK*, 'The Siege of Gondor', 800). Surprisingly, this statement seems to imply that Denethor thinks of Sauron as a great lord, and that Sauron's willingness to utilize others is a laudable use of his power. The use of the word 'spending' here is also interesting – implying a sense of economics as well as resource management.

It is interesting that, upon first meeting Denethor, Pippin observes some degree of similarity between him and Gandalf – an inner fire and a sense of power that is revealed in the palpable tension between these two stewards. At first, "Denethor looked indeed much more like a great wizard than Gandalf did, more kingly, beautiful and powerful" but Pippin soon perceives that this is only on the surface. Despite the more simple outward appearance, Pippin sees that Gandalf "had the greater power and the deeper wisdom, and a majesty that was veiled" (*RK*, 'Minas Tirith', 740). Gandalf has no need to appear majestic; when power is used only in the service of others there is no need to wear it as openly as Denethor does. Despite the tension between the two, and regardless of their differences of opinion, Gandalf still offers Denethor his help and support, telling him "you shall have all the aid that you are pleased to ask for" (741). This shows the extent of the disparity between these two conflicting visions of stewardship, with only Gandalf showing any great level of care regarding the potential consequences for the whole of Middle-earth of either a hard-won victory, or a bitter defeat at the hands of Sauron's dark forces.

In contrast to his father, Faramir seems to fulfil all of the requirements of a faithful and loyal steward. He cares for the land as a whole and has a deep sense of responsibility for it. His one desire is to preserve and to protect, a fact which helps to make him immune to the call of the Ring. In *Two Towers*, Faramir states unequivocally: "I would not take this thing, if it lay by the highway. Not were Minas Tirith falling in ruin and I alone could save her, so, using the weapon of the Dark Lord for her good and my glory" (*TT*, 'The Window on the West', 656). As Jane Chance remarks in her work *The Lord of the Rings: The Mythology of Power*: "[t]o resist the desire for the Ring proves the excellence of one's stewardship – proves indeed one's humility and lack of selfishness" (2001, 89). In a scene that emulates the Middle English Breton lai of Sir Orfeo, king of Tracience, who returns from a quest to find his kingdom preserved by a faithful steward who gladly surrenders authority to his king, Faramir cedes power to Aragorn and declares him king of Gondor. In *Return of the King* we are told that "Faramir met Aragorn in the midst of those there assembled, and he knelt, and said: 'The last Steward of Gondor begs leave to surrender his office" (*RK*, 'The Stewart and the King', 945). Aragorn immediately returns the staff of office to Faramir, declaring that the position of Steward would remain in his keeping. This bodes well for the future of Gondor as Faramir, already described by his father as a "wizard's pupil" (*RK*, 'The Pyre of Denethor', 836), seems to hold a similar view of stewardship as Gandalf, his childhood mentor.

When those who are placed in a position of stewardship, or guardianship, fail to use their position wisely and well, or lose sight of their responsibility, there are grave consequences. Denethor, prepared to sacrifice even his sons to maintain his position, is weakened by his struggle with Sauron through the palantír. He refuses to listen to Gandalf's wise counsel and, as a result of his pride and his actions, loses everything. There are other characters who also illustrate this point to a greater or lesser degree: Saruman, who was sent into Middle-earth with Gandalf to be a guide and counsellor, seeks power for himself. He betrays the White Council, he also betrays Sauron and, as a consequence of his actions, has his staff broken by Gandalf and suffers an ignoble death. Gandalf casts him out of the order of wizards and the White Council, recognising that Saruman could never be the kind of steward that he ought to have been and stating that: "He will not serve, only command" (*TT*, 'The Voice of Saruman', 570).

In *Two Towers*, King Théoden of Rohan allows himself to fall under the influence of Gríma Wormtongue and Saruman; as a result, he loses hold on power and places Rohan in great danger, during which time his only son, Théodred, is killed by Orcs. Dickerson and Evans remark that in his despair, Théoden has "lost sight of the far-reaching impact of his decisions and of the fact that he has allies [...] Wormtongue would blind him to this; Gandalf must remind him of it" (2006, 47). Théoden has to be restored to power and, in so doing, be brought to appreciate that, good steward of his people, horses and grasslands though he may be, yet he must also see the value of other peoples and also of the forests that he has previously feared and avoided.

Clearly, it is Gandalf who represents what it means to be a good steward. He protects, defends and preserves the land on behalf of all living things, whilst challenging others to act. When in *Fellowship of the Ring* Frodo laments his fate and wishes that these terrible things had not happened in his time, Gandalf refuses to allow Frodo to indulge in self-pity. Instead, Gandalf's reply articulates Tolkien's own view of stewardship: "So do I, and so do all who live to see such times. But that is not for them to decide. All we have to decide is what to do with the time that is given to us" (*FR*, 'A Shadow of the Past', 50). Gandalf cannot act on Frodo's behalf, nor will he make decisions for him. He may sympathise with Frodo, but this does not change the fact that it is Frodo's responsibility to decide and to act. In this, Gandalf shows that he is a steward unlike even the benevolent managers that the Elves appear to be. He will not order as he sees fit, nor exercise control.

Most telling is the episode in Book V, Chapter IX, in which Gandalf advises the Captains of the West to continue in their battle against Sauron. In a passage that reiterates the guidance he gave to Frodo, and which resonates with environmental imagery, Gandalf counsels the Captains to draw Sauron's forces out of Mordor, to allow Frodo a greater chance of reaching Mount Doom to destroy the Ring, thus maiming Sauron forever and removing a great evil from the world:

> Other evils there are that may come; for Sauron is himself but a servant or emissary. Yet it is not our part to master all the tides of the world, but to do what is in us for the succour of those years wherein we are set, uprooting the evil in the fields that we know, so that those who live after may have clean earth to till. What weather they shall have is not ours to rule. (*RK*, 'The Last Debate', 861)

This explanation of what Gandalf sees as their duty uses natural metaphors that reflect his view of good stewardship: one that cares for all of the land, uprooting evil as if uprooting weeds, and leaving clean earth for others to till. Gandalf's role is to protect all of Middle-earth from the evil that Sauron brings, as is represented by the blighted land of Mordor. If Sauron were to prevail, all of Middle-earth would become a wasteland beneath his rule. It is therefore imperative that the stewardship of Gandalf is the one that prevails.

What is evident is that Tolkien intends for the reader to perceive the importance of a Gandalfian-style stewardship to the ultimate survival of Middle-earth. Gandalf's selfless approach to his task is a model that other figures of authority are meant to follow, suffering dire consequences when they do not. Gandalf exists solely to serve the world; his purpose is to protect and preserve all that is good in that world. As a steward, Gandalf embodies the ecological concept of respect for all living things, celebrating their unique nature and grieving over any loss of life. Stewardship of the land is interconnected with the battle against Sauron – to defeat the Dark Lord is to protect the natural world from being despoiled – implying that the responsibilities of stewardship have inevitable environmental consequences. The significance of these responsibilities is therefore clear: a system of caring management may be good for the land, but the suffering of the world would be immeasurably increased if it were not for those few who conceive of their duty as one of servanthood stewardship, placing the needs of the natural world on an equal footing with our own.

Bibliography

Brook, N., 'Notebook: War Cabinet Minutes 6th July 1945' British National Archives, CAB/195/3

Chance, J. *The Lord of the Rings: The Mythology of Power*, (Lexington: University Press of Kentucky, 2001).

Dickerson, M. & J. Evans, *Ents, Elves and Eriador*, (Lexington: University Press of Kentucky, 2006).

Hammond, W.G., 'All the Comforts: The Image of Home in *The Hobbit* and *The Lord of the Rings*' in *Mythlore*, 14.1 (1987) 29-33.

Malpas, S., 'Home' in *Reading The Lord of the Rings: New Writings on Tolkien's Classic*, ed. by R. Eaglestone (London: Continuum, 2005) 85-98.

Tolkien, J.R.R., *The Hobbit,* (London: Harper Collins, 1991).
— *The Silmarillion,* (London: Harper Collins, 1992).
— *The Lord of the Rings,* (London: Harper Collins, 1995)

Willink, H.U., 'Memorandum to the Cabinet 6th October 1945' British National Archives, CAB/129/3

Willink, H.U. 'Conclusions of a Meeting of the Cabinet' Wednesday 18th July 1945' British National Archives, CAB/65/53/15

The Geopolitics of Tolkien's Legend

Dr. Lamont Colucci

The point of this paper is to utilize Tolkien's works to analyse international politics and geopolitics. Geopolitics is a field that tries to reconcile the demands of a nation within the limits and benefits of its geography, abilities, and resources. Geopolitics combines all the academic fields that are no longer considered in favourable terms today. These are military strategy, diplomatic history, (which used to be called great man leadership or personal leadership), and geography. Some people have called Tolkien's works, especially *The Lord of the Rings*, a geopolitical literary work; others have called it fantasy cartography. Those are all interesting, but we must remind ourselves of the famous 1954 letter to Naomi Mitchison, where Tolkien said, "In any case, this is a tale about a war" (*Letters*, Letter 154, 198). This is a critical point. It is useful to illustrate some generalizations about how one can use geopolitics and international relations to view his work. The wars in Middle-earth generally favour fixed fortifications, such as Angband, Minas Tirith, Fornost, and Dol Guldur. They all serve as focal points for much of the stories concerning any warfighting. Second, the evil side uses wave tactics without concern for the loss of life. If one looks at many of the battles and many of the stories, it is one of the biggest problems for the side of good, because there is no concern about life on the other side. This can be analysed by studying the implications in human history where one nation used human wave tactics with dire consequences for all concerned. The third is the idea of perversion in the case of Númenor or deception in the case of Saruman, both of which produce horrible outcomes, and, when combined, produced the One Ring.

In history, international relations and geopolitics categorize geopolitical ages, which we can apply to Tolkien's work as well. In the First Age, there are four of them. First was a hegemonic attempt to create a superpower or hyperpower by Morgoth. This is followed by the battle of powers – of the Valar vs. Melkor, then the kinslaying over the Silmarils and finally the Fall of Nargothrond, Gondolin, and the intrigue of the Noldorian princes.

The Second Age, in international affairs terms, would be called bipolarity or a bipolar world. The first bipolar incarnation is the conflict between Númenor (then Gondor) and Sauron, as well as Sauron vs. the Elves. This is all within the context of the complicated plans of the Númenóreans, culminating in their destruction and then wrapping up with the dynastic politics of Gondor. The Third Age is dominated by the war of the Last Alliance, which in geopolitics would be called a multi-polar world where there is no single power that has more control than any other, or at least not a world supremacy power. This era is dominated by Sauron's attacks against Gondor. Finally, in the Fourth Age, we end up with a hegemonic or unipolar situation with the imperial reunited kingdom under Gondor's King Aragorn and his ally Éomer. Although the war continues even after the return of the king, we should return to the 1954 letter to Naomi Mitchison, "but in any case, this is a tale about a war and if war is allowed at least as a topic and it's setting it is not much good complaining that all the people are on one side or against those on the other" (198). This is a powerful quotation, and if you use a geopolitical lens, you can summarize the entirety of *The Lord of the Rings* as a bipolar battle between the forces of Gondor and the forces of Mordor.

Another method of studying international politics is levels of analysis. There are three basic ones to consider. These are the individual-level analysis, the nation state-level analysis, and the world-level analysis. The individual level of analysis in the real world focuses on an individual and their actions and their interactions in international affairs both historically and in the contemporary world. If you do that, you could focus all your attention on Elizabeth I or Vladimir Putin and argue that what moves geopolitics is individual people (rulers/generals/philosophers) and their actions. In the case of *The Lord of the Rings*, one would emphasize Denethor and his weakness, Sauron and his evil, and Aragorn and his heroics.

The second-level analysis in geopolitics is the nation-state, today focusing on the great powers like the United States, Japan, and the UK. In Tolkien's world, it would be Gondor, Mordor, Rohan, Mirkwood, and the Shire, studying their characteristics as a nation, their history, culture, and their motivations. In geopolitics, we ask, 'why do they do what they do?'. What separates Germany from Russia or Russia from China? This level of analysis is probably the most common historically in the field of geopolitics. Finally, there is the world-level analysis where IR scholars talk about this concept of world anarchy. In the majority of world history there is no single power that influences world affairs, and of course, there are three exceptions to that. The three exceptions would be the Pax Romana, the Pax Britannicus, and the Pax Americana. We are currently living in the third age, the Pax Americana; where today's youth have known nothing other than this, where the United States is the supreme power, the world hegemon, and the order-maker, and it is very different from the other two attempts at this in world history. Nonetheless, it is not to be confused with a cartoon depiction of world domination. It can be expressed by the question, who (which nation) keeps the sea lanes open? The U.S. Navy keeps them open, which does not mean the U.S. Navy is everywhere: that would be a cartoon. In Tolkien's Fourth Age, it is the Pax Gondorian, which is achieved by King Aragorn.

Other international relations concepts illustrated in Tolkien's world are band wagoning, represented by a train. As bystanders get excited by the train's success, they jump on to the train wagon to ride to the perceived success. Nations want to be on the side of victory. This is represented by Saruman and the Southrons following of Sauron. Another concept in international affairs is called balancing, where one nation is not in favour of any particular side; they simply know that if one of the parties wins, it will be a worse outcome. One can argue this is demonstrated by the Ents and their decision making. A final concept in this section we can examine in IR is nonstate actors. A nonstate actor in today's world could mean one of two very different things.

On the one hand, you have benevolent nonstate actors; those are people and groups acting transnationally across borders, and they do something good. There are many modern examples, such as Doctors Without Borders. That is a benevolent example of a non-state actor. On the opposing end is the malevolent non-state actor, such as groups like ISIS and Al Qaeda. In Tolkien's world, non-state actors are expressed by Túrin Turambar, the Rangers, the Corsairs, and the Wainriders.

Geography is a titanic subject in international affairs, and naturally, geopolitics. It is simply impossible to understand these in any real depth without geography. The same can be said for Tolkien's epic. His epic is dependent on both natural and created geographic problems and opportunities such as the Misty Mountains, Mirkwood, Fangorn Forest, the River Anduin, Weathertop, Moria, the Argonath, Amon Hen, Orthanc, the Gap of Rohan and the Black Gate.

Another way of applying international relations is a geopolitical theory, which in the modern age has been dominated by three schools: realism, liberalism, and Marxism. There have also been a lot of additions of theories such as constructivism and the school of feminism and many others. The debate specifically in the Anglosphere has primarily been between realism and liberalism and democratic realism. But, because that does not exist in Tolkien's world for the most part, we can use what predates democratic realism as a level of analysis which is sometimes referred to as moral realism. Thus, in Tolkien's sphere, we can utilize realism, liberalism, and moral realism. Realism boils down to the belief that nations make choices regardless of rhetoric on two things, and two things only: Do my actions serve my vital interest? Do my actions serve my national interest? Vital interests are very simple, as opposed to national interest which tends to be a little more complicated. Vital interests are existential threats that the choice or action presented will determine a civilizations' existence or what the other side does to a nation will put into question that nation's existence. Nations tend to allocate all available resources to ensure vital interest. Realists believe in the worst about human nature, that it is at best selfish and at worst evil. Power is the only currency that matters and a nation's life is determined by the struggle to avoid extinction and or subjugation.

For example, the United States in 1965 looked at the world and knew that the Soviet Union's nuclear arsenal was a vital interest. The fact that the USSR could destroy the United States within 15 to 20 minutes, depending on its launch ability was clear. Vital interests are not very debatable. There is more debate over national interest. National interests are those interests that ensure a nation's standard of living, its prosperity, its political position, its strategic position, and its trajectory for the future.

Another example in the modern era concerned the United States in the 1990s. The USA was very heavily criticized by some for not intervening in the Rwandan genocide. From a realist perspective, one cannot make a utilitarian argument that it was either in American vital or national interests to intervene, and realists often defend that decision.

Who would be a good realist in the world of Tolkien? Many would say Sauron is the ultimate realist. This is mostly true, but perhaps not as true as on the first impression. Sauron makes one major mistake that a true realist leader would not: he enjoys cruelty, sadism, and torture. Realists are not interested in that; they are interested in simply how they can achieve what they need to achieve. If cruelty creates more enemies and thus more than one would otherwise have, there is no reason to pursue it. One of the cartoons that we see in our world regarding realism is that realists are warmongers; they are not, in fact, quite the opposite. If realists can achieve their national and vital interests without war, they would do so. Peace costs fewer resources and time. Thus, Sauron is mostly a realist, but the Ents and Saruman are much better examples.

What about liberalism? Liberalism in IR theory refers to those who believe the best about human nature. For liberals, human nature is, by definition, good, and history is really about the story of progress. And, every age is a leap into better things, so they heavily emphasize the trajectory of democracy, free markets, toleration, the rule of law, international law and peace. It is a very positive view of international affairs and says if we could only harness that attitude, whether it is more democracy and more human rights, then we will have a better world. Some have suggested that perhaps Rivendell and the Shire are some possible ways to look at liberalism through Tolkien's world. However, just like many modern liberals, for example, the United States in the 1930s, liberals mixed their liberalism and their good-natured view of the world with an aspect of isolationism.

Finally, there is moral realism, which is this idea that prioritizes vital and national interests but also attempts to ensure that decisions are made along with a moral compass and a moral compass has to exist. This is primarily expressed today as democratic realism and in the pre-democratic age by historical and important figures like St. Thomas Aquinas whose Christian worldview accepted the reality of human nature while attempting to regulate behaviour along Christian lines as in his ideas on Just War, Justice in War, and even before Aquinas, the Peace of God and the Truce of God. If one applies that to Tolkien's world, we can witness that at the nation-state level with Rohan and Gondor and the individual level with Gandalf and Galadriel.

A very important measurement in geopolitics is done through an analysis of political systems. In other words, how does a nation's internal political system help to determine their foreign policy behaviour? The most prevalent system in Tolkien's world is the feudal monarchy, which is demonstrated by much of Gondor's history, Arnor, Rohan (a client state of Gondor), Dwarven kingdoms, Elven kingdoms (dominated by immortal personalities) and Dale. There is also an example of an imperial monarchy in Gondor, one before the events of *The Lord of the Rings* with King Hyarmendacil I and at the end with Aragorn. There is an example of rule by the aristocracy in Rivendell and a benevolent dictatorship in the case of Lórien. There is one system that comes close to representative democracy with the Shire where the mayor has a ceremonial role with some responsibility, like the mail service, coupled with a Thain who was Captain of the Shire muster (hence a militia instead of a standing army) who in times of emergency could take power. He was also Speaker of the Shire Parliament. Tolkien himself indicated that this devolved level of power found in the Shire, where decisions were made at the most local level, was the best use of political power. Naturally, there would be no War of the Ring without the totalitarian theocracy under Mordor, a corrupt system built on slavery and expansionism. Evil creatures served Melkor and Sauron out of fear, loathing and misery. There are tribal governments with Easterlings and essential anarchy with the Ents; they are more of a sense of being than a political system or even philosophy. The quasi-democratic anarchy of the Ents almost leads to their extinction.

There is an example of oligarchy under the Masters of Lake Town, and of course, the free city of Bree ruled by humans and hobbits.

There are three final general ideas concerning geopolitics: diplomacy, alliances, and the issue of war. The purpose of an alliance, regardless of whether it is from a liberal or realist perspective, is to maintain some aspect of power. A nation manages allies and deters adversaries. One can hope that the threat leading to the creation of the alliance can be built on for greater and farther-reaching cooperation and partnerships. NATO is a good example of this in our age. It is very interesting what Tolkien does with alliances. He was very good at illustrating how hard alliances are to create and maintain. He emphasizes how all of the kingdoms are focused on their own borders instead of the wider world. This, again, is very parallel to our situation today. Gondor feels bitter disappointment and a sense of abandonment due to the concept in International Relations that is called the free-rider problem. This is often illustrated by negative attitudes about spending money on defence and security with the expectation that someone else will take care of it. One could almost write an entire textbook in IR regarding Gondor and this idea that everyone is a free rider. And, the worst example of this, not because they are doing it on purpose, is the Shire. Without the Rangers, and Gondor, so without a non-state actor with the Rangers and a state actor with Gondor, the Shire's existence is probably non-existence. We have this in our world too. And, of course, many Americans feel as though they are Gondorians. American soldiers are doing the work that others probably should. Then there is Rohan, a victim first of a horrible, denial and deception campaign. Once that has been lifted, they fear entanglement. Rohan is supposed to be allied with Gondor but feels this is not their fight after all; maybe, they ponder, they will try to protect their own borders and be done with it.

Wars in Middle-earth are primarily won or lost, not by the supernatural and magic. They are primarily won or lost by medieval-style strategies and tactics, using the geopolitics of whatever age we look at in Tolkien's works to one's advantage. If one looks, for example, at the Wars of the Last Alliance, it is a perfect case study of Tolkien and war, of specific battles.

Further, just as in our history, specific battles that are won or lost completely change the geopolitical picture. Examples of this are Dagorland, Gladden Fields, Fornost, Khazad-dûm, and the Greenfields. In the War of the Ring, many battles had lost their real significance but were pivotal to the overall story. Again, these battles were won or lost based on medieval-style strategy and tactics alone, such as the battles of Isen, Siege of Lórien, Mirkwood, Dale, and again in the Shire, the battle of Bywater. These are Holy Wars. On the side of evil is Mordor pursuing a dark storm. The forces of light are engaged in a crusade to stop evil from enveloping the entire world. The decisive battles at places like Helm's Deep, Osgiliath, the Pelennor Fields and the Black Gate all include missions of morality and justice. Important to the good side is that the goodness of their cause and the justice of their cause will overcome the incredibly absurd odds that the good side always faces. In conclusion, the parallel between the historical geopolitical world and Tolkien's legendarium is spectacular and one can utilize Tolkien's works to illustrate aspects of geopolitics and international relations and international theory that is both striking and very instructive.

Bibliography

Tolkien, J.R.R., *The Letters of J.R.R. Tolkien*, ed. by H. Carpenter with the assistance of C. Tolkien, (London: HarperCollins, 2006).

IDENTITY

Cultural perspectives on the Elves in *The Lord of the Rings*

Lauren Brand

As we read *The Lord of the Rings* we are exposed to characters from different species, races, and cultures. In one of his letters J.R.R. Tolkien apologised modestly "I am a philologist, and much though I should like to be more precise on other cultural aspects and features, that is not within my competence" (*Letters*, Letter 144, 174-5). But with great skill Tolkien makes characters and cultures come alive. We end up deeply immersed in these characterisations and the consistency and depth of Tolkien's creation is unsurpassed.

Steve Walker said "One of Tolkien's most efficient techniques for exposing depths of character in short space is his presentation of a series of individual reactions to the same stimulus" (2009, 13-4). This paper will illustrate the wonder of Tolkien's work through a mini ethnographic study of a tiny slice of his creation: how the characters of different races and cultures who meet Elves in *The Lord of the Rings* understand and react to them, particularly through the words chosen by each character.

Paul Kocher said that in *The Lord of the Rings* what the individual characters say is very revealing: "Being thoughtful people, though, they say quite enough in the process to give a good idea of the kind of order in which they believe and the nature of the planner operating through it" (2000, 11).

Walker further summarised reactions to Tolkien's work, Tolkien's characters seem

> not folk-tale 'types' […] but beings […] often as complex psychologically as any in world literature: no individual, and no species, seems to exist only for the sake of the plot. All exist in their own right, each one perfectly realized. (2009, 17)

I hope to show the depth and layering of Tolkien's creation. Characters have individual personalities formed within their own culture, race, and life experience. Characters express beliefs and opinions about Elves based on this underlying formation. And depending on what happens when characters meet Elves, their lives and beliefs are either changed or remain the same.

Tolkien seems to have amazing insight about his creation and cross-cultural experiences. In a letter referring mainly to the Silmarillion he explained that if we, humans, tried to write stories about Elves we would turn them into men (*Letters*, Letter 212, 285). We will see in what follows that each character and race or culture has a tendency to understand or know Elves from their own perspective, even though they are not aware of it.

1 – Frodo

Frodo is the Hobbit most familiar and at ease in elven culture as Bilbo has educated him well. He is an exceptional Hobbit as book learning is quite rare. His upbringing was unusual: his parents died while he was young and he was adopted by an eccentric uncle who told tales of unbelievable adventures and of meeting Elves. He marvelled at Bilbo's songs, poetry, and stories about Elves. Frodo's knowledge of Elves is exceptional in his community and this made the average Shire Hobbit cringe.

Before the journey begins, Frodo demonstrates an academic but naive knowledge of Elves. When Sam first sees Gildor's band Frodo acts as the elder Hobbit explaining to the younger about the High Elves and their departure from Middle-earth.

When succumbing to his injury from the Morgul blade Frodo glimpses the real elvish magic shining in Glorfindel and reports this to Gandalf. He further defies the Nazgûl himself by invoking that same power when he cries out to Elbereth and Lúthien. Frodo's deeper appreciation of Elvendom starts to grow when he gets to Rivendell; he marvels that the great lords, Elrond and Glorfindel, should care for him.

In Lothlórien, the feeling of magic or power is even stronger and Frodo says "You can see it and feel it everywhere" (*FR*, 'The Mirror of Galadriel', 380). And recognising real power and grace, he offers Galadriel the Ring. As he leaves Lothlórien he mourns that he is parted from the power of the Lady.

Later in the journey, Frodo's survival depends on his new belief in the power of the Elves, their language and magic, and their deep connection to the powers of the world. In Shelob's lair words of power come to his mind in the elvish tongue and the phial shines out and drives the monster away. And he then wields his elvish blade, knowing that it was made in an age of elvish power in Beleriand.

The Ring is finally destroyed and Frodo returns home. But his life has changed forever and he cannot return to a simple Hobbit life. Imprisoned and tortured in the tower of Cirith Ungol he had despaired that only Elves could escape from the horrors of the reign of Sauron.

But maybe greater powers knew that Frodo's life would change because of the Elves? Gildor, Goldberry and Faramir had noticed something special about Frodo. For example, Goldberry said to him "I see you are an elf-friend; the light in your eyes and the ring in your voice tells it" (*FR*, 'In the House of Tom Bombadil', 139). And then Arwen gave him her hope by allowing him to take her place and leave for the West where he would find healing and rest.

Frodo didn't understand that his early exposure to, and comfort with, elvish culture had already made him an exceptional Hobbit. Then the gifts and power of the Elves would change him forever. He will depart his home, friends, country and culture to dwell with the Elves in Tol Eressëa where he can be healed.

2 – Samwise

Sam is a good example of Lionel Basney's observation that many times in the work "Legend is fulfilled as a character suddenly recognizes that some reality he has known only in legend stands before him in actuality" (2004, 183).

Sam is a hardworking country gardener. He has never left the Shire or seen any other race except for Hobbits. But Bilbo taught him his letters and told him tales of the Elves and he developed an enthusiasm for all things elvish, especially their magic. At the beginning of the journey he longs to see Elves, and on the journey to Rivendell he explains that he used to love hearing about the Elves from Bilbo.

When Sam finally meets Elves, he starts to make sense of what he has seen in his own way, in terms that a gardener would understand. Of Gildor's band he says "if I could grow apples like that, I would call myself a gardener" (*FR*, 'Three is Company', 96). He shows that he has really started to comprehend the way Elves are when he says "They seem a bit above my likes and dislikes, so to speak [...] It don't seem to matter what I think about them. They are quite different from what I expected – so old and young, and so gay and sad, as it were" (*FR*, 'A Shortcut to Mushrooms', 100).

As evil draws closer on the journey to Weathertop, Sam has a feeling that the elvish virtue will help against fear and begs Strider to fill the darkness with a story of Elves from the old days. In Rivendell, when Sam is immersed in elvishness, he bubbles over with enthusiasm.

And in Lothlórien Sam feels the depth of elvish power even more and describes the experience in nature's terms again. Rather than being wanderers, he notes their intimate relationship to the land they live in and comments, as only a gardener could, "If there's any magic about, it's right down deep, where I can't lay my hands on it" (*FR*, 'The Mirror of Galadriel', 380).

Sam initially has a naive idea about elvish magic and imagines that Galadriel might be able to show him some. When he is exposed to Galadriel's magic he is discomforted and wants to return home. After looking in the Mirror, Sam regrets ever coming to Lothlórien or wanting to see elvish magic. However, Lothlórien changes Sam and his naiveté is replaced with deep love for the elvish land and he expresses his desire to stay there rather than travel on.

Sam is now an ambassador for the Elves. When Faramir regrets that he has never met Elves nor the White Lady, Sam explains, in his unique language, that she is like:

> a great tree in flower, sometimes like a white daffadowndilly, small and slender like. Hard as di'monds, soft as moonlight. Warm as sunlight, cold as frost in the stars. Proud and far-off as a snow-mountain, and as merry as any lass I ever saw with daisies in her hair in springtime. (*TT*, 'The Window on the West', 706)

He goes on to demonstrate his new understanding when he responds to Faramir's concern that Galadriel must be dangerous. He explains that people bring their own danger to Lórien and that Galadriel is so strong you could "dash yourself to pieces on her, like a ship on a rock; or drown yourself, like a hobbit in a river" (706).

As the journey becomes more dangerous Sam finds real hope and strength in the power of the Elves. When Sam faces Shelob himself he cries out for aid to the Elves and their heavenly queen. When Sam then finds he is too late to save Frodo he prays for the Lady to help him come back and find Frodo. Then when he is reunited with Frodo and dresses him in the elven cloak that he recalls she made.

The Elves are no longer a fantasy for Sam. He has passed through their lands. They have aided him. Their magic and love have kept him going and saved his world. He is not the same Hobbit. Even as Galadriel and Celeborn take their leave of the party returning to the Shire, Sam wishes he could go back to Lórien. But his place has always been in Hobbiton.

Galadriel, more than any other, understands Sam and the transformation he undergoes. She hands on her magic to him before she leaves Middle-earth and elvish power fades away. Perhaps this is because Sam has become the Hobbit who understands and can use elvish magic best. He spreads the soil of Lothlórien throughout the Shire and plants the Mallorn seed. Sam won't see Galadriel in Lothlórien again, but part of Elvendom will always be on his doorstep and in his heart. And legends say that Sam even followed Frodo and the Elves into the west.

3 – Gimli

Gimli is the son of Glóin, one of the band of displaced Dwarves who recovered the kingdom of Erebor. Although we know from the long history of Middle-earth that Dwarves and Elves often don't get on, there are multiple polite and respectful exchange between the two races:

1. Glóin explained that he came to Rivendell to seek Elrond's advice.
2. Gimli explained that:
    2.1. Ori, one of the thirteen adventurers, wrote with Elvish characters,
    2.2. that the Dwarves helped make the elvish halls in Mirkwood, and
    2.3 that his ancestor, Durin, walked the earth in the middle of elvish history in the days of Nargothrond and Gondolin.

However, it is clear that Gimli lacks knowledge about the Elves. Near the borders of Lothlórien Gimli wonders aloud if Elves still live there and he finds that the hostility between the races is still real when treated with distrust by the Galadhrim, even though he objects that he is no more dangerous to them than Legolas.

Gimli also knows that Elves are strange and different to Dwarves (who prize material treasure so greatly). He tries to express this when he says on physically leaving his beloved Lothlórien "Memory is not what the heart desires […] Elves may see things otherwise. Indeed I have heard that for them memory is more like to the waking world than to a dream" (*FR*, 'Farewell to Lórien', 399).

The dwarvish desires of Gimli are transformed into reverence for the power and beauty of Galadriel and her land. When Galadriel reminds him of the beauty of Khazad-dûm in his own language he replies in the language of a dwarvish artisan that "the Lady Galadriel is above all the jewels that lie beneath the earth" (FR, 'The Mirror of Galadriel', 375).

Indeed, Gimli makes a pledge that the hostility between Elves and Dwarves will end. He takes Galadriel's gift and promises he will treasure it as a pledge of friendship. His dwarvish love of precious metal and jewels is abandoned and he proclaims that nothing will ever be as fair as her gift. Later, when Éomer expresses superstitious views about the Lady of the Golden Wood, Gimli confronts him angrily.

Gimli's meeting with Legolas and other Elves is life changing. When Legolas speaks of sailing to the West, Gimli begs him not to leave as the world will not be the same without the Elves. His legendary friendship with Legolas has become unbreakable. Gimli leaves his own culture and people forever – to go with Legolas into the West.

4 – Gandalf

Gandalf has a unique appreciation of the Elves because he is a Maia who has dwelled in Aman with the Calaquendi and spent his time in Middle-earth closest in the Elves' council. He is the mentor and teacher to the members of the Fellowship and shares his privileged understanding of Elves with them.

He knows that the Elves, including Glorfindel, are more powerful and noble than Hobbits or Men can imagine and has a unique understanding of the "Lords of the Eldar from beyond the furthest seas" (*FR*, 'Many meetings', 238). He explains to Frodo that the Calaquendi have great power against the dark forces, that in Hollin, hundreds of years after the Noldor left, there is still benefit from the presence of the Elves, and that evil cannot enter the elvish land of Rivendell.

Nevertheless, Gandalf knows their limitations. He warns, for example, that:

1. against Sauron's darkness, the Elves cannot prevail,
2. even Elrond can't foresee the future for Frodo, and
3. men will eventually replace the Elves.

Gandalf the Grey is reborn through his journey and becomes Gandalf the White and his strategies help free Middle-earth from Sauron. In the end, after waiting so long to see Tirion the Fair again, he returns to Aman to dwell once more in this hallowed land side by side with the Caliquendi.

Boromir, Saruman, and Gollum reject elvish culture even though the door is opened to each of them and, had they accepted the offer, they would have been saved. All three are corrupted by the power of Sauron and their inability to understand or modify their egocentric behaviour.

5 – Saruman

Saruman is also a Maia from Aman, and would have had as much exposure to Elves as Gandalf. However, he never felt the same closeness to them. Saruman, as the greatest of the Istari formerly taking counsel with the Elves, grows to value his own intellect, machines, and growing military might. Trapped by the lies of Sauron, he holds the powerless Elves in contempt and says to Gandalf that their days are over, thus elevating the wisdom of his own great plans.

After his downfall he must reframe and externalise his failure. He believes the Elves are the source of his destruction and that they wish to humiliate him and exact revenge. When he meets Galadriel for the last time, he accuses her of wanting to gloat over his fall. He curses her return to the West. He completely rejects reconciliation with the Elves and orders Wormtongue, with twisted words, "If these fine folk are going our way, then we will take another" (*RK*, 'Many Partings', 1020). His rejection of mercy and refusal to accept his own guilt lead to his ruin.

6 – Gollum

Gollum began life as a river dwelling hobbit many centuries before, and may have had tendencies to selfishness and petty crime. The Ring magnified the negative aspects of his personality. He was totally corrupted by it and became almost completely evil, living a life in darkness and want. Gollum's corruption cannot tolerate anything elvish, because the Elves represent goodness and light. Even when Frodo and Sam try to turn Gollum back to a wholesome life, he rejects this.

Gollum's utterances are the perfect example of Walker's observation that "In Middle-earth, the style is the creature. Language in its every aspect reveals character" (Walker 2009, 144).

For Gollum Elves are terrible and when touched by an elvish rope he screams "It freezes, it bites! Elves twisted it, curse them!" (*TT*, 'The Taming of Sméagol', 642). He even rejects lembas when he is starving because it stinks of the elvish country.

Gollum is destroyed by the corruption of the Ring having rejected hobbit and elvish kindness and a chance for redemption.

7 – Boromir

Of the Elves, Tom Shippey says:

> It is in fact the strong point of Tolkien's 're-creations' that they take in all available evidence, trying to explain both good and bad sides of popular story; the sense of inquiry, prejudice, hearsay and conflicting opinions often gives the Elves (and other races) depth. (1982, 55)

Boromir initially knows little of Elves and was sent to find Elrond the Wise in Rivendell by his father. But his desire to find knowledge is soon transformed into suspicion as the Ring plays on his mind. He distrustfully recalls disturbing tales about Elves and when hearing that the Fellowship must journey through Lothlórien he asks if there is any other way. He has heard that the land is perilous and none "have escaped unscathed" (*FR*, 'Lothlórien', 356).

Whereas Gimli and Sam are transformed by their Lothlórien sojourn, Boromir's fears and suspicions are confirmed. He dwells on his meeting with Galadriel and concludes "I do not feel too sure of this Elvish Lady and her purposes" (*FR*, 'The Mirror of Galadriel', 377).

Boromir tries to cajole Frodo into taking the Ring to Gondor and in doing so reveals his growing contempt for the Elves, wondering if they are weak.

Kocher commented on his attitude:

> The coexistence of the free peoples of Middle-earth with one another is founded on mutual respect and appreciation. Radically incompatible with these is the kind of contempt Boromir expresses for all Halflings, elves, and wizards, not to mention Aragorn, in the scene when he tries to take the Ring from Frodo at Parth Galen. In this context his saying, 'Each to his own kind', is in effect a proclamation of the superiority of men over other species, of Gondoreans over other men, and eventually of Boromir over other

> Gondoreans. In some degree some members of all the other species are smirched by this sense of the alienness of other peoples and the peculiar excellence of their own. (1972, 155)

This is a very common belief system when people find themselves in cross cultural situations.

Although Boromir is exposed to the wisdom and goodness of the Elves, the seeds of distrust and paranoia grow. The journey for Boromir ends at Parth Galen. His body is consigned to Anduin with an elven cloak cushioning his head and the golden belt of Lothlórien around his waist.

8 – Faramir

Faramir is quite different from his brother. He is a scholar first, rather than a warrior, and although he has never met an Elf, he has a more realistic idea of what they are like. His words mix reverence and doubt. He explains to Frodo that he has heard that "Elves are wondrous fair to look upon" (*TT*, 'Of Herbs and Stewed Rabbit', 683). He knows a little of elvish history and language and observes the Gondorian custom at mealtimes to look towards Elvenhome and beyond.

But Faramir reports the same superstitious fears of the Elves, and particularly of the Golden Wood, as Boromir. The death of his brother gives credence to these superstitions. When learning about Frodo's journey through Lothlórien he muses that it was perilous to go there. And when he hears how his brother died, he laments that Boromir ever entered the land.

But although Faramir is wary, he expresses some potential to learn and recognises his own ignorance. He apologises that he is not "learned in Elven-lore" and expresses his confusion by explaining "I deem it perilous now for mortal man wilfully to seek out the Elder People. Yet I envy you that have spoken with the White Lady" (*TT*, 'The Window on the West', 706). He asks Frodo to tell him more of the Elves of Lothlórien.

Faramir will meet his first Elf, Legolas, after the battle of the Pelennor Fields. He will not be destroyed by the meeting, as he fears Boromir was. This is in part due to his openness to the possibility that Elves are both magical and virtuous. His life will change in ways he did not expect. He will marry Éowyn and become Prince of Ithilien. Some of the Elves of the Greenwood will move to the Ithilien and, as Legolas promised, "it shall be blessed" and transformed into Faramir's own haven of elvish peace and beauty, just like the mythical Elvenhome (*RK*, 'The Field of Cormallen', 992).

9 – Éomer

Lionel Basney captures the experience of many characters very well:

> The general pattern of this repeated incarnation is as follows: an individual character, often on his home ground and thus confident of his ability to judge rightly, suddenly recognize as that some reality of which he had known only in legend now faces him in broad daylight, or is attested to by authority he cannot gainsay. The character's response

> is normally a blend of surprise, assent, and wonder. For the reality he confronts does not thereby lose its mythical fascination. Rather the myth merges with experience, or into experience, its wonder intact, but having gained empirical solidity. (2004, 188)

A good example of this is Éomer. The Rohirrim, just like Boromir and Faramir, have never met the Elves and know even less about them, they only know what they have heard in half remembered legends, told in song, like the songs of the slaying of Scatha the Worm, and of the taming of Felaróf. True to this culture of awe and the supernatural, on first meeting the three hunters in the plains of Rohan, Éomer is so surprised that he asks if they are Elves. When told that they have passed through Lothlórien he shows his superstitious beliefs about Elves by saying "Then there is a Lady in the Golden Wood, as old tales tell! [...] Few escape her nets, they say. These are strange days! But if you have her favour, then you are also net-weavers and sorcerers, maybe" (*TT*, 'The Riders of Rohan', 453). Éomer also explains that all of the Rohirrim believe the same things.

Éomer is not aware that his beliefs about Elves are destined to change but he recognises the tides of change when he finds Elves and Dwarves walking together and "folk speak with the Lady of the Wood and yet live" (458). He is also open minded enough to rethink his assessment of Elves and the Lady of the Wood, and seeks Gimli's pardon.

As his story comes to a close Éomer has indeed learned better. He has met, befriended, and fought side by side with Elves and knows they are no sorcerers. Instead, he warns Gimli that he will battle anyone who does not judge Queen Evenstar to be the most beautiful woman in Middle-earth.

10 – Aragorn

Aragorn is unique amongst the race of Men because his view of the Elves is formed by his upbringing in Rivendell and Lórien, surrounded by elvish and half-elvish culture. His attitude to Elves is first hand and is untainted by fear and superstition. Aragorn is a keeper of elvish history and wisdom shown by his telling of the tale of Beren and Lúthien and use of *athelas*.

Aragorn rightly sees elvish communities as havens of safety, friendship and love – his home. Early in the journey he tells the hobbits to look forward to reaching Rivendell. And he looks forward to entering Lothlórien even in Winter. He also tries to correct Boromir about the loveliness of Lothlórien which he calls "the heart of Elvendom on earth" (*FR*, 'Lothlórien', 371).

After Frodo is wounded on Weathertop Aragorn confirms the power of elvish words by explaining that they were the best defence against the Nazgûl. He later bases his decision to cross the bridge on the Mitheithel on a small elvish stone. Even on the border of Lothlórien he believes they will be safer under its eaves. On the departure of the company from Lothlórien he knows that they will be blessed by the Lady, and this is confirmed later when he finds Merry's broach and knows "Not idly do the leaves of Lórien fall [...] This did not drop by chance" (*TT*, 'The Riders of Rohan', 444).

Aragorn also understands the mystical power of the Elves. When Boromir fears that the Fellowship will not pass through Lothlórien unscathed, Aragorn clarifies the real risk that they might be changed by the experience, rather than harmed. He warns Boromir to "Speak no evil of the Lady Galadriel" and that evil can only come to Lothlórien if it is brought by an outsider (*FR*, 'The Mirror of Galadriel', 377).

Aragorn joins the Fellowship to save Middle-earth and the people he loves, knowing that he won't be able to remain in Rivendell. To save them he must take up his heritage as the King of Men. He never sees Lothlórien again, but Arwen joins him to bless his reign.

11 – The Ents

Walker comments:

> The aura of internal consistency is in part the product of Tolkien's penetrating vision of his world, in part a dividend of its detailed buttresses to coherence as his stylistic system of internal allusion, of cross-referencing to his world as if it were reality. (2009, 13)

Treebeard's utterances are interesting because he is absorbed in his own culture and thoughts, and when thinking and speaking about other peoples such as Elves, ends up going full circle and speaking about them and himself without seeming to notice. He cross-references with his own world constantly.

What stands out about Entish culture is their love for the forests that they care for, their language that they use to order the world, the loss of the Ent-wives, and their solitary contentment.

Treebeard likes Elves, or rather, his memory of Elves. He is so old that time has little meaning anymore and he probably can't remember exactly when he last met an Elf. This particular fondness for Elves comes first from their language. He explains that the Elves gave the Ents the gift of speech and that this cannot be forgotten. Treebeard does indeed speak a long-winded version of *Quenya.*

Treebeard regrets that his friendship with the Elves failed when the Elves crossed over the sea and hid themselves away, making "songs about days that would never come again" (*TT*, 'Treebeard', 489). He echoes this by also making songs about days that would never come again.

Treebeard *Ent-thropomorphises* Elves and in doing so he reveals great self-absorption, possibly because of his long isolation from most of the peoples of Middle-earth. He describes his species and Elves in a complex and confusing way:

> For Ents are more like Elves: less interested in themselves than Men are, and better at getting inside other things. And yet again Ents are more like Men, more changeable than Elves are, and quicker at taking the colour of the outside, you might say. Or better than both: for they are steadier and keep their minds on things longer. (489)

He also reflects on the dangers of Celeborn's woods in a way that sounds remarkably like how others would perceive the dangers of Fangorn.

And perhaps because he has lost contact with Elves for a very long time, he also appears to criticise Elves for not caring for the woods enough! And then he can't help but complain even about elvish songs, compared to the beauty and verbosity of his own: "It is Elvish, of course: lighthearted, quickworded, and soon over. I daresay it is fair enough" (499).

After the Ents topple Saruman from power and restore the gardens of Isengard, little changes for Treebeard who returns to the care of his woods. He is not required to change his own framework for understanding the world and I doubt that his view of Elves changes either. But he does reveal to us his insight when he is reunited with Galadriel, Celeborn and Elrond, who he respectfully calls the "Great ones" and "Beautiful Ones" (*RK*, 'Many Partings', 1015, 1017). As only a tree can do, he feels in the water, in the earth, and in the air, that he won't meet Galadriel, Elrond, or Celeborn again.

To conclude, in *The Lord of the Rings*, a protagonist's character and culture of origin strongly influence how they perceive the Elves. Initial beliefs and later conclusions are different for each character we meet. Whether, or how, these characters are changed by the experience of knowing or meeting Elves differs. Some utterly reject the goodness and wisdom of the Elves and are destroyed. Some change from being distrustful to showing a willingness to see things differently. A few find such beauty and peace in the elvish communities that after their journey concludes they hold on to the goodness they have found and long not to be separated from it. In a remarkable transformation, some even leave their culture and take the Straight Road to spend the rest of their lives with the Elves that they have come to love. There they find true healing.

Galadriel has almost the last word. She says to Sam as she passes through the Shire on the way to the Havens "I hear and see that you have used my gift well. The Shire shall now be more than ever blessed and beloved" (*RK*, 'The Grey Havens', 1066-7).

Behind Galadriel's comment is a truth: the Elves we meet are beings of light, far seers and gift givers. Where travellers who meet them use that experience well, the Elves pass on their blessings and part of Elvendom stays in their hearts forever.

Bibliography

Basney, L., 'Myth, History, and Time in *The Lord of the Rings*', in *Understanding The Lord of the Rings*, ed. by R.A. Zimbardo and N.D. Isaacs (New York: Houghton Mifflin Company, 2004).

Kocher, P.H., *Master of Middle-Earth,* (Harmondsworth: Penguin Books, 1972) .
— 'Cosmic Order' in *Modern Critical Views: J.R.R. Tolkien*, ed. by H. Bloom (Philadelphia: Chelsea House Publishers, 2000).

Shippey, T.A., *The Road to Middle-earth,* (London: Harper Collins Publishers, 1982).

Tolkien J.R.R., *The Letters of J.R.R. Tolkien*, ed. by H. Carpenter with the assistance of C. Tolkien (Boston: Houghton Mifflin Company, 1981).
— *The Lord of the Rings* (London: Harper Collins, 1991).

Walker, S., *The Power of Tolkien's Prose,* (New York: Palgrave Macmillan, 2009).

"We should look at green again": of magic, Green Elves and the battle of good vs evil

Aurélie Brémont

Colour symbolism is a social construct and as such, it varies according to time and space. A colour can have an obvious meaning to Westerners in 2021 and mean the complete opposite in other cultures or at other periods of history (in the nineteenth century for example, pink was the colour of boys, being a watered down version of red, the colour of manhood). Nowadays, we associate green with nature, clean ingredients, durability, the preservation of wildlife, but we can safely assume that it has not always been so. Exploring how an author uses certain symbols allows us to find their working perspective, which is particularly interesting with medievalist authors: do they operate from a strictly medieval standpoint? Is it possible for a modern author to completely steer clear of their contemporary perspective and the symbolism inherited from their culture? Or is good medievalist writing a skillful blend of old and new?

These are the question I will apply to Tolkien's works in this paper. The first part of this paper will set the groundwork by examining the symbolism of the colour green in the Middle Ages and how it differs from earlier periods in history.

In the second part, I will explore Middle-earth to try and determine what period of time was used to create its natural landscape and what cultural imagery lies behind the characters' perspective. We will also question the presence of modern ideas into a medieval fantasy story and see the importance Tolkien gave to nature in his writings, and to what purpose.

Finally, the colour green in Middle-earth cannot be examined without studying the Green People, the Sylvan Elves, and I will briefly venture into older creative material to explore their origin, their story, what it means to call them Green, and how art can sometimes imitate history.

1 – The nature of green in the Middle Ages and in Middle-earth

1.1 – Medieval green

Michel Pastoureau, French historian and specialist in heraldry, devoted an entire series of books to colours and their history. The third instalment, *Vert, Histoire d'une couleur*, retraces the various symbolisms and uses of green from Antiquity to Modern times, and shows that the history of green essentially began in the Middle Ages. Before that time, green was mostly a discarded colour: first, because to the classical eye, nature is not only fields and forests but the entire natural world which contains way more than one colour. Secondly, because the complex rules of fabric dyeing made it very hard to obtain: mixing colours was a highly codified operation that made it virtually impossible to mix yellow and blue.

But during the first half of the Middle Ages, green takes on a more defined identity, albeit clearly two-sided: on the one hand, a very positive symbolism associated with youth, love, chivalry and romance (*vert gai* "gay green") and on the other, a very negative connotation linked to treachery, sorcery, the devil and the Other World (*vert perdu* "wasted green") (Pastoureau 2013, 99).

1.1.1 – Gay green

The positive symbolism of green, *vert gai*, is embodied by the emergence of an important locale of the medieval landscape: the orchard. Medieval orchards were square, enclosed spaces, recalling the Garden of Eden, and organized according to precise patterns: squares of grass, flowers, trees, fountains and brooks, every inch was highly codified in order to serve a purpose. Orchards were places where people would come to meditate or court. It is the first direct association of green with nature and it naturally follows that green has its own season, Spring. Gay Green is about birth, youth, love and life, but in a very neat, chaste and organized way. The Latin word for green, *viridi*, allowed for a phonetic link with *veritas*, truth, but also with strength, *viribus*, while in French there is an homophony between green and glass (*verre*), linking green with transparency and honesty (66). In French romance, when a green knight appears in a tournament, it is a code for a young, inexperienced, spirited man. Tristram, the tragic hero of one of the most famous and popular love stories of the Middle Ages, is the epitome of the green knight (93-5). The tragedy of Tristram and Isolde is full of associations with the green world: from the herbed wine that seals the lovers' fate to the orchard where the lovers meet and the forest they flee into once they can no longer keep their love secret, green is everywhere.

Just as Tristram goes from garden to forest as his love story becomes tragic and he is cast away from society, we now leave the positive associations of *vert gai* to go into *vert perdu*. As opposed as those two semantic fields are, it is quite logical that they should be linked to one another: youth is but a fleeting stage and all that is green must decay and rot. Thus green is also the colour of treachery, duplicity, fickleness, it is the colour of the greatest traitor of all times, Judah. And as naturally as death is the counterpart of birth, wilderness is the counterpart of order, dividing the green world between well-ordered enclosures of carefully designed gardens and mysterious sylvan mazes of forests where it is easy to lose oneself, be it physically or spiritually.

1.1.2 – Wasted green

The threatening image of forests goes back to the Roman conquest, since forests were sacred and used as temples by several people conquered by Caesar. Writers such as Lucan describe forests in German lands as being sanctuary to ancient gods where humans were sacrificed and where no Roman soldiers would dare to enter, while the druids of Gaul and Ireland could enchant trees and turn them into soldiers.

In the Middle Ages, forests are first and foremost seen as "outside of society": hermits want to escape the mundane world, and heroes like Merlin and Lancelot take shelter in the forest when their madness makes them unfit to live among others. Woods are places out of time and space where Arthurian knights enter to seek adventure and where you can stumble upon a magical hunting party, or see a fairy maiden comb her hair by a stream.

In early medieval texts, fairy people are ambivalent, meeting them can be a blessing or a curse, but Christian authorities were quick to assimilate figures such as the Green Man, a symbol of fertility and renewal, with the devil, by painting his skin green and casting an evil hue on all things pagan. However, while green skin remains a token of evil right into modern times (see the Wicked Witch of the West for reference), fairy folks retained their ambiguity in medieval poems with characters such as the Green Knight whom Gawain must meet in the forest. He is a scary character throughout the story but in the end, he does not harm Sir Gawain and reveals himself to be the victim of a curse by Morgan (Pastoureau 2013, 113-7). In *Sir Orfeo*, another famous medieval fairy tale, the King of Faery stays true to his word and gives Heurodis back to Orfeo, even if his decision to kidnap her early in the tale seems cruel and unfair.

The Middle Ages are definitely a turning point in the symbolic history of the colour green when it becomes associated with nature in all its aspects and ambivalence: birth and young love blossoming in the garden at spring time, magic, decay and evil lurking in the dark forests outside of the civilized world. Did Tolkien use this ambivalence in the forests of Middle-earth or does he adopt an earlier (or later) perspective?

1.2 – Green in Tolkien

Woods and forests in Arda are very strongly inspired by pagan lore and pre-Christian traditions. Mirkwood, the Old Forest, Lothlórien or Fangorn are scary places where all sorts of enchantments and otherworldly encounters happen, and even when heroes come out of the woods unscathed, they are not "unchanged" (*FR*, 'Lothlórien', 329). Forests are home to ancient, primeval, mysterious creatures such as Tom Bombadil or Treebeard who are so removed from the affairs of the world that their moral alignment can be hard to fathom. Be it Pippin on the edge of the Old Forest, Boromir in Lothlórien or Gimli entering Fangorn, there is always a voice of fear and distrust upon going into the woods, and several mentions of tales or testimonies attesting to the scary atmosphere under the trees. In Mirkwood, Bilbo and the Dwarves witness a fairy hunt and a magical banquet reminiscent of *Sir Orfeo*, and in Lothlórien, the members of the Fellowship experience glitches in moon phases that suggest time operates differently in Galadriel's realm. Forests in Middle-earth answer every characteristics of the woods in ancient times.

1.2.1 – Gardens in Arda

However, if we go back to Pastoureau's description of nature in medieval societies, it is not so much scary pagan forests that we must look for, but gardens, and in Middle-earth, gardens can be found in the most unexpected places. We will set aside the Shire and its gardeners for the moment and go first to Lothlórien.

While our heroes are resting in Galadriel's realm, Sam and Frodo are invited to follow the Elven Lady "through a high green hedge [...] into an enclosed garden", with a stream running through it (*FR*, 'The Mirror of Galadriel', 352). There, in a hollow where no trees grow, directly under the stars, lies the Mirror of Galadriel. It is at once the heart of her kingdom, the sanctuary of her magic and a garden that fits all the criteria of the Middle Ages. It is also worth noting that Galadriel is the only character in the book to be the subject of a chaste and pure courtship echoing what used to take place in medieval gardens.[1]

The separation of the natural world between forest and garden is nevertheless nowhere more obvious than in Fangorn and the story of the Ent people. As Treebeard tells Merry and Pippin, the Ents are shepherds of the forest "the great trees, and the wild woods, and the slopes of the high hills", while the Entwives gave "their minds to lesser trees, and to the meads in the sunshine beyond the feet of the forests [...] the wild apple and cherry blossoming in spring" (*TT*, 'Treebeard', 464). Tolkien differentiates Ents and Entwives by describing how the former "drank of the mountain-streams, and ate only such fruit as the trees let fall in their path [...] spoke with the trees" while the latter "did not desire to speak with these things; but they wished them to hear and obey what was said to them (464). The Entwives ordered them to grow according to their wishes, and bear leaf and fruit to their liking" (464). These differences led to an estrangement, the Ents "lost the Entwives", they grew apart, but they remain parts of the same species, they branched out of the same tree (464). The story of the Ents is the very illustration of the evolution of the place of nature in medieval times, the sundering of the green world into two spaces, two visions that cannot be reconciled, because one sees nature as the primeval force and the other puts outside intervention at its core.

There is however little doubt as to which direction the world is taking since by the end of the book, Ents have started to create their own garden in Saruman's former stronghold: "All the stone-circle wall had been thrown down and removed, and the land within was made into a garden filled with orchards and trees, and a stream ran through it [...] Welcome to the Treegarth of Orthanc' [Treebeard] said" (*RK*, 'Many Partings', 957). The very word garth means an enclosed space and while the Ents could have left nature to take back its right in the ring of Orthanc, they designed a garden following the rules of medieval landscaping. Thus, in the end, all Ents have decided that nature should be ruled and organized.

1.2.2 – The Shire

When speaking of orderly nature, it is only logical that we should now turn to a part of Middle-earth that we had left aside so far, and that is the Shire. It is the first place that comes to mind when mentioning gardens in Middle-earth, both because gardens are an essential feature of the Shire and its restoration after the War of the Ring and because one of the four Hobbits of *The Lord of the Rings* is a gardener who takes great pride in his status. However, the point of the demonstration so far was to compare medieval symbolization of nature and how Tolkien described nature in his medievalist writings. The Shire and its inhabitants are an anachronism as they are modelled on nineteenth century rural England and constitute an oddity within the medieval-inspired world of Middle-earth.

1. The courtship of Galadriel by Gimli is studied, for example, in J.G. Wollock's *Rethinking Chivalry and Courtly Love* (2011, 239).

Finding gardens in 19th century England is not an exciting discovery, but it allows us to mention another way in which Tolkien depicts nature: in opposition to industry. This seems to be at odds with what we just demonstrated regarding the Ents, where Tolkien leans towards the idea that some amount of control over nature is a good thing, but the solution to this conundrum lies in the personal history of the author.

Tolkien grew up in the country before moving to Birmingham and he kept a love of rural life that made him mourn every tree that was cut and hate every new car that he saw in the streets throughout his life.[2] The Shire represents the ideal balance of a society that has enough control over nature to be comfortable even when living in holes but still respects the green world and does not seek machines and productivity. How much of a fantasy such an image of nineteenth century rural England is the subject for another paper. But the fact remains that nature and the place of humans (and Hobbits) within it is an essential aspect of Tolkien's ideas, albeit a late one to surface: the author had to make significant changes to his narrative to fit that purpose.

1.2.3 – Perfect balance

Tolkien first imagined Middle-earth as a pre-medieval world, with a predominance of the natural world as a threatening space: forests in Middle-earth are scary. Whether they are legendary like Fangorn, Mirkwood or Lothlórien, or familiar like the Old Forest, they are considered dangerous, even by those who know them: Tom Bombadil is aware of the danger of the Old Man Willow, Beorn warns the Dwarves at length about straying into Mirkwood and Celeborn thinks of Fangorn as "a strange land, and is now little known" (*FR*, 'Farewell to Lórien', 364). They are sanctuaries of magic, filled with mystery, places out of space and time, home to witches (as Galadriel is perceived in Rohan) and monstrous spiders and even walking trees that can eat up Orcs escaping from Helm's Deep.

Upon exploring the Old Forest or Lothlórien, our heroes will go from fear to relief by entering shelters at the heart of the woods, places where they will receive rest, solace, protection from the dangers of the outside world and ample supplies of food and equipment to resume their journey. Those shelters, the house of Tom Bombadil and Caras Galadhon are places where nature is orderly, where the inhabitants live in harmony with the green world. From a human perspective (be it the heroes', the author's or the reader's), nature is fundamentally hostile and needs to be tamed to a certain degree.

Fangorn is used to tell us where the limit is, and for that, Tolkien completely transformed the character behind this name. Originally, Treebeard was not benevolent, but "pretends to be friendly, but is really in league with the Enemy" and is the one keeping Gandalf captive while the Hobbits are trying to reach Rivendell (*Shadow*, 384). Tolkien never explained this radical change, but it is hard to not link this to the poetic defeat of Saruman and his mind of wheels by the forces of nature in order to transform the breeding factories of Isengard into a beautiful garden.

---

2. See for example Letter 181 to his son Michael about the destruction of Oxford to make way for technology and industry (*Letters*, Letter 181, 232).

The depiction of the green world in Middle-earth is complex and fascinating as it becomes a catalyst for Tolkien's mastery of ancient and medieval symbolism as well as his personal and modern ideals of natural and human balance. In the War of the Ring, when walking trees or wildmen come into play, they fight against evil, and while entering a forest can be daunting, you can trust that you will find shelter and help inside, instead of the entrapments and curses of treacherous pagan creatures answering to Satan.

Tolkien offers us a truly medievalist perspective, away from the fears and beliefs of the Middle Ages but with a sense of nostalgia and regret that only a man living in a world where nature has been controlled beyond reason can have. So now that we no longer fear to enter the forests of Middle-earth, it is time to go from green leaves to Greenleaf, to meet those who dwell under the trees, the Green Elves, the people of Legolas.

2 – The Green People of Middle-earth

Most of the Elves we meet in *The Lord of the Rings* are Green Elves and we know next to nothing about them. The great Elves of Middle-earth are the Noldor and Sindarin of *The Silmarillion*, and very few are left in Middle-earth by the War of the Ring, only Galadriel (and Celeborn, though his origin varies greatly), Cirdan, Glorfindel, Elrond remain. However, they rule over Elves that never went to Valinor.

2.1 – Why Green Elves?

All the tales of the First Age are about Elves, their origins, fights and fates. So why did Tolkien need to add yet another Elven people in the Third Age? *The Lord of the Rings* contain several people or creatures that have no origins in the earlier material, such as Hobbits and Ents, but they serve a literary purpose: Hobbits need to be outsiders in order for the reader to identify themselves with the heroes and discover the world outside the Shire along with the heroes. As for Ents, the first idea behind their creation was Tolkien's dissatisfaction with Shakespeare's *Macbeth*.

The use of Green Elves in *The Hobbit* and *The Lord of the Rings* also has a literary origin: when writing *The Hobbit*, Tolkien used Elves, because he had used Dwarves and Dragons and was pulling in all the available folkloric material at his disposal. But even if the first Elves we see (when the Company arrives in Rivendell) are closer to the whimsical Victorian fairies that permeate 'The Book of Lost Tales', he soon introduced Elrond, and then the Elven King (Thranduil), wise and formidable Elves, closer to the King of Faery of *Sir Orfeo* than to Shakespeare's Puck.

He then had to tie in the bow-wielding, green-clad forest dwellers that the readers had encountered in his first book with the Noldor and Sindarin heroes of the First Age and decided that the latter would be High Elves, ruling over the anonymous Green Elven people. He then had to answer two questions to make his creation coherent: where do Green Elves come from and why are they a lesser people ruled by a minority of Noldor and Sindarin lords?

2.2 – History of the Green Elves

Green Elves are literally a footnote in the history of the Elder Days and their history has to be pieced together from scarce mentions in *The Silmarillion*. We are told that during the great migration towards Valinor,

> one arose in the host of Olwë, Lenwë he was called. He forsook the westward march and led away a numerous people, southwards down the great river and they passed out of knowledge of their kin until long years were passed. Those were the Nandor and they became a people apart, unlike their kin, save that they loved water, and dwelt most beside fall and living streams. Greater knowledge they had of living things, tree and herb, bird and beast, than all other Elves. (*Silmarillion*, 63)

As the fell beasts of Morgoth awoke, those Elves, led by Denethor, son of Lenwë, fled their homes, and settled in Ossiriand, land of the Seven Rivers. But when Morgoth and Ungoliant came back to Middle-earth and war came to Beleriand, Denethor was killed by Orcs. Some of his people thereafter refused to go to war and became secret and secluded, and they were called the Laiquendi, the Green Elves, because of their raiment of the colour of leaves. But many went north and entered the guarded realm of Thingol, and were merged with his people (111). They are sparsely mentioned in *The Silmarillion* afterwards, we mostly know that when Beren and Luthien returned from the Halls of Mandos, they settled on Tol Galen with Laiquendi, who accepted Beren the One-Handed as their leader, and the island became known as the Land of the Dead that Live (226).

The Silmarillion does not give us more information, but in *The Lost Road* and *Morgoth's Ring*, we learn that Lenwë was also called Nanô, or Dan in his people's language and this people is called Nandor, or Danas (*Lost Road* 112; *Morgoth* 89, 163). The people of Danas, led by a one-handed chief, dwelling on an island between the world of the dead and the world of the living: Tolkien took the Green Elves straight from Irish mythology and barely changed anything to integrate them in Middle-earth.

It should not come as a surprise as Irish mythology is an important part of the folklore of Western Europe and something that Tolkien was very well-versed in. Furthermore, the Grey Elves of Middle-earth are heavily inspired by Welsh culture, as is their language, Sindarin. It would not make sense to have Welsh folklore and language in Middle-earth without any trace of its Gaelic cousin. However, the tales and languages of the Green Isle predate those of Wales, so the Green Elves should be more ancient and somehow wiser than their Sindarin cousins, and there is no justification for them to be ruled by Thingol and its people.

2.3 – A moral spectrum

The reason lies not in history, but in morality and in order to understand it, we must now turn to a book that is absolutely essential to understand Tolkien's creation: *Splintered Light* by Verlyn Flieger. This essay explains the theories of Owen Barfield on poetic diction and how Tolkien used them in his own mythology. To try and summarize the idea, there is a direct link between Truth, the Divine Word and Light, Good, Wisdom, the purpose of Eru; and the further one is removed from the Word, the further they are from the Light, and vice-versa.

Thus, *The Silmarillion* is the struggle of the Elves to come close, possess, lose and regain the Divine Light, and each splintering of the Light results in a new people and a new language one step removed from the original Word of Eru. This is why the first great division of the Elven tribes is between the Calaquendi, the Elves of Light, who went to Valinor, and the Moriquendi, the Elves of Darkness, who stayed in Middle-earth away from the Trees.

The Grey Elves, the people of Thingol, never completed the journey to Valinor but Thingol was one of the three emissaries that first went west and saw the Trees. On leading his people westward, he met Melian, a Maia, who lived in Valinor until that meeting. Together they share a wisdom far beyond anything that can be found east of Valinor, which is why their people are called Grey and are counted among the High Elves.

But what of the Laiquendi, the Green Elves? Where does green stand in the spectrum from light to dark? Green Elves never crossed the sea to go to Valinor but were victims of Morgoth and its creatures. They never took an active part in the Quest for the Silmarils, be it for good or bad. Nothing of what is told of their history places them in Light or in Darkness, so we have to look at other material, more specifically the linguistic material presented in the History of Middle-earth, to try and find which moral alignment Tolkien assigned to the Laiquendi.

In *The Lost Road*, 'The Lhammas' contains some information about Green Elves, especially the parts that Christopher Tolkien labelled Lhammas A, Lhammas B and Lhammasethen. In Lhammas B, Green Elves are said to be

> of Noldorin race, but not counted among the Eldar, not yet among the Lembi (Moriquendi). Nor was their tongue like the tongues of the Lembi, different from the tongues of Valinor and of the Lembi, and most like that of Doriath, though not the same. But their speech has now vanished from the earth. (*Lost Road*, 176)

Christopher Tolkien then explains that his father's first idea was to count them as Lembi, but they are among the Eldar in Lhammas A and in neither group in the Lhammas B.

In the two versions of the Tree of Tongues that can be found in *The Lost Road*, the language of the Laiquendi is a branch of Quendian language that sprang before some Elves became Eldar and separated into three branches (169-70). But we are also told very clearly in the Lhammas that "though they had turned back, the Green elves had yet heard the call to the West, and were still drawn thither at times in unquiet and restlessness; and for this reason they are not among the Lembi" (175).

Christopher Tolkien concludes that the Laiquendi are an anomaly, and we are left with this, trying to solve a riddle that even the author could not unravel.

Tolkien was well-versed in Irish mythology and used it throughout his creation of Middle-earth.[3] He also used Welsh language and culture as a foundation for the Sindarin

3. Brémont, A., 'Les Celtes en Terre-du-Milieu' (Unpublished PhD thesis, Université Sorbonne Paris, 2009).

people. However, he had no affinity for Old Irish, but loved Welsh, so it would make sense that he would want to include material from Irish mythology but gave superiority to Welsh material. The overall impression is that he wanted some Irish influence in his history of the Elves but was not interested enough in Laiquendi to give them more than a supporting role.

As a result, he was able to include Green Elves in *The Hobbit* and *The Lord of the Rings* without having to reconcile earlier material from *The Silmarillion* with the narration of the War of the Rings, and since he never imagined that readers and critics would have access to his notes, he did not care to decide which moral alignment to give them.

But the result is a mysterious aura, an ambiguity of the Elves in the Third Age that leaves heroes and readers unsure of what they are going to face when Elves approach: whimsical woodland creatures who will sing silly songs when Bilbo and the Dwarves approach, evanescent figures feasting in the dark trees of Mirkwood or wise and powerful heroes of the Eldar such as Glorfindel who shine with the light of the Valar and can face the Nazgûl without fear?

Whether by design or unconscious influence, Tolkien created his Elves to be as paradoxical and unfathomable as the symbolism of green in the Middle Ages, both good and bad, young and old, honest and treacherous, pure and decaying. Medieval theologists wanted all pagan things to be attributed to Satan and branded as evil, but the literature of the time shows that fairies were not perceived that way in texts like *Sir Orfeo*, *Sir Gawain and the Green Knight*, Marie de France's *Lais* and many others. At worst, fairy people sometimes act threateningly or cruelly, but more often than not, if the hero is true and righteous, he will be rewarded, unscathed, if not unchanged.

Tolkien mirrored this ambiguity with the Elves in the Third Age, along the lines of the 13th century poem *The Early South English Legendary* quoted by Tom Shippey in *The Road to Middle-earth* "in the war between God and Satan for men's souls, there may be neutrals […] These are called Elves" (1982, 211-2).

"We should look at green again and be startled anew by blue and yellow" (*TL*, 57). This quote, used as a title for this paper, comes from Tolkien's essay 'On Fairy-stories' in which he explains how fairy stories can re-enchant the world and help the reader find magic in the mundane. It would probably be a mistake to imagine that this example was random or that it simply means that green is a wonderful mix of blue and yellow. The story of green in the modern era is indeed one of disenchantment: after holding a primary place in the medieval society, green was relegated to an inferior colour by the advances of science that proved it was but a mix of two primary colours and not a primary colour on its own (Pastoureau 2013, 141). But Tolkien invites us to go beyond this primary/secondary reading of the natural world and remember the mystery and magic that lurk in the woods.

As a skilful medievalist writer, Tolkien had a mastery of ancient and medieval material that enabled him to create a green world with a landscape and inhabitants perfectly fitting a medieval perspective, while seamlessly integrating modern ideas and concerns into the narrative, and giving us stories that enchant the reader, the critic and the world around us.

Bibliography

Flieger, V., *Splintered Light: Logos and Language in Tolkien's World,* (Kent: Kent State University Press, 2002).

Lucan, *De Bello Civilli (The Pharsalia)*, trans. by E. Fantham (Cambridge: Cambridge University Press, 1992).

Pastoureau, M., *Vert, Histoire d'une Couleur,* (Paris: Editions du Seuil, 2013).

Shippey, T., *The Road to Middle-earth,* (London: Allen & Unwin, 1982).

Tolkien, J.R.R., *The Hobbit,* (London: HarperCollins, 1993).
— *The Lord of the Rings,* (London: HarperCollins, 1995).
— *The Silmarillion,* (London: HarperCollins, 1994).
— *Tree and Leaf,* (London: HarperCollins, 2001).
— *The Letters of J.R.R. Tolkien*, ed. by H. Carpenter with the assistance of C. Tolkien (London: HarperCollins, 1995).
— *The Lost Road and Other Writings*, ed. by C. Tolkien (London: HarperCollins Publishers, 2002).
— *Morgoth's Ring*, ed. by C. Tolkien (London: HarperCollins Publishers, 2002).
— *The Return of the Shadow*, ed. by C. Tolkien (London: HarperCollins Publishers, 2002).

Wollock, JG., *Rethinking Chivalry and Courtly Love,* (Westport: Praeger Publishers, 2011).

Leaving the homeland and finding a home: An exploration of migration in Tolkien's works

Ellen Duncan

My research has previously focused on nostalgia; exploring migration seems a natural progression. 'Nostalgia' literally means a longing for home, and the theme of home, and the difficulty of defining and finding one, is the starting point for this paper. The notion of homesickness and homecoming in Tolkien's work have garnered a lot of critical attention, and obviously journeys away from home are significant – *The Hobbit* is subtitled 'There and Back Again' after all. The search for and abandonment of homes has a far wider scope within the texts however, involving whole peoples and societies, migrating to and away from what might be considered 'a homeland'.

The idea initially came to me while re-reading *The Fellowship of the Ring*, specifically 'Concerning Hobbits', for the umpteenth time. The section that details the history of the Hobbits and their movements stood out to me, noting as it does that "like many other folk Hobbits moved westward [...] Why they later undertook the perilous crossing [...] is no longer certain. Their own accounts speak of the multiplying of Men in the land, and of a shadow that fell on the forest" (*FR*, 'Prologue', 3-4). One area of nostalgia that I've previously explored is how it ties in with the movement of people, my focus being particularly on *The Silmarillion*. Seeing this passage about the history of Hobbits highlighted how ubiquitous it is as a theme across Tolkien's works, and this is what I will be investigating here.

According to Massey, "Humans are a migratory species. Indeed, migration is as old as humanity itself" (Massey et al 2009, 1). For the purposes of this paper, I will expand the definition of humanity to include all the races found in Tolkien's work, and I think it becomes clear that we see something similar play out there. Although many of the factors typically described within migration theory are not overt within the text, it is worth touching on the notion of 'push and pull' dynamics in migration (Mayo 2017, Loc 298). Usually this is used in economic terms when discussing migration, but although rather simplistic and reductionist, it has a much wider applicability that I will be using here – even if we're not talking labour market forces, there are still broader positive and negative states that affect migration. A 'pull factor' is a positive incentive of some kind that encourages movement towards a place – for example, the promised paradise of Valinor would constitute a pull factor. Conversely, a 'push factor', is a negative state, such as war or poverty, that drives someone away from their home –an example of this would be in Númenor, when the Elendili are summoned by Ar-Gimilzôr but choose to sail for Middle-earth and the kingdom of Gil-galad. This certainly has flavours of some of the political push factors that can be seen in migration today.

In the very worst of situations, we might call migration precipitated by a push factor 'impelled migration', where a person or people are forced from their homes due to the seriousness of the threat caused by remaining there. These people would typically be referred to as refugees, and this expression has indeed been used in connection with

Tolkien's work, for example in John Garth's review of *The Fall of Gondolin*, describing "Tuor leading the refugees from Gondolin" (Garth 2018).

Another example of this – worth mentioning if for nothing more than the sheer scale – would be the migration of Elendil and his few followers back to Middle-earth when Númenor sinks into the sea. You don't get a much more compelling 'push factor' than that. Similarly, at the end of *The Silmarillion* proper, Beleriand is physically ruined, displacing a vast majority of the people living there and forcing them either Westward to Valinor in the case of some of the Elves, or Eastward into the Middle-earth familiar to us from *The Hobbit* and *The Lord of the Rings*. The majority of overt 'impelled migrations' occur in *The Silmarillion* – though neither of the two great Elven migrations would be considered this – but there is also 'impelled migration' in the other texts. When the Dwarves are forced from the Lonely Mountain by Smaug, in the words of Rateliffe, they "have been driven from their homeland and suffered a diaspora; settling in scattered enclaves amongst other folk, yet still preserving their own culture" (2011, 146). Impelled migration and diaspora is something that Dwarves suffer throughout the texts; Moria is of course the other significant example of this, though the quest to return to it has a far worse outcome for them than the Dwarves' return to the Lonely Mountain.

According to Malpas, "home is a category under threat from technological innovation" and the "resonance of the term 'home' has not remained stable in the face of restless processes of modernization and conflict" (2005, 86). The impelled migrations discussed so far could certainly be seen as related to this threat, the (often seemingly literal) instability of home resulting in migration. However, in contrast with these emphatic and purposeful migrations, there is also the notion of 'wandering', which appears at a few points in Tolkien's work, when the Elves who do not travel to Valinor "wander" and indeed the Men after their awakening "spread and wandered, and their joy was the joy of the morning before the dew is dry, when every leaf is green" (*Silmarillion*, 96). 'To wander' is defined as 'to ramble without a definite purpose or objective'. Modernity is typically synonymous with notions of progress, bringing to mind a journey along a single and definite path. Conversely then, the directionless, purposeless 'wandering' seems to be attached to notions of innocence, part of a pre-modern, pre-lapsarian world. The Elves after their awakening, Men wandering after their own awakening, even the Ents' wanderings arise out of an interest in the world, receiving knowledge and wandering without desire to impose any order, unlike the Entwives. Alongside this is the fact that, in our own world, humans were originally nomadic, with a hunter-gatherer lifestyle (Balter 2005). Verlyn Flieger has previously made the connection that "This mythology in process shows Tolkien deliberately mirroring the presumed migrations of the Indo-European peoples, with a concomitant fragmentation and differentiation into a multitude of languages and myths" (2002, 77). Although this was noted primarily in relation to the Elven migrations in Middle-earth, we see it rippling out through the other texts as well.

The concept of a fixed 'homeland' is therefore part of the general notion of progress – the Hobbits typify a middle-state in their agrarian culture, whereas Gondor is more closely linked to the modern world, being largely based around the city of Minas Tirith. More broadly however, as time passes, the 'wanderings' discussed become more purposeful, less innocent, often typified by homelessness and displacement. This is the case with the Dúnedain. The last remnants of a broken kingdom, they wander the lands – the general feeling created here is one of loss, though the benefits of their position as wanderers are also evident, in their relationship with the wider world around them, and the knowledge and wisdom they possess that is not only due to their Númenorean lineage, but also to their engagement with the wider world.

In discussing notions of migration and homelessness, it also becomes necessary to define the concepts of 'home' and 'homeland'. These terms seem clear and simple, relatively straightforward in comparison to other related themes; however, the moment the theoretical notion of a homeland encounters all the vagaries of reality it becomes rather more complex. In the words of Femke Stock,

> The concept of home emerges as a highly contextual and ambivalent notion, referring to multiple places and spaces in past, present and future in various ways. Home can be remembered, lived, longed for. Notions of home are fluid and bound to change as one moves in time and space. (2010, 26-7)

We see this fluidity and ambivalence play out within the texts, and it feeds very much into the contradictions and tensions that typify Tolkien's treatment of many of the themes in his work. As Carpenter puts it, Tolkien was a "man of antitheses" (2011, 95). Love for the history, culture and traditions of the past and a 'homeland' oppose his apparent philosophy that we should engage with the wider world.

The further you look back through history in our own world, the blurrier a concept of 'homeland' becomes for a nation or culture. As already discussed, at our earliest stage, humans were nomadic, and over the expanse of our history we have moved, colonized, been colonized, seen the immigrations and emigrations of people, until nations are typically a layer of historic mixing and intercultural and ethnic traditions that have come to be part of what we see as 'home'. This complexity and contingency can be seen in Tolkien's work. Arguably, Middle-earth is the 'homeland' of the Elves. We read that "By the starlit mere of Cuiviénen, Water of Awakening, they rose from the sleep of Ilúvatar" (*Silmarillion*, 37). However, there is a general feeling that although this is the place of their origin, it is not their true home. Although the discrepancy arises when the Valar first summon the Elves, the conflict of differing ideas of 'home' for the Elves is woven throughout their story, a complex layering of nostalgia, myth-making and nationhood.

This comes into focus when Fëanor initially rallies the Noldor to make the journey back to Middle-earth, crying "shall we return to our home? In Cuiviénen sweet ran the waters under unclouded stars, and wide lands lay about, where a free people might walk. There they lie still and await us who in our folly forsook them!" (73). His words foreground the birthplace of the Elves as their homeland, and one true home, despite the fact that neither Fëanor himself, nor presumably the vast majority of the Noldor whom he addresses, had ever lived there. How then can it be called 'home'? The first factor is the discontent with the current situation, often coming from a sense of disconnect or lack of belonging. Then there is the inherited nostalgia that creates an idealized notion of that original homeland, with the connection to that homeland becoming a central part of that identity, even if the characters never had direct experience themselves. You can argue about how self-aware Fëanor is when he uses this rallying point, but aware or not, the notion of 'home' is used as a political point to sway people to his side. By using it in this way, Fëanor essentially influences the nation of Elves who travelled to Valinor, changing the narrative so that they become far closer to what we might understand as a diaspora. According to Stock,

> behind the concept of diaspora lies the image of a remembered home that stands at a distance both temporally and spatially'. It can 'encompass both relations to the 'homeland' and feelings of being home; both physical localities and metaphorical symbolizations of belonging. (2010, 24)

Prior to this, there is little sense that their origins in Middle-earth had been considered relevant; now, the notion of home and where it might be found is brought into focus. It remains a core point of the Elves from this point forward, though the direction of this focus changes.

As we see, very soon after the Elves arrive in Middle-earth, the longing to return to Valinor and the West arises, and never really goes away, if anything steadily increasing as the Ages pass in Middle-earth. It can be seen in Galadriel, and in the general notion that all Elves will eventually sail West, returning to or finally arriving at their true 'home'. It becomes an almost physical yearning even if the Elves have never been there – we see it directly when Legolas first encounters the sea in Return of the King. Increasingly there is a sense that Elves no longer belong in Middle-earth, that the world no longer has a place for them. This is actually addressed explicitly in the Akallabêth, when the Valar address the discontent of the Númenoreans, telling them that Elves are "bound to this world, never to leave it so long as it lasts, for its life is theirs" (*Silmarillion*, 272-3). In this sense then, Valinor is simply the culmination of the whole of Arda as we know it being the homeland of the Elves.

In contrast, there are Men. However much they love the world they live in, they are not intended to remain there. The Valar go on to tell them "your home is not here, not in the Land of Aman, nor anywhere in the Circles of the World" (273). Men are therefore quite literally homeless in the world; it is a stopping point for them on the journey elsewhere. Regardless of whether this ties in with notions of a 'Kingdom of Heaven', the point stands, and it makes sense that we never see any kind of 'true homeland' for Men in the same way that we do for Elves. The closest we get is Númenor – but even that ended, and in disastrous fashion.

It seems logical then, that the borders of Men are generally more porous than those of the Elves. They are not erected or defended by magic – they stand far closer to the land borders that we know in our own world, hard to guard, and changeable depending on the social and political times. Different peoples can live within the same borders – for example Wild Men, Dunlendings and Púkel-men in Rohan alongside the Rohirrim, and the mingling of people in Bree. This is in contrast with the Elves, where we see a very pronounced sense of borders created – often involving some form of magic in order to keep outsiders away – in the case of Doriath, Gondolin and Lothlórien – not to mention Valinor itself.

These borders of Elvish homes are typically intended to isolate and prevent the encroachment of the outside world via change and the march of time, leading to a kind of stasis and Tolkien's description of Elves as 'embalmers'. This leads to the connection between isolationism and the general reaction against progress, suggesting that there is a time and place that is pure and perfect, that the encroachment of the outside world and the 'future' will diminish this. For all that Elves are considered the greatest of the races in Tolkien's world, and for all that they are generally shown as wise and good, this aspect of them is generally depicted as being tempting, seductive, but ultimately their one of their greatest flaws, and perhaps their greatest downfall.

Furthermore, this isolationism interferes with the Elves' relationships with the other people of Middle-earth. As they withdraw from the wider world behind their own borders, suspicions arise. Lothlórien is described as a "perilous land", for example, and various characters raise misgivings about Elves in the time of *The Lord of the Rings* (*FR*, 'Lothlórien', 440). One result of this is that it makes a true alliance between the various races far less likely – and certainly no alliance such as that of the Second Age – so their position against Sauron is vastly weakened. Further to this, as the Elves leave Middle-earth to sail West to Valinor – to their 'home' – we see something akin to the notion of 'brain drain', one of the concerns about migration currently. It may not be a direct parallel, but the feeling of loss at their departure and the general sense that their leaving has weakened Middle-earth as a whole is very similar. The combination of an outflow of many Elves, and divisions between those who remain behind and the other races of Middle-earth, is seen as something that naturally weakens Middle-earth as a whole, though Tolkien – and many characters within the text – sympathise with and often enact the desire to maintain borders and prevent change. However, it is in fact an Elf who acknowledges the problems of isolation, and the fluid nature of homeland, when Gildor tells Frodo: "But it is not your own Shire [...] Others dwelt here before hobbits were; and others will dwell here again when hobbits are no more. The wide world is all about you: you can fence yourselves in, but you cannot for ever fence it out" (*FR*, 'Three is Company', 109).

There is the temptation to give into the idea of a static notion of home; that to move away from it is a loss from which we cannot recover, that to have someone enter our home undermines it. However, in Tolkien's work, we also see the broadest definition of home – that it constitutes the whole world – and all the greatest victories are won through the collaborative efforts of all the races and peoples of Middle-earth. Alliances, and the interaction and collective effort of all, is what makes victory possible.

To conclude, as much as may be possible for a short paper on such a large topic – the treatment of home and migration in Tolkien's texts is as varied as the reality of it in our own world, shown neither solely positively nor negatively. Rather, it reflects the complexity of existing in a world with others, some of whom may welcome you into their home, others who may force you out of your own. Migration is both the loss of a home and the finding of one; the journey may destabilize, but it also creates the potential for a different – or perhaps even greater – whole.

Bibliography

Balter, M., 'The Seeds of Civilization', *Smithsonian Magazine* (May 2005) <https://www. smithsonianmag.com/history/the-seeds-of-civilization-78015429/ > [Accessed 9 July 2019]

Carpenter, H., *J.R.R. Tolkien: A Biography,* (London: HarperCollins Publishers, 2002).

Flieger, V., *Splintered Light: Logos and Language in Tolkien's World*, rev. edn. (Ohio: Kent State University Press, 2002) [Kindle Edition].

Garth, J., 'Review: The Fall of Gondolin by JRR Tolkien — the last tale from Middle-earth', *The Times*, 24 August 2018 <https://www.thetimes.co.uk/article/review-the-fall-of-gondolin-by-jrr-tolkien -the-last-tale-from-middle-earth-dwl5qdjts> [Accessed 7 June 2019].

Malpas, S., 'Home' in *Reading The Lord of the Rings: New Writings on Tolkien's Classic*, ed. by R. Eaglestone (London: Continuum, 2005).

Massey, D., and others, *Worlds in Motion: Understanding International Migration at the End of the Millennium,* (Oxford: Oxford University Press, 2009).

Mayo, M., *Changing Communities: Stories of Migration, Displacement and Solidarities,* (Policy Press: Bristol, 2017).

Rateliff, J.D., *The History of the Hobbit,* (London: HarperCollins Publishers, 2011).

Stock, F., 'Home and Memory' in *Diasporas: Concepts, Intersections, Identities*, ed. by K. Knott and S. McLoughlin (London: Zed Books, 2010).

Tolkien, J.R.R., *The Silmarillion,* (London: HarperCollins Publishers, 1999) [Kindle Edition].
— *The Hobbit,* (London: HarperCollins Publishers, 2001).
— *The Letters of J.R.R. Tolkien*, ed. by H. Carpenter with the assistance of C. Tolkien (London: George Allen and Unwin, 1981).
— *The Fellowship of the Ring*, 50th anniv. edn. (London: HarperCollins Publishers, 2005).
— *The Two Towers*, 50th anniv. edn. (London: HarperCollins Publishers, 2005).
— *The Return of the King*, 50th anniv. edn. (London: HarperCollins Publishers, 2005).

Four Brethren Heroes of the Gondothlim – Egalmoth, Ecthelion, Glorfindel and Legolas: A mythic and linguistic exploration

Dr. Andrew Higgins

Before his very sad passing, Christopher Tolkien gifted scholars and students of his father's legendarium one more time with *The Fall of Gondolin* (2018). Like its immediate predecessor, *Beren and Lúthien* (2017), in this last of his edited volumes of his father's legendarium, Christopher Tolkien presents the real world chronological development of the first great tale of his father's world-building – the legendary cycle known as 'The Fall of Gondolin' which Tolkien first recorded in his 'Book of Lost Tales' notebooks in c.1917 as he recovered from his activity in the First World War.

In the preface to *The Fall of Gondolin* volume, Christopher Tolkien cites the introductory remark that his father made when he delivered one of the versions of this developing tale to the Exeter College Essay Club in 1920.

> It has of course never seen the lights before. A complete cycle of events in an Elfinesse of my own imagining has for some time past grown up (rather, has been constructed) in my mind. Some of the episodes have been scribbled down. This tale is not the best of them, but it is the only one that has so far been revised at all and that, insufficient as that revision has been, I dare read aloud. (*FoG*, 22)

In his introduction, Christopher Tolkien also indicates that one of the key characteristics of this earliest and sadly only completed version of this great tale is the vivid description Tolkien evokes of the invasion of Melko's forces and the valiant but unsuccessful defence of the doomed city of seven names – Gondolin.

> In the original version of the Tale the overwhelming attack on Gondolin with its unimagined new weapons is seen with such clarity and in such detail that the very names are given of the places in the city where the buildings were burnt down or where celebrated warriors died. (14)

However, it is not just the names of places that Tolkien spent considerable time constructing from his emerging Elvish language invention. In this first narrative from his emerging story-world Tolkien also used a similar linguistic process to construct the names of celebrated and valiant warriors who defended the city of Gondolin as it fell to the invading forces of the first Dark Lord. In this paper I want to focus on the names of four of these fallen heroes and explore how Tolkien employed his creative use of "lit and lang", the conceptual foundations of philology, to enshrine these characters in the memory of his legendarium and perhaps in doing so receive some consolation and release from the loss of the real life heroes, some of them his best friends, who had just perished on the battlefields of Europe. As I will explore, Tolkien did such a good job at inventing these particular names that they would persist in different forms and in varying degrees in later conceptual layers of his legendarium; in some cases as the names of different characters and in one clear case as the same characters reborn in a later time to fight in another battle against a second Dark Lord. Therefore, this paper also explores how Tolkien invented, embedded, niggled with and ultimately kept a good well-made name – a key creative jumping off point for Tolkien – in his world-building.

Each of the four names I will be exploring first appear in the earliest fall of Gondolin narrative as members of the Twelve Houses of Gondothlim; remembered as those who came to the aid of city after Melko discovered its location and launched a massive invasion force of goblins, dragons and balrogs to take this last bastion of the Elves. Tolkien describes the standards and individual characteristics of the Twelve Houses of Gondolin in great depth and detail. As several Tolkien scholars, including John Garth, have noted this detailed description of the Houses of Gondolin suggests influence from the works of William Morris; especially his historic-fantasy novel *The House of the Wolfings* (1889) which describes tribes with folk-names like the "Wolfings", the "Hartings", the "Elkings" as well as the Men of the Vine, Men of the Sickle and Men of the Bridge – all Germanic tribes who defended their lands against the invading Romans (Garth 2003, 219). When Tolkien read his *The Fall of Gondolin* to the Exeter Essay Club in March 1920 the records note that Tolkien's work was "a staunch follower of tradition, a treatment indeed in the manner of such typical romantics as William Morris, George McDonald, de la Motte Fouque, etc." (Scull and Hammond 2017, 799). Tolkien signified this sense of "houses or even folk" as well in one of the other para-textual documents Tolkien compiled during the composition of the 'Book of Lost Tales' stories which later became known as 'The Official Name List' and in which Tolkien invented names for the people, places and items in the Lost Tales in both Qenya (also known at that time as *Eldarissa*) and Gnomish (and known at that time as *Noldorissa*). Tolkien signifies these band of warriors with the Gnomish world "thlim" which is glossed in c. 1917 The Gnomish Lexicon as "kind, species, sort" and has a cognate in the Qenya suffix "ilqa" signifying the adverbial "-ly" or like and is also used as a collective suffix as in the Gondo-thlim (Tolkien 1995, 77). Therefore this Gnomish word suggests that those "thlim" was a group or sort and this could be extended to a band as in band of brothers.

1 – Egalmoth, the Divine Lord of the Bow

The first of these heroic names is *Egalmoth* which is Gnomish and first appears to signify the Elf Lord whom Tolkien describes as the "Chief of the Heavenly Arch; one of the wealthiest of the twelve houses" (*FoG*, 74). On the emblem for the house of the "Heavenly Arch" there is a multi-coloured rainbow which, given its associations with both Egyptian mythology[1] and *The Old Testament*,[2] signifies a divine sign. In 'The

1. In Egyptian mythology the goddess of the sky Nut is portrayed as a rainbow (or heavenly arch) spread over the earth.
2. According to the book of Genesis after Noah saved the animals from the Great Flood a rainbow appeared as a sign by God that he would never send another flood to destroy the world.

Official Name List', Tolkien indicates that Egalmoth is also associated with another aspect of divine nature and another type of bow; in this case bows and arrows.[3] In the name list he is recorded as "Egalmoth Lord of Thlim Quing Ilon" (Tolkien 2001, 104) which according to the Gnomish Lexicon means "The Lord of the Band/Group of the Divine Bow" (Tolkien 1995, 32). In the entry for Egalmoth in 'The Official Name List' he is referred to with the epithet "Ilqingi" (divine bower) which combines the divine name "Ilu"with the Qenya root "qinqi" meaning "twang, thrum of strings, harps" and from which the word for bow "qinqa" is constructed (Tolkien 1998, 77). The association of this specific house with divine things may also be signified by the colour the house is associated with which is blue; as when Tolkien vividly describes in the house of the divine bow's shields:

> blue of the heavens and its boss a jewel built of seven gems, rubies and amethysts and sapphires, emeralds, chrysoprase, topaz and amber but an opal of great size was set in their helms. (*FoG*, 71-2)

Egalmoth himself is said to have worn a blue mantle upon which stars were embroidered in crystal (71). In the legendarium, the Lord of the Valar Manwë is very associated with the colour blue. Manwë is said to have blue eyes and appeared dressed in long blue robes – he also said to ride in a blue chariot (*Lost Tales I*, 107).

However, in the diegetic world the memory of the actual meaning of the name "Egalmoth" seems to be a point of contestation. This becomes apparent in another name list from this period – the para-textual "The Name List to the Fall of Gondolin" which reflects Tolkien's early portal framework of the mariner Eriol recording the following philological argument about the meaning of his name as the story of the fall of Gondolin is being told to him for ultimate transmission.

> Egalmoth is a great name, yet none knew clearly its meaning – some have said its bearer was so named in *that he was worth a thousand elves (but Rumil says Nay)* and other that it signifies the mighty shoulders of that Gnome, and so saith Rumil, but perchance it was woven of a secret tongue of the Gondolithim, yet he was lord of the house of the Heavenly Arch, and got even out of the burning of Gondolin and dwelt ever after at the mouth of Sirion, but was slain in a dire battle there when Melko seized Elwing. (Tolkien 2004, 23; emphasis mine)

In addition to recording his brief history, Eriol also records three potential origins of Egalmoth's name. First "some say" that Egalmoth signifies he was worth "a thousand Elves". This interpretation is based on a reading of the name coming from a variation of the Gnomish name for Elf "egla" which in the Gnomish Lexicon is glossed as "a being from the outside name of the Fairies given by the Gwalien (Valar) and adopted largely by them" (Tolkien 1995, 32) and the interesting Gnomish words "Moth (in) and Moth (wen) signifying 1000 and related to the word for flock and sheep (possibly suggesting the large flocks of sheep the Noldoli may have seen in their wanderings in the great

3. An interesting link between rainbows and bows and arrows can be found in Hindu mythology where the god of thunder and war Indra uses the rainbow to shoot arrows of lightning.

lands)" (58). However, the local Elvish philologist Rumil counters this with a reading of the name which is much more grounded in the suggested meaning coming from the older Qenya language which Rumil remembers and has written philological essays on.[4] Rumil draws his suggested meaning from the Qenya word "aika" signifying "broad or vast" and posits the cognate name "Aikaldamor" literally meaning "broad back" which through the various sound changes of Gnomish would become "Egalmoth" listed in the Qenya Lexicon as "the hero of the defence of Gondolin" (Tolkien 1998, 29). Then there is a third possible origin to the name focused on a "secret tongue of Gondolin", a tongue Tolkien would also evoke for the possible origin of the name Earendel (*FoG*, 62). While the character of Egalmoth Lord of the Arch does not appear in any of the later published texts it appears that Tolkien did continue to niggle with the name. In the Noldorin Word-Lists of the 1920's there is an entry for Egallmoth which retains Rumil's hypothesis that the name means broad shoulders "Eka-jalda-mbod-t he of the broad shoulders" which now appears to be based on a reconstructed asterix name (Tolkien 2001, 142). The name Egalmoth, but in this case seemingly not the same character, reappears in the Appendix A to *The Lord of the Rings* which itself is an interesting repository of several names that Tolkien invented in earlier phases of his creative development of the legendarium. In this case, the name Egalmoth is given to a mortal man, the 18th Ruling Steward of Gondor whose reign is recorded as being fairly uneventful – excepting for the Orcs renewing their attacks on Gondor. This Egalmoth is recorded as having died at the age of 117 years after ruling forty-five years and was succeeded by his son Beren. In one of the drafts to his attempted sequel to *The Lord of the Rings* 'The New Shadow' Tolkien thought of calling one of the young men of Gondor Egalmoth (later changed to Saelon) (*Peoples*, 419). There is also an intriguing example of a form of this name appearing in the corpus of legends around another hero who was know for using a bow; namely Robin Hood.[5] The English Dramatist's Ben Johnson contributed to the Robin Hood story-cycle in 1640 with his unfinished play *The Sad Shepherd, or a Tale of Robin Hood.* [6]In this play the name of the sad shepherd who is mourning the loss of his beloved wife Earine is Aeglamour. Earine has been reported to have drowned while passing over the River Trent and Aeglamour asks Robin Hood and his band of merry men to help find her. In addition to the associate with Robin Hood and bows and arrows, the River Trent also has a Tolkienian association as this is the river which flows underneath the Essex Bridge in Great Haywood which Tolkien mythologised incorporated as the Grey Bridge of Tavrobel in his early 'Heraldic Device of Tol-Etherin' (Tolkien 2001, 94).[7]

---

4. In addition to inventing the "sarati" writing system, Rumil was also said in the legendarium to be the author of Ainulindale, the Annals of Valinor, Lhammas and Lhammasethen, Ambarkanta and I Equessi Rumilo (The Sayings of Rumil).
5. For an interesting survey of the Robin Hood legends and Tolkien's works see Alex Voglino's "Middle-earth and the Legend of Robin Hood" in Amon Hen vol 284 (July 2020).
6. The play can be found here https://d.lib.rochester.edu/robin-hood/text/jonson-sad-shepherd (last accessed 27/8/2020).
7. Intriguingly in a late note on the name Egalmoth Tolkien indicated that the name Egalmoth is "a late popular form or archaic Aegamloth, Aegthelion" (*Jewels*, 118) which brings it even closer to the name Johnson's play.

2 – Ecthelion, the Lord of the Fountain

The next heroic name Ecthelion is also Gnomish and first appears to signify the valiant leader of House of the People of the Fountain who are described as arrayed in diamonds and silver (*FoG*, 75). This heroes association with fountains can be seen in his entry in "The Official Name List" which indicates part of his name being derived from the Gnomish word for fount or fountain "ecthel" (Tolkien 2001, 104). This Gnomish word for fountain derives from the Qenya root KELE, KELU meaning "flow, run, ooze and trickle" and from which Tolkien constructed a series of related words (Tolkien 1998, 246).[8] Tolkien embeds Ecthelion's connection to fountains into the fall of Gondolin narrative in two key places; perhaps suggesting how this character was given his name in the recording of this key event in Elvish history. First when he is wounded fighting off goblins and Balrogs, Ecthelion regains his strength by drinking from the fountain of the King (*FoG*, 87). Then as described in his final fight with the Lord of the Balrogs, Gothmog, Ecthelion literally perishes with the Balrog in the king's fountain.

> Then leapt Ecthelion lord of the Fountain, fairest of the Noldoli, full at Gothmog even as he raised his whip, and his helm that had spike on it he drove into that evil breast, and he twined his legs about his foeman's thighs and the Balrog yelled and fell forward; but those two dropped into the basin of the king's fountain which was very deep. There found that creature his bane; and Ecthelion sank steel-laden into the depths, and so perished that lord of the Fountain after fiery battle in cool waters (90-1)

However, in later developments it is the very spike that Ecthelion used to kill the Balrog which seems to have caused Tolkien to re-think the etymology of this name and move it away from the earlier ideas of fountain. In the c. 1938 *Etymologies* his name is now said to be composed from the words "ehte" spear and "thela" point (of spear) which put together would translate to something like "Spear Point" or "Spear Head" (*Lost Road*, 355). Tolkien kept this idea for the meaning of his name in his sadly unfinished attempt to re-write *The Fall of Gondolin* in the 1950's (200). The name Ecthelion, but again as with Egalmoth not the same character, re-appears twice in the Appendix A to *The Lord of the Rings*. First, the name is given to the Steward of Gondor Ecthelion I who in the last year of his rule (2698 TA) rebuilt Minas Tirith's White Tower which was known as the Tower of Ecthelion. Then to Ecthelion II (2886 –2984) a son of Turgon who was known for strengthening Gondor's defences against the encroaching power of Saruman. Aragorn served Ecthelion II in these endeavours under the name Thorongil. He died at 98 succeeded by his son Denethor II – the last of the Stewards of Gondor before the return of the King.

---

8. These Qenya words are kelata (a trickle), kelu/kelume (stream), kektele (fountain), kelusindi (a river), kektelu- (bubble up) and kelta (draw water). All of these words suggest a sound-sense of water running or trickling. This name also appears on the aforementioned "Heraldic Devices of Tol-Etherin" in the third device down this page for the town of Celbaros which seems to be Tolkien mythical imaging of the town of Cheltenham where after his 21st birthday he resumed his relationship with Edith Bratt. This device includes the image of a fountain (for which Cheltenham is well known for its Neptune Fountain) with the Gnomish word Ecthelin – a variant of the word for fountain.

3 – Legolas Greenleaf, the Man or Elf with keen sight

The name of the next of our four heroes is arguably the most well known of our four heroes to Tolkien readers. However, before the name signified one of the Fellowship of the Ring, the name "Legolas" appeared in the earliest fall of Gondolin cycle narrative for a hero who is said to come from The House of the Tree. One key characteristic of Legolas in the earliest fall of Gondolin narrative is that he is said to have been sharp eyed and night-sighted and could thus help the survivors of Gondolin escape in the dark as demonstrated in these three passages.

> But the others, led by Legolas Greenleaf of the house of the Tree, who knew all that plain by day or by dark, and was night sighted, made much speed over the vale for all their weariness, and halted only after a great march. (*FoG*,100)

> Galdor and a band of men spear-armed went ahead, and Legolas was with them, whose eyes were like cats in the dark, yet could they see further. (103)

> Galdor's men were beset in the dark suddenly by shapes leaping from behind rocks where they had lain hidden even from the glance of Legolas. (105)

The entry that Eriol records in the name list to the Fall of Gondolin is as follows and note that while retaining the memory of his keen sight. Legolas is referred to here as a man not an elf

> LEGOLAS or Green-Leaf was a man of the Tree, who led the exiles over Tumladin in the dark, being night-sighted and he liveth still in Tol-Eressea named by the Elder there *Laiqalasse*, but the book of Rumil saith further hereon. (Tolkien 2004, 28)

Why Eriol recorded this name as being a "man of the tree" is not clear and indeed in the latest list that Christopher Tolkien provides in the new edition of *The Fall of Gondolin*, the entry for Legolas Greenleaf is listed as "an Elf of the House of the Tree in Gondolin, gifted with extraordinary night sight" (*FoG*, 276). We do have of course another example of a character changing from elf to man in the case of his earliest version of Beren who in the Book of Lost Tales "The Tale of Tinúviel" was first a Noldoli Elf and then became a mortal man (*Lost Tales II*, 59). As with Egalmoth, although this time not recorded, the name Legolas suggests several different origins. The "green-leaf" meaning comes from the Qenya Lexicon "lassë" meaning leaf deriving from a root LAYA – be alive, flourish combined with the word "laiqa" meaning green (Tolkien 1998, 52). However, there is also the suggestion that name comes from another Qenya root "LAIKA" meaning "keen, sharp" (50) from which derives the Gnomish words "Leg" and "last" meaning "a look, glance" (Tolkien 1995, 53). In the Gnomish Lexicon there is following philologically focused note on this name.

> note Laigolas = green leaf, becoming archaic because of final form becoming 'laib' gave Legolast ie. keen sight but perhaps both were his names, as the Gnomes delighted to give

> two similar sounding names of dissimilar meaning as Laigolas, Legolast, Turin Turambar, etc. Legolas, the ordinary form, is confusion of the two. (53)

In this passage, as like the one for Egalmoth, Tolkien seems to be allowing for there to be different or disputed meanings of names which were recorded into memory from the transmission of the Lost Tales from the Elves to Eriol. Also, as with Egalmoth and Ecthelion, Tolkien would continue to niggle with the name Legolas until it eventually became the name deriving from the Silvan dialect of Sindarin meaning "green-leaf" and signifying a different character who would retain two aspects of the Legolas *Laiqalasse* from the fall of Gondolin narrative (Tolkien 2007, 84). Before deciding to re-use the name "Legolas" in his new Hobbit, Tolkien thought of instead re-using the name of his House of Tree comrade Galdor; as can be seen in Tolkien's drafts for The Council of Elrond (*Treason*,114-6). When Tolkien decided to use the name Legolas for this new Elvish character who would become part of the fellowship of the Ring he retained the attribute of this Legolas being keen-sighted. For example, as Aragorn, Legolas and Gimli are approaching the plain of Rohan, Legolas sees an eagle very high in the sky. When Legolas asks Aragorn if he can see the eagle, Aragorn who is said to have keen sight as well replies, "no not even my eyes can see him, my good Legolas, he must be far aloft indeed." (*TT*, 'The Riders of Rohan', 423) However, while they share certain characteristics – the first age Legolas *Laiqalasse* and the Third Age Silvan elf and member of the Fellowship do not appear to be the same person.[9]

4 – Glorfindel, the Hero who came back

When we come to the last of our four heroes of Gondolin, Tolkien not only re-uses this "well made" name but also later in The Lord of the Ring brings back both the name and the character. In "The Official Name List" the entry for this Gnomish name is listed as "Glorfindel Lord of thlim losgloriol" which means Lord of the Folk of the Golden Flower (Tolkien 2001, 104). Tolkien also cites Qenya cognate names that all have associations with Golden Hair such as "laurifindi" (golden-lock of hair), "kulufindi"(gold hair) and "loter kuluinai" (flower of gold) (104). In *The Fall of Gondolin* Tolkien describes this house and its leader.

> There stood the house of the Golden Flower who bore a rayed sun upon their shield, and their chief Glorfindel bore a mantle so 'broidered' in threads of gold that is was dispersed with celandine as a field of spring, and in his arms were damascened with cunning gold (*FoG*, 74).

In the invasion of Gondolin, Glorfindel and his diminishing army defended the rear of the force – "but Glorfindel held the rear manfully and many more of the Golden Flower

---

9. It is interesting that there is another member of the Fellowship of the Ring whose name also first appears in *The Book of Lost Tales* and that is Legolas's dwarf companion Gimli – a name which first appears in the c.1917 *Tale of Tinúviel* as the name of an aged blind Gnome with sharp hearing (as Legolas had sharp sight) who Beren encounters in the kitchens of the evil cat Tevildo (*Lost Tales II*, 29).

fell there" (95). Also, like his comrade Ecthelion, Glorfindel has an epic fight with a Balrog.

> Then Glorfindel leapt forward upon him and his golden armour gleamed strangely in the moon, and he hewed at the demon that it leapt again upon a great boulder and Glorfindel after. Now there was a deadly combat upon that high rock above the folk, and these, pressed behind and hindered ahead, were grown so close that well nigh all could see. [...] Now had he beaten a heavy swing upon its iron helm, now hewn off the creature's whip-arm at the elbow. Then sprang the Balrog in the torment of his pain and fear full at Glorfindel, who stabbed like a dart of a snake, but he found only a shoulder and was grappled, and they swayed to fall upon the crag-top. Then Glorfindel left hand sought a dirk, and this he thrust up that it pierced the Balrog's belly nigh his own face (for that demon was double his stature) and it shrieked, and fell backward from the rock, and falling clutched Glorfindel's yellow locks beneath his cap, and those twain fell into the abyss. [...] and Thorondor himself, a mighty bird, descended to the abyss and brought up the body of Glorfindel' (106-7)[10]

The name and character of Glorfindel and the remembrance of this fight with the Balrog persisted in Tolkien's work on the legendarium. His fall appears in the fragment alliterative 'Lay of Earendel' composed by Tolkien in the 1920's.

> how Glorfindel the Golden/in the gap of the Eagles
> battled with the balrog/and both were slain. (*Lays*, 142)

Moreover, in Tolkien's 1926 'Sketch of the Mythology' the valour of Glorfindel is also marked.

> In the fume of the burning Tuor leads his company into the mountains into the cold pass of Cristhorn (Eagles Cleft). There they are ambushed but saved by the valour of Glorfindel (chief of the house of the Golden Flower of Gondolin, who dies in a duel with the Balrog upon a pinnacle). (*Shaping*, 37)

The same heroism appears in both the version of the 'Quenta Simarillion' and is briefly mentioned in the earliest 'Annals of Beleriand' from the 1930's.

> Then dreadful was their plight, and hardly would it have been saved by the deathless valour of yellow-haired Glorfindel, chief of the House of the Golden Flower of Gondolin [...] Songs have been sung of the duel of Glorfindel with the Balrog upon a pinnacle of rock in that high place. (145)

10. There is an interesting parallel here with Gandalf's fight with the Balrog in Moria. In both cases in the last minute of the fight both Glorfindel and Gandalf are clutched and dragged into the abyss by the Balrog. Compare above with "the thongs lashed and curled about the wizard's knees, dragging him to the brink. He staggered and fell, grasped vainly at the stone, and slid into the abyss. 'Fly, you fools!' he cried, and was gone." (*FR*, 'The Bridge of Khazad-dûm', 431) It is also interesting that both Glorfindel and Gandalf, although dragged into the abyss, return from these battles with their respective balrogs.

> Glorfindel was there slain in an ambush. (308)

Like the names of his heroic companions, the name Glorfindel would reappear in *The Lord of the Rings*. However, unlike the others, in the case of Glorfindel it was not just the name that reappeared but the character from the fall of Gondolin himself. Perhaps this was because Tolkien had (as explored above) persisted in keeping the memory of this character alive in the various and shifting conceptual versions of his mythology. The Glorfindel who appears to Aragorn and the Hobbits on their perilous journey to Rivendell is clearly the "reborn" character from the fall of Gondolin. The first indication that we have that this Glorfindel is the same character is in a note Tolkien made which appeared in *Return of the Shadow* "Glorfindel tells of his ancestry in Gondolin" (*Shadow*, 214). The most definitive proof we have that Tolkien thought these two characters to be one and the same is in some very late notes he made on Glorfindel which was published in *The Peoples of Middle-earth* where Tolkien grappled with this very concept of the reappearance of Glorfindel in the War of the Ring.

The name is in fact derived from the earliest work on this mythology – The Fall of Gondolin composed in 1916-1917, in which the Elvish language that ultimately became that of the type called Sindarin was in a primitive and unorganised form and its relation with the High-elven type (itself very primitive) was still haphazard. It was intended to mean "Golden-Tressed" and was then the name given to the heroic 'Gnome' [Noldo], a chief-captain of Gondolin, who in the pass of Cristhorn ('Eagle-Cleft') fought with a Balrog [>Demon], whom he slew at the cost of his own life' (*Peoples*, 379).

In these notes Tolkien indicated that there are some difficulties in fitting this name into the new phonological structure of Sindarin (379). There are indications that he did think, like Legolas, of making these two different Glorfindels (Glorfindel of Gondolin and Glorfindel of Rivendell). He dismissed this though with this very interesting and revealing statement.

> this repetition of so striking a name, though possible, would not be credible. No other major character in the Elvish legends as reported in *The Silmarillion* and *The Lord of the Rings* has a name borne by another. (379)

Christopher Tolkien indicates that his father made a subsequent note "Why Not?" (379). Christopher suggests that this question is answered in the following sentence of the text with the emphasis on the word "Elvish" which if we go back to the name Legolas suggests that perhaps Tolkien meant the First Age character of Legolas to be a man of the tree and not an elf – and, therefore, there would not be any repetition of an Elvish name (as Gimli in *The Lord of the Rings* was now a dwarf). Tolkien then writes that by accepting the reality that the Glorfindel of the First Age and of the Third Age are one and the same it will not only strengthen the inner consistency of reality of his place in Tolkien's world-building but also open up the opportunity to tell a better story about him and how he existed in both narrative time bands.

> Also it may be found that acceptance of the identity of Glorfindel of old and of the Third Age will actually explain what is said of him and improve the story. (380)

Thus Tolkien proceeds to weave together a story of how due to his valiant act of defending the survivors of the fall of Gondolin, including Tuor, Idril and their son Earendel, from the Balrog Glorfindel's body (hroa) and spirit (fëa) were restored by Manwë and he became a living incarnate whose spiritual power "had been greatly enhanced by his self-sacrifice" (381). He becomes a friend of Olorin (Gandalf) and returns to Middle-earth in the Second Age with the rise of Sauron and leads a force against the evil kingdom of Angmar. He causes the Witch-king to flee and proclaims to king Eärnur the prophecy of the Witch-king's ultimate fate that not by a man's hand will he fall. Glorfindel then plays his part in the War of the Ring including again, as he did in the fall of Gondolin (*FoG*, 85), bringing up the rear in the defence at the Ford of Brulnen (*FR*, 'Flight to the Ford', 213).

5 – Conclusion

We can therefore, put these four "well made" names[11] that Tolkien first introduced as valiant heroes in the First Age narrative cycle of the fall of Gondolin on a spectrum of name and character use and re-use. The first name, Egalmoth of the Heavenly Arch, only appears in the earliest version and not in any of the other known conceptual versions of the mythology up to the time Tolkien started work on *The Lord of the Rings*. Therefore, in his need to come up with names for his appendices, Tolkien seems to have come back to his 'well sounding' name of Egalmoth to re-use it for an entirely different mortal character of one of the ruling stewards of Gondor and then thought of using the name again for a completely different character in his sequel 'The New Shadow'. In the case of Ecthelion there is evidence from his language work in 'Etymologies' that Tolkien continued to work on the meaning for this name and that he intended the Elf character to reappear in the 1950's version of the Gondolin story; even though Tolkien would use the name twice for two different Gondorian stewards including the father of Denethor II. With Legolas Tolkien re-used the form of the name but while the two characters clearly share some traits which may be signified in their names, the evidence seems to indicate that these were not the same characters and perhaps the original character from the earliest fall of Gondolin narrative was not an elf but a man. However, it is with the well sounding name of Glorfindel that Tolkien not only re-uses the name but creates a mythic narrative that explains how the Glorfindel of the First Age is the same character who appears in *The Lord of the Rings* as a great Elf Lord who is pardoned for being an exile by the Valar and returned to Middle-earth to fight in the next great battle with evil. A character who Frodo sees as "a white figure that shone and did not grow dim like the others" and who Gandalf calls "one of the mighty of the firstborn. He is an Elf-Lord of a house of princes." (*FR*, 'Many Meetings', 223).

Thus the four names Tolkien first invented from the building blocks of his earliest

11. Christopher Tolkien notes that there is a very late note that his father wrote on one of the texts that constitute chapter 16 of the Silmarillion ("Of Maeglin") which seems to indicate that his father was thinking of making the three lords of the household whom Turgon appointed to ride with Aredhel from Gondolin – Glorfindel, Ecthelion and Egalmoth. Tolkien notes that Ecthelion and Egalmoth "are derived from the primitive F[all of]G[ondolin] but they are well sounding and have been in print" (*Lost Tales II*, 212). Subsequently he decided against naming Aredhel's escorts with these names.

Elvish language invention to perhaps mythically reflect and commemorate the known and unknown fallen heroes of the First World War, would each, in varying degrees, live on and reappear as either name forms and in some cases similar characters in the later conceptual versions of the legendarium. As Tolkien himself said "it gives me great pleasure, a good name. I always in writing start with a name; give me a name and it produces a story, not the other way about normally."[12] The four names of the heroes of Gondolin – Egalmoth, Ecthelion, Legolas, and Glorfindel – are all shining examples of a group of well sounding names which both remembered and evoked the one of the great tales of Tolkien's legendarium – a story itself forged in the war and deaths of so many unnamed and unremembered heroes on the battle fields of Europe and beyond.

Bibliography

Garth, J., *Tolkien and the Great War: The Threshold of Middle-earth,* (London: HarperCollins, 2003).

Gerrolt, D., "*Now Read On*" BBC Radio 4, Tolkien Gateway, January 1971, <https://tolkiengateway.net/wiki/1964_BBC_Interview>

Johnson, B., *The Sad Shepherd: or, A Tale of Robin Hood,* <https://d.lib.rochester.edu/robin-hood/text/jonson-sad- shepherd> [Accessed 27 August 2020].

Scull, C. and W.G. Hammond, *J.R.R. Tolkien Companion and Guide: Readers Guide Part II: N-Z*, (London: HarperCollins, 2017).

Tolkien, J.R.R., *The Letters of J.R.R. Tolkien*, ed. by H. Carpenter with the assistance of C. Tolkien (London: George Allen & Unwin, 1981)
— *The Book of Lost Tales, Part One*, ed. by C. Tolkien (London: George Allen & Unwin, 1983).
— *The Book of Lost Tales, Part Two*, ed. by C. Tolkien (London: George Allen & Unwin, 1984).
— *The Lays of Beleriand*, ed. by C. Tolkien (London: George Allen & Unwin, 1985).
— *The Shaping of Middle-earth*, ed. by C. Tolkien (London: George Allen & Unwin, 1986).
— *The Lost Road and Other Writings*, ed. by C. Tolkien (London: Unwin Hyman, 1987).
— *The Return of the Shadow*, ed. by C. Tolkien (London: Unwin Hyman, 1988).
— *The Treason of Isengard*, ed. by C. Tolkien (London: Unwin Hyman, 1989).
— *The War of the Jewels*, ed. by C. Tolkien (London: HarperCollins, 1994).
— 'I-Lam-na-Ngoldathon: The Grammar and Lexicon of the Gnomish Tongue', ed. by C. Gilson and others, *Parma Eldalamberon*, 11 (1995).
— *The Peoples of Middle-earth*, ed. by C. Tolkien (London: HarperCollins, 1996).
— 'Qenyaqetsa: The Qenya Phonology and Lexicon: Together with The Poetic and Mythologic Words of Eldarissa', ed. by C. Gilson and others, *Parma Eldalamberon*, 12 (1998).
— 'The Alphabet of Rúmil and Early Noldorin Fragments', ed. by P. Wynne and others, *Parma Eldalamberon*, 13 (2001).

— 'Si Qente Feanor and Other Elvish Writings', ed. by P. Wayne and others, *Parma Eldalamberon*, 15 (2004).
— *The Lord of the Rings: The Fellowship of the Ring,* (London: HarperCollins, 2005).
— *The Lord of the Rings: The Two Towers,* (London: HarperCollins, 2005).
— *The Lord of the Rings: The Return of the King,* (London: HarperCollins, 2005).
— 'Words, Phrases and Passages in *The Lord of the Rings*', ed. by Christopher Gilson, *Parma Eldalamberon*, 17, (2007).
— *The Fall of Gondolin*, ed. by C. Tolkien (London: HarperCollins, 2018).

12. Interview with Dennis Gerrolt, first broadcast on the BBC Radio 4 programme "Now Read On" (January 1971) – accessed here https://tolkiengateway.net/wiki/1964_BBC_Interview

Knife, Sting, and Tooth: The Lasting Effects of Frodo's Wounds

Jamie McGregor

As *The Lord of the Rings* nears its denouement, Frodo increasingly understands that the toll his journey has exacted is such that he will never truly recover in his lifetime, saying to Gandalf, "I am wounded with knife, sting, and tooth, and a long burden" (*RK*, 'Homeward Bound', 967). The specific details here are not, of course, random, but summarise the chief causes of Frodo's suffering; other than the primary and continuous cause, the 'long burden' of the Ring itself, they are all the results of physical attacks upon him at key points of his journey. His stabbing by the Witch-king on Weathertop fails in its object of turning him into a wraith, but not completely, heightening his senses and partly detaching him from the world of the living. His poisoning by Shelob plunges him into "darkness and foul dreams", symptoms that recur – like those of the knife-wound – upon its anniversary (*RK*, 'The Tower of Cirith Ungol', 890). More ambiguously, Gollum's biting off his finger proves to be his (as well as the world's) salvation, but leaves him with a permanent reminder of his own ultimate – and continuing – failure. This paper offers a reading of Frodo's three wounds as distinct but cumulative contributions to his penitential, if not wholly tragic, experience.

My starting-point is taken from a passage that occurs towards the end of *The Lord of the Rings*, after the quest to destroy the One Ring has been achieved and the hobbits are returning home with Gandalf, who notices that Frodo is in pain and says "Alas! There are some wounds that cannot be wholly cured." To this Frodo's full reply is, "I fear it may be so with mine. [...] There is no real going back. Though I may come to the Shire, it will not seem the same; for I shall not be the same. I am wounded with knife, sting, and tooth, and a long burden. Where shall I find rest?" and the passage ends: "Gandalf did not answer" (*RK*, 'Homeward Bound', 967).

This is obviously a key passage in setting up the book's bittersweet ending – but what stood out for me when I read this was that Frodo enumerates the three wounds ("knife, sting, and tooth") in the order he received them. For the purposes of this paper, there is no room to consider the full effects of the "long burden", but this is obviously the primary and overarching cause of Frodo's suffering, as well as the root cause (and sometimes the direct and immediate cause) of the other wounds mentioned here. Each of these three is nonetheless of interest in its own right, and the aim of this paper is to discuss each in turn.

Taking them in order, the first is the one I will have the most to say about, Frodo's stabbing by the Witch-king on Weathertop. This takes place very early in the story, less than a fortnight into the hobbits' journey – when the Black Riders, the Ringwraiths that have been hunting them, finally catch up with them, and their leader, as Gandalf later clarifies, attempts to stab Frodo in the heart with his accursed Morgul-knife, an evilly enchanted weapon that would not simply kill its intended victim but rather bring about his transformation into a creature of the same type and render him subject to their will, so that he would ultimately have submitted to them and been made to surrender the Ring to their master. In other words, the knife functions as a means of infecting one with the unnatural death-in-life that is the normal state of the Ringwraiths. Frodo only escapes this fate because he resists the attack for long enough to deflect his enemy's stroke and suffer a wound to the shoulder instead.

Despite this seeming setback, the wraiths are nonetheless content to withdraw at this point, knowing that the splinter remaining in the wound will continue to work its way in until Frodo succumbs to it, and we are told this is what would have happened but for the fact that Elrond succeeds in locating and removing the splinter.

And so Frodo has what Gandalf calls "a terribly narrow shave, so to speak", but as their later conversation indicates it is by no means a complete escape (*FR*, 'Many Meetings', 216). In fact, he suffers permanent side-effects, which tellingly indicate that he has taken on disturbingly wraith-like characteristics, as if he is no longer quite in the land of the living. These symptoms first become noticeable, as one would expect, immediately after the stabbing, and throughout the ensuing period, when his companions are desperately trying to get him to Rivendell in one piece. One symptom is the sensation of unnatural cold already associated with the mere presence of the riders. The stabbing itself is described as "a pain like a dart of poisoned ice", the next day Frodo feels "a deadly chill [...] spreading from his shoulder to his arm and side" and, after nearly two weeks of this, and at the end of an especially gruelling day's climbing, he "threw himself down, and lay on the ground shivering (*FR*, 'A Knife in the Dark', 191). His left arm was lifeless, and his side and shoulder felt as if icy claws were laid upon them. The trees and rocks about him seemed shadowy and dim" (*FR*, 'Flight to the Ford', 198). Here, in addition to the cold, we have what at first appears to be a blurring of Frodo's vision but is an early sign of his slipping into the wraith-world. During the same phase, he has ominous dreams in which, for example, "he walked on the grass in his own garden in the Shire, but it seemed faint and dim, less clear than the tall black shadows that stood looking over the hedge" (197).

This inversion of reality is of course an extension of what happens to Frodo when he wears the Ring – when he is magically rendered invisible, but ironically becomes more markedly visible to the eyes of the wraiths, just as their true forms are then revealed to him in place of the shrouded, faceless figures they present to normal sight. The knife-wound thus serves to amplify, and render permanent, the effects of the Ring itself. As the symptoms worsen, Frodo seems to slip more easily into the other world without needing to wear the Ring – such as when the riders again catch up with him at the Ford of Bruinen, and he is described as being able to see them clearly, whereas his own friends have now become "small shadowy forms waving flames, that flared red in the grey mist that was falling over the world" (209).

As we have seen, this process is halted and even reversed by Elrond's intervention, but not completely. In an especially telling passage, the reader is given access to Gandalf's private assessment of Frodo's condition during his recovery in Rivendell:

> to the wizard's eye there was a faint change, just a hint as it were of transparency, about him, and especially about the left hand that lay outside on the coverlet.
> 'Still that must be expected,' said Gandalf to himself. 'He is not half through yet, and to what he will come in the end not even Elrond can foretell. Not to evil, I think. He may become like a glass filled with a clear light for those to see who can.' (*FR*, 'Many Meetings', 217)

So, if Gandalf is right, Frodo resists evil, resists succumbing to the will of his enemies, but does not wholly resist the process of fading, of passing – almost imperceptibly – from the living world into some otherworldly dimension, and it is also clearly being suggested that this process will continue and increase.

And this is exactly what we find as the story continues, though Tolkien tends to employ great subtlety in presenting this, scattering clues like breadcrumbs for the reader to pick up at tantalisingly rare intervals. The most obvious recurrence of Frodo's symptoms is whenever he is again in close proximity to a wraith, as this literally causes the cold pain to return to his shoulder, but others are less obvious and are often not overtly linked to the wound at all. When the Company are travelling through the Mines of Moria, we are told that

> Frodo began to hear, or to imagine that he heard, something [...] like the faint fall of soft bare feet. It was never loud enough, or near enough, for him to feel certain that he heard it; but once it had started it never stopped, while the Company was moving. But it was not an echo, for when they halted it pattered on for a little all by itself, and then grew still. (*FR*, 'A Journey in the Dark', 304)

It is eventually revealed, five long chapters later, that this is the first of a handful of clues that Gollum has picked up the Company's trail and is following at a safe distance. But it's only other member to have noticed this is Aragorn, the professional ranger and tracker, and he is mildly surprised to find that Frodo has also done so. Nothing further is said about it, but the point has nonetheless been made, albeit with great delicacy, that Frodo's senses have been subtly enhanced; and there are further, equally understated, instances of this as the narrative progresses. No explicit cause is ever identified, but an attentive reader is invited to suspect that an ability to hear faint noises in the dark may just be a long-term side-effect of the process Tom Shippey has suggestively termed "the wraithing process" (2001, 125).

By the time we get to the homeward journey and the passage we began with, where Frodo refers to the wounds of "knife, sting, and tooth", it is the first-named that is uppermost. I have already quoted the closing lines; it is now worth paying attention to those preceding them. The passage begins:

> At last the hobbits had their faces turned towards home. They were eager now to see the Shire again; but at first they rode only slowly, for Frodo had been ill at ease. When they came to the Ford of Bruinen, he had halted, and seemed loth to ride into the stream; and they noted that for a while his eyes appeared not to see them or things about him. All that day he was silent. It was the sixth of October. (*RK*, 'Homeward Bound', 967)

At this point Gandalf asks if Frodo is in pain, and he admits that he is, before adding "It is my shoulder. The wound aches, and the memory of darkness is heavy on me. It was a year ago today" (967).

The symptoms of the knife-wound, then, recur on their anniversary, and this is the first of many sobering signs in the closing chapters that the successful completion of the quest, the downfall of the enemy and the return of the king are no guarantee of lasting universal happiness, and that a price remains to be paid. It is especially chilling that Frodo here exhibits markedly wraithlike qualities, not only an inability to see the physical reality he inhabits, or his own companions, but a strange reluctance to cross the water – something formerly, and exclusively, associated with the Ringwraiths themselves.

A week or so after the crossing, they pass the actual site of the stabbing – amid a good deal of significantly autumnal imagery:

> it was then drawing towards evening and the shadow of the hill lay dark upon the road. Then Frodo begged them to hasten, and he would not look towards the hill, but rode through its shadow with head bowed and cloak drawn close about him. That night the weather changed, and a wind came from the West laden with rain, and it blew loud and chill, and the yellow leaves whirled like birds in the air. When they came to the Chetwood already the boughs were almost bare, and a great curtain of rain veiled Bree Hill from their sight. (967)

The elegiac tone is evident but there are suggestions of transcendence here too. Throughout the text, a wind from the West is consistently associated with the beneficent influence of the Undying Lands beyond the Great Sea, Tolkien's version of the Garden of the Hesperides, so that this passage can be seen to foreshadow the ending, where Frodo's only hope of healing is shown to lie across the sea and outside of this mortal world altogether. This reading is supported, albeit with great subtlety, by the reference to the curtain of rain, an effective Tolkienian image for the ephemerality of this world, almost akin to the Buddhist conception of the Veil of Māyā. It echoes the prophetic and visionary dream Frodo had in the house of Tom Bombadil, in which he hears "a sweet singing running in his mind: a song that seemed to come like a pale light behind a grey rain-curtain, and growing stronger to turn the veil all to glass and silver, until at last it was rolled back, and a far green country opened before him under a swift sunrise" (*FR*, 'Fog on the Barrow-downs', 132).

But before this vision can be fulfilled another two years pass, and Frodo's symptoms recur on the next anniversary of his stabbing, when we are told how

> One evening Sam came into the study and found his master looking very strange. He was very pale and his eyes seemed to see things far away.
> 'What's the matter, Mr. Frodo?' said Sam.
> 'I am wounded,' he answered, 'wounded; it will never really heal.'
> (*RK*, 'The Grey Havens', 1002)

Here again the nature of his symptoms suggests that he no longer fully belongs in the land of the living. And there is a further suggestion of this in the hobbits' conversation when they first return to the Shire, having taken their leave of Gandalf. Merry remarks "Well here we are, just the four of us that started out together. [...] We have left all the rest behind, one after another. It seems almost like a dream that has slowly faded" and Frodo's response to this is "Not to me. [...] To me it feels more like falling asleep again" (*RK*, 'Homeward Bound', 974).

The knife-wound, then, is consistently tied to Frodo's growing otherworldliness. The remaining wounds can be addressed more simply. The second, the sting, is that of the monstrous spider Shelob, which makes him, in Shagrat's memorable phrase, "go as limp as boned fish" (*TT*, 'The Choices of Master Samwise', 723) so that Sam mistakes him for dead. But the poison wears off, leaving Frodo only with a sense of falling "into darkness and foul dreams" (*RK*, 'The Tower of Cirith Ungol', 890), and seems to have no further effect on him. Its symptoms nonetheless recur, like those of the knife-wound, on their anniversary, in this case the thirteenth of March. After the first year, for example,

> Farmer Cotton found Frodo lying on his bed; he was clutching a white gem that hung on a chain about his neck and he seemed half in a dream.
> 'It is gone for ever,' he said, 'and now all is dark and empty.'
> (*RK*, 'The Grey Havens', 1001)

The white gem is the gift of Arwen, given to aid him, as she says, "When the memory of the fear and the darkness troubles you" (*RK*, 'Many Partings', 953). But what shocks the reader here is the intimation that at some level, presumably unconscious, Frodo actually laments the loss of the Ring. It will be remembered that Sam, on thinking his master dead, had finally worked up the courage to take the Ring and continue the quest alone, and that Frodo, on waking, had mistakenly believed the enemy had taken it and that all was lost. So the implication is that his dreams take him back to that experience; at the same time it is hard to shake the unsettling impression that it may be the real and lasting destruction of the Ring for which Frodo feels a lingering regret, as irrational as that would be. (As is often the case, such implications, again often made with great subtlety in the text of *The Lord of the Rings*, are made explicit when Tolkien writes to answer readers' enquiries. In one such letter, he refers to Frodo's words quoted above and describes them as revealing his having been "tempted to regret [the Ring's] destruction, and still to desire it", going on to suggest that his passing to the Undying Lands must consequently be a purgatorial as well as a healing experience) (*Letters*, Letter 246, 328)

These bouts of illness always take place, significantly, during Sam's absence – as on the original occasion of Frodo's stinging – and his full recovery from them coincides with Sam's return twelve days later, on March the twenty-fifth, the anniversary of the third wound (and the fulfilment of the quest): Gollum's desperate act of biting off his finger. Of all the three, this wound is the simplest, the most straightforwardly physical and least associated with anything supernatural. It is also, in marked contrast to the others, redemptive, the deus ex machina that suddenly and unexpectedly intervenes to deliver both Frodo and the world from the burden of the Ring. Its anniversaries, then, are marked not by illness but recovery – and, on the second occasion, by the birth of Sam and Rosie's first child. This makes it all the more revealing, then, that Frodo nonetheless numbers it among the wounds he has suffered and that he feels will never really heal. With his usual restraint, I believe Tolkien here has in mind something to which the text makes no overt reference: that while, from a simply physical point of view, Frodo's missing finger is the least troubling of the scars he bears, psychologically on the other hand it is the permanent reminder of his failure. It is therefore humbling, chastening, and – presumably, in the long run – ironically necessary to his healing.

Bibliography

Shippey, T., *J.R.R. Tolkien: Author of the Century,* (London: HarperCollins, 2001).

Tolkien, J.R.R., *The Letters of J.R.R. Tolkien*, ed. H. Carpenter with the assistance of C. Tolkien (New York: Houghton Mifflin Co., 2000).
— *The Lord of the Rings,* (London: HarperCollins, 2001).

Not at Home: Liminal Space and Personal Identity in *The Hobbit* and *Coraline*

Kristen McQuinn

Liminal space plays a prominent role in fantasy literature as a genre. The otherworldly sensations the reader experiences, the surreal settings, unsettling or uneasy feelings, are all functions of liminal space. Very often, liminal space is physically portrayed by a portal or a door, and the act of opening a door and stepping through can have lifelong consequences as well as rewards. In most fantasy tales, there are always consequences, whether good or bad, whenever a door is opened and a threshold crossed. When characters cross through the door to Wonderland (*Alice in Wonderland*), Platform 9 ¾ (*Harry Potter* series), or even the door to the hidden garden (*The Secret Garden*), they will never be the same again, nor will the ordinary world hold quite the same shine for them. By examining J.R.R. Tolkien's *The Hobbit* and Neil Gaiman's children's novel *Coraline*, an analysis of the function of doors and liminal spaces as necessary catalysts for evolving personal identity in fantasy literature will highlight the importance of liminality. In both *Hobbit* and *Coraline*, the act of physically passing through doors becomes the literal means by which liminality enters the narrative, allowing the characters to enter their own liminal spaces, begin their rites of passage, grow as individuals, and discover new aspects to their identities within the action of the story.

Liminal space is, by definition, an in-between place, whether physical or metaphorical. Deriving from the Latin term *limen*, or threshold, liminal spaces are transformative or transitional, often serving as places where one waits between one point and the next. These spaces often engender feelings of unease or discomfort, or the sensation that something is not right. Physical places that embody liminality can include the beach (neither land nor sea), stairwells (between two different levels of a building), schools during summer break (where there should be many people but it is empty except for you), or doorways (neither indoors nor outdoors, as Bilbo is when he is caught by his coat buttons in chapter 5, or at the back door in chapter 11). Adolescence is another liminal space, since one is neither a child nor yet fully adult. This applies especially to Coraline; although her age is not specified, it is clear that her adventures in the novel are a coming of age of sorts based on the arc of her development and character growth throughout the novel. Adolescents in various cultures often undergo rites of passage, another form of liminality, before they can become fully adult. In literature, liminality often takes a more ephemeral tone, though it is not always necessary. As Klapcsik states, in liminal space, "the fantastic is no longer interpreted as a realm different and distant from consensus reality" (2008, 317). Some narratives such as the *Hobbit* or *Coraline* are written such that the fantastical elements common to liminal space are made ordinary yet are vital to the development of plot and characters. Thus, normal doors become portals, or evil Other Parents with button eyes are accepted without second thought. Every story needs liminality in some form because that is the space in which character growth takes place.

The first door the reader encounters in *Hobbit* is Bilbo's front door. Indeed, it is the third line Tolkien pens in the novel, implying its importance right from the start. Tolkien writes, "[The hobbit hole] had a perfectly round door like a porthole, painted green, with a shiny yellow brass knob in the exact middle" (*Hobbit*, 'An Unexpected Party,' 1). When the reader first meets Bilbo himself, he is standing just without the door, smoking his pipe. His position is telling, for although he is outdoors, he is in ready distance of the threshold and may quickly return inside if he desires. Initially, this doorway serves for Bilbo as a safeguard or barrier to the outside world, keeping him safe within and the frightening things of the world locked out. In fact, that is exactly the door's role after Bilbo's encounter with Gandalf: "With that the hobbit turned and scuttled inside his round green door, and shut it as quickly as he dared" (6). However, once Gandalf enters the picture, Bilbo's worldview begins to be challenged, and the front door undergoes a change from the ordinary to liminal space. Crossing the threshold back indoors after his initial encounter with the wizard no longer offers the safety it once did.

Once Gandalf "scratched a queer sign on the hobbit's beautiful green front door," (6) he initiates the opening of Bilbo's liminal space. Arguably, Gandalf himself is the one who intentionally transforms the door into a portal through wizardry; sometimes a door is just a door. After Gandalf's intervention, Bilbo's door becomes less a door than a portal into what is, for him, another place altogether: the wide world beyond the narrow borders of the Shire. It has become the entrance into his own liminal space where he will become a different version of himself than he was when he set foot out the door on the path with Thorin and company. Appropriately, liminality is about being on the verge of something, and as the reader knows, Bilbo is about to embark upon the adventure of a lifetime. This kind of gateway is a necessary element in liminality that allows the protagonist to launch and either thrive or fail.

Liminality can also encompass ambivalence; Bilbo embodies his own liminality at first, for he is ambivalent about change, adventure, and going to new places. When Thorin and company arrive and begin making their plans, Bilbo is resistant to joining them. He thinks,

> something Tookish woke up inside him, and he wished to go and see the great mountains, and hear the pine-trees and the waterfalls, and explore the caves, and wear a sword instead of a walking-stick. [...] Suddenly in the wood beyond The Water a flame leapt up – probably somebody lighting a wood-fire – and he thought of plundering dragons settling on his quiet Hill and kindling it all to flames. He shuddered; and very quickly he was plain Mr Baggins of Bag-End, Under-Hill, again. (15-6)

Bilbo's yearning yet reluctance to join the company is a reflection of his liminal state, his desire to be in two places at once. Although he has crossed the threshold and taken the initial step into his adventure, he does not yet understand that the liminal space is a place he cannot enter and then choose to leave unscathed. His resistance reflects his new status; much like adolescence, when a person is no longer a child but not yet fully adult, Bilbo is entering a similar state of growth. This journey will become his rite of passage, and as most adolescents before have done, Bilbo feels conflicted, uneasy, scared, and eager, all emotions which bring about a reflexive resistance. Eventually, although he still has understandable and normal fears, Bilbo stops resisting his liminality and instead leans in. “Then Mr Baggins turned the handle and went in. The Took side had won. He suddenly thought he would go without bed and breakfast to be thought fierce” (18). He is still of two minds at multiple points during his journey, but it is at this moment, when he barges into Thorin’s meeting in Bilbo’s own parlour, that he makes up his mind fully to lean in, enter his liminal space, and embark on a life-changing adventure.

Beorn’s liminal space is the among the strangest Bilbo encounters in his journey. Beorn himself is neither fully human nor fully beast, a liminal state which is unsettling to Thorin’s entire party. As a skin-changer, Beorn lives his whole life in a liminal state, which Gandalf explains to the company before crossing the threshold into Beorn’s home. He says, “He is a skin-changer. He changes his skin: sometimes he is a huge black bear, sometimes he is a great strong black-haired man with huge arms and a great beard. I cannot tell you much more, though that ought to be enough” (*Hobbit*, ‘Queer Lodgings,’ 116). The lack of information about their fierce host creates a separate liminal space, for it is apparent that he inhabits some ill-defined place between friend and foe.

Once Beorn allows Bilbo and the dwarves to enter his home, the differences between his liminal space and Bilbo’s becomes more apparent. When Thorin’s party reaches Beorn’s Hall, they first pass through a plain wooden gate and into a farm-like setting, which at first seems normal, but beyond are Beorn’s giant bee pastures.

> They soon came to a wooden gate, high and broad, beyond which they could see gardens and a cluster of low wooden buildings […] barns, stables, sheds, and a long low wooden house. Inside on the southward side of the great hedge were rows and rows of hives with bell-shaped tops made of straw. The noise of the giant bees flying to and fro and crawling on and out filled all the air. (117-8)

The gate through which they pass separates Beorn’s liminal space from Bilbo’s, and its liminality is even more pronounced than many other places in *The Hobbit*. The bee pastures highlight immediately the fantastical elements of Beorn’s liminal space, so different from Bilbo’s. Once Bilbo passes through the hall and the “dark door that opened out of the courtyard into the house” (119), it becomes clear that Beorn’s home itself is liminal in a number of ways, incorporating elements of the wilderness into the construction of the building and blurring the lines between indoors and outdoors.

> Though it was summer there was a wood-fire burning […] They passed through this dim hall […] and came through another smaller door into a sort of veranda on wooden posts made of single tree trunks. It faced south and was still warm and filled with the light of the westering sun which slanted into it, and fell golden on the garden full of flowers that came right up to the steps. (119)

The forest and the outdoors are all worked into the making of the home and there seems to be little distinction, in some places, between the outside and inside, both of which are full of trees and flowers. It is interesting that Bilbo spends his entire visit at Beorn’s so anxious, since hobbits are known to love plants and things that grow. Beorn’s house seems like a setting that ought to make Bilbo perfectly at ease, yet the clash of liminal experiences sets him on edge. Beorn’s liminal space is more pronounced than Bilbo’s, necessarily so in order that the lessons Bilbo learns in that place are not overlooked.

The liminality of Beorn's home is enhanced by his admonition not to go outside at night. Night time is often a liminal space, for it is at night that we dream, and Beorn's home has a dreamlike, or possibly nightmarish, quality to it. At night, Bilbo notices that the house seems magical:

> The dark came on outside. The fires in the middle of the hall were built with fresh logs and the torches were put out, and still they sat in the light of the dancing flames with the pillars of the house standing tall behind them, and dark at the top like trees of the forest. Whether it was magic or not, it seemed to Bilbo that he heard a sound like wind in the branches stirring in the rafters, and the hoot of owls. (116)

Later in the night, Bilbo wakes to the sound of animal noises scuffling near the door, and growling; he wonders if it is Beorn in bear shape, coming to kill them all. Bilbo's interpretation of Beorn's house is intriguing because it highlights the conflict between Bilbo's liminal space and Beorn's. Whereas Bilbo's space is uncomfortable to him alone because it is unfamiliar and takes him far outside his comfort zone, Beorn's space is a danger and uncomfortable to everyone, including Beorn himself. There is no becoming accustomed to Beorn's liminal space for anyone in the night.

Beorn's animal servants also add to the liminality of the place, for it is clear they are sentient, yet they do not speak, and they act very differently than their fully animal counterparts with which Bilbo and his companions are familiar. When Bilbo first encounters Beorn's animals, the horses take a good look at him and Gandalf and run off to alert their master of strangers on his land. Later, during the feast, dogs, horses, and sheep set the table, rearrange the furniture and trestles, and serve food to Beorn and his guests. Before the company ever set foot in Beorn's realm, Gandalf tells them that Beorn's animals "are nearly as marvellous as himself. They work for him and talk to him. He does not eat them" (116). The animals are just another element in Beorn's liminal space to which Bilbo must adapt in his own journey. The concept of home is upended at Beorn's, made into a place that is dangerous and strange, wholly foreign to Bilbo, who associates home, to which his identity is closely tied, with safety and stability. It is therefore extremely important that Bilbo encounter the liminality of Beorn and his home, which are so different from his own, for it is here that Bilbo begins to understand, perhaps at an unconscious level yet, that his identity is changing in key ways. In Beorn's home, Bilbo truly crosses the threshold from the last trace of everything he has held familiar and comfortable in preparation for entering the wholly liminal space of Mirkwood Forest. In the forest, Bilbo's identity evolves from a person who is often frightened or in need of rescuing to a person who must take charge and rescue his companions. He would have been unable to make this transition without having first encountered Beorn and entering his liminal space, the effects of which have a profound impact upon Bilbo's identity. It is here that Bilbo begins to find the connection between his inner self and who he is outwardly.

The Back Door in the Lonely Mountain offers yet another entrance into liminal space for Bilbo. At first, the company is confused by the door since it will not open. Bilbo physically enters a liminal state when he sits at the doorway, as he calls it, to ponder the dilemma.

> there was not a doorstep, of course, really, but they used to call the little grassy space between the wall and the opening the 'doorstep' in fun, remembering Bilbo's words long ago at the unexpected part in his hobbit-hole, when he said they could sit on the doorstep till they thought of something. (*Hobbit*, 'On the Doorstep,' 207-8)

Bilbo physically occupies a liminal place before entering the metaphorical space presented once the Back Door is opened. The space acts as a waiting room for both the dwarves and Bilbo; the dwarves are waiting to reclaim their lost kingdom and this is the last stop before they can do so, and Bilbo is waiting to fulfil his role as burglar and ultimately as a person who learns more about himself than he ever thought possible. The Back Door is the gateway to each. The liminal space offers creative room for Bilbo to think. It is only when Bilbo figures out its secret, after reflecting in his liminal space, that the door opens, even though it was built by dwarves and ancestors of Thorin.

When Bilbo realizes the Door must open under moonlight, the door at that point reflects said moonlight and reveals itself to the company. Thorin is then able to use his key and reveal the actual passage into the Lonely Mountain.

> A door five feet high and three wide was outlined, and slowly without a sound swung inwards. It seemed as if darkness flowed out like a vapour from the hole in the mountainside, and deep darkness in which nothing could be seen lay before their eyes, a yawning mouth leading in and down." (210-1)

This dark tunnel is very much a physical manifestation of liminal space, leading Bilbo into another place. His liminal experiences up to this point have already made a profound change upon his identity, which is noted when he states,

> 'Perhaps I have begun to trust my luck more than I used to in the old days' – he meant last spring before he left his own house, but it seemed centuries ago – 'but anyway I think I will go and have a peep at once and get it over.' (*Hobbit*, 'Inside Information,' 212-3)

Before entering his liminal space, it would have been impossible for Bilbo to take the initiative like this or to be bold enough to go into a dark tunnel. The narrator clearly acknowledges this change as well, stating, "He was trembling with fear, but his little face was set and grim. Already he was a very different hobbit from the one that had run out without a pocket-handkerchief from Bag-End long ago" (214). Bilbo's changing identity is linked inextricably with the time spent in liminal space. Indeed, without that time, he could not have changed as he had.

While in Smaug's lair, Bilbo also dons the ring he found in Gollum's cave; thus for a large part of the time during his dragon encounter, he occupies the liminal space of invisibility. When one is in a liminal state, it can create a sense of invisibility because this type of space often exists only for the individual experiencing it, outside the observation of others who may be experiencing liminality of their own. Much of Bilbo's journey has passed in this way, whether by being overlooked or underappreciated. Wearing the ring and actually becoming invisible is the literal physical manifestation of his liminal state of being overlooked or underappreciated. In his conversation with Smaug, Bilbo says, "I am he that walks unseen" (223). His state of being unseen is not simply because he is wearing his ring of invisibility; Bilbo has passed unseen in many situations without being noticed, such as when he escaped unnoticed from the trolls in chapter two, or even in his own home at the beginning of the book, when Thorin and company discuss him as though he is not there. Being in that kind of liminal state allows Bilbo to reflect on events in ways that may not be open to others who are viewed as more central, more seen, than he is. It gives him a unique insight that later allows him to become one of the most seen people of Thorin's company. Passing through the Back Door into that specific liminal space allows Bilbo to take the final step in becoming the brave person he is just prior to the Battle of Five Armies. It is unlikely that Bilbo could have acted so bravely were it not for his experiences in the liminal space beyond the Back Door.

Bilbo's narrative presents liminality as seen in an adult journey. However, children and especially adolescents also have to go through liminal stages of their own. This is evident in Neil Gaiman's children's novel *Coraline*. As with *Hobbit*, liminal space is the vehicle for character growth and personal identity, and indeed, "*Coraline* is centrally concerned with how one negotiates one's place in the world; how one is recognised in one's own right" (Rudd 2008, 160). The very first line of the book is about the door in the drawing room: "Coraline discovered the door a little while after they moved into the house" (Gaiman 2002, 6-7). Immediately, the reader is alerted to the door's importance in the narrative, and it will be through the door in the drawing room that Coraline enters her own liminal space. Unlike in *The Hobbit*, there is only one door in Coraline which is truly of significance, and it is of appropriate impressiveness. Gaiman writes,

> Of the doors that she found, thirteen opened and closed. The other – the big, carved, brown wooden door at the far end of the drawing room – was locked. [...] [Coraline's mother] reached up and took a string of keys from the top of the kitchen doorframe. She sorted through them carefully, and selected the oldest, biggest, blackest, rustiest key. They went into the drawing room. She unlocked the door with the key. The door swung open. Her mother was right. The door didn't go anywhere. It opened onto a brick wall. (2002, 6-7)

Coraline is intensely curious about the door and there is a sense of fate that she is meant to find her liminal space there. Her parents are utterly disinterested, both in the door and, apparently, in Coraline herself. Her feelings of neglect and abandonment create the framework for her to desire different parents, which ultimately highlights the importance of the door specific to Coraline and her evolving identity (Vargas and Vargas 2014, 83). That she feels invisible to her parents also creates a liminal space similar to Bilbo's; both are characters who are overlooked by others.

When Coraline is left to her own devices, she attempts to open the door once more. Instead of finding the brick wall again, she discovers a long, dark hallway.

> The bricks had gone as if they'd never been there. There was a cold, musty smell coming through the open doorway: it smelled like something very old and very slow. Coraline went through the doorway. [...] Coraline walked down the corridor uneasily. There was something very familiar about it. (Gaiman 2002, 24-5)

When Coraline reaches the end of the corridor, she discovers another flat mirroring her own, darkly, right down to the same carpet, wallpaper, and parents. Coraline's liminal space displays many traditional qualities, such as the feelings of unease or creepiness that are often associated with liminality. She is being primed to enter her space purposefully so that she will be receptive to the tasks she needs to complete and the lessons she needs to learn along the way. Part of Coraline's liminal space includes the Other Mother and Other Father who want to keep her with them. She quickly learns that this liminal space tests her ability to think on her feet and outwit her Other Mother, honing her independence and critical thinking in ways previously unavailable to her in the regular world. Tolkien's influence on Gaiman shines throughout this novel: Coraline's journey mirrors Bilbo's in its essence – she leaves the comfort of her home, she undertakes an adventure she is not entirely sure she wants, she performs heroic actions along the way, and returns home changed in meaningful ways from her quest. The lessons children and adults learn in their liminal spaces are both necessary to their development as individuals. Gaiman, perhaps drawing further influence from Tolkien, creates a journey through liminal space for Coraline that is similar to Bilbo's, albeit for a much shorter duration, a necessary concession to Coraline's young age.

Unlike *Hobbit*, there is only one door in *Coraline* that is a threshold into true liminal space within the story; however, its function alters each time Coraline crosses it. Initially, the 14th door offers Coraline adventure, excitement, and a little bit of creepiness, nothing more than something to do to pass a boring, rainy afternoon. The door itself serves as her call to adventure, offering the liminality for her to explore a necessary new aspect of her identity. The function of liminal space to explore identity is underscored when Coraline meets the talking cat:

> 'Please, what's your name?' Coraline asked the cat. 'Look, I'm Coraline. Okay?' The cat yawned slowly, carefully, revealing a mouth and tongue of astounding pinkness. 'Cats don't have names,' it said.
> 'No?' said Coraline.
> 'No,' said the cat. 'Now, you people have names. That's because you don't know who you are. We know who we are, so we don't need names.' (35)

It is here that Coraline starts to consider how the Other Place will influence her relationship to her own identity. The discussion of names is continued during Coraline's second trip into the liminal space. First, the cat accompanies her and she recognizes him even though he startles her. "'Oh. It's you,' she said to the black cat. 'See?' said the cat. 'It wasn't so hard recognizing me, was it? Even without names'" (63). Identity is found or evolves in one's liminal space, but it can also be lost if care is not taken, as Coraline learns from the three ghostly children she meets. She asks who they are, and one replies, "Names, names, names […] The names are the first to go, after the breath has gone, and the beating of the heart. We keep our memories longer than our names. […] But I have forgotten the name of my governess, and of the tulips, too" (81). These children teach Coraline one of the most important rules for being caught in liminal space, at least in fantasy literature: "Remember your name" (21). The thread of identity and discovery continues to be woven through Coraline's liminal space in this way, reminding her to reflect upon who she is, who she is becoming, and to hold on to that burgeoning self with both hands.

Coraline continues to evaluate her identity, though unconsciously, when her Other Parents ask if she likes it there. Coraline honestly admits that it is more interesting than her real home, but balks at committing to staying there "forever and always" (43). She returns to her own home and locks the door behind her, blocking the other world and resisting the call into her own liminal space as Bilbo similarly did. Resistance is futile, however, and once it becomes clear that the Other Mother has taken Coraline's real parents, her identity becomes entangled with the liminal space beyond the door in the drawing room. Crossing that threshold is now linked to the success of her quest to find her parents and bring them back to their own world. Coraline heads back through the door, telling the cat, "when you're scared but you still do it anyway, *that's* brave" (57). She, like Bilbo in Smaug's lair, goes back down the dark corridor to face a monster despite her terror. When she crosses the threshold into her liminal space this time, it is far more sinister, dangerous than before, something she knows will have repercussions of far more import than just providing her with some entertainment for a day. Her ability to do so is a result of her time spent in liminality, examining her identity and understanding that, even though she is young, she is brave, worthy of notice, and a person who is going to take matters into her own hands.

Once Coraline's quest is complete, her parents safe in her pocket along with the souls of the three ghostly children, the return from her liminal space is just as fraught as the rest of her experiences had been. Coraline has to return through the dark corridor, past the Other Mother who is determined to keep her in the other world. Because her experiences have prepared her and taught her about a valuable new aspect of her identity, Coraline is able to take command of the situation and return safely to her world, along with her parents, the ghostly children, and the black cat. Returning from her liminal space is as difficult as entering it the first time was easy. Coraline struggles to shut the door behind her, but, "[i]t was heavier than she imagined a door could be, and pulling it closed was like trying to close a door against a wind" (131). The lessons she learns and hardships she endures are being physically manifested in the battle with the door, which can be seen as a struggle against herself and her former desires as well as a struggle of good against evil.

Liminal space is a place to discover new parts of characters' identities. Bilbo finds that he is courageous and adventurous even while he yearns for home. At Thorin's deathbed, he proclaims that he is glad he has been able to share in their adventures, a wholly opposite position from when the dwarves first encountered him at his home at Bag-End. Coraline learns to be self-reliant, to make others see her, and that no one actually wants whatever they want because it would have no meaning otherwise. The lessons they each learn are appropriate to their ages and stage in life, and that is reflected in the structure of their liminal space itself. All of these discoveries happen from the simple act of opening a door and stepping through into that liminal space. As author Seanan Maguire states, "Doors are important. What we find on the other side matters even more" (Maguire 2016).

Bibliography

Amison, A., 'An Unexpected Guest', *Mythlore*, 25.1/2 (2006) 127-136.

Buckley, C.G., 'Psychoanalysis, "Gothic" Children's Literature, and the Canonization of Coraline', *Children's Literature Association Quarterly*, 40.1 (2015) 58-79.

Gaiman, N., *Coraline,* (New York: HarperCollins, 2002).
— 'Mythcon 35 Guest of Honor Speech', Mythopoeic Society Conference, 30 July – 2 August 2004, University of Michigan, Ann Arbor, MI <http://journal.neilgaiman.com/2012/ 01/speech-i- once-gave-on-lewis-tolkien-and.html> [Accessed 25 January 2024].

Hallam, A., 'Thresholds to Middle-earth: Allegories of Reading, Allegories for Knowledge and Transformation', *Mythlore*, 30.1/2 (2011) 23-42.

Klapcsik, S., 'Neil Gaiman's Irony, Liminal Fantasies, and Fairy Tale Adaptations', *HJEAS: Hungarian Journal of English and American Studies*, 14.2 (2008) 317-334.

Maguire, S., 'Opening Doors: The Chosen Children of Portal Fantasy', *Tor.com*, 4 April 2016, https://www.tor.com/2016/04/04/opening-doors-the-chosen-children-of-portal-fantasy/ [Accessed 19 April 2019].

Norbert, G., 'Fantastic Liminality', *Anachronist*, 17.4 (2012) 319-323.

Rudd, D., 'An Eye for an I: Neil Gaiman's Coraline and Questions of Identity', *Children's Literature in Education*, 39 (2008) 159-168.

Tolkien, J.R.R. *The Hobbit,* (New York: Ballantine, 1937).

Vargas, J.R.S., and J.C.S. Vargas, 'A Girl in the Dark with Monsters: The Convergence of Gothic Elements and Children's Literature in Neil Gaiman's Coraline', *Revista De Lenguas Modernas*, 21 (2014) 77-94.

Clothing in Tolkien's World and What Can Be Seen through its Analysis

Dr. Torredelforth

When in a hospital we find a man in a white robe and another in shirt and jeans: who is the doctor? Who is the patient? Clearly, nobody would hesitate when trying to identify them. Thanks to what? Clothing. This, since the origins of humanity, has been a symbol, a tool of basic semiotic, because it shows us what we are like and says a lot about the person wearing them, as many scholars have argued in this regard (Squicciarino 1990, 17) Even J.R.R. Tolkien himself mentions in *The Silmarillion* that "even as with us male and female may be shown by the raiment but is not made thereby" when referring to the ability of the dress to show the qualities of the being that is wearing it (*Silmarillion*, 11).

Since Tolkien was aware of this, what did he want to tell us with the numerous references to clothing he made? Whenever we approach Middle-earth is made, an imminently medieval atmosphere can be perceived. Generally, these types of aspects are transmitted to the reader through more than just the preconceived knowledge of Tolkien's taste for the Middle Ages. This type of perspective is achieved through the visual aspects described, and, among them, clothing stands out. This is due not only because through clothing we may read many symbols that Tolkien did not mention explicitly, but also because he shows us the extensive knowledge he had as a medievalist, which even exceeds his own remarkably extensive knowledge on medieval philology.

In this analysis, we cannot fathom all the clothing information we see in his work basically because it is too extensive and would comprise a whole series of articles. Nevertheless, it would be interesting to analyse in detail some examples of Middle-earth races and how their clothing shows the professor's knowledge of medieval fashion, as well as a couple of examples of how far one could go in a deep analysis of each one of these aspects with its references, symbolisms and medieval background.

Dwarves, for example, are widely described in the Hobbit; they wear stockings made in different colours (*Hobbit*, 'Roast Mutton', 40), caps that even have tassels – like the one Thorin wears, which has a silver one (*Hobbit*, 'An Unexpected Party', 11). Jewels among Dwarf nobility are very common even in belts and even in necklaces (*Hobbit*, 'A Warm Welcome', 182), the latter being worn by men throughout the Middle Ages more ostensibly than nowadays (Carmen de Arechaga Rodriguez Pascual et al. 1989, 60). Nonetheless, the most renowned of all these may be the Nauglamír necklace, made with Valinor gems. Regarding the wide use of belts of all kinds (well adorned with pearls and crystals such as the one Bilbo had on his mithril chainmail) they were commonly used not only to decorate clothes, but also to support their well-known broad beards. In the Middle Ages, belts were considered one of the main jewellery accessories of the moment, on which jewels and protective gems of high value were profusely inset (Bohen 1951, 224-5).

Flexible breeches seem one of the central characteristics of dwarven attire. They are also described as being made of a flexible and fine material that only the Dain people knew (*Hobbit*, 'The Clouds Burst', 256). A good historian can only think of the breeches that were first created in the High Middle Ages during the seventh century and that were established as one of the most important garments of the moment, even in posterior centuries (Boucher 2009, 460). It is curious to note the technical innovation created in 1589 by William Lee, who invented an elastic and flexible fabric that would be mostly used for the production of socks and man breeches. Was this a subtle reference Tolkien made to the technical innovation in fashion? It may be impossible to know, but at least we can guess that he would not be ignorant of such historical facts.

Elves, as a people, are described in detail on many occasions. In most descriptions, the general tendency seems to portray them as dressed in green, brown, gray and white. Simplicity seems to be one of the general features that define everything related to their costumes, as well as many of the relevant characters in other stories. For example, the queen of fairyland does not wear a crown that identifies her as such in *The Smith of Wootton Major* (*SWM*, 40).

An academic effort should be made in order to understand the concept of simplicity that surrounded the mind of the professor because, generally, when looking back, one tends to make the mistake of projecting in the past the ideas and perceptions of the present. It should be born in mind that Tolkien grew up in the fashion context of the early twentieth century, where the concept of simplicity (with its corseted dresses, wide hats and refined manners) were far from what may be seen nowadays. A medieval brial, by comparison, might have seemed to him the simplest of the garments.[1]

Tolkien invents his own clothing, similar to mithril, such as cloaks made of elven fabric that, despite being silky, light and warm, allow the company to move stealthily through all kinds of natural environments. It stands out that the fabric's ability to change colour is a positive aspect of the design, which seems to be the counterpoint to what Tolkien describes in Saruman's clothing. The wizard, who once was 'white' changes the fabric of his clothing to one that changes colours.[2] Gandalf understands this change as a sign that the white (a symbol of his past wisdom) has been tainted and lost, and even accuses the wicked wizard in this regard. Greg Harvey explains that Saruman's

> reference to becoming a wizard of Many Colors seems to point toward his ability to put his extensive knowledge to use in the pursuit of particular [...] Gandalf, on the other hand, seems to respond to Saruman of Many Colors with the idea that knowledge put to the use of a particular application is no longer pure knowledge (white) but more what one would call skill (particular colors in the spectrum of white light). Applied knowledge is no longer pure, which Gandalf says he prefers, and a wizard seeking it is in danger of leaving the path of wisdom (something Saruman is guilty of in contrast to Gandalf). (Harvey 2003, 155-6)

1. Nancy Martsch showed a really good study in this direction in her article: "The Lady with the Simple Gown and White Arms" or Possible Influences of the 16th and Early 20th Century Book Illustrations on Tolkien's World.
2. Herman A. and M. Cagiano di Acevedo, in their publication "Farbe" (431-434), clearly explain the ambiguity present in the symbolism of colours and how white has been related in Western cultures to purity and perfection. These ideas are repeated by Pastoreau.

Saruman's multicolour fabric is understood as something negative in contrast to the elven fabric, the colour range of which is absolutely elvish (with gray, greens and earth tones) which are understood as something positive, perhaps because they reflect nature.[3]

In line with colour symbolism, some of the most used colours give us clues regarding the characters that make use of them[4] (Parker 2006, 106-7). Green, related to celestial sun-light by Hidlegard in medieval times, could be one of Tolkien's favourites (Dronke 1972, 84). The general tendency seems to be to use it in those characters of importance in close relationship with nature, either because they wander in it, like Strider, or because they are people of hidden value like kings. Aragorn wears these colours when he appears for the first time as a strider (*FR*, 'At the Sign of the Prancing Pony', 153), and also the king of the fairyland kingdom in Smith of Wootton Major (*SWM*, 43). Green is also the dress of Goldberry (*FR*, 'In the House of Tom Bombadill', 121), and of Yavanna, the powerful Vala (*Silmarillion*, 17). It is closely related to a spectrum of brown, which in general is related to the Elven race, and is one of the characteristic colours of their culture.

Blue is one of the most popular colours of the Middle Ages according to Pastoreau studies (Pastoreau 2010, 85).[5] It seems to relate to characters linked to the original wisdom of the Valar in some aspects. For instance, Tom Bombadil wears blue (*FR*, 'The Old Forest', 117). Manwë, the most powerful of the Valar, is also dressed in blue (*Silmarillion*, 33), and even Lúthien also wears blue (193). It is fascinating how original characters of great antiquity are related to blue, and how, later on, others of great wisdom show it in the headdress. For example, in *The Hobbit*, Thorin's cap is blue, as well as Gandalf's (*Hobbit*, 'An Unexpected Party', 24). We must also mention the French historian, and scholar in fashion philosophy, Alison Laurie, when regarding the symbology of the headdress. She affirms that we can perceive the author line of thought and how it establishes blue as a symbol of the mind which is beneath the ornament that covers the head (Laurie 1994, 25, 192).

Different from clothing, jewels seem to show a general tendency to imitate plant patterns very much in the style of Art Nouveau of the late nineteenth and early twentieth centuries. Thranduil wears a crown of fences and reddish leaves which, in spring, changes to a crown of forest flowers with green leaves that frame his golden hair (*Hobbit*, 'Barrels out of Bound', 160). The gems mentioned in these descriptions are mostly green and white (*Hobbit*, 'Flies and Spiders', 144). These kinds of designs go beyond the elven race, as Goldberry wears a golden belt shaped like a chain of irises, and a dress full of beads that imitate dew as well.

In general, there seems to be no use of gold-made jewellery by elves, except for the description of Lúthien's mantle, which is said to have pure gold flowers on its cloak

3. A really good explanation is given in Greg Harvey's work *The origins of Tolkien Middle-earth for Dummies* regarding the colors of Saruman and the origins of the wizards Tolkien created (151-161).

4. Yet we should not be dogmatic about the theme, because there is always a point of ambiguity.

5. In this regard, the research of Michelle Pastoreau must be mentioned, with a corpus of publications regarding the history of colour that stands out today with books such as *Azul: historia de un color*, or *Las vestiduras del diablo: Breve historia de las rayas en la indumentaria* among others.

(*FR*, 'A Knife in the Dark', 187). The description of some of the female jewels would fit perfectly in what is understood as 'medieval' jewellery. For example, in the poem of Nimrodel, it is mentioned that she had a brooch on her forehead. This type of ornament was very common in the Middle Ages, especially in the kingdoms of Castilla and Aragon during the fifteenth century, and it can be found in an innumerable amount of paintings. Actually, it was usually worn as a ribbon inset with a jewel called a 'head strap'", which also helped to decorate maidens' hair (Bernis 1978, 131).

In all of Tolkien's works jewels seem to be given great importance, and their symbolism as an ornament, as well as their magical power, certainly stands out. The Silmarils are used by Fëanor as a jewel on the head in the Noldor festivities, in the same way the Rings of Power are created, or the Arkenstone has exceptional properties. Once again, such a feature cannot go unnoticed. The attribution of powers to jewels and stones beyond its decorative aspect very likely comes from the Middle Ages. Nobles would, as often as they could, have inset gemstones in their clothes which were attributed magical effects. Many of them were believed to have protective or beneficial effects not only for the bearers, but also for those surrounding them. For example, sapphires were apparently one of the most valued gemstones for their magical powers, as they had both physical and psychic properties. It was considered to have the ability to influence the feelings of the people surrounding the wearer positively. Sapphires would make their requests more likely to be accepted, eliminate envy, promote peace, or even protect against the art of necromancy or sorcery. Physically, it was believed that sapphires not only favoured the health of the members, but also healed heart disease, sore throats, wounds (if placed on them), and so on. These beliefs were so widespread that they were synthesised in the so-called lapidaries or handbooks of the use of gems in this regard (Gili 1977, 1-4, 5, 12).

There are the diamond buttons that Gandalf gives to the Old Tuck, whose rare feature was to buckle and unbutton just at the owner's order (*Hobbit*, 'An Unexpected Party', 7). Importance may not be given to buttons nowadays, but in the Middle Ages they were considered a piece of jewellery and were made with noble materials such as gold and pearls (Maranges I Prat 1991, 15).

In this respect, the invention of mithril by Tolkien is certainly fascinating, as it stands halfway between the noble material, the jewel and the metal which extraordinary and ideal properties are attributed to. In many chivalry novels of the Middle Ages, such ideal characteristics are also attributed to other noble materials. For example, in a fifteenth century Catalan novel titled *Tirant lo Blanc*, the use of strips made of gold to tie clothes when going to battle is mentioned under the belief that they were unbreakable (Martorell 1490, 254-5).

Opulence shown in certain pieces cannot be overlooked, such as the necklace of five hundred green emeralds that Girion, Lord of the Valley, made to inset in his son's mithril chainmail (*Hobbit*, 'Inside Information', 215). These types of extravagantly opulent elaborations are not fiction surprisingly. In the late Middle Ages at the height of the late fourteenth and early fifteenth centuries, there was a burst of luxury after the outbreak of the Black Death, during which even higher elaborations can be seen. As an example, it would be interesting to mention Hipólita Sforza, who married Alfonso de Aragón in 1464. The bride received as a present, among other items, a robe embroidered with 8,966 pearls and 70 pounds of silver, which is breathtaking even nowadays (Perrot 1992, 176).

As a conclusion, perhaps the following question should be asked: Can it be affirmed that there is a carefully crafted symbolism behind the clothes that are described in Tolkien's works? Nothing can be stated in this regard, but it has been possible to analyse in depth a couple of details that show that few aspects in the professor's work seem left to chance, and clothing certainly does not seem to be among them. It is also an open door to his knowledge as a medievalist; through examples such as jewellery, it can be seen that Tolkien was aware of the dynamics of medieval fashion as well as its changes and customs.

Not all the details that support these claims have been provided, but an interesting topic of growing interest nowadays has been pointed out: the analysis of the power clothing – and medieval clothing – holds as a symbol not only in the present, but also in fantasy literature. This fascinating subject is still lacking a profound investigation regarding Tolkien's work.

Bibliography

Arechaga Rodriguez Pascual, C., and others, *Orfebrería de los siglos XV y XVI,* (Barcelona: Planeta-Agostini, 1989).

Bernis, C., *Trajes y modas en la España de los Reyes Católicos*, 2 Vol. II. (Madrid: Instituto Diego Velásquez, CSIC, 1978)

Bohen, M., *La Moda: historia del traje en Europa desde los orígenes del cristianismo hasta nuestros días / por Max von Boehn; con un estudio preliminar por el Marqués de Lozoya, 12 Vols.*, trans. by María Luz Morales (Barcelona: Salvat, 1951).

Boucher, F., *Historia del traje en Occidente: Desde la antigüedad hasta nuestros días*, trans. by A. de P. Kuhlmann Thomann (Barcelona: Gustavo Gili, 2009).

Dronke, P., 'Tradition and Innovation in Medieval Western Colour- Imagery', in *Eranos Jahrbuch* 41 (Leiden: Brill, 1972) 51-107.

Duby, G., and M. Perrot, *Historia de las Mujeres: La Edad Media, II* (Madrid: Taurus ediciones, 1992).

Harvey, G., *The Origins of Tolkien's Middle-earth for Dummies,* (Indianapolis: Wiley Publishing, 2003).

Herman, A., and M. Caguiano di Acevedo, 'Farbe', *Reallexicon für Antike um Christentum*, ed. by T. Klauser, VII (1969) 358-447.

'Introduction', in Lapidari: Tractat de pedres precioses, ed. by J. Gili (Oxford: The Dolphin Book,1977) <https://bruixes.mhcat.net/images/stories/pdfs/lapidari.pdf> [accessed 25 January 2024].

Lurie, A., *El lenguaje de la moda: una interpretación de la forma de vestir,* (Barcelona: Paidós, 1994).
Maranges i Prat, I., *La indumentària civil catalana: Segles XIII-XV,* (Barcelona: Institut d'Estudis catalans, 1991).

Martorell, J., *Tirant lo Blanch,* (Barcelona: Edicions 62, 1984).

Martsch, N., 'The "Lady with the Simple Gown and White Arms" or Possible Influences of 19th and Early 20th Century Book Illustrations on Tolkien's Work', in *Tolkien in the New Century: Essays in Honor of Tom Shippey*, ed. by J.W. Houghton and others (North Carolina: McFarland, 2014) 29-40.

Parker, V.L. 'Colours' in *J.R.R Tolkien Encyclopedia, Scholarship and Critical Assessment*, ed. by M.D.C. Drout (New York: Taylor Francis, 2006), pp. 106-107.

Pastoureau, M., *Azul: Historia de un colour,* (Madrid: Paidós Ibérica, 2010).

Squicciarino, N., *El vestido habla,* (Madrid: Ed. Cátedra, Signo e Imagen 1990).

Tolkien, J.R.R, *The Hobbit,* (London: Harper Collins, 1999).
— *El ferrer de Wotton Major*, trans. by D. Udina (Barcelona: Punt de lectura, 2002).
— *The Lord of the Rings,* (London: Harper Collins, 2001).
— *The Silmarillion*, ed. by C. Tolkien (London: Harper Collins, 1999).

Fruitless Victories: The Life and Times of Elrond Half-elven

Dr. Stuart Whitehouse

Perhaps the most famous quotation about Elrond is from Bilbo, in *The Hobbit*: "He was as noble and as fair in face as an elf-lord, as strong as a warrior, as wise as a wizard, as venerable as a king of dwarves, and as kind as summer" (*Hobbit*, 'A Short Rest', 48). This paper builds up evidence for Bilbo's description as we go through Elrond's life. Bilbo's brief character sketch of Elrond is indeed accurate. Elrond was clearly one of the Wise; he was a member of the White Council. He had good judgement, for example in denying Annatar access to Lindon in the Second Age, and he was skilled in many things, such as healing, and matters of lore – it is Elrond who recited the story of the Second Age and the Rings of Power in the Council of Elrond. He also has the gift of foresight, and he had some power over the river Bruinen. Elrond was venerable in that he clearly commanded respect amongst Elves, Dwarves, Men and Wizards; Boromir, in spite of his attitude, accepts correction from Elrond, and even Gandalf consults with him. Elrond's kindness is perhaps best demonstrated by the "Last Homely House", which was a refuge for those in need of counsel. He gave sanctuary and hospitality to thirteen Dwarves and a Hobbit after their encounter with trolls, and took in Frodo and his companions, possibly even knowing the risk of temptation from the One Ring, which he rejected.

One theme which comes across consistently is persistence in the face of adversity. Elrond says "I have seen three ages in the West of the world, and many defeats, and many fruitless victories" (*FR*, 'The Council of Elrond', 316). Elrond lost his parents, his brother, his wife, and in the end his daughter, but he does not give up and take the ship to Valinor until Sauron is finally defeated, at which point Elrond finally sails west and is (presumably) reunited with his wife.

1 – Early Years

Elrond was born in the year 532 of the First Age, to Eärendil and Elwing in the Havens of Sirion. He had the blood of the Three Houses of the Edain through his paternal grandfather Tuor; Tuor was the grandson of Galdor of the House of Hador and Hareth of the Haladin, and his mother was Rían of the House of Beor. Elrond also had the blood of the three kindreds of the Eldar – the Noldor through his great-grandfather Turgon of Gondolin, the Vanyar through Turgon's wife Elenwë, and the Teleri as his mother Elwing was granddaughter of Thingol of Doriath. This also makes Elrond a descendant of Melian the Maia. Somewhat unusually amongst Tolkien's writings on the First Age, his parentage was never modified, though initially he was an only child, and it was only in a subsequent rewrite that his twin brother Elros came into existence.

By the time Elrond and Elros were born, Morgoth's ascendency was seemingly inexorable. The Havens of Sirion were founded by refugees from Doriath and Gondolin, which had both been destroyed (as had Nargothrond some years earlier). Eärendil and Elwing did possess Beren's Silmaril. However, this meant that the Sons of Fëanor felt obliged to fulfil their Oath to recover the Silmarils from whomever had them.

When Elrond was only six years old, while Eärendil was away on a voyage, they attacked the Havens of Sirion in the Third Kinslaying to recover the Silmaril. Elwing threw herself into the Sea with the Silmaril and was turned into a white bird, which came to rest of Eärendil's ship Vingilótë, and they voyaged to Valinor to seek the aid and pardon of the Valar. The young twins were captured by the forces of Maedhros and Maglor; the sons of Fëanor. Maglor felt sorry for the twins and they eventually began to care for each other. At some point Elrond and Elros were rescued, released, escaped or maybe even elected to stay with Maglor; one can imagine Maglor releasing them – after it was clear that Elwing had dived into the Sea with the Silmaril, there would be little point in holding hostages.

Elrond and his brother would have reached maturity during the War of Wrath. Whilst it is unclear whether the Elves of Beleriand fought alongside the Host of the Valar, it's hard to believe that the Eldar did not while their Edain allies joined the fight: "and such few as such remained of the three houses of the Elf-friends [...] fought upon the part of the Valar" – and if that was indeed what happened, Elrond, as the descendant of many famous names amongst both Elves and Men, could well have taken part (*Shaping*, 38). Elrond also remembers the host assembled when Thangorodrim was destroyed, as he compares the army of the Last Alliance to it in the Council of Elrond: "And yet not so many, nor so fair, as when Thangorodrim was broken" (155). This is potentially the first evidence we have for Elrond as a warrior.

After the final defeat of Morgoth, the Elves of Beleriand were summoned to leave Middle-earth (*Silmarillion*, 297). However, some refused to go, including Elrond. Elrond and Elros were also given the same choice as their parents due to their half-elven nature: to share the fate of Men, or join the Eldar in their immortality. "Elrond Halfelven chose, as was granted to him, to be numbered amongst the Eldar; but Elros his brother chose to abide with Men" (302). Hence the twins were separated permanently, with one eventually destined to die and the other bound within the Circles of the World forever. By the end of the First Age in 590, Elrond had lost both of his parents, and effectively his brother too. The concept of Elrond having to choose his own end was present even in the earliest version of the narrative. Interestingly, Tolkien once stated that this Choice by Elrond was not irrevocable, and Elrond could change his mind and become mortal. This notion does not seem to be pursued any further though, and Tolkien later wrote that the Choice was irrevocable.

It seems that the default option of the half-elven was to be counted as Elves until they made their Choice. The evidence suggests that they aged at a faster rate than full Elves before they stopped ageing, "not until the fiftieth year did the Eldar attain the stature and shape in which their lives would afterwards endure and for some a hundred years would pass before they were full-grown" (303). Eärendil and Elwing (both half-elves) were both only 29 years old when Elrond and Elros were born (which is a reasonable age for Men to start a family), so they were mature enough to have children at an earlier age than a full-blooded elf. Once half-elves reached maturity they seem to have stopped ageing – Arwen lived for nearly three thousand years before making her Choice, and if she had been counted as mortal she would have died of old age in this time.

Elrond is described physically in Lord of the Rings;

> the face of Elrond was ageless, neither old nor young, though in it was written the memory of many things both glad and sorrowful. His hair was dark as the shadows of twilight, and upon it was set a circlet of silver; his eyes were grey as a clear evening, and in them was a light like the light of stars (*FR*, 'Many Meetings', 295)

Bilbo calls him "as noble and as fair in face as an elf-lord" (*Hobbit*, 'A Short Rest', 48). It seems harder to sustain that the half-elven grew old in the same way Men do and then revert back to a less aged appearance if they choose to abide with Elf-kind than the other way around. This combined with the brief idea from Tolkien that Elrond could alter his choice and die, leads to the conclusion that half-elves matured as Men until adulthood, then stopped and were treated as Elves with their ageing "paused", until they decided otherwise – the choice could be delayed, as Elladan and Elrohir did, but not forever.

Elrond never claims to be High King of the Noldor – the title passes from Turgon to his cousin's son Gil-galad rather than his daughter Idril, or her grandson Elrond, and after the death of Gil-galad the title is never claimed, either by Elrond or by Galadriel; this implies that the title cannot be inherited through the female line.

2 – The Second Age

Elrond was one of the Eldar who refused to travel to Valinor after the War of Wrath, and he lived with Gil-galad the High King in Lindon, while his twin brother Elros became the first King of Númenor. There is no evidence either way whether Elros visited Lindon after becoming Tar-Minyatur, the first king, or whether Elrond visited Armenelos on Númenor, but news of Elros' death in SA 442 presumably reached him somehow. Elrond remained in Lindon when Celeborn and Galadriel founded the Noldorin realm of Eregion around 700 taking with them Celebrimbor, a grandson of Fëanor.

For the next four centuries, Elrond remained with Gil-galad and Círdan. This lasted until around SA 1200 when Annatar sought entrance to Lindon. Annatar claimed to be an emissary of the Valar, and offered to aid the Elves in their endeavours. However, both Gil-galad and Elrond mistrusted him and "though they knew not who in truth he was they would not admit him" (*Silmarillion*, 343). It is unclear what position Elrond had in Lindon at this point; presumably he was someone with great authority since he is noted alongside Gil-galad as mistrusting Annatar and having the power to refuse him entry, showing wisdom and foresight from Elrond and Gil-galad.

The first mention in the story of the Second Age of Celebrían, Elrond's future wife, comes during this period. Celebrimbor and the smiths of the Gwaith-i-Mírdain in Eregion, welcomed Annatar (over Galadriel's objections), and together they forged sixteen Rings of Power. Annatar also encouraged Celebrimbor to rebel against the rule of Galadriel and Celeborn around SA 1350, and Galadriel took her daughter Celebrían and travelled through Khazad-dûm to settle in Lothlórien. Celeborn remained behind, not wanting to travel through the realm of the Dwarves.

Elrond's actions during Sauron's invasion of Eregion shows his prowess as a warrior – even by the end of the Third Age, he was "hale as a tried warrior in the fullness of his strength" (*FR*, 'Many Meetings', 295). Sauron prepared to invade Eregion in SA 1697 to capture the Rings of Power, and Gil-galad sent Elrond with an army to assist

Celebrimbor, "but Elrond had far to go, and Sauron turned north and made at once for Eregion" (*UT*, 237). Celeborn sortied and drove off Sauron's scouts, but whilst he managed to reach Elrond's force, Sauron had the advantage of numbers, and could both hold them off and assault Eregion at the same time. Sauron's forces broke through into Ost-in-Edhil and sacked the halls of the Gwaith-i-Mírdain and killed Celebrimbor. Sauron then turned his army's attention to Elrond, who had gathered the few survivors of Eregion. Some timely aid from the Dwarves of Khazad-dûm and Elves of Lórinand, whose combined forces took Sauron's forces in the rear, enabled Elrond to escape.

3 – Rivendell

Elrond retreated northwards with the remnants of the elves of Eregion, including "many Noldorin lords" together with Celeborn (*Peoples*, 79). He established a refuge in a valley on the west side of the Misty Mountains, named Rivendell (Imladris in Sindarin). Elrond's house was "refuge for the weary and oppressed, and a treasury of good counsel and wise lore" (*Silmarillion*, 357). It became known as the Last Homely House East of the Sea, and "upon [Elrond's] house the stars of heaven most brightly shone" (358). One can imagine this is due to Eärendil, Elrond's father, who carries a Silmaril across the night sky.

The main part of Sauron's forces overran Eriador and marched towards Lindon but he left a detachment to beseige Rivendell. In SA 1700 the combined forces of Gil-galad and the Númenoreans sent by Tar-Minastir defeated Sauron's forces at Sarn Ford, and Sauron's forces retreated to meet reinforcements only to find more Númenórean troops in their rear at Tharbad, as a Númenórean admiral had dropped off a second force at the mouth of the Gwathló. In the resulting battle Sauron's forces were routed, and the army besieging Rivendell, caught between Gil-galad and Elrond, was destroyed. At this point a Council was held in Rivendell, and Gil-galad gave Elrond Vilya, the Blue Ring. This is clear evidence of wisdom, Gil-galad would not entrust Vilya to someone he did not believe was wise enough to use it (or not use it, as at the time Sauron wore the One Ring). Gil-galad also appointed Elrond his vice-regent in Eriador, though it is unclear what that entailed. There were Mannish settlements in the Bree-land, and the Númenorean harbours at Lond Daer and Tharbad, but whether Elrond's authority extended to those is never stated. One can imagine Elrond ruled with a light touch and local officials would have acknowledged his wisdom, but as relations between the Elves and Númenóreans soured the Númenórean settlements may have become effectively independent. Elendil presumably created Arnor with the permission of Gil-galad and Elrond, since they nominally controlled that region.

One year later, Galadriel and Celebrían visited Rivendell, searching for Celeborn, "and it was then that Elrond first saw Celebrían, and loved her, though he said nothing of it" (*UT*, 240). This was the first meeting of Elrond and his future wife, although it would be many centuries before they were married. The various facts Tolkien stated allow us to put bounds on her year of birth – if she was born before the founding of Eregion, Elrond would surely have already met her in Lindon, and she certainly was born by SA 1350 as she passed through Khazad-dûm with her mother, so she was born between SA 700 and 1350.

During the next centuries Sauron gave the Nine to men, three of whom were Númenoreans. Ar-Pharazôn, the last King of Númenor travelled to Middle-earth, landing at Umbar, and called forth Sauron to swear fealty to him. This he did, and accompanied Ar-Pharazôn back to Númenor, where he urged the King to cut down the White Tree and worship Morgoth. Eventually Ar-Pharazôn took a fleet west to Valinor, seeking immortality for himself precipitating the drowning of Númenor. The folk of Elendil, who had remained faithful to the Valar, sailed to Middle-earth and established the realms of Arnor and Gondor.

Sauron also survived the Downfall of Númenor, and upon returning to Middle-earth found that Gil-galad's power and influence had grown to the borders of Greenwood the Great. Sauron prepared for War against the Dúnedain and the Elves, and Gil-galad and Elendil formed the "Last Alliance", gathering a great host of Men and Elves and stopping for a while at Imladris, in SA 3431. Valandil son of Isildur was born there. After a few years they crossed the Misty Mountains and marched down the Vale of Anduin. Elrond was "the herald of Gil-galad and marched with his host" (*FR*, 'The Council of Elrond', 316), took part in the Battle of Dagorlad, and crossed into Gorgoroth and laid siege to Barad-dûr. Sauron himself came forth to fight Elendil and Gil-galad, and both were slain, but Isildur cut the One Ring from Sauron's hand, and Sauron was temporarily defeated.

Elrond, once again showing his wisdom, advised Isildur to destroy the One Ring in Mount Doom where it had been forged but Isildur refused to surrender it to Elrond and Círdan, taking the Ring for himself. The armies then disbanded. Isildur travelled to Minas Anor to instruct his nephew Meneldil, and Elrond returned to Rivendell. Isildur was slain shortly afterwards and the One Ring lost in the Disaster of the Gladden Fields, as he travelled back to Rivendell where his wife and youngest son resided.

4 – Family Life

The Third Age began with Sauron's power and influence greatly diminished, but there were many casualties on the victorious side, including Gil-galad the High King. In TA 109 Elrond wed Celebrían, daughter of Celeborn and Galadriel. It was the custom of the Eldar to wed in their youth, soon after they were fifty, but in this Elrond was certainly bucking the trend, as at this point he was just over three thousand six hundred years of the Sun old! It is unclear how long the courtship and betrothal lasted, nor who stood with Elrond, if anyone, as his closest living relatives in Middle-earth were probably his future father- and mother-in-law. However, Elrond and Celebrían had children not long afterwards (in Elvish terms), this time in accordance with the customs of the Eldar, with the twin sons Elladan and Elrohir being born in TA 130, followed by their daughter Arwen in TA 241. The early years of bringing up children are supposed to be some of the merriest in the life of an Elda, so we can presume that Elrond spent the early Third Age bringing up his family and ruling Imladris.

Events in the world outside Rivendell continued onwards, with the realm of Arnor fragmenting into three successor kingdoms in 861. In the year 1000, a shadow started growing in Greenwood the Great, soon to be renamed Mirkwood, ruled by the Necromancer in the former Elven stronghold on Amon Lanc, now renamed Dol Guldur.

This was followed by the arrival of the Istari (Wizards), who were Maiar from Valinor. Elrond may have been one of the few to know where the Istari came from: "it was not known whence they came (unless to Círdan and Elrond)" (*Peoples*, 228). It is clear from the narrative in *The Hobbit* and *The Lord of the Rings* that Gandalf was welcome whenever his wanderings took him to Rivendell. Saruman, as a member of the White Council, would have visited Rivendell, and as stated by Elrond, "we trusted him and he is deep in all our counsels", so it seems that he too was a colleague of Elrond, and trusted and respected by him (*FR*, 'The Council of Elrond', 345).

During the fourteenth century of the Third Age a new realm arose north of the Ettensmoors in Angmar48, practically on Elrond's doorstep, and the Witch-king was later found to be the chief of the Ringwraiths. Rivendell was again besieged for a time as the people of Angmar took the lands east of the Weather Hills, the Great East Road, and the lower River Hoarwell. In 1409 a great host from Angmar sacked the tower on Weathertop, but the men and orcs of Angmar were subdued for a time by Elves from Lindon, Rivendell and, at Elrond's request, Lórien.

The final end of the Dúnedain kingdoms of the north came in 1974 when the Witch-king captured Fornost towards the end of winter. The following year, Eärnur of Gondor allied with an army of Elves from Lindon sent by Círdan and routed the forces of Angmar. At the same time Glorfindel led a force from Rivendell from the other direction. This is the last time mentioned in the texts that Rivendell sent out a military force; presumably the Elves in the later Third Age were so few in number as they left over the Sea that Rivendell no longer had the numbers to field a regular army. Aranarth, the heir of Arvedui, the last king, claimed the title of Chieftain of the Dúnedain, and his heirs were brought up in Rivendell by Elrond and his household.

It was the custom of Celebrían (and Arwen after her) to visit her parents in Lórien, travelling south from Rivendell to Eregion, crossing the Misty Mountains by the Redhorn Gate and travelling down Dimrill Dale to Lórien. In TA 2509, however, Celebrían was attacked by Orcs bearing poisoned weapons on her way across the Redhorn Gate. Celebrían returned to Rivendell, but Elrond, despite all his knowledge of healing, could not cure his wife, and the following year she went over the Sea to Valinor. This is the first time Elrond is noted as a healer. Learning healing was an unusual skill for a warrior, for "the Eldar deemed the dealing of death […] diminished the power of healing" (*Morgoth*, 213). It is possible that Elrond became a healer after the wars which punctuated the Second Age – in the Third Age it seems to be Glorfindel who leads the military forces of Rivendell, or maybe Elrond ignored Eldarin custom and learned both skills, in a similar manner to his ignoring Eldarin custom and waiting many centuries to get married.

5 – The Watchful Peace and the War of the Ring

A number of events of note occurred in the twenty-fifth century of the Third Age. Firstly, the Necromancer returned to Dol Guldur, and the White Council was formed shortly afterwards. This was a group of many of the Wise, including Elrond, Galadriel, Saruman and Gandalf. Elrond's inclusion in this group is evidence for venerability; he was clearly respected by others of the Wise and counted amongst their number. Despite

Galadriel's objections, it was led by Saruman. Secondly, Déagol found the One Ring in Anduin near the Gladden Fields, and was murdered by his cousin Sméagol. Four centuries later, in TA 2851, the White Council met again in Rivendell, and discussed an attack on Dol Guldur. Gandalf had previously infiltrated Dol Guldur and suspected the Necromancer was Sauron, but Saruman spoke against attacking him. During the events of *The Hobbit*, Elrond attended another meeting of the White Council, and the debate went Gandalf's way, and Elrond, together with the rest of the White Council, drove out the Necromancer from Dol Guldur.

In 2933, Arathorn II, the current Chieftain of the Dúnedain, was shot whilst hunting orcs with the sons of Elrond, and his young son Aragorn was fostered in Rivendell. Elrond loved Aragorn as much as his sons. When he was twenty, he revealed to Aragorn his true ancestry, and gave him the Shards of Narsil, the sword of his distant ancestor Elendil. Aragorn first met Arwen in the woods around Rivendell at this time, after she returned from visiting her grandparents in Lothlórien. Aragorn went out into the Wild. In TA 2980 Aragorn and Arwen were betrothed on Cerin Amroth, and in doing this Arwen chose to die as a mortal, rather than go over the Sea with her father to spend the rest of the lifetime of Arda in Valinor. This pained Elrond, who was now faced with the prospect of losing his daughter forever, in the same manner as his brother had been lost to him. Elrond correctly foretold that Arwen would lose all she made her choice for before she died.

In TA 2941 thirteen dwarves and Bilbo Baggins arrived in Rivendell with Gandalf, on the Quest of Erebor. Elrond, "grieved to remember the ruin of the town of Dale", and read the moon-letters on Thorin Oakenshield's map, thus giving them a vital clue on how to access the Lonely Mountain without making the dragon Smaug aware of their presence (*Hobbit*, 'A Short Rest', 49). Bilbo, by then bearing the One Ring, returned through Rivendell the following year, after the death of Smaug and the victory of the Free Peoples at the Battle of Five Armies. Just after the turn of the millennium, Elrond invited Bilbo to stay in Rivendell. This is good evidence for Elrond's kindness; there was no compelling reason for Elrond to let Bilbo settle in Rivendell, doing so was an act of simple generosity.

The Third Age was drawing to a close when Gandalf discovered the One Ring was in the possession of Frodo Baggins. Frodo and his friends made their way to Rivendell and they encountered Gildor Inglorion and his Wandering Company, who sent messages far and wide that Frodo was abroad without aid with the Ringwraiths in pursuit, and that Gandalf was missing. These messages eventually came to Rivendell. It is not clear just how much Elrond knew about Frodo's business at this point; Gandalf and Aragorn had passed through Rivendell in April on their way west (Elrond gave them fresh horses), and Gandalf may have disclosed his suspicions about Frodo's Ring to Elrond. Alternatively Elrond may just have been disturbed by the pursuit of the heir of Bilbo Baggins (or for that matter anyone) by the nine Black Riders.

Either way, Elrond was concerned enough by the news to send out parties in all the likely directions of travel between the Shire and Rivendell. Glorfindel took the Road, and encountered Frodo in mid-October. They hurried to the Ford of Bruinen with the Ringwraiths in pursuit, and Frodo crossed the Ford. The Ringwraiths, attempting to pursue him, set foot in the Ford, and Elrond caused a great flooding of the river, which was under his power. This is probably the most "magical" thing Elrond does in the whole legendarium. Interestingly, according to Return of the Shadow, the original version of the chapter had Gandalf creating the flood, rather than Elrond. This deliberate change implies that Tolkien envisaged Elrond being able to perform such "magical" acts, even if he did so rarely.

Frodo was retrieved from the riverbank, and Elrond healed him, extracting a fragment of a Morgul-knife which was slowly turning Frodo into a Ringwraith. After Frodo had recovered, Elrond held a Council in Rivendell, attended by folk from all over the north-west of Middle-earth, who had arrived in Rivendell. Here the fate of the One Ring was debated, and it was agreed that Frodo and eight others would attempt to destroy the Ring by dropping it into Mount Doom in Mordor. At this point Elrond rejects the One Ring in a much less dramatic fashion than Galadriel later does: "I fear to take the Ring to hide it. I will not take the Ring to wield it" (*FR*, 'Many Meetings', 349). It is possible that, in contrast to Galadriel who had left Valinor seeking power in a realm of her own, Elrond was less tempted by the prospect of dominion over Middle-earth. Having grown up in Beleriand as Morgoth was winning the fight against Elves and Men, his earliest memories would include how the sons of Fëanor, and the forces of the Shadow, exercised power, rather than the somewhat better example of the Valar in Valmar that Galadriel would remember. In rejecting the Ring, Elrond shows nobility as well as wisdom. It is also interesting that Elrond chairs the Council and picks Frodo's companions, rather than Gandalf (though Elrond was wise enough to listen to Gandalf's advice), which could show the respect and dignity Elrond was held in, and hence is evidence of venerability.

Something present in early drafts of the Council of Elrond which was lost in later versions was Elrond's sense of humour. Elrond's smile was "like the summer sun" and he laughs when Bingo (predecessor to Frodo in early versions) realises his age (*Shadow*, 213, 215). This is removed in the final version; presumably Tolkien felt that the gravity of the situation required a more solemn council. Elrond was definitely approachable to his people though, to the extent that Bilbo feels able to joke with him and sing songs about his father in his house.

Elrond furnished the party with winter clothes, and also gave Gandalf Miruvor, the cordial of Imladris, which was crucial in helping the Fellowship withstand the snowstorms of Caradhras and the subsequent warg attack. This must have been a nervous time for Elrond, as there was a significant chance that the One Ring would be recovered by Sauron, and Elrond, as bearer of Vilya, would be vulnerable.

After the destruction of the One Ring, Elrond took Arwen to Minas Tirith to be the bride of Aragorn, now King of the Reunited Kingdom. It was not recorded what happened in his final interview with Arwen, but Elrond returned to Rivendell with Frodo and his friends, and foretold that Bilbo would accompany him and the other Ringbearers over the Sea shortly. Two years later, Elrond, together with Galadriel, Bilbo and a large number of Elves, left Rivendell, met Frodo and Sam in the Shire, and together they travelled to the Grey Havens. After 6,520 years of the sun, Elrond left Middle-earth on the White Ship, and "passed on into the West" (*RK*, 'The Grey Havens', 1348).

6 – Conclusion

It can be seen that Elrond demonstrates all of the qualities Bilbo gives him over the course of his lifetime. He is clearly one of the Wise, known for his wisdom and knowledge, and he had skill both as a warrior and a healer. He was greatly respected by his peers, and he played a crucial role in the eventual victory against Sauron. In particular, his assistance to first Bilbo and then Frodo on their respective quests was in the form of counsel and knowledge rather than military might, but both quests would probably have failed without his help. For Elrond the final victory is rather bittersweet, losing his daughter to mortality even though he eventually travelled over the Sea and was reunited with Celebrían, and possibly his mother Elwing, who was by now living on the shores of Eldamar.

There were indeed many defeats during his lifetime, and some of the victories were not the best outcome imaginable. However, as Elrond then goes on to say, his victories were not wholly fruitless, and little by little each victory added up, and in the end led to the downfall of Sauron.

Bibliography

Tolkien, J.R.R., *The Hobbit,* (London: HarperCollins, 1989).
— *The Shaping of Middle-earth*, ed. by C. Tolkien (London: HarperCollins, 1989).
— *Unfinished Tales*, ed. by C. Tolkien (London: HarperCollins, 1993).
— *The Return of the Shadow*, ed. by C. Tolkien (London: HarperCollins, 1994).
— *The Letters of J.R.R. Tolkien*, ed. by H. Carpenter with the assistance of C. Tolkien (London: HarperCollins, 1995).
— *The Silmarillion*, ed. by C. Tolkien (London: HarperCollins, 1999).
— *Morgoth's Ring*, ed. by C. Tolkien (London: HarperCollins, 2002).
— *The Peoples of Middle-earth*, ed. by C. Tolkien (London: HarperCollins, 2002).
— *Sauron Defeated*, ed. by C. Tolkien (London: HarperCollins, 2002).
— *The War of the Jewels*, ed. by C. Tolkien (London: HarperCollins, 2002).
— *The Lord of the Rings,* (London: HarperCollins, 2005).

ART AND MUSIC

Artists in Middle-earth: illustrating *The Lord of the Rings*

Marie Bretagnolle

Thinking about *The Lord of the Rings* often brings to mind visuals created by artists such as Alan Lee, Pauline Baynes, John Howe, and many others. They have helped make J.R.R. Tolkien's Secondary World more real by adding the power of images to that of the words through their illustrations published within the books or in calendars, the covers they designed, and, in the case of Lee and Howe, the movie adaptations they contributed to. For a time, Tolkien considered providing illustrations for *The Lord of the Rings* himself, as he had done for *The Hobbit*. However, as time went by and the story grew, he dropped the idea, because his priority was to publish the text. Given the size and scope of the narrative, to illustrate it is a challenge, even for professional artists.

This presentation deals with interior illustrations, published within the book and not only on the cover. In the first British illustrated edition of *The Lord of the Rings*, published in 3 volumes by the Folio Society in 1977, Eric Fraser redrew the illustrations created by Ingahild Grathmer (who was in fact the Princess and then Queen of Denmark). In later years, only Alan Lee illustrated this text again, for the 1992 Centenary edition featuring 50 of his watercolour paintings. His pictures have been so well-received that they are now a reference and are part of the collective imaginary.

This paper will focus on these two editions, looking at the illustrations, how they interact with the text, and shed light on it, as well as on the artists' reading of the story. The differences in the making of the volumes guided some of the artists' choices, but it was also a question of how to adapt their style to this complex narrative. I will also examine the artists' own sources of inspiration, and how looking at past artworks helped them shape their visual interpretations of Tolkien's story.

1 – Two editions, two visions

1.1 – The Folio Society edition

The Folio Society edition of *The Lord of the Rings* features black & white illustrations: one illustration for each of the 62 chapters, one for each of the 6 books and one for each of the 3 volumes, which makes up a total of 71, in addition to the cover design. The pictures are always positioned in the same way: at the opening of each section, above the text, for the chapter headings, or in full page in the case of the frontispieces. One of the most remarkable things about these illustrations is that they were created by two artists. The princess of Denmark, who later took the pseudonym of Ingahild Grathmer, made pencil sketches, some of which she sent to Tolkien himself, as a thank you for the story that she had become passionate about. It seems to have been a hobby in the first place, without intention of publication. When the Folio Society decided to publish an illustrated *Lord of the Rings*, Eric Fraser then redrew the sketches as ink, black-and-white illustrations. Some research is still to be done on the circumstances of this endeavour and the place of each artist in the making of the finished illustrations. However, we can already find some clues in the pictures themselves.

1.2 – Two artists for one edition

Some of these sketches were displayed in the correspondence section of the 2018 Bodleian exhibition in Oxford, 'Maker of Middle-earth', and are reproduced in the catalogue. To compare them with the finished illustrations reveals the extent of Fraser's touch.

In some cases, he stayed as close as possible to Grathmer's design, for instance with 'A Conspiracy Unmasked'. Illustrating the bathroom at Crickhollow, Fraser kept the general composition designed by Grathmer, as well as the placement of each element. He only added some texture to the walls (suggesting the surface with a scattering of dots), floor and wooden objects (with parallel lines) in order to bring more depth to the picture and to make the steam cloud stand out.

In other cases, he made some alterations to the original sketch. In 'Fog on the Barrow-downs', for which Grathmer drew four stones in a circle shrouded in mist, Fraser kept the frontal viewpoint but changed the number and the design of the stones from four to two, so that in the final illustration they suggest a passage leading the Hobbits to a terrifying episode.

1.3 – Placing illustrations within the text

In the Folio Society edition, the artists had to follow the storyline regularly in their pictures, with the exception of the frontispieces. These are detached from the text, placed on a full page before the story begins. Three of them feature more or less recognizable characters, and the other six are landscapes with a romanticist touch: they offer a view on a land that the reader can identify, but some are not exactly accurate, or are tinged with symbolism, so that they depict both a natural scene and the emotions of the characters walking across these landscapes. In these editions, frontispieces set the tone for the readers.

In the 1992 edition embellished by Alan Lee, although each picture does not correspond to a particular chapter (since there are 50 pictures and 62 chapters), their placement was not left to chance. Given the way a book is bound, the thicker paper for the images could only be placed at regular intervals throughout the text. Alan Lee turned this constraint into an opportunity to pick the subjects of his illustrations more easily. To make the reading experience as smooth as possible, he chose to illustrate the passages closest to where the images would be positioned, so that the readers would neither be spoiled by an illustration placed too soon in the text, nor find one that referred to a scene three chapters before. In that way, they can go from text to image seamlessly, without having to turn pages.

2 – The artists' reading of the text

The Lord of the Rings is a multi-facetted text, encompassing an adventure novel, an epic narrative, dozens of songs and poems, etc. It begins, after a prologue that wasn't illustrated by the artists, by a rather light-hearted chapter focusing on life in the Shire, where Hobbits are quite oblivious to the state of the outside world. However, the illustrations offer a first clue to the reader that the narrative is not going to stay light-hearted for long.

2.1 – Ominous figures and weather in the first illustrations of *The Fellowship of the Ring*

In the Folio Society edition, the book begins with two frontispieces. The first one faces the title page and is a rather surprising, almost abstract illustration, giving the impression that we are watching a piece of cloth billowing in the wind. However, looking closely, one may identify a series of nine hooded figures echoing the number of the Black Riders.

The second frontispiece comes between the prologue and the first chapter and shows without ambiguity a Black Rider coming towards the reader through the page. The rider and his horse are drawn in negative: white on black instead of the usual black on white. On the horse's legs, this technique gives the impression that its bones are visible. The place where the Rider's face should appear, looks like an empty void, according to the text that specifies, when Frodo meets him for the first time, that: "his face was shadowed and invisible" (*FR*, 'Three is Company, 74). This encounter takes place in chapter 3, some 93 pages after the beginning of the book, making this frontispiece a visual prolepsis. However, the absence of contextualisation in the picture, which offers no indication of place for instance, abstracts the representation from any specific moment in the narration.

These two frontispieces suggest a lurking danger that the text has not yet introduced.

A similar view is conveyed through one of Alan Lee's first illustrations of the 1992 edition. In the picture facing the first page of 'A Long-expected Party', although Alan Lee paints a landscape that may feel familiar to English readers, the atmosphere is not exactly comforting: wind is blowing, and dark clouds are gathering on the horizon, as a line in chapter 8 suggests: "A shadow now lay round the edge of sight, a dark haze above which the upper sky was like a blue cap, hot and heavy" (*FR*, 'Fog on the Barrow-downs', 136).

In the first images of both editions, the artists suggest the dark tone that makes *The Lord of the Rings* very different from *The Hobbit*.

2.2 – Where is the Ring?

In the following chapters, in their own style, they underline the tremendous importance of the little ring that Bilbo once found in a cave.

In Fraser and Grathmer's 'The Shadow of the Past', the hooded figure holding a Ring between crooked fingers is probably Sauron just after he forged the One. He is never shown in the text, but his presence permeates the dialogue between Gandalf and Frodo in this chapter. Around the figure's left elbow, the folds of his cape, drawn in white on black, merge with the volutes in the background, black on white. In this area where the eye does not necessarily linger, the character tends to blend into the decorative background as if it did not quite belong to this world.

In this picture, the Ring is almost at the centre of the composition, and the serpentine lines of the cloak converge toward it as if to provide a visual representation of the Ring's irresistible attraction on people's minds.

In Alan Lee's illustration for the same chapter, the Ring seems at first absent, although it is at the heart of Gandalf's explanations which Frodo is listening to, eyes on his hands. *The Hobbit* appears to be holding the Ring on his lap, and yet we cannot see it. The composition draws the eye in its direction, too: Frodo's head, bent toward it; the wizard's pipe and his matchstick, creating white lines standing out against the dark background; and last but not least the window frame, leading right to Frodo's hands. The illustration transposes the growing hold of the Ring on the young Hobbit's mind.

The detailed description of the Ring in the text may be the key to its absence in the image. Alan Lee may have wanted not to transpose, though in a different medium, what the writer has already stated. His illustration shows the atmosphere of the scene, made almost claustrophobic by the beams on the ceiling, which create a frame within the frame of the picture, and the fire standing as an obstacle in the foreground. And yet it is also familiar and cosy, thanks to the same fireplace and the library which may be glimpsed at the back of the room.

Alan Lee builds his illustration on what the text doesn't say in this chapter, making Frodo's posture mirror that of Gollum, head bent, arms cradling the object as if it was much bigger than it really is. In both editions, the illustrations for this particular chapter go beyond the text to play on the idea of appearance and disappearance, of the visible and the invisible, the better to highlight the Ring's influence.

2.3 – A very close reading or a looser interpretation?

The illustrations by these three artists show a tension between a desire for the image to follow the text very closely, or to interpret it more loosely. It is an issue that resurfaces again at the beginning of *The Two Towers*.

Alan Lee's first illustration for this volume is a double picture, highlighting the contrast between the long distances of Middle-earth in the upper panel, where the Three Hunters are catching their breath in the plains of Rohan, and the lower panel, in which Merry and Pippin are surrounded with enemies. This part especially mirrors the effects of repetition found in the text:

> hundreds of hideous orc-faces grinned at him out of the shadows, hundreds of hideous arms grasped at him from every side (*TT*, 'The Uruk-hai', 444)

> Immediately in front were bowed backs, and tough thick legs going up and down, up and down, unresting, as if they were made of wire and horn, beating out the nightmare seconds of an endless time. (452)

To represent these figures of speech, the artist chose a very tight frame and crowded it with Orcs and Uruk-hai, so that not the slightest bit of landscape is visible. It contrasts with the open panorama of the upper panel. With this one picture, Alan Lee illustrates two chapters at the same time, something that Grathmer and Fraser could not do.

Their picture for chapter 3, 'The Uruk-hai', is one of the rare instances of character depiction. And yet, the liberties it takes with the text leads us to think that something else is at stake here. Tolkien is very specific at this moment of the story, writing: "He had a black knife with a long jagged blade in his hand" (445). Instead, Grathmer and Fraser drew a wide and curved blade. The intricate arabesques in the background, suggesting a lack of space, are another clue that this particular illustration is more about the danger and tension at the heart of the chapter than it is about the portrait of an Orc.

3 – Pictures and narration: illustrating the time of the story

3.1 – A study in mushrooms

Grathmer and Fraser often chose a symbolic representation on the chapter headings. Some examples in which they illustrated a specific element of the narrative reveal how the placing of pictures within the book can be a problem. Indeed, each artwork is supposed to illustrate a part of the text, but is placed right before, as a sort of pre-text element. It means that the reader can find clues about the story before it is even told by the author. The relation between text and image would have been quite different if the pictures had been placed at the end of the chapter they were supposed to illustrate, because the text would have pre-conditioned them. For instance, the image for 'A Short Cut to Mushrooms' is a wink at the title, but the title is already a teaser since the mushrooms in question only appear at the very end of the chapter. In this case, the picture is out of step with the time of the narrative. It anticipates and announces the pleasant surprise awaiting the Hobbits.

3.2 – Illustrating chapters with a complex temporality

On other occasions, the illustration needs to keep up with the complexity of a chapter, as is the case in 'The Council of Elrond'. This is a key chapter gathering together several narrative threads, and to illustrate the complex temporality created by the many different accounts, Alan Lee combined two pictures into one. The background features the council, in the lower part, in which most of the characters can be identified, and in the upper part the airy architecture of Rivendell.

In the centre part of the composition is an inset image featuring Gollum on a tree, chewing a bird he has just caught. It relates to Legolas's account of how Gollum escaped from the Elves of Mirkwood. In this regard, the central panel is both anchored into the narrative, and detached from it, opening as it does on a different time. It brings depth to the representation, echoing in a double image the embedded narratives of the members of the Council.

In the Folio Society version of this illustration, the artists opted for the opposite approach, and drew an empty hall in the middle of which a fire is producing an ominous, black smoke. Despite the characters' gathering being the justification for this chapter, Grathmer and Fraser's picture hides them from view. As far as the architecture is concerned, they may have taken inspiration from Tolkien's illustration of Beorn's Hall from *The Hobbit*. Both rooms feature two lines of columns bearing a wooden framework. The fireplace is set in a pit in the middle of the floor, and the smoke curls towards an unseen opening in the roof.

In the text, the room where the council gathers is not described, because the attention of the characters and of the readers is focused on all that has happened and is still happening in the outside world. The picture is then a negative of the chapter, showing what the writer did not describe. It works as a theatre stage before the actors enter, showing the empty room waiting to be filled with tales and conversations, but for the roaring fire in the middle and its clouds of ominous black smoke, which turn the image into a more symbolic representation of the chapter.

The question of time cannot be avoided when we talk about illustrations. By opening a window onto the world created by the author, an artist suspends the narration – after all, an illustration is not a movie, and it actually demands that one stops reading for a moment. The pictures for this particular chapter show how the artists deal with the representation of time at a moment of the story when past, present and future are mingled.

4 – Complementary illustrations and the power of the text

4.1 – In landscapes

A common trait of these two editions is the limited number of character depictions. On the reverse, the landscapes and locations of Middle-earth are given centre stage, mirroring their importance in the text. These pictures are the visual equivalent of the textual descriptions, but they are not merely a repetition in a different medium, first and foremost because a text and an image cannot do the same thing and have the same effect on the reader or viewer. Each has its own tools, and in their turn each artist has his or her own interpretation of the same chapter. However, some illustrations show a remarkable similarity.

For instance, the illustrations for the chapter 'The Passage of the Marshes' in both editions are composed following the rule of thirds, which is a common rule in visual arts, stating that you should organise the elements of an image along imaginary lines cutting it in three horizontal and/or three vertical parts. Here, despite the different orientation of the images, the artists used this rule to depict the landscape: in the lower horizontal third are herbs and reeds, then the marshes in the middle third, drawing the eye toward the upper third where the Mountains of Shadow stand as the border of Mordor.

Many things happen in this chapter, with Sam eavesdropping on Gollum having a conversation with himself, Frodo feeling the weight of the Ring getting heavier and heavier, and the little group being terrified by a Nazgûl flying over them. And yet, it is the foul and foggy landscape that captured the imagination of the illustrators who then depicted it following a similar composition. The main difference between the two comes from the artists' techniques, ink in Eric Fraser's case, and watercolour in Alan Lee's.

4.2 – And in narrative scenes

Another example of an echo between the two editions is given in 'The Passing of the Grey Company'. Both Grathmer and Fraser on the one hand, and Alan Lee on the other hand, chose to picture a moment both solemn and tinged with emotion, when Aragorn and Éowyn share a cup before his departure for the Paths of the Dead.

Grathmer and Fraser, in the limited space of the chapter heading, opted for a close-up on the four hands and the cup, leaving the rest of the scene off-frame. Here, the artists play with the angle of view. Choosing a three-quarters view creates a negative, empty space between Éowyn's right hand and Aragorn's left, where their hands are not touching. However, because of the same viewpoint, Éowyn's left hand and Aragorn's right appear to be touching, perhaps suggesting the shieldmaiden's unrequited feelings.

Alan Lee also chose to picture this particular scene in the Centenary edition. He made full use of the vertical format of his picture to paint the characters almost full-length, facing each other. Their arms are extended in front of them to share the cup, in a posture whose rigidity is enhanced by the strict profile in which they are painted. The arms form a broken, almost architectural line, here too creating an interesting negative space between their bodies. Despite the apparent fixity of the composition, the artist introduced an element of imbalance. He did not centre the characters exactly in the composition, but rather placed Éowyn a little bit forward, so that she is in full view, whereas Aragorn is standing back and his figure is cut by the frame. This may suggest that Aragorn has chosen a path that will lead him to the border of the realm of the Living, whereas Éowyn embodies a life force, moving forward to save her people and to declare her feelings.

Again, this is a chapter in which many things happen, but the artists chose to focus on the same passage and to isolate the characters from the rest of the world. The very tight framing of this illustration in the Folio Society version is also a way for the artists not to tell too much before the scene actually takes place. When readers flip the page and find this picture, they cannot yet tell who the two characters are – the illustration is only complete when the corresponding text is read.

4.3 – Mirroring the history of Middle-earth

Upon reading *The Lord of the Rings*, one cannot help but notice the rich history hinted at throughout the text. Three examples show how illustrators replicate this in their pictures.

In Book 4, Alan Lee depicted the city of Osgiliath. In the text, it is never described, only mentioned as "the ruined city", which gives the artist complete agency (*RK*, 'The Siege of Gondor', 817). He used this opportunity to create an image detached from the immediate action and related to the vast legendarium created by Tolkien. To do so, he introduced the idea of the past in the representation of the city itself. The two full-length statues are inspired from classical and medieval art. For instance, the male figure is reminiscent of Roman sculpture. His posture mirrors that of an emperor with his arm in the air and his contrapposto (meaning that he is standing on one leg with the other slightly bent to suggest movement). As for the female figure, her demure attitude, head slightly bent, covered in an elegant drapery, with an arm bent, evokes that of the Virgin on French Gothic cathedrals.

The parapet shows another nod at the history of Middle-earth. Its bas-relief depicts a ship on a stormy sea, fleeing a city being submerged. To a learned reader, this sounds familiar. The story of Númenor is only hinted at in the corresponding chapter, 'The Window on the West' but through the illustration, another clue is given.

In the Folio Society edition, the illustration for this chapter is more straightforward, depicting the cave where Faramir takes Frodo, Sam and Gollum. To find a reference to the past, one must move to *The Return of the King*, in the chapter 'The Ride of the Rohirrim', in which Théoden and his men make their way toward Minas Tirith in the Drúadan Forest. Grathmer and Fraser depict a paved road leading into a dark forest with trees shaped like crooked fingers. In the foreground, huge rocks frame the road. Upon close examination, one notices Greek-inspired columns, almost swallowed by the rock. We can guess that the artists did not mean to suggest that the army was actually in Greek territory, but that these shapes would instantly suggest an antique past to the viewer. By referring to a symbol of the past that was not imagined by Tolkien, but that many readers will identify, the artists create echoes between the present times of Middle-earth, its past and the past of the Primary World – our world – that is still visible in our present. In this respect, we can trace a similar inspiration in Alan Lee when he paints statues inspired by Antiquity or the Middle-Ages to suggest that Osgiliath is a very old city, although Tolkien does not describe it visually.

A similar theme is woven in one of Alan Lee's last watercolours for the Centenary edition: *Bilbo in Rivendell*. This illustration works as a summary of the artist's work, bringing together a portrait, a still life, a landscape and decorative work. It evokes a French medieval manuscript, *The Very Rich Hours of the Duke of Berry*. The upper part of Alan Lee's composition, which could be a very decorative piece of architecture or an elaborate border design, borrows its spatial organisation from that manuscript, in which a series of arcs frame a representation of the sun – a figurative element in the Limbourg Brothers' work, but geometrical in Alan Lee's picture.

All these illustrations work in continuous echoes, evoking elements from both the Secondary and the Primary world, to mirror the rich cultural basis of Tolkien's texts.

5 – Interlacing images: variations on a similar theme

Other pictures create echoes within their corpus, and this is particularly visible in the Folio Society edition.

5.1 – Visual parallelism

These links can be made through visual parallelism, as in 'The Muster of Rohan' and the chapter just following it, 'The Siege of Gondor'. J.R.R. Tolkien's narrative is built in parallel, with the former chapter told through Merry's point of view, and the latter through Pippin's. Here Grathmer and Fraser chose to mirror the narrative process by drawing a strong visual link in the use of iconography: both illustrations are still lives of objects that are representative of the realm at the centre of the chapter. By repeating the picture's subject matter, with a variation due to the cultural identity of each realm, the artists highlight the closeness of the chapters, which is also a chronological simultaneity.

These illustrations are also the occasion to introduce the artists' version of the emblems of Rohan and Gondor, emblems which the reader will encounter again, in the chapters 'The Last Debate' and 'The Field of Cormallen'. Showcasing them first separately, gives the reader a chance to become familiar with them, and recognise them when they appear later in the book.

5.2 – Echoes of composition

Another type of interlacing consists in composing two pictures similarly. It is for instance the case of 'A Conspiracy Unmasked' and 'The Houses of Healing'. Both illustrations are composed around a steaming basin of water at the centre of the composition. The other elements are organised around the basin and are seen in a three-quarters perspective: a tea pot or water jug, white towels, and a bench or bed. Each time, the floor is drawn after a geometrical pattern.

Both illustrations convey the comfort found after hardships. In 'A Conspiracy Unmasked', the Hobbits have only just started their journey, but they revel in the idea of a hot bath. In 'The Houses of Healing', three characters slowly heal from physical and psychological wounds thanks to Aragorn and his knowledge of *athelas*.

These illustrations create links that the reader may not perceive, given the sometimes wide interval between the two images. However, they participate in unifying the book as a whole, text and image, by creating variations on a similar theme.

6 – Conclusion: "The road goes ever on". Further illustrations for Tolkien

In its 65 years of existence in published format, *The Lord of the Rings* was given interior illustrations twice in British editions. The artists took care to show in their pictures that this story is not a mere adventure tale: it spans different genres and more than the 14 months it takes for the Hobbits to bring the Ring to Mordor and come back.

Ingahild Grathmer and Eric Fraser had to consider the fact that their pictures would come before the text they were supposed to illustrate. Thus, they did not give too many details, but rather focused on landscape or used a very tight framing to keep most of the information out of frame.

Alan Lee was presented with a very different configuration, since his pictures did not depend on a specific placement within a chapter. He was then free to create images which either immersed the readers in the landscapes of Middle-earth, or spanned several different chapters in illustrations which, to attentive readers, may weave references to the rest of the story or even the rest of the legendarium.

Both Eric Fraser and Alan Lee went on to illustrate *The Hobbit*: in 1979 for Fraser, in a Folio Society edition that works as a companion to their *Lord of the Rings*, and in 1997 for Alan Lee, the same year that the Folio Society published an illustrated *Silmarillion*, this time with Francis Mosley.

Bibliography

Hammond, W.G. and C. Scull, *J.R.R. Tolkien: Artist & Illustrator,* (Boston: Houghton Mifflin, 1995).

Lee, A., *The Lord of the Rings* Sketchbook, (London: HarperCollins, 2005).

McIlwaine, C., *Tolkien: Maker of Middle-earth,* (Oxford: Bodleian Library: 2018).

Nash, P.W., *Folio 60 : A Bibliography of The Folio Society, 1947-2006,* (London: Folio Society, 2007).

Tolkien, J.R.R., *The Hobbit,* (London: Unwin Paperbacks, 1979).

Tolkien, J.R.R., I. Grathmer and E. Fraser, *The Lord of the Rings*, 3 vols (London: Folio Society, 1977).

Tolkien, J.R.R. and E. Fraser, *The Hobbit,* (London: Folio Society, 1979).

Tolkien, J.R.R. and A. Lee, *The Lord of the Rings,* (London: HarperCollinsPublishers, 1992).
— *The Hobbit* (London: HarperCollins, 1997).

Setting *The Silmarillion* to Music

Paul Corfield Godfrey

This talk, as originally delivered at the Tolkien 2019 event in Birmingham, was illustrated with extracts from the Prima Facie recordings of the 'epic scenes from The Silmarillion' as well as newly prepared examples. These have here been replaced by additional material derived from other contemporaneous talks given to the University of Oxford Tolkien Society in 2019 and during 2020 to the Tolkien Society seminar and Oxonmoot. Full references are provided at the end of the text.

It is well established that Tolkien took a highly jaundiced view of adaptations of his works, especially those involving dramatic presentation. In 1955 he commented that *The Lord of the Rings* was "quite unsuitable for dramatization" (*Letters*, Letter 144, 175), and he assumed a similarly dismissive attitude towards other adaptations for the stage such as A.A. Milne's *Toad of Toad Hall*, based on Kenneth Grahame's *The Wind in the Willows*, in an appendix to his essay 'On Fairy-stories' where he trenchantly described one would-be realistic production as an example where "disbelief had not so much to be suspended as hung, drawn and quartered" (*P&S*, 181, 185). He never appears to have committed himself to any observations on musical settings of literary material, although he seems to have disliked Wagner's *Ring* cycle and its treatment of Norse mythology. The principal difference between musical settings and purely spoken ones is, of course, the fact that the former inevitably proceed at a much slower pace than the latter (unless the words are reduced to quasi-spoken recitative); and that in consequence the abridgement of the text, already necessary for the practicalities of film or theatre performance, has to be even more extreme. This is all the more so in the case of a work like *The Silmarillion*, where much of the action proceeds in the form of narrative description and reported speech rather than the more conversational tone found in *The Hobbit* or *The Lord of the Rings*.

At the time that I began work on my cycle of 'epic scenes from *The Silmarillion*' I had been seeking permission to undertake some musical composition on *The Lord of the Rings*, but this had been confounded by confusion over the copyright resulting from Tolkien's sale of film and subsidiary rights (Corfield Godfrey 1996). But it did seem to me that *The Children of Húrin*, taking into account the large quantity of new material available following the publication of *Unfinished Tales*, could form an individual operatic treatment in its own right. I wrote accordingly to Rayner Unwin as Tolkien's publisher, but was told in no uncertain terms that the Tolkien family would refuse any rights unless they were able to hear some of the musical material and approved it. Faced with that challenge, I corralled a friendly pianist and produced a recording of the prologue to *The Children of Húrin*, myself both singing the role of Morgoth (with my head in a bucket to provide amplification) and speaking the role of the defiant Húrin. Much to my amazement, now as well as then, both Rayner Unwin and Christopher

Tolkien appreciated what I was driving at and were positively co-operative in helping me to sculpt a useable libretto from the alternative versions of the material, including some manuscript drafts that were at the time unpublished; this was of course before *The History of Middle-earth* had begun to emerge into print. Now we have a full recording of that prologue, with Laurence Cole as the implacable Morgoth and Julian Boyce as the hapless Húrin, we can perhaps appreciate what those unsuspecting listeners heard back in 1981 with the very opening of a work which is deliberately designed to shock the audience. (Full details of the singers and their roles in the recordings played during the presentations are at the end).

An additional problem now presented itself. I had originally thought of the proposed work as a straightforward opera, presented in conventional scenes; but it soon became clear that, since some excision of the various episodes in the original story was essential to keep the work within reasonable bounds (in *The Children of Húrin*, Mîm and the outlaws were early casualties) there was also a need for a narrative element which might provide some continuity. This was resolved by incorporating some choral episodes into the interludes between scenes. The result is something of a hybrid; although *The Silmarillion* could well be staged as a series of operas, it could also be performed in a purely concert version and thus might be attractive to choral societies as an alternative to similar semi-dramatic works such as *The Dream of Gerontius* or *The Damnation of Faust*. The chorus thus assumes the role of the teller of the tales, filling both a functional and explanatory. Against this background the soloists assume the dramatic function.

When the score for *The Children of Húrin* was completed, the Tolkien Society of Great Britain arranged for a performance of excerpts – with piano accompaniment – as part of the festivities at their 'Oxonmoot' in 1983. We rehearsed for the recital at Priscilla Tolkien's house in Oxford, using the piano that had belonged to Tolkien's wife Edith, and with Priscilla herself in the chorus. At that time I had no intention of proceeding further with any settings of texts from *The Silmarillion*, but was immediately besieged with requests that I should undertake such further work; and I was sent a draft libretto by Dénis Bridoux for a proposed *Beren and Lúthien*. This was wildly different in almost every way from the final text as used in the cycle, which derives from my own drafts made at that time; scenes that he had included, I had omitted, and vice versa; and the two versions had not even been able to agree in a three-act structure where the breaks between acts should fall. Nonetheless this in its turn set me thinking, and expanded my thinking in a somewhat alarming direction. I had already been perturbed by the sheer weight of explanation which had perforce been omitted from *Húrin* and, idly toying with the idea, sketched out in one evening a complete four-opera cycle. Between them these four legends contained a brief summary of the whole history of the First Age of Middle-earth. I immediately dismissed the idea as nonsense; I wrote to Helen Armstrong, then secretary of the Tolkien Society, in January 1983 that there was nothing like enough text for a first act of *Fëanor* and far too many characters involved for straightforward explanation to be possible; also that there was no text at all for the end of *The Fall of Gondolin* (unless one returned to a wholesale reworking and rewording of the early 1917-1920 drafts), and that there were dreadful gaps in structure everywhere. But I was assured by Priscilla that among her father's manuscripts there were substantial amounts of further material that might be employed.

And so indeed it proved, as over a period of more than ten years Christopher Tolkien produced *The History of Middle-earth* series which featured unpublished poetry and prose which expanded upon his father's legends in a manner that yielded the words for three further sets of what I called 'epic scenes,' making up at that time a complete cycle of four evenings (although my labours in the field were not even then concluded, as I will explain). The three 'great tales' (as Tolkien called them) of *Beren and Lúthien*, *The Children of Húrin* and *The Fall of Gondolin* were preceded by a largely narrative work entitled *Fëanor* which served as an introduction to the legends, and indeed to the Silmarils themselves. The final agreement between the Tolkien Estate and myself granted me wide-ranging permission to make use of the author's words in a "cycle of musical works" (and Christopher Tolkien kindly agreed to accept the dedication of the score of *The Children of Húrin* in acknowledgement of his assistance).

The composition of the music to explicate all this took me some fifteen years, during which I was also of course involved in the writing and performance of other works. When in 1996 I finally completed my massive set of 'epic scenes', I realised of course that I had created a work which was always going to prove a major challenge to would-be performers. The music extended over four full evenings, and involved a collection of solo singers which would have defied the casting abilities of most opera houses, as well as a chorus and orchestra of full-scale romantic proportions. It was at an early stage pointed out to me that it was the largest single work of classical music written in Wales during the twentieth century.

However, I was not altogether prepared for the decidedly unenthusiastic reception that the complete cycle would receive when it was finished. The very name of Tolkien appeared to conjure up the notion of a massively unperformable construction on a gargantuan scale – similar considerations seem to have deterred the many attempts made over the years to film *The Lord of the Rings* until Peter Jackson took up the challenge later – and although I attempted to meet these objections by preparing smaller-scale versions of individual sections, nobody seemed to be willing to even attempt to tackle any part of the whole.

Even when Simon Crosby Buttle approached me regarding the music in 2016, we initially only considered the performance of some sections of the score with chamber accompaniment; and it was not until three further factors entered the equation that our ambitions began to expand. In the first place Simon discovered the potential of the sampled orchestra and suggested that we should look at the possibility of using these sounds as the basis of recordings. The first segment recorded, Tuor's song recalling his encounter with the Vala Ulmo during the storm (*Shaping*, 216-7), certainly illustrated what could be accomplished.

Then Simon's enthusiasm for the work began to attract the attention of other singers in the Welsh National Opera, several of whom were willing to take part in these recordings – purely as an attempt to realise the music, and not with any thought of commercial profit. And the final part of the equation came from Prima Facie Records who, agreeably surprised by the level of sales of their CD featuring some of my chamber music and songs (including some of Tolkien settings) agreed to release new recordings on an international market. Quite suddenly other elements began to fall into place: Ted Nasmith, who had already produced sets of illustrations for various published editions of *The Silmarillion*, agreed to provide cover artwork as part of a profit-sharing exercise, and arrangements were made to recompense the singers for their time and effort (originally freely volunteered) from any profits that arose from the sales of the CDs. *The Fall of Gondolin* was released in 2018, and received enthusiastic reviews; we have subsequently recorded and issued both *Beren and Lúthien* and *The Children of Húrin*, with further instalments to follow.

The world of *The Silmarillion* comprehends a vast swathe of texts and dramatic scenes, and as a composer I have had to pick my way selectively through many different versions of Tolkien's sketches and legends in order to produce a cohesive musical whole. Although *The Children of Húrin* contained a considerable amount of dramatic material which could be treated in a relatively conventional manner, there were sections of the story elsewhere – including passages which Tolkien himself had left in an unfinished state – where the progress of the tale could only really be carried forward by narration, using Tolkien's own words assigned to a chorus of what I dubbed 'unseen voices.' This narration became an even more significant element in the other evenings of the cycle, to the extent that the first triptych in *Fëanor* consists entirely of this explanatory material in a choral setting, with no soloists at all appearing until the second triptych – nearly an hour into the music. Indeed, it was the sheer volume of choral writing in *Fëanor* which has led to the work being the last of the cycle to be recorded; but in one of the crucial solo scenes the Curse of Mandos is proclaimed in trenchant tones by Julian Boyce to the host of the Noldor seeking to come to Middle-earth.

In the great tales the element of the narrative chorus is not so prominent, but it is nevertheless significant in a manner that precludes the description of my *Silmarillion* as an 'operatic cycle' in the manner of Wagner. It is more akin to the notion of a 'choral drama' proposed by Rutland Boughton for his work *The Birth of Arthur* (Boughton & Buckley 1911) and which was designed to launch his own Arthurian cycle, a projected series of similar proportions to my *Silmarillion* but of which the last two evenings remain unperformed to this day.

And the process of adaptation of Tolkien's original texts in itself goes well beyond that. In the love scene when Beren first encounters Lúthien dancing in the forest of Neldoreth, the sung words derive not only from the description found in the published editions of *The Silmarillion* and *Beren and Lúthien*, but also draw from earlier sketches for the *Lay of Leithian* and later revisions, as well as Aragorn's song at Weathertop when he describes this meeting to an audience of uncomprehending hobbits. There Aragorn describes the verses as being "in the mode that is called *ann-thennath* among the Elves" (*FR*, 'A Knife in the Dark', 210). Whole essays have been written on the metrical rhythms and rhymes of this *ann-thennath* mode, but none of these have sought to define precisely what the mode might be in melodic terms; I attempt to reflect it in a tune that is close to an old English folksong with some slightly unusual and alien twists. At this crucial juncture in the drama we hear the words of Aragorn sung by the chorus as a frame to Angharad Morgan's rapturous delivery of Lúthien's Elvish hymn (from the revised *Lay of Leithian*) and its sudden interruption as Beren appears through the trees (*Lays*, 354).

There are other elements, of course, one of which is the illustration of the landscape. Tolkien's depiction of the realm of Beleriand is nowhere as elaborate as that to be found in *The Lord of the Rings*; but he does provide detailed descriptions of the realm of

Doriath, of the forest of Brethil, and of Tuor's first encounter with the sea, which provide in their turn for miniature tone-poems evoking the scene. One such is the prelude to Act Three of *Fëanor*, describing the Haven of the Swans at Alqualondë in a repetitively rocking sea-like theme.

Another of the most distinctive features of *The Silmarillion*, and one which sets the text apart from *The Lord of the Rings*, is the close involvement of the Valar with the mortals and Elves whom they encounter and seek to influence. In the primal world of the First Age this gives rise to a whole series of confrontations such as those between Tuor and Ulmo, between Morgoth and Lúthien, between Mandos and Fëanor, or indeed between Morgoth and Húrin.

Such extracts perhaps serve best to illustrate the wide variety of styles which are demanded by any attempt to encompass the realm of *The Silmarillion*, let alone to reflect the changing emphases of the dialogue between the various characters. It is also an essential part of the whole to allow for points of repose when individual singers are given space to reflect lyrically on the situation of the drama. Tolkien himself did of course provide liberal amounts of verse for this in *Beren and Lúthien*, but elsewhere it was necessary to incorporate material from other Tolkien sources; and nowhere more so than in the final sections of *The Fall of Gondolin*, where Idril would otherwise have found herself severely short-changed for anything at all to sing. She and Tuor took the text for their love duet from the poem *The Nameless Land*, where in the recording Anitra Blaxhall and Simon Crosby Buttle reflect on the prospect of the shores of Valinor beyond the seas.

And of course the lovers Beren and Lúthien have a whole series of love duets scattered through the length of their own opera, one in each of the three Acts, which form a contrast to the brutality of the scenes between Sauron and Gorlim, between Sauron and Finrod, and finally and most cataclysmically between Morgoth and Lúthien. The first encounter between the two lovers forms a sudden moment of stillness at the centre of Act One, as Daeron's flute is heard offstage and the chorus begin to sing Aragorn's ballad about the lovers from *The Lord of the Rings*. The theme of Aragorn's ballad recurs throughout the score and at the end of Act One, as Lúthien falls into Beren's arms, it forms a slowly moving meditation where Daeron's flute is contrasted with the remainder of the orchestra playing the music associated earlier with Beren.[1]

But of course *Beren and Lúthien* is more than simply a love story, it is the mythic tale of the Quest for the Silmaril; and the encounter between Lúthien and Morgoth in the Halls of Angband is the dramatic climax of the work. Here, as elsewhere in the cycle, the lead role is taken over by the chorus who narrate the story in Tolkien's own words. They describe Lúthien plunging Morgoth into slumber, Beren cutting the Silmaril from the Iron Crown and the resulting crack of thunder which rouses the forces of Angband from sleep, until the scene ends as the wolf Carcharoth swallows the Silmaril which sears his inward flesh.

The conclusion of *Beren and Lúthien*, too, brought particular problems resulting from Tolkien's failure to complete the *Lay of Leithian*. When Angharad Morgan as Lúthien sings before Mandos, she takes her text from the sketch that Tolkien entitled "a

1. I have discussed the construction of the music of these three love duets in greater detail in a half-hour illustrated talk which may be heard on YouTube (Corfield Godfrey 2019).

fragment from the end of the poem" (*Lays*, 308), and the restoration of Beren to life is then succeeded by the final verse of Aragorn's song of the lovers from *The Lord of the Rings*. The music, of course, recalls the initial meeting of the lovers two Acts before.

The text for *The Children of Húrin*, more complete in itself and more wholly finished by Tolkien both as published in *The Silmarillion* and later as a full-length prose narrative, required much less intervention in order to produce a musically and dramatically coherent setting. Nonetheless there were places where the dialogue provided by Tolkien simply failed, and even in the original version of the story in the *Book of Lost Tales* we were vouchsafed precious little in the form of dialogue for a crucial episode such the death of Beleg. I could simply have rendered the drama in visual terms, but the involvement of the chorus describing the scene and the action adds an additional dimension.

As the drama proceeds, and the description of the action by Tolkien becomes more continuous, the narrative role of the chorus disappears altogether. But with the advent of The Fall of Gondolin the situation changes again. There are some elements of continuous narrative and dramatic dialogue, especially in the stories of Maeglin and of Tuor's coming to Gondolin, but elsewhere the story is carried forward almost exclusively in terms of annalistic prose with occasional scraps of dialogue which can be derived from the very early 'lost tale' written in 1917. Any lyrical expansion has to come from the use of Tolkien's poetry written on or about the subject over a period of many years, and much of this too requires adaptation before it can be employed in a musical context. At the end of *The Fall of Gondolin*, I provided an Epilogue that combines two of Tolkien's poems. One is *The Happy Mariners*, written originally in 1915 but continually revised until at least 1940, which seems to have been identified as the "song of the Sleeper in the Tower of Pearl" (*Lost Tales II*, 275-6). It is a poem addressing those voyaging beyond the seas from one who has been left behind, a situation that in some ways anticipates that at the end of *The Lord of the Rings*; and, just as Frodo there hears "the sound of singing that came over the water", here a distant semi-chorus gives us the Elvish poem *The Last Ark* written in 1931 but revised much later (*RK*, 'The Grey Havens', 310).

Such wide-ranging conjunctions of material were of course necessitated by the scarcity of material for the narrative of the legends which conclude Tolkien's mythology of the First Age of Middle-earth; and they became even more extreme in the case of *The War of Wrath*, the final conclusion of the cycle which I long regarded as unachievable, and indeed only completed writing in the spring of 2020 after prompting from Simon Crosby Buttle. In assembling the textual material I made considerable use of the setting I had earlier made for solo voice and orchestra of Bilbo's *The Lay of Eärendil* in an attempt to supply a conclusion for the originally tentative ending of the *Silmarillion* cycle; this was now expanded into choral narrative which framed the dramatic setting of other material from the concluding pages of the text as sketched by Tolkien in the 1930s. Other material, including the ruin of Doriath, drew on passages from the published *Silmarillion* mixed with my own adaptation of the *Tale of the Nauglafring* and passages illustrating the Second Age of Middle-earth drawn both from *Of the Rings of Power* and *The Lord of the Rings* itself (*Lost Tales II*, 231-2).[2]

2. Preliminary recordings of brief sections of the score can be heard in a YouTube video by Simon Crosby Buttle discussing the work and cited among the references below.

But work on the recording of *The War of Wrath* had hardly commenced before the onset of the worldwide viral pandemic brought the whole process to an abrupt halt. We very much hoped in 2020 to return to the recording not only of *The War of Wrath* but also *Fëanor* (which had largely been completed before the process halted) and then to furnish an appendix including fragments and episodes from my projected cycle on *The Lord of the Rings* (written before *The Silmarillion* and which later found echoes within it). We expect that these instalments of the project will continue to appear during 2021-2022 and beyond; but in the meantime my 'cycle of musical works' based on Tolkien is also continuing to expand, and the original material for *The Lord of the Rings* has also acquired momentum of its own binding the material of *The Silmarillion* into a musical unity with *The Lord of the Rings*. In this new writing, for example, we find that the music of Gondolin is closely reflected in that for Lothlórien, some six thousand years later in the history of Middle-earth. In the same way Galadriel's '*Namarië*' as envisaged by Tolkien had already made its way into *Beren and Lúthien*, quite apart from Aragorn's song; and Bilbo's version of 'The Lay of Eärendil' is redolent of themes from *The Silmarillion* which combine into ever-new counterpoints and developments.

The texts which comprise *The War of Wrath* indeed come from widely extended intervals throughout the whole of Tolkien's creative career. They include the poem 'The Shores of Faery', which Tolkien himself identified as the "first poem of my mythology" which is sung during the prologue to the work, and the immediately succeeding scene where Círdan seeks to follow the other Elves to Valinor and is prevented by Ulmo – a text written some sixty years later (*Lost Tales II*, 271).

The parallels are underlined by the use of the original Anglo-Saxon verse couplet about Earendel which had first inspired the author, given in the Elvish translation which he had contrived for use by Frodo in *The Lord of the Rings*; this returns to frame the later verses, which set the drama in the context of a mortal existence. At one stage I contemplated the use of 'Bilbo's Last Song', either in the form that Tolkien revised it in the late 1960s or in its earlier 1930s version as Vestr am haf, but eventually I concluded that the poem itself was too bound up with the events of *The Lord of the Rings* to be satisfactory in a *Silmarillion* context. I accordingly took up a suggestion by Wayne Hammond and Christina Scull that I should investigate the possibilities of using some of Tolkien's other early poems, and I saw potential in the lengthy poem *Kortirion* which he had written in 1915 but had subjected to later revision including a final overhaul in the 1960s when the verses were considered for inclusion in the published collection *The Adventures of Tom Bombadil*. Tolkien himself rejected such an idea – "they would upset the boat" – but it seemed to me that some selections from the lengthy poem, celebrating the continuing presence of the ideals represented by the Elves in the modern world, would make a perfect conclusion to a cycle which sought to encapsulate *The Silmarillion* as a whole, and to *The War of Wrath* in particular (*Lost Tales I*, 32).

By its very nature then *The War of Wrath* is less dramatically conceived, more episodic, than the other segments of the *Silmarillion* cycle, but nonetheless it has a theatrical validity; and, as in the other works, stage directions are included in the score. But even so the work, like the other 'epic scenes', can perhaps be viewed as a sort of secular cantata which may indeed best be encountered through the medium of sound recording, where listeners can mentally supply their own visual images to counterpoint the aural effect. Such a recording, which allows for the detailed interweaving of the choirs to be fully appreciated, would inevitably be very difficult to realise in the context of live performance.

At the same time the medium of recording does serve to obviate Tolkien's own objections to dramatic adaptation; a sympathetic treatment of the text can assist readers to come to terms with a narrative that may be relatively unfamiliar to them, and at the same time both expand the emotional range of that narrative and make it more accessible. And it also has the merit of simultaneously avoiding the crude representation of events and the simplification of the author's intention. At least, that appears to be the view of some of those, most notably Chris Seeman of the *Tolkien Music List*, who has commented on and reviewed these 'epic scenes' (2019).

When I presented excerpts from my cycle of "epic scenes from *The Silmarillion* after the mythology of J.R.R. Tolkien" in Birmingham at the Tolkien 2019 event and again during the 2020 seminar of the Tolkien Society, I was asked by members of the audience if I could give some explanation as to the manner in which I had approached the musical setting. To give any such comprehensive description would be a mammoth task, since all nine hours of the music are so closely interwoven; but I might perhaps be permitted to address one particular aspect of the music here, with the suggestion that for more detailed investigations listeners might be referred to the thematic analysis on my website as well as the booklet notes for the currently available recordings.

It is inevitable that in such a large-scale piece of writing the melodic themes will assume dramatic significance in the same way as Wagner's use of *Leitmotive* in his *Ring* cycle. Similar techniques were, for example, employed by Elgar in his projected triptych of oratorios beginning with *The Apostles* and *The Kingdom*. But in *The Silmarillion* I have gone farther, attempting to suggest the conflict between the various realms of the mythology by a contrast in the harmonic language employed. This too was anticipated by Wagner. In the *Ring* the joyous acclamations of the Rhinegold by the Rhinemaidens are transformed during Hagen's Watch in *Götterdämmerung* into a baleful theme representing the power of the Ring which has been forged from the gold, to chilling effect. Wagner, uncharacteristically bashful when it came to describing his own compositional procedures, was particularly proud of this effect, drawing attention to it in a published essay (Wagner 1879). But it was Deryck Cooke who showed how it was even more closely bound into the whole by illustrating the manner in which the new and darkened harmonies were drawn from the notes of the very theme of the Ring itself (Cooke 1967).

In my setting of *The Silmarillion* I began, as all music does, from a single tone which was then expanded harmonically in a manner which was designed explicitly to colour the character of the music and the essence of the thematic material. At the very beginning of *Fëanor*, the first of the set of epic scenes, in music that derives directly from my third symphony *Ainulindalë*, we hear a chord that is intended to represent the primal chaos from which Ilúvatar begins his work of creation. This begins with a single note played by all the double-basses, which is then elaborated with a series of major thirds in the divided cellos, a series of *minor* thirds in the similarly divided violas, a superimposed scale of *major* seconds in the second violins (a sort of whole-tone scale of the kind espoused by Debussy and the impressionists) and finally a cluster of solo first violins playing every tone in the chromatic scale (an effect familiar from Ligeti's *Lux aeterna* as used in the film 2001), to represent the ultimate in chaos. The extreme disharmony then resolves itself back into the single note, and this same process is then repeated at a faster and more urgent speed before the theme of Ilúvatar himself emerges, constructed on a series of open fifths and fourths – the ultimate in consonance – to resolve the complexity with his creation of the Valar.

The Valar themselves have a whole series of themes which serve to define their characters and attributes. The Elder King in *Fëanor*, for example, adheres as solidly as a rock – or as Nature itself – to a single note for all his utterances. Morgoth attempts to emulate that sense of power and immutability; but he is constantly drawn to a new pitch a semi-tone higher or lower, and his vassal Sauron seems to exist in a realm consisting almost entirely of these semi-tonal drifts. Against these, Mandos also adheres to a single note underpinning a pair of changing chords which shift like ghosts from one key to another with the unrelated dichotomy between major and minor modes exposed. At the end of *Beren and Lúthien*, as Lúthien undertakes her pilgrimage to plead before Mandos, this alternation becomes the only element to be heard in the music, and it is this theme, now expanded and developed, which returns as Beren is restored to life.

Ulmo similarly takes a single note and shades it by reference to the fifth above and the fifth below to provide a sense of shifting reflections on water. This elemental succession of chords is first heard in *Fëanor* as he raises a storm against the Kinslayers; but it also manifests itself as a brief tag of five notes which underpins many passages of the music and perhaps reaches its apotheosis during the epilogue to *The Fall of Gondolin* where, as Tuor departs on his voyage over the seas, it is heard superimposed upon itself in three different rhythmic patterns which underlie the main melodic material. Yavanna in her creation of the Two Trees similarly employs the interval of a fifth to separate two individual iterations of her theme, although when the idea recurs later it is usually reunited into a single strand of melody.

The Elves in turn expand this harmonic basis into a modal inflection, like a free-flowing folk version of mediaeval plainchant. This is heard at its most elemental in the hymn to Ilúvatar sung by the people of Gondolin to greet the arrival of summer; it is this same musical material which will then recur in the music for Lothlórien. But similar folk modalities also underpin the melody of Aragorn's song about the meeting of Beren and Lúthien. (By the way, it may be noted that even when Tolkien himself comes closest to approximating English folk style in his writing, he is often startlingly iconoclastic about his approach. Frodo's song in the *Prancing Pony*, for example, not only has verses each consisting of five rather than the anticipated four lines found in the original nursery rhyme, but the prosody of each of these verses falls without any sense of artifice into eleven bars instead of the normative twelve – and folk interpretations of the song have therefore not uncommonly to resort to some stretching of the natural rhythm simply in order to make the words fit.)

The Men who interact with the Elves are more romantically modern, with chromatic shifts that give a sense of impermanence and instability. Thus the main theme associated with mortal Men as the Second Children of Ilúvatar (which also originated in my *Ainulindalë* symphony) forms the principal subject of the duet between Tuor and Idril following their wedding in Gondolin. This all sounds terribly technical, I know; but it does hopefully serve also to bring a sense of unity to the contrasts of the music, in which the implacable declamation of the Elder King and the shifting chromatic thrustings of Ungoliant can exist together.

I have briefly alluded earlier to the manner in which Morgoth attempts to imitate and subvert the harmonic structure which has emerged from the primal chaos. This begins from the very outset of the cycle, where his already highly chromatic themes are often set against the more concordant tonality which surround them: "thoughts of his own unlike those of his brethren," to quote Tolkien's own words in the *Ainulindalë* (*Silmarillion*, 4). The results of these contrasts are graphically described by Tolkien – "straightway discord arose about him" which "rose in uproar and contended with" the music of Ilúvatar – and lead in their turn to still more extremely discordant clashes (16). The same basic elements are also to be found in the music for Glaurung, who is described in Tolkien's text as "speaking by the evil spirit that was in him" (213). And, as I have observed earlier, the music of his servant Sauron takes this same minor second and winds it around in a serpent-like chromatic writhing. As such Jasey Hall's probing is contrasted with the nervous interjections of Simon Crosby Buttle as Finrod Felagund in his attempts to impersonate a disguised Orc, using Morgoth's own themes and harmonies without (it must be confessed) much conviction. And when Morgoth in the shape of Laurence Cole does finally encounter Lúthien as an unexpected guest in his halls, something even more unexpected happens. The immortal Vala suddenly finds himself conceiving a passion for the beauty of the Elven maiden, and his bold upthrusting theme (first conceived for the opening of *The Children of Húrin*) is transformed into a delicate rising wistful phrase at first on the clarinet and then on the violins. And then, hesitantly, a slow waltz-like theme makes its presence felt, although it is continually being thwarted by a more brutal martial beat which derives from the music where he had earlier removed her disguise from Lúthien. And the characteristic semitonal clashes of his music elsewhere are totally banished until the very end of his lyrical effusion, where they are reintroduced by the seductive tone of a solo violin as Lúthien offers to dance for him. The slothful gardens of Tolkien's poem have an insidious venom.

That sense of venom is of course an ever-present menace in *The Silmarillion*, far more so than in the more optimistic *Lord of the Rings* – although of course that is not to gainsay the ultimate sadness and sense of loss of the latter work. Even when Julian Boyce as Húrin salutes the courage of Helen Greenaway as the dying Morwen at the end of *The Children of Húrin*, his sense of challenge – as the melody associated with mortal Men dies slowly away – is closed by the theme associated with the narration of the Narn itself, in which Morgoth's semitonal discords are a perpetual if transitory element. I was understandably delighted when Brian Wilson in a recent review of the recording of *The Children of Húrin* (Wilson 2020) drew particular attention to this passage, and underlined the parallels with the same point in the score of Wagner's *Götterdämmerung*. Which brings us back full circle to where we began.

Bibliography

Boughton, R. and R. Buckley, *Music Drama of the Future,* (London: William Reeves, 1911).

Buttle, S.C., *The Beginning and the End,* Volante Opera productions (YouTube, 2020) <https://youtu.be/77jg4X7UnnI?si= RgZCxLPUSXaABFS0>.

Cooke, D., *Der Ring des Nibelungen*: An Introduction, (Decca, 443 581-2, 1967).

Corfield Godfrey, P., *Words on Music,* (Cardiff: Zarathustra Press, 1996). Preface to *The Silmarillion* available on the website https://sites.google.com/site/paulcorfieldgodfrey/the-silmarillion
— *Epic Scenes from* The Silmarillion *after the mythology of J R R Tolkien.* [1] *Fëanor*, Prima Facie (2 CDs, forthcoming): [2] *Beren and Lúthien*, Prima Facie PFCD 110/11 (2 CDs, 2019): [3] *The Children of Húrin*, Prima Facie PFCD 126/27 (2 CDs, 2020): [4] *The Fall of Gondolin*, Prima Facie PFCD 092/93 (2 CDs, 2018): [5] *The War of Wrath*, Prima Facie (2 CDs, forthcoming). Booklet notes by the composer. Principal singers: Anitra Blaxhall, soprano (Idril): Julian Boyce, baritone (Beren, Mandos, Húrin, Gwindor, Voronwë, Eöl, Círdan): Simon Crosby Buttle, tenor (Fëanor, Túrin, Tuor, Finrod, Eärendil, Elrond): Michael Clifton-Thompson, tenor (Gorlim, Saeros, Dorlas, Olwë, Maglor): Laurence Cole, bass (Morgoth): Helen Greenaway, mezzo-soprano (Morwen): Jasey Hall, bass (Sauron): Helen Jarmany, mezzo-soprano (Melian): Emma Mary Llewellyn, soprano (Finduilas, Elbereth): Huw Llewellyn, tenor (Curufin): Martin Lloyd, bass (Thingol, Ulmo): Philip Lloyd-Evans, baritone (Beleg, Brandir, Ecthelion, Eönwë): Angharad Morgan, soprano (Lúthien, Niënor, Galadriel): George Newton-Fitzgerald, bass (Turgon, Glaurung, Elder King): Louise Ratcliffe, mezzo-soprano (Aredhel): Stephen Wells, baritone (Maeglin, Mablung, Maedhros), Sophie Yelland, mezzo-soprano (Elwing)
— *Beren and Lúthien*: an analysis, Volante Opera Productions (YouTube, 2019) <https://youtu.be/DCzPkOJTwJo?si= TimvKuulfFzxpmi9>.

Seeman, C., *The Tolkien Music List,* (2017-2020) <www.tolkien-music.com>

Tolkien, J.R.R., *The Fellowship of the Ring*, 2nd edn. (London: George Allen and Unwin, 1967).
— *The Two Towers*, 2nd edn. (London: George Allen and Unwin, 1967).
— *The Silmarillion,* ed. by C. Tolkien (London: George Allen and Unwin, 1977).
— *Poems and Stories,* (London: George Allen and Unwin, 1980).
— *Letters of J R R Tolkien,* ed. by H. Carpenter with the assistance of C. Tolkien (London: George Allen and Unwin, 1981).
— *The Book of Lost Tales* Part One, ed. by C. Tolkien (London: George Allen and Unwin, 1983).
— *The Book of Lost Tales* Part Two, ed. by C. Tolkien (London: George Allen and Unwin, 1984).
— *The Lays of Beleriand,* ed. by C. Tolkien (London: George Allen and Unwin, 1985).
— *The Shaping of Middle-earth,* ed. by C. Tolkien (London: George Allen and Unwin, 1986).

Wagner, R., *On the application of Music to the Drama,* (1879), trans. by D. Cooke, in *I Saw the World End* (London: Oxford University Press, 1979) 44.

Wilson, B., "Review: *The Children of Húrin*", Music Web International (2020) <ww.musicweb-international.com/classrev/2020/ Jun/Godfrey_Hurin_PFCD126.htm>

"Independently real, but viewed by a different eye": Tolkien's reactions to others' Middle-earth art

Jeremy Edmonds

J.R.R. Tolkien provided the illustrations for *The Hobbit* himself, and in 1956 stated he was "not myself eager to have an illustrated edition" of *The Lord of the Rings* (Scull and Hammond 2017, 518). In 1961, Cor Blok said that Tolkien "did not want readers to see his characters through the eyes of any individual artist, as we see Alice through the eyes of John Tenniel or Don Quixote through those of Gustave Doré" (2011, 15). With the exploding popularity of the *Hobbit* and *The Lord of the Rings*, it was inevitable that other artists would illustrate the world of Middle-earth whether as professionals working for the publishers, or fans who were drawn to share their own visions.

Tolkien himself saw many of these artistic impressions, and had much to say about them. including how important he felt it was for illustrations to be accurate to his text in tone and feeling. In a 1962 letter to Rayner Unwin, Tolkien pointed out that "there is an illustrative as well as a pictorial side to take into account" when illustrating a book (Scull and Hammond 2017, 628). Tolkien once told Rayner Unwin "I wish the commonest reaction of admirers was not the desire to tinker with it!" (546) Tolkien seems to have had two types of reaction to others' illustrations of Middle-earth. Either it completely missed the mark and was in his words "horrible", "mordoresque", or "frightful", or he found many details to like. His exposure to these illustrations was primarily through foreign publications, and his first introduction to these illustrations was when he received complimentary or gift copies soon before or even long after they were published. Almost always his only recourse to complain was to Rayner Unwin or other staff at George Allen & Unwin, but he also often corresponded with the artists, as well.

Tolkien found many published Middle-earth illustrations he didn't like. In 1947 the first translation of *The Hobbit* was released in Sweden, illustrated by Torbjörn Zetterholm. In various letters Tolkien says Zettgerholm took "impertinent and unwarranted liberties with the text", that the illustrations are "frightful" and "quite out of tune with the tone of the text" (584-5) and that he "makes [Gollum] look huge" (348). He writes to a friend that he does not approve of the cover art for the 1959 Swedish translation of *The Fellowship of the Ring* which he thinks contradicts the text – Scull and Hammond describes this illustration as "somewhat in the style of archaic Greek paintings" (590). In 1960, he said of the simplistic, childlike illustrations in the Polish *Hobbit* drawn by Jan Młodożeniec that they are "mordoresque" (595). The 1962 Portuguese *Hobbit* illustrations by António Quadros he regarded as "horrible" (Kilby 1976, 23). He thinks the cover of the 1963 Polish *Return of the King* is of a "Mordor hideousness" (Scull and Hammond 2017, 643). For proposed illustrations for the 1957 German edition of *The Hobbit* he says they are "too 'Disnified' for my taste: Bilbo with a dribbling nose, and Gandalf as a figure of vulgar fun rather than the Odinic wanderer that I think of" (*Letters*, Letter 107, 119). In 1964 Princess magazine published a Ferguson Dewar illustrated version of *The Hobbit*.

Tolkien says of these "I should myself wish at least that Gandalf were less fussy and over-clad and had some dignity. He should not be styled 'magician' but 'wizard'" (Scull and Hammond 2017, 654). Also in 1964, Houghton Mifflin considered Maurice Sendak (author and illustrator of, for example, *Where the Wild Things Are*) as the illustrator for a proposed deluxe *Hobbit*. The project eventually fell apart, but Rayner Unwin wrote that Tolkien was "not wildly happy about the proportions of the figures" that Sendak had drawn (724).

For the Italian *Lord of the Rings* published in 1967 illustrated by R. Conti, Scull and Hammond say Tolkien was horrified by the cover, "based on and even degraded from the frightful Ballantine cover" (753). To understand more of what Tolkien is referring to here, a bit of history about the Ace Books controversy is needed. In 1965 in the USA, Ace Books felt that the copyright for Tolkien's *The Lord of the Rings* was not covered and the books were in the public domain, and began preparing to release a paperback version. They used Jack Gaughan, a well known graphic arts style illustrator, for the cover art and frontispieces. *The Fellowship of the Ring* came out in May of 1965 but Ace's plans had leaked and Rayner Unwin and Tolkien were aware of it a few months before. A race was under way, with Ace rushing to get the second and third volumes in print quickly and Ballantine (under agreement with Houghton Mifflin and George Allen & Unwin) charged with getting the authorized editions in print as soon as possible.

Barbara Remington was an in-house artist for Ballantine. Without any advance warning or time to read any of the books, "she had to produce the *Hobbit* cover in only three hours, and was then instructed to put an animal (the offending lion) in an empty space" (745). In response to his first viewing of this *Hobbit* cover, Tolkien writes to Ballantine saying he "will not enter into a debate about taste – (meaning though I did not say so: horrible colours and foul lettering) – but I must ask this about the vignette: what has it got to do with the story? Where is this place? Why a lion and emus? And what is the thing in the foreground with pink bulbs? I do not understand how anybody who has read the tale (I hope you are one) could think such a picture would please the author" (*Letters*, Letter 277, 362). Summarizing a phone call that Betty Ballantine had with Tolkien soon after, he writes to Rayner "With regard to the pink bulbs she said as if to one of complete obtusity: 'they are meant to suggest a Christmas tree'" (363). It is important to note that Tolkien is clearly focused on what will please the author, while Betty is focused on what will sell more copies of the book. It is a rare occasion where any author is pleased with the cover illustration that they are given, or even if it is accurate to the text.

Soon after, and again without time to read the books, Remington had to quickly paint covers for all three of *The Lord of the Rings* paperback volumes, and decided to do one large painting that could be divided into thirds by Ballantine for the cover illustrations. Barbara has since said, "If I read *The Lord of the Rings* first, I don't think I could have drawn the cover art" (Hage 2007).

On the other side of the race, Humphrey Carpenter writes "Ace Books for all their moral 'piracy' had employed a cover artist who knew something about the story" (Carpenter 1977, 228). Ace cover illustrator Jack Gaughan recounts his side of the story – he was given a weekend to read *The Fellowship of the Ring*, and he "was afraid that should I have illustrated the stories as I think they *should* be illustrated, we'd miss the market. [...] So I chose scenes wherein I could minimize the fairy-tale visual qualities and play up those which related to S.F. as it was now being sold" (Gaughan 1965, 47). He chose yellow for Gandalf "for display reasons" and even offered to fix this mistake when the proper color was pointed out, but it was too late in the publishing process (47). A few weeks afterwards, rumors emerged that Ballantine was also going to release the books, and Gaughan was again given a single weekend to read both *The Two Towers* and *The Return of the King*, and to paint the covers for them. He of course could not possibly do all of this in that amount of time, so he had his very good friend Lin Carter come over and give him a short synopsis of both books from which he painted his cover illustrations. Gaughan sums up by saying "I myself do not like the covers I did for Ace. They are not illustrations of the story" (49). In one specific example in regards to the flying horse instead of pterodactyl, he says "the error on *The Two Towers* cover is mine alone" (65, 38).

Beyond book covers and interior illustrations, there was other art that bothered Tolkien for one reason or another. One infamous question that Tolkien asked in reference to the 1958 movie script from George Zimmerman was "Why does Z put beaks and feathers on *Orcs*!? (*Orcs* is not a form of *Auks*)" (*Letters*, Letter 210, 274). Tolkien had many strong critiques of this script outside the scope of this paper but according to Rayner "he actually liked the specimen artwork" which was done by Ron Cobb (Unwin 1999, 107). While Cobb's artwork for the *Lord of the Rings* project has been lost, a small *Hobbit* figure he later drew was published in Mythlore survives, along with a portfolio of other film concept art he produced later in his quite successful career working on dozens of films such as *Star Wars*, *Alien* and *Raiders of the Lost Ark*. "He thinks that the artist Ron Cobb and the model-maker Jon Lackey have real talent. [...] the chief and special talent of the group obviously lies, and will lie, in the scenic, & pictorial" (Scull and Hammond 2017, 545-6). Another artist named Marc Simont also drew orcs with feathers and beaks in his 1954 review of *The Fellowship of the Ring* (Simont 1954, 106). Perhaps it is possible that Zimmerman and Simont, both American, had been exposed to L. Frank Baum's *Wizard of Oz* books, where the ninth book, *The Scarecrow of Oz*, features a race of creatures called "Orks", which can be best described as scrawny, four-winged feathered beasts with a prominent beak and a propeller for a tail. The later Oz books were not popular at the time in England, and thus these Orks were not at all likely to be known to Tolkien – for example, no Baum books are mentioned in Oronzo Cilli's *Tolkien's Library*.

Tolkien found a few more opportunities to critique Middle-earth related art in his later years. For example, when commenting on Robert J. Lee's illustrations for *The Hobbit* extract that appear in the 1966 volume titled *The Children's Treasury of Literature*, Tolkien says that they seem "vulgar, stupid and entirely out of keeping with the text" (Scull and Hammond 2017, 720). For a 1972 Gollum poster with hot pink orders and a lime green Gollum centered in a curving stone block wall, he says "I provided Miss Hill with a copy of a fearful thing bearing in enormous letters GOLLUM [...] they are even on sale in reputable bookshops like Blackwell's" (807).

Tolkien found other artists more appealing. He had a decades-long warm relationship with Pauline Baynes as an illustrator and a friend. For the 1961 Puffin *Hobbit*, he tells Joy Hill that "[h]e likes it very much" (602). In regards to *The Adventures of Tom*

Bombadil, Tolkien writes to Baynes that he "thought of you, because you seem able to produce wonderful pictures with a touch of 'fantasy', but primarily bright and clear visions of things that one might really see", and "I have vivid visual pictures of those pieces that are narrative, but I cannot communicate them. Nor will they be the same as those awakened in the mind of readers. But I believe that yours will be of the order and mode which I should like, and will in fact probably enrich my own imagination" (613, 625). After seeing her *Bombadil* illustrations, he writes again to say "I do not think they could have been more after my own heart. I am not surprised: I felt certain that anything you produced would delight me – and make me deeply envious of your skill" (627). He has been quoted as saying she would not be a suitable illustrator for *The Lord of the Rings* – while she cannot, he says, "rise to anything more noble or awe-inspiring" (761) than her lighter hearted illustrations for *Tom Bombadil* and *Farmer Giles*, he did end up liking her illustration for *The Lord of the Rings* deluxe boxed set – Rayner writes to Baynes to tell her Tolkien "was enchanted and said you had exactly his eye for landscape and asked if, when we had finished using it for technical reproduction, he could have your original on permanent loan in his study" (653). Also, for her *Map of Middle-earth* Tolkien tells her that "some of these pictures agree remarkably with my own vision: especially the first four on the right (Minas Morgul is almost exact)" (McIlwaine 2018, 384). He does write "a private memorandum critical of Paunline Baynes' poster-map, especially her rendering of characters in *The Lord of the Rings*. Among other points, he notes the relative heights of Hobbits and of the Company of the Ring. But he praises her lettering and some of her vignettes, and excuses her for not knowing details the text does not reveal or make clear" (Scull and Hammond 2017, 783).

In 1956 Doris Elizabeth Sykes sent some samples of her artwork to Tolkien that she hoped could be used for an illustrated edition of *The Lord of the Rings*. While these illustrations have not been seen publicly since, we know Tolkien writes that they are "extremely good […] they not only in many cases correspond closely to my vision, but even enrich it. I was particularly delighted by Treebeard with Merry and Pippin in his arms; but all your hobbits are admirable, and also the orcs, and Gimli (Tolkien 1956). I also thought the scene under 'Weathertop' and the Witch-king powerful. It was tackled in the only possible way: making Frodo and the King visible and the other Companions shadowy […] Aragorn alone does not closely correspond to my vision […] I think of him as sterner, keener and in face less 'Greek' and straight-nosed, more Roman" (Scull and Hammond 2017, 511). Also Tolkien gives her advice that "the best way of doing hobbits is to make them absolutely ordinary human beings (except for a neat gaiter or buskin of hair), and not too childlike, roundeyed, etc." (Tolkien 1956)

Cor Blok sent paintings to Tolkien around 1961, and also visited him personally. Tolkien wrote to Rayner about the first pieces he saw that he "thought them most attractive […] I should very much like to see some more, in the hope that some more will be as good as 'The Battle of the Hornburg'. The other four I thought were attractive as pictures, but bad as illustrations. But I suppose it is impossible to hope, nowadays, that one might come across an artist of talent who would, or would even try to depict the noble and the heroic" (Blok 2011, 7). While Blok's artwork is definitely not realistic, Tolkien was drawn to some of the pieces quite strongly. The ones he liked most had very small figures and did a good job representing the events in the text.

In 1963, Virgil Finlay was considered for a deluxe edition of *The Hobbit* by Houghton Mifflin in the United States. Tolkien was sent a sampling of this art for his approval, and he wrote back that "[t]hough it gives prospects of a general treatment rather heavier and more violent and airless than I should like – I thought it was good, and actually I thought Bilbo's rather rotund and babyish (but anxious) face was in keeping with his character (up to that point)" (Scull and Hammond 2017, 641).

According to Clyde S. Kilby, Tolkien definitely liked the first Japanese edition of *The Hobbit*. He found it "in many ways astonishing" and "showed [Kilby] with particular satisfaction the frontispiece which portrayed Smaug falling convulsively over Dale" (Kilby 1976, 23).

Tolkien also told Charlotte and Denis Plimmer in an interview discussing filming and illustrating *The Lord of the Rings* that he felt "Arthur Rackham would be good for the treeish parts" (Plimmer 1966). Tolkien "was impressed by visualizations [...] by artist Ron Cobb, whom Tolkien compared favourably to Arthur Rackham" and "[s]ome of Tolkien's own art has Rackhamesque qualities" (Scull and Hammond 2017, 19, 106).

In 1968 Mary Fairburn sent some of her paintings to Tolkien, which he enjoyed very much. After seeing Mary's artwork, however, he not only offered to purchase some, he changed his mind about the possibility of having an illustrated edition of *The Lord of the Rings* and approached Rayner about using her art. Enough of her artwork has survived or she made new versions of that HarperCollins was able to feature her art in their 2015 calendar. For her illustration titled 'Galadriel' Tolkien says that it "attracts me because it so very nearly corresponds to my own mental vision of the scene" (772).

Ted Nasmith sent his illustration 'The Unexpected Party' to Tolkien in the summer of 1972, showing Gandalf revealing Thráin's map to an expectant party of Dwarves and Bilbo gathered around a single lamp in a dark room. Tolkien replied with generally quite positive feedback "both praising the work and making the comment that Bilbo seemed too childlike" (Nasmith).

Princess Margrethe wrote to Tolkien to express how much she liked *The Lord of the Rings*, and included some illustrations she had made for it. Tolkien, mindful that he was writing back to Danish royalty, wrote back "At times I have been struck by a resemblance between them and attempts of my own (unpublished); but more often by their unexpectedness – as if the story and the landscapes were independently real, but viewed by a different eye. The device of illustrating the theme or 'air' of chapters instead of particular events or characters is successful, especially in providing a running contrast between glimpses of sinister darkness and homely simplicity, which is characteristic of the tale" (McIlwaine 2018, 106). In a 1979 interview, Queen Margrethe said "when I read Tolkien's book, the tale so moved me that I thought: Oh, if only it was real! If only something like that existed in real life!" (Margrethe 1992, 11). Her illustrations were later used, slightly modified for publication by Eric Fraser, in the Folio Society illustrated editions of *The Lord of the Rings.*

Tolkien was repeatedly moved by the illustrations of many artists and his internal vision of what Middle-earth looked like in landscape, atmosphere, and panoramic views was often matched or exceeded by these other artists, lending some credence to the conceit that Middle-earth was real and just discovered by Tolkien. Perhaps "other minds and hands" were catching glimpses of the fantastic world that he has shared with us all (*Letters*, Letter 131, 145).

Bibliography

Baum, L.F., *The Scarecrow of Oz,* (Chicago: Reilly & Britton, 1915).

Blok, C., *A Tolkien Tapestry,* (London: HarperCollins, 2011).

Carpenter, H., *Tolkien: A Biography,* (Boston: Houghton Mifflin, 1977).

Cilli, O., *Tolkien's Library: An Annotated Checklist,* (Edinburgh: Luna Press Publishing, 2019).

Gaughan, J., 'Laiskai', Niekas, 13 (1965).
— 'The ACE Tolkien Covers', *Niekas*, 16 (1966).

Hage, N.M., 'Connecting with History – An Interview with Barbara Remington', *Tolkien Collector's Guide* (2007) <https://www.tolkienguide.com/modules/wiwimod/index.php?page=Brem%20Interview> [accessed 13 Sep 2020].

Kilby, C.S., *Tolkien & The Silmarillion,* (Illinois: Harold Shaw Publishers, 1976).

Margrethe II, Queen of Denmark, 'From an Interview Conducted by Thorkild Hansen in 1979', *Tolkien Centenary Conference Souvenir Book,* ed. by W. Hammond (Oxford: Tolkien Society, 1992).

McIlwaine, C., *Tolkien: Maker of Middle-earth,* (Oxford: Bodleian Library, 2018).

Nasmith, T., 'The Unexpected Party', *Ted Nasmith,* <https://www.tednasmith.com/tolkien/the-unexpected-party/> [Accessed 13 Sep 2020].

Plimmer, C. and D., [unpublished interview notes for] 'The Tolkien Phenomenon', *Sotheby's Fine Books and Manuscripts Catalog*, 16-17 May 1984, lot number 704.

Scull, C. and W. Hammond, *The J.R.R. Tolkien Companion and Guide: Chronology, rev. and exp. edn.*, (London: HarperCollins, 2017).
— *The J.R.R. Tolkien Companion and Guide: Reader's Guide, rev. and exp. edn.*, (London: HarperCollins, 2017).

Simont, M., 'Books', *Newsweek,* (29 November 1954) 106.

Tolkien, J.R.R, *Drużyna Pierścienia (The Return of the King),* (Warsaw: Spółdzielnia Wydawnicza "Czytelnik", 1963).
— *Härskarringen (The Fellowship of the Ring)*, (Stockholm: Gebers, 1959).
— *Hobbit, czyli, Tam i z powrotem (The Hobbit, or There and Back Again)*, illus. by J. Młodożeniec (Warsaw: Iskry, 1960).
— *The Hobbit* (serialized), *Princess Magazine,* (London: Fleetway Publications, 1964-1965).
— *Hompen, eller, En resa dit och tillbaksigen (The Hobbit, or There and Back Again)*, illus. by T. Zetterholm (Stockholm: Kooperativa Förbundets Bokförlag, 1947).
— *Kleiner Hobbit und der grosse Zauberer (The Hobbit)*, illus. by H. Engels (Recklinghausen: Paulus Verlag, 1957).
— 'Letter to Doris Elizabeth Sykes (July 1956)', *Tolkien Gateway* <http://tolkiengateway.net/wiki/Letter_to_Doris_Elizabeth_Sykes_(July_1956)> [accessed 13 Sep 2020].
— *O gnomo (The Hobbit)*, illus. by A. Quadros (Porto: Loivraria Civilização, 1962).
— *Il Signore degli Anelli (The Lord of the Rings)*, illust. by R. Conti (Milan: Bompiani, 1967).
— *The Letters of J.R.R. Tolkien*, ed. H. Carpenter with the assistance of C. Tolkien, (London: George Allen & Unwin, 1981).

Untermeyer, B. and L.,*The Children's Treasury of Literature,* (London: Hamlyn, 1966).

Unwin, R., *George Allen & Unwin: A Remembrancer,* (Ludlow: Merlin Unwin Books, 1999).

Hompen as the source text for Tove Jansson's illustrations for *The Hobbit*[1]

Sonja Virta

1 - Introduction

Tove Jansson, the famed creator of the Moomins, illustrated J.R.R. Tolkien's *The Hobbit* for a Swedish translation in the early 1960s. A key issue that comes up in critiques of Jansson's work is her presumed ignorance of certain details in Tolkien's story. While certain aspects of the problem, i.e. the dissimilarities between Tolkien's text and Jansson's illustrations, are the result of Jansson's conscious and deliberate decisions, and others are due to artistic licence, I argue that the text Jansson most probably used as her source material has contributed to the differences between her vision and Tolkien's. Jansson's illustrations were commissioned for the second Swedish translation of *TH*, translated by Britt G. Hallqvist and published in 1962 as *Bilbo. En hobbits äventyr.* However, there has been some speculation among scholars interested in both Jansson and Tolkien that Jansson may have used as her source text an earlier translation, the 1947 Swedish translation called *Hompen, eller En resa dit och tillbaksigen* by Tore Zetterholm, with illustrations by Torbjörn Zetterholm and Charles Sjöblom. This earlier translation is known for, in Tolkien's own words, "unwarranted liberties" and omissions (Scull & Hammond 2017c, 1322). In addition, due to its timing, it is based on Tolkien's original published version of *TH*, i.e. before he made considerable revisions to the text (the revised edition published in 1951). In this paper, I will present some textual influences from *Hompen* that appear in Jansson's final illustrations. Her sketches and notes as well as her comments in some of her letters also show the possible influence of the Zetterholm brothers' work.

Björn Sundmark, who has studied both contemporary reviews and later fan critiques in Sweden, notes that Jansson was critiqued for her illustrations, especially with respect to the illustrations not having enough danger but, moreover, resembling her Moomin pictures too much (Sundmark 2014, 9-10). Her characters, Gollum for example, were also critiqued due to them not being true to the text (9, 10, 11).

While the Moomin style was not intentional – Jansson deliberately tried to steer away from her the illustration style she used with the Moomins (Westin 2014, 349) – can some of Jansson's choices be explained by the source text she might have used when illustrating? What aspects point to her having used a version of *The Hobbit* that mispresents the text, i.e. the first Swedish translation of *The Hobbit*, i.e. *Hompen*, instead of the *second* translation she was illustrating? How might the source text have affected Jansson's work with the illustrations? I will argue that Jansson used *Hompen* as her source text for the illustrations and that the choice of source text could have affected her illustrations in an important way.

1. All translations from Swedish and Finnish into English are mine unless mentioned otherwise.

The importance of choosing the source text is first demonstrated when discussing Tolkien's different versions of *The Hobbit* as well as the way *Hompen* differs from them. It also helps us understand the web of texts at play. Certain possible effects that the chosen text may have had on Jansson's illustrations are also remarked upon when discussing the possible source texts.

There has been some speculation among scholars about whether Jansson might have used *Hompen* as her source text when illustrating. The speculation has centred upon the Swedish terms for elves and goblins that Jansson used in a letter of hers when mentioning her illustration work: these terms are identical to the ones used in *Hompen* (Sundmark 2014, 16). Without more information from Jansson, such as her notes or unpublished letters,[2] the question of the source text has been difficult to answer.

On the other hand, in order to demonstrate that Jansson probably did use *Hompen* as the source text for her illustrations, I compare Jansson's notes to *Hompen* both on a terminological level as well as when it comes to page numbers. Additionally, I look into the mystery of Jansson's own copy of *Hompen* and whether she could have owned it at the time of illustrating *The Hobbit*.

In this article I will look at the indications that suggest that Jansson may have used *Hompen* as well as some of the consequences. Section 2 will present the material in more detail, introducing the possible source texts, i.e., different published versions and translations of *The Hobbit*. Section 3 deals with facts that imply *Hompen* would have been Jansson's source text. It also adds unpublished material, i.e. Jansson's sketches and notes – which, to my knowledge, have barely been studied before – as well as the final published illustrations, and discusses the indications found in Jansson's possible source material. Additional information includes a list of books from Tove Jansson's Home Library as well as Tove Jansson's own copy of the possible source text, *Hompen*. Section 4 looks at some criticism Jansson's illustrations have faced and tries to explain some of Jansson's decisions through her use of *Hompen*. Finally, section 5 delves into a special case of criticism, horror, and how this theme, a favourite of Jansson, could have been influenced by *Hompen*.

2 - Material

Tove Jansson (1914-2001), a Swedish-speaking Finnish painter, illustrator and writer most well-known for her self-illustrated Moomin books and comics, illustrated J. R. R. Tolkien's 1937 *The Hobbit, or There and Back Again* for the second Swedish translation of the book, translated by Britt G. Hallqvist and published in 1962 as *Bilbo. En hobbits äventyr* by the publisher Rabén & Sjögren.

The source texts used in this essay consist of the following four texts: the first edition facsimile of Tolkien's *The Hobbit, or There and Back Again* (1937/2016) (which will later be referred to as *The Hobbit* 1937), a 1993 edition of the novel (henceforth: *The Hobbit* 1993), the first Swedish translation of the book by Tore Zetterholm (illustrated

2. The book *Letters* from Tove or the original Swedish *Brev från* Tove Jansson (compiled and edited by Boel Westin and Helen Svensson) unfortunately do not include letters dealing with *The Hobbit*.

by Torbjörn Zetterholm, cover and maps by Charles Sjöblom) as *Hompen, eller En resa dit och tillbaksigen* (1947) (henceforth: *Hompen*), and the second Swedish translation of the book by Britt G. Hallqvist as *Bilbo: en hobbits äventyr* (1962) (henceforth: Bilbo), i.e. the text where Jansson's illustrations were first published.

Jansson, however, had not seen Tolkien's own illustrations (Sundmark 2014, 5), which would rule out an edition of *The Hobbit* illustrated by Tolkien. Despite this, I compare *The Hobbit* 1937 – with Tolkien's illustrations – and *Hompen*, as the former is the direct source text for the latter and it becomes important to compare them to one another.

On the other hand, the reason for including two editions of *The Hobbit* in English is due to the changes Tolkien made to his text after the publication of the first edition and the fact that this has had an effect on the Swedish translations mentioned. As the harmless-seeming magic ring Bilbo find in *The Hobbit* turns into The One Ring, a central device of evil in Tolkien's *The Lord of the Rings* (published in English in 1954-1955), Tolkien rewrote large parts of Riddles in the Dark, i.e. Chapter 5 in *The Hobbit*, in order to make the storylines fit. The revised second edition was published in 1951. Smaller revisions were made for later editions, e.g. for the third edition, published in 1966, but these are not relevant to the topic at hand (Scoville 2007, 278-9; Anderson 2003, 118).

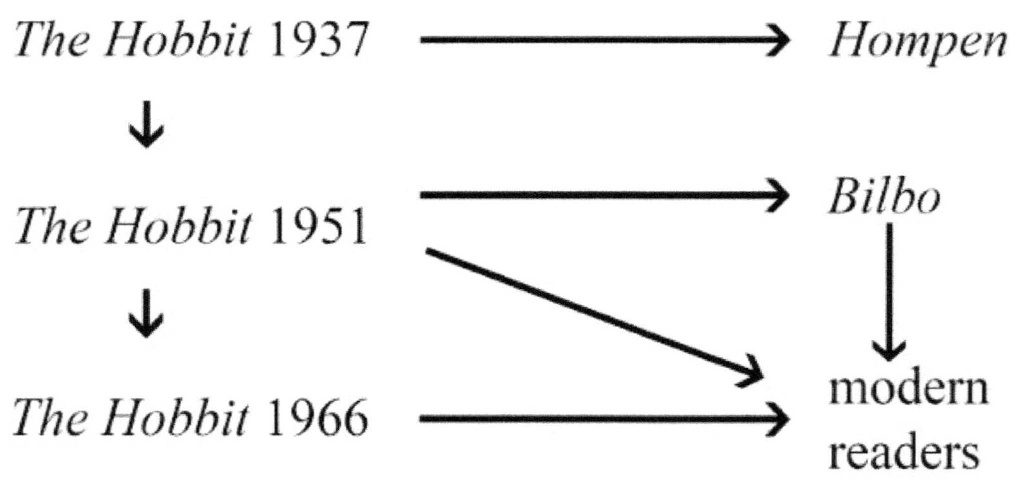

Figure 1 displays the relationships between the texts discussed. The original 1937 edition of *The Hobbit* functioned as the source text for *Hompen*, while the 1951 edition is the source text for *Bilbo*. Most modern readers are, however, likely to know the 1966 edition or, perhaps, the 1951 edition.

3 - *The Hobbit* 1937

The Hobbit, or There and Back Again was originally published in 1937. However, due to Tolkien's later revisions, most readers know the story in a form slightly different from the original. In addition to a number of smaller changes and revisions in the next decades, Tolkien partially rewrote Chapter 5, 'Riddles in the Dark', in the late 1940's when he was working on *The Lord of the Rings*. He realized he needed to change certain aspects of *The Hobbit*, especially regarding Gollum's behaviour and the importance of The Ring, in order make the story better in line with the logic of *The Lord of the Rings*. The revised second edition was published in 1951 (Scoville 2007, 278). This was followed by a third edition in 1966 with, among other things, an added mention about Gollum's small size. While the changes in the second edition were made due to the internal logic of Tolkien's epic, the small revision concerning Gollum in the third edition was due to Tolkien being unhappy with several illustrators depicting Gollum as far too large in size. Therefore, when first introducing Gollum in the text, he added the words "a small slimy creature" (Anderson 2003, 118).

4 - *Hompen*

The first Swedish – or any – translation of *The Hobbit*, published in 1947 as *Hompen, eller En resa dit och tillbaksigen* by Kooperativa Förbundets Bokförlag, was translated by Tore Zetterholm, and illustrated by his brother Torbjörn Zetterholm and by Charles Sjöblom, who was in charge of the cover and the two maps. As it was published in 1947, the Zetterholm translation was based on the first edition of *The Hobbit*, the revised second edition being published some years later in 1951. Additionally, Zetterholm has omitted both major and minor parts of the text as well as making word choices that do not quite fit with Tolkien's intentions. This has an effect on the tone and the atmosphere of the text (Nilsson-Lång 2002, 28).

5 - Bilbo

The second Swedish translation, for which Jansson's illustrations were commissioned, was translated by Britt G. Hallqvist and published by Rabén & Sjögren in 1962 as *Bilbo. En hobbits äventyr* (Westin 2007, 356, 358, 361). As this translation was published a decade after the revised second edition of *The Hobbit* but several years before the third, it is based on a different version of Tolkien's text than *Hompen* – but has slight differences from *The Hobbit* currently on sale.

When Tolkien's publisher Allen & Unwin were making a contract for *The Hobbit* with Rabén Sjögren, Tolkien noted on 12 February 1960 to Alina Dadlez, a representative of Allen Unwin, that he hoped that the illustrations used in *Hompen* would not be used again (Scull & Hammond 2017a, 584-5). Dadlez responded on 26 February, probably after hearing back from the Swedish publisher, that the publishing house Rabén & Sjögren would not be using the illustrations or the translation by the Zetterholms (585). It is not certain based on Scull & Hammond 2017a alone whether Rabén & Sjögren had already come to this conclusion on their own or whether Tolkien's opinion had an effect.

Astrid Lindgren, who worked as an editor at Rabén & Sjögren, commissioned Jansson to illustrate *The Hobbit* in November 1960 (Westin 2014, 346). Jansson sent the finished illustrations to Lindgren in the summer of 1961 (347) or, more specifically, in July (Sibley 2015, 2). While Westin provides a crude timeline for Jansson's work, it is unclear how

Hallqvist, the translator, fits into the picture. It is unclear if Hallqvist was translating and Jansson illustrating at the same time or if Hallqvist had already begun her work when Jansson's illustrations were commissioned. I am assuming, however, that at least a finished translation by Hallqvist would not have been available for Jansson to read.

6 - Indications that Jansson may have used *Hompen* as her source text

While there is no definite proof available as to which version of *The Hobbit* Jansson used when illustrating the book, there are indications that point to her having used *Hompen*. This section begins with Tolkien's revisions for Chapter 5 and how using *Hompen* would have meant that Jansson would have only been familiar with the original version, which would have prevented her from knowing several relevant details when illustrating. From Tolkien's changes I will move on to the changes made by Tore Zetterholm, the translator of *Hompen*, and the effect these could have had on Jansson's work. After this, I will discuss the revelatory nature of two terms Jansson mentions in a letter of hers. Finally, I will look into Jansson's sketches and notes for *The Hobbit* illustrations, and present several pieces of textual evidence that link Jansson's notes to *Hompen*.

7 - Revisions for Riddles in the Dark

In his revisions, Tolkien rewrote Chapter 5 and Gollum's nature to better suit the ring's importance in *The Lord of the Rings*. Tolkien's original "Riddles in the Dark" features a somewhat less scary Gollum. While he still would like to eat Bilbo, he does not attack or chase the hobbit. Neither does Bilbo have to jump over the creature. In this original version, if Bilbo won the riddle game, Gollum would give him a present – i.e. the ring. Yet Bilbo had already found Gollum's precious, but wisely keeps quiet about it. After losing the riddle game, the good loser Gollum cannot find the ring to give to Bilbo, and instead he shows the hobbit the way out. They say goodbye on amiable terms – even if Bilbo is relieved to get rid of the slightly creepy creature (*Hobbit* 1937, 83-94).

The revisions resulted in a far more vicious, dangerous and suspicious Gollum, who means to attack Bilbo despite losing the riddle game. The 'good loser' version of Gollum is gone. When he cannot find the ring, the enraged Gollum attacks and chases Bilbo and inadvertently shows him they way out of the caves. Finally, Bilbo has to jump over (the crouching) Gollum to escape (*Hobbit* 1993, 77-91).

Hompen, having been translated before 1951 and the publication of the revised second edition of *The Hobbit*, features the relatively nice Gollum from the first edition of *TH*, and hence the text does not include Gollum's more dangerous nature, Gollum's attack on Bilbo or Gollum chasing Bilbo through the caves. After the revisions Gollum is more dangerous than before and "the encounter [is treated] in a less light-hearted manner" (Roberts 2013, 99). If Jansson, then, used the text in *Hompen* when illustrating, she would not have known of Gollum's viciousness.

Indeed, in a full-page illustration of Gollum and Bilbo, Jansson's Gollum looks quite passive. The illustration depicts Gollum and Bilbo in a stalactite cave facing one another. Gollum stands in the water and hovers over Bilbo, looking down at the hobbit. Bilbo, standing on rock, has raised his sword and points it at Gollum, looking at him suspiciously. While Bilbo is pointing at him with his small sword, Gollum simply stares at Bilbo with his big, lamp-like eyes, his arms and hands resting at his sides. In the illustration, Gollum is perhaps grinning eerily, perhaps baring his teeth in a growl, and while the grin is very much reminiscent of the Groke, an antagonist from Jansson's Moomin books, the look on Gollum's face is not exactly evil or aggressive.

While the Swedish critics in the 1960s do not mention Jansson's illustrations of Gollum, at least not in the reviews gathered by Sundmark, Gollum's large size has been an issue for many fans (2014). Jansson's Gollum is approximately 2.5-3 times the height of Bilbo. While *The Lord of the Rings* would reveal Gollum to be a hobbit and hence of similar size with Bilbo, the first edition of *The Hobbit* – and, hence, also *Hompen* – does not reveal this information, making it difficult for the reader, or Jansson, to correctly estimate Bilbo's and Gollum's respective sizes (Scoville 2007, 278).[3] Jansson was not the only one to fall into this trap, as Gollum's size and appearance has been a common problem for illustrators in decades past. Of Jansson's Gollum, Florence Vilén writes that his size is a mistake and that "a devoted Tolkienist would know" (which probably explains why the Swedish reviewers in the 1960s, not being Tolkienists, did not comment upon on it) that Jansson's Gollum is far too tall and big (Vilén 1992, 85). Vilén does, however, admit that the mistake is understandable due to *The Hobbit* not being very clear about Gollum's appearance.

Yet, Tolkien gives the readers a tip about Gollum's size when he writes in the later editions of *The Hobbit*: "Straight over Gollum's head he [Bilbo] jumped, seven feet forward and *three in the air*" (*Hobbit* 1993, 90; emphasis mine). The first edition, however, does not contain this scene, because Gollum does not attack Bilbo and hence Bilbo need not escape. The same is true for the text in *Hompen*. If Jansson's source text indeed was *Hompen*, we must presume she did not see the words revealing (the possibly slightly crouched) Gollum's height being under a metre. It is worthwhile to note that Hallqvist's Swedish translation does contain Tolkien's entire renewed the "Riddles in the Dark" storyline, including "Straight over Gollum's head he jumped, seven feet forward and three in the air", i.e., "Rakt över Gollums huvud hoppade han, sju fot framåt och tre fot över marken" in Swedish (*Bilbo*, 95). Hence Jansson's illustration of Gollum, far too large, is published only 10 pages before the Swedish text hinting to Gollum's smaller size, underlining how unfortunate the mistake in his height is (85).

Additionally, modern readers would know the sentence "Deep down here by the dark water lived old Gollum, *a small slimy creature*." (emphasis mine). The words "a small slimy creature" take a clear stand on Gollum's size, but they were only added in the 1966 third revised edition (Anderson 2003, 118). Jansson's illustration therefore precedes this information: the addition simply could not have been available to Jansson when she was working on the illustrations. Moreover, Hallqvist's translation understandably does not include the added words but only states "Här djupt nere vid det mörka vattnet bodde gamle Gollum" (*Bilbo*, 78), (literally: 'Here deep down by the dark water lived old Gollum'), while Zetterholm has almost identical sentence: "Djupt nere vid detta mörka vatten bodde gamle Gollum" (*Hompen*, 76), (literally: 'Deep down by this dark water lived old Gollum'). As mentioned before, it is claimed that Tolkien added the words on

3. Jansson's notes on this chapter would shed light on the matter, but I have not yet seen her notes for 'Riddles in the Dark'.

Gollum's size because many illustrators had illustrated Gollum as being far larger than he should be (Anderson 2003, 118).

Jansson's and Zetterholm's full-page illustrations on Gollum and Bilbo have some similarities: Gollum's large size compared to Bilbo (Gollum being approximately 2.5-3 times Bilbo's size), Bilbo standing in the front pointing a sword at Gollum who hovers in the background, the cave and the water, the general composition of the picture. The main differences are the fact that Jansson's illustration is a mirror-image of Zetterholm's composition (Jansson's Gollum is on the left while Bilbo is on the right; the other way around for Zetterholm), that Zetterholm's Gollum takes about half of the space in the illustration while Jansson's is much smaller, and that Jansson's Gollum is more detailed than Zetterholm's blob. Jansson's stalactite cave also has more details. Bilbo, on the other hand, has his back turned to the viewer's in Zetterholm's picture while the viewers have more of a side/back view of Jansson's Bilbo. On the other hand, Jansson's illustration bears clear similarities with an illustration of her own. In a two-page illustration in *Vem ska trösta knyttet?* (1960), i.e. *Who Will Comfort Toffle?*, Jansson depicts the encounter of the scary Groke and the brave Toffle (Jansson 2014, 22-3). The composition is similar to Jansson's illustration with Gollum and Bilbo, even if the illustrations are, again, mirror-images of one another.

In English-speaking countries Jansson's illustrations to *The Hobbit* have only been seen in the official Tolkien Calendar 2016, published by HarperCollins. In the introduction to the calendar, Brian Sibley writes that Jansson's illustration of Gollum would be the most important – if not the only! – reason Jansson's work has not been published in English in any edition of *The Hobbit* (Sibley 2015, 2). When looking at the illustrations chosen for the calendar, the omission of Gollum is hence noteworthy. In addition to two different published cover images, there are 12 black-and-white full-page illustrations in *The Hobbit*, i.e., 14 large illustrations altogether. In addition to smaller illustrations throughout the calendar, each month features one full-page illustration – 11 black-and-white, one is in colour – and the centre spread has a large version of one of the two covers. There are, therefore, 13 full-page illustrations in the calendar, which means that one published large illustration did not make the cut. The illustration that was left out is, indeed, the one with over-sized Gollum and small Bilbo. In his foreword to the calendar, Brian Sibley suggests that Gollum is the reason Jansson's illustrations for *The Hobbit* have never been published in English – or, indeed, even outside of Sweden and Finland – suggesting that the omission of Gollum, who is not present even in the smaller illustrations throughout the calendar despite Jansson also including a smaller illustration of him in the book, was no coincidence.

Sibley writes that it is not known what Tolkien thought of Jansson's illustrations (Sibley 2015, 2). Indeed, no comments from Tolkien can be found. E.g. Christina Scull and Wayne Hammond give a detailed account of comments Tolkien made in his letters regarding more than a dozen different illustrated publications – or plans for such – of his work from the 1940s to the late 1960s (Scull & Hammond 2017b, 559-65). Despite fitting this time range, Jansson's work is not mentioned, except in a list of illustrators (Scull & Hammond 2017b: 566). Therefore it is unclear if Tolkien ever put his opinion in writing or whether such a letter or note has been lost – or if he ever even saw Jansson's work to begin with.

8 - Changes made by Zetterholm

Tolkien was not pleased with *Hompen*, and complained on the "unwarranted liberties" Zetterholm had taken "without consultation or approval", nonetheless. The text "was also unfavourably criticised in general by a Swedish expert, familiar with the original, to whom I submitted it" (Scull & Hammond 2017c, 1322). Tolkien neither took a liking to the illustrations by Torbjörn Zetterholm, but considered them, with the rare exception, "frightful", "dreadful" and "quite out of tune with the tone of the text". He also complained that the illustrator had ignored the text and drawn Gollum to look like a monster and far too big in comparison to Bilbo (Scull & Hammond 2017a, 585; Scull & Hammond 2017b, 560).

While it appears that a thorough list of the omissions and changes Zetterholm has made does not exist, Lena Nilsson-Lång notes that omissions to the text occur in every chapter and that Zetterholm "frequently deletes major and minor elements in the text" (2002, 28-9). Nilsson-Lång argues that Zetterholm's target group is clearly young children and that *Hompen* is more of a children's book than Tolkien's *The Hobbit* is (29). She lists the censoring of language, the absence of fierce and frightening elements, possibly "tedious" parts of the texts being removed as examples of her theory, as well as the narrator's avuncular style being maintained to the very end (29). It should be noted, however, that Nilsson-Lång has not had the chance to use *The Hobbit* 1937 as her source text and is hence comparing *Hompen* to a later, revised edition of *The Hobbit*.[4] Hence her results may be slightly misleading.

While the reasoning behind the omission of scary material is clear, the reasons for other changes are less so. Zetterholm has fused the two last chapters, Chapter 18 'The Return Journey' and 19 'The Last Stage', into a single chapter, *Resan Hem* ('The Journey Home'), omitting the return to Rivendell as well as the travel with the Elven-king and his host (Nilsson-Lång 2002, 9). Nilsson-Lång considers it possible that Zetterholm regarded the omitted parts unnecessary to the story, or that it was a matter of lack of time or inspiration (9). The omission of such a large part of text, approximately 6 pages, could have had an effect on Jansson's work: Jansson only has one illustration (the vignette starting the chapter) in Chapter 18 and two illustrations (the starting and ending vignettes) in Chapter 19. This is fewer than the average, which is slightly shy of three per chapter, but not unheard of: Chapter 16 also has only a single illustration while Chapters 4, 9, 14, and 15 have two. Two of these three illustrations are clearly textual and both refer to points in the text present in *Hompen*. The opening vignette for Chapter 18 has Bilbo, on a pony, waving goodbye to a group of dwarves (*Hobbit* 1937, 297; *Hompen*, 263).

The end vignette to Chapter 19 – and the whole book – shows Bilbo, probably at home, eyeing his coat of mail. This illustration refers to the sentence: "His coat of mail was arranged on a stand in the hall (until he lent it to a Museum)" (*Hobbit* 1937, 308), or in Swedish: "Rustningen sattes upp på en ställning i hallen (tills han lånade ut den till ett museum)" (*Hompen*, 268).

---

4. It is slightly unclear which edition of *The Hobbit* Nilsson-Lång is using, exactly.

The third illustration is more difficult to place textually. It has an empty helmet with a face lying on the ground with its mouth ajar and with birds in the sky behind. The illustration is placed as the opening vignette for chapter 19. There does not seem to be an exact referent to the illustration, unless the reference is in Bilbo's words "But I have a helm and a hard skull" (*Hobbit* 1937, 293), i.e., "Men jag har en hjälm och en hård skalle" (*Hompen*, 258), but those words are found in Chapter 18 instead of Chapter 19.

Not all of Jansson's vignettes have exact textual counterparts, however, but they do still clearly refer to the people, events and places in the text.

It is noteworthy, yet could also be coincidental, that the three illustrations in Chapters and 19 exclude the elves and, hence, nothing Zetterholm has omitted appears in the illustrations. Perhaps more revealingly, however, all 19 chapters have an opening vignette, and 18 vignettes are clearly wider than they are tall. The only exception is the helmet vignette in Chapter 19, which is almost square-shaped. As Jansson was very particular with how the illustrations should be positioned (see section 4), this opening vignette being the odd one out could be taken as evidence that Jansson read Zetterholm's *Hompen*, which only has 18 chapters, and hence she only made 18 opening vignettes. When a 19th opening vignette was needed, perhaps a vignette meant to be placed either mid-chapter or as an ending vignette – most of which are not of the wide kind – was used instead.

9 - Zetterholm, elves, and goblins

In a letter to Tuulikki Pietilä in the spring of 1961, Jansson refers to some of Tolkien's characters using the Swedish terms (in plural) "älvor" and "svartalfer" (Westin 2007, 359, 551). This is yet more evidence that Jansson could have used *Hompen* as her source text. Björn Sundmark notes that these are exactly the terms that Zetterholm has chosen for *elves* and *goblins*, implying that Jansson may have been familiar with Zetterholm's *Hompen* (Sundmark 2014, 16, note 4). Conversely, Hallqvist's translation employs "alver" and "vättar", respectively.

Stenström notes that both "älva" and "alf" are cognates with the English *elf*, yet with different connotations: "älva" brings to mind fairies, i.e. not the types of elves that Tolkien was after. *Svartalf* ("black-elf"), consisting of the words "*svart*" and "*alf*", on the other hand, refers to "a malign underground being" and hence is quite similar to Tolkien's goblins (Stenström 2011, 110). The terminology Jansson has used can both be an indication of her having used *Hompen* as her source text, but also that she could have been misled by terms not consistent with Tolkien's intentions.

Jansson's elves have indeed faced some critique: "the barrel-dumping wood-elves have horns like cattle" (114). But Louise Svensson also argues that the Zetterholm translation may be misleading. Svensson notes that "älvor" would refer to "fairies" or "sprites" and that the term has negative connotations. "Älvor" are malevolent creatures that were believed to spread diseases, and people sacrificed to these spirits to cure these illnesses (Svensson 2016, 11-2).

Svensson also notes that the term "älvor" is not compatible with the wood elves being "a good and kindly people" at the end of Chapter 14 in *The Hobbit* (11-2). However, this quote is omitted in Zetterholm. In fact, the last four paragraphs of Chapter 14, 'Fire and

Water', have been omitted. These are scenes in which the wood elves help the people of Lake-town instead of continuing to the Lonely Mountain to claim the mountain's riches. Yet Jansson can't have been very misled, as her Thranduil is more elf-like than an evil sprite. Her illustration of a beautiful and serene elf with leaves and berries in his head is compatible with the words "A woodland king was there with a crown of leaves" (*Hobbit* 1937, 156, *Hompen*, 142).

10 - Jansson's copy of Hompen

The Tove Jansson Collection at The Finnish Institute for Children's Literature (Finnish: Lastenkirjainstituutti) in Tampere, Finland, houses 410 books donated in 1989 by Jansson herself from her personal library. The collection includes children's literature and studies on literature and illustration (Tervaharju 2014, 5; Raiskio 2018). One of the books Jansson donated is Zetterholm's *Hompen*[5] – a fact that is not widely known (despite the speculations about Jansson possibly having used *Hompen*), possibly because the Institute only catalogued the collection for the public in the summer of 2018. There are no other Tolkien books in the collection (Onnet database 2018), but the collection houses only a (small?) part of Jansson's personal library.

It is unclear where or when Jansson bought or received her copy of *Hompen* as while the book has Jansson's name and her bookplate, there is no handwritten date in the book. There are no notes in margins, either, or any other definite proof that Jansson used the book when illustrating *The Hobbit*. There are, however, the names of previous owners as well as their address and a bookplate of theirs.

The first spread of *Hompen* has Sjöblom's map (*Thror's* [sic] *karta* for *Thror's map*) as well as the institute's own markings. More interestingly, the first spread has the handwritten name of CAJ as well as his address near Stockholm, Sweden. On the second spread, there is CAJ bookplate, Tove Jansson's handwritten name – added when she donated the books to the institute (Nordling 2018, personal communication) – but also the name MJ, who shares her last name with CAJ. Finally, the third spread has Jansson's black-and-white ex libris with the decorative mirror-image monogram 'TJ'. The ex libris with Jansson's initials was designed by her mother Signe Hammarsten-Jansson (Kruskopf 1992, 143-4).

The two owners, CAJ and MJ, share a last name and they may have been a father and a daughter. As there is a CAJ ex libris in the book, the copy may have been a fairly permanent part of his book collection. MJ's name appears in two different handwritings: in capital letters partially erased and, overlapping it, a signature in cursive. Due to the evolving handwriting of MJ, it is likely that MJ had the book in her possession as a child for several years.

Päivi Nordling from the institute suggests that Tove Jansson's 'TJ' ex libris used in the book could have been designed after 1955 (Nordling, personal communication). This is because Jansson's mother, Signe Hammarsten-Jansson, also designed an ex libris in similar style, with the decorative mirror-image monograph 'TP', for Tuulikki Pietilä, Tove

5. My thanks to the Finnish SFF author Maria Turtschaninoff, whose blog post originally alerted me to this fact. <http://turtschaninoff.blogspot.com/2015/10/tammerforstampere.html>

Jansson's partner. Jansson and Pietilä only became better acquainted in late 1955, and if Hammarsten-Jansson's designed both bookplates at around the same time, then *Hompen*, published in 1947, would predate Jansson's ex libris by several years (Karjalainen 2014, 193). Additionally, the ex libris Jansson had in use before the monogram was designed by Jansson herself in about 1950 and had an illustration of a stormy sea, but this ex libris is not found in Jansson's copy of *Hompen* (Kruskopf 1992, 143-4).

While it is of course possible that the 'TJ' ex libris could have been added later, it is worth noting that many books in her collection often do have both the 'stormy sea' and the 'TJ' ex libris, the latter having been added later. The lack of the 'stormy sea' ex libris could be indeed be interpreted as her copy of *Hompen* not having reached her before at least the mid-1950s.

I am arguing that it is likely that Jansson did not gain her copy of *Hompen* that soon after its publication in 1947. The several scribblings by the previous owners of Jansson's copy and the possible dating of Jansson's ex libris would suggest Jansson would not have received her copy before the mid- to late 1950s. This would make it quite probable that she would have received it when illustrating the second Swedish translation of *The Hobbit*.

11 - Jansson's notes: page numbers, word choices and other details

Jansson's notes and sketches for *The Hobbit* are in the collections of the Moomin Museum in Tampere, Finland. Only the occasional note/sketch has been on display or published before spring 2018 when some of them were on display in Finland at the Vantaa Art Museum Artsi as a part of their exhibition PAX – *Puhutaan rauhasta*, "PAX – Let's talk about peace". In addition to several final illustrations, the exhibition included five large frames with Jansson's notes and/or sketches. While some of the exhibited sketches were from other chapters, the exhibition included notes from six chapters: Chapter 3 'A Short Rest', Chapter 4 'Over Hill and Under Hill', Chapter 6 'Out of the Frying-Pan into the Fire', Chapter 7 'Queer Lodgings', Chapter 14 'Fire and Water', and Chapter 15 'The Gathering of the Clouds'. When it comes to the hypothesis of her using *Hompen* as her source text, it is worth noting that her handwritten "title" to the sketches "Skisser för ill. av J. R. R. Tolkiens 'Bilbo' (*The Hobbit*)", meaning "Sketches for ill[ustrations] to J. R. R. Tolkien's 'Bilbo' (*The Hobbit*)" does not refer to *Hompen*, but to Bilbo, the name of the publication she was illustrating. Yet she could have known the intended name for the publication despite having *Hompen* as her source text.

The notes are written in Swedish, i.e. Jansson's mother tongue. The notes include possible illustration ideas (some of which were abandoned), the placing of certain illustrations (such as the end vignettes), details from the text, and sketches. The notes include some page numbers which may help to identify Jansson's source text: Jansson's notes to a chapter begin with the chapter number and the number of pages in the chapter, e.g., "Kap. 6. (17½ sidor)", i.e., "Ch. 6 (17½ pages)" (emphasis original).

Comparing these two, however, does not result in absolute certainty. Jansson could have used another edition of TH, or, at least theoretically, Hallqvist's translation or a draft of it. Nevertheless, the comparison gives us an idea on whether to further entertain the *Hompen* hypothesis or not.

	Number of pages in Jansson's notes	***Hompen***	***The Hobbit* 1937**	**Page numbers Jansson mentions**	***Hompen***	***The Hobbit* 1937**
Chapter 3	81/2	81/2	91/2	–	52-60	56-65
Chapter 4	11/12	**12**	131/2	–	61-72	66-79
Chapter 6	17/12	**19**	201/2	95, 96, 98, 103, 106, 109	91-109	97-117
Chapter 7	23	**24***	28	111, 114, 116, 124, 125, 130	110-133	118-145
Chapter 14	9	**10**	10	–	220-229	252-261
Chapter 15	9	9	101/2	234	230-238	262-272

* *The Hobbit* 1937 facsimile mistakenly says *Chapter VI* for 'Queer Lodgings', but this has been taken to mean Chapter VII.

Table 1: Number of pages in different chapters of Hompen *and The Hobbit 1937, compared with the number of pages in Jansson's notes, and the page numbers of these chapters in* Hompen *and The Hobbit 1937 compared to the page numbers mentioned in Jansson's notes.*

Looking at Table 1, it is clear that not all of the page numbers in *Hompen* line up cleanly with Jansson's notes. While Chapters 3 and 15 are a perfect match with 8.5 and 9 pages, respectively, Chapters 4, 6, 7 and 14 are less clear. Yet the explanations seem simple: when counting the pages, Jansson has left out some full-page and half-page illustrations in the book. Chapter 4, for instance, has a half-page illustration which could explain the slight disparity between Jansson's 11.5 pages to the book's 12 pages. Similarly, Chapter 6 has a full-page illustration Jansson seems to have left out, leaving only 17.5 pages instead of 18.5 pages. Chapter 7 only has 6 lines on its 24th page, which explains why Jansson has marked it down as 23 pages. Finally, Chapter 14 has one full-page illustration, which is probably the reason Jansson's notes say 9 pages instead of 10. Despite these slight differences, it is clear that the page numbers in Jansson's notes are much closer to *Hompen* than to *The Hobbit* 1937.

The page numbers Jansson mentions in her notes disclose perhaps even more. While page numbers appear in only half of Jansson's chapter notes, they match up perfectly with the chapter page numbers in *Hompen*. *The Hobbit* 1937, on the other hand, does not: while some page numbers Jansson mentions with reference to a certain chapter do match with the numbering in *The Hobbit* 1937, others do not.

More importantly still, the content reveals more than the simple numbers. In Jansson's notes, she refers to bracken when describing page 96: "under ormbunkar" meaning 'under bracken'. To match this, page 96 in Chapter 6 of *Hompen* includes the sentence ”stenarna dråsade ner bland ormbunkar och tallrötter långt där nedanför.” This corresponds to *The Hobbit* 1937, page 104, “the disturbed stones went bounding and spinning among the bracken and the pine-roots far below” (all emphases mine). Similarly, Jansson makes plans of making a full-page illustration for page 98 for a scene in which everyone is up in trees (“Helsida allihop i träden (98)” i.e. ‘Full page everyone in the trees (98)’, emphasis original). This correlates exactly with page 98 in *Hompen*, which describes the company having climbed up trees – except for Bilbo, who is still trying to make it up a tree – to take shelter from the goblins and wargs. In *The Hobbit* 1937, the corresponding scene is on pages 101-102. In both these cases, Jansson’s notes match perfectly with *Hompen*. All in all, the page numbers in Jansson’s notes are either perfect or near-perfect matches with the page numbers in *Hompen*, making it quite likely that she used *Hompen* as her source text.

Some word choices may also be revealing. When it comes to Mirkwood, Jansson uses the term *Mörkskogen* in her notes and refers to page 130. On page 130 in *Hompen*, *Mörkskogen* is mentioned. In Hallqvist’s translation *Bilbo*, Mirkwood is translated as *Mörkmården*, and it is not mentioned on page 130. However, page numbers for *Bilbo* are less useful as Jansson could not have used a published copy of *Bilbo* when illustrating the book. One could argue that *Mörkskogen* is a direct translation for Mirkwood – indeed, also Åke Ohlmarks has made the same choice in his translation of *The Lord of the Rings* – and Jansson could have come up with the word herself while reading *The Hobbit* in English (Nilsson-Lång 2002, 24). However, in *The Hobbit* 1937, Mirkwood is not mentioned on page 130, unlike in *Hompen*.

In her notes, Jansson refers to Bilbo as “H.”. This could be either “hobbit”, which both Tolkien and Hallqvist use, or “hompe”, which Zetterholm coined for *Hompen*. Even “hob”, coined by Åke Ohlmarks, is a possibility as the *The Lord of the Rings* translation by Ohlmarks had already been partially published (*FR* in 1959, *TT* 1960, *RK* 1961) by 1960 and 1961 when Jansson was working on the illustrations. Jansson referring to Bilbo as “H”, therefore, does not reveal anything about the source texts she might have used.

Another textual example of Zetterholm’s probable influence in Jansson’s notes is that, like Zetterholm, Jansson’s notes do not distinguish between the ponies and the horse that Beorn lets the company use. Both *Hompen* (128, 130) and Jansson’s notes simply talk of horses, *hästar*, while *The Hobbit* 1937 (138, 142-3) makes clear that Gandalf was given a horse while the others had ponies.

Additionally, Jansson makes notes on the items that Beorn gives the company – skin pouches for water, bows and arrows – and notes that ’The horses will be left at the end of the ch. ’ (“Hästarna lämnas i kap. slut.”) (*Hompen*, 128, 131; *Hobbit* 1937, 139, 143-4).

12 - Critique and Jansson’s notes

The critique on Jansson’s illustrations centred on Jansson’s perceived ignorance of the details in the text, which goes hand-in-hand with the complaints on Jansson’s characters not being consistent with the textual details. Additionally, not everyone like Jansson’s perceived Moomin style nor the lack of horror in her illustrations. In this section, I will concentrate on the details and the characters, while part 5 focuses on horror and (partially) the Moominesque style.

While the illustrations in Moomin books are more concentrated on the events while leaving the landscape to the background (Aejmelaeus 1994, 36), *The Hobbit* is different. Jansson was not interested in Tolkien's characters but concentrated on landscapes. "The characters are commonplace [...] but the scenery is seductive in its macabre ferocity", Jansson wrote in a letter. She also considered inventing new goblins and elves for the illustrations (Westin 2014, 348). While Jansson appears to not have invented new characters, her lack of interest in the characters has not escaped the attention of reviewers or readers. One of the Swedish reviewers Sundmark refers to, wrote that Jansson had not concerned herself with the details in the text with respect to the characters despite the details being numerous and significant (Sundmark 2014, 9). This could be compared to Tolkien's comment on Robert J. Lee, who had illustrated the first chapter of *The Hobbit* for an anthology: Tolkien thought Lee did "not seem to have read [the text] with any care" (Scull & Hammond 2017b, 564). Somewhat similarly, Björn Sundmark writes that Jansson's illustrations do not always fit with the details in the text and that Jansson's Moominesque imagery perhaps overshadows and obscures Tolkien's vision (Sundmark 2014, 9).

When studying Jansson's work ethic and her notes for the illustrations, it becomes clear, however, that critics could not be further from the truth when thinking that Jansson had not read her source text with care. Firstly, "[i]n her usual way" Jansson "soon provided a work plan: the number, size, execution and placing of the illustrations, 'slender' introductory vignettes should extend horizontally at a certain distance along the title of each chapter. Her instructions were to the point, precise and practical" (Westin 2014, 348). She had also asked for a plenty of time for finishing the assignment (346). Both the methodical planning and the need for enough time suggest that Jansson wanted to do good work and meant to work closely with the book.

Secondly, Jansson's notes reveal how particular she was about the text and her illustrations. When planning the full-page illustration of the company up in trees in Chapter 6 'Out of the Frying-Pan into the Fire', her notes say, among other things:

> Lärkträd (2) tallar (5 \1)[6] (4) gran (2)

Meaning:

> Larch tree (2) pines (5 \1)[7] (4) fir (2)

Here Jansson is jotting down not only the types of trees the company has climbed, but also the number of people in each tree. The larch tree hosts two people (Fili and Kili), the two pines originally have five (Dori, Nori, Ori, Oin, Gloin) and four (Bifur, Bofur, Bombur, Thorin), but Jansson has added number one on top of the number five to demonstrate that Bilbo will up this first pine tree as well. Finally, there is a fir tree with two dwarves (Dwalin and Balin). It is worth noting, however, that Gandalf, sitting

6. The number 1 has been added on top of the number 5.
7. As previously.

alone in a large pine, appears to be missing from this note. This may be because he is said to be "quite hidden in its boughs", although his eyes are visible (*Hobbit* 1937, 106; *Hompen*, 98). Therefore Jansson may have intended to stay true to the text and not to have Gandalf visibly appear in the illustration.

Another case in Jansson's notes where she is very particular with the details is regarding Beorn's looks. Referring to Chapter 7, 'Queer Lodgings', she writes:

> Beorn: stor lång svarthårig man med långa \nakna armar och stort skägg. Ylledräkt till knäna, stor yxa.
>
> [above the text] (med hästar?),
>
> Svarta ögonbryn. (116)

Meaning:

> Beorn: big tall black-haired man with long \naked arms and big beard. Wool outfit to knees, big axe.
>
> [above the text] (with horses?)
>
> Black eyebrows. (116)

When comparing Jansson's notes with both *Hompen* and *The Hobbit* 1937, it is evident that she has included all details on Beorn's appearance from the scene where the company meet him. In *The Hobbit* 1937, page 124, Tolkien writes:

> Standing near was a huge man with a thick black beard and hair, and great bare arms and legs with knotted muscles. He was clothed in a tunic of wool down to his knees, and was leaning on a large axe. The horses were *standing by him with their noses at his shoulder.*
>
> "And what's this little fellow?" he said, stooping down to frown at the hobbit with his bushy black eyebrows."
>
> [all emphasis mine]

The details underlined in the passage have been mentioned by Jansson directly in her notes. The bolded details are not present in the notes, but instead are clearly visible in Jansson's illustration of Beorn and his horses: despite the illustration being relatively small and drawn in a sketch-like style – and hence not very detailed – it is obvious that Beorn is leaning on his axe and that the horses, standing behind him, have their noses at Beorn's shoulder.

Jansson's eye for detail is evident also earlier in the story when the dwarves are making music at Bag End. Jansson's illustration to Chapter 1, 'An Unexpected Party', shows six dwarves, everyone with an instrument. Tolkien is particular in mentioning what instruments each of the dwarves play (*Hobbit* 1937, 23; *Hompen*, 18), and, as M. Lee Alexander notes, Jansson has likewise stuck with the correct instruments in her illustration (Alexander 2016, 217). The illustration shows one dwarf with a clarinet (either Bifur or Bofur per Tolkien's text), one with a drum (Bombur), one with a harp (Thorin), one with a flute (either Dori, Nori or Ori) and two with little fiddles (Kili and Fili), while the viol-playing Dwalin and Balin have been left out of the illustration. Additionally, Thorin, Kili and Fili bear a striking resemblance to one another in Jansson's illustration, and the most likely explanation is that Jansson, having read the book, knew Kili and Fili to be brothers and Thorin their uncle. Alexander argues that the correct instruments – and, I would add, the appearance of Thorin, Kili and Fili – could mean Jansson was indeed familiar with the text.

When it comes to the criticism of Jansson's illustrations missing the mark when it comes to certain details, it is true that the text and the illustrations do not always correspond to one another (Sundmark 2014, 9). This is typical for Jansson, however. In her six first Moomin books, Jansson's illustrations are more detailed than the text, and the images, e.g., have additional creatures that the text does not mention (Aejmelaeus 1994, 36). On the other hand, Sundmark argues that Tolkien's text differs from the way fantasy was written previously: the predecessors were more symbolistic and dream-like while Tolkien's take on fantasy is more realistic (Sundmark, 2014, 2). Nowadays there is an expectation of realism and faithfulness to details when it comes to illustrating fantasy, but Jansson was illustrating in an era when the expectations were only beginning to shift, and there was space to illustrate more expressively (3-4). Indeed, the "illustrations were an impressionistic rather than a literal response to Tolkien's story" (Sibley 2015, 1). This expressiveness is also present in Jansson's short-story collection *Det osynliga barnet* (in English: *Tales from Moominvalley*), which was published in 1962, i.e. the same year as Bilbo with Jansson's illustrations. Unlike in previous Moomin books, the illustrations in the short-story collection go less hand-in-hand with what happens in the story and, instead, the illustrations focus on creating the atmosphere (Moomin Museum 2017, 148).

All in all, while Jansson's illustrations are not always detailed, it is clear that the reason is not that she would have ignored Tolkien's details. Instead, she has jotted down a plethora of meaningful facts in her notes when reading the text. Her interest in landscape instead of the characters has probably had an effect on the resulting illustrations, making the characters less detailed, as also has the expressive and symbolistic style that would have still been considered the norm in previous decades.

13 - Horror in the eyes of Jansson and her critics

While the characters bear the brunt of the criticism Jansson's illustrations faced, another issue often remarked upon is horror. Swedish reviewers in the 1960s mostly liked the illustrations but some criticised that the horror, or the lack of it. Sundmark mentions how a critic noted that in Moominvalley, evil is not "real", while in Middle-earth evil with its dark powers is the frightening reality. According to the reviewer, the distinction is unfortunately visible in the illustrations (Sundmark 2014, 10). The characters, especially, resemble the Moomins too much and thus fail to be Tolkienesque enough (10). Indeed, several writers have commented upon how, although not always negatively. Bilbo appears to have many Moominous sides, depending on the image and the viewer: he can look like a whomper[8] (Kruskopf 1992, 321), Snufkin[9] (Hołownia 2014, 11; Sibley 2015, 2), Toffle (Metso 2004, 29; Alexander 2016, 217; Sundmark 2014, 9) or Too-ticky (Sibley 2015, 2), while Gollum resembles the Groke (Hołownia 2014, 11; Sibley 2015, 2). This is despite Jansson deliberately changing her illustration technique in order for the illustrations to be different from the Moomins (Westin 2014, 349).

Aside from the Moomins, another critic complained that goblins should look more dangerous: "they have a more dangerous countenance and sharper teeth later in the saga" (Sundmark 2014, 9). Additionally, the first critic complains that in the cover Bilbo looks as if he was dressed for play (10).

This is where Zetterholm's omissions become relevant again. When it comes to the goblins, Zetterholm has omitted several lines describing the goblins' potential raiding of villages near the goblin caves in Chapter 6. *The Hobbit* 1937 (108) says: "If their plan had been carried out, there would have been none [=villagers] left there next day; all would have been killed except the few the goblins kept from the wolves and carried back as prisoners to their caves", but this bit has been omitted from *Hompen* (100). Similarly, when describing the raids, the words "especially to get food or slaves to work for them" (*Hobbit* 1937, 107), have been slightly truncated: "slaves to work for them" has been translated as "fångar", i.e. "prisoners" (*Hompen*, 100). The original text underlines the fierce cruelty of the goblins. The changes make the goblins' actions less concrete and, hence, less scary. Changes like this can have an effect in the illustrations as the characters involved may not be portrayed in a manner scary enough when compared to the original text.

Zetterholm's changes are not restricted to the bad guys. As Nilsson-Lång (2002) notes, Zetterholm's The Battle of the Five Armies ends with only "Then dismay fell on the Goblins and they fled in all directions. Victory had been assured before the fall of night" (*Hompen*, 261). Approximately 10 lines have been omitted in between the two sentences (cf. *Hobbit* 1937, 295-6), including the goblins being pursued closely and driven into the Running River, and "those that came hardly to the Wood-elves' realm were there slain, or drawn in to die deep in the trackless dark Mirkwood", but also "the coming of new hope" (*Hobbit* 1937, 295-6; *Hompen*, 261).

An even more gruesome example is when it comes to Beorn's extermination of the goblin and the warg. While *The Hobbit* 1937 reveals that "A goblin's head was stuck outside the gate and a warg-skin was nailed to a tree just beyond" (131), *Hompen* simply has Beorn mention that they live no longer ("De lever inte längre!", 127), omitting the details of Beorn's cruelty (Svensson 2016, 15). Zetterholm probably "considers the original text too frightening" for his presumed child audience (Nilsson-Lång 2002, 8). He also "alters the perception of Beorn's character. [...] we are not told how brutally he has killed them, we do not perceive how vicious Beorn can be" (Svensson 2016, 15).

8. The Finnish translation of Kruskopf's book claims Bilbo looks like the Hemulen, but the Swedish original says "en homsa", i.e., a whomper from e.g. Jansson's book *Moominsummer Madness*. Moreover, I would argue that many characters in Jansson's illustrations to Lewis Carroll's *The Hunting of the Snark* do resemble the Hemulen, but Bilbo does not.

9. While writing this article, a stranger on public transport asked me why my Bilbo canvas bag had an image of Snufkin on it although the bag stated (in Finnish) "The Finnish Tolkien Society".

This is probably due to concern for children: protecting children from issues regarding death and grief (15).

Lena Nilsson-Lång argues that Zetterholm has censored horror and "offensive" expressions, perhaps to make the book more suitable for children (2002, 8, 12). Furthermore, Zetterholm "conforms the register by exchanging 'offensive' expressions" for less 'offensive' ones (12). When the trolls complain that they haven't had any manflesh for a long time, Zetterholm translates the verbs as not "having seen" instead of referring to eating like the original (11-2). Swearwords also get censored: "What the 'ell", uttered by one of the trolls, is rendered as "Vad sjutton" where "sjutton" is a more minor swearword than "hell" (11-2).

The omissions, however, cannot explain everything. In *Hompen*, Torbjörn Zetterholm's illustration of goblins barging in on the company sleeping in a cave features some scary and angry goblins – with the sharp teeth that a reviewer is looking for – ready to whack them into pieces with the axes, spears and swords they are holding. Jansson has an illustration of the same scene with a similar point of view, i.e. the company's, but her goblins are more like friendly-looking yet slightly shy dogs who are crouching by the mouth of the cave, curiously looking at the company (who are not pictured). While we cannot know which text the illustrator Zetterholm has read – *The Hobbit* 1937 or *Hompen* – Jansson would nevertheless have seen his illustration. This begs the question of why Jansson's goblins are so much more toned down compared to Zetterholm's.

Not all critics and commentators have, however, found the horror lacking. The illustrations were described as horrible (in the horror sense) and several reviewers in the 1960s mentioned nature mysticism or described the images being mystical (Sundmark 2014, 8). Other writers have described the full-page illustrations as having a mysterious atmosphere, with terror and horror (Björk 2003, 128), and even a fervent critic finds the landscapes and "townscape" of Lake-town interesting and scary (Vilén 1992, 85). Elsewhere the illustrations are said to be dramatic, and the full-page ones of Lake-town and the Battle of the Five Armies are described as exciting and intriguing (Nummelin & Sisättö 2014, 218).

The expectations of critics have also differed. Sundmark argues that the reviewers who are familiar with *The Lord of the Rings* seem to have more "adult" expectations than *The Hobbit* in itself would create (2014, 10). Even the publisher's opinion had an effect on this: Jansson's original cover for the book seemed "too adult" for the publisher, and Jansson had to create a new, more childish cover, despite being against the idea (Westin 2014, 349-51).

Additionally, despite critics thinking of Moominvalley as idyllic and safe, one could argue that there are dark undertones that the critics have missed. As Ty Burr writes (2001): "But surely it was [Jansson's] knowledge of paradises lost that speaks to the lonely corners of every child's heart." Or, as Lisa Allardice notes (2019), "It is striking how much fear shadows the [Moomin] novels: for all the sunshine and picnics, menace lurks behind every bush" which, in the end, does not sound too different from the idyllic Shire and dangerous Middle-earth outside it. Moreover, Ali Smith remarks how Jansson writes in her semi-autobiographical short story The Dark that "danger, when you're a child, 'lies in wait everywhere'" (2013, xii). Additionally, Allardice quotes Jansson herself: "I wonder if the nursery and the chamber of horrors are as far apart as people think" (Allardice 2019).

Jansson herself indeed looked forward to illustrating the horror in *The Hobbit*: "Forests of living horror, coal-black rivers, moonlit moors with fiery wolves – a whole world of catastrophe that I know I can respond to in pictures", she wrote (Westin 2014, 348). Jansson loved Edgar Allan Poe and considered Tolkien even "more gruesome". (348). On the other hand, she considered Tolkien almost as horrid as Lewis Carroll (Sundmark 2014, 5). A main reason why she took the job of illustrating *The Hobbit* was because she saw it as a chance to make illustrations in a "world of catastrophe". The horror spoke to her just like it had when illustrating *The Hunting of the Snark* by Lewis Carroll (Westin 2014, 348). Granted, "the note of melancholy that emerges towards the end of *The Hobbit* [...] would most certainly have chimed with her own explorations of fear, loneliness and sadness in the Moomin books" (Sibley 2015, 1).

Horror is often subtly visible in Jansson's illustrations. Jansson, like Tolkien, had "a sense of the 'personality' of landscape with its vast immensities and ever-present dangers, and a concept of catastrophe constantly poised to overwhelm the characters" (1). As mentioned in section 4, Jansson was far more interested in Tolkien's landscapes than his characters, and found horror in the scenery. In her illustrations for *The Hobbit*, the characters often disappear into the landscape. The characters are framed as spectators, marginal observers, while the dangers take the main stage (Hołownia 2014, 9-10). By making the characters very small in relation to their surroundings, Jansson emphasizes the peril and the immensity of the quest (Sibley 2015, 2). This as well as the tight framing, dark colours and many details create an ominous atmosphere (Hołownia 2014, 9-10): "The creation of this intense atmosphere seems to be the most successful element in Jansson's take on *The Hobbit*" (11).

Excitingly, the tight framing that creates immensity is a device shared by Jansson, the legendary Swedish illustrator John Bauer, as well as Tolkien himself. In her short story *The Bays*, Jansson memorably describes a Bauerian forest as not including the tops of trees or the sky, but only straight tree-trunks and the ground, and with everything being roughly the same colour (Jansson 2013, 57). This description matches to a degree Jansson's illustration of the company in Mirkwood, but even more so Tolkien's own Mirkwood illustration for *The Hobbit* (*Hobbit* 1937: The illustration between pages 146 and 147). While this illustration is black-and-white, its predecessor – originally meant as Taur-na-Fúin but later renamed "Fangorn Forest" – is of brown and grey shades (Hammond & Scull 2011, 74-6).

On the other hand, if Jansson's illustrations do not reach the degree of horror many people see in the novel, one can argue that the differences between *Hompen* and both *The Hobbit* 1937 and *The Hobbit* 1993 and the modern reader's expectation of epicness in the style of *The Lord of the Rings* pile up into a greater issue. Adam Roberts suggests that through the reconceptualization of the novel, making it a part of the legendarium, *The Hobbit* pre-*The Lord of the Rings* and post-*The Lord of the Rings* are quite different in terms of seriousness. Originally the novel was "homely, funny, a little bit slapstick and a little bit wondrous". After the revisions the novel is "grand-verging-on-grandiose, theological, epic" and "the great dramas of the age" (Roberts 2013, 95-6). I would argue that the reconceptualization of the novel also applies to horror and how an illustrator might deal with the theme. Jansson, having read a version of *The Hobbit* preceding the revisions and most probably not being familiar with *The Lord of the Rings*, could not have reacted to the epic scale nor the seriousness of the drama and horror, possibly resulting in illustrations that do not fit with the expectations of readers familiar with Tolkien wider legendarium.

Suitably, a Finnish interviewee mentions appreciating Jansson's illustrations as "they give the work a touch of accessibility and lightness" (Alexander 2016, 218-9). These features fit exactly with what Roberts describes *The Hobbit* having been before its reconceptualization: down-to-earth, being accessible to the reader, using a lot of comedy. Similarly, a Finnish reviewer notes that the familiar Moomin-style of Jansson's illustrations underline the fairytale aspects of the story in a nice manner, making a clear distinction to Peter Jackson's "demonic orcs and other scary things" (Metso 2004, 29). It is interesting that the reviewer not only refers to *The Lord of the Rings*, but specifically Peter Jackson's films. His familiarity with the films did not create expectations that would have prejudiced him against Jansson's work. Moreover, two Swedish reviewers from the 1960s noted that familiarity with the Moomins might have made readers, in Sweden at least, more open to a story like *The Hobbit* (Sundmark 2014, 8). Whether or not they are referring to Jansson's illustrations within the book or only to Moomin books in general, these statements do remind us of the accessibility to the reader that Roberts' talks about when discussing *The Hobbit* before its role as a part of Tolkien's legendarium.

14 - Conclusion

When comparing *The Hobbit* 1937, *Hompen* and Tove Jansson's notes for her illustrations, a relatively clear picture emerges. Despite some inconsistencies, the page numbers and word choices in Jansson's notes appear to refer to *Hompen*, leading to the assumption that *Hompen* was her source text for the illustrations. The changes made to *Hompen* by the translator Tore Zetterholm may have had an effect on Jansson's illustrations. While Zetterholm censored the more horrible elements of the text, Jansson nevertheless relished in them. Jansson's Gollum, on the other hand, may have suffered from Tolkien's own revisions as *Hompen* precedes these changes. Jansson's notes reveal a detail-oriented artist instead of one who has not bothered with the particulars of the book.

Bibliography

Aejmelaeus, S., *Kun lyhdyt syttyvät: Tove Jansson ja muumimaailma,* (Finnish Institute for Children's Literature, 1994).

Allardice, L., 'It is a Religion': How the world went mad for Moomins, *The Guardian*, 6 April 2019: <theguardian.com/books/2019/apr/06/it-is-a-religion-how-the-world-went-mad-for-moomins> [Accessed 17 July 2019].

Anderson, D.A., *The Annotated Hobbit*, rev. And exp. edn. (London: HarperCollins, 2003).

Alexander, M.L., 'Tolkien and the Illustrators: Visual Representations of *The Hobbit*', in *Critical Insights: The Hobbit*, ed. By S.W. Potts (Ipswich: Salem Press, 2016) 201-224.

Björk, C., *Tove Jansson: mycket mer än Mumin,* (Stockholm: Bilda Förlag, 2003).

Burr, T.,. 'Moomin Struck: Tove Jansson: 1914-2001', *Entertainment Weekly*, 27 July 2001, 66. <https://ew.com/article/ 2001/07/27/moomin-struck/> [Accessed 31 January 2024].

Hammond, W.G. and Scull, C., *The Art of the Hobbit by J.R.R. Tolkien*, (London: HarperCollins, 2011).

Hołownia, O., '"Hell, what a chance to have a go at the classics": Tove Jansson's take on Alice's Adventures in Wonderland, The Hunting of the Snark, and *The Hobbit*' in *Barnboken – tidskrift för barnlitteraturforskning*, 37 <http://dx.doi.org/10.14811/clr.v37i0.191>.

Jansson, T., Sculptor's *Daughter: a Childhood Memoir*, trans. by K. Hart (London: Sort of Books, 2013).
— *Vem ska trösta knyttet?*, (Stockholm: Rabén & Sjögren, 2014).

Karjalainen, T., *Tove Jansson: Work and Love*, trans. by D. McDuff (London: Particular Books, 2014).

Kruskopf, E., *Bildkonstnären Tove Jansson*, (Helsinki: Schildt, 1992).

Kuinkas sitten kävikään? Muumikirjojen tarina, ed. by M. Honkasalo, 166 (Tampere Art Museum Publications, 2017).

Metso, P., 'Hobitti eli Sinne ja takaisin' *Ortodoksinen kulttuuri*, 23 (2004) 29.

Nilsson-Lång, L., *Hompen v. Bilbo: a study of two Swedish translations of Tolkien's The Hobbit*, (Master's Thesis, Lulea Technological University, 2002).

Nordling, P., email to the author, 9 April 2018.

Nummelin, J. and V. Sisättö, *Tolkien – elämä ja teokset*, (Helsinki: Avain, 2014).

'PAX – Puhutaan rauhasta: Tove Janssonin Hobitti' at Vantaa Art Museum Artsi, 16 March –3 June 2018.

Raiskio, N., 'Tove Janssonin kotikirjasto', *The Finnish Institute for Children's Literature* (31 July 2018) <lastenkirjainstituutti.fi/kirjasto/kirjakokoelma/ erikoiskokoelmat/tove-janssonin-kotikirjasto> [Accessed 12 October 2018].

Roberts, A., *The Riddles of The Hobbit*, (London: Palgrave Macmillan, 2013).

Scoville, C. N., 'Hobbit, The', in *J. R. R. Tolkien Encyclopedia: Scholarship and Critical Assessment*, ed. by M.D.C. Drout (New York: Routledge, 2007) 277-279.

Scull, C. and W.G. Hammond, *The J. R. R. Tolkien Companion and Guide I: Chronology, rev. and exp. edn*., (London: HarperCollins, 2017a).
— *The J. R. R. Tolkien Companion and Guide II: Reader's Guide, part 1: A–M, rev. and exp. edn*,. (London: HarperCollins, 2017b).
— *The J. R. R. Tolkien Companion and Guide III: Reader's Guide, part 2: N–Z, rev. and exp. edn*., (London: HarperCollins, 2017c).

Sibley, B., 'From Moominland to Middle-earth' in: *The Official Tolkien Calendar 2016*, (London: HarperCollins, 2015).

Smith, A., 'Introduction', in *Sculptor's Daughter: a Childhood Memoir*, by T. Jansson, trans. by K. Hart (London: Sort of Books, 2013) vii-xxi.

Stenström, A. "Beregond", 'Tolkien in Swedish Translation: From Hompen to Ringarnas herre', in *Translating Tolkien: Text and Film*, ed. by T. Honegger, 2nd edn. (Zurich: Walking Tree, 2011) 109–118.

Sundmark, B., '"En hobbit och ett mumintroll skulle kunna mötas i bästa sämja": Receptionen av Bilbo, en hobbits äventyr (1962)', in: *Barnboken – tidskrift för barnlitteraturforskning*, 37 (2014) <http://dx.doi.org/10.14811/clr.v37i0.186>.

Svensson, L., *Lost in Translation? – A Comparative Study of Three Swedish Translations of J.R.R. Tolkien's The Hobbit,* (Lund University, 2016).

Tervaharju, M., 'Tove-juhlaa ja kokoelma-aarteita', *Onnimanni*, March 2014, 4-6.

Tolkien, J. R. R., *The Hobbit, or There and Back Again*, 1st edn. Facsimile. (London: HarperCollins, 2016).
— *Hompen, eller En resa dit och tillbaksigen*, trans. by T. Zetterholm, illus. by T. Zetterholm and C. Sjöblom. (Stockholm: Kooperativa Förbundets Bokförlag, 1947).
— *Bilbo. En hobbits äventyr*, trans. by B.G. Hallqvist, illus. by T. Jansson, 1st edn. (Stockholm: Rabén & Sjögren, 1962).
— *The Hobbit, or There and Back Again,* (London: HarperCollins, 1993).
— *Bilbo. En hobbits äventyr*, trans. by B.G. Hallqvist, illus. by T. Jansson. 2nd edn. (Stockholm: Rabén & Sjögren, 1994).

The Tove Jansson Collection (2018) in Onnet Database <prettylib.erikoiskirjastot.fi/lib4/src?DATABASE=4&PBFORMTYPE =01001&PROFILESET=SNKF&MAX=50&DEPARTMENT=0&LOCATIONID=12&FREETEXT=&Hae=Hae&MULTISRC=4&MULTITEXT=&MULTISRC=5&MULTITEXT=&Year1=&Year2=&TITTYPE=-1&Language=&SORT=1&SSS=2> [Accessed 12 October 2018]

Vilén, F. (Aldamírie), 'Mumintrollets broder – Tove Janssons bilder till *Bilbo* & English summary', *Arda* 1987 (1992) 84-88.

Westin, B.,*Tove Jansson: Ord, bild, liv* (Stockholm: Bonniers, 2007).
— *Tove Jansson: Life, Art, Words: The Authorised Biography*, trans. By S. Mazzarella (London: Sort of Books, 2014).

RECEPTION, FANDOM, AND LEGACY

Tutoring Key Stage 5 Students in Tolkien: A Priceless and Hilarious Experience on Sharing My PhD Project with 16-Year-Olds

Aslı Bülbül Candaş

Dear reader, if you are reading this, you most probably have already read some literary works of J.R.R. Tolkien. Reading Tolkien's texts and getting familiar with his world-building must have been so much fun for you, or perhaps even a life-changing experience on its own like it is with some of us. If you are also a teacher, that is another common ground between you and me (unless you think it is impossible for you to teach Tolkien because of your eccentric subject, in that case do not ever worry and e-mail me so we may discuss this further and I will dissuade you with my Half-elven powers). It may be stating the obvious, but reading and teaching Tolkien are completely different experiences by letting a person see different aspects of world-building in opposite ways: one is unshared and the other is interactive at first glance, and while reading, you may preferably want to adapt your mindset to be immersed in literary belief whereas before, during and probably after teaching, you need to adapt the relevant text to the needs of students.

When I first started to work for a charity which aims at increasing the number of pupils from under-represented backgrounds progressing to the Russell Group universities, I used to see this as a challenging and right-minded experience. Soon I realised in shock how quickly my sweet students could turn out to be little Melkors, on their way to mar the imaginary worlds their classmates had just started to create. The seven-week-long tutorial scheme swiftly turned into a psychological experiment just after the second week, and no matter what I did, not to mention the fact that I had carefully planned all the tutorials beforehand, I had to watch my Melkors create fantastic artefacts to destroy the artefact of one another. I ended up feeling like the Godhead Eru Ilúvatar, obviously with some basic differences–my students did not originate from my thought, and I had not kindled them with the Flame Imperishable, apparently, they had already been kindled by some kind of secret fire that I could not yet name.

In the end, the tutorial project revealed a strange way of thinking, which came as no surprise when common human traits were considered. I am not a psychologist but all I can say is when a creative process was triggered in my students' mind, they immediately started to seek ways to elaborate it, and when they reached the boundaries of one another's creation, they desired more space without doubt and gave more meaning to their own creations simply by destroying the artefact of one another. It was almost as if they naturally felt that the loss on one side would be a gain for the other. The coexistence of polarities was a must; it was my mistake to rule this out in the first place.

Before demonstrating how the tutorial scheme progressed, I would like to note that it was the charity policy to adapt our PhD projects to the level of Key Stage 5 students. Therefore, the contents of the KS5 Programme did not necessarily go in parallel with the main chapters of my thesis; however, it was customised to give an idea about the hypothesis and main aims of my PhD. Here is a summary of what aspects of my PhD thesis were taught each week.

- Tutorial 1 – Launch Trip, 06 November 2018, "Building a Fantasy World": The concepts of the Primary and secondary world, the meaning of world-building and the function of art in Arda
- Tutorial 2, 13 November 2018, "The Rings of Power as Artefacts": Fantastic features of the Rings, their overall significance in surpassing the boundaries of space and time (particularly the Three and the One Ring)
- Tutorial 3, 20 November 2018, "The Two Lamps, the Two Trees (Part I) and Their Fantastic Features": Their role in the legendarium and the mythopoetic characteristics of Arda, the concept of 'light' in artefacts
- Tutorial 4, 27 November 2018, "The Two Trees (Part II), the Silmarils, and the Relationship between Them": The connection between the Trees and the Silmarils, the transmission of light and the beginnings of time perception
- Tutorial 5, 04 December 2018, "What Is the Purpose of All These Artefacts?"
- Tutorial 6 – 1:1 Feedback, 11 December 2018
- Tutorial 7 – 1:1 Feedback, 30 January 2019

At this point, I would like to make it clear what I mean by "artefact". In my doctoral thesis, I study the concepts of art and light in Tolkien's secondary world, and my hypothesis is that the artefacts which capture a ray of the Godhead Eru Ilúvatar's light echo perfection. I thus study miscellaneous things–the Two Trees, the Silmarils, the Moon, the Sun, stars etc.–as artefacts. Whether handmade or natural, they are all practically "made" from the materials coming out of Arda's nature, there is artistic creativity in their making, and more importantly, they are not uniform like the "machinery" of Melkor, Sauron or Saruman. In his letter to his son Christopher Tolkien, while talking about Christopher's flying course experiences, Tolkien differentiates art and machinery thus: "There is the tragedy and despair of all machinery laid bare. Unlike art which is content to create a new secondary world in the mind, it attempts to actualize desire, and so to create power in this World" (*Letters*, Letter 75, 87). Because of the inescapable relationship between the primary and the secondary world, there are both art and machinery to be found in Arda. As for the Silmarils and the One Ring, both of which are completely arguable to be classified as "artefacts" when it comes to Tolkien's own claims of the actualisation of desire and creation of power, during the tutorial scheme, we studied their differences to the machinery of the "evil" in Arda, their artistic qualities, and the reasons why they were exceptional by passing the boundaries of space and time or transmitting light.

Based on these descriptions and differentiation, throughout the whole scheme, I designed the Course Rationale to enable my pupils to rediscover their humane desire to create an imaginary world and to discern the function of literature in sparking our imagination and the role of art in Tolkien's world-building. In his essay "A Changeling Returns", Michael Swanwick remembers how he started to become a writer after he read *The Fellowship of the Ring*:

> Oh, how that book shook and rattled me! It rang me like a bell. Even today, when I am three times as old as I was then, I can still hold my breath and hear the faint reverberations from that long, eternal night. That reading made me a writer, though it took me forever to learn my craft. It showed me what literature could do and what it could be. (Haber 2003, 34)

My intention was not only to expose the pupils to Tolkien's subcreation but also to spark the inspiration to write something of their own. As Mark Wolf suggests: "For many, the desire for imaginary worlds does not change over time, only the manner in which those worlds are constructed and experienced" (2012, 4), and I wanted my pupils to see how effective and significant the role of literature was in the construction of imaginary worlds. Cynthia Freeland points to the central role of art in cognitive theories:

Both the expression and cognitive theories of art hold that art *communicates*: it can communicate feelings and emotions, or thoughts and ideas. Interpretation is important because it helps explain how art does this. Art acquires meaning in part from its context. (2001, 149)

And this was my third aim: I desired to share with my pupils how art communicated both in the secondary world and within the class. Of course it was neither rational nor practical for me to expect from them to invent their secondary worlds just in 7 weeks, so I made it clear every single week that their inventions could be limited with artefacts that may match well with Arda's inner consistency and ontological infrastructures of space and time, meanwhile leaving them with the option to introduce their fantastic artefacts in a completely different setting that was similar to Tolkien's subcreation.

At this point, I feel the necessity to clarify it for the readers the reason why I call my lovely pupils "little Melkors", as the desire to imagine and create are not only natural but also it is to be found with the rest of the Valar. To do this, I should first remind how Melkor is introduced in "Ainulindalë":

> But as the theme progressed, it came into the heart of Melkor to interweave matters of his own imagining that were not in accord with the theme of Ilúvatar; for he sought therein to increase the power and glory of the part assigned to himself [...] He had gone often alone into the void places seeking the Imperishable Flame; for desire grew hot within him to bring into Being things of his own [...] being alone he had begun to conceive thoughts of his own unlike those of his brethren. (*Silmarillion*, 16)

This is a subjective observation rather than a justification of whatever destruction is to follow on Melkor's part but actually, in the beginning, the only explicit difference of Melkor to the others is his lack of teamwork skills. He is always "alone", thus is isolated and left with his own thoughts, which misleads him to assume that there is more space for him to expand the boundaries of his assigned part. When his melodies clash against those of the Valar, he can only think of and desire for subverting the Music to create more space for his creations. So this is it: lack of realisation and appreciation that a medium of creative power is shared with others. And this is exactly what happened with my students: they could not have a proactive strategy while inventing their artefacts as they were allocated some alone time for this–just to come back to the following tutorial to discover that their inventions had to share the same time and space with some other artefacts of their classmates. Immediately, issues of practicality were raised and there started the Battle of Artefacts by revealing the survival strategy of their inventions.

To understand this escalation better, I should repeat the parallelisms between the primary and secondary world. These two phrases were coined and thoroughly discussed by Tolkien in his essay 'On Fairy-stories'. To narrow it down for this paper, the secondary world needs to have physical boundaries like the primary one to maintain its own inner consistency. In his essay, under the concept of "literary belief", Tolkien describes the art of story-making thus: "What really happens is that the story-maker proves a successful 'sub-creator'. He makes a Secondary World which your mind can enter. Inside it, what he relates is 'true': it accords with the laws of that world" (*OFS*, 52). "That world" also needs its "laws" in the way our world does. In my understanding, these laws are nothing but boundaries set for the readers to have a complete understanding of the secondary world in their own terms. As Wolf points out: "The automatic filling in of gaps by an observer was first noted in Gestalt psychology, which began in the early twentieth century and saw the whole as being more than the sum of its parts", and this is the true essence lying at the heart of invented worlds and enabling them to reach a sense of completeness that gives them the name "world" (2012, 51). For two weeks, we particularly studied the concepts of space and time as the ontological boundaries in Arda, and my pupils tried to fill in the gaps in their minds to make sense of the secondary world. Wolf goes on by answering the question of what a world is constructed from: "Similar systems of relationships hold a world's elements together and define its structure; maps, timelines, histories and mythologies [...] and those involving nature, culture, language, and society. When a large enough number of elements from these systems are combined in a consistent fashion, a kind of 'world logic' starts to form" (53). These systems of relationships bring inescapable boundaries, and my pupils' previously created artefacts had to be reformed, destroyed or left alone to survive. And they chose the most practical way, to destroy the other.[1]

I can remember the first time I started reading *The Lord of the Rings*–I was 14. Although I could have been considered as an age-mate of my pupils, I never had the chance to be in a tutorial scheme covering Tolkien's legendarium back then, let alone practising to invent my own fantastic artefacts or to build my secondary world. The overall tutorial scheme thus has led me to understand how different and interesting viewpoints the youngsters may have about world-building and its boundaries. It has also revealed how honestly, clearly and naturally they can bring the chaos of the secondary world back to the primary one–and that sets an example of the connection between the two worlds which Tolkien suggested and developed, and many Tolkien scholars have studied and discussed further.

Bibliography

Freeland, C., *But is it art?*, (Oxford: Oxford University Press, 2001).

1. During my presentation I shared several examples of my students' writing that I cannot replicate here.

Haber, K., *Meditations on Middle-earth,* (London: Simon & Schuster UK Ltd, 2003).

Tolkien, J. R. R., *The Silmarillion,* (New York: Houghton Mifflin Harcourt, 2001).
— *The Lord of the Rings,* (London: HarperCollinsPublishers, 2004).
— *The Letters of J.R.R. Tolkien,* ed. by H. Carpenter with the assistance of C. Tolkien. (London: HarperCollins Publishers, 2006).
— *Tolkien On Fairy-stories*, ed. by V. Flieger and D.A. Anderson (London: HarperCollins, 2008).

Wolf, M.J.P., *Building Imaginary Worlds: The Theory and History of Subcreation,* (New York: Routledge, 2012).

Over Hill and Under Hill

Erick Carvalho

When Tolkien's works were first published in Brazil in the 1970s, almost nothing was known - not only about the author but also about what we now call Tolkien's legendarium. We can certainly say that it is not easy to trace a history of academic or fandom perceptions of Tolkien's works in Brazil. In fact, it looks like a journey with ups and downs and that's the main reason why I call this presentation 'Over Hill and Under Hill', because, indeed, our Brazilian journey is surrounded by difficulties and misconceptions but also good and fierce groups committed to make Tolkien canon literature amongst Brazilians.

I quote the first lines of chapter four of *The Hobbit* to illustrate my perceptions of it, because as the main title of this presentation suggests, our Brazilian readers and scholars face some problems worthy of dwarves and hobbits trying to reach The Lonely Mountain. And if I could compare it in the same way,

> There were many paths that led up into those mountains, and many passes over them. But most of the paths were cheats and deceptions and led nowhere or to bad ends; and most of the passes were infested by evil things and dreadful dangers. The dwarves and the hobbit, helped by the wise advice of Elrond and the knowledge and memory of Gandalf, took the right road to the right pass. (*Hobbit*, 'Over Hill and Under Hill', 70)

Well, I'm not saying that our scholars or fandom group leaders are as wise as Elrond or Gandalf, I'm trying to say that they make mistakes and achievements and they have helped to build a large Tolkien community in Brazil. Some of them are very popular on the internet and others more well known in academic circles. But they all contribute in a way to make Tolkien's writings popular and canon in Brazil, even when they're fighting for different sides and interpretations.

To reach that point of our explanation, we first need to understand the very beginning of 'Tolkienism' in Brazil, its different periods and, of course, the different perceptions for scholars and the general public of readers. In the end, this is a cultural and social memory analysis, of how a great literary figure attracts different feelings and social actions and interactions within a specific culture, in this case our Brazilian culture.

1 - The Road goes on

In the very beginning there were few who actually read Tolkien in Brazil. Some may find it interesting to know that our first Brazilian edition of *The Lord of the Rings* came between 1974 and 1979, divided into six books and published by 'Arte Nova' editors (which means 'New Art'), a group with no official rights to translate Tolkien and therefore with no knowledge of the names or any idea how to translate it. The result, with the translation of the 1976 *The Hobbit* as well, was a very rare group of books known by a few fantasy addicted people by that time and no more.

By the 1980s the majority of Tolkien's readers in Brazil were introduced to Tolkien by the Portuguese version of the books and by that time the first academic research was made as well: "*O Senhor dos anéis: estrutura e significado*" ("The Lord of The Rings: structure and meaning") by Lucia Lima Polachini in 1984. At the end of the decade the now renowned translator Ronald Kyrmse founded *Heren Hyarmen*, the "Order of the South", the very first Tolkien Society affiliated Smial in Brazil (and also in Latin America) and therefore the Brazilian fans became more and more organized in groups. It's interesting to mention that Ronald Kyrmse is the oldest Tolkien Society member in Brazil and thereafter a real "Tolkien Reference" in our country.

Despite those initiatives, Brazilian readers lacked a very important thing: a proper translation in our language. This began to change in the 1990s when the first official translations came to be published by Martins Fontes editors, starting with Humphrey Carpenter's biography in 1992, followed by *The Lord of The Rings* in 1994, *The Hobbit* in 1995 and *The Silmarillion* in 1999. By that time, in 1997, the very first PhD thesis was written by Rosa Sílvia López, entitled "*O narrar ritualístico em o Senhor dos Anéis de J.R.R. Tolkien*" ("The ritualistic narrative in J.R.R. Tolkien's *The Lord of The Rings*").

With real Brazilian translations we started to build up a large community at the end of the 1990s and, of course, different fans from different parts of Brazil started to fight for representation, affiliations and other minor elements (even sometimes among each other). The advent of the internet was, in this specific case, a double-edged sword because different groups started to gather larger audiences just to be isolated in their own social bubble.

So, we had groups being created, for example, the very informative and academic website and internet forum Valinor (still working today with a large archive of the very best texts in Portuguese language), The STB (Brazilian Tolkien Society), The White Council (a large Tolkien society promoting events in different parts of Brazil), and so on.

Eventually through the 2000s those groups became more and more intertwined and the explanation was, in fact, two distinct things. First, Peter Jackson's *The Lord of The Rings* movie trilogy, a huge box-office success in Brazil that helped to change the way Brazilians view Fantasy productions as a profound form of adult entertainment. Second, the professionalisation of the fans who started to publish academic books, to study Tolkien at universities and to promote it with a Brazilian way of reading Tolkien. This professionalization is responsible for organizing different academic events such as symposiums, expos and even open classes in large Brazilian universities in Rio de Janeiro and São Paulo.

Translators like Reinaldo José lopes and Gabriel Brum came from that background and nowadays they're responsible for the current translations of *The Silmarillion*, *The Hobbit*, *The Letters of J. R. R. Tolkien*, etc.

By the time the new books and translations arrived in bookstores, new fandom groups and scholars began to appear within the internet. Just to mention a few of them: The website and Facebook page *Tolkien Brasil* (which started with good reading guides despite the isolationist posture it has assumed nowadays), the YouTube channels *Tolkien Talk* (today the most watched and polyvalent channel in Brazil with very interesting and diversified videos from video dramas to academic coverage) and O Bolseiro (with some reviews); and the website *Tolkienista.com* (with texts from different authors but organized by the Brazilian scholar Cristina Casagrande, who recently published one of the very best studies in Portuguese language about the friendship in *The Lord of the Rings*). And, of course, the creation of two new Latin America Smials: The Toca in Rio de Janeiro followed by Imladris in São Paulo, promoting public readings and everything Tolkien.

2 - There and back again: Contemporary questions

Talking about how this Tolkien community was built up through the past decades inevitably leads to a discussion about Memory and the perception of 'Tolkienism' among Brazilians. First, we need to define what kind of memory we're talking about here and then we need to understand what kind of methods the scholars or the general readers use to define their perceptions.

The first point we need to understand comes from the fact that the academic community of Tolkien scholars and Tolkien's general readers are intertwined. Both groups communicate among themselves and also produce a sort of Communicative Memory passing through them among the past decades. The Communicative Memory here is a kind of collective memory based on the historical experiences in a framework of individual biographies, informal and everyday interactions, personal experiences with and readings of Tolkien's literature, book launches, public readings, free academic lectures and, more recently, internet interactions with posts and live videos on social media.

In the Brazilian Tolkien community, this kind of communicative memory is defined by two models. The first, more linked with a generational exchange of ideas and a second one closer to specific and contemporary witnesses within a proper group committed to a specific activity such as a book club, Role Playing Games, video games or Music fans. Together, both groups create a very Brazilian way of reading Tolkien based on the reading of the text itself but linking academic analysis with good and popular humour.

At the same time, we can see a huge growth of the Tolkien community in the past two years and that happens because , as we already said, both academic and general reader groups seems to be intertwined for their own survival, and also because of the efforts of these groups to make Tolkien a more popular author in Brazil.

Among those groups, we must agree that the new Brazilian editors of Tolkien's books, Harper Collins Brasil, took an important role. After all, since the new contract came along and new and more accurate translations are being published, new doors are being opened for Tolkien's readers (whether a Tolkien scholar or a member of the general public). The editors are promoting links among the more traditional fan based groups, the youtubers and even the scholars (since their own translators are scholars themselves) and with that, more and more of the public is attracted to Tolkien's works. Just to mention an example, the past four Tolkien books published by Harper Collins Brasil reached the top ten list of the best sellers in Brazil, a surprising status for a fantasy book in our country.

3 - And whither then? I cannot say: But let's draw some conclusions anyway.

The Tolkiendil future in Brazil seems bright. Future Tolkien readers will be well served with new academic publications, new books with new, and more accurate, translations and even the prospect of *The History of Middle-earth* being published in our country is now on the horizon.

But all these efforts rely on solid communicative memory built up through the past decades and constantly reaffirmed with the close relationship between the Brazilian Tolkien scholars and the general public. Of course, there are some controversies. After all, nothing concerning humans and intellectuals is easy to comprehend. But, despite a few dissonant and sometimes snobbish voices within the more fanatic groups of fans, the majority of Tolkien readers in Brazil seems to be aligned with a bigger cause. In other words, the future of Tolkien studies in Brazil seems to follow a reliable path.

Over the past decades, history was the base for the development of a complex multi-layered Tolkien memory culture, both communicative and multidirectional, forged to assume a very Brazilian way of reading and interpreting this kind of literature. Tolkien could be labelled as the great and 'generic' form of fantasy literature that already "altered reading tastes" in Brazil. This is mostly because of the efforts of Tolkien scholars and fandom groups who have created this memory culture that surrounds Tolkien's work's reception in our country.

In comparison with English speaking countries, of course, Tolkien studies in Brazil are still in their infancy. But based on the "wise advice" coming from the new Tolkien scholars and the knowledge and memory from our well established groups of fans, the future should be promising.

Bibliography

Tolkien, J.R.R., *The Hobbit,* (London: HarperCollins, 1996).

The TARDIS in Middle-earth

Joel Cornah

Two of the most well-known and well-loved imaginary worlds to come out of the last century have been Tolkien's Middle-earth, and the *Doctor Who* universe. These two creations walk in parallel, cross paths, and reflect one another; they delve into the inner fire of fairy stories and pull at something that sparks the imagination.

Doctor Who is a science fiction family drama that started in 1963. It is the longest running science fiction drama and has spawned an awful lot of iconic imagery, from the police-box-time-machine, to the pepper-pot-like Daleks and their obsession with "extermination". The show follows the adventures of a time travelling alien called the Doctor as he faces monsters, tyrants and even dinosaurs across all of history. The Doctor often takes companions from contemporary earth (mostly) and shows them the wonders of time and space.

The inspiration for this talk came from some of the tiny references and parallels I noticed over the years of watching. I remember seeing the 1981 story *The Keeper of Traken* with the Fourth Doctor, Tom Baker. On the planet Traken evil cannot enter. If it tries, an evil source would be turned to stone and left standing as a motionless monument to Trakenite peace. These evil statues were called Melkurs. The Master's TARDIS took the form of this red-eyed monster and became a Melkur who terrorised the people and sought to take the secret of eternal life from them.

Tolkien's first Dark Lord was, of course, Melkor. The similar names are quite striking: a dark and evil creature seeking domination and mastery over the universe, searching for the secret fire, and generally making a nuisance; that sounds very much like the Master.

The first Doctor wore a signet ring of which he was very protective. It was a ring of power. He could use it to open the TARDIS doors, hypnotise and manipulate others and it even protected the Doctor from electrical shock. He was incredibly possessive of it until he regenerated. This little parallel sparked my imagination and I started looking for other ways in which the show mirrored Tolkien more substantially.

And so, with rumours abounding that Peter 'film adaptations' Jackson will possibly be directing an episode or two of Doctor Who, it seems that now is a good time to delve into this topic. I want to talk about how we can see Tolkien through the lens of *Doctor Who* and vice versa. I want to look at how we can examine the way these two works build on the same foundations and tap into the same creative tools.

For Tolkien, one of the profound effects of fantasy and fairy stories was the way in which one can see again mundane, familiar and every-day things and find something else to see in them. To look again at the world with renewed wonder and strangeness;

> We need, in any case, to clean our windows; so that the things seen clearly may be freed from the drab blur of triteness or familiarity—from possessiveness. Of all faces those of our familiares are the ones both most difficult to play fantastic tricks with, and most

> difficult really to see with fresh attention, perceiving their likeness and unlikeness: that they are faces, and yet unique faces. [...]
> Creative fantasy, because it is mainly trying to do something else (make something new), may open your hoard and let all the locked things fly away like cage-birds. (*OFS*, 68)

Tolkien was talking often of 'recovering' a truth about what may have always been true about a thing in the mundane and familiar. To pull back the veil to reveal what had been lost to time or distorted. To turn off the chameleon circuit and see the true underlying reality once again.

Bilbo Baggins housed many familiar characteristics of the bourgeois and yet he was still something else entirely. He was a Hobbit, with furry feet, diminutive stature, and a thirst for adventure, which, though hidden, eventually came roaring out. A ring may be a mundane item, or it may be the very soul of a dark lord. A tree might be a tree, or it may be an old man with a black heart, or a bearded shepherd. Likewise, a blue phone-box may be a phone-box, or it may be a vast, alien time machine.

The Doctor's time machine, the TARDIS, is able to disguise itself as anything. When it first appeared on our screens in 1963 it took the form of a battered old Police Public Call Box. However, it malfunctioned and got stuck on this image from that moment on. Though the Doctor attempted to fix it a couple of times, he never really succeeded. As the Eleventh Doctor explains in a deleted scene from the 2010 series;

> Every time the TARDIS materializes in a new location within the first nanosecond of landing it analyses its surroundings, calculates a twelve dimensional map of everything within a thousand mile radius and determines which outer shell would blend in best with the environment. [...]
> And then it disguises itself as a Police Telephone Box from 1963. It's probably a bit of a fault. (Smith 2010)

At the time, a Police Box was a fairly mundane item one would see on street corners or, as it happened, in a junkyard. For the audience of the 1960s, to think that an old police box could be an alien machine from the future would have been a thing of wonder in and of itself.

The TARDIS appears as a small blue phone box, but within is a vast interior. It is bigger on the inside than it is on the outside. Existing in a different dimension, the TARDIS's interior goes on, seemingly forever. It is quite literally another world existing beyond the doors of a simple, battered, wooden phone box.

Statues, shadows, plastic mannequins, trampolines and pepper pots – *Doctor Who* has always taken the familiar and given them shades of the unusual, the otherworldly, and the frightening. Sometimes the show takes the same track as Tolkien – living trees for example turn up multiple times.

Back in the 2005 story *The End of the World*, the Ninth Doctor encounters the Forest of Cheem, an intelligent and inquisitive world leader who witnessed the end of the planet Earth. She also helped save the people on Platform One by sacrificing herself. Much like the Ents and their sacrificial attack on Isengard. In the 2011 Christmas special, *The Doctor, The Widow and the Wardrobe*, we were introduced to the Androzani Trees. An intelligent species of trees that were able to shapeshift into humanoid forms that somewhat resembles Ents. The Wooden King even had a beard. A Tree-Beard, you might say. The idea of the woods taking over, becoming sentient and living did not stop there. In the 2014 episode *In the Forest of the Night*, Peter Capaldi's Doctor faced a worldwide invasion of trees. Ultimately, the trees were benevolent, rescuing the earth from impending destruction, acting as guardians and sentinels.

Trees taking back the world, defending themselves, or causing mischief is something you will find throughout Tolkien as he said

> Every tree has its enemy, few have an advocate. (Too often the hate is irrational, a fear of anything large and alive, and not easily tamed or destroyed, though it may clothe itself in rational terms.)
> (*Letters*, Letter 241, 321)

This seems very much like something the Doctor would say about many of the monsters he has encountered. So often his reaction is to reason with them, to seek out peace and understanding. For the Doctor, the wonder of the world - discovering and helping people - is one of his great motivators. He is eternally fascinated with people, with their little lives and their great destinies. For the most part, he doesn't see simply a young woman working in a shop, but an adventurer who can have more life in a few years than many have in decades. He doesn't see just a tired medical student, he sees someone who can walk the earth and bring down a tyrant. He doesn't just see a temp working job after job, but the most important woman in the universe.

Likewise, Gandalf does not see just a little hobbit with funny quirks and a peaceful life, he sees the potential to change the world and bring down a dark lord. He too is a wanderer, a traveller from a distant, otherworldly realm and his powers are beyond those of the people around him.

The wise old wizard figure is so often used in fantasy as the mentor and guide, but in *Doctor Who*, he is the hero. However, the Doctor does not see himself as a hero and seems to actively resent the idea at times. He is offered praise and power several times – he brings down regimes and dethrones tyrants, often to be offered the throne, and yet turns it down. He does not see himself as one suited to power, perhaps because he has seen what it does to people so often.

In a special extra scene for the 2010 episode *Flesh and Stone*, the Doctor refers to himself as a 'space Gandalf'. The comparison makes sense when you see it from the Doctor's point of view. They are both wise beyond human capabilities, a little eccentric and silly at times, and possess abilities that many would call magical. Also, they both come back from the dead in a new, slightly changed persona and costume.

The Time of the Doctor (2013) had the Doctor facing his ultimate demise. He sends his companion away so that he might face the enemy alone. He fought an exhausting battle that left him at the end of his life, no more regeneration possible. Clara, his companion at the time, is essentially told 'Fly you fool!' as the Doctor fights on. Yet, when his death finally hits, he is given a new life cycle by the Time Lords who have deemed that, much like Gandalf, his task is not yet complete.

A criticism the Doctor often receives from his own people is that he is too fond of and familiar with the people of Earth. Much like Saruman's dismissive and derogatory attitude towards Gandalf's view of Hobbits and pipe-weed.

> I know well enough that you have become a curious explorer of the small: weeds, wild things, and childish folk. Your time is your own to spend if you have nothing worthier to do; and your friends you may make as you please. But to me the days are too dark for wanderers tales, and I have no time for the simples of peasants. (*UT*, 350)

The Time Lords set themselves up as passive, sworn only to watch and never interfere, much like the Valar. However, they do occasionally meddle by sending envoys. For the Time Lords this often comes in the form of the Celestial Intervention Agency (CIA), who often snatches the Doctor up for covert missions. They exiled the Doctor to earth as punishment for his meddling, accepting that there was evil in the universe and he had a part to play in combating it. The Valar, similarly, send their envoys in the form of the Istari, rather than interfering directly.

Gandalf's rivalry with Saruman might be compared to the Doctor's eternal struggle against the Master. A fellow renegade from Time Lord society, the Master was once a close friend of the Doctor's; some have speculated they were brothers, lovers, or otherwise closely bonded.

The Master is generally considered somewhat more intelligent than the Doctor, though his lust for power and control are his foils. They ask one another for help when needed, and respect each other, albeit grudgingly and masked by petty insults and jabs. Much like Saruman, the Master possesses superior technology to the wandering Doctor; a running joke through the original series was that the Doctor's rackety old Type-40 TARDIS was little more than junk when he stole it, while the Master's newer model had all the bells and whistles.

While the Master has his superior apparatus, the Doctor is a vagabond, a wanderer and (in his second incarnation especially) a cosmic hobo. Much like Gandalf, he is an underdog within the scope of his own people. The Master, like Saruman, raises armies, builds engines of war, and does so from a more secure seat of power.

But the Doctor's aims are never about power. He goes from place to place, helping where he can. He never stops, and he never stays, he never waits to be thanked. He fights the good fight and moves on. He is offered kingships and power, even the presidency of the High Council of Time Lords, but he runs away. Gandalf could have taken the keys to Orthanc, the rods of the five wizards, and the crowns of seven kings, but he did not. He is no king and has no desire to be one.

It is perhaps worth pointing out that Sylvester McCoy, who played the seventh incarnation of the Doctor, was also cast as Radagast the Brown in Peter Jackson's adaptations of *The Hobbit.* McCoy's Doctor was mysterious, a game player, a chess master, and even a sinister character at times. His relationship with his companion, Ace, was one of a teacher and student, but she was never afraid to call him out on his questionable morals and methods.

Radagast's brief appearance in *The Lord of the Rings* and brief mentions elsewhere do not paint a detailed picture. He was certainly able to befriend birds and beasts, able to make friends across the animal kingdom. Radagast is not the only character within Middle-earth to have an affinity with animals and birds. Beren son of Barahir was also famous for this ability to commune with nature, and it saved his skin on almost as many occasions as Lúthien did.

The Doctor, similarly, has tremendous language skills and is seemingly able to communicate with beasts of thousands of species. From minotaurs to babies. McCoy's Doctor even took to making birdcalls on multiple occasions.

Why choose this figure for a hero? I think it's because in Tolkien's works and *Doctor Who* we are encouraged to look beyond the familiar and rediscover what might be there. An old man with a walking stick may be a wizard from across the sea, or he may be an alien from across the stars.

Heroes are more than just stories, they are people, and people are complicated. People are strange. Heroes and the stories they inhabit can inspire, they can bring hope, and they can set you thinking. In Tolkien, one of the great tools of fairy stories and fantasy was the eucatastrophe.

> I coined the word 'eucatastrophe': the sudden happy turn in a story which pierces you with a joy that brings tears (which I argued it is the highest function of fairy-stories to produce).
> (*Letters*, Letter 89, 100)

The Eagles arrive at the battle of the five armies, and at the Black Gate; the Ring is destroyed though Gollum's fall; and the voyage of Eärendil into the West brings about the cataclysmic end of the War of the Jewels. It is when disaster appears inevitable that triumph is achieved.

For Tolkien, things are never perfect and there are always challenges in life, but he insists we never give up hope for the chance things will take a sudden turn from bad to good. The Daleks are defeated, the monster is sent home, or the war has ended – time and time again the solution comes at the last moment when all hope seemed lost. For the Doctor, saving the day comes when the potential for tragedy is at its highest. One of the moments that stands out to me as a great example of the eucatastrophe comes at the conclusion to the 2008 story, *Journey's End*. Here the Daleks, thanks to their creator Davros's malicious machinations, are about to literally destroy the entire universe. All of the Doctor's friends are incapacitated or imprisoned.

It is in the moment when all seems lost that companion Donna Noble rises. Previously she has been dismissed by many (including herself) as a useless temp, as a loud figure of no importance. But in the moment of ultimate tragedy, she becomes the most important woman in all the cosmos.

Davros, having shot her with a bolt of electricity, thinking to kill or stun her, has in actuality triggered a Human-Time-Lord-Meta-Crisis in her, meaning that Donna now has the power to deactivate the Daleks' weapons and save the universe. This is a common theme. The crisis will build and build, but then the day is saved. Donna's heroics fit eucatastrophe better than most, I feel, because it is a direct result of the crisis itself that the solution is made. Without the malicious actions of Davros, she may not have had the power to stop him.

But sometimes things do not work out. All too often in the case of the monsters known as Silurians (the former inhabitants of the earth before humans came along) the result is devastating. In most of the Doctor's encounters with the Silurians it ends with humans killing them and effectively committing genocide, despite the Doctor's attempts to avert such an eventuality.

In the 1984 serial, *Warriors of the Deep*, the Doctor has failed to make peace between humans and Siluraians and almost everyone is left dead in the sea base. Sadly, regretfully, the Doctor laments: “there should have been another way” (Roberts 1984).

Because that is the Doctor’s outlook (there should be a resolution), there should be another way. Death and destruction are final, almost unthinkable solutions for him. The Doctor seeks out the eucatastrophe, so when it does not come, he is devastated.

Tom Baker, the Fourth Doctor, was fond of calling *Doctor Who* not science fiction, but science fantasy. In the show’s history we see mythologies taken on, subverted or revealed true. From Atlantis to Father Christmas, *Doctor Who* is rarely afraid to look into human creativity and have a new way of imagining it.

Beyond myth and legends, we see the familiar turned suddenly alien. Within Tolkien’s works, and within *Doctor Who*, we see cakes and forests become keys to other worlds, we see showroom dummies become soldiers, and we see old raggedy vagabonds become the stuff of legend.

The familiar regaining lost awe, the old becoming new, and the discovery of new meanings; all these things are threads that weave both Middle-earth and the Doctor’s universe. The fifty-year-old science fiction show more than likely owes a lot to Tolkien, and whether intentional or otherwise, both sources give us reason to look again at the world. Because you never know, the world might be bigger on the inside.

Bibliography

‘The Doctor, the Widow, and the Wardrobe’, *Doctor Who*, dir. by Farren Blackburn (BBC, 2011).

‘The Eleventh Hour’, *Doctor Who*, dir. by Adam Smith (BBC, 2010).

‘The End of the World’, *Doctor Who*, dir. by Euros Lyn (BBC, 2005).

‘In the Forest of the Night’, *Doctor Who*, dir. by Sheree Folkson (BBC, 2014).

‘Journey’s End’, *Doctor Who*, dir. by Euros Lyn (BBC, 2008).

‘The Keeper of Traken’, *Doctor Who*, dir. by John Black (BBC, 1981).

Tolkien, J.R.R., *Unfinished Tales*, ed. Christopher Tolkien (London: Harper Collins, 1980).
— *The Letters of J.R.R. Tolkien*, ed. H. Carpenter with the assistance of C. Tolkien (London: HarperCollins, 2006).
— *Tolkien On Fairy-stories*, ed. by V. Flieger and D. A. Anderson (London: HarperCollins, 2008).

‘Warriors of the Deep’, *Doctor Who*, dir. by Pennant Roberts, (BBC, 1984).

Reputations: Their rise, their fall, both and neither

David Doughan

In 1964, in a letter to Christopher Bretherton, Tolkien mentions a book by a fellow Brummie, one Joseph Henry Shorthouse. Like Tolkien, he was an "amateur" author; his day job was producing sulphuric acid for industrial purposes, but he also wrote a long, odd book, which in the late 19th century had a definite vogue, although, as Tolkien says, "few now find it possible to read" (*Letters*, Letter 257, 348). It was called *John Inglesant.* Published in 1876, it takes place in the 17th century: the hero finds himself at the court of Charles 1, then fighting in the Civil War, wounded at Edgehill and back again for Naseby – involved in plotting over Ireland, sentenced to death, reprieved literally on the scaffold. Then his brother is murdered, and Inglesant pursues the murderer to Italy, where among much else he witnesses a papal conclave – he gets married, has a son – both wife and child die of the plague, and so on. An action-packed historical novel? Not quite. About every page of briskly-dealt-with action is followed by two pages of disquisitions on subjects such as theology, philosophy, suppression of the Quietists, why Bologna got a better deal from the Vatican than Ferrara, the community at Little Gidding etc. A wordy book even by mid-Victorian standards, and his vogue was over well before the First World War. Tolkien feared that his reputation might suffer a similar fate, as the author of just one long, odd book which was once the subject of a craze.

Does this have any relevance to Tolkien? Hoping for illumination, I decided to consider some other instances of reputations undergoing popularity and decline – some initially also as vogues, or crazes.

To begin with, let's take the opera *The Immortal Hour*, by Rutland Boughton, which in its day was extremely popular. It's based on the Irish legend of Etain and Eochaid, and in 1922 it ran for 216 consecutive nights, followed by another 160 in 1923 – which must be a record. Craze or not? It is certainly a remarkable work.

Boughton also wrote a charming light Nativity opera, *Bethlehem*, based somewhat freely on the Coventry cycle, which also was popular in the early 1920s. However, things changed in 1926, the year of the General Strike. That Christmas Boughton staged Bethlehem with Mary and Joseph and the baby Jesus in a miner's cottage: Herod wore a top hat, frock coat and spats, and his troops charged with killing baby boys were British bobbies. It turned out Boughton was a dyed-in-the-wool Communist, the revelation of which brought the craze of *The Immortal Hour* to a sudden end, so that the only thing remembered from it is the Fairy Song. *The Immortal Hour* has of course been staged numerous times since then, but without catching fire, which is a pity, because it is indeed a remarkable work – full of memorable tunes and choral action, with opportunities for inventive staging, and even, in an appropriate production, for some cosplay.

Moving on, and speaking of cosplay, another vogue in the 1920s and 1930s involved *Hiawatha.* It was staged annually in the Albert Hall, with scenery and dancing, and the large choir, and many of the audience, in what they imagined to be "Red Indian" costume. Tents for changing had to be erected in Kensington Gardens. Cultural appropriation?

Well yes, if you can work out exactly whose culture is being appropriated. But definitely a craze – except that it was for the presentation, rather than the work itself, which already had an established reputation. The first part, *Hiawatha's Wedding Feast*, had been premiered in 1898, when it was an immediate hit, and the appearance shortly afterwards of the other two parts – the *Death of Minnehaha*, and *Hiawatha's Departure* – had established the composer's reputation, both in Britain and the USA. The composer came from South London (South Norwood, to be precise). He was Samuel Coleridge-Taylor who in fact had died in 1912 at the age of 37. Despite being of mixed race, he had a solid reputation with his musical contemporaries (Elgar liked his music) as well as with the public; for example, Tolkien heard *The Death of Minnehaha* in 1912, at Exeter College (Garth 2015, 36, 38). In addition to *Hiawatha*, much of his orchestral music achieved popularity – for instance, his Petite Suite was regularly broadcast on BBC Radio - and it's ironic that his music didn't really go out of fashion until the racially-conscious 1960s. Recently there has been a bit of a revival of interest in his music; and *Hiawatha's Wedding Feast* at least has never quite disappeared, being kept alive by occasional performances by amateur choirs.

So much for the music of *Hiawatha.* The words, of course, in their Kalevala metre, were by the poet Henry Wadsworth Longfellow, who died in 1882, and whose reputation during his lifetime could hardly have been higher, although more in the USA than elsewhere. He was a contemporary of the New England Transcendentalists: Emerson, Thoreau, and Alcott. He made lots of money, had a big house, and he was a big name. A classic. After his death his reputation began to decline, though only gradually. Some of his works were still well known in my youth, such as "Under a spreading chestnut tree / the village smithy stands, "Excelsior", "Evangeline" etc. He still has something of a reputation, though again more in the USA than in Britain. Still, he isn't forgotten.

About the time of Longfellow's death, in Britain, a composer had made a cantata based on a poem by Longfellow called *The Golden Legend*: a deeply serious work. It had a degree of popular success – but, to the composer's mild discomfiture, nothing like the success of his series of comic operas in collaboration with a writer, with titles like *The Pirates of Penzance*, *HMS Pinafore*, *Iolanthe* and of course *The Mikado.* For yes, the writer was W.S. Gilbert, and the composer was Arthur Sullivan.

Well, the reputation of these comic operas may not be what it was in their lifetimes, but it remains constant at a moderate level of appreciation. I'm bringing them in for the sake of a reference they make in *The Mikado*, whose object all sublime, you may remember, was to make the punishment fit the crime. Bach, Beethoven, and Spohr are all mentioned. Bach and Beethoven are both well known. We're certainly among the Greats here. But what about Spohr?

Louis Spohr was a younger contemporary of Beethoven – 14 years younger: he lived until 1859. He was widely regarded in his lifetime as Beethoven's successor, though of a different character. He completed 9 symphonies, wrote 18 violin concertos (he was also a violin virtuoso), ten operas, four oratorios and much more. The decline in his reputation began almost immediately after his death; by the time that Mikado mentioned him, he was a name to be revered, but in practice not much more. By the end of the 19th century he was almost entirely forgotten, except by amateur choral societies, and even they seem to have abandoned him by 1918 or so. Throughout most of the 20th century his music was almost completely ignored. In the past 20 years there have been attempts to revive interest, though without great success. He went from universal adulation to relative neglect quite quickly and ended in almost total obscurity.

So that's a reputation that goes just about all the way down. And before I pass on the reputation that concerns us most, I'll just mention a sort of mirror image of Spohr: the case of Thomas Traherne, a 17th century clergyman whose writings don't seem to have attracted much attention during his lifetime, were totally neglected after his death, and rediscovered fortuitously in the 1890s, since when they've had quite a revival – for example, from his *Centuries of Meditation*, recalling an infant's view of the world:

> Certainly Adam in Paradise had not more sweet and curious apprehensions of the world than I. All appeared new, and strange at first, inexpressibly rare and delightful and beautiful. All things were spotless and pure and glorious.
> The corn was orient and immortal wheat, which never should be reaped nor was ever sown. I thought it had stood from everlasting to everlasting. (Traherne 1908)

Here we have several different examples of the way reputations develop. First, the classic ephemeral craze: reputation goes up like a rocket, comes down like the stick. Or a rapidly established reputation goes into a long decline. Or a secure solid reputation dwindles away to nothing. Or a reputation declines but stabilises at a relatively high level. Or a forgotten work is rediscovered. A variety of outcomes – one we haven't had yet is an uninterrupted rise.

Tolkien has had various reputations. In 1955 his main reputation was academic, as a great but dilatory and unmethodical scholar from whom had been expected a great work of philology, but who instead had wasted his time and talents writing a long very odd fairy story. In fact, philology itself was in decline, under attack, first from the "lit" branch of English studies – people like the Leavises regarded it as a sort of Casaubon-style piling up of useless data, not at all life-enhancing (see *Scrutiny* passim). Well, this wasn't new. What was new was the attack from the "lang" side, with the science of linguistics shifting the emphasis from the study of words and their histories to an emphasis on structures, particularly grammar. Generative Grammar. Transformational Grammar. Philology came to be seen as not merely out-dated, but positively reactionary. We shall return to this.

As for that fairy story: the publishers were soon relieved to know that sales were breaking even, and becoming positively profitable, and went on increasing. By the time Tolkien wrote that letter about Shorthouse, in 1964, it was doing very respectably indeed, which is why Tolkien had become mildly concerned about his "vogue". Well, that was 1964. In 1965 there was the War of the Paperbacks, which alerted young America to the existence of *The Lord of the Rings* and ushered in the Days of the Craze: "Go go Gandalf" "Gandalf for President" "Frodo Lives" etc., all of which is documented elsewhere. Then, just as the craze appeared to be passing its peak, Tolkien died. As we've seen, this sometimes presaged a decline in a reputation, but not with Tolkien, partly because we were all waiting for the Silmarillion – and that was followed by all the posthumous publications. However, there was also the fact that many new readers, particularly Americans, were involved in science-fiction fandom, and had started creating a Tolkien fandom along similar lines, with conventions, fanfic, filking, cosplay and especially gaming: board games, role playing games, LARPing and eventually video games. This all helped to make money, especially for official trademark holders, who of course had a financial interest in promoting *The Lord of the Rings* and *The Hobbit.*

By the end of the 1990s there were several polls of which *The Lord of the Rings* either came top or very nearly, to the surprise of many, to the delight of others and to the dismay of yet others, some of whom had actually read the books. This showed that it was not merely an advertising and merchandising boom, and Tolkien became the Author of the Century – and that meant that there was finance for the films. Of course, with the advent of the films marketing and all the non-book activities went into a different gear, and Tolkien was no longer an author, but a franchise. In many circles nowadays the books mainly seem to be used as references to check people's lore and see whether it is canon or not – and even that may be on the way out, with new Amazon Prime developments. Tolkien has become a phenomenon. Or is it Tolkien anymore? There was almost certainly a reason for Tolkien Enterprises changing its name to Middle-earth Enterprises. It's interesting that the recent biopic seems not to have attracted mass audiences. Tolkien-the-phenomenon seems to be in danger of disappearing behind his own creation of Middle-earth. A sort of literary Col. Sanders.

But there's still another aspect of Tolkien: as an influence. Now I'm not thinking here of the scores of pale imitations, the whole sub-genre of pseudo-tolkienian fantasy. I'm thinking of the very different issue of world-building, with particular reference to language.

First, conlangs. At the time *The Lord of the Rings* was published, if a writer gave an alien a name, or quoted a word or two of Alien, it was usually alphabet soup, or at best something that looked superficially like a real language, e.g: "Egz pra strastischek Maria!" (*Earthman, Come Home*, by James Blish). Tolkien changed all that. Now, to be credible, you have to make some effort at language creation. Hence we have a collection of more-or-less credible conlangs, from Klingon to Dothraki and beyond. Granted, they tend to be two-dimensional, compared to Tolkien's Elvish languages, which are three-dimensional, with a crucially important diachronic approach – in other words Tolkien's languages have their own essential history and development as part of the languages. The purely synchronic (in the main) conlangs lack this dimension - though this can be an advantage, in that they stop developing long enough for people to learn how to speak them, which a problem with Tolkien's Elvish only partly solved by David Salo's 'neo-Sindarin', as used in Peter Jackson's films.

Of course, Elvish is the mother of all conlangs, and a study of the Elvish tongues is in itself a good grounding for studying languages generally. However, there is more to Tolkien than Elvish. There are real world languages too: some Old Norse, even a hint of Gothic, but above all English, especially its development. To take an example, when I first read *The Lord of the Rings* I knew the words meet and moot, and the connection between them, but although I also knew the words deem and doom, it had not occurred to me that a doom was something you deemed, therefore a judgement. Doomsday is indeed the Day of Judgement, and the Judgement itself, at the end of the world, is heralded by a sudden sharp trumpet note: the Crack of Doom, which also used to be called the Last Trump. Tolkien of course knew this perfectly well and used "Doom" in its original sense as well as the modern and made the Cracks of Doom the fissures in Mount Doom.

These words are not exactly archaic, but certainly not in everyday use. Similarly with place-names – for example Michel Delving. "Delve" is in that same not-quite-archaic category – when Adam delved and Eve span, who was then the gentleman? – but "Michel" goes further and is definitely archaic. So is, for example, 'mathom'. Those who investigate further will discover that these words are in fact not just archaic but Old. Old English, in fact, otherwise known as Anglo-Saxon.

Now there is a considerable leap from discovering this interesting fact to looking at the hangings in Edoras and quoting 'The Wanderer'. Still, it seems that some people go at least part of the way towards that. The decline in Anglo-Saxon studies, very marked even 50 years ago, seems at least to have been halted, and possibly even reversed – and this is generally ascribed to Tolkien, and the influence of *The Lord of the Rings*.

Anyway, we seem to be back to words and their significance. Not that we've abandoned structures. Chomsky famously made up the sentence "Colorless green ideas sleep furiously" as an example of something grammatically irreproachable which is nonetheless devoid of semantic significance: nonsense (1957). Well, Chomsky had green ideas; Tolkien had a green dragon. A green *great* dragon, which is just about the converse of Chomsky: a phrase the meaning of which is clear, but which is an offence against word order. Still, he was after all a lover of words – a philologist – and the term "philology" is no longer in the shadows (Carpenter 1978, 30–1). Perfectly respectable people are happy to call themselves Doctor of Comparative Philology – and this I think is at least partly due to Tolkien. However, I'm not really one of those who think that *The Lord of the Rings* is indeed the great work of philology that Tolkien had been expected to produce. Still, his work in the field is appreciated, and not just by academics. For example, collectors with no academic background not only seek out relevant issues of *The Year's Work in English* but read them and make intelligent comments. A number of readers are inspired by the books to study Old and Middle English, and Old Norse – it's difficult to say just how many, but as I've mentioned their impact does seem to have been noticeable.

So where does all that leave Tolkien's reputation? Has Middle-earth really taken over from Tolkien? Or will his main reputation be academic? Well, I suspect he will indeed continue to be vaguely respected as the Father of the Fantasy Genre, and his academic reputation will be pretty solid, and as more than a gateway to medieval literature.

Still, that appeals to a relatively limited circle. However, leaving aside the Phenomenon and academia, what's left is the books. For staying power, my money is on Tolkien the Storyteller. *The Lord of the Rings* is above all a Rattling Good Yarn – it holds your attention, whether read from the page or heard in a reading. I would bet on Tolkien's reputation surviving above all as the great storyteller, and the books will endure after the merchandise, the gaming and so on. have moved on.

Bibliography

Carpenter, H., *J.R.R. Tolkien: A Biography,* (London: Unwin Paperbacks, 1978).

Chomsky, N., *Syntactic Structures,* (Berlin: Mouton & Co., 1957).

Garth, J., *Tolkien at Exeter College: How an Oxford Undergraduate Created Middle-earth,* (Exeter, 2015).

Tolkien, J.R.R., *The Letters of J.R.R. Tolkien,* ed. by H. Carpenter with the assistance of C. Tolkien (London: HarperCollins, 2006).

Traherne, T., *Centuries of Meditation*, ed. by B. Dobell, (1908).

The formation of Tolkien fandom in the US, the UK and France

Laura Martin-Gomez

1 - The birth of Tolkien fandom

Getting into fan studies, I realised most case studies were about either media fandoms (TV series or films), music or sports. When it comes to the written word, science-fiction fandom attracts most of the attention, legitimately.[1] But in that area, studies almost never focus on just one work of fiction. You have to turn to literary studies to see a focus on the reception of one specific author, like Shakespeare, Jane Austen or Arthur Conan Doyle.[2] In that sense, my research stands at a fascinating and original crossroads.

Let us now dive into fandom history and tell the story of how the work of fiction of an English don[3] came to be such an important part of many readers' lives and the heart of vibrant and long-standing communities of fans.

2 - The US

The Fellowship of the Ring was published by Houghton Mifflin in the USA barely three months after its outing in the UK, in 1954. Our first fan texts related to Tolkien's work appear only in 1959 but in a context in which it seems that most of the fanzine readers' seemed to have already read or heard about *The Lord of the Rings*, which indicates some sort of reception was already in place especially in the science-fiction fandom.[4]

It seems that the first surviving texts dedicated to Tolkien in a fanzine were by Ted Johnstone. In November 1959, he published what has been called the first fan poem on Middle-earth, 'The Passing of the Elven-kind', in *All Mimsy*.[5] Around the same period, he also published a series of articles in *Psi-Phi* about adapting *The Lord of the Rings* on the screen.[6] Barely a few weeks later, Doc Weir, an English fan, published 'No Monroe

1. See the groundbreaking study by Henry Jenkins, *Textual Poachers: Television Fans and Participatory Culture*, 1992.
2. An interesting case in point, we usually refer to Sherlock Holmes' fandom rather than to the author of most of his adventures, Arthur Conan Doyle. This fandom has been around since the thirties.
3. Even though the invented fictional world of Middle-earth is what brought Tolkien to fandom, I find it noteworthy that societies have focused more on being dedicated to the author than specifically Middle-earth, which shows a specific hold of the author's position over his own fictional creation.
4. For example, the earliest *The Lord of the Rings* costumes recorded to my knowledge appeared at the science-fiction World Convention in 1958, as Ruth Berman recalled in her text 'Costume fandom A Rough Echo' in Marion Zimmer Bradley's fanzine *Andúril* published in 1962.
5. *All Mimsy* no. 5, Minnesota, November 1959.
6. I have not yet been able to read these articles. In my oral presentation at *Tolkien 2019* I got confused and mistakenly cited the source as *Cry of the Nameless*. Still, this fanzine has interesting

in Lothlórien' in *Triode* no. 17, also about filming *The Lord of the Rings*. Up to now, I have not been able to determine whether Doc Weir had read Ted Johnstone's texts, he did not mention them anyway. Regardless, his beautifully written text has remained as one of the founding texts for Tolkien fandom and has been repeatedly reprinted.[7] Thus, science-fiction fandom, which was well anchored and had a well-connected network of fanzines thanks mostly to the APAs,[8] seems to have been the first recipient of the yet-to-be Tolkien fandom.

Actually, the discussion around *The Lord of the Rings* as a film seems especially to have been a topic among members of the LASFS,[9] to which Ted Johnstone belonged, but also Bjo Trimble and Bruce Pelz. Incidentally, Bruce Pelz also published his own personalzine, *Glamdring*, in 1960: in its pages, he commented on the impending creation of *The Fellowship of the Ring* as well as on the fanzines he received and their content. The pages of this fanzine, whose title is the only actual Tolkien-content, show how a specific group dedicated to Tolkien's work came to be. The name of the group itself was specifically subject to a debate, in which Doc Weir and Joe Patrizio participated: they thought it was presumptuous to dub a group from the most noble and brave beings in Middle-earth while Bruce Pelz defended the phrase as having a broader sense. The idea of this group seems to have been the product of several people's drive, including Bjo Trimble or Leslie Nirenberg and it was supposedly going to imitate the structure of the Baker Street Irregulars,[10] which shows how from the outset Tolkien fandom owed its identity to more than just science-fiction fandom.

The Fellowship of the Ring eventually got off the ground with the publishing of *I Palantir* no. 1 in 1960 and the second issue the next year. Yet, it did not really take root, probably because the two main founders, Ted Johnstone and Bruce Pelz, were two young fans with multiple interests in fandom who did not feel like concentrating all their efforts in just one group and fanzine. The fourth and last issue of *I Palantir* was published in 1966. In these first few years of Tolkien fandom, there were some short-lived publications or one-shots like *Andúril* edited by Marion Zimmer Bradley in 1962 or *Grimoire* by David Hall in 1964 for example. Yet, no specific fandom group took hold in that first period.

As is well-known among Tolkien fans, it was the Ace Books affair in 1965 that sparked a 'campus craze' and helped Tolkien fandom take root with a fully-fledged identity – even though many students had read Tolkien before the whole scandal

---

discussions about *The Fellowship of the Ring*'s creation by its editors F. M. and Elinor Busby.

7. In *Eldritch DreamQuest* no. 3 (1961), *I Palantir* no. 3 (1964), in *I Palantir* no. 4 (1966), in *The Tolkien Scrapbook* (1978).

8. 'APA' stands for 'Amateur Press Association' and consists of a group of people who self-publish material. Each person sends his or her fanzine to the whole group and then receives the others' production in return.

9. Los Angeles Science Fantasy Society. It was a very active science fiction society in California at the time.

10. 'Baker Street Irregulars' is a literary society devoted to Sherlock Holmes' stories and was founded in 1934. The reference to this group was not made by any of the organizers of the Fellowship of the Ring but by f. M. Busy, editor of *Cry of the Nameless* in issue no. 138. There seems to have been a competitiveness about who would launch a Tolkien-related club.

happened. A very short summary of what happened will do here: Ace Books published a paperback edition of *The Lord of the Rings* in 1965, which sold well, but it came to Tolkien's and Allen & Unwin's attention that they were not paying royalties, so a protest campaign was launched by fans at the same time as an "authorized" edition was prepared by Ballantine. The commercial success attracted the attention of mainstream press on the phenomenon which was dubbed 'the war on Middle-earth' and attention was also brought to the student image and a strong comparison with hippies was made.[11] Even though these mainstream articles sometimes fell wide off the mark, it is undeniable that that period saw a huge investment of students on campus around *The Lord of the Rings* and Tolkien's fiction in general, with examples of groups discussing his works in Harvard or in Smith College.[12]

In that same crucial year of 1965, Dick Plotz decided to create the New York Tolkien Society – soon to be renamed the Tolkien Society of America. Based in New York when Dick Plotz was a senior student in high school, the society began editing the *Tolkien Journal* with very academically oriented content. The society even famously welcomed W. H. Auden in its meetings.[13] Quite soon due to his own student's responsibilities, Dick Plotz handed the society over to Ed Meskys who kept it going for a few years before becoming blind and having to resign in 1972. The TSA was then merged into the newly-founded Mythopoeic Society – which had been created in 1967 in California by Glen GoodKnight around a Frodo & Bilbo's Birthday Pique Nique in Los Angeles. Since the Mythopoeic Society had slightly different goals – the studies of Tolkien's works but also Lewis' and Charles Williams' – it is interesting to see how the necessity for strong leadership inside a young society seems to have led to this merge.

Outside of the traditional science fiction fandom circles, the media burst and the book's fame led to a surge in number of readers and to very varied approaches. There were politically active fans (mostly students and/or hippies with very catchy slogans like "Gandalf for President" or "Frodo Lives"), enthusiasts who were inspired by the fiction (with costumes, songs, meetings) or academics from highbrow culture who participated in the Tolkien Conference at Belknap College in 1968 for example.

Through the late 60s, Tolkien fandom gradually took hold and a characteristic identity: first born from a branch of science-fiction fandom, it was then enriched with personal initiatives by (mostly young and literate) enthusiasts editing fanzines all around the country and with the creation of societies like the TSA and MythSoc. Other societies and numerous fanzines cohabited throughout the 70s and 80s, which Gary Hunnewell has been collecting minutely for decades,[14] showing all sorts of approaches to the works

11. Articles were published in *Esquire, Los Angeles Times, New York Times Book Review.*
12. An article in the *New York Times Book Review* in January 1965 shows that students were already numerous in those universities in reading *The Lord of the Rings* even before it was published in paperback. This could also explain the speed at which it became a commercial and campus success afterwards.
13. *Letters*, Letter 284.
14. It is now the S. Gary Hunnewell Collection at the Raynor Memorial Library of Marquette University. He collected hundreds of fanzines which are microfilmed and belong now to Marquette's huge Tolkien collection.

of fiction of Tolkien. Still, the dominant structure of MythSoc tends to pull American Tolkien fandom towards a serious and literary approach to Tolkien's work.[15]

3 - The UK

The first traces of British fandom go as far back as 1960: Ken Cheslin, an English science-fiction fan, was involved in *The Fellowship of the Ring* from its inception, and he edited *Nazgûl's Bane* as a companion fanzine for *I Palantir* and in the quality of 'British correspondent' for the American group. A few other fanzines around the same period, like *Eldritch DreamQuest*, a fanzine about sword and sorcery, evoke Tolkien in their pages. From Tolkien's *Letters* we also know that there were student groups reading and discussing his work, like Rhona Beare's one in Exeter.[16] Yet, all these signs of activity remained transient and left few traces.

It was in 1968 that the first real drive for a British organized fandom appeared.[17] Science-fiction fan Archie Mercer launched *The Middle Earthworm* in October 1968 as a British correspondent for the Tolkien Society of America, then led by Ed Meskys. The TSA soon disappeared with its merger in MythSoc but Archie Mercer's fanzine, in the shape of a letter column, took hold and gained its own community of readers and enthusiasts. So, it's not surprising that it is in those pages that the call for a British society arose. There were actually several local initiatives that sprouted all at the same time and looked up at Archie Mercer and his experience as a fan to give them advice. There were also student groups like the Hobbit Society at University College London which had existed for a while and got publicized in those pages.[18]

Eventually, the much discussed British society was founded at the very end of 1969 by Vera Chapman, a retired lady with a typing machine at home, who, as many of the correspondents in *Middle Earthworm*, did not belong to the science-fiction fandom circles. After a rough first few years, probably as a consequence of the first committees' inexperience in handling a society or lack of communication skills,[19] it gradually became the reference for all things Tolkien-related in Britain. *Mallorn*, the society's fanzine, had trouble finding its feet at first because of unreliable and changing editors, but then it began to gain consistency. The appearance of *Amon Hen* as early as 1972

15. This does not mean that an academic approach is the only one present in the Mythopoeic Society – the Society publishes *Mythic Circle* for art and poems and costuming is common at gatherings – or that the Mythopoeic Society is the only important structure in the USA today.

16. Tolkien wrote to her in 1958 to answer a few questions she had asked him about his work (Letter 211).

17. Given the media coverage of the Ace Books in 1965, it is quite surprising not to see any strong British reaction on the other side of the Atlantic. More interesting still, the first stable signs of reception, be it with *The Middle Earthworm* or *Gandalf's Garden*, coincide precisely with the publication of *The Lord of the Rings* in paperback in the UK (a one-volume edition by Allen & Unwin came out on October, 10th 1968).

18. According to Charles Noad, the 'HobbitSoc' must have existed since 1966 or 1967. I have not found confirmation of this in the UCL student newspaper *Pi*. Alex Holdschmidt was one of its members in 1969, he helped to lead a collaboration between the two groups.

19. There was a long debate around the Constitution and the handling of the treasury was a bit hectic until Archie Mercer cleared the mess up.

also helped give shape to the group as it was more frequent and became quite regular under the editorship of Stuart and Rosie Clark. Due to the dispersion of its members, the idea of creating "smials", local branches, was soon put in place. While American fandom was celebrating Frodo & Bilbo's Birthday Party as an annual festive meeting in the third week of September, the Tolkien Society launched the idea of Oxonmoot. The first gathering happened in 1974 and it helped tighten the emotional link with the fictional work of Tolkien as well as strengthen the important place that the author and his life would have in the society.

From the outset, the Tolkien Society took advantage of its geographical proximity with the family and the editors to create links that helped to contribute to its position today as the reference society around the world. Vera Chapman contacted Tolkien through Allen & Unwin to announce the creation of the Society in May 1970, she actually met Tolkien himself in 1972 and asked him to become an honorary president of the society. Also, gifts were sent for Tolkien's birthday and later on when he had passed away and Oxonmoot got in motion, there were visits to his tomb and also to Priscilla Tolkien's house.[20] Thus, the society reached a noble status and privileged position that led to the attraction of international members, a growth of membership and the organization of bigger events such as the Centenary Conference in 1992 to which Christopher Tolkien himself attended.

Given the mixed origins background of the Tolkien Society and its geographical closeness to the author, his life and his editors, it is not surprising to observe this different relationship to the family, at the same time more familiar and more respectful.[21] Also, the will to broaden its perspectives and include everyone shows in the fanzines' pages as a push for a very varied content, from academic style articles to poems and artwork or games.

4 - France

France's reception of Tolkien's work has been much more discreet in those early decades and only had a real fan reception towards the end of the 1980s. There has been a slight academic interest in Tolkien's work since the 1950s, but still, *The Hobbit* was not translated before 1969 – just when the Tolkien Society was founded – and *The Lord of the Rings* in 1972-1973 by the editor Christian Bourgois to whose attention it had been brought by the publishing of Jacques Bergier's *Admirations*. There have been some individual links between French fans and the English-speaking fandom in the 1970s, which shows a will to connect with other readers, but there is no documented society or group from that period.[22]

20. Priscilla Tolkien was Tolkien's only daughter and youngest child.

21. The current situation may have evolved slightly since the Tolkien Estate has taken a very strong stand against Peter Jackson's adaptations of *The Lord of the Rings* to the screen (2001-2003) while the Tolkien Society has broadened its views to accept and welcome adaptations in their discussions.

22. Philippe Bechennec, in one of the French fans' testimonies I gathered, explains that with a group of friends from high school, he published a fanzine called *Horizons de la Terre du Milieu* between 1977 and 1982, which largely predates surviving sources and shows that some sort of

Actually, the first French society that has left a trace was only founded in 1987 by French fan and linguist Edouard Kloczko and a group of friends including mathematician Sébastien Ferenczi. It was called 'La Faculté des Etudes Elfiques' or Faculty for Elvish Studies. During the first years, a few issues of *Féérik* came out but it was more or less supplanted by *Le Gollum Illustré* which was meant as a more frequent newsletter than the original thicker fanzine. The structure of the society was settled on subjects of interests, decided by the leader Edouard Kloczko, rather than geographically, similar to MythSoc or the Tolkien Society have done. These branches were called 'chairs' and were on 'Monsters', 'Elvish Languages', 'Geography', etc. This shows a will for an academic structure – also noticed in the announcement of a 'certificate' that would be delivered to those who attended the first seminar in 1993. That year also saw the project of an encyclopaedia circulate among a close circle of members, but the project never got off the ground. After thriving for the first few years, there was a progressive seclusion and isolation of the historical leader who lost all of the founding team and could not manage to get active members to bring life to the different "chairs" for a long period of time.[23]

To be fair, it seems that the FEE experienced the same difficulties as any new society. An added obstacle may have been the discrepancy between the leader's wishes and expectations – an academically-oriented structure with a high-level of knowledge of Tolkien's works – and the grass root members' expectations – rather an introduction to Tolkien's work or a social structure to get to know each other. The strong leadership personality, which most of the time helps a society gain stability and identity, may have led to the demise of that group due to the slow and small changes towards what most members of the society aspired to. Still, Edouard Kloczko's activity was impressive and managed to sow the seeds for a nascent French fandom, which he advertised by connecting to foreign societies (there were letters sent to Nancy Martsch of *Beyond Bree*, and exchanges with Polish and Belgian fanzines for example).

Even though that society did not survive after a few years of activity, the arrival of the internet around those same years, led to the formation of a more stable and lasting fandom online with 'Tolkien en VF' created in 1996 – it became Tolkiendil later on and today is one of the most active societies in France – and JRRVF created in 1998.

Through this quick overview of how different national fandoms came to be, we see that there are vast amounts of published material with widely different societies existing at different periods of times and in different countries. Yet, what is of interest to me is to try and show how similarities between these Tolkien fandoms can be spotted and commented upon.

5 - National fandoms: same difference?

Following this presentation of three national fandoms, my goal is to analyse how they relate to each other and how they differ in their dynamics. These conclusions are very

---

fan reception existed before.

23. One of the few exceptions is Didier Willis, who published his fanzine *Hiswelóce* (later *Hiswelókë*) for the 'Chair of Geography' and continues to work and publish on Tolkien to this day. His personal collection of fanzines is the greatest source of documentation I have had access to for French fandom.

early in my research process since I have not yet worked through all of my material, yet I hope that they're representative of what my final conclusions will be.

5.1 - Similar patterns: wherever you are fandom is fandom

Reading through the pages of these Tolkien fanzines from various periods and countries, what first strikes the researcher is the similar patterns in how fandom works. It seems that the constraints linked to the nature of fandom activities (based on volunteering) and the types of initiatives launched by Tolkien fans are the same regardless of the culture.

Let us first look at the constraints of volunteer activities. Most fan groups or structures revolve around and rely on very few individuals, which has very direct consequences: the activity and liveliness of a group depends entirely on these fans' free time or changes in personal life. In most cases, changing addresses, going from high school to university or from single to married life can have a dramatic impact on a group. For example, Dick Plotz, the founder of the Tolkien Society of America in 1965, had to pass on the leadership quite soon when he felt in 1969 that as a student at Harvard that he could no longer take care of the society. In that case, the 'change of hands' seems to have gone quite smoothly with Ed Meskys taking charge. Yet, a few years later, when Ed Meskys became blind, the society had to merge with the Mythopoeic Society, for lack of volunteers inside the TSA itself, which shows the frailness of these fan groups which depend highly on a strong leadership to survive. Most fanzines live as long as their editor has the means to publish, and even societies' fanzines have had trouble getting out sometimes. For example, the Tolkien Society's fanzine *Mallorn* has had complicated first years. In charge of issue no. 7, the Númenórean group actually lost track of the second issue they had to publish since the members of the group had all been scattered across various British universities and could not meet easily. The Committee had to take charge of the editing using bits and pieces of what they had managed to take hold of and print the issue in a complete rush so that Tolkien Society members would not be completely at a loss to understand what was going on with the society.

Other constraints on these volunteer activities are material: to produce a fanzine, one needed access to specific material like a typewriter, a mimeograph and a lot of stationery. This meant sometimes the sudden break of publishing of some fanzines if the typewriter broke down or on the contrary allowed some would-be editors to turn into one. Obviously, this is directly linked to the financial issue of editing fanzines. Fanzines are a labour of love most of all, with a lot of hours dedicated to typing, mimeographing, collating and sending them to subscribers or friends. As such, some editors had trouble keeping up the printing when financial issues occurred. Most 'independent' editors depended on their own resources but societies' fanzines can depend on subscriptions and the funding of the expenses caused by the production of the fanzine itself. For instance, Phil Spencer, recently arrived in the Tolkien Society, took in charge the editing of the first version of the society's newsletter, *The Tolkien Society Bulletin*, but he soon decided to stop editing it because he was not receiving from the TS the promised funding that should have covered all the expenses, due to organizational issues inside the society itself. Obviously, these material constraints have reduced as technology has improved through the last decades of existence of Tolkien fandom.

Similar patterns can also be noticed when it comes to what fans actually do to express their passion. Tolkien fans create societies dedicated to the study of Tolkien's work, they gather in these societies or loosely shaped groups of friends, they edit and circulate fanzines dedicated to Tolkien and his fiction, and they organize parties or reading meetings. The human experience inside those groups seems to have been similar too: small in-groups last as long as those belonging to it stay close friends or as long as the person who is at the centre of it remains active (and it can be a very long time, see Nancy Martsch's *Beyond Bree*) while most university or high school groups are short-lived, like the Michigan State University Tolkien Fellowship for example. As for societies, they seem to have grown or died depending on their ability to change hands, to become not a one-person's product but a full structure that can evolve.

5.2 - A global network – fandom as a precursor to the web

Most fanzines provided members and fans a space for communication: often, letters were sent to the editor who then either printed them all and thus gave way to people's opinions without much editing (like with *The Middle Earthworm* for example, called a 'letterzine') or were compiled in a 'lettercolumn' inside the fanzine itself. This system, which goes back to the very beginning of fandom and fanzines in the thirties,[24] gives fans an opportunity to chat, get to know each other and to create a feeling of community. Following the example of its predecessor the science-fiction fandom, the Tolkien fandom reuses some acronyms like 'LoC' or specific words like 'gafiate'[25] which baffle newcomers to fandoms, especially Tolkien readers who had not been involved in fandom beforehand. Thus, fanzines allowed members to have a sense of belonging and identity despite the geographical distance, sometimes even with the Atlantic in the way.

Thus, it does not really come as a surprise to see that international links are a core element in Tolkien fandom. From the outset, American and British fans have been in touch and tried to tighten the links inside the newly born Tolkien fandom. Actually, as early as 1960, Ken Cheslin was a correspondent for The Fellowship of the Ring – a position that led him to edit the first ever British Tolkien fanzine, *Nazgûl's Bane* – while Archie Mercer was a correspondent for the Tolkien Society of America in 1968 when he launched *The Middle Earthworm*. Fans also crossed the ocean on some occasions, following the tradition of TAFF in science-fiction fandom, one of the candidates in 1960 was actually nicknamed 'Bilbo Bentcliffe Baggins'[26] and the bid for WorldCon 1964 was nicknamed 'Mordor' which stood for Los Angeles or the Bay Area. Later on, fans who had got to know each other through paper, travelled to meet each other or participate in foreign events, like for example Nan C. Scott who stayed in the UK in 1973 and met Vera Chapman.[27]

---

24. An interesting analysis of the role and history of letter columns was made by Michael Saler in *As If, Modern Enchantment and the Literary of Prehistory of Virtual Reality*.
25. An interesting analysis of the role and history of letter columns was made by Michael Saler in *As If, Modern Enchantment and the Literary of Prehistory of Virtual Reality.*
26. Eric Bentcliffe was the editor of science fiction fanzine *Triode*.
27. Nan C. Scott had already been in the UK as early as 1966 and she had met Tolkien, who expressed his gratitude for her help in campaigning against the Ace Books pirate edition.

As the vision of a global network of fans emerges, it becomes apparent that these links are mainly between English-speaking communities.[28] Yet, some French fans have got in touch with British or American fanzines,[29] long before the appearance of a real French fandom: contacts have thus existed but as individuals who reached to a community in a foreign language and country, like Jean Chausse, a French fan who participated in Tolkien Society events in the mid-1990s. Moreover, English-speaking societies themselves have been interested in foreign editions and translations of Tolkien's work from the beginning. When *The Hobbit* was translated into French in 1969, a French journalist contacted Vera Chapman to discuss Tolkien, plus the translations were all reviewed. When the Faculté des Etudes Elfiques was active, Edouard Kloczko also followed all the new publications in English, reviewing the different volumes of the *History of Middle-earth* as they came out. During that period, around the turn of the nineties, it seems that Edouard Kloczko got in touch with several societies or fan groups (like *Beyond Bree* for example), but most of them were not in English.[30] It seems that from that time on, links have existed but were rather the result of French fans reaching out to English-speaking fandom, while French fandom and British or American fandom barely seem to know each other's existence. Thirty years onwards, the situation has slightly evolved towards more awareness and communication, despite the language barrier, but tighter links are still a goal.

5.3 - Global trends with 'local colour': ideas/opinions of fandom

Beyond the idea of similar structures and international connections, there seems to be an undercurrent (and ongoing?) dilemma in Tolkien fandom, which gets its expression in the constant search for a balance between a fannish approach of Tolkien's work – which more or less includes all adaptations – and a stricter academic approach.

Actually, approaches tend to evolve in groups or tend to flow towards a middle ground approach in order to please and attract more members. Yet this is not always the case, as we can see with the Tolkien Society of America for example: from the outset, it published very serious and academically oriented texts in its fanzine, adequately entitled 'journal'. Even though it started with Dick Plotz scribbling in runes on New-York subway walls just a few weeks or months before the whole 'campus craze' began, the TSA remained very academic in all its activities and bearings up to its merging into the Mythopoeic Society. We find a similar position in the French society, la Faculté des Etudes Elfiques, whose name and structure (in chairs rather than smials) already point at an academic endeavour. The articles published in *Féérik* seem to reach for this ideal.

---

28. There are some examples of an early Australian fanzine too for example, with fanzine *Carandaith* published by 'Alpajpuri' between 1968 and 1972.

29. There are some examples of an early Australian fanzine too for example, with fanzine *Carandaith* published by 'Alpajpuri' between 1968 and 1972.

There were also contacts with Swedish, Dutch, German, Japanese, Spanish fans, etc. but these are not included in my research topic. The earliest recorded contact from a French fan dates back to 1974, J. Sabourin wrote to *The Middle Earthworm* (letter printed in no. 22).

30. Exchange of fanzines with Dutch, Polish.

Nevertheless, the president of the society Edouard Kloczko eventually had to publish a newsletter *Le Gollum Illustré*, with a much lighter content. It seems that the readers and members of the FEE pushed for more accessible contents, even though 'fannish' activities were reduced and cornered to the 'Chair of playful studies' (note still the use of the term 'studies') for people who did role playing games. Still, most fan groups in our research either choose to follow a middle road from the outset or end up taking it by following a general and mostly unspoken wish of its members. This is specifically the case of the MythSoc and the Tolkien Society: these two societies had a very different onset – rather fannish for MythSoc, rather amateurish but serious-minded for the TS – but gradually got to a similar stand towards Tolkien's work in general.[31] In the 90s, their stand was a very broad approach that included fannish activities, academic articles and a general acceptance of by-products and adaptations – without making it the centre of their interests.

Another interesting point is how debate is essential in the building of fan group identity. From the outset and as soon as there were reader columns (we can assume that reading groups and meetings got to the same point), questions were mooted that led to endless debates on specific topics in Tolkien's fiction. A few examples that would not surprise any Tolkien fan are the questions of Tom Bombadil's identity and age (Is he really the Eldest? What would be his race, or is he Eru himself?), whether Balrogs have wings or not, the exact shape of Elves' ears, etc. Even though some of these questions have been answered by Tolkien himself in his letters and made available to the readers as soon as the selected collection was published by Humphrey Carpenter in 1981, new comers in Tolkien readership or fandom arrive regularly and raise the same questions, again and again. Incidentally, this strengthens the implicit hierarchy that can be made between newcomers and more 'mature' fans, who will likely be erudite on these matters and patiently quote texts or references to enlighten the green fan. Interestingly to us, these endless and repeated debates almost never wander towards the field of political debate, except for a few exceptions that show how outlandish it actually felt to the community. This was the case with the 'Hippie-Hobbit' controversy during the first years of the TS existence in which Belladonna Chapman pushed for a conservative stand towards drugs and the magazine *Gandalf's Garden*,[32] which she felt was giving Tolkien bad press. A few members reacted to this and it was rapidly decided that the debate had nothing to do inside the pages of the society's fanzine. Another example might be when Nan C. Scott raised the racial question inside *The Lord of the Rings* in one of her letters to *The Middle Earthworm* and that no one actually reacted to her words: this silence sounds to me like a definite stand towards the political consensus.

31. Again, this statement seems more valid for the period preceding Peter Jackson's adaptations than today. My impression is that MythSoc has rather turned its back to anything derived from Tolkien's work and taken a very literary point of view – without completely disregarding creativity – while the Tolkien Society has embraced all kinds of approaches to Tolkien's work including cinema adaptations.

32. *Gandalf's Garden* was a hippie magazine published in London by Muz Murray in 1968-1969. Most of its content was not about Tolkien's work, even though they were occasional references showing that the authors and readers were quite familiar with the book.

Still, debates are an essential part of fandom activity, and what looks from the outside as a pointless quibbling, is actually a very formative experience for fans who thus practise their debating and argumentative skills as well as their text analysis skills.[33]

If we wanted to quickly brush a portrait of national fandoms, it would still be possible and it would go like this. The American fandom is composed of a variety of groups and publications even today, which makes sense given the size of the country – both the geographical divide and the amount of people – and also the existence of some non-reconcilable attitudes. It is obvious that there is a huge divide between the exclusive stand to the 'Professor's' work taken by the National Tolkien League led by Louis Epstein and The Tolkien Fellowships of Bernie Zuber which openly embraced adaptations.[34] Another possible explanation for this multiplicity of groups, despite the predominance of the MythSoc, is the fact that this helps preserve a "human" size of fan communities, to keep a sense of fellowship inside the fan group itself. In the UK, the predominance of the Tolkien Society is obvious, and its hegemony is clear despite its "late" appearance compared to some American societies. To me, it seems that this unique position comes from the middle ground line of conduct of the society, which was made possible mainly thanks to its mixed origins (fans and non-fans) but also the creation of the privileged link with the Tolkien family and Oxford. France's position is less clear in part because its fandom is much younger and the search for a form of legitimacy has been prevalent for years. Still, the general trend seems to have been moving from an aspiring academic attempt at first (with the FEE) to a more grassroots approach that is closer to the TS middle ground and was helped by the internet without excluding the academic-like work of many fans inside French fandom.

6 - Identity & interests of Tolkien fans

With this last part of my study, I reach the point of my personal and ongoing attempt at canvassing what makes Tolkien fandom what it is.

6.1 - A varied number of groups and attitudes towards the works of Tolkien (example of the US)

To have a broader vision of the variety of attitudes towards the works of Tolkien and of fan socialization, let us have a closer look at American fandom. Thanks to Gary Hunnewell's Collection at Marquette University, it is possible today to draw a quite complete map of the different types of fan organizations through their fanzines. The diversity of societies that have existed also allows us to canvas most of the types of interests in the work of Tolkien.

The most influential and numerous society in America has been, since its creation, the Mythopoeic Society. It was founded by Glen GoodKnight and was so successful that it quickly got organized into local branches for meetings. Each branch has its own

33. See Michael Saler, *As If.*

34. Bernie Zuber was actually hired by Saul Zaentz' company Tolkien Enterprises – today Middle-earth Enterprises – to promote the films and Zuber's fanzine *The Westmarch Chronicle* thus actively helped promote Bakshi's adaptations for example.

reading programme and members discussed these chapters (taken from Tolkien's work, but also from C. S. Lewis's and Charles Williams' works). Moreover, the Society has been publishing *Mythlore* since 1969 – almost without interruption – and *Mythprint*, a thick academic-style fanzine and a newsletter. Clearly, the Mythopoeic Society is not the only Tolkien-related society, there is also the American Tolkien Society that has been run by Phil Helms since the end of the 60s and whose fanzine *Minas Tirith Evening Star* has been published since 1967.[35] Also in the 1970s, Renée Alper efficiently ran the American Hobbit Association and published *The Rivendell Review* for a few years. Even though these groups could apparently be very similar, it appears that their structure is mostly centered on the leader for ATS and AHA while despite the strong presence of Glen GoodKnight for decades, Mythopoeic Society has managed to reach out to many active members. It would seem that the declared and official status of a group as a "society' gives it more credential, it also looks to the newcomer as a stable and reliable structure. At least it is interesting to note that, given the drive and activity of its leaders, there was some recognition, from the general press for *Mythlore* – a few articles – or from politicians – the ATS received several letters from senators and even from Ronald Reagan to acknowledge the importance of Hobbit Day.

With a similar structure but very different paths, there were many student groups dedicated to Tolkien and his works. Because of their transient nature – students only stay for a short period of time – these groups did not not always leave a trace and were not necessarily 'structured'. Still, a few of them, led by motivated students, produced fanzines, like the Michigan State University Tolkien Fellowship which published several short-lived and light-hearted fanzines in the late 60s, including the wondrous *Magic Bagel*. In a completely different approach but around the same period, the University of Wisconsin Tolkien Society published *Orcrist*: edited by Richard West,[36] it had a much more academic layout and contents.

More loosely organized groups have also existed and relied most of the time on a circle of friends and their meetings. The New England Tolkien Society founded by Gary Hunnewell in the 1970s seems to fall in that category. It is long-lived thanks to its steadfast leader and editor of *Ravenhill*, yet the tone is more familiar than the usual one we can find in other publications, probably because the fanzine's outreach is similar to the traditional fanzines from the 1960s with a limited number of copies sent out to faithful readers.

Traditional reading groups are more strictly organized but still targeted at a small group of related people. Gary Hunnewell's collection only includes one such group, but we may safely assume that others have existed, and may have cohabited with fandom without ever meeting it. The Tolkien Society of Peekskill for example, was a group animated by Sister Pauline Johnson, who published the fanzine *News from Bree*, mainly composed of minutes of the society's meetings. Interestingly, this group is the most feminine one encountered, as there were no male members at the beginning and just a few "imported" from the National Tolkien League at the end of existence of the society.

35. Issues were first on wargames with a circle of friends. It only became a Tolkien fanzine in 1975. The society has been less active these last few years, but the fanzine still comes out now and again in a digital version.

36. Richard C. West later on published *Tolkien Criticism: An Annotated Checklist.*

The National Tolkien League stands apart from the other societies for its specific policies, just as the Kingdom of Gondor and Arnor does, in a very different way. The NTL published *Frodo Fortnightly*, a fanzine that respected its name and thus a great many number of issues exist. Louis Epstein was the leader and he made his society very selective and exclusive: each person who wanted to become part of the society had to pass a test – trivia questions about Tolkien's works. It also organized several 'TolCons' which seem to have been rather simple group meetings and promoted a 'Tolkienic University'. Moreover, the tone used also created a distinctive fanatic atmosphere since everything and everyone who criticized Tolkien were called 'heretics'. An amateurish video game called *Kill the Tolkien Hater* was even publicized in its pages. In a very different vein, The Kingdom of Gondor and Arnor chose to communicate solely as though it were actually part of Middle-earth, with a mock-chivalrous style and a flourish of titles and names. Even though it automatically creates some sort of exclusivity, it also stands as a very original form of communication around what was mostly a group of friends who liked to gather and have fun.

As we have seen, Tolkien groups exist in very different forms, structures and sizes. Though most of these groups display a general interest for Tolkien's work and leave a space for all sorts of interests to express themselves, some groups also focus on just one aspect of Middle-earth. When it comes to participating in fandom, fans' interests get very different 'shapes'. Most groups allow for a general text analysis, be it through meetings or through discussions in letter columns, but there is also a great amount of creativity shown in either writing (poems and fan fictions) or artwork (drawing, but also music, knitting, costuming etc.). This creativity also finds its outlet in the many fun activities, games and trivia quizzes that have been invented and circulated inside fandom from its beginning. Finally, another approach of these varied interests, can be on the discussed themes, that is to say on what aspect of Middle-earth fans feel like discussing the most. Some groups may show a specific interest to a designated people (Hobbits, Elves or Dwarves most likely) or to a specific area of expertise, the main and most famous one being the invented languages, their grammar and also the styles of writing.

6.2 - Identities

Studying fandom through fanzines leads to the curiosity – many times expressed in these fanzines themselves – about what led Tolkien fans to read and like Tolkien. I have made such an analysis inside French fandom, using as source the fanzines in my corpus but also many testimonies gathered online.[37] It appears that Tolkien fans are a very motley crowd with widely different original interests beforehand.

Going back to the very beginning of Tolkien's work's reception in France, we come across an article by Louis Bouyer, published in a magazine called *La Tour Saint-Jacques*: the magazine was mostly dedicated to spiritual and esoteric questions and the author was a Catholic priest. A few years later, Philippe Marlin, a French reader of

37. I have collected testimonies online, mainly on Tolkiendil's and JRRVF's forums for French fandom. I have received a few testimonies by email too.

Tolkien, became the editor of Œil du Sphinx, an edition mostly interested in esoteric and spiritual questions.[38] On a very different spiritual branch, there were also hippie gatherings dedicated to the discussion of meaning in *The Hobbit* for example as early as the 1970s in Rouen. This can find another expression in the usual student and social gatherings, that find their expression in high school fanzines for example.

Some fans come from a 'high brow' cultural background, nurtured on traditional French literature, Classic literature and epic tales, they usually discovered Tolkien by chance when a reference came up in a press article or when they read Jacques Bergier's *Admirations* in Christian Bourgois' catalogue. From another field of literature, many readers have come to Tolkien from science fiction or genre literature like detective fiction. For example, the first professional magazine that dedicated a whole issue on Tolkien was *Les Cahiers de L'Imaginaire*: this 1982 issue was initiated thanks to the initiative of Jacques Baudou, a journalist specialized in Sherlock Holmes literature.

As Tolkien's work's reception really began to take off ground in the 1980s, it is quite unsurprising to see a lot of fans being initially wargame players and even more commonly RPG players, be it of *Dungeons & Dragons* or others. Actually, the oldest Tolkien reference I have found in a French fanzine comes from an RPG fanzine called *Runes* and published in 1983. It clearly pictured his work as a well-known world of fiction that was considered as being familiar to its readership. At the very end of our timeline study, a few readers were video game players before becoming Tolkien readers.

As our few sidestep examples show, French fandom seems to mirror – maybe with different proportions – the composition of Tolkien fandoms in the UK and the US. We can also notice that most participants in fan groups are young or at least get into fandom at a young age, most fans are high school or university students at their arrival in a society or a fanzine community. If those fans who remain gradually age within the community, there is usually this strong trend of young membership, probably for the practical reason that they have more free time. Interestingly, most letter columns and societies show a mixed membership, most of the time there are almost as many women as there are men, which stands in contrast with the science fiction fandom that was mostly composed of men, even though it got more feminized through time.

As a final reminder, let us not forget that Tolkien fans are readers – whether from the outset or as a side effect – who became engaged and took an active stand. A fan necessarily engages in a more "personal" relationship with the author (see all the letters that were sent to the Professor, or the campaign captained by Nan C. Scott against Ace Books) and it also entails a will to create (fiction, art or fanzines and projects) and to meet like-minded people. To me, a fan becomes fully one from the moment he reaches out to other fans, but I acknowledge the reality and depth of a reader's passion even before he connects with other fans and fan communities.

6.3 - Interests

Reading through so much material – spanning over five decades – for my research and having been myself part of French fandom for almost two decades now has gradually

38. Archie Mercer's wife, Beryl, also evoked such interests in *The Middle Earthworm*.

led me to this first synthesis on Tolkien fans. I have identified two main trends, not exclusive of one another, among Tolkien fans: an intellectual curiosity or thirst for knowledge and a drive for creation.[39] These complementary psychological traits find different branches of expression.

The first and most visible branch is the 'knowledge' one. To me, this can be visible with the countless encyclopaedias and lexicons that have been published from the beginning of fandoms for example. The first lexicon dates back to 1962 and was published by Al Halevy in *Rhodomagnetic Digest* and reprinted in Niekas the same year. The same fanzine printed Bob Foster's lexicon in 1967 which was going to be published by an editor later on. A lot of fans confess their own attempt at listing names, places, creating glossaries, etc. which corresponds to a drive for accumulation and quantity of information but also a will for order. Two main fan figures belong to this trend: the linguist who will go through every possible detail to analyse, understand and learn about the invented languages, and the collector who will try and gather everything that exists in the field of collection he has defined.

The creative branch is more visible inside fanzine pages and at social events. Creative fans will find in Tolkien's work an endless source of inspiration for writing poems, stories, songs or composing music.[40] Obviously visual creation also has an important existence in Tolkien fandom with illustrations, but also knitting, calligraphy, costuming.

The middle ground position between these two branches would be the fan with a "playful mind". In that case, creativity is mingled with knowledge: one's knowledge about the works of Tolkien is tested through countless quizzes, puzzles, riddles. These imply most of the time knowledge but also form a competition, where fans would rival to show the highest level of knowledge. This (friendly) rivalry also surfaces in a very common fan declaration of being 'the greatest fan' or of bragging about the number of times they have read *The Lord of the Rings*. Another mingled attitude towards the works of fiction is the important trend of fan naming things or people with Tolkien's invented names or even names fabricated thanks to Tolkien invented languages. It seems that part of Middle-earth's magic comes from the unending source of inspiration given by its nomenclature.

A third and complementary trend in fan characterization is the social inclination. For some fans, it seems that the urge for creativity gets its expression in the editing of a fanzine, the organization of events and activities for example and their knowledge is more pragmatic as the knowledge of Tolkien's works is mostly used to determine what other fans will want to do and see. Also socializing among other Tolkien fans is sometimes a sort of first step for becoming oneself a fan – what must have happened to many of the first Tolkien Society members. A devoted reader may come across a fanzine or an announcement for an event and step into fandom 'by chance' before getting completely involved in fandom and steeped in Tolkien's works.

As my research analysis and results deepen, I should be able to draw a subtler portrait of fans and fandoms. As for now, I want to express my deepest gratitude towards those who have my work possible by generously sharing what they had on their hands and

39. Aspect mostly studied by my PhD supervisor Anne Besson.

40. Varied interesting testimonies are gathered in the volume *Meditations on Middle-earth*.

collections – showing how Tolkien fans around the world will always go the extra mile to make sure Tolkien scholarship can reach new heights.

Acknowledgments

My research would not have been made without the invaluable help of Bill Fliss at Marquette University, Charles Noad of the Tolkien Society, and Didier Willis. Thank you also to Bill Fliss, Jeremy Edmonds and Marcel Aubron-Bülles for their insightful feedback and proofreading. My deepest thanks to them.

Bibliography

Jenkins, H., *Textual Poachers: Television Fans and Participatory Culture,* (Routledge, London: 1992).

Besson, A., *Constellations : des mondes fictionnels dans l'imaginaire contemporain,* (Paris: CNRS éditions, 2015).

Blackwelder Collection, Milwaukee, Raynor Memorial Library at Marquette University.

Noad, C.E., 'The Tolkien Society – the early days., *Mallorn,* 50 (2010) 15-25.
— Personal Collection.

Saler, M., *As If, Modern Enchantment and the Literary of Prehistory of Virtual Reality,* (Oxford: Oxford University Press, 2012).

S. Gary Hunnewell's Collection, Milwaukee, Raynor Memorial Library at Marquette University.

Tolkien, J.R.R. *The Letters of J.R.R. Tolkien: A Selection*, ed. by H. Carpenter with the assistance of C. Tolkien (London: Allen & Unwin, 1981).

Willis, D., Personal Collection.

'Not Worth Doing': Fan fiction writers and the Fourth Age

Dr. Una McCormack

1 - Tolkien and 'The New Shadow'

Expansions of Tolkien's world are a truly fascinating idea, as interest in the forthcoming Amazon Prime series shows. Such expansions are a chance to explore further the geography, history, and politics of Middle-earth; a chance to spend more time with beloved characters, discovering where else their story may have led, which roads they may have walked along, which paths they may have taken.

This paper concerns fan fiction stories set during the Fourth Age, which act in some way as 'sequels' to *The Lord of the Rings*. For some of us, this is a delightful prospect. What might the Fourth Age look like? How might Elessar have ruled? Did he give up the crown and form an anarcho-syndicalist commune? What alliances needed to be made, and how? What is it like to be the child of parents who fought – and defeated – monsters? After the war is over, what do we do with peace?

Tolkien, inevitably, was there first. His story fragment 'The New Shadow', which appeared in volume 12 of *The History of Middle-earth*, is set in Gondor 'in the days of Eldarion', when the story of the Ring War 'was little heeded now by most of the people of Gondor, though a few were still living who could remember the War of the Ring as a shadow upon their early childhood' (*Peoples*, 410-11). This reminds me of World War 2 veterans: many of these were alive when I was a child in the 1970s and 1980s; there are fewer and fewer remaining.

The story of 'The New Shadow' follows Borlas, the son of Beregond, who is now an old man. In a conversation with Saelon, a younger man and friend of Borlas' son, they discuss the wanton felling of trees (sure signifier of evil in Tolkien's work); Saelon talks about Men's dissatisfaction since the death of the King. Then the name 'Herumor' is mentioned, a renegade Númenórean during the Last Alliance. Borlas conceals his shock; Saelon, departing, offers to tell him more, if Borlas meets him at full dark, dressed in black. What could possibly go wrong? After Saelon leaves, Borlas thinks about his son, and reflects on the news he has received of disappearing ships. He considers this new 'canker':

> [Borlas] halted in the narrow passage that ran through the house, and it seemed that he was wrapped in a blackness: not a glimmer of twilight of the world outside remained there. Suddenly he smelt it, or so it seemed [...] he smelt the old Evil and knew it for what it was (418).

It's an exciting start. Unfortunately, this is also where the story stops. Tolkien abandoned 'The New Shadow', and we know why, from Letter 256, written in May 1964.

> I did begin a story placed about 100 years after the Downfall [...] but it proved both sinister and depressing [...] [T]he people of Gondor in times of peace, justice and prosperity,

> would become discontented and restless – while the dynasts descended from Aragorn would become just kings and governors – like Denethor or worse. I found that even so early there was an outcrop of revolutionary plots, about a centre of secret Satanistic religion; while Gondorian boys were playing at being Orcs and going round doing damage. I could have written a 'thriller' about the plot and its discovery and overthrow – but it would be just that. *Not worth doing*' (*Letters*, Letter 256, 344; emphasis mine).

This is a fairly cutting dismissal of his own efforts, and, while one can imagine that Tolkien's publishers would quite happily have printed and promoted this novel, one can understand why Tolkien decided that this story was 'not worth doing'. Novel-writing is not a task to be undertaken lightly, and after *The Lord of the Rings*, the production of a mere 'thriller' must surely have felt pointless: the reduction of the complex tapestry of the Third Age into the more mundane conflicts that he believed would characterise the Fourth Age. In a recently auctioned letter, written in 1961, Tolkien wrote:

> I shall not write a sequel to *The Lord of the Rings* because, as is clearly stated in the course of the story, it is the end of the kind of world about which I write: the twilight in which mythology and history are blended. After that there is only history. (cited in McIntyre 2019)

Why tell a 'sinister and depressing' story about the wars and intrigues of petty dynasts? You could turn to a history of the later Roman Empire – or simply open the newspapers. Nevertheless, many people have found Fourth Age stories very much 'worth doing', and in the rest of this talk I am going to outline a handful of these, and suggest some reasons why we might want to write stories set during the 'King's Peace'.

2 - Fan fiction writers and the Fourth Age

I've written extensively elsewhere how fan fiction can act as a form of 'reparative reading' for women readers of *The Lord of the Rings* (McCormack 2015). Fan fiction can allow women readers to inscribe female presences, queer presences, and urban working-class presences in a text chiefly concerned with the masculine and heroic. A text, that is, from which women are largely absent.

It is no surprise therefore to find post-Ring War stories which bring female characters to the fore. An exemplary story, to my mind, is 'Keepers of the Hearth' by Alawa. This story follows the 'change of the home guard' in Meduseld after the War of the Ring. The point-of-view character, an original character, is named Winfrith. She has been housekeeper for Théoden since the death of his wife, Elfhild. We follow Winfrith, like Mrs Dalloway, through the course of a single day, during which the wedding of Éomer and Lothíriel occurs, restoring a Queen to the Golden Hall. During this day, Winfrith recalls the long years of her service through the decline of Rohan, first as wet-nurse to Théodred, then as nanny to Éomer and Éowyn, and last as housekeeper to Théoden. Domesticity – the keeping of the hearth; the lives, cares, and unceasing responsibilities of women – is brought to the fore. The story culminates not in the wedding, that traditional payoff, but in a beautiful ceremony at the evening feast at which Winfrith hands over her keys – and her charge – to Lothíriel. The following, adapted by the author from a Celtic blessing, is said during the ceremony:

Keeper of the Hearth kindle us
Gather us up under your mantle
And restore to us remembering.
Mothers of our mother remind us how
Foremothers strong show us the way
To kindle the hearth keep it bright
Preserve the flame's flicker in darkness.
Your hands upon ours our hands within yours
Day and night now keep light kindled.

Kings may return, the piece seems to argue, but true restoration – true regime change – is not complete until the arrival of a fully powerful Queen and all she symbolises. The story quietly and subversively asserts the significance of women in the making of any new realm. The subject changes from the King's Peace to the Queen's Peace.

As part of this shift towards domesticity, many authors construct families for characters, i.e. families that are at best sketched but not detailed by Tolkien. Characters who are no more than a name are fleshed out; new characters are created.

(Again, my focus is on Gondor in the Fourth Age, and particularly Faramir and Éowyn.) The author Nesta, for example, in her story 'Thorn in the flesh', gives the couple two more children after Elboron (who we know of from Tolkien): one of these is a character very like Denethor, causing significant stresses within the household, and making Faramir reflect on parenting a child very different from oneself.

Sian22 has created an extensive household around the first Prince and Princess of Ithilien: not just more children, but a memorable housekeeper character, Nera. Sian's stories are often concerned with the transmission of memory: Faramir, the sole survivor of his immediate family, has only fragmented stories of, for example, his mother to pass on. But Nera, who has known him since he was a boy, is a repository of knowledge that cannot be learned through books of lore. In the very fine story 'Emyn Arnen Yule', set at the beginning of the Fourth Age, this wisdom acts a means of healing an emerging rift between the newlywed couple, and became the means by which they establish a new shared custom for the new principality to celebrate the turning of the year. In 'The Battle of the Beds', an ostensibly light-hearted story about a family misunderstanding has a serious and poignant undertone: Faramir, woken from sleep by the cries of his young children, immediately has the household up in arms, but he has mistaken a simple children's game for an Orc attack. Peace has not been easily earned, the story suggests; the transition from the war footing of the Third Age to the gentler perils of the Fourth Age requires adjustment – and requires ongoing healing.

In my own stories, under my penname Altariel, I've also created further children for Faramir and Éowyn. Many of my stories dramatize the transmission of knowledge about the reality of the horrors of the Ring War. In 'We Need to Talk about Denethor',

Faramir and Éowyn tell the story of the death of Denethor and his attempted murder of Faramir to their adolescent children in such a way that the trauma is not inherited. In my very short story 'Safekeeping', in which Faramir's children find buried Haradric bones, that care cuts the other way: "We never told Father. It would only worry him." Ithilien, in my stories, becomes the site of the healing and regeneration necessary to transform a wounded land back into the Garden of Gondor.

Another source of storytelling shifts away from the start of the Fourth Age to the end – to the old age or death of one of the main characters. By this means an author is able to reflect upon the whole trajectory of the King's Peace. In my story 'The Stewards', an elderly Faramir and Samwise Gamgee meet in Ithilien, shortly before Rose's death and Sam's passage West. The story posits an ongoing tradition, whereby a tree is planted in Ithilien each time Sam visits. In the past, this has involved large parties of family members – this time, only Sam's son, and Faramir's grandson are present. Some memories are already disappearing (Faramir knows what is buried under each tree, while his grandson wonders), but an ongoing tradition has been established. The story gestures forward to the moment when stewardship of the land must be handed on.

Sian22, in her exceptional story 'Winter's Balm', also documents the passing of the guard to the children. Faramir, on his death bed, waits for the arrival of each of his children: "*It is peacetime*, he thought, and *my children are fighting other battles*." When at last they are, and he can let go. The story concludes:

> Faramir rose then and the man who took to his feet had no grey upon the raven waves and wore the white tree upon his leather jerkin. No sound did his footfalls make as his worn boots paced across the floor. The hand that touched each of them in blessing bore the many cuts and blemishes of battle once again.
>
> Yearning had made his spirit nearly solid; the night birds chattered in surprise as he crossed the veranda and walked out into the snow-bound garden.
>
> Suddenly Faramir was in her arms, the place he had ached to be again for every minute. His lips rested upon her hair. Poised again as if upon the walls, the snow devil whirled around them; gold and raven strands mingled together in its swirl.
>
> 'Come my love, tarry no more. Lay your duties down.' Gladly now he did.
>
> He swung up onto Windfola's back and lifted Eowyn before him. Together they took reins in hand and turned to westward. They set their path: to follow Earendil's star throughout the dim, unto the Doors of Night.

In this very fine conclusion to a beautiful story, we see a whole life brought to fulfilment. We recall Gandalf's words to Denethor, spoken at the pyre: "To me it would not seem that a Steward who faithfully surrenders his charge is diminished in love or in honour" (*RK*, 'The Pyre of Denethor', 888). In Sian22's story, Faramir passes his duties on to his son: "blemished" by war, but certainly undiminished. It is up to the children to fight the battles of peacetime.

This paper can only give a glimpse of the wealth of storytelling out there: there is a great deal, and what is most interesting to me is how often these visions of the Fourth Age are assembled as *mosaics*: constructed by individual authors from numerous short stories that shift back and forth across the Fourth Age, perhaps in response to specific challenges, building up an overall effect of how the Fourth Age might be. These aren't lengthy, plot-driven 'thrillers': they're threads of tapestries, pictures of the Peace woven from many threads, stories upon stories of renewal, healing, restitution, growth, and change. They are often gentle but poignant, bringing to mind what Ursula K. Le Guin wrote about storytelling:

> Modernist manuals of writing often conflate story with conflict. This reductionism reflects a culture that inflates aggression and competition while cultivating ignorance of other behavioral options. No narrative of any complexity can be built on or reduced to a single element. Conflict is one kind of behavior. There are others, equally important in any human life, such as relating, finding, losing, bearing, discovering, parting, changing. Change is the universal aspect of all these sources of story. Story is something moving, something happening, something or somebody changing. (Le Guin 1998, 123)

These Fourth Age stories, in their shifts and movements forwards, show the process of making and establishing the Peace.

3 - Epics of peace and odes to joy

At the start of 2019, as I was conceiving of this paper, the German actor Bruno Ganz died. Most people know Ganz from his performance as Hitler in *Downfall* (and the online memes, of course), but news of his death sent me, for the first time, to watch another mesmerising performance, in Wim Wenders' *Wings of Desire*. In this film, Ganz plays Damiel, an invisible and immortal angel, who wanders the streets of West Berlin, listening to the thoughts of humans – who seem solitary, isolated from each other, often in great psychological pain – and he tries to bring them comfort. In the course of his wanderings, Damiel encounters an old man named Homer, who dreams of an 'epic of peace'. In voiceover, we hear the following: "No one has so far succeeded in singing an epic of peace. What is wrong with peace that its inspiration doesn't endure? That its inspiration doesn't endure?" As I reflected on this, and on the stories set in the Fourth Age that I've read, it seemed to me that this impulse might lie behind some of the fiction I have discussed here.

The Lord of the Rings, of course, is an epic of war – its pain and its passion born in the mud of Flanders. At the end of that epic, we are offered the peace. But what about those of us born to this peace, those of us who have inherited it – the children of a kindlier West – how might we sing an epic of peace? How might we make its inspiration endure?

Tolkien was not optimistic that the peace earned during the War of the Ring would last. In 1972, not long before his death, he wrote about 'The New Shadow' to his friend Douglas Carter:

> I of course discovered that the King's Peace would contain no tales worth recounting; and his wars would have little interest after the overthrow of Sauron; but that almost certainly a restlessness would appear about then, owing to the (it seems) inevitable boredom of Men with the good; there would be secret societies practising dark cults, and 'orc-cults' among adolescents. (*Letters*, Letter 338, 419)

In 'The New Shadow', the memory of the old war is slipping beyond human memory; the Enemy is emerging as a source of children's games – and the schemes of older men who should know better. Through these means, the 'old lie' is beginning once again to propagate. What stories can be offered in response to this lie? In these tales of healing, growth, regeneration, the setting down of weapons and the building of a new world, what these stories of the Fourth Age suggest is how we might sing an epic of peace – or perhaps, as we might call it, an ode to joy.

Bibliography

Alawa, 'Keepers of the Hearth', *Archive of Our Own*, 19 April 2015 <https://archiveofourown.org/works/3784218/chapters/8417169> [Accessed 31 January 2024].

Altariel, 'Safekeeping', in *Garden of Gondor, Archive of Our Own*, 13 September 2011 <https://archiveofourown.org/ works/252903/chapters/392830> [Accessed 4 October 2019].
— 'The Stewards', in *Garden of Gondor, Archive of Our Own*, 18 July 2019 <https://archiveofourown.org/works/ 19862527> [Accessed 4 October 2019].
— 'We Need to Talk About Denethor', in *Garden of Gondor, Archive of Our Own*, 18 August 2018 <https://archiveofourown.org/works/15720888/chapters/36544944> [Accessed 4 October 2019].

Downfall, dir. by Oliver Hirschbiegel (Munich: Constantin Film, 2004).

Le Guin, U.K., *Steering the Craft: Exercises and Discussions on Story Writing for the Lone Mariner and the Mutinous Crew,* (Portland: The Eighth Mountain Press, 1998).

McCormack, U., 'Finding Ourselves in the (Un)Mapped Lands' in *Perilous and Fair: Women in the Works and Life of JRR Tolkien*, ed. by J. Brennan Croft and L. Donovan (Altadena, CA: Mythopoeic Press, 2015) 309-326.

McIntyre, A., 'JRR Tolkien letter sells at auction' *Dorothy House Hospice Care* <https://www.dorothyhouse.org.uk/ blog/jrr-tolkien-letter-sells-at-auction/> [Accessed 4 October 2019].

Nesta, 'Thorn in the flesh.', *FanFiction*, 29 September 2005<https://www.fanfiction.net/s/2598604/1/Thorn-in-the-flesh> [Accessed 4 October 2019].

Sian22, 'The Battle of the Beds', *Archive of Our Own*, 29 July 2019 <https://archiveofourown.org/works/20032891> [Accessed 4 October 2019].
— 'Chapter 8' in *Emyn Arnen Yule, Archive of Our Own*, 7 January 2016 <https://archiveofourown.org/chapters/ 13772446> [Accessed 4 October 2019].
— 'Winter's Balm', *Archive of Our Own*, 16 September 2014 <https://archiveofourown.org/works/2316719> [Accessed 4 October 2019].

Tolkien, J.R.R., 'The New Shadow' in *The History of Middle-earth, Volume XII: The Peoples of Middle-earth,* (London: HarperCollinsPublishers, 1990a) 409-421.
— *The Letters of J.R.R. Tolkien*, ed. H. Carpenter with the assistance of C. Tolkien (London: HarperCollins, 1990b).
— *The Lord of the Rings,* (London: HarperCollinsPublishers, 1991).

Wings of Desire, dir. by W. Wenders (Berlin: Basis-Film-Verleih, 1987).

Le Nere Lame – The Black Blades

Marco Scicchitano

'The Black Blades' (Nere Lame) is the name of an innovative learning project for teenagers aged 14 to 21 using tabletop and live-action role-playing games in settings inspired by Tolkien's fiction. With this project Tolkien's world comes out of the circle of enthusiasts and scholars to become part of life and the construction of the identity of the current generations of young people, as we will see later.

The aim is to achieve psychological and social objectives that are significant to every age group, and crucial during adolescence, such as: developing cooperation and friendship skills, improving emotions management, increasing self-awareness. The project runs from September to June in two-hours sessions once a week. The most exciting aspect of this project is the fact that it provides teenagers with a non-pathologising alternative to a strictly clinical therapeutic setting, to help them face the issues of such a critical time as adolescence in a creative, ludic and entertaining environment.

The background to this project dates back to 2012, when it all started as an original workshop activity for young people on the high-functioning autism spectrum, with the aim of achieving results in the development of social skills, emotions management, and social cognitive flexibility using tabletop role-playing games. In this step, we don't use a Tolkienian setting. Given the success of this venture, a team came together, other clinical centres were involved, and the target was widened beyond the autism spectrum to include young people with different clinical diagnoses, such as social anxiety and behavioural disorders.

'The Black Blades' project started in 2018, introduce the live action role-playing and the Tolkienian setting, and includes, in addition to boys with clinical diagnosis, also young people with no clinical diagnosis who, nevertheless, would benefit from the workshop formulation and were interested in role-playing or becoming part of a Tolkien-themed LARP group. In the various steps we have chosen increasingly inclusive goals

The project group, composed of the young participants and RPG Workshop professionals, was spontaneously joined by other people who were attracted by the project and by Tolkien's world. A feature of the LARP Group is, therefore, its high level of diversity, as its ludic dimension demolishes barriers and levels out differences, thus offering a real inclusion. A true fellowship.

We are happy with the results achieved so far. After two years, most parents think that taking part in the project was useful or very useful to their child. Positive feedback also emerged from an internal assessment using standardised tests that allowed us to identify a significant improvement in skills, such as: listening, achieving external perspective, turn-taking, and overall cooperation.

The effectiveness and originality of the project can also be ascertained by the welcome it received from the wider community. We have already received requests for our work to become the topic of dissertations; we have been interviewed as a case study of excellence in the educational use of RPG. We have been asked to provide, and we have already provided, training programmes to fellow psychologists who would then apply the RPG Workshop Method in their healthcare field area, and for Master's Degree Courses including role-playing games and wanting to achieve a higher educational sensitivity. We also received invites from academia: the Pontifical Holy Cross University in Rome (Università Santa Croce) invited us to an expert meeting in October, and the Philosophical Institute for Thomistic Studies (Istituto Filosofico Tomistico) of Modena in November.

The experience of these past few years also allowed us to significantly gather theories and procedures to develop a Method, the RPG Workshop Method, which we explained in a book to be published in November by Franco Angeli, one of the most important publishing houses in Italy, which will be officially presented during the Lucca Comics & Games convention.

What is this project? The project presupposes a Tolkienian setting, which is a pivotal element, and the use of a specific tool, the role-playing game, in its tabletop and live-action formats.

The Tolkienian setting is used not only to create the backdrop and to name the characters, but also as a value system enabling the identification of themes that can be used from a psycho-educational standpoint, such as, for example, fellowship and friendship, both very important in Tolkien's work.

We tried to actualise this within the workshop through exchange, attention to others, ludic moments and activities developing sensitivity to care about the suffering of others.

Another value that is very important is courage, and the ability to recognise and face evil always and at any cost, and this is a very important value for teenagers, exactly because it stimulates them to confront difficulties and not to feel overwhelmed by problems.

We stimulate them through grit and the invite to confront and relate to one another also through conflict and they do so in different ways, all the way to actual clashing.

Another value that is very important for Tolkien is the clear distinction between good and evil, which is not an immutable kind of distinction but rather a dynamic one and, above all, a personal choice, experienced within the inner dimension of each individual. For Tolkien each character, or at least each of the characters whose inner dimension he outlines, has an ethical dimension, choices that need to be made, and this is very important to us because teenagers too must make choices in the course of their lives.

So we encourage reflection in teenagers by means of classroom presentations through which we provide them with a compass to understand good and evil, but – above all – by means of practical experience where they can see evil as portrayed by the characters played by actors who come and work with us in this workshop. Reflection is also encouraged as part of a personal inner research experience, by practising mindfulness meditation, to consciously get in touch with themselves. This activity is carried out outdoors with a professional mindfulness teacher. Teenagers face evil also through fighting, understanding that life entails challenges, that there are borders to be defended, and that fighting helps to channel energy in a positive way and direct it towards an objective. We were satisfied to notice that parents, most of whom didn't already know Tolkien when we started, have learned to appreciate and better understand Middle-earth so much that 64% of them think that Tolkienian values are useful or very useful for learning purposes.

Actually, we were able to codify the game also thanks to the work of Francesco Nepitello, author of role-playing games such as One Ring (Unico Anello) and Adventures in Middle-earth (Avventure nella Terra di Mezzo).

We also received a huge support from the community of enthusiasts gravitating around the Italian Association of Tolkien Studies (Associazione Italiana Studi Tolkieniani), thanks to a precious and enriching debate. The Association is a sponsor of the project.

Besides the Tolkienian setting, the other distinctive feature is the use of the RPG Workshop Method, which intentionally uses play, simulation and interactions among participants. Making them work in sync.

Playing is a very important activity. In mammals, ludic activity favours learning, and it is not by chance that all cubs play and, in doing so, they learn social rules and adaptive behaviour patterns. The same brain circuits that support ludic activity in children are also active in adults, and indeed playing does facilitate learning and collaboration processes in adults too.

Simulation, which is of course a leading feature of role-playing games, is essential precisely because it creates imaginative backdrops, fantasy narratives and imaginary characters that enable the creation of situations where teenagers can move and experiment, and they are allowed to test themselves in different ways, sometimes very useful from an identity development standpoint.

Also essential are interactions, because there is a group – there are rules to be observed. These rules are observed and agreed on together. In the group, both during the game and out-of-game, conflict can happen and it can be managed. It is therefore possible to organise ad hoc moments when professionals can intervene and reformulate, putting into words episodes of conflict that can occur among teenagers or between teenagers and professionals. Another very important thing is the appreciation of the position of each individual and of group dynamics, because professionals can promote camaraderie and help teenagers to drive the group forward in the most collaborative way. Psychologists interact with teenagers not in the closed environment of their office, but rather by observing them and being at their side during real-life dynamics, while they relate with their peers or clash with them – or with the psychologists themselves, who then help them to become aware of themselves, and to experience themselves in a new way within the group.

The Black Blades are set in the North of Middle-earth, during the Third Age. We are in a defined historic period, i.e. 2952 (twenty-nine fifty-two), 10 years after the Battle of the Five Armies, and we are a fellowship wanting to reform a secret elite platoon, that had been founded during the Second Age in Nùmenor by Tar Palantir, with the aim to try and kill all remaining dragons. After the fall of Arnor, the fellowship became extinct, but our Captain found a book telling the story of ancient deeds and tales and decided to reform it. The fellowship is called Mormegiliath, 'all the black Blades'.

Let's now explain the features of this fellowship, starting with its *motto*: 'to assuage the pain of the world'. How can the pain of the world be assuaged? It can be assuaged by elevating man through art, culture, wisdom and beauty, represented by the seven stars, which are the seven soothsaying stones that the Eldar gave to the men of Nùmenor. Elevation is a way to heal the world because through culture and art, and taking care of nature, Man can create antidotes and elevate himself so as not to be taken in by pain and evil. The pain of the world is assuaged by fighting, because this allows to face evil directly, and to defeat it; the pain of the world is also assuaged through care and compassion for all suffering creatures that endured the effect, the wound of evil. One member, who is a wonderfully talented musician, has composed an original melody, so he says, inspired by the Black Blades.

Elevation, grit and care are the three vectors through which we carry on the in-game action of the black blades. We approach these through specific, identified objectives. For example, self-awareness develops in-game from the creation of a character and attribution of shadow points. Out-of-game, this means that the teenager can develop self-consistency and identify their fragility. In-game, we teach teenagers to form a *fellowship*, to create a bond of fellow soldiers and friendship through play, and this allows us to develop their ability to collaborate and their sense of belonging to a group. Another objective of the project is also the practice of *music* that, in-game, takes the shape of music lessons, spell-bounding tunes, or the composition of an anthem for the fellowship, while it also takes on an out-of-game value by enabling artistic expression, entertainment, and harmonious cooperation.

This year's RPG Workshop was organised in three phases: Autumn, with both outdoor live-action and indoor activities; Spring; and Winter, when the weather cools down and light fades off, so we remained indoors using table top role-playing games. The latter was also a rather inventive activity because we managed to bring into the tabletop format the characters played by teenagers during the live-action game.

These are activities carried out in the Autumn phase: storytelling lab, acting, music and comic strips drawing. We also have live action sessions where, surrounded by nature, teenagers used purpose-designed maps. This is a map of a public park area in Rome. We also had actors and extras.

Then we had our tabletop session. The team is made up of RPG Workshop professionals and professional master players from Giano Academy. We divided the group into 3 different sub-groups, each with a master player and an RPG Workshop psychologist who would lead the sessions.

All the teenagers engaged in a final multi-tabletop session. During the 4-months tabletop phase in Winter, we created a live-action session to break the rhythm and we did it on the 3rd of January, so that it would coincide with Tolkien's birthday and afterwards we made a toast to the Professor.

In Spring we started live-action sessions. We had a professional actor teaching acting techniques to the teens. We asked him to focus on the self-aware and expressive use of the body to oppose the relationship drift of digitally-mediated interactions via smartphone and social media. We had Elvish classes that were surprisingly very popular leading up to the Battle for Vilegis, the biggest LARP event in Italy, attended by 1400 players and to which we took part as a group of 20 for 5 days in a row.

Here you can see the teens in action with myself and other players. We were able to experience an extensive camp- and characters-immersion, having many adventures and educational experiences, wearing armour, but also exchanging views and learning together with others who were also there with us to have fun, all the way to a very important moment, that we organise every time, using the circle-time technique to reflect on what we experienced. This is because we think that reflection and expression in words give teenagers the opportunity to think something over and get in touch with themselves, to make contact with their fragility and difficulties in order to be able to overcome them, because in order to smoke out evil it's important to strike it where it's weaker, and remove it to free up the space previously infested by its presence, fighting evil and making way for good.

Young Readers, *The Lord of the Rings*, and the Question of Genre

Luke Shelton

In my PhD project, I asked several questions concerning genre and type in order to gain information about how young participants classify *The Lord of the Rings*. The first question of this kind simply asked participants 'what type of story is *The Lord of the Rings*'? The goal of this question was to be as open-ended as possible so that participants could emphasize the aspects of the story that they thought were most important in determining what kind of story the book is. A different approach to discussing how young readers identify the genre or type of story of *The Lord of the Rings* was made in the next two questions of the survey. Question seven gave participants twelve genres and asked them to pick the 'kind of story *The Lord of the Rings* is'. A follow-up question asked participants to justify their selection of one of the genres. This was an open-ended 'what' question that allowed for a wide variety of feedback. In this presentation, I will limit my comments only to the two most popularly selected genres: fantasy and quest. I have decided to address these two genres today because they are evenly indicated as the most prevalent opinion for the genre of *The Lord of the Rings* for this sample of readers. By discussing these two genres with you, I hope to share two trends that developed in the study and indicate some of the implications of these trends.

The genre 'fantasy' was selected by eight of the thirty participants in the study. This makes it one of the most recognized genres for the text, tied with the 'quest' genre. Many participants who chose the fantasy genre also mentioned the genres of epic or myth in their discussions. For instance, one participant saw the story as 'an epic, high-fantasy tale, and in some ways, it is like a tribute to the mythologies and epics of the past'. Similarly, another participant described the book as 'an epic fantasy story focusing on good versus evil, but also as a part of a whole mythology that Tolkien created'. A couple of these participants also thought the idea of a quest was important; for example, called it 'a fantasy quest story'. Most of these participants also indicated that the setting played an important role in their decision to classify the story as a fantasy. One participant provided a good overview of this perspective when he explained that 'I chose "fantasy" because, even though it has elements from the other categories, it takes place in a fantastical setting'. How other people classify the story was also a consideration for about half of the participants who consider it a fantasy. One noted how 'it's typically categorized as a fantasy novel or an epic fantasy'. Another went so far as to claim that 'it like literally defines the fantasy genre'.

It is difficult to compare and contrast the responses of young readers to scholarship defining the fantasy genre because this is a definition that scholars have had a hard time pinning down. One of the most influential attempts to do so comes from Brian Atteberry's *Strategies of Fantasy* (1992). In the text, Atteberry defines fantasy by using the concept of a fuzzy set that he borrows from logicians. In essence, he contends that a genre is defined by the texts that are most consistently placed at the centre of the genre and is made up of texts that have similar features or techniques to these central texts. This results in genres that have unclear boundaries, rather than fixed walls. While this definition is helpful to combat overly-rigid ideas of genre, there are some complications that arise from this concept when compared with the current study.

Initially, Atteberry places *The Lord of the Rings* at the centre of the fantasy genre based on fourteen responses to a questionnaire that he developed for critics of fantasy literature. The current study has more than double the sample size and, arguably, includes a more representative population in terms of the popular ideas about fantasy literature than did Atteberry's. Since only eight out of the thirty participants in this study rated *The Lord of the Rings* as a fantasy text, this could potentially undermine Atteberry's case by contesting the one piece of objective evidence that he presents. If, however, we still follow Atteberry's model of the fuzzy set based on his own insights in the book rather than the results of his questionnaire, there are still problems to be found with regard to the current study.

This is significant, since as recently as 2012, scholars such as James Edwards and Farah Mendlesohn have cited Atteberry's work in their introduction to *The Cambridge Companion to Fantasy Literature* as "the most valuable theoretical text for taking a definition of fantasy beyond preference and intuition" (2014, 1). For now, it is important to note that less than a third of the study participants indicated that *The Lord of the Rings* belonged in the genre of fantasy. The question still remaining is whether these conversations give any indication of how *The Lord of the Rings* position within the fantasy may have shifted since Atteberry's definition. We will come back to these points in the conclusion of this presentation.

The other most commonly chosen genre for *The Lord of the Rings*, also being chosen by eight participants, was the genre of quest. Many participants who chose the quest genre initially talked about the story as a fantasy. In fact, six of the eight participants who ultimately labelled the story a quest said something similar to this: "[the book is] an adventure story. And it's obviously very thought-out, too. It's actually kind of like a fantasy history-book". Most of them suggested that the story is *more than* a fantasy. These observations reflect a complex understanding of genre. Most of these participants demonstrated a preference for discussing the plot of the story *after* they decided that it is a quest. One participant demonstrated this tendency when she described how "when you break down the story, you end up with the quest to destroy the Ring". Another participant went a little further than the others. He indicated that there is more than one quest portrayed in the story:

> I think the part with Frodo, Sam, and Gollum, to me, it seems more like the main story because it deals specifically with the Ring and that's… more like a quest to go destroy the Ring. I also think a little bit of the part with Aragorn. He's kind of on a quest to regain his mantle of king.

Instead of attempting to find a more inclusive genre for the entire story, like the participants who chose the fantasy genre, these participants focus on a specific element within the text that they perceive to be the most important. In all instances, participants who chose quest as the genre for the story focused primarily on plot elements rather than character elements or setting elements.

The tendency to focus on the plot rather than the characters or setting of the story is well attested in scholarship. One of the first reviewers to become captivated with Tolkien's use of the archetypal quest narrative was W.H. Auden. In his essay 'The Quest Hero' he begins by defining a quest. He claims that "to go in quest means to look for something of which one has, as yet, no experience; one can imagine what it will be like but whether one's picture is true or false will be known only when one has found it" (Auden 2004, 31-2). This definition provides the foundation for the remainder of his explication of *The Lord of the Rings* and several other works. To lend more specificity to his argument, Auden enumerates six 'essential elements' of a quest. He then traces how these elements are portrayed over the course of *The Lord of the Rings*, focusing on Frodo as the main character of the quest. Importantly, while Auden mentions characters in this list of essential elements, he discusses them more in the context of narrative function than their actual portrayal. This aligns with the kinds of observations made by participants as they focus more on the plot than the characters or settings.

In *There Would Always Be a Fairy tale: More Essays on Tolkien* (2017), Verlyn Flieger revisits the concepts of journey and quest. She argues that "in the most general sense, both [*The Hobbit* and *The Lord of the Rings*] follow the traditional romance trajectory – a hero's journey and return" (210). She goes on, though, to distinguish between the two texts as illustrating different kinds of journey:

> Bilbo had *adventures* – dangerous escapades exciting for their own sake, ending in peace and prosperity for the Elves, Men, and Dwarves, and for Bilbo himself. Frodo goes on a quest – a journey as careless for soul as for body – with a fixed purpose, a goal beyond itself. (210)

While her ultimate goal in this section is to illustrate the way in which French romance influenced Tolkien's writing, along the way Flieger expertly explains how the different archetypes to which Tolkien appeals in his two works change the way that readers respond to the texts. The adventure of Bilbo has several contained, discrete episodes which are magnifying in intensity as the book continues, whereas Frodo's journey has a singular mission, but also has to overcome obstacles along the way. The former focuses on the way in which the action changes the character, the latter focuses on the way in which the action changes Middle-earth.

One scholar who expands the understanding of the quest structure employed throughout *The Lord of the Rings* is Anna Caughey. In her essay 'The Hero's Journey' (2014) she claims that "the text works successfully in both the adventure-story and elegiac modes because *The Lord of the Rings* offers the reader not one quest-narrative or Hero's Journey but several, which run simultaneously in a number of registers and at a number of levels" (404). She argues that the way Tolkien employs these multiple narratives helps the work appeal to multiple audiences, including various age ranges. Not only does Caughey indicate Tolkien's employment of multiple quest narratives, but she also postulates how these narratives function to engage the attention of readers at differing levels of maturity. Such an analysis helps to reveal one of the appeals that the text has for younger readers. This resonates with some of the findings of my larger study. Caughey's arguments are also reminiscent of the way that participants recognize that the narrative surrounding the Ring represents a quest. A further similarity is how one participant also recognised that both Frodo and Aragorn have their own quests to complete over the course of the text. In all, there are many similarities between the scholars who discuss the theme of the quest and the observations made by this group of participants.

Participants chose fantasy and quest with equal frequency in the study. Between them, these two genres represent the preferred classification of more than half of the participants in the study. There are a few conclusions, then, which seem significant about this group. The most significant trend that arises from this analysis is the tendency for participants to choose whatever genre they perceive as the most inclusive option available to them when they try to categorize *The Lord of the Rings*. This tendency occurs in discussions about almost every genre chosen by participants. It is interesting that this trend developed across the genres, demonstrating that participants often used the same kind of justification to support their decision, regardless of what genre they chose. Participants who chose very different genres all claimed that they selected their genre because it is more inclusive than the others provided.

The other tendency, though it is present far less often, is for participants to choose one element and base their conclusions about the type of story that *The Lord of the Rings* is based on that element. This trend is particularly strong in the genres of threatened homeland and quest. What follows is a brief discussion of these two tendencies and how they either conform to or defy the way that texts are usually classified. The second, and less common, tendency would seem to align more readily with the pre-existing system of categorizing books within genres. Participants find an element that they deem is important to the book, and they find a genre that that element fits within. The largest complication of this tendency comes up when what young participants deem to be the most significant element of a story is different from what older readers perceive to be the most significant element. This certainly doesn't seem to be the case very often with *The Lord of the Rings*, since this process leads many readers to assume that the story follows a quest narrative, which is one of the most discussed topics by Tolkien scholars.

The larger trend in these responses, however, presents a more liberating approach to classifying the story within a given genre than is traditionally used by critics, publishers, and older readers. Perhaps this indicates that, to these young readers, *The Lord of the Rings* is a broad text that defies pigeonholing in a specific genre. When they were forced to choose a genre for the story, most of them simply chose the term that they found to be the most inclusive. Many of the participants specifically referenced other genres in the discussion as a means of demonstrating that their chosen genre did not preclude the story from being interpreted as fitting into other categories.

This may demonstrate that the preconceived notions that scholars have when they discuss genre are either not universally accepted among young readers or, in fact, that there is an over-eagerness to apply clean labels to a text that defies such an easy categorization. It also indicates that the way *The Lord of the Rings* is perceived as a standard for fantasy literature by older readers may be a disservice to the text and to other books. Since this text is often considered to be paradigmatic of fantasy literature, one would expect a majority of young participants to choose this as the genre for the story; however, that is not what happened. Instead of allowing *The Lord of the Rings* to define the fantasy genre, as many critics, writers, and readers have, these results demonstrate that *The Lord of the Rings* does not hold such a stable identity to this group of young readers.

These responses indicate that we should approach proposals like Atteberry's centring of *The Lord of the Rings* within the fantasy genre with trepidation. If critics and scholars build a genre around this text, it appears that the genre will not only have liminal edges, but an unstable centre. Readers are free to interpret texts in a number of ways and to see commonalities that critics may overlook in their classification. Because of this, we cannot state with certainty that *The Lord of the Rings* shares more in common with certain texts than others for all readers at all times. When one considers how young readers may classify books as they are exposed to them, it is entirely possible that they may not perceive the story as fitting within the genre of fantasy as they have experienced it. Perhaps, then, this analysis serves to help us keep in mind a very important caveat stated by Flieger: "I do not propose to assign *The Lord of the Rings* to a particular genre, such as fairy tale, epic, or romance. The book quite clearly derives from all three, and to see it as belonging only to one category is to miss the essential elements it shares with the others" (2004, 123).

These young readers inspire critics to keep their minds open to new possibilities and connections that they may overlook if they are too quick to assign the story to a single genre. Instead of finding ways to limit our perspective and clean up the lines surrounding the story, let us revel in the messiness that great writing can achieve. Let's celebrate the various influences, overlaps, transmissions, and transmutations that we find in this story and in many others.

Bibliography

Atteberry, B., *Strategies of Fantasy,* (Bloomington: Indiana UP, 1992).

Auden, W.H., 'The Quest Hero' in *Understanding The Lord of the Rings: The Best of Tolkien Criticism*, ed. by R.A. Zimbardo and N.D. Isaacs (New York: Houghton Mifflin, 2004) 31-51.

Caughey, A., 'The Hero's Journey', in *A Companion to J.R.R. Tolkien*, ed. by S.D. Lee (Malden, MA: John Wiley & Sons, 2014) 404-417.

Flieger, V., 'Frodo and Aragorn: The Concept of the Hero' in *Understanding The Lord of the Rings: The Best of Tolkien Criticism*, ed. by R.A. Zimbardo and N.D. Isaacs (New York: Houghton Mifflin, 2014) 122-145.
— *There Would Always Be a Fairy tale: More Essays on Tolkien,* (Kent, Ohio: Kent State University Press, 2017).

James, E. and F. Mendlesohn, 'Introduction' in *The Cambridge Companion to Fantasy Literature*, ed. by E. James and F. Mendlesohn (Cambridge, UK: Cambridge University Press, 2014) 1-4.

Tolkien's Legacy[1]

Tom Shippey

I would like to begin by noting the slogan of the German Tolkien Society, or Deutsche Tolkien Gesellschaft, which is this: *Ohne Tolkien Keine Fantasy*, or 'Without Tolkien, No Fantasy'. It is a good slogan, but not 100% true. There was fantasy before Tolkien, and independent of Tolkien, as we can see for instance from Douglas Anderson's 1995 collection *Tales before Tolkien: The Roots of Modern Fantasy*. So what exactly is it that Tolkien did for fantasy, and what was the great difference that he made?

I think what he did was reconcile two things, or two traditions, which till then had seemed completely incompatible. There was ambitious literary fantasy, mostly British. And there was popular mass-market fantasy, mostly American. Tolkien made literary fantasy mass-market, or if you prefer, he made mass-market fantasy ambitious and literary.

The point about ambitious literary fantasy is probably no longer well understood, and I would like to stress it, because it's very clear to me, for well-remembered personal reasons. British fantasy in the 1950s and before was ambitious and it was literary, and I will add one other adjective – it was expensive.

One example of this is a book by a fantasy author who made a considerable impact on me before I ever read Tolkien, both book and author now all but completely forgotten. The author was Richard Garnett, and the book was a collection of short stories called *The Twilight of the Gods*. It was originally published in 1888, but the edition I now own is the 1924 reprint published by John Lane, The Bodley Head, in London. It's a big heavy hardback, with a gilt cover, and a dedication in the native language of the British Establishment, which is of course Latin. The Introduction to it was written by T.E. Lawrence, otherwise known as Lawrence of Arabia. It's upper-class in every way, a book very suitable for a gentleman's library, but not at all the kind of book you find in a student's bed-sit. I have no idea what it would have cost in 1924. Garnett moreover, like M.R. James the ghost-story writer, was actually a learned man from the British upper class, his day job being Keeper of Printed Books at the British Library.

Consider now my old first edition of *The Fellowship of the Ring*. Also hardback, all three volumes even heavier than Garnett, gold stamp on the front of the first volume – though that is an accident, explained below – and also, of course, expensive. Too expensive for me when it came out in 1954, and that is the point I am trying to rub in.

What did this book cost in the late 1950s, when I was trying to find a copy to read? It cost a guinea. Many of us now probably do not know what a guinea was, but in our old currency there were 12 pennies to a shilling, 20 shillings to a pound – and 21 shillings to a guinea. (Pricing in guineas was a way of saying "this is upper-class material, so we are charging an extra 5% for it".)

Meanwhile, as I well remember, back in the late 1950s in Birmingham, a pint of Mitchells and Butler's mild beer in the public bar at the Country Girl pub in Selly Oak,

1. Please note: this is a slightly revised version of a talk given at theTolkien Society Conference in Birmingham on August 7th, 2019. PowerPoint slides have been incorporated into the text, and a long footnote has been added in response to valuable criticism.

cost one shilling and tuppence, 14 old pence. If you have been following my arithmetic, you will recall that a guinea, the price of one volume of *The Lord of the Rings*, was 252 old pence. One volume of *The Lord of the Rings*, then, was in 1954 the same price as 18 pints of beer.

Mild beer is rarely sold now, not even in the *Country Girl*, but if you can get it it would cost you at least £4. In other words the equivalent price for one volume of *The Lord of the Rings* in modern money would be £72, or £216 for all three volumes – which, as you can well understand, as a teenager back in the late 1950s, I had not got.

So how did I get hold of *The Lord of the Rings*? I had to win a book prize, King Edward's School, form prize Modern Languages Division, 1959. That is when they put the gold stamp on the front of volume one, and I wish they had not at the same time removed the dust jacket. Anyway, for me it was *Ohne Preis Kein Tolkien*, 'No Prize, No Tolkien'.

Literary. Ambitious. Expensive. That was the British tradition. Meanwhile, of course, there was also mass-market fantasy, by people like Robert E. Howard and Jack Vance, nothing to do with Tolkien, and published in the old pulp fiction magazines, like *Weird Tales*. They sold very widely, and a magazine only cost 25 cents, or in England, back then, one and thruppence (not tuppence). Even I could afford that. But these had no prestige at all. The two fantasy traditions just had no contact with each other.

But then came the pirate Ace edition of Tolkien in 1965, followed very quickly by the authorised Ballantine paperback in the same year, and as we all know, Tolkien took off. Not only did he become mass-market – he made *the whole fantasy genre mass-market*! Back in the 1960s, every publisher was crying out for a new Tolkien, and there were plenty of people ready to supply one.

Two anecdotes here: I was talking years ago to an American publisher, with whom I was on good terms – so he would be honest with me – and I asked him why he had published a particularly derivative Tolkien-imitation (the name of which I forbear to mention) which had followed The Lord of the Rings not merely in general outline, but character for character, scene for scene. "He replied, "We didn't publish it because we thought it was good. We published it because we knew we could sell it."

On another occasion I was talking to a British publisher and I asked him what he would like someone to write for him. Historical novel? Science fiction? Fantasy? And he replied: "Fantasy. These days only fantasy is mass-market. Everything else is just genre fiction." He thought for a bit and added: "that includes mainstream."

So, the Booker Prize does not matter anymore. The only people who care about that are professional literary critics in London and in academia. Whatever wins the Booker Prize will not sell enough copies to matter. Fantasy has swept them all aside. Because, as I have just declared, Tolkien mated ambitious-fantasy with mass-market fantasy.

One final anecdote: after I published *Tolkien: Author of the Century*, to the fury of my literary-critic "colleagues", I was asked to debate "author of the century" with a most distinguished literary critic, but he refused to come to the telephone, and I heard him shouting at the interviewer: "Author of the century! Has the fellow never heard of Proust?"[2]

2. At this point in the talk as delivered, I started asking for shows of hands on the issues of: had anyone read Proust? How many people had read Joyce's *Ulysses*? What, all of it? Answers confirmed what I was saying, though admittedly this was a highly skewed audience.

I wonder how many people in the modern world have ever read *A la Recherche du Temps Perdu*, or indeed even a single page of it? Very very few. Once again, the judgement of professional literary critics and that of the reading public are so far apart as to have no connection at all.

One unfortunate result of this is that, despite the dominance of fantasy in the world of general readership, there are few literary studies of it, and as far as I know there is no account of the great change that took place post-Tolkien. It would be good to have a history of this major literary event, as well as some sort of taxonomy of fantasy.

The problem is that this is a job beyond any single person. There is just too much of it. I'm told that some 700 works of fantasy are published every year in English, all aiming at the mass market. Now, I am the reviewer of fantasy and SF for *The Wall Street Journal*, so I get sent a lot of them. In fact not long ago I rang my editor at the WSJ and told him that I had just piled up on my desk all the heroic fantasies sent to me *for the coming month* and measured them, and the pile was two feet high! I begged him to tell me that I didn't have to read them all, and added. "and they have all got the same kind of title! They're all variations on X of Y ! Can they not think of another kind of title?"

What caused that, of course, was George R.R. Martin and the HBO series *Game of Thrones*. But would Martin be there at all if the pattern had not been set by Tolkien? *Ohne Tolkien, Kein Martin*. (And by the way, Martin knows that. He is very respectful to Tolkien.)

Nevertheless, what I would once have liked to do was produce a collective volume of commentaries on the major post-Tolkien writers of what we might as well call Tolkienian fantasy. We would try to indicate what had become hegemonic within the tradition, and what was original. We would try to trace the threads of the Tolkien legacy.

Because, after all, this is a major literary phenomenon. Maybe the most important literary phenomenon of the twentieth and twenty-first centuries. It deserves a history, and a cultural explanation. Somebody should be writing a PhD about it.

Needless to say, my literary-critic former "colleagues" would not have anything to do with it, they are all too busy reading Proust and James Joyce (or pretending to read Proust and James Joyce. Some years ago I had to give a lecture on *Ulysses* and I got the new revised edition and noticed as I read through the philological chapter "The Oxen of the Sun" that it was full of obvious typos. So I sent a list to *James Joyce Quarterly* and waited for the editor's letter of grateful acceptance and heartfelt thanks for this contribution to Joycean scholarship. Which did not come. Because what I had just proved, of course, was that no-one had ever read that chapter of *Ulysses* with any attention. I wonder how many people have read the critics' favourite *Ulysses* even with limited attention? I suspect the answer would be, many fewer than have claimed to do so.)

Nevertheless, my idea for a history / taxonomy of modern fantasy broke down on two problems. First, I would need a list of the 20 or so top authors. Then I would need a list of 20 people who could write a well-informed essay on each of them. (It was the second list which proved impossible to generate.)

Who, however, would I put on the list of authors? And, most important question, *what is distinctive about each of them?*

I have only space here to mention three: Stephen Donaldson, Michael Swanwick, and George Martin. All admirable, all distinctive, all posing questions about the nature and purpose of fantasy, and their relationship to Tolkien.

First, Stephen R Donaldson. He was born in 1947, he began to publish his *Chronicles of Thomas Covenant* in 1977, and it is now up to 10 volumes, the last one being *The Last Dark*, in 2013, as follows:

The First Chronicles of Thomas Covenant
1. *Lord Foul's Bane* (1977)
2. *The Illearth War* (1978)
3. *The Power That Preserves* (1979)

The Second Chronicles
1. *The Wounded Land* (1980)
2. *The One Tree* (1982)
3. *White Gold Wielder* (1983)

The Last Chronicles
1. *The Runes of the Earth* (2004)
2. *Fatal Revenant* (2007)
3. *Against All Things Ending* (2010)
4. *The Last Dark* (2013)

I should say that Stephen is a friend of mine, as is Bill Senior, who wrote an important book about him (Senior 2005). But that means Stephen is going to be completely honest with me, and that applies to the first of three things I have to say about him.

What is his relationship to Tolkien? Now, Stephen is quite definite that he never had any intention of imitating Tolkien, and for the reason just given, I believe him. But at the start of the *Chronicles*, it *looked* as if he was imitating Tolkien. Just to run through a few similarities, here is a list of Donaldson characters or locations, which can readily be matched to a Tolkien list:

- Cavewight Drool Rockworm
- Old hero Berek Halfhand
- Giant Saltheart Foamflower
- The horse-tending Ramen
- Tree city of Revelwood
- Caerroil Wildwood, a Forestal of Garroting Deep
- Climax scene on Mount Thunder

So, how to reconcile this contradiction? Briefly, I think it is very likely that if you read Tolkien in early life, it does not leave you. You may forget it up here in the head, but it stays down here in the heart. So similarities may be unconscious.

But in any case there are very marked differences between Tolkien and Donaldson. Just to be awkward, I will point to one more similarity. It struck me years ago that many of the most important 20th-century writers of fantasy were traumatised authors, often guys who had been shot, or shot at very seriously. I will not go through my list, but note especially Kurt Vonnegut, author of *Slaughterhouse 5* (he was in Dresden the night it was firebombed, in the cellar of an abattoir).

But there are more kinds of trauma than being shot, and here I think Donaldson comes in again. Like me, but like very few Americans, he spent his childhood in India, and in fact he spent it in a leprosarium – a home for lepers – run by his parents. This childhood experience may not have been exactly traumatic, but it does mean that Stephen has personal knowledge of levels of suffering which are most un-American.

So many of the derivative fantasies I have to read are written by people with – shall we say, politely – very limited social experience outside safe, cosy white-flight American suburbs. Just to give one example, I was reading one of these which was the usual scenario: medieval world, young woman discovers she is a princess in a kingdom threatened by invasion and dark forces. So how does she set about dealing with this situation? She sets up a nation-wide system of public libraries, so everyone is converted to the life of virtue. This seems unlikely to have much effect in even a fantasy world.

Donaldson is different. Just to start with, his hero is a leper himself. Tolkien's hobbits were one bold switch on the traditional Conan-type hero, but Donaldson's is another. Being a leper means Thomas Covenant not only cannot solve matters by physical confrontation, *he also has to be constantly careful.* The lost nerve-endings do not grow back. Cuts, burns, structural damage may go unnoticed. For lepers, self-monitoring becomes a way of life: not an ideal start for heroic action.

Covenant moreover carries from the start a burden of guilt quite alien to hobbits, in forms which are readily recognisable in our own real world. In some fantasies characters escape from their griefs into a world which presents more manageable challenges. But as his series has progressed, Covenant has taken more and more of his relationship issues with him into his Other World, 'the Land.'

There is his ex-wife Joan, consumed with anger and desire for revenge, perhaps as a result of her own guilt in abandoning a sick husband. There is his new partner Linden, who is also a kind of leper, not physically but mentally. Leprosy makes you numb, untouchable, unaffected, and Linden — terribly traumatised in youth — has cut herself off emotionally.

Very briefly, the fantasy world is a kind of mirror of Covenant's remarkably dysfunctional family back in the real world. A sick Land which cannot heal itself, that's Covenant. The abused and injured females in the Land – they are Joan and Linden.

And here is another thing. One of the few books that have studied fantasy in general, and I think the most successful of them – Farah Mendelsohn's *Rhetorics of Fantasy* (2008) – has suggested four basic types of fantasy:

1. Portal quest (e.g. Narnia)
2. Immersive (e.g. Terry Pratchett's Discworld series)
3. Intrusive (e.g. Susan Cooper's *The Dark is Rising* series)
4. Liminal (*The Hobbit*?)

The first is quite easy – a little girl goes through the wardrobe, she finds herself in Narnia. The second is fairly easy – *The Lord of the Rings,* you are in the fantasy world and centered already on fantasy characters. The third – well, something comes through from outside, or some old dark force is revived, as in Susan Cooper.

And the fourth? Well, *The Hobbit* looks like an immersive fantasy: we start off in the Shire and that is that. But the fact is that Bilbo is completely unfamiliar with the world outside the Shire – he is just like us. He doesn't understand about trolls, he can't hoot twice like a barn-owl and once like a screech-owl, he is used to having his meat supplied to him by the butcher – just like us. His journey to the Lonely Mountain is a portal-quest fantasy *for him*, and we go along with him.

Donaldson's *Chronicles* look initially like portal fantasy. The hero just finds himself in the strange world of "the Land", quite unfamiliar to him and with rules and conditions he does not understand. But he keeps moving *backwards and forwards*. The connection between his real-world problems and his fantasy-world problems keeps being made clearer and closer. So, one thing you can be quite sure of is, this is not escapist. Like Tolkien, Donaldson is confronting what he sees as the vital issues of our time, and playing them out in fantasy.

Again very briefly, if the underlying bass-note of Tolkien's work was the traumas of the early 20th-century, industrial war and the corruptions of totalitarianism, then the bass-note of Donaldson's "Chronicles" is pollution: toxic dumping, physical pollution, medical and psychic disease. He is saying, if we want to save the whales, and the polar bears, and the Earth, then we need to look inside first.

Because we are lepers. We are falling to bits but we don't notice it.

Second, Michael Swanwick. The series I focus on is this one:

Industrialised Faerie
The Iron Dragon's Daughter (1993)
The Dragons of Babel (2008)
The Iron Dragon's Mother (2019)

Could there be anything less Tolkienian than "Industrialised Faerie"? Tolkien would have shuddered if you even said the phrase to him! Nevertheless, I think that Swanwick is in one way at least closer to Tolkien, and to Tolkien's original inspiration, than any other writer.

It is now known that hobbits turn up only once before Tolkien, in a strange pamphlet from the 19th century, the "Denham Tracts", which lists some 196 kinds of folklore creature, almost all of which have vanished from memory (for which see further Shippey 2011). Here are just a few of them:

Strange creatures from the Denham Tracts:

cauld-lads, death-hearses, goblins, hob-headlesses, buggaboes, kows, or cowes, nickies, nacks, waiths, niffies, buckles, gholes, sylphs, guests, swarths, freiths, freits, gy-carlins, pigmies, chittifaces, nixies, Jinny-burnt-tails, dudmen, hell-hounds, dopple-gangers, boggleboes, bogies, redmen, portunes, grants, HOBBITS, hobgoblins, brown-men, cowies, dunnies, wirrikows, alholdes, mannikins, follets, korreds, lubberkins, luricanns, kobolds, leprechauns, kors, mares, korreds, puckles, korigans, sylvans, succubuses

To be brief, Swanwick uses a lot of these, and some perhaps of his own invention. He has got: knockers and hobthrushes, shellycoats and cluricauns, spunkies and chittifaces, boggarts and haints and wodewoses and hulders. Billy Bugaboo is a named character, and 'the cauld-lad' is another one.

What I like about this is that Tolkien's choice of species has become all too hegemonic in modern fantasy. Everyone these days has elves and dwarves and trolls and even Tolkien's own invention orcs, as well as ent-variants and halflings. Swanwick, however, has realised there is a wider selection available from the goblin-universe, and he uses it heavily.

Moreover, going back to Farah's taxonomy of fantasy types. *The Iron Dragon's Daughter* looks like an immersive fantasy – a child trapped in a dragon-factory run by elves, constantly threatened and beaten and half-starved (it reminded me vividly of my Scottish boarding-school).

But she is a changeling, in training to be a dragon-pilot, or a breeder for dragon-pilots, because she can endure cold iron, which her elf-owners cannot. And she retains connections with her early life, which is us. So it is a portal fantasy, but for her, *the portal goes the other way*.

The whole series is a kind of negotiation between Faerie and Reality, and the two leak into each other all the time. And it is also, in its way, a grim commentary on politics, not in the twentieth century, like Tolkien, but in the twenty-first.

Finally, there is the most prominent example, George R.R. Martin, and I have only two things to say about him.

One is that I think he changed his name at the age of 13 to be more like Tolkien. His real name was just George Raymond Martin. He added the Richard of his own accord, aged 13, to become George R.R. Martin, just like J.R.R. Tolkien. Surely that was deliberate.

The other thing – and this is not my idea, but I was immediately convinced by it: Is it not the case that (despite significant qualifications mentioned below) in Tolkien, characters are good or bad? Nothing in the middle. No shades of gray. You may say, hah, but what about:

- Boromir (no, he is a good character who is momentarily corrupted by the Ring)
- Denethor (no, he is a bad character, suicide, son-murderer: but not corrupted by the Ring)
- Gollum (no, he is two characters, Gollum, corrupted by the Ring, and Smeagol, who was made into a murderer by the Ring)

My best example of a morally ambiguous character, shades of grey is:[3]

3. [An aside: after I delivered this paper, I was contacted by Nils-Ivar Agøy, who objected strongly to what I had said about "no shades of grey". He pointed out that this sounds far too much like the old and patronising criticism made by people like Edmund Wilson, that *The Lord of the Rings* is basically non-adult, morally over-simplified. I agree with Nils-Ivar, of course, that (as Gandalf says in 'The Council of Elrond', "nothing is evil in the beginning. Even Sauron was not so" (*FR*, 'The Council of Elrond', 267). In the same way, even Frodo in the end gives way and declines to

- Lobelia Sackville-Baggins (she stole Bilbo's spoons, and she cannot stand the Bagginses, but she went for Saruman's gang with her umbrella, and was eventually released from the Lockholes to great applause, after which she becomes popular for the first time in her life and bequeaths all her property to charity).

With Martin, however, surely the case is much clearer. There are plenty of people who are absolutely horrible, like Reese Boldon, who hunts girls with man-eating dogs, and Cersei, and Walder Frey, and Tywin Lannister, and King Joffrey. But is there anyone who can be called good?

Admirable (?) characters in Martin

Sansa Stark – feeds husband to the dogs
Arya Stark – trained assassin, feeds his own sons to Lord Frey in a pie
Daenerys Targaryen – crucifies people, burns them alive
Jon Snow – hangs a child
Tyrion Lannister – shoots his own father
Jaime Lannister – commits incest, attempts child-murder to cover this up

You notice, the only character fit to take the Iron Throne in the end is Bran the Broken, "first of his name": because he hasn't done anything during the whole sequence.

Do you think that is deliberate? Was Martin perhaps thinking, Tolkien created a world of moral certainty, I am going to create one of total moral uncertainty?

And if so, what does that tell us about the way things have changed between 1954 and now? I suspect there have been far-reaching changes in our collective psyches.

I will not speculate about what these changes may have been, or how they are reflected in fantasy, but I will say this about Tolkien's legacy. First, as I've said, he made fantasy the dominant literary tradition of our time, both mass-market and ambitious. It is true my 'critic-colleagues' have not noticed, but they are like economists and bankers: experts whose expertise is now discredited.

Second, Tolkien has now become part of most people's mental and emotional world, at any rate (but not only) within Western culture. I live deep in the countryside, about as

---

destroy the Ring. So there is (originally) good in evil and (potentially) evil in good.
Another way of putting this is to say that in Tolkien, corruption is always a possibility, and is at the root of all problems. His world, like ours, is a fallen world, as Nils-Ivar puts it. So much we can agree on.
Nevertheless, and with all the caveats and qualifications above, it seems to me that we rarely if ever have any doubts in Tolkien's work about which characters we are able to sympathise with, and which of them are – at their present state of corruption – non-negotiable. This opinion is seconded in the modern urban fantasy by Jim Butcher, *Changes*. At the end of chapter 39, *The Lord of the Rings* is described as "a world of blacks and whites with precious little in the way of grey, where (my emphasis) *you could tell the good guys from the bad guys with about two seconds of effort*." That is how it seems to even a sympathetic commentator.

close to the Shire as you can get. The other day I saw in the window of the single village shop, a diorama, titled 'Middle-earth mice'. It was hand-made mouse figures, made to look like *The Lord of the Rings* Gandalf, Théoden, the hobbits, etc. They were all recognisable, but none of them were labelled. They did not need any explanation, none was given, and the diorama certainly had nothing to do with me. Even in the depths of the countryside, far from any literary centre, Tolkien needs no introduction.

And third, that is exactly what Tolkien wanted. Nearly 70 years ago he wrote this:

> Once upon a time [...] I had a mind to make a body of more or less connected legend, ranging from the large and cosmogonic, to the level of romantic fairy-story [...] I would draw some of the great tales in fullness, and leave many only placed in the scheme, and sketched. The cycles should be linked to a majestic whole, and yet leave scope for other minds and hands (*Letters*, Letter 131, 144-5)

He went on, "Absurd" and remarked "my crest has long since fallen" (145).

Well, his crest did not need to fall. What he wanted is what has happened, is happening, and is going to happen. Everything from Middle-earth mice to whole TV series.

I called Tolkien "author of the century", and I meant the 20th century, and as I have said my "critical colleagues" were furious. But he is going to be the author of the 21st century too. I have called him "the English Grimm". But now he looks like "the English Homer" as well, the creator of epic for a new millennium: a starting-point, not a termination.

Bibliography

Butcher, J., *Changes,* (London: Orbit Books, 2010).

Garnett, R., *The Twilight of the Gods,* (London: Bodley Head, 1924).

Mendelsohn, F., *Rhetorics of Fantasy,* (Middletown, CN: Wesleyan University Press, 2008).

Senior, W.A., *Stephen R Donaldson: Variations on the fantasy tradition,* (Kent, OH: Kent State University Press, 1995).

Shippey, T., 'The ancestors of the hobbits: strange creatures in English folklore', in *Lembas-extra*, ed. by C. van Zon (Tolkien Genootschap Unquendor, 2011) 97-106.
— 'The Faërie World of Michael Swanwick', in *Sub-creating Arda: World-building in Tolkien's work, its precursors and legacies*, ed. by D. Fimi and T. Honegger (Zurich and Jena: Walking Tree Press, 2019) 417-29.
Tales Before Tolkien: The Roots of Modern Fantasy, ed. by D.A. Anderson (New York: Ballantine, 1995).

Tolkien, J.R.R., *The Letters of J.R.R. Tolkien*, ed. by H. Carpenter with the assistance of C. Tolkien, (London: HarperCollins, 2006).
— *The Lord of the Rings,* (London: HarperCollins, 2007).

www.ingramcontent.com/pod-product-compliance
Ingram Content Group UK Ltd.
Pitfield, Milton Keynes, MK11 3LW, UK
UKHW010143010325
455692UK00008B/43